D1455062

George Harrison

Printed in the United Kingdom by MPG Books Ltd, Bodmin

Published by Sanctuary Publishing Limited, Sanctuary House, 45-53 Sinclair Road,
London W14 0NS, United Kingdom

www.sanctuarypublishing.com

Distributed in the US by Publishers Group West

Copyright: Alan Clayson 1996 as *The Quite One: A Life Of George Harrison.*
This edition, 2003.

Cover photograph: © Redferns

All rights reserved. No part of this book may be reproduced in any form or by any
electronic or mechanical means, including information storage or retrieval systems,
without permission in writing from the publisher, except by a reviewer, who may quote
brief passages.

While the publishers have made every reasonable effort to trace the copyright owners
for any or all of the photographs in this book, there may be some omissions of credits,
for which we apologise.

ISBN: 1-86074-489-3

George Harrison

Alan Clayson

Sanctuary

"*Like most clever young men, hurrying home with a pile of books and glowering at the passers-by, he magnifies the gulf between men of genius and ordinary stupid people... He cannot believe that stockbrokers may have strange dreams, that butchers cutting off chops may be touched with intimations of mortality, that the grocer, even as he hesitates over the sugar, may yet see the world in a grain of sand.*"

JB Priestley on Colin Wilson's The Outsider

November 2001

George Harrison could not permit himself the luxury of hope after a syndicated photograph from Tuscany reached the media. He smiled his old smile, but, ashen-faced and grey-haired now, he seemed to have aged shockingly. Those well-wishers in closest contact – including Ringo and Paul – became as uneasily aware as George was that there might be less than six months left.

As if blowing sparks of optimism, he marshalled enough energy to record "Like A Horse To Water", a new opus by himself and Dhani. Yet outward evidence of respite from gathering infirmity ended when a brain tumour developed, requiring weeks of chemotherapy in a specialist clinic in Switzerland. Prescribed a course of drugs and avoidance of stressful situations, he convalesced in Kuppaqulua – where he continued to practice guitar and tease songs from nothing more than the ghost of a lyric or melody.

Being awash with medications for a debilitating illness wasn't the soundest footing from which to consider another Cloud Nine-sized comeback. A final desperate strategy was an admission to New York's Staten Island University Hospital for what George had been convinced was a "revolutionary" new radiotherapy technique that had bought time for other cancer sufferers. There was, however, little that could be done.

Coming to terms with what was inevitable, George resigned as director of Harrisongs, and, with characteristic black humour, created "RIP Ltd.", an outlet for "Like A Horse To Water" and other latter-day compositions. He also affirmed a wish to be cremated without ceremony, and for the ashes to be scattered on the Ganges.

A further onslaught of symptoms brought him to UCLA Medical Centre in Los Angeles for care rather than cure. The light was fading, but he discharged himself and took refuge in the house of Gavin de Becker, head of the most proficient Hollywood security service money could buy. As it had been in Switzerland and New York, there wasn't a newspaper editor on the planet who wouldn't promise a fortune for a Harrison exclusive or an up-to-date picture. Nevertheless, de Becker's home was as off-limits as Howard Hugues's Las Vegas penthouse. For George Harrison, it was there, with imposition on his treasured privacy as low as it could be, that the light went out in the early afternoon of Thursday, 29th of November 2001.

About The Author

Described by *The Western Morning News* as the "AJP Taylor of pop", Alan Clayson is the author of many books on music, including the best-selling *Backbeat*, subject of a major film. He has contributed to journals as disparate as *Record Collector*, *The Independent*, *The Beat Goes On*, *Mojo*, *Mediaeval World*, *The Guardian*, *Folk Roots* and, as a teenager, the notorious *Schoolkids Oz*. He had also written and presented programmes on national radio and has lectured on both sides of the Atlantic.

Before he became better known as a pop historian, he led the legendary Clayson And The Argonauts and was thrust to "a premier position on rock's Lunatic Fringe" (*Melody Maker*). Today, his solo cabaret act remains "more than just a performance; an experience" (*Village Voice*). "It is difficult to explain to the uninitiated quite what to expect," adds *The Independent*. There is even an Alan Clayson fan club, which dates from a 1992 appearance in Chicago.

Alan Clayson's cult following continues to grow, along with demand for his production skills in the studio and the number of versions of his compositions by such diverse acts as Dave Berry – in whose Cruisers he played keyboards in the mid 1980s – and (via a collaboration with Yardbird Jim McCarty) Jane Relf and new age outfit Stairway. He has also worked with the Portsmouth Sinfonia, Wreckless Eric, The Pretty Things and Screaming Lord Sutch, among others.

Born in Dover in 1951, Alan Clayson lives near Henley-on-Thames with his wife, Inese, and sons, Jack and Harry.

To Alan Peacock

Contents

Prologue
The Invisible Man

I'm not certain how many people know this, but George Harrison – along with Paul McCartney, John Lennon and various others – used to be a member of a Merseyside pop group whose act went down well with local teenagers. Later, quite a few of their gramophone records got into the hit parade. George was the readiest of the four to venture beyond pop music through his explorations of Indian culture and, after the group disbanded, the underwriting of HandMade Films, now a pillar of British cinema. More subtly than John Lennon, he rode out the 1970s as the most self-contained – and oddest – ex-Beatle. Nevertheless, despite a career blighted with stimulant abuse, marital ructions, religious obsession and proven artistic plagiarism, muckrakers would be hard pressed to ravage a distinguished, charitable and humorous middle-aged musician whose character – in contrast to those of John, Paul and Ringo – was rooted in a secure family background.

Following the success of 1989's album, *Cloud Nine*, fans await George Harrison's next album with more anticipation than at any time since the celebrated *All Things Must Pass* triple LP of 1970. His growth as a composer was one of the pressures that caused the sundering of The Beatles in that same year, notably when his 'Something' – along with McCartney's 'Yesterday' – emerged as one of the most covered songs of all time.

Harrison's sojourn as a Beatle and its repercussions will always remain central to any consideration of him as a figure in time's fabric. Unlike in a biography of some Dark Ages king, we are embarrassed with too much information – an idle afternoon in 1968 when George and Klaus Voorman painted a friend's 1966 Citroën 2CV was deemed worthy of a half-page of speculation in one Beatle fanzine in which no piece of information was without value, no item too insignificant to be interesting. As the Bible can prove any religious or moral theory, so the millions of words chronicling and analysing his every trivial act (to which I shall be adding) can warp the Harrison saga to any purpose.

In one empty moment, I thought of writing it as a calypso, but, as I'd arrived at many (although not all) of the same conclusions as other Beatle-related authors, I decided it would be misleading to be too "original" or to disguise nostalgia as social history. With a bit of perverted logic, I could have been mischievous enough to intimate that George indulged in bondage sessions with Dora Bryan or that he paid a Mafia hit-man to bump off Roy Orbison. One of Lennon's biographers did worse.

· Lately, many well-known heroes have gone down. Richard the Lionheart, Robin Hood and Bonnie Prince Charlie are three who have been transformed respectively into a sadistic homosexual, a non-existent thug and a wife-beating alcoholic. Edward the Confessor, apparently, turns out to be A Right Bastard. Indeed, if one American author is to be believed, there is a case for Adolf Hitler to be re-assessed as Not Such A Bad Bloke After All. A similar reappraisal has been applied to the notorious pop manager Allen Klein, "the Robin Hood of pop", whose questionable financial machinations were excused by Rolling Stone Keith Richards as "the price of an education".[1] Nonetheless, it is feasible that more "new and rediscovered" evidence may prompt a restoration of earlier assumptions until they are again amended.

While the deeds and personalities of the illustrious become more nebulous and ambiguous in retrospect, I have taken care to define as widely as possible the myriad social, cultural, economic, environmental and other undercurrents and myths that polarise and prejudice what we know about George Harrison and The Beatles. Often, pop biography has tended to shy away from these areas, even though they form a more tangible basis for investigation than treating a subject's flippant remarks as gospel or squeezing a few paragraphs from, say, an encounter between Paul McCartney and Dave Dee, Dozy, Beaky, Mick And Tich in a Cromwell Road pub: "All he said," recalled Dozy, "was, 'I've seen you lot on the telly,' and we said, 'We've seen you on the telly as well.'"[2]

This is a fair example of the depth to which those who happen to be in the same profession know each other, although in showbusiness it's easy to get a different impression. Entering a Southsea hotel bar one evening in 1988, a puzzled Dave Berry was embraced by Gerry of The Pacemakers, who'd become buoyant with rose-tinted enthusiasm for the Swinging '60s. Dave hardly knew Gerry then. "People can only see each other from their own state of consciousness," expounded George Harrison. "The press' state of consciousness is virtually nil, so they never get the true essence of anything they write about."[3] During The Beatles' only Australasian tour, was George "outgoing and friendly", as the singer Johnny Devlin found him, or "deeply introspective and hard to know",[4] the view of radio personality Bob Rogers?

As Horace reminds us, "*quandoque bonus dormitat Homerus*" – even the wisest can make mistakes. In his own autobiography, George is guilty of factual error, such as when he states that his family was living at Mackett's Lane when he first visited Hamburg. (A recording agreement that he signed during his second trip to Germany clearly gives his home address as 25 Upton Green, Speke.) Those whose lives are devoted to collating information about The Beatles could alight on lesser mistakes and omissions, as they might while scrutinising *The Quiet One*. To them, I can only say that it's as accurate as I was able to make it.

They might also take into account that I'm the sort who has to screw himself up before talking to complete strangers at a moment's notice. My nerve failed completely when I noticed Jane Asher, McCartney's former girlfriend, two seats to the left of me in a London theatre. During the interval, it didn't seem the time or place to actuate a dialogue with her about Paul's ex-colleague. At times, I was riven with self-disgust when wheedling an interview from someone who only wanted to crawl away and hide. I spent a lot of time while in Liverpool wandering the streets with pangs of muttered nostalgia for locations to which I'd hitherto never been but only drunk in second hand as germane to The Beatles' legend – Litherland, Penny Lane, the ferry 'cross the Mersey, *et al.* In 1977, my group Clayson And The Argonauts played at Eric's, a club in Mathew Street where the spirit of '77 faced the ghost of '62. While The Argonauts busied themselves in the adjacent pub – the Grapes – after our usual harrowing soundcheck, I crossed the road and climbed through a gap in the fence to pay my respects on that patch of unofficial countryside that had surfaced on the site of the Cavern. If it had been a film, you'd have heard the ranting abandon of 'Twist And Shout' as a spooky drift, as if through a seashore conch.

Ten years later, Merseyside, in recession, had fallen back on its cradling of The Beatles, just as it had so long fed off its past as a great port. While it was entirely fitting that the city's university should have founded Britain's first Institute of Popular Music, other by-products of The Beatles weren't as anxious to foster research. A "Cavern" had been reconstructed down Mathew Street next to Cavern Walks shopping mall. Propping up the bar in the John Lennon pub opposite, tourists on the scent of The Beatles might have been regaled by John's late Uncle Charlie or, more reluctantly, former Beatles "manager" Allan Williams with endless reminiscences about what Ringo said to Rory Storm down the Blue Angel in 1962.

In the aftermath of Albert Goldman's infamous portrayal of Lennon, I could understand why Williams and others either refused to talk altogether or demanded payment for so doing. According to his secretary, The Beatles' record producer George Martin was sick and tired of retelling the old, old story. Many of Harrison's former employees were legally bound not to discuss life in the offices of HandMade Films or at Friar Park, George's estate in Oxfordshire.

After weighing every word of it, I delivered a letter to Friar Park by hand. Requesting George's co-operation, it assured him that I wasn't a scum reporter but an *artiste* like himself. *The Quiet One* was to be a respectful account, concentrating mainly on his professional career and artistic output. Unlike certain other tomes about musicians with whom he was (and is) associated, it would not peter out after a rehash of Those Fabulous '60s. I wanted him to like it. Six weeks later, I received a charming reply from California. It advised me that "Mr Harrison does not have the least interest in having his biography done again".[6]

By then, however there was no turning back. I'd accumulated a filing cabinet of Harrisonia, exercise books full of scribble to decipher, interview tapes to transcribe and a deadline I'd never meet. More material was arriving with every post. To get closer to him, I'd attended a Hare Krishna evening and waded through numerous religious tracts that led me to research myself as much as George Harrison.

His not granting me just one little interview was galling with me living "just up the road", so to speak, but this isn't a scissors-and-clippings job; I've drawn a lot of information from press archives – some of them quite obscure – because we can learn a lot from verbatim accounts that recreate the feeling of being there. Unlike people, they are not influenced by the fact of being observed – *litera scripta manet*[7]. For most of my secondary research, I went first and last to my good friend Ian Drummond, who, as a scholar and observer of The Beatles and George Harrison, commands the highest respect. I wish to express my deepest gratitude to him for his encouragement and practical help with this project.

I'd like you all to put your hands together for Peter Doggett, who saw me over the final hurdle. I am also grateful to Brian Cresswell, Pete Frame, Spencer Leigh, Steve Maggs, Colin Miles and John Tobler for their faith and very real assistance, especially as consultants over apparent trivia. For example, dear sub-editor, I'm told it's HandMade rather than Handmade or Hand Made. I also owe a particular debt to Dave and Caroline Humphreys for accommodating me whenever I was on Merseyside, and for Dave being Dr Watson to my Sherlock Holmes.

Special thanks are in order, too, for Susan Hill, Amanda Marshall, Carys Thomas, Helen Gummer and the rest of the team in Museum Street, plus a special "hello" to my original editor, Hilary Murray. Let's hear it too for Penny Braybrooke, who authorised this reissue, as well as Jeffrey Hudson, Eddy Leviten, Alan Heal, Dan Froude, Chris Bradford and especially Michelle Knight, whose patience and understanding went beyond the call of duty.

For their advice and for trusting me with archive material, let's have a big round of applause for Phil Cooper (of Radio 210), Ron Cooper, Lesley Dibley, Mark Ellen, Ann Freer, *The Henley Standard*, David Horn (of the University of Liverpool Institute of Popular Music), David Humbles, Allan Jones (of *Melody Maker*), Fraser Massey, Steve Morris, Darrell Paddick, Jill Pritchard, Charles and Deborah Salt, Jonathan Taylor-Sabine and Michael Towers.

I have also drawn from conversations with the following musicians: Ian Amey, Don Andrew, Roger Barnes, Andre Barreau, Alan Barwise, Cliff Bennett, Dave Berry, Barry Booth, Allan Clarke, Terry Clarke, Frank Connor, Eric E Cooke, Tony Crane, Daniel D'Arcy, Spencer Davis, Dave Dee, Wayne Fontana, Freddie Garrity, Gary Gold, Eric Goulden, Mike Hart, Rick Huxley, Garry Jones, Billy Kinsley, Graham Larkbey, Kenny Lynch, Stephen MacDonald, Kevin Manning, Jim McCarty, Zoot Money, Adrian Moulton, Sandy Newman, Ray Phillips, Ray Pinfold, Brian Poole, Gail Richards, Mike Robinson, Twinkle Rogers, Jim Simpson, Larry Smith, Norman Smith, the late Vivian Stanshall, the late Lord David Sutch, Mike Sweeney, John Townsend, Paul Tucker, Chris Warman, Norman Warwick, Val Wiseman and David Yeats. Invaluable too was a long chat with Bill Harry.

It may be obvious to the reader that I have received much information from sources that prefer not to be mentioned. Nevertheless, I wish to thank them.

Thanks are also due in varying degrees to Veronica Armstrong, B&T Typewriters, Robert and Janice Bartel, Colin Baylis, Stuart and Kathryn Booth, Carol Boyer, Rob Bradford, Eva Marie Brunner, Gordon and Rosemary Clayson, Hilary Cresswell, Greg and Debi Daniels, Doreen Davidson, Nancy Davis, Kevin Delaney, Tim and Sarah Fagan, Kathi and Rick Fowler, Caroline Freyer, Ian Gilmore, Stanley Green, Tom Hall (of the Spinning Disk), Louise Harrison, Virginia Harry, Paul Hearne, Martin Hockley, Matt Holland, Graham Humphreys, Oliver Johnson, Sarah Knake, Graham and Yvonne Lambourne, Mark and Carol Lapidos, Brian Leafe, Bill Mielenz, Coy Ness, Russell Newmark, Sarah Parish, Carolyn Pinfold, Evan and Lyn Reynolds, George Rowden, Steve Rowley, Steve Shiner (of the Reading Hare Krishna Society), Maggie

Simpson, Andrea Tursso, Kathryn Varley and Ted Woodings – plus Inese, Jack and Harry, who are now more knowledgeable about George Harrison and The Beatles than they ever needed to be.

Alan Clayson, July 2001

1 The Rebel

With middle-aged candour, he'd insist, "I'm just an ordinary fellow."[8] Certainly, the occupations of George Harrison's immediate forebears were the kind you'd expect an ordinary fellow to have. Merseysiders all, they came and went and in between they earned livings as joiners, able seamen, bricklayers, engine drivers and similarly honourable if unlettered professions. Edward Harrison, George's great-grandfather, had inscribed a mark rather than a signature on the parish register when he wed Elizabeth Hargreaves, a carter's daughter, in 1868 when both were under age. As well as bearing the stigma of his illegitimacy, Edward had been launched into life at the height of a cholera epidemic that had struck Victorian Liverpool.

From peasant stock with such solid-sounding tributary surnames as Shepherd and Thompson, the Harrisons had lived in the predominantly working-class South Liverpool district of Wavertree for perhaps two centuries when Edward's grandson, Harold Hargreaves Harrison, was born in a house off one of its main junctions in 1909. By the time 17-year-old Harold threw in a job selling mangles to go to sea as a White Star Line steward, new tangles of terraces – raw red brick rather than ancient sandstone – were beginning to impinge upon the area's surviving parks and tree-lined avenues. The largest patch of green, Wavertree Playground, had long been slashed along its western side by the clattering railway connection to Lime Street Central, three miles away in the heart of the city.

To outsiders, Wavertree was already becoming indistinguishable from any other Merseyside suburb when Harold Harrison began a two-year courtship of Louise French, a greengrocer's assistant and daughter of the uniformed commissionaire at New Brighton's grand Tower Ballroom, the most capacious seaside dance palais in the northwest outside Blackpool. Within a year of their marriage in 1931, Harold and Louise were blessed with their only daughter, who was named after her mother, as their eldest son, born three years later, was named after Harold.

His job being the only impediment to family stability, Mr Harrison left his ship to take a chance on finding work in the mid-1930s' recession. For months, he drew dole money until taken on as a Corporation bus conductor in 1937. By the outbreak of the Second World War, he'd been promoted to driver and was also an active member of his depot's union and social committee. In 1940, Goering's Luftwaffe pounded the Liverpool docks, and Louise gave birth to another child, Peter, in the two-up/two-down family home along a small, neglected cul-de-sac within the clang of the High Street fire station.

With its front door opening straight onto the pavement, 12 Arnold Grove had no garden, apart from a minuscule square of flower-bed that was less prominent in the paved back yard than the outside toilet and the zinc tub that was carried indoors and set down before the fireplace in the lino-floored kitchen whenever sufficient hot water had been accumulated for the family to bathe. Water was boiled either on the open coal fire or a gas cooker that boomed when lit. It was generally lukewarm by the third immersion in the tub. Babies were washed in the sink. The kitchen apart, the house in winter was cold enough for the windows to ice up and goose-flesh to rise on those who'd neglected to warm their freezing sheets with a hot-water bottle before retiring.

Into this household of shared bedrooms and bathwater, plumpish 33-year-old Mrs Harrison's final confinement would produce the remarkable George – named after King George VI – on 25 February 1943, a mild, dry night.[8.1] The worst of the war was past, although barrage balloons still hung over the docklands where giant chimneys and cranes were trained on the sky like anti-aircraft guns.

Both Peter and George took after their father, with his slim build, jug-handle ears, angular features and eyebrows that, thickening towards the nose, tinged their lopsided smiles with gravity. George inherited some Irish blood from Louise, and there was the hint of a leprechaun about him, but one that carefully deliberated its impishness. Growing from babyhood, his blond hair darkened to brown, and he caught and held a dry and "common" Scouse drawl that would be with him always, rendering "care" as "cur" and splitting "bringing" into "bring-ging".

His earliest memory was of the buying of three chickens to fatten in a back-yard coop for Christmas. He also recalled the hard wooden kneelers in the church down nearby Chestnut Grove, where he'd been baptised and where his Roman Catholic mother would take her youngsters to Mass. George has said, "[Although] I almost became a Catholic when I was eleven or twelve, I couldn't relate to Christ being the only son of God. The only things that made an impression were the oil paintings and the Stations of the Cross." Reacting against "the Catholic trick" of indoctrinating young minds, he also questioned the motives of adult communicants: "They go to church and it's all that thing about, you know, Tommy Jones has got a brown suit on, and here comes Mrs Smith with her new hat. It's a bore."[9]

None of the Harrison offspring were forced to attend church. In any case, Harold was a lapsed Anglican. Neither he nor Louise pressured the children to do well academically, either, although Harold was pleased when "Our Kid" (as youngest Merseyside siblings were often nicknamed) passed the Eleven Plus examination to gain a place at a grammar school rather than a secondary modern where Peter went. Perhaps to beef up a self-image of one streetwise beyond his years, George has told tales of being allowed, while still at primary school, to "stay out all night when I wanted to and have a drink when I wanted to".[10] Such excessive licence seems at odds with both George's later destruction of unfavourable school reports before they reached his parents' eyes and the moderation and hard work incumbent upon Mr and Mrs Harrison to keep their young family fed and clothed.

Harold was the firmer of the two, but in practice the Harrison household was more liberal than might be expected in an age when "spare the rod and spoil the child" was still a much-quoted maxim.

Nonetheless, until the age of 13, when he was hospitalised for seven weeks with nephritis,[11] George's upbringing was as undramatic and free from major traumas as that of any other "ordinary fellow" from Liverpool.

"It is one big family," Jimmy Tarbuck, one of Liverpool's many famous comedians, would say. "No matter where a Scouser goes, he never stops being a part of it."[12] Liverpool looks after its own. The Saturday after the Hillsborough disaster, I just happened to be there when the entire city, with every traffic light on red, observed a silence for those crushed to death in the bulging stadium during a Liverpool football team away match. The quiet was so absolute you could almost listen to it. When the two minutes were up, a Salvation Army band pierced the heavy air at the crowded Anfield ground, from where a symbolic chain of football scarves stretched across to Goodison Park, home of Everton, the rival club in this city formed of overlapping towns.

Southern settlements in Britain lack the fiercer sense of regional identity and loyalty – even fair play and compassion – peculiar to areas like Liverpool, Glasgow and Newcastle. There is a common unconsciousness that bonds Liverpudlians more strongly than, say, the inhabitants of Dover or Guildford. I would dare to hint that tolerance towards minorities is more pronounced than elsewhere in this, one of the most cosmopolitan of cities. As well as containing the largest Chinatown in Europe, Liverpool is referred to facetiously as "the capital of Ireland". This is traceable to the ingress from across the Irish Sea and through the murky sweep of the Mersey that led to Irish dockers becoming the foundation of the 19th-century merchant prosperity when a third of Britain's exports went through Liverpool.

Prosperity was thin on the ground when George Harrison and those born in the war years came to consciousness. Food and clothing continued to be rationed well into the 1950s. To further alleviate the plight of poor families – of which the Harrisons were typical – the government introduced "Utility" goods. Although not expensive, a garment or item of furniture thus marked was deemed to be functional and hard wearing. The same could not be said of the homes in which many Utility consumers on Merseyside had to dwell, however. It hadn't been practical to erect more than the most essential buildings during the war, and in peacetime a lot of those still standing cried out for modernisation. Even in 1960, thousands of Liverpudlians were still living without bathrooms and hot water in dark terraces with front rooms cold and tidy for funerals, and grim side passages leading to outside lavatories.

As an economic base, Liverpool had been overlooked since the gouging of the ship canal to Manchester. To the affluent south, it had become a corner of the map where penury and unemployment clotted. It was assumed that the further north you voyaged, the more primitive the natives, just as the Roman historian Tacitus had stated. Past Birmingham, people still wore clogs, didn't they?

Disregarded by the rest of the country, "the pool of life" – as Jung had tagged it – had bubbled in its isolation and built-in resilience. "A good cry and a good laugh were never far apart,"[12] playwright Carla Lane wrote of her home city. What else can you say about a place where, beneath a hoarding inquiring, "What would you do if Jesus came to Liverpool?" a hand had taken the trouble to scrawl "Move St John to inside right."[13] Liverpool spawned a crop of that strain of comedians who relied on cheeky forthrightness to get laughs and conveyed the feeling that everyone knew him and he them, although most were compelled to go south for national acclaim.

More buffoons than other types of artists emerged from the city, but festering in the streets to the immediate east of the unfinished Anglican cathedral was a Scouse bohemia teeming with poets, painters and the like eking out a living or feeding off college grants in studio flats within crumbling back-to-back Victorian town-houses with peeling pillars, off-white window ledges thick with pigeon droppings, thunderous door-knockers and rubbish clogging behind railings. One day, the adult George Harrison would be asked if Liverpool was like New York's vibrant beatnik district, Greenwich Village. "No," he replied, considering the area as a whole. "It's more like the Bowery."[14]

From the perspective of poky Arnold Grove, you could appreciate the comparison with the Big Apple's most run-down corner. For the Harrisons, things could only get better, and during the family's 18th year on the council housing list they did. Assisted partly by the Luftwaffe, an urban renewal programme was under way, which was evidenced by the erection of churches like dental surgeries and the box-like dwellings that spread across slum overspill estates like that in Speke, where the Harrisons moved when George was six.

25 Upton Green was unquestionably an improvement, with a hallway, bathroom and extra bedroom. The prospect of a refrigerator replacing the meat safe did not seem as far fetched here as it had in Wavertree. Not so remote, either, were such luxuries as a washing machine and a telephone. However, while Our Kid, in his excitement, "just ran round and 'round it all"[15] that first day, his mum soon missed the cosier domesticity of Arnold Grove. She felt uncomfortable in the terrace circling the roundabout of scrappy grass where the forlorn side road came to its dead end. Some neighbours glared with gormless menace as the newcomers unloaded their furniture. Louise blamed their brats for the nocturnal theft of shrubs she planted in the small front garden. Such was the consequence, she concluded, of the council mixing "the good and the bad families together, hoping the good would lift the rest".[10]

Thrust to the city's outskirts, the Harrisons' home was in the middle of what had once been fields but was now a sprawling peninsula of residential streets built by the book for those who had no choice. To the south and west, Liverpool airport droned by the windswept mudbanks of the river, while the A561 ran along the northern border, lined with belching chimneys. Chemical waste fouled the air and waterways. Harold Harrison had to pass through this industrial zone to reach Speke Bus Depot.

Harold's youngest sons were prevented from enrolling at Alderwood Junior School, directly opposite Upton Green, because its roll was full. Instead, Peter and George were bussed five miles back towards Wavertree to Herondale Road, where stood Dovedale Church of England Primary, the only school with vacant desks, when the gaberdine-raincoated and short-trousered brothers' formal education began.

Under the unimaginative regime of chanted multiplication tables and spelling tests, George made steady progress. To his father's fury, he was once caned for quite a minor misdemeanour, but headmaster Robert "Pop" Evans and his teachers had to struggle on termly reports to write anything that made Harrison Minor remotely extraordinary. He was sound enough in most subjects, his retentive memory and methodical tenacity facilitating a mature and sometimes encyclopaedic understanding of people and places, interactions and outcomes. As well as a solid grasp of mathematics, there were also indications of a flair for art and creative writing, although he was loath to take literary risks for fear of getting into trouble. For the same reason, he was rather a shrinking violet when obliged to approach the teacher's desk with his exercise books. However, George was talkative enough with his playground pals and needed little coaxing to participate – and even to sing solo – in class assemblies.

A younger child asserting himself, George also loved to entertain at home. Louise remembered her husband giving him glove puppets on the Christmas before his tenth birthday and how, "from that day on, whenever we had visitors, he always insisted on giving a little show kneeling behind the settee. George was always full of fun when he was a child. He never caused any big trouble, and even the neighbours liked him a lot, which is unusual with a little boy."[15]

A different George had cringed with embarrassment when, after delivering him for his first day at school, Louise had lingered outside with the other mothers. The next morning, he implored her to let him and Peter walk the mile from Arnold Grove to school unescorted. Even at five, he resented any personal intrusion that her gossiping at the gate with other parents might precipitate.

Yet another George would later turn his back on the Speke estate to roam the farmland, woods and marshes of the Cheshire plain to the east on foot or bicycle: "There's a part of me which likes to keep quiet, and I do prefer wide, open, quiet spaces to traffic jams."[15]

He endured plenty of those after he started at Liverpool Institute High School For Boys in September 1954. Self-conscious in the regulation uniform of black bomber shoes, grey flannels, blazer, white shirt and tie, the first-former boarded the number 86 bus to school from the stop on Speke Boulevard for a trek which, in the morning rush hour, took just under an hour to reach the dropping-off point in Mount Street, within earshot of the cathedral bells. A compensation for living so far away from the school was that he was generally able to secure a seat before the vehicle filled to standing room only. He quickly came to detest this cramped, jolting commuting, with its banal chit-chat, body pressure and "some old man breathing down your neck".[16] For the return journey, he discovered that other pupils from Speke preferred to walk through the bustling city centre to catch the bus home from the Pier Head terminus.

From the outset, the long journey to and from the Institute dogged George's involvement in the extra-mural activities that the school offered. To attend a swimming gala at the usual venue in Walton meant hanging about for hours after the 4pm dismissal. Unless they were held during the lunch break, attending meetings of the many worthy societies devoted to chess, modelling, archaeology *et al* meant arriving back at Upton Green in the middle of the evening, ravenous, tired and with homework to do. That Peter's mixed secondary modern was only a ten-minute dawdle from home made up for any intellectual inferiority he may have felt through Our Kid going to a grammar school. Needless to say, the family's limited finances forbade a week in Ireland with the Canoeing Club and school trips further abroad.

Because his participation was so restricted, George nurtured a resentment of the Institute's hearty clubbism, with its slide shows, "eminent speakers" and patronage by masters who either dressed down in cardigans or, to drill those daft enough to enlist in the Combined Cadet Force, donned dung-coloured regimentals. Yet, at a time when many English grammars were a cross between daytime borstals and homosexual dating bureaux, the Liverpool Institute wasn't too bad, although you might not have thought so at first glance. Old enough for Dickens to have given readings there, the building behind the imposing Greek façade was in poor repair, despite having escaped major damage by enemy action. An ink-welled desk mutilated with the initials of comedian Arthur Askey was still in general use 40 years after he had collected his leaving certificate.

The Institute was adjoined by a sister school, the Dance and

Drama Academy and the grimy looking Art College. Perhaps its proximity to these establishments and the city's Bohemian oasis bestowed upon it an attitude less shrouded in the draconian affectations and futile rigmarole prevalent in newer Merseyside grammars such as the Collegiate or Quarry Bank over in Calderstones, nicknamed "the Police State". Nevertheless, academic streaming was in full force and, rather than a cry of "Quiet!", the Latin "*Cave!*" would hush a noisy classroom when a gowned master was sighted. Religious education was of the Old Testament persuasion and, technically, the tone-deaf could get by in music lessons by adhering to quasi-mathematical rules of harmony. Prefects were permitted to cuff recalcitrants for such ghastly crimes as entering the school via its main door. Other than masters, that privilege was reserved for sixth formers, a select number of whom were allowed to attend life classes next door and watch "art" movies under the aegis of the Film Society. Moreover, an Institute pupil wasn't automatically threatened with expulsion for talking to a girl.

The headmaster in George's day was Jack Edwards, a round-faced Oxbridge type who stared appraisingly at whoever spoke to him. "In his own work," so it was written, "only excellence satisfied him. The second rate wasn't good enough."[17] Though his school cradled an impressive number of university graduates, the perfectionist Mr Edwards did not neglect – so his valediction in the Institute magazine attested – "its traditional quota of competent, hard-working but less brilliant boys, as well as some slower people. Mr Edwards kept a watchful eye on all three groups and, from time to time, he was minatory as seemed appropriate."[17]

With more than 1,000 "Liobians", as pupils were dubbed, under his wing, Edwards was "minatory" more often than his anonymous hagiographer implied. He was, however, amused despite himself when Ivan Vaughan, a gifted classical scholar, spent a morning impersonating a new boy at Quarry Bank. Other eccentric japes were also excused, including Vaughan's appearance at the Institute with his shoes painted yellow.

George Harrison was little more to the headmaster than a name in a register. As a second former, George was remembered by another master as "a very quiet if not even introverted little boy who would sit in the furthest corner and not even look up. I'm not saying he was unintelligent, but Harrison hardly ever spoke."[18] In the previous year, George had settled down almost eagerly to schoolwork, proud to be the brainiest member of the family. Two terms transformed him into a capable but uninvolved student, unblinking in the monotony of, say, geography teacher "Frankie" Boote's chalky exposition of Latvia's inner waterways.

Next came homework copied shakily off someone else on the bus, orders to spit his chewing gum into the classroom litter bin, even more passive disinterest in school and a report that concluded that he "seeks only to amuse himself".[10] The signature on the chit supposedly confirming that his parents had received the report was forged by the obliging mother of Arthur Kelly, a friend in the same class. As well as Arthur and, intermittently, a bespectacled boy named Charlie Shaw, George's circle of Institute ne'er-do-wells included Tony Workman, who'd tried to pick a fight with him on first acquaintance. With such allies in delinquency, George "found the wit, not the brain"[19] to cheek even the head boy, "Pontifical Pete" Sissons – later a well-known television broadcaster[20] – during Sissons' harassed efforts to enforce school rules in lunch queue and quadrangle.

Workman, Kelly and Harrison became known as truants, sharers of smutty stories and initiates of a caste who'd graduated from the innocence of tooth-rotting Spangles to the lung-corroding evil of Woodbines. Not standing when he could lean, that Harrison boy, with his bad attitude, "would not have wanted to be a prefect" in the understated opinion of Jack Sweeney, head of modern languages, "because he was against everything. I think George may have felt lost in the academic environment."[21]

His extra-curricular pursuits had little bearing on what he was meant to be learning at the Institute. To afford them, he'd taken on a Saturday morning delivery round for Quirk's, a local butcher. For George, the longest lasting of his diverse hobbies was motor racing. Attracted by a poster advertising the 1955 Grand Prix at the Aintree circuit, he journeyed by bus and internal railway almost twice as far as school to see the great Argentinean driver Fangio and his team-mate Stirling Moss dominate the event. Soon, he would be as ever present at Aintree as other boys were at Anfield: "I had a box camera and went 'round taking pictures of all the cars. If I could find an address, I wrote away to the car factories, and somewhere at home I've got pictures of all the old Vanwalls, Connaughts and BRMs."[22] With help from his father and eldest brother, driving was second nature to George and Peter long before they were officially entitled to take a car on the public highway.

George's enthusiasm also extended to motorcycle scrambles, and as far as he ever had a boyhood sports hero, it was Geoff Duke, perhaps the best professional biker of the 1950s. If short of cash, George would watch the kick-starting panorama from the railway embankment adjacent to the race course with a packed lunch at his side.

In most of his pastimes, he was a spectator rather than a doer. Throughout the 1950s, he and a million other children would queue for Saturday-morning cinema sessions and a weekly diet of Walt Disney, cowboys and injuns and swashbuckling "historical" epics. Though he was never as keen on films as he was on racing, "It was just nice to get out of the house and go somewhere where there were all nice golden lights and goldfish swimming in the foyer."[23] It was always fun there – the convulsions of laughter at the same joke; telling yourself that they're only acting in the sad bit; the lump in the throat giving way to giggles at mawkishness; the Pearl & Dean commercials; the involuntary dip into the rustling packet of Murray Mints or popcorn; the choc-ice; the Kia-Ora; and the muted buzz as the house-lights dimmed before the main feature.

When truanting, George's gang would frequently seek refuge at the Jacey Cinema in Clayton Square. They were particularly fond of the more escapist horror flicks about outer space "things". This period also saw the apotheosis of Hollywood's film noir and its Ealing Studios antithesis of hello-hello-hello policemen, monocled cads, kilted Scotsmen and happy endings. "I liked the way things looked in those 1940s films," said George, "when the streets weren't crowded and the chemist shops had nice signs over them."[24]

In a haze as rosy, he would hark back also to the time "when I used to go to the Liverpool Empire. It used to be ninepence up in the back upstairs, and I'd watch all the variety shows – whatever came in there."[25] The Harrisons went regularly to the city's most ornate theatre, whether to Christmas pantomimes or to those presentations that marked the passing of the music hall. To perform at the Empire was nearly as high an aspiration as Drury Lane for any up-and-coming juggler, ventriloquist and feathered dancing girl. There, too, onlookers like the Harrisons could shut off – however fleetingly – the nastier realities of post-war economies – the repellent housing estates where they'd been put, the dingy jobs they had to do. George could forget about school in the reverie of a magician sawing his buxom assistant in half and Max Miller telling the one about his wife and the nudist come to use the telephone.

It was called "music hall" because each artist was expected to make use of the pit orchestra, if only for a rumble of timpani as a rabbit was produced from a top hat. Usually the bill would contain an entirely musical act – a singer, more often than not. In those days, you'd be less likely to be serenaded with 'Danny Boy' or 'The Road To Mandalay' than 'How Much Is That Doggie In The Window?', 'Mambo Italiano' or something else from the newly established *New Musical Express* record and sheet-music sales charts.

"That was my contact with the musical or entertainment world," said George of the Empire, "because it was before the days of TV – *before* we had TV – and the only other thing was the radio."[25] Most of the music heard on the BBC's three national radio services before about 1955 was directed at the over 30s. Otherwise, there was *Children's Favourites* – record requests aired by "Uncle Mac" – on the Light Programme. For the adolescent listener, there was *Quite Contrary*, a show built around the light operatic style of Ronnie Hilton, a former apprentice engineer form Leeds, who, for want of anyone better, was cited by the *NME* as the most popular British vocalist of 1955.

Disturbing Uncle Mac's red-nosed reindeers and Davy Crocketts as that year drew to its close was a disc by Bill Haley And The Comets, a North American dance band. Like all but the most serious-minded children of the 1950s, Peter and George Harrison were superficially thrilled by the metronomic clamour of 'Rock Around The Clock'. A more profound impression was created by Elvis Presley's hillbilly-blues shout-singing that the USA only dared televise from the waist up. Presley was not married and paunchy like Haley, but, as the first photograph of him published in Britain[26] testified, a hoodlum type whose brilliantined but girly cockade was offset by sideburns down to his earlobes. Garbed in outrageous "cat" clothes – pink socks, hip-hugging slacks, checked shirt and box jacket – this "unspeakably untalented and vulgar young entertainer" (as a US television guide described him) made adult flesh creep. Unlike Bill Haley, he made no apologies for his on-stage frolics, which involved hip-swivelling, doing the splits and rolling about as if he had a wasp in his pants.

How could he miss? "At school, there was all that thing about Elvis," George enthused. "You never wanted to go to school; you wanted to go out and play or something. So when some record comes along like Elvis' 'Heartbreak Hotel' and you had this little bit of plastic... It was so amazing. Now, it's hard to realise that there are kids like I was, where the only thing in their lives is to get home and play their favourite record."[27]

It went without saying that George's growing record collection did not conform with Institute dictates of what was "good" music. Infinitely less meaningful to him than the heart-stopping second guitar break of 'Hound Dog' was the Music Club's "appreciation" of Brahms' *German Requiem*, its outings to hear the Liverpool Philharmonic play Beethoven and, for light relief, a master choosing *Desert Island Discs*, like real celebrities did on the Home Service. In Upton Green, "classical music" meant string-laden Muzak sometimes oozing from the Light Programme by the orchestras of Mantovani or Geraldo: pruned-down arrangements of Handel's 'Largo', 'Tales Of Hoffman' and the *Lone Ranger* theme.

Even wilder than Presley was shrieking black Little Richard in billowing drapes, beating hell out of a concert grand in the movie *The Girl Can't Help It*, which arrived in Liverpool in 1957. Every week seemed to bring another American rock 'n' roll wildman into the British hit parade – Chuck Berry, with his crotch-level electric guitar; Jerry Lee Lewis, a piano-pumping fireball from Louisiana; crippled Gene Vincent, "the Screaming End"... Britain hung onto the new craze's coat-tails with strict-tempo supremo Victor Sylvester's sanitised "rock 'n' roll" sequence, and certain jazz musicians forming contingent groups in the Haley image. More attractive was 'Sweet Old-Fashioned Boy' by Terry-Thomas Esq and his Rock 'n' Roll Rotters, notable for the distinguished character actor's haw-haw interjections of "dig those crazy sounds, Daddio", "see you later, *alma mater*", *ad nauseum*. Liverpool was represented by Clinton Ford's rocked-up 'Nellie Dean'. As pathetic in its way was the Best Guitarist category in a *Melody Maker* popularity poll being won by Tommy Steele, England's answer to Elvis, who was "just as talented or just as revolting, according to the way you feel".[28]

Thus spake *Everybody's Weekly* in an article entitled, "Are we turning our children into little Americans?" Still a principal port of embarkation for the Americas, Liverpool was more prone to such a metamorphosis than other cities. Many teenagers within the Merseyside hinterland knew transatlantic seamen – "Cunard Yanks" – who would import Davy Crockett caps, otherwise unobtainable records, checked cowboy shirts and other treasures long before they filtered even to London. George's source was Arthur Kelly's sister, Barbara, whose fiancé, Red Bentley, was a ship's engineer.

For a while, a crew-cut like Red's bristled on George's scalp, but eventually he adopted a closer-to-home look. On desolate estates like his and down in the docklands, pedestrians would cross streets to avoid fearsome clusters of hybrid Mississippi riverboat card sharps and Edwardian rakes out for more than boyish mischief. The first Teddy Boy murder had taken place in 1954. Less overtly violent was the secretive slitting of cinema seats with flick-knives while young women jived in gingham to the musical interludes in Presley's movies. Thanks in part to Elvis, the word "teenager" had been coined by the media to denote all 'twixt twelve and 20 who were deciding whether or not to grow up. However, although teenagers had become a separate target for advertising since the war, a girl still wore socks well into her teens, and a sure sigh of growing up was when she pulled on nylon stockings held up with a suspender belt.

At the Liverpool Institute, boys were still supposed to dress like little men, men like English master Alfred J "Cissy" Smith, very smooth in his 1950s "quiet" style of dark business suit with baggy trousers. Mr Smith's white hair was thin, matted and actually quite long at the back, which is why it was odd that he should poke fun at Harrison of the Fourth's lavishly whorled Teddy Boy quiff. Actually quite short at the back – cut in a "Boston" – George's oiled coiffure was not the sole butt of teachers' sarcasm. Just short of openly flaunting school rules, he'd customised his uniform to seedy-flash Ted-cat standards. He seemed top-heavy on thin legs that, from a distance, gave the illusion that they'd been dipped in ink.

His father had eventually seen the funny side of George's enterprise in drainpiping a pair of new flannels on Louise's sewing machine. For a blazer, he'd dyed one of his eldest brother's cast-off box jackets black, although to his glee the check pattern was still discernible. From Harold, too, came a custard-yellow waistcoat that alternated with a black double-breasted one with drape lapels. With his Quirk money, George bought a white shirt, as ordained, but it was pleated down the front and was stitched with black embroidery. On his feet were winkle-pickers of dark-blue suede and, costing nine shillings and sixpence ($47^1/_2$ pence), fluorescent socks with a rock 'n' roll motif.

In all his finery and with his lips curled in an Elvis half-sneer, he'd slouch last into class. Oblivious to the jibes of both wrinkled senior master and trainee on teaching practice, he lounged in the back row, dumbly insolent and indifferent to logarithms and the Diet of Worms. In reciprocation, he was ignored by most teachers now, as long as he didn't disturb other pupils. Relieved when he was absent, they were as anxious for him to leave the Institute as he was. About the only master to warm to Harrison was Stanley Reid, head of Art. Significantly, art was the only subject in which George did not fail among the few GCE "O"-level examinations he was considered able to sit.

Academically, George may have coped better with the comprehensive system's concept of "education for all", then so new that schools of this ilk were comparatively unknown north of Birmingham. Combining elements of both grammar and secondary modern, these skirted around the Eleven Plus and, theoretically, enabled children to follow what best suited their inclinations and abilities as they developed. So open-minded was the outlook in some comprehensives that skiffle – a British offshoot of rock 'n' roll – was seen not as a plague but as a more effective means of arousing adolescent interest in music than Brahms and his *German Requiem*.

Although it was derived from the rent parties, speakeasies and dustbowl jug bands of the American Depression, skiffle had never gripped the imagination of young America. Rockabilly, its closest American equivalent in primeval rowdiness, employed conventional rather than home-made instruments. While retaining a thimbled washboard for percussion, even those British skiffle outfits that made the hit parade tended to abandon the makeshift, too, thereby adulterating the form for purists, who were still divided over the policy of London's Chris Barber Jazz Band, in which an ex-serviceman named Tony Donegan had been allowed to sing a couple of blues-tinged American folk songs

With his very stage name lifted from that of Lonnie Johnson, a black blues singer, "Lonnie" Donegan was, more than Tommy Steele, a British "answer" to Elvis in his vivacious processing of black music for a white audience. Sung in an energetic whine far removed from the gentle plumminess of other British pop stars, his first hit, 'Rock Island Line', was from the repertoire of walking musical archive Huddie "Leadbelly" Ledbetter. As exemplified in the titles of later chart strikes such as 'My Dixie Darling' and 'Battle Of New Orleans', Donegan delved deeper into Americana to embrace also bluegrass, spirituals, Cajun and even Appalachian music, which in its minimal melodic variation was the formal opposite of jazz. Backed by his Skiffle Group, Lonnie bossed the form throughout its 1957 prime as he brought a vigorous alien idiom and transmuted it into acceptability onto an impoverished and derivative UK pop scene.

George Harrison had been aware of pop since his infancy but, Elvis apart, had had no real allegiance to any specific star (although particular records, like Hoagy Carmichael's 'Hong Kong Blues', twisted his heartstrings now and then), but "Lonnie and skiffle seemed made for me."[29] Like punk after it, anyone who'd mastered basic techniques could have a go: "It was easy music to play, if you knew two or three chords, and you'd have a tea chest as a bass and a washboard, and you were away... [sings] 'Oh, the Rock Island Line is a mighty good road...'"[29]

The idea was to find an individual style, even with well-known material. Hence Dickie Bishop and his Sidekicks' 'Cumberland Gap' deviated from that of Donegan and his Skiffle Group in its substitution of slashing acoustic guitar with a jigging fiddle. Most such outfits were formed for the benefit of performers rather than audience, but nationwide there were thousands of skifflers thrumming tea-chest-and-broom-handle basses, tapping washboards, singing through nostrils, rasping comb-and-paper, clanking dustbin-lid cymbals and thrashing the E chord on finger-lacerating guitars for all they were worth.

Once the guitar had been associated mainly with Latinate heel-clattering, but now it was what Elvis and Lonnie played. In April 1957, *The Daily Mirror* cracked "Springtime Is Stringtime" as 'Cumberland Gap' became Donegan's first Number One and a London musical instrument firm with 2,000 unfilled orders for guitars indented a West German manufacturer for a further 6,000 One found its way (via several owners) to the hands of Peter Harrison for the knockdown price of five shillings (25p). "Some of the lads," believed leading guitar tutor Ivor Mairants, "are buying them just to hang on their shoulders."[30] Groups often had an embarrassment of guitarists, most of them just strumming chords, but this rudimentary rhythmic impetus could be overlaid by a "lead" guitarist, sometimes crudely amplified, plucking obligatos and solos.

There also evolved vague regional shades of skiffle. Birmingham leaned towards jazz, while in the West Country groups like The Avon Cities Skiffle and Salisbury's Satellites – led by a youth who would assume the stage name "Dave Dee" – betrayed roots in Morris dance bands in their respective uses of mandolin and piano accordion.

Merseyside, meanwhile, had more of a country-and-western bias, which was understandable, because within the area abounded more such artists than anywhere outside Nashville. On any given weekend, you could guarantee that plenty of the 300-odd venues affiliated to the Liverpool Social Clubs Association had booked The Dusty Road Ramblers, The Hillsiders, The Ranchers or any other band from a legion of outfits also playing the kinda music folk like a-tappin' their boot-leather to. Notable among young skifflers favouring a C&W

approach were The Red Mountain Boys, who adapted the "hard" style of the legendary Hank Williams. From Oak Hill Park, sporting cowboy suits, The Texan Skiffle Group acquired local eminence by winning a Butlin's Holiday Camp contest. A Wild West influence was also felt by The James Boys, featuring Edward "Kingsize" Taylor, a singing guitarist whose powerful build and knockout punch was a reassuring asset at more unrefined engagements.

The city's thriving folk tradition left its mark, too, as skiffle groups began to plunder its motherlode of sea shanties, like 'The Leaving Of Liverpool' and 'Maggie May'. From the ashes of The Rivington Ramblers rose The Gin Mill Skiffle Group, which was later to mutate into The Spinners, a professional folk quartet for almost 30 years.

Some of the chaps that George knew at school had been bitten as hard as he by the skiffle bug. Two older lads with guitars, Don Andrew and Colin Manley, had their own group, The Viscounts. With "Ive the Jive, the Ace on the Bass" painted on his tea chest, even madcap Ivan Vaughan was among the mutable pool of players that made up The Quarry Men, formed by his friends at Quarry Bank. They were a cut above a lot of groups, in that they had a drummer with a full kit.

While appearing casually knowledgeable, George drank in accounts of his contemporaries' progress. Fired by envy, he'd turned over an idea of starting a skiffle group with Peter. As his brother had a guitar, George wondered aloud about the humble washboard while trailing along with Arthur Kelly and his grandmother on a shopping expedition in the city centre. Passing through Cazneau Market, Arthur's soft-hearted grandma paused at a hardware stall to hand over a threepenny bit for George Harrison's first musical instrument.

This kind gesture was much appreciated, until his mastery of the washboard surpassed that of Peter's with a guitar now in the evening of its life. George wished that he had a guitar and expressed his longing by tracing its shape in the condensed vapour on windows and in illicit doodlings at school. Through overspending on his provocative clothes, George had nothing saved up when someone at the Institute offered him a second-hand guitar with f-holes and a movable bridge for half its cost price of £5.

His mother came to the rescue with the required cash transfusion, and he brought home a battered, stringless model with a damaged neck. Trying to mend it, he removed a connecting screw that he then failed to re-insert. Dismayed, he thrust the disjoined instrument into a cupboard, hoping that Louise would forget what had been rather a Jack-and-the-Beanstalk episode. For nearly three months, the guitar gathered dust in a darkness broken only when George opened the door to peer wistfully at it. Finally, he begged Peter, now an apprentice welder, to see if it could be fixed.

George then made two depressing discoveries. Firstly, the repaired guitar – ill made, anyway – could only be restrung so high above the fretboard that holding down a barre chord was painful and single-note runs were impossible on high frets. Secondly, like the rest of the family, George was no natural musician. He was, however, handsomely endowed with a capacity to try, try again. Boosted by his mother's jocund encouragement, he laboured over his guitar late into the evening, to the detriment of even that modicum of homework necessary to avert a detention the next day. Positioning yet-uncalloused fingers on the taut strings, he'd pore over 'When The Saints Come Marching In' (sic), 'Simple Blues For Guitar', 'Skiffle Rhythms' and other exercises prescribed in *Play In A Day*, a tutor book devised by Bert Weedon, guitarist with Cyril Stapleton's BBC Show Band and on Tommy Steele's records.

After commendable effort, George moved on to a more advanced manual. His fingertips hardened with daily practice, and it occurred to him – and Louise, egging him on over the ironing – that he'd become a better guitarist than Peter. He might even be not that far behind Colin Manley and Don Andrew, or even Johnny "Guitar" Byrne of The Texan Skiffle Group, whom he'd seen in action at a dance in Garston, a grim Liverpool suburb a couple of bus stops from Speke. Both George and his mother saw that the next step was the purchase of a worthier instrument. Between them, they scraped up enough for an electric model from Hessy's, a central Liverpool music shop that boasted "our easy terms are easier". Compared to his first guitar, George's new £30 Hofner Futurama cutaway was as a fountain pen to a stub of pencil.

From a kit advertised in *Melody Maker*, it was feasible to solder together an amplifier "with a ten-watt punch" that was transportable in a school satchel. Neither was it laughable for a skiffle group warily magnifying its volume to wire guitars into the workings of a record player. George fed his semi-solid Hofner through an amplifier of unspecifiable make mounted on an unpainted chipboard speaker cabinet when the skiffle outfit he'd dreamed of leading made its first public appearance.

He, Arthur Kelly and Peter were the guitarists, with the remaining personnel being two other lads on mouth organ and an inaudible tea-chest bass decorated with wallpaper gnomes. Rehearsals took place either in a Harrison bedroom or back at Arthur's in Wavertree, where Mrs Kelly served percolated coffee, a rare treat to the Speke contingent. They called themselves The Rebels, a name duplicated by other groups throughout the country, including one in South Wales containing future political leader Neil Kinnock and another that recorded for Parlophone, a subsidiary of EMI, one of London's four major record labels.

George's Rebels had no such aspirations, but with two songs at their command they began at the bottom by procuring an audition at a British Legion club on Dam Wood Road, a few hundred yards from Upton Green. On that night of nights, the quintet assembled at number 25. In honour of the occasion, the word "Rebels" had been daubed in red across the front of the tea chest. At the moment of departure, George advised that they sneak from the house, crouching with their instruments behind the hedge before dashing down the road one after another. In case their debut was a flop, he wanted the least possible number of people to know about it.

At the Legion Hall, a surprise awaited them: the booked act hadn't materialised. Clutching at straws, the social secretary bundled The Rebels on stage and hoped for the best. Courageously, they stretched out their limited repertoire for the whole evening, the bass player's fingers bleeding by the finish. Cheered for their youthful nerve, The Rebels tumbled through the Harrisons' front door afterwards, wild with excitement, each recounting the eventful engagement at the top of his voice and flourishing the ten-shilling note he'd been given from the grateful club's petty cash.

The first time was the only time, however, and The Rebels didn't spoil the greatest night any of them could ever remember with a repeat performance. Besides, Peter was fed up with the guitar, and Arthur's parents didn't want him to think of skiffle as a career. Even George conceded that it had lost its flavour on the bedpost overnight. Among the nails in its coffin was growing approval by grown-ups. "Never before have so many young people made their own music,"[31] chortled one aged television pundit on the BBC's *Six-Five Special* magazine programme, in which self-improving features on mountaineering, ornithology *et al* were slotted in between the pop items.

A hastily assembled skiffle group at Scott Base went to town on 'My Bonnie Lies Over The Ocean' to greet Dr Vivian Fuchs after his historic trans-Antarctic trek in 1958. With this *Boys Own Paper* incident as the spur, Sunday schools and youth clubs saw skiffle as a potent medium for instilling the Lord's Holy Word into teenagers. However, bored silly by ping-pong, "Brain Trusts" and now abominations like a Camberwell vicar's "Skiffle Mass", formerly tractable adolescents had taken to either loafing about the streets or frequenting coffee bars that, although thickest in the city centres, had penetrated even the furthest-flung suburbs.

Even Donegan, the genre's figurehead, had hacked "Skiffle" from the name of his Group, and in the teeth of much criticism was broadening his appeal with 'Knees Up Mother Brown' and other music-hall gems, scoring his third Number One with an adaptation of the Liverpool folk ditty 'My Old Man's A Fireman On The Elder-Dempster Line'. Lonnie Donegan and his Group also included a comedy routine in their act when they topped a variety bill at the Empire. Yet, if he did nothing else, Donegan made skiffle homogenously British by fusing black rhythms with pub singalong and folk music, the ripples of which spread across decades of British pop.

At the end of skiffle's brief but furious reign, some of its exponents turned to traditional jazz. On Merseyside, however, there was a greater tendency to backslide via amplification to classic rock and an increasingly more American Top 20. "I think a lot of people dropped the idea of being musicians," commented an ex-Rebel, "but the ones who didn't, like the washboard players, progressed into snare drums, and the tea-chest players bought bass guitars."[25] To reflect their new leanings, groups re-emerged with new handles – The James Boys, for example, were now Kingsize Taylor And The Dominoes and Gerry Marsden's Skiffle Group evolved into Gerry And The Pacemakers.

The remnants of The Texan Skiffle Group wasted no time in relaunching themselves as just The Texans, and auditions for new members had been held at leader Alan Caldwell's home. In this tidy Victorian house in West Oakhill Park, Caldwell's parents, Ernie and Violet, backed his activities with a zest that even Louise Harrison may have thought excessive. Alan's group was, therefore, welcome to rehearse there at all hours, despite moans from the neighbours.

When George Harrison came to try for The Texans, he was already a familiar figure to the Caldwells. After his first girlfriend, Ruth Morrison, moved to Birmingham with her family, he had paired off with Alan's sister, Iris. This became a foursome when Arthur Kelly dated her best friend. Violet Caldwell apparently nicknamed the two boys "Arthur and Martha".

It was her duty to tell 14-year-old Martha that, for all his experience as a Rebel, he was too young to quit school and go professional, as The Texans intended to do at the earliest opportunity. This had been a foregone conclusion for her son and Johnny Byrne, no matter how well George played and sang the ballad 'Wedding Bells' – Gene Vincent's 1956 arrangement – for them. Another disappointed hopeful was Graham Bonnet, a singer destined for modest fame ten years later as a member of The Marbles and then Ritchie Blackmore's Rainbow.

George was less concerned with The Texans' impression of him than with Jack Edwards' testimonial, which each leaver received as he filed out on his last day at the Institute. An inkling of what George's would say was detectable in Edwards' acidic remark that he'd "made no contribution to school life". Sure enough, George read on the bus home that the headmaster "cannot tell you what his work is like because he hasn't done any". A play that captured George's imagination later was David Halliwell's *Little Malcolm And His Struggle Against The Eunuchs*, in which an expelled student gets his own back on the headmaster.

A postscript to George's bursting free of the Institute was his return in September to repeat the "O"-level year, so some mortified teachers assumed. Only an hour in class, however, convinced him that slacking until the following summer among boys a year his junior was an uninviting prospect that would give him no more time to find an opening as a musician than if he followed his father's advice to get proper work.

The War Office, anxious about the stalemate in North Korea, had sent for Harold Harrison junior. Although Harold completed his National Service without complaint, the regular army figured nowhere in his unqualified youngest brother's vocational stock-taking. Our Kid was, nevertheless, contemplating travel of some kind, perusing job opportunities in Australia, Malta and Canada. After all, sister Louise had emigrated, following her marriage in 1954 to an American named Caldwell. Waiting, like Mr Micawber, for something to turn up, George stayed where he was as month succeeded jobless month, playing for time, in every sense of the phrase, until, to placate his displeased father, he submitted half-heartedly to a written test for eligibility to work for the Liverpool Corporation. Botching this, he then underwent a humiliating interview at the Youth Employment Centre.

The YEC sent him to Blackler's, a largish department store opposite Lime Street Station, where there was a vacancy for a window dresser. While George was sauntering over there, however, it went to someone quicker off the mark. It was probably just as well as, in order to publicly adorn dummies in sober clothing, you have to dress soberly yourself. Nonetheless, he was found a job under Mr Peet, Blackler's maintenance supervisor, as a trainee electrician. Dusting strip-lights with a paintbrush wasn't exactly showbusiness, but it would do for now. Although George had failed at the Institute, his Dad was delighted at his respectable overalled apprenticeship. In George's stocking that Christmas was a magnificent set of electrical screwdrivers. With young Harold a mechanic, Peter a welder and George an electrician, Mr Harrison's daydreaming ran to a family business – a garage, maybe.

Window-gazing in Blackler's, George realised how far removed his own notion of self-advancement was to one who'd borne the brunt of the Depression. Rigging up Santa's Grotto in December or laying cables in the firm's Bootle warehouse had been among few highlights of a workaday routine as dull as school. Already he'd absorbed habits of his idler co-workers, stopping the service lift between floors for a quiet smoke or enjoying rounds of darts on a board hung in the basement. During an under-age drinking session one lunchtime, he showed the others what a hell of a fellow he was by managing – so he bragged later – to hold down two hamburgers, three rum and blackcurrants and 14 pints of ale.

2 Carl Harrison

The audition with Alan Caldwell's Texans hadn't been George's only attempt to "be in a band, as opposed to having a job".[32] Along Hayman's Green, a leafy thoroughfare in West Derby Village, was the Lowlands, a skiffle club in uncertain transition, where he'd scraped acquaintance with some lads more his own age who were forming a group. One of its guitarists, Ken Brown, was committed enough to invest in a Hofner and a new ten-watt amplifier. He and George became the instrumental backbone of The Les Stewart Quartet, with Les taking most vocals and hacking a third guitar. General factotum – mainly percussion – was his friend Geoff Skinner. With a tuneful if rather bland voice, George came to the fore to sing only for a prescribed time, as Lonnie used to with Chris Barber.

Regular bookings at the Lowlands seemed to be the fullest extent of the Stewart combo's ambitions. Therefore, while religiously attending rehearsals, George had no conscience about playing with other musicians whose outlook might prove more attractive. Around the time that his school career began its decline, he'd discovered that another boy who boarded the number 86 at Speke also had a guitar. This Paul McCartney was in the year above George, but could exculpate himself from criticism of hob-nobbing with a younger pupil as Mrs Harrison had once met him on the bus and had lent him the money to pay his forgotten bus fare. From then on, Paul felt obliged to be civil to her son George.

Because of the academic gulf between co-operative pupil and form captain McCartney in the A stream and C-stream hardcase Harrison, Institute masters were surprised later that the two even knew each other, although Frankie Boote had expressed his disapproval of Paul's interest in skiffle. Unheeding, Paul had seen Donegan at the Empire and begged his father to buy him a guitar.

A cotton salesman by trade, Jim McCartney had taken his place on many a local palais bandstand during the 1920s with his own Jim Mac Jazz Band. After family commitments and the war effectively put paid to his charlestons and square tangos, he relived the old days in anecdote and seated at the upright piano in his house on Western Avenue, to the west of Speke estate. Of Jim's two sons, dark-haired Paul, the eldest, was the more fascinated listener. Sensibly, neither Jim nor his wife goaded the boys to formalise their innate musical strengths.

When Paul was 13, the family moved to Forthlin Road on the more up-market council estate of Allerton, which bordered on the mock-Tudor colonies, golf courses and boating lakes of Woolton, a village-like suburb that aligned itself more with Lancashire than Merseyside. After only a year in the new semi-detached, Mrs McCartney died suddenly. Various aunts and neighbours rallied around to help Jim cope with housework and what remained of his sons' childhood.

Jim was glad enough to give a few pointers when Paul took up the guitar. Skiffle, even jazz, was harmless, as long as it didn't interfere with school. Jim, like Arthur Kelly's parents, understood that, unless you'd been born into showbusiness, it was unwise to see it as a viable career. This rock 'n' roll was all very well, but it wouldn't last, any more than previous crazes, like the Jitterbug or the Creep. Presley, Vincent, Donegan – they'd jumped the gun, because, by Jim McCartney's book, popular musicians were generally well into their 30s before achieving worthwhile recognition after servitude in an established band who played the good old ones, such as the silent-movie classics 'Charmaine' and 'Ramona'. His son would recall that "My dad gave us some of the worst advice ever. 'It's all right on the side,' he'd say, 'but, Paul, it will never last.'" "Remember," added George, "he always wanted us to sing 'Stairway To Paradise'."[33]

After the McCartneys left Western Avenue, Paul and George's friendship lapsed until George consulted the older boy about a manual exercise by jazz guitarist Django Reinhardt. Cycling over to Speke that evening with his guitar on his back, Paul, with his greater theoretical insight, was able to make sense of the piece. He in turn was stunned by his host's advanced fretboard expertise. Either at Upton Green or Forthlin Road, the two began practising together, frequently truanting to do so. They even lugged their guitars with them when, on the spur of the moment, they disappeared on a three-week hitch-hiking expedition along the south coast one summer holiday.

Usually, Paul sang to his acoustic as George picked at his Futurama. Discussions during these sessions drew to light George's liking for Carl Perkins, a rockabilly artist from Tennessee whose harsh guitar style was as cutting as his singing on his best-remembered hit, 'Blue Suede Shoes'. Much admired, too, was Duane Eddy, a New Yorker who'd pioneered the "twangy guitar" approach by booming the melodies on his instrumentals solely on the bass strings. Jauntier, but still highly regarded, was Chet Atkins, heard on countless Nashville country-pop recordings, including some by Elvis Presley.

As far as he could, chubby Paul modelled his appearance on Elvis, although he was also fond of The Everly Brothers, a quiffed duo with delinquent-angel faces whose double-edged bluegrass harmonies had propelled them into charts beyond their native America. Repeated listening to 'Bye Bye Love', the *risqué* 'Wake Up, Little Susie' and subsequent smashes brought home to Paul how rock 'n' roll could be simultaneously forceful and romantic.

He and George were in complete agreement about Buddy Holly, a singing guitarist from Texas, who dominated his group, The Crickets. George was the later convert, through borrowing Holly singles from Tony Bramwell, son of a family to whom he delivered meat. Making up for a manifest deficit of teen appeal, gangling Buddy possessed other creative talents, not least of which was an ability to compose – with various Crickets – simple but atmospheric songs tailored to his elastic adenoids.

Of all the elements that coalesced to produce the British beat boom of the 1960s, perhaps the single most influential event was when fated young Holly and his Crickets – second guitarist, double bass and drums – undertook a British tour in March 1958. "How these boys manage to make such a big, big sound with such limited instrumentation baffles me,"[35] remarked a reviewer after the Holly outfit closed the show at a Kilburn cinema with a loud half-hour mixture of their own and rivals' hits. Among those schoolboys of George and Paul's age who found Buddy's stage act and compact sound instructive were Mick Jagger, Dave Clark and Brian Poole, who, from Kent, London and Essex respectively, caught The Crickets at Woolwich Grenada. At the Manchester stop were two Salford boys, Allan Clarke and Graham Nash, who sang together as Ricky And Dane. Reading of Buddy's death not quite a year later, a member of Dave Dee And The Bostons, Trevor "Dozy" Davies, "cried all the way home. Yes, he was a big hero."[2]

After The Crickets had played the Empire, Paul suggested to a less enthusiastic George the idea of writing their own songs. Paul had already made up a few on his own. To George, nothing could be up to American standards, but he didn't mind being Paul's sounding board.

A study of chord charts on sheet music revealed that three basic structures recurred in rock 'n' roll: the "three-chord trick", the twelve-bar blues and the I-minor VI-IV-V ballad cliché. More often than not, these were complicated by a "middle eight" or bridge passage. This understanding was the foundation of Paul and George's first efforts at composition. A collaboration that survived into 1960 was 'Hey Darlin'', a doctored twelve-bar piece much in a lovelorn Everly Brothers mould.

Through Ivan Vaughan's sponsorship, Paul had joined The Quarry Men in July 1958. Nonetheless, despite this and George's fealty to Les Stewart, George and Paul may have toyed with the notion of being a double act, like The Dene Boys, The Allisons and other Britons who imitated Don and Phil Everly. When they performed during the lunch hour of George's last full day at school, Charlie Shaw remembered only "the vibrant sounds of electric guitar"[34] as George gave 'em his party piece, 'Raunchy', a morose jogalong by Bill Justis and covered for the British market by The Ken Mackintosh Orchestra.

Such syndication was anticipated, even welcomed, by US pop stars, as it brought their music, if not their performances, to another country full of teenagers with money to waste. Rather than pre-empting Elvis, wiser British acts gave themselves a more sporting chance by mechanically reproducing records by lesser-known Americans. On the radio, these could sound virtually identical to the originals. There were no takers for the medley of nursery rhymes by canine vocal group The Singing Dogs, but a veritable pack of Britishers fought over Marty Robbins' 'The Story Of My Life'. The war was won by Liverpool-born Michael Holliday, who, with Robbins on the other side of the Atlantic, was better able to promote his version in concert and on television. Tommy Steele had a more unfair advantage with his 'Come On Let's Go', originally by Ritchie Valens, who was killed in the same aeroplane crash as Buddy Holly.

After a controversial tour in 1958 by Jerry Lee Lewis, Sir Frank Medlicotte, MP, pointed out in Parliament that "We have enough rock and rollers of our own without importing them." In quantity, at least, Britain had more than enough duplicates of almost every US pop sensation.

After Tommy Steele abdicated by appearing on the *Royal Variety Show*, the role of English Elvis was assumed briefly by Cliff Richard, until he shaved off his sideburns at the behest of producer Jack Good, who'd also insisted that Gene Vincent array himself in biker leathers before setting foot on the inspired Jack's ITV pop showcase *Oh Boy!*. With a more electric atmosphere than *Six-Five Special*, its pious predecessor, *Oh Boy!* was a parade of vocalists following each other's spots so quickly that the screaming studio audience, urged on by Good, scarcely had pause to draw breath – although screams became cheers for the resident Vernons Girls, a troupe of choreographed singers recruited from employees of the Liverpool Football Pools company.

From the *Oh Boy!* stencil came more televised pop: *Drumbeat*, *Cool For Cats*, *Boy Meets Girls*. Implied in the last title was the emphasis on male stars. Most were studs from the stable of the celebrated manager Larry Parnes, who tended to give them names which juxtaposed the run of the mill with the descriptive, hence Vince Eager, Dickie Pride, Marty Wilde and so on. As expected, these specialised in American covers plugged on the "scream circuit" package tours of Britain's cinemas and theatres.

A regular spectator whenever such a show hit Merseyside, George Harrison noted the similarity in presentation to *Oh Boy!*: "They'd have ten or 15 different people on the show [who'd] all just go on and sing a couple of tunes each."[25] Backstage, there'd be squabbles over who'd do Ray Charles' 'What'd I Say', wherein a vocalist could, over ten minutes, take it down easy, trade "heys" and "yeahs" with the audience, build the tension to raving panic and finally sweep into the wings, leaving 'em wanting more. Time limitations truncated such exhibitions on television and the Light Programme's new *Saturday Club*, a two-hour pop show hosted by Brian Matthew, who was as "with it" as an ex-announcer in his 30s could be without being called to task by his staider superiors.

Saturday Club was recorded in Birmingham, which in 1959 was where the motorway from London terminated. It was also the geographical limit of the pool from which the entertainment industry centred in the capital was usually prepared to fish for its talent. Although Manchester, with its radio and television stations, was "entertainment capital of the north", it had still been necessary for the likes of Clinton Ford, Michael Holliday and The Vernons Girls to head south to Make It. "In the noise and heat of a tailor's shop," cooed *Everybody's Weekly*, "a 19-year-old negress from Liverpool thinks of crooning in a West End night club."[36]

The same impossible visions appeared before George, Paul, Alan Caldwell, Ted Taylor, Gerry Marsden and scores of other Scouse rock 'n' rollers as Cliff Richard's image flickered from *Oh Boy!*. Spurred on by his mate Jimmy Tarbuck, an unemployed Mersey tugboat hand by the name of Ronnie Wycherley cut corners by insinuating his way into Marty Wilde's dressing room at Birkenhead's Essoldo Theatre. There and then, he played songs he'd written to Wilde and Larry Parnes. Enthralled by Ronnie's prominent cheekbones and restless eyes, Parnes squeezed him into the show. Wycherley's knees knocked and his voice was tremulous with terror, but the girls all thought it was part of the act. An overnight sensation, he joined the tour as "Billy Fury". Next, Parnes dressed him in gold lamé, and his metamorphosis from nobody to teen idol was set in motion. Billy-Ronnie rarely spoke to fans. Apparently, he was ashamed of his "yobbish" accent.

John Lennon was very much the opposite. As leader of The Quarry Men, he was given to brutalising his Lancashire intonation to facilitate a "common touch" at bookings in districts rougher than Woolton, where he'd been brought up in middle-class comfort. His father had deserted the family when he was an infant. While John's mother would visit him daily, her complicated domestic arrangements made it more convenient for him to grow up in the semi-detached villa of her childless sister, Mary, whom John would always call by his cradle articulation "Mimi".

Lennon, too, might have fared better at a comprehensive school, for, like George Harrison at the Institute, he left Quarry Bank an academic failure and with a reputation as a square peg in a round hole. He was also an incorrigible rock 'n' roller in appearance, in attitude and in the musical style of his Quarry Men. In character, however he resembled the unique Ivan Vaughan, his friend at the Institute. On an annual holiday with Scottish cousins, Lennon, affecting a piping Highland trill, went shopping in Durness clad in a kilt he'd found in a chest of drawers. That he wisnae a *bona fide* Scot became obvious when he forgot to take his change in a tobacconist's.

More so than Harrison and McCartney, Lennon and Vaughan were fans of BBC Radio's *Goon Show*. Starring Spike Milligan, Peter Sellers, Michael Bentine and Harry Secombe, its parodies – 'I Was Monty's Treble', 'Bridge On The River Wye' *et al* – and incongruous connections not only made it different from other comedies like *The Clitheroe Kid* and *Hancock's Half Hour* but also ushered in the "offbeat" strata of humour that was to culminate in *Monty Python's Flying Circus*.

A habit of Lennon's that intensified with exposure to The Goons was scribbling lines of nonsense verse and surreal stories, supplemented by cartoons and caricatures. As Aunt Mimi wouldn't hear of him entering the world of work without qualifications, she fastened onto John's skills as an illustrator to get him into the Art College. There he matured not so much as an artist but as a would-be hardened Teddy Boy in an establishment where girls, hiding their figures inside baggy sweaters annexed from "existentialist" boyfriends with bumfluff beards, were more likely to be "sent" by Lewis, Meade Lux than Lewis, Jerry Lee.

Moreover, the new student was a lecture-disrupting wit, made more aggravating by an illusion of perpetual mockery in the short-sighted eyes that he was then too vain to protect with spectacles. His tutors' names were inserted irreverently in 'When You're Smiling' (sung in a Goon voice) and other items by The Quarry Men, whom he'd brought with him from school. Regarded as the college band, they were heard often enough in both midday sessions in the Life Room and dances in the main hall. Sometimes, they'd support one of the traditional jazz outfits that were nowadays finding favour with intellectual types living in the shadow of the Bomb – or, more precisely, of the Anglican cathedral.

For longer than he could possibly have anticipated, George Harrison would live in John Lennon's shadow. At Dovedale Primary, John had been in the same form as Peter Harrison (as well as Jimmy Tarbuck and Peter Sissons), but George was first aware of him as a rather sharp-featured boy who lived in one of the posher houses on his meat round. They were formally introduced by Paul in February 1958 at a Quarry Men engagement at the same Garston hall at which George had seen The Texan Skiffle Group. If out of context in Ted attire, George was still only the errand boy, and so was granted only an irresolute nod as John turned away to continue chatting with someone else.

The turnover of personnel within The Quarry Men had abated, and in the more fixed set-up Paul had surfaced as John's lieutenant. He was therefore well placed to champion George as Ivan Vaughan had championed him. The group's next booking was on 13 March at the Morgue, a club run by Alan Caldwell in the starkly-lit cellars of a large semi-derelict house in Oak Hill Park. If George brought his guitar along, Paul would do what he could.

In the Morgue, George lifted his Futurama from its case. It was a splendid instrument, compared to any owned by The Quarry Men and other local combos entertaining that night. Lennon was among those who gathered around in admiration. Feeling obliged to do a turn,

George was too overwhelmed to sing before older lads bunched so closely around him like friendly if over-attentive wolf hounds. In a quandary, he picked out 'Raunchy' and a Bert Weedon number that some listeners recognised from the harder tutorial book. As his notes hung in the musty air, even Lennon was impressed by this pale slip of a lad's virtuosity, lowering himself to actually speak to George. The display was not, however, sufficient for the great Lennon to consider George as an official Quarry Man, but he became a reliable understudy whenever the regular lead guitarist, Eric Griffiths, didn't turn up.

Neither did John object much when George came too whenever Paul cut classes at the Institute to attend rehearsals in the Life Room. Like Scullion of Tom Sharpe's *Porterhouse Blue*, George knew his place and tried not to put his foot in it with some inane remark that showed his age. "With George, you'd get virtually nothing going between you," observed Bill Harry, one of Lennon's cronies. "I think George was just extremely shy. He kept in the background so much in those days, he was almost the invisible man." Tagging behind when the Lennon gang went lunaticking around central Liverpool, his reserve would drop when John's butterfly concentration alighted on him. One remarkable Rag Week stunt had George and Paul garbed as vicars who, with Lennon as referee, would start a wrestling match on tables in chain-store restaurants until staff intervened.

Before he realised that John was making fun of him, George would pluck 'Raunchy' at his request in the oddest setting. Quoted most frequently by Beatle biographers was a performance on a bus. "Knowing John," reflected Bill Harry, "I can imagine him taking the mickey out of George mercilessly in private. He'd try it on you, and if you stood up to it, fine. If you put up with it, he'd keep on." Although he learned rejoinders, nothing in George's eyes could belittle John, even when it transpired that he was related to Cissy Smith by marriage. "Living with good and bad," he'd write later of Lennon, "I always looked up to you."[37] George was enchanted to be in the court of a fully-fledged rock 'n' roller who'd had sex and was on the verge of moving into a flat in beatnik Gambier Terrace, fount of wild parties, stolen street furniture, afternoon trysts and bare floorboards. John might have been less able as a guitarist than he, but he was a marvellous Presley-derived vocalist with instinctive if indelicate crowd control.

Then more Lennon's disciple than friend, George was sometimes a bit of a pest with his "Look! I've worked out this new chord" and his guileless arrival at Aunt Mimi's doorstep to ask her nephew to go to the pictures with him. Wishing that the floor would swallow him up, John pretended to be too busy. Still some inches short of his adult height of just under six feet, George was conscious that John, mature enough to have luxuriant sideburns, was "a bit embarrassed about that, because I was so tiny. I only looked about ten years old."[32]

George's hero-worship and machinations to be a Quarry Man also encroached on Lennon's amour with Cynthia Powell, another art student. Because John liked her, so did George – although, as he confided to John, man to man, "She's got teeth like a horse."[38] With the insensitivity of puberty, he'd wait outside the college portals for the couple to emerge after lectures. At first, he'd follow at a distance as John and Cynthia quickened their pace, intending to get up to he knew not what. When he caught up, neither had the heart to tell him to get lost. Growing bolder, he'd greet them with a trademark piercing whistle and once more, with their hearts in their boots, they'd be stuck with George for the afternoon. Cynthia's patience finally broke when she was hospitalised with an ill-humoured appendix. Anticipating an hour of sweet nothings during John's first ward visit, she burst into tears when he approached the bed with his admirer in tow. This time, George was told to go away.

An only child, John couldn't appreciate how much lack of privacy was the way of things at the Harrisons'. Young Harold and his fiancée, Irene, understood during their courtship that there'd nearly always be someone sewing, practising guitar or sweating over homework, should they choose to canoodle on the front-room settee at number 25. Fortunately, Irene had a soft spot for Our Kid. Although four years his senior, she and he had "hung out together"[39] while Harold was in the army. She'd even accompanied him to some pop shows at the Empire. Naturally, George was called upon to entertain with one of his groups at her and Harold's wedding reception.

For this and similar family functions, George preferred The

Quarry Men to the more dour Les Stewart Quartet. With fond pride, he was gratified that his mother and John got on so well, despite an inauspicious start when Mr Harrison entered to find his wife and Lennon seemingly entwined on the sofa. About to shake her hand, John had tripped and fallen towards her.

Although less eventful, George's first meeting with strait-laced Aunt Mimi had been frosty. However, her disapproval of his "common" manner and mode of dress was a point in his favour, as far as John was concerned. He was also touched when George – admittedly forced by Louise – went around to commiserate with him after his mother was killed in a road accident on 15 July 1958.

There were more pragmatic reasons for Lennon to finally accept Harrison as a Quarry Man. As Paul sensibly pointed out, "George was far ahead of us as a guitarist...but that isn't saying very much, because we were raw beginners ourselves."[15] In addition, George's training at Blackler's ensured that overloaded amplifiers with naked wires would be rendered less lethal and less likely to fall silent midway through a number. Of equal importance was the availability of Upton Green as a place to rehearse, where Mrs Harrison's welcome sometimes extended to tea and beans on toast. Furthermore, George's dad was such a power on various depot social committees that he could swing it for The Quarry Men to play in clubs like the one in Wavertree where he and Louise taught ballroom dancing. Indeed, some of these clubs were quite prestigious, and tin-pot skifflers considered themselves lucky if booked for a bill that also included The Merseysippi Jazz Band, that side-splitting Knotty Ash comic Ken Dodd, The Hillsiders and local speciality dancer Lindsay Kemp.[40]

Even with George in their ranks, however, such engagements were few and far between, despite The Quarry Men's willingness to perform for as little as a round of drinks. In the months before they disbanded, bookings were confined mainly to "a few parties at night. Just silly things – John, Paul and I, and there were a couple of other people who kept coming and going."[32] Going for good was Eric Griffiths, very much a spare part after the more skilled George joined. The job of telling him was assigned to drummer Colin Hanton, his best pal. Shortly after a foolhardy expedition to Manchester to audition for a spot on television, Colin himself packed it in after some beery unpleasantness at Picton Lane social club. And then there were three.

Len Garry, the most consistent of their bass players, had long departed through illness, agreeing, as everyone did, that groups who still used instruments made of household implements looked amateurish nowadays. At a Butlin's camp ballroom, Alan Caldwell had seen a band called Rory Blackwell And The Blackjacks using one of those new-fangled electric bass guitars. A few weeks later, Alan's singing bass player, Lou Walters, had bought one on credit from Hessy's. Not only did it have an infinitely greater volume and depth of sound than a broomstick bass but, as George noted, "it was much easier to get around. [You could] do more gigs and carry it in a case."[25]

All local groups not wishing to be anachronisms now had to have a bass. However, John's proposal that George switch to one had as much effect as if he'd suggested an Indian sitar. As a compromise, George dangled the carrot of a place in The Quarry Men before Arthur Kelly, as long as he could muster up £60 for an electric bass.

This was a dubious carrot, now that the group were so desperate for work. George was better off with Les Stewart, even if the Lowlands, like the Morgue, was about to close. Through Ruth Morrison, the Quartet had become known to the brothers Peter and Rory Best, who, with a team of helpers, had spent most of the summer of 1959 converting the spacious basement of their family home into a coffee bar-cum-club.

At 8 Hayman's Green, just up the road from the Lowlands, the club was to be like the Gyre and Gimble, the 2I's and like London venues where Harry Webb and Reg Smith used to sing before changing their respective names to Cliff Richard and Marty Wilde. "As certain sections of the adult population go to the public house for relaxation," sniffed *Liverpool Institute* magazine, "so the younger generation goes to a coffee bar to contemplate the weird and exotic vegetation."[41] These new havens made it possible to sit for hours, conversing with other teenagers, for the price of a transparent cup of frothy coffee. Entertainment was usually coin operated, but, as a change from the juke box, some bars would book a live act. Sunday-press condemnation of such houses of ill repute, where boys smoked and girls were deflowered, may have been justified in the case of the Morgue, where neighbouring gardens were receptacles for cigarette butts and used rubber johnnies.

Peter and Rory would not have their mother, invalid grandmother or any of the lodgers so offended. This was West Derby Village, not Oak Hill Park. Their father was almost permanently away, and the atmosphere in the Bests' 15-room Victorian property – with its enamelled Hindu goddess depicted in the hall – reflected their mother Mona's upbringing in India, where Peter had been born in Madras in 1941. From voluptuously handsome Mona had come his own sultry good looks, similar to those that had made Cliff Richard so popular. Girls who initiated conversations with Peter were further charmed by his modest bemusement at their interest in him. The impression that he was the strong-but-silent type was enhanced by his broad shoulders and slim waist of an athlete, which were evident when he posed for the team photograph during a football season at Liverpool Collegiate, where he also distinguished himself academically. With hardly a murmur, he went along with advice to apply to teacher training college after the cache of "O"-levels his teachers expected him to pass.

Whatever the school thought he should do, Mrs Best would support with all the vivacity of a Violet Caldwell any more glamorous ambitions that could be teased from her reticent son. When he and his friends began spending hours listening to pop records in the basement, it was she who suggested turning it into a club. It was Mona, too, who christened it "the Casbah Coffee Club".

Partly because Ken Brown and, less often, George Harrison had assisted in the redecoration, The Les Stewart Quartet were asked to play for £3 – a generous fee in 1959 – on the Casbah's inaugural evening on Saturday 29 August, when a huge attendance was expected. A week prior to this engagement, the four met at Stewart's house to run through the set. A tense mood came to a head when Les rounded on Ken for missing rehearsals. The accused guitarist protested that the group would have nothing to rehearse for if it wasn't for the time he'd put in at the Bests'.

Lines were drawn as the quarrel boiled down to Stewart washing his hands of the Casbah. Keeping his peace throughout, George elected to side with Ken. Outside Stewart's banged front door that afternoon, he tried to assuage worries about letting Mrs Best down with the idea of amalgamating with "two mates I sometimes play with".[42] For two hours, Ken fretted in the Casbah until George reappeared with Paul, John and Cynthia. After casing the joint, Lennon decided that The Quarry Men, augmented by Brown in his Buddy Holly glasses, would perform in front of the juke box. To save dragging more than their guitars over to Hayman's Green, they'd all plug into Ken's pristine amplifier, as he lived nearest. Entering the discussion, Mona pushed paint-brushes on the new arrivals and energetically put them to work.

Paul's brother, Michael, was spectacularly sick after swigging some noxious liquid from a bottle marked "lemonade" when The Quarry Men played before a full house of 300. Except for the guitarist whose turn it was to sing, the group were seated rent-party style in deference to Ken, who was a skiffle purist. Drawing protracted salvos of applause were Paul's race through Little Richard's 'Long Tall Sally' and John's growled insinuation in The Coasters' dolefully comic narrative 'Three Cool Cats'.

What Les Stewart's unit had been to the Lowlands The Quarry Men were to the Casbah for several weeks, until a dispute with Mrs Best and Ken Brown – present but unable to perform through illness – over the division of one night's £3. Ken had been the key to the Casbah, but musically he was as superfluous as Eric Griffiths had become. He wasn't missed when the remaining three took their brief turn under the Empire's proscenium in a "Search For Stars" talent contest organised by Carroll Levis, spiritual forefather of fellow Canadian Hughie Green, of *Opportunity Knocks* fame. In an earlier heat, the ubiquitous Alan Caldwell and his group, Al Storm And The Hurricanes, had scrambled to second place, and even if they weren't able to seize the ultimate prize of a spot on "Mr Starmaker" Levis' ITV series, at least they'd come out of it with a fuller, more lucrative date-sheet.

Although it's debatable whether or not The Quarry Men's decision to change their name made a difference, the fact remains that Johnny (Lennon) And The Moondogs qualified for the next and then final round of the contest, which was held at the Manchester Hippodrome. Up against such disparate acts as a blindfolded knife-thrower and Three-Men-And-A-Microphone comedy impersonators, the Liverpool trio went down sufficiently well to eat their hearts out when obliged to catch the last train back to Lime Street before they could be judged by volume of applause in the finale. The winners, so they learned later, were Ricky And Dane, who had played an Everly Brothers number.

Although John let George duet with him on Buddy Holly's 'Words Of Love', Johnny And The Moondogs' principal asset was the vocal interplay between Lennon and McCartney. Fans attempting to describe it found it simpler to say that it sounded like The Everly Brothers. That power structure, in which George was subordinate to John and Paul for as long as they stayed in the same group, was founded not so much on vocal compatibility as the handshake that had formalised the Lennon-McCartney songwriting partnership during John's last term at Quarry Bank. Between the two older boys, it was understood that, should the group fold, they would make a go of it purely as composers.[43] After all, jobbing tunesmiths were staples of the record business. In New York's Brill Building, there was even a songwriting "factory" where such combines as Goffin and King, and Mann and Weill churned out assembly-line pop for the masses. Although musically untrained, a London printer named Lionel Bart and actor Mike Pratt had together written hits for Tommy Steele and Cliff Richard. Why too couldn't a pair of Liverpudlian schoolboys called McCartney and Lennon?

While Johnny And The Moondogs survived, songwriting was more of a sideline. Paul's 'In Spite Of All The Danger', with slight help from George and sung in shooby-doo-wah style, had been recorded on a demonstration disc by The Quarry Men. This had been the tide-mark of McCartney's collaboration with Harrison, for whom composing was incidental to his artistic self-image. Made to feel intellectually (as well as chronologically) inferior to Paul – who was soon to sit his "A"-levels – and Art School John, he felt he had neither the knack nor the inclination to compose. Where did it get you, anyway? The Dusty Road Ramblers' 'Sweet Liverpool' was a rare example of a band performing an original in public, but, as George and everyone else knew, if anything more than the familiar was attempted, dancers would be inclined to either sit it out or go to the toilet. It just wasn't done.

However pointless it seemed, the increasing exclusiveness of his two friends' creative alliance must have been a wellspring of emotional confusion for George. Where it had once been George and Paul, it was more Paul and John. During 1960's summer holiday, those two had spent a week down south in Paul's married cousin's Berkshire pub, even performing as a duo in its bar. It wasn't as easy to absent himself from his job at Blackler's as it had been from school, but when he could, George would accompany the two students on similar expeditions and sit in, as their lyrics and melodies took form. All the same, as Cynthia concluded, "George, being younger and not writing songs, didn't have the same communication with them, but John and Paul couldn't stop playing together."[44]

For an audible but private gauge of John and Paul's efforts alongside that of professionals, they and George committed 'Hello Little Girl', 'The One After 9.09', 'You Must Lie Every Day', 'I'll Follow The Sun' and others into McCartney's Grundig tape recorder, rigged up in Forthlin Road living room. On a muffled tape of one such session, the three guitarists are anchored by the plonk of a simplistic bass line supplied by Stuart Sutcliffe, a gifted painter in John's year at college whom he had befriended. With dress sense peculiar to himself and a beard that hadn't really taken, Sutcliffe's yardstick of cool was Modigliani, rather than Presley. Although all were the most heterosexual of males, George was anxious and Paul frankly jealous of the vice-like grip that slight, sensitive Stuart appeared to have on John. Lennon in turn fascinated Sutcliffe because he wasn't like most of the others at Art College. Therefore, it wasn't surprising when Stuart bought an electric bass and John told a consternated Paul and George to welcome a new Moondog. At John's decree, too, George and a student called Dave May took turns in teaching Stuart the rudiments of his new instrument.

Prior to Sutcliffe's arrival, Paul had thought of taking up bass himself, as, no matter how contrasting his and John's chord shapes could be, the group had one rhythm guitarist too many. On the likely conjecture that the greater number of lead vocals, the higher a member's rank in the group hierarchy, Paul was several cuts above George, who was well ahead of Stuart, who had only 'Love Me Tender' to sing. As well as a handful of Perkins, Holly and Presley favourites, George – with a voice not long broken – was now carrying the tune of 'Three Cool Cats', a gift from John, who, with Paul, just harmonised on key lines. Lennon had gone off the song after the trio of Marty Wilde, Cliff Richard and Dickie Pride had massacred it on *Oh Boy!*. Later, John nobly surrendered his lead-guitar *pièce de résistance* – Duane Eddy's 'Ramrod' – to George.

Much as he professed to despise the synchronised footwork with which Cliff Richard's backing quartet, The Shadows, decorated their instrumental airs on stage, Lennon would admit that, as a guitarist, he'd "vamp like Bruce Welch [of The Shadows] does".[44] Recording in their own right, The Shadows would become nearly as famous as Richard himself, especially when their tune 'Apache' was voted Top Record of 1960 in the *NME* readers' poll. Although a butter-finger phrase on their follow-up, 'Man Of Mystery', went unchanged to EMI's pressing plant, The Shadows' Hank Marvin remains the most omnipotent of British lead guitarists, given those fretboard heroes like Jeff Beck and Ritchie Blackmore, whose professional careers started in outfits who copied The Shadows.

While their line-up – lead, rhythm and bass guitar plus drums – consolidated the pop group stereotype, few assumed that there were openings for The Shadows and their imitators beyond instrumentals and accompanying some pretty boy like Cliff. The main attraction of being in a group was, perhaps, the implied camaraderie, whereby – in the words of Jimmy Page, then a guitarist backing Cliff soundalike Neil Christian – "some of those Shadows things sounded like they were eating fish and chips while they were playing".[45] Also, glancing at four-eyed Hank and stunted fellow Shadow Jet Harris, you didn't have to be a Charles Atlas to join a group.

Other group leaders might have done, but Lennon did not entice Stuart to peroxide his hair like Jet's or cajole George into sporting lensless Marvin horn-rims. Nonetheless, sniffing the wind, he and his

Moondogs began rehearsing more instrumentals. In the forefront of these was George, loud and clear on 'Ramrod', Weedon's 'Guitar Boogie Shuffle' and faithful old 'Raunchy'. Trickier, but with as little scope for improvisation, were several group originals like 'The Guitar Bop', developed from a passage in Chuck Berry's 'Brown-Eyed Handsome Man'.

Almost as strong an influence as Berry was Eddie Cochran, a multi-talented Elvis from Oklahoma. His 'Summertime Blues' and other singles that outlined the trials of adolescence had already garnered a plenitude of British covers when, co-starring with his pal Gene Vincent, his first "scream-circuit" tour of the country reached Liverpool's Empire in March 1960. Although all of Johnny And The Moondogs attended, George – with his working-man's wage – was able to follow Eddie to other northern cities to learn from a distance what he could of the American's terse, resonant lead-guitar technique. Joe Brown, an English intimate of Cochran's, later told George about Eddie's practice of using an unwound, extra-light third string. This was the secret of his agile bending of middle-register "blue" notes.

The indigenous supporting bill included Billy Fury and other charges of Larry Parnes, and it was through Larry's contact with Allan Williams, a local agent, that Vincent and Cochran were scheduled to return to Merseyside on 3 May to head a three-hour extravaganza at a 6,000-seat sports arena near Prince's Dock. The rest of the bill would be filled by an assortment of Parnes acts and two Liverpool groups: Cass And The Cassanovas and Rory (formerly Al) Storm And The Hurricanes. Williams added Gerry And The Pacemakers and four more bands to the bill after Eddie Cochran couldn't make it, incapacitated as he was by his death in Bath's St Martin's Hospital on 17 April.

Pulled from the same car crash was Gene Vincent, who, despite broken ribs and collar bone, plus injuries to his already callipered leg, insisted with characteristic obstinacy on honouring existing British dates. Using the microphone stand as a surgical support, Gene paid tribute to Eddie with a mournful 'Over The Rainbow', which in Liverpool only just upstaged Gerry Marsden's equally plaintive 'You'll Never Walk Alone' and Rory Storm's riveting 'What'd I Say'.

With his aversion to signing groups, Larry Parnes abstained from leading more Scouse musicians to his stable that night, but he was sufficiently awed by both the local boys' impact on the frenzied audience and former plumber Allan Williams' competence as a promoter to discuss a further – albeit less ambitious – joint venture. After the show, he'd been invited back to the Jacaranda, Williams' late-night coffee bar a stone's throw from Central Station. Watching them from an outermost table were Johnny And The Moondogs – minus Paul, usually the most willing to picket on the group's behalf. None of the other three summoned the courage to approach Parnes, but in the cafe two nights later John lodged a plea with Williams to "do something for us".[46] Thick-set and black-bearded Allan had known them as customers before realising that they were also a pop group of lesser standing locally than those he'd procured for the Gene Vincent spectacular. Mainly because he was something of a curt agony aunt to Stuart and his artistic sufferings, he there and then began acting for Johnny And The Moondogs in a quasi-managerial capacity, in exchange for whatever non-musical services he felt that they could provide. Under Stuart's direction, they painted murals in the Jacaranda basement, which had a dancing area and a space for groups to set up their equipment.

Before Lennon's outfit reached a high enough standard for Williams to let them perform there, a steel band played alternate evenings to Cass And The Cassanovas, whose leader, Brian Cassar, allowed Lennon to sit in on the night of his negotiation with Allan Williams. John mentioned that his group was thinking once more of changing its name. Buddy Holly had his Crickets and Gene Vincent had been backed by The Beat Boys, so he and Stuart had come up with Beetles, Beatles or Beatals. An adherent to the 'Somebody And The Somebodies' dictate of the 1950s, Cassar howled with derision, and with Robert Newton's role in the film version of *Treasure Island* (lately extended into a television series) in mind suggested Long John And His Pieces Of Eight. Warming to his theme, he next put forward Long John And The Silver Beetles. Cass stopped being facetious long enough to help secure John the drummer that the group – whatever they called themselves – had been lacking since Colin Hanton's exit.

A forklift truck driver at Garston Bottle Works, Tommy Moore started rehearsing at the Jacaranda with The Silver Beatles, although it was understood that, with his heart in jazz, 26-year-old Tommy would never quite fit in among arty youths whom certain of the Cassanovas derided as "posers". Chief among them was drummer Johnny Hutch, who nonetheless saved the day for Lennon *et al* on occasions when Moore and the sticksmen who came after him were unavailable.

Hutch first stepped in when Tommy was late for the group's make-or-break ten-minute spot during auditions held a week after the Vincent show for Larry Parnes, who was after an all-purpose backing combo for his solo stars. It was assumed that the singer he had immediately in mind was Billy Fury, now with a hat-trick of modest hits to his credit, who accompanied his manager that afternoon to the auditions. These were held in premises that Williams would open as the Blue Angel night club later that year.

Their drummer's tardiness exacerbated The Silver Beatles' collective feeling of inadequacy as the other groups that Allan had called up to play for Parnes tuned their Hank Marvin Stratocasters, positioned gleaming cymbals on pearly drum sets and brushed non-existent specks of dust from costumes that gave each a neat, professional identity. Despite a pep talk from Williams, The Silver Beatles were too aware of being the least probable contenders. Over in Derry Wilkie And The Seniors' corner, Howie Casey adjusted the reed in his lustrous silver saxophone to the purring note of a two-tier Hammond organ. In another recess, Gerry and his Pacemakers chatted idly. They were saving up for "GP"-monogrammed blazers. Over there lounged Rory Storm, a blond Adonis in hair lacquer and Italian suit, as much a star on Merseyside as Fury was in the Top 20. He and the Hurricanes were shortly to begin a residency at Butlin's in Pwllheli for £25 a week each – not a bad deal when £500 a year was thought to be a good salary for a young executive.

After Mrs Kelly had refused to let George have the silver-grey curtains of her French windows as material for The Silver Beatles' stage outfits, they performed for Larry Parnes in two-tone plimsolls, jeans, black shirts and cheap pendants. Prudently, they concentrated mainly on instrumentals and, while they toed no conventional line with fancy dance steps, at least they weren't slick to the point of sterility, like other bands that Parnes surveyed that day. "Silver Beetles – very good," he jotted on a pad. "Keep note for future work." He recalled the sensation at Bradford Gaumont recently when Marty Wilde experimented by taking the stage with The Wildcats, who'd backed him when he was still Reg Smith, rather than the "corny and square" session musicians foisted on him by his record company. "It takes youngsters," he'd announced, "to play and feel the rock beat." Apart from their drummer, The Silver Beatles, with George just turned 16, were young enough. Furthermore, they weren't encumbered with a flamboyant non-instrumentalist who might agitate to get in on the act.

"Future work" came sooner rather than later. On 14 May at Lathom Hall, a dilapidated Victorian monstrosity in Seaforth, they'd completed their first true semi-professional engagement. Less than a week later, group and equipment were hurtling from Lime Street to an eight-day tour of Scotland, beginning in Alloa. It wouldn't be Billy Fury they'd back there but a square-jawed hunk on whom Larry Parnes had bestowed the *nom du théâtre* Johnny Gentle. A-twitter with excitement and childish swagger, the three youngest Silver Beatles straightaway gave themselves stage names too, George's being "Carl" Harrison, in recognition of Carl Perkins. While the stratagems Stuart "de Stael", Paul "Ramon" and John Lennon used to obtain release from college and school were not entirely honest, all Tommy had to do was take an early summer holiday from the bottle works, while "Carl" – who'd never acknowledged that he'd one day be a department supervisor like Mr Peet – went the whole hog by resigning altogether from Blackler's.

Only the swiftest rehearsal was feasible before star and group trooped on at Alloa Town Hall to entertain with mutually familiar rock 'n' roll standards, plus the simpler side of Gentle's four singles, such as self-penned 'Wendy', a four-chord ballad – "Wendy, Wendy, when? Wendy, Wendy, when?" *ad nauseum* – that must have made Paul and John wonder what they were doing wrong. Whatever they thought of him, Johnny was delighted with The Silver Beatles as musicians, especially George, and said as much when he called

Parnes with progress reports. The story goes that he presented George with one of Eddie Cochran's old shirts.

The light-heartedness of such a gesture was atypical of the prevalent atmosphere of the tour, which after Alloa zigzagged along the north-east coast with its brooding sea mists and dull watchfulness when the van in which the party huddled stopped at lonely petrol stations. In the grim digs where The Silver Beatles would repair late each night, Lennon would authorise who slept where, ensuring that he had the least crowded bedroom. Good-natured Tommy or the acquiescent Stuart would sleep on the floor if ever they were a bed short.

Stuart and Tommy were also the prime targets for abuse when the spurious thrill of "going professional" gave way to stoic cynicism as each man's £18 for the week's work dwindled. Rumbustious repartee became desultory and then suddenly nasty as, led by John, Paul and George – swimming with the tide – poked ruthless fun at whomever of the other two seemed likelier to rise to it. With malicious glee, Sutcliffe and Moore would be snubbed as the rest sat on a separate table for breakfast.

Well, it helped pass the time as they trudged around Scottish venues where Gentle's past appearances on *Drumbeat* guaranteed top billing over a diversity of local acts, from tartan-clad *ceilidh* bands to Alex Harvey, "Scotland's own Tommy Steele". The most northerly engagement, Fraserburgh Town Hall, was notable for the estranged Moore drumming with his head in bandages, fuzzy with sedatives and missing several teeth. He'd been the sole casualty when the van had crashed into a stationary Ford Popular earlier in the day. Not of Gene Vincent's "the show must go on" persuasion, Tommy had been semi-conscious in hospital when the group and hall manager barged in as showtime approached. They weren't laden with grapes and sympathy either.

Larry Parnes had a homily that ran, "Take care of the pennies and the lads can take care of themselves." Well before they steamed back to Liverpool after the final date, Tommy Moore – with only £2 left to show for his pains – had had more than his fill of being a Silver Beatle. They all had.

3 Das Liebschen Kind

"The Germans were just coming to the end of their jazz era," remembered Dave Dee, "and the American rock 'n' roll thing had really taken off. For the Germans to bring in all these stars from America would have cost a fortune, and there they had, just across the Channel, these English blokes that were copying the Americans and doing it very well. So it was easy to bring them in for 20 quid a week and work them to death, so all the English bands were in Germany doing two- or three-month stints."[47]

Britain in 1960 was in the thick of its own jazz era, which to the man in the street meant a bowler-hatted Somerset clarinettist called Acker Bilk, plinking banjos and "dads" who'd boo if a "trad" outfit deviated from defined New Orleans precedent by corrupting their toot-tooting with amplification. In the Cavern, Liverpool's principal jazz stronghold, proprietor Ray McFall would dock the fee of any band who dared to launch into a rock 'n' roll number within its hallowed and rather mildewed walls. With trad jazz's stranglehold on such venues and classic rock denounced as kids' stuff by most collegians, it was small wonder that Dave Dee's Bostons and others keeping the rock 'n' roll faith were open to offers from abroad.

One of the first West German impresarios to put action over debate was an ex-circus clown called Bruno Koschmider, who in spring 1960 set off with his interpreter for London and the Soho coffee bar that seamen visiting his Hamburg clubs had assured him was still the shrine of British pop. From the 2I's, Herr Koschmider raked up a ragbag of out-of-work musicians to transport across the North Sea for re-assembly as The Jets on the rickety stage of his

Kaiserkeller, a nightspot down a side street of Die Grosse Freiheit, a main thoroughfare of the Reeperbahn area, an erotic Blackpool notorious as the vice capital of Europe. A hitch over work permits caused a delay on the Dutch border, but with Bruno's unbothered string-pulling they were on their way.

Although pianist Del Ward was The Jets' nominal leader, they were licked into shape by the better of their two singing guitarists, Tony Sheridan, an ex-art student who'd flowered momentarily on *Oh Boy!* before being consigned to an obscurity largely of his own making. Twenty-year-old Sheridan's self-destructive streak did not, however, tarnish his ability as a performer. His wanton dedication to pleasing himself rather than his audience resulted in a sweaty intensity rarely experienced in British pop before 1960. Seizing songs by the scruff of the neck and wringing the life out of them, Tony and the other Jets were an instant and howling success with a clientèle for whom the personality of the house band had been secondary to boozing, brawling and the pursuit of romance.

Rival club owners cast covetous eyes on Koschmider's find, and soon Tony and his boys were administering their rock elixir at the Top Ten, a newer and bigger night spot, where they were protected by its manager's henchmen from any reprisals for deserting the Kaiserkeller.

When he'd calmed down, Bruno returned to London armed with a cast-iron contract for any attraction likely to win back the many customers who'd followed Sheridan to the Top Ten. Through one of those chances in million, he and Allan Williams froze in mutual recognition across the kidney-shaped tables of the 2I's.

Earlier that year, the Jacaranda's steel band had been seen by a German sailor, and it was on his recommendation that, with Deutschmarks and mention of affectionate *frauleins*, the West Indians were poached by a Reeperbahn club agent. Quite unashamed of their perfidy, letters from them arrived at the Jacaranda, telling of the recreational delights of Hamburg. The opportunist Williams found himself soon afterwards on the Grosse Freiheit, sampling an evening of music and loose money. With amused contempt, he listened to the inept Kaiserkeller band who were destined to be displaced by The Jets. Before the night was out, Williams and

Koschmider, entrepreneur to entrepreneur, had had an exploratory talk about the possibility of bringing to Hamburg some of the Merseyside outfits held in esteem by no less than Larry Parnes. The discussion ended on a sour note, however, when a tape of the fabulous groups in question that Allan proudly threaded onto the club recorder had been rendered a cacophonous mess through demagnetisation, probably as it passed through customs.

Back in Liverpool, Williams shrugged off this embarrassing episode to concentrate on the possible. A group without a permanent drummer was no use to anyone, and so after Tommy Moore's disgusted resignation from The Silver Beatles it had fallen upon Cass And The Cassanovas to trek up to Scotland for the next leg of the Johnny Gentle tour and another with Duffy Power, whose second single had been an arrangement of the ragtime standby 'Ain't She Sweet', whereby he'd planted unfruitful feet in both the trad and rock 'n' roll camps.

It reached Larry Parnes' ears that Brian Cassar had been prone to pushing off the star that his Cassanovas were backing in order to commandeer the central microphone himself. A tarring with the same brush may explain why Derry Wilkie And The Seniors' forthcoming summer season in Blackpool was cancelled by Parnes just as the gentlemen concerned had given up their day jobs and spent a loan on new stage uniforms. Looking for a scapegoat, they marched to the Blue Angel, from whence all their woes had emanated. "Well?" demanded burly Howie Casey of its owner. Thinking fast, the intimidated Williams threw a slender lifeline. The next day, he drove Derry And The Seniors the long miles down to the 2I's. To his amazement, room was made for them to do a turn that very evening. Even more incredible, Koschmider was there. The group showed London what Scousers could do with such unbottled exuberance that three days later they were on their way to Germany.

To Reeperbahn pleasure-seekers, Wilkie And The Seniors proved a comparable draw to Sheridan. With the Kaiserkeller thriving again, Bruno's thoughts turned to the Indra, his strip club at the dingier end of the *Strasse*. With only a few onlookers there on most nights, it could only be more profitable to put on pop.

Of a like mind was Les Dodd, who ran "21-plus" nights in two dance halls in the Wirral, on the opposite bank of the Mersey to Liverpool. For half a crown, adult dancers could savour Tuesday evenings with (as Dodd's advertisements stressed) "No Jiving! No Rock 'n' Roll! No Teenagers!" Yet it would be these undesirables that would give his profit graph an upward turn when, grudgingly, he began to promote Saturday night "swing sessions" with "jive and rock specialists" like The Silver Beatles, who appeared last after busier groups – like those led by Gerry Marsden and Kingsize Taylor – finished and left to play further engagements elsewhere on any of the given evenings.

Maybe middle-aged Dodd excused his cashing-in on the grounds that it was a moral crusade to bring the scum to the surface in order to dissipate it so that decent music could reign once more. At the Grosvenor Ballroom, especially, there was immediate trouble, with youths pushing their way in *en bloc* without paying, usually just after closing time. Narrow-eyed bouncers were hired to keep order, but if delegations from rival gangs showed up then there was at least the threat of a punch-up. Fighting and vandalism outside the premises was a matter for the Merseyside constabulary, who started paying routine calls towards the end of Grosvenor swing sessions.

Fists often swung harder than The Silver Beatles, who felt compelled to maintain ghastly grins as their music became a soundtrack for beatings-up. At Neston Institute, Dodd's other concern, a boy was half-killed before their eyes and beneath kicking pointed shoes. Musicians weren't immune, either, and a table was hurled at Paul McCartney during one enbattled evening. The provocation would be either catching the eye of some roughneck's girl or not playing enough slow ones (or fast ones) to facilitate the winning of a maiden's heart. There were a few close shaves but, mercifully, only one serious assault on The Silver Beatles, when, at Seaforth's Lathom Hall in the following February, the gentle Stuart received head injuries that were at first be thought to be minor.

Certain agents weren't above using stink bombs and hiring strippers to disrupt proceedings at a rival venue, thus blackening its reputation with local burghers, but it was an exposé in a local newspaper that led to Dodd resuming his earlier policy of strict tempo only. As if the rowdiness of the patrons hadn't been enough, what wasn't reported was the trouble he'd had with groups turning up with only half their equipment or a player short. The Silver Beatles had been the limit, with their shabby amplifiers and no drummer for most of their bookings. *In extremis*, Paul bashed away with bad grace, but once a hulking Liscard gangleader had volunteered. Not liking to say no, they'd let him inflict untold damage on Tommy Moore's kit, which was still in their possession, even if Tommy himself wasn't. When they'd lost Moore's successor, Norman Chapman, to the army after only three weeks, Allan Williams was forced to pass the chance of another Parnes tour – backing Dickie Pride – to another group.

With the end of their employment with Les Dodd, all that The Silver Beatles' future appeared to hold was Jacaranda nights for one fizzy drink and a plate of beans on toast per man, plus odd engagements at less public Williams venues. "Odd" was the word for the week in which, twice nightly, they tried to keep their minds on their job of accompanying the cavortings of a Mancunian stripper at Allan's new Cabaret Artists club, a well-concealed ledger in his accounts. Allegedly, the lass took a fancy to George ("that nice boy with the bony face"[46]) as, without looking up, he fingered the smoochy melodies of 'Begin The Beguine' and Gershwin's 'Summertime'.

Because they'd so gamely gone through with this tasteless assignment, Williams was finally convinced that the group, now defiantly trading as plain Beatles, were no longer, as George would say, "hopefully messing around".[32] When Rory Storm, Brian Cassar and other possibilities with a full complement of musicians demurred, the Indra contract was theirs, if they could enlist a drummer.

The Beatles' campaign for work had driven them back to the Casbah, where, about to disband, was the club's resident quartet, the Blackjacks – nothing to do with Rory Blackwell but formed by Ken Brown with Peter Best, whose adoring mother had bought him an expensive drum kit with skins of calf-hide, rather than plastic. No more was Pete harbouring thoughts of being a schoolmaster. The news that he wanted to drum for a living provided the answer to The Beatles' dilemma over Hamburg. Following a cursory audition at the Blue Angel, Best became a Beatle and, to many who heard him play with them, would always remain so.

Pete packed his case with Mona's blessing. John, Paul and Stuart's guardians and teachers raised quizzical eyebrows but, after grumbling about the opportunities they were wasting, didn't stand in their way either. With no ties, academic or otherwise, George met hardly any opposition from his parents for this, his first trip abroad, although Harold was still a little reproachful about his losing a chance to Make Good at Blackler's. Unlike his big brother on National Service, George would have no old job waiting for him when he got back to the real world. His mother, who'd seen the group play, felt that, if he kept at it, he might just make a reasonable living as a musician.

Hazy impressions of a Germany of bomb sites and lederhosen were rudely shattered on entering Hamburg, a port that had recovered more thoroughly from the war than Liverpool ever had. They climbed from Allan Williams' exhausted minibus outside the Kaiserkeller, vaster and plusher than any club or ballroom they'd seen on Merseyside. It was therefore a disappointment when Mr Koschmider showed them around the tiny Indra, which had the tell-tale signs of having known better days: the dusty carpeting and heavy drape curtains; the padded wallpaper peeling off here and there; the depressed forbearance of its staff.

Ist gut, ja? Nein, not really. Worse were the three windowless holes at the back of a cinema where they were to sleep – coats for blankets, naked light bulbs, shampooing in a washbasin in the moviegoers' toilet and waking up shivering to Stuart snoring open-mouthed on a camp-bed a yard away. Until now, George's only taste of roughing it had been a fortnight at Gambier Terrace in the first flush of his wonderment at John. "It was us living in squalor with things growing out of the sink," he said. "'Where's my share? Why can't I have some?' That sort of attitude."[24]

With martyred nobility, The Beatles let themselves be pushed in whatever direction fate, Williams and Koschmider ordained. The living conditions of Derry's Seniors were as poky, but they were talking of staying on as a strip-club band when their contract with Bruno was up. The Beatles, therefore, could hope to step into their shoes at the Kaiserkeller. There was token sullen mutiny when the season began, but, forgetting the misery of their position, they perked up, quite tickled when anyone cried encouragement to them.

The Beatles endured the Indra for seven weeks, six hours a night, an hour on and 15 minutes off. Up at the Kaiserkeller, Derry And The Seniors' intermissions caused patrons to drift away, Bruno presumed, to the hated Top Ten and entrapment by Sheridan for the rest of the evening. It was a bit unreasonable to expect Wilkie's group to work around the clock without a break, but, discontinuing the juke box, Koschmider bridged the gaps with an instrumental group he created by extracting Sutcliffe from The Beatles and Howie Casey and pianist Stan Foster from The Seniors and luring a German jazz drummer from another club.

This quartet's disparity, plus the related umbrage of the depleted Seniors and Beatles, combined with complaints about the noise and change of programme at the Indra, but it was the situation's false economy that led Koschmider to reconstitute the two groups and move The Beatles uptown to the Kaiserkeller.

Not a word of moral protest was raised when the Indra's gartered erotica was restored. Striptease, clip joints and brothels were to the Reeperbahn as steel was to Sheffield. Naked before their conquerors, Germans of all sexes would wrestle in mud, have sex with animals and perform all manner of obscene tableaux, frequently inciting their audiences to join in the fun. "Everybody around the district," George would recount fondly, "were homosexuals, transvestites, pimps and hookers, [and I was] in the middle of that when I was 17."[32] Back home, he might have fled if accosted by a prostitute in a dark doorway, but with Mum not looking a young Merseysider might abruptly lose his virginity in the robust caress of a bawd who'd openly exhibited her seamy charms in a bordello window. "They usually arrived knowing it all, poor sods," sighed Iain Hines, one of the Jets, "taking no advice that I offered them and, sure enough, would return to the good old UK with crabs, pox, 'Hamburg Throat' – you name it, they had it."[48]

More knowingly self-inflicted were the headaches, rashes and other side-effects of stimulants swallowed to combat exhaustion during the last sets of the night. "The only problem with that," warned Dave Dee, "was that, when we finished work, we couldn't sleep and went through the next day waiting for the pills to wear off. Of course, we were knackered again at four o'clock, so we asked for more pills."[47] Lennon might have crowned this with, "What with playing, drinking and birds, how could you find time to sleep?"[49] He and Stuart had been introduced to benzedrine – a stimulant extracted from Vicks inhalers – through the beat poet Royston Ellis, whose declaimed verses The Beatles had once framed musically at the Jacaranda. New to both of them, however, were Preludin tablets, amphetamice-laced appetite suppressants that, although recently outlawed in Britain, were easily available over counters in German pharmacies. A supply of Preludin was stocked for employees' use in every all-night establishment along the Grosse Freiheit for purposes other than fighting the flab.

In the Kaiserkeller, Bruno's musicians could also avail themselves of a nightly quantity of free beer and salad. A virtue of both was that they could be consumed in instalments on stage if need be. Outside working hours, breakfast was "*Cornflakes mit Milch*" in Freiheit cafes. At the British Seamen's Mission along Johannis Bollwerk in a dockside suburb of Davidswache, lunch was something with chips. For young George, at least, this unvaried diet was a psychological link with home.

On hot afternoons, there were excursions to Timmendorf on the North Sea, where The Beatles would recharge their batteries on the beach for the night's labours. Otherwise they might take pot luck on a tram to an unknown part of Hamburg and whatever diversion it might hold. From a bric-à-brac shop in one such district, John and Paul returned to the Reeperbahn with jackboots and Afrika Korps *kepis* decorated with swastikas.

The less extrovert George was, however, the first Beatle to walk on stage in cowboy boots and a lapel-less leather windcheater bought from a club waiter, garments that became central to the group's look for the next two years. At the Indra, their uniform black had been broken by grey winkle-pickers and mauve jackets, but on transference to the bigger club they earned the nickname "Little Black Bastards"[48] from the Top Ten's UK contingent. In acquiring black-leather trousers, too, they certainly became very beetle-like in colour and texture, but their precarious pompadours, glistening with grease, caused more of a stir at a time when veterans of both the Somme and Dunkirk still wore their hair shaved halfway up the sides of their skulls.

Also worth seeing now was The Beatles' stage act. After a week's petrified inertia on the expansive Kaiserkeller podium, they had slipped into gear when Allan Williams' exasperated yell of "Make a show, boys!" was taken up as "*Mach schau!*" by club regulars. This chant – later corrupted to "Let's go!" – infused each of the group's front line with the desire to outdo each other in cavortings and skylarks. John made the most show of all, with much bucking and shimmying, like a composite of every rock 'n' roller he'd ever admired, an act that – so they and other outfits observed – always elicited a wild response. "They go in for movement," The Spencer Davis Group's leader said later of Reeperbahn patrons. "Musical ability doesn't matter so much."[50]

Suddenly, The Beatles found themselves home and dry as involved onlookers rushed towards the stage or clambered onto crammed tables, worrying when the five flagged, cheering when they rallied, glowing when they went down well. Driven by the new fans' enthusiasm, as well as the fizz of amphetamines, The Beatles' last hour each morning was often as energetic as the first had been at 7pm. Now that they had the knack, there was no stopping them, although, as George would recall, "All we really were was thump-thump-thump."[27] Abandoning his instrument, McCartney might appeal to dancers to clap along to Pete's bass drum, snare and hi-hat, now simultaneously stomping every beat in the bar.

The most active participants were male "Rockers" in uniforms of real or imitation leather jackets, jeans, motorbike boots and T-shirts. The girls sometimes dressed the same, but more frequently it was flared skirts, stilettos and beehive hair-dos. Had they been British, the boys' Brilliantined ducktails would have been in direct descent of the Teds'. Their taste in music and hostility towards interlopers into the Kaiserkeller certainly were.

In comparison, the Grosvenor in the Wirral was a vicarage fête. While up to a dozen waiter/bouncers hacked and struck at single *Schlager* – a chap actively looking for fights – amidst upturned furniture and shattered tankards, a ragged cheer would ensue when Koschmider himself bounded from his office with his ebony truncheon to pitch in, too. *Pour encourager les autres*, the unresisting, blood-splattered victim would then be raised aloft, weight-lifter style, and chucked into the street. A man once staggered from the Top Ten with a stevedore's baling hook embedded in his neck. More conventional aids to keeping the peace could be purchased from a Reeperbahn store called simply "the Armoury" which – as well as the usual coshes, flick-knives and pistols – once displayed a submachine gun, a bargain at 350DM.

All this was a trifle unsettling to a youth of George's temperament, for, guest workers or not, The Beatles' well-being depended on their standing among "all these gangster sort of people".[32] With fear spreading from them like cigar smoke, a midnight *demi-monde* of Mr Bigs and the wealthier madames clumped table-tops to Pete's *mach schau* beat rather than demean themselves by dancing among the Rockers. This fortunate and unquenchable partiality for Bruno's new band was manifested in crates of liquor and even trays of food being sent to sustain them while on stage, or as prepayment for requests.

The Beatles all knew better than to show less than the fullest appreciation of these gifts. In between reprising some parochial Capone's favourite song seven times, they each swigged liberally at a bottle of champagne. An advantage of being so frighteningly honoured was extra-legal protection if ever they ran into trouble within such an admirer's sphere of influence. Descending on a clip joint that had fleeced another approved British group, a *polizei* squad smashed every bottle, mirror and tumbler in the place before boarding it up.

Through Koschmider, George was unofficially exempted from the curfew regulation that forbade those under 18 from frequenting

Reeperbahn clubs after midnight. Bruno had noticed a placard daubed "I love George" – the first of its kind – being hoisted as a fair cross-section of Kaiserkeller females, and males, shouted for *das liebschen kind* – "the lovely child" – to take a lead vocal. Waved in by Lennon, George would evoke desultory screams with Presley's throbbing 'I Forgot To Remember To Forget' or Carl Perkins' 'Your True Love', singing close to the microphone with concentration on every phrase lighting his face.

Sending frissons through more nervous systems was Pete Best, toiling at his kit, his eyes not focused on anyone. He kept in trim by denying himself Preludin and too much booze, and his need for natural sleep emphasised a gradual isolation from the others. Although an improvement on Tommy Moore, Pete's hand in The Beatles' on- and off-stage frolics was dutiful, rather than hedonistic. They'd remember later the longer conversations he had with fellow drummers such as The Seniors' Jeff Wallington or, from the group who replaced them, Ringo Starr of Rory Storm's Hurricanes.

Although George was initially indifferent, even antipathetic, to Ringo, "the nasty one with this little grey streak of hair",[10] as he'd rhyme more than 20 years later, "Dislike someone and will not bend/Later they may become your friend."[51] It was hardly Ringo's fault, either, that his group, direct from Butlin's, received a higher wage than The Beatles. With this intelligence, John immediately solicited Rory to lend him the balance for a new guitar.

Fraternising more with the Storm combo than they had with the rather supercilious Seniors, George, John and Paul gladly helped out when Allan Williams financed Lou Walters' recording of a couple of numbers in a minuscule studio behind Hamburg's central station. Able to reach a bass grumble and falsetto shriek with equal precision, Walters – another who borrowed from the Buddy Holly pin-up aesthetic – was backed by Ringo and the three Beatles (with Paul on bass) on a version of 'Summertime'.

By this time, the Kaiserkeller's stage, creaky in The Jets' day, had become downright unstable, and the two groups conspired to damage it beyond repair and force Bruno to buy a new one. Much stamping and jumping during a spirited performance by Rory And

The Hurricanes did the trick, but rather than provide a new stage Koschmider felt entitled to deduct an amount from the culprits' pay. He'd grown somewhat leery of these British imports of late and, although he couldn't prevent The Beatles from paying their respects to Tony Sheridan, he was damned if any Top Ten defectors were going to pollute the Kaiserkeller. Two Jets got as far as a front table disguised as matelots in false moustaches and striped jerseys before they were frogmarched out. The Beatles had spotted them from the playing area and Lennon, with perverse humour, had announced them ceremoniously and, for the benefit of the knuckle-dustered waiters, in pidgin German.

Pete and Paul knew some schoolboy German, but all of them picked up enough to get by, despite that insular arrogance peculiar to certain Britons abroad that would come to a head in the soccer hooliganism of the 1980s. John was at the forefront of the on-stage cursing, mock-Hitlerian speeches and jibes about the war to an audience uncomprehending, disbelieving or shocked into laughter. Although tittering behind him, George would cry off at the last fence of his hero's habitual shoplifting sprees and one ineffectual attempt to mug a drunken marine who had been sufficiently impressed by the group to stand them a meal.

Mention of The Beatles in Hamburg still brings out strange stories of what people claim they heard and saw. Many of the escapades later attributed to them had taken place under the alibi of a stage act, were improved with age or were originated by others. More shocking than a nauseated memory of a Beatle loudly breaking wind in a Top Ten dressing room is a member of Johnny Hutch's new group The Big Three stepping onto a club stage in nothing but pinafores or one of The Undertakers donning a gorilla suit and emptying several Freiheit bars.

However much The Beatles made themselves out to be frightful pranksters and desperados, to Tony Sheridan, "They weren't that rough at all."[52] As bigoted a southern chauvinist as ever walked the planet, Norwich-born Sheridan gave them credit as "brighter, more intelligent then most of the northern Liverpool people, who are not famous for their intelligence".[52] In corroboration, George would suggest that The Beatles resulted from an English grammar-school interpretation of rock 'n' roll, and who could have disagreed in 1960, when all five were products of such establishments? Although clothed as Rockers, that they were of the so-called academic elite may have been a subliminal lure for the "existentialist" element, who were afraid of Rockers (with good reason) but dared to trespass into the Kaiserkeller to see The Beatles. "Up north, we'd be reading *On The Road* and they'd be reading *On The Road*,"[53] noticed McCartney. "We'd be looking at the same kind of things."[54]

Thanks to the prevalent atmosphere at Liverpool Art College, The Beatles were aware of existentialism. Lennon, especially, was a fan of Juliette Greco, one of its icons. *The Rebel*, a period Tony Hancock film vehicle, represented its adherents as pretentious, middle-class beatniks – all berets, ten-day beards, white lipstick and old sweaters – going about their action-painting, free-form poetry and scat-singing in Paris, the traditional home of bohemianism.

The first German existentialists – nicknamed "exis" – to stumble on The Beatles were an illustrator named Klaus Voorman and his photographer girlfriend, Astrid Kirchherr. It's tempting to imply that they fell for the group like the mock-up "Parisian set" did for abstract artist Hancock's Infantile school, but it was more likely that the Hamburg students were tacitly bored with the coolness of Dave Brubeck, The Modern Jazz Quartet and other hip music-makers whose LP covers were artlessly strewn around their pads. Exposure to the uproarious abandon of the English groups and their trashy rock 'n' roll in the Reeperbahn mire inspired in the city's young intellectuals a horrified urge to reject coolness altogether. Beyond specific songs, all that counted was the rhythmic kick. *Mein gott*, let's dance.

Slumming it at first, sombrely garbed exis cowered near the sanctuary of the stage, hiding behind the piano when, squinting their way now and then, the Rockers commenced their nightly brawl. Little by little, the exis sat more comfortably in the Kaiserkeller and, later, the Top Ten, partly because they'd adopted Rocker dress but mainly because of the friendship they'd struck up with the musicians. "They wanted to know what made us tick," said Tony Sheridan, "and we found them entertaining. Rather than associating with the real tough characters, we just sort of fell together. They showed us the ropes and a lot of things we otherwise wouldn't have seen."[52]

For Klaus and Astrid, the most enigmatic Beatle was not Pete but Stuart, the tortured artist whose eyes were usually hidden behind sunglasses unnecessary in the overcast German autumn. It was no coincidence that bass guitar was the instrument that Klaus began to teach himself. He also felt no loss of face or admiration for Stuart when Astrid and the younger Stuart became lovers.

Astrid's disarming Teutonic directness might have put him on his mettle, but the intelligent rather than intellectual George was also drawn to her. Part of the fascination was her daunting independence – her own car, a separate annex in her parents' house, the ease of her switching from Voorman to Sutcliffe. Her refusal to be an adjunct to Stuart, like Cynthia was to John, was very different to what George had known of women in northern England, who overcooked the cabbage for their dart-throwing husbands.

Like everybody else, including the lad himself, Astrid acknowledged that George was the "baby" of The Beatles. After she presented John with an edition of the works of de Sade for a Christmas gift, George enquired whether his contained comics. A decade later, however, Astrid would express the opinion that the baby had become the most talented Beatle.[29]

As Astrid and Stuart's affair blossomed in 1960, George – not so naïve now – didn't hover around them to the obtrusive extent that he had with John and Cynthia. Of his own age among the exis was another photographer, Jurgen Vollmer, who was also the maker of the "I love George" sign. Vollmer's most abiding memory of the youngest Beatle was of adolescent narcissism, after George had to be roused for an afternoon's boating on a Hamburg lake. While understanding his guest's need to stay dry, Jurgen was amused at how much persuasion was required before, in order to stabilise the vessel, George would remove his long winkle-pickers, stuffed with cardboard so that they didn't curl up. Back on shore, he carefully combed his wind-blown hair into place before he and Vollmer caught the tram back to the Freiheit evening.

Jurgen, Klaus and Astrid's *pilzenkopf* ("mushroom-head")

hairstyle, commonplace in Germany, would be emulated by Stuart and then George during a second trip to Hamburg, although it would be restored to its old shape before George went home. Even if Adam Faith, a new British pop star, was the darling of the ladies with the similar Henry V cut, a male so coiffured would be branded a "nancy boy" on the streets of Speke when even a Presley quiff was still regarded as a sure sign of effeminacy. Funny looks from Kaiserkeller Rockers and open laughter from the other musicians were bad enough, but within a year, said McCartney, all of The Beatles bar Best would get Vollmer "to try and cut our hair like his".[53]

Questions of haircuts may have been as yet unresolved, but at the club George reckoned that "We got to be very good as a band because we had to play for eight hours a night [sic]. We got together a big repertoire of some originals, but mainly we did all the old rock things."[55] A bouncer's typical recollection of the group's Freiheit period was of John and Paul composing in a backstage alcove while George drank his pay, chatted up girls and let the exis lionise him. Few, if any, Lennon-McCartney compositions were then unveiled publicly, but the monotony of stretching out their Merseyside palais repertoire up to four times a night at the Indra had been sufficient impetus to rehearse strenuously even the most obscure material that could be dug from their common unconscious.

The hoariest old chestnuts were tried, though preferential treatment was given to those covered by artists they rated, such as 'Over The Rainbow'. However, bearing a closer likeness to Duffy Power's treatment than Gene Vincent's was The Beatles' 'Ain't She Sweet'. Also, because it had been recorded rock 'n' roll style by US comedian Lou Monte in 1958, The Beatles even had a go at the vaudeville novelty 'The Sheik Of Araby', with Harrison on lead vocal. Neither had they inhibitions about deadpanning standards such as 'September Song' and – an eternal favourite of George's – Bing Crosby and Grace Kelly's 'True Love', from the 1956 movie *High Society*.

In the days when vocal balance was achieved by simply moving back and forth on the mike, the three-part harmonies of John, Paul and George were hard won but perfected in readiness for what lay ahead. Even John's rhythmic eccentricities were turned to an advantage. "We learned to live and work together," said George, "discovered how to adapt ourselves to what the public wanted and developed our own particular style – and it was our own. We developed along the lines we felt suited us best."[56]

Musical progress didn't correlate with personal relationships within The Beatles, however. Once amusing but now annoying its target was the ragging of "baby George" about notices forbidding minors from entering certain red-lit streets. More serious than this and the imperceptible alienation of Pete was Paul's furious jealousy of Stuart as John's closer intimate – so close now that Lennon's inner ear ignored the hard truth that his best friend's bass playing hadn't got far past the three basic rock 'n' roll forms after all these months. Had Paul acquired a bass before Stuart had had the chance, the group would have been less cluttered, Sutcliffe might not have gone to an early grave and the more musical McCartney wouldn't have felt so redundant, often just singing and dancing about with a disconnected guitar around his neck or impersonating Little Richard at the abused Kaiserkeller piano, from which irritating Stuart would snip wires to replace broken bass strings.

A short-lived opportunity for Paul to contribute more would occur sooner than any Beatle contemplated, when history repeated itself. In the face of Bruno's reprimands, the group's visits to the Top Ten had gone beyond merely watching The Jets. When The Beatles joined them on stage during Kaiserkeller breaks, Top Ten proprietor Peter Eckhorn heard not casual jamming but a new resident group, after The Jets' stint ended on 1 December. As well as higher wages, Eckhorn also offered bunk-bed accommodation above the club that, if plain, was palatial compared to the dungeons of Koschmider. Furthermore, The Jets found Peter an affable employer from whom bonuses and other fringe benefits could be expected when business was brisk. Also, rather than racketeers, sailors and tearaways, the Top Ten tended to cater for tourists and *Mittelstand* teenagers.

After he'd secured Sheridan, Eckhorn had next charmed away key members of Bruno's staff, including his formidable head bouncer, Horst Fascher. Reading Eckhorn like a book – and an avaricious publication it was – Koschmider acted swiftly. Firstly, The Beatles were given a month's notice and reminded of a contractual clause that forbade them from working in any other Hamburg club without his permission, which he withheld. Aware that Eckhorn could grease enough palms to circumvent such legalities, Bruno struck harder by withdrawing whatever immunity he'd arranged concerning the youngest Beatle's nightly violation of the curfew.

With less than a fortnight to go at the Kaiserkeller, The Beatles were ordered to present their passports for police inspection. As George was a good three months short of his 18th birthday and had so flagrantly disregarded the law, he was to be deported from West Germany forthwith.

He spent much of the day before his exile giving Paul and John a crash course in lead guitar the Harrison way, as they seemed quite willing to continue in his absence. Indeed, after a month at the Top Ten, there were prospects of playing a season in Berlin. Another possibility was a stint at Le Golf Drouot in Paris, after the departure of its British house band, Doug Fowlkes And The Airdales. Despite government efforts to ban subversive rock 'n' roll, a Gallic species of Rocker – *le yé-yé* – had bred entertainers such as Les Chats Sauvages, Les Chausettes Noires and a Parisian Presley in the form of 17-year-old Johnny Hallyday.

Because the French weren't as rigid about youngsters up past their bedtimes, perhaps George could rejoin The Beatles if they went to Le Golf Drouot. This hypothesis was cold comfort, however, as he gathered his belongings for the voyage back to Upton Green. He also carried with him the heart-sinking conjecture that the others were managing without him. Eric Griffiths had been dumped by The Quarry Men, so what would stop The Beatles recruiting another lead guitarist, if need arose? There were plenty to choose from among the many Merseyside groups now flooding into Hamburg. "A lot of really good guitarists came over from Liverpool," estimated Bill Harry. "Nicky Crouch of Faron's Flamingos...Paddy Chambers – he could have stepped in."

Only Astrid and Stuart saw him off from Hamburg railway station. Bewildered, subdued and very young, George flung his arms around the couple before heaving his suitcase, amplifier and guitar into the second-class compartment of the long, high, foreign train. An inexperienced traveller, he wouldn't be reckless enough to get out to stretch his legs as others did during the painfully slow disembarkations from stops *en route* to the Hook of Holland. Babble penetrated from outside as he stared moodily at the flat landscape, where the exposed cold from the Westarweg hit like a hammer.

The pallor of dawn gleamed dully as he walked stiffly from the ship with his luggage across the concrete desolation of the customs post at Newhaven. After the connection to Liverpool jolted forward, he may have slipped into the uneasiest of slumbers, now that he was more assured of getting home. Hours later, George Harrison climbed down into the vastness of Lime Street's glass dome. Near the taxi rank, an elderly pipe-smoking road sweeper pushed a broom along the gutter. A newspaper vendor in his kiosk barked the headline of Tuesday 22 November 1960's edition of *The Liverpool Echo*.

4 *The Cave Dweller*

Over a few days' convalescent sloth, George pondered. With every reason to believe that The Beatles would remain indefinitely in Europe, who could blame him if he joined another group? Since he'd been away, the Merseyside music scene, while not yet exploding, had grown immensely. From The Pathfinders in Birkenhead to Ian And The Zodiacs in Crosby, each vicinity seemed to have a group enjoying parochial fame. Either active or in formation were outfits of every variety and size, including sextets and octets. Some were all female, others all black. A couple were even all female and black. Most were in it (as The Quarry Men had been) for beer money and a laugh with a "Bert-can-play-bass" attitude. However, as their hire-purchase debts at Hessy's demonstrated, some meant business, among them The Remo Four, who, emerging from Don Andrew and Colin Manley's Viscounts, were recognised as Liverpool's top instrumental unit.

No more an amateur, George might have been welcome in a band of like standing, perhaps Lee Castle And The Barons, which contained his old colleague Les Stewart. Nonetheless, such a consideration proved academic as, by the second week of December 1960, all of The Beatles except Stuart Sutcliffe – by now betrothed to Astrid – had come home, their Top Ten enterprise scotched when Best and McCartney were ordered out of the Fatherland on a trumped-up charge of arson, courtesy of Herr Koschmider.

With ex-Blackjack Chas Newby deputising on bass, The Beatles regrouped for an exploratory booking at the Casbah, followed by another on Christmas Eve at the Grosvenor, cautiously re-opened for pop business. Because of their sojourn in Hamburg, the "successful German tour" of pre-engagement publicity, they were an unknown quantity locally, but not for long. They were a last-minute addition to a bill at Litherland Town Hall on the 27th, and John Lennon would recall The Beatles "being cheered for the first time"[57] in Liverpool after a casually cataclysmic performance that their spell in Hamburg had wrought. Whereas the customers had jived to The Searchers and the two other groups engaged, there'd been a spontaneous rippling stagewards when the curtains swept back a few dramatic bars into The Beatles' first number. As Sheridan would, they behaved as though they couldn't give a damn about the audience and were just up there having fun amongst themselves. "And so many people really dug the band," exclaimed George, "and they were coming up to us and saying, 'Oh, you speak good English.'"[32]

The Beatles' Litherland wipe-out was food for thought for many of the hip Merseysiders who witnessed it. One of Kingsize Taylor's Dominoes, Bobby Thomson, "could see that they were going to be big and I wanted them to be. It was a funny feeling for blokes to want that. Everybody loved them."[58] Actually, it wasn't quite everybody, because to some The Beatles were a scruffy lot who smoked on stage and made, in Don Andrew's view, "a horrible, deafening row". You couldn't deny their impact on the crowd, yet musically they were a throwback, now that pop was at its most harmless and ephemeral. "In England," recounted George, "Cliff Richard And The Shadows became the big thing. They all had matching ties and handkerchiefs and grey suits, but we were still doing Gene Vincent, Bo Diddley...you know, Ray Charles things."[32]

At this time, most of the fiercest practitioners of classic rock were either dead (Buddy Holly), gaoled (Chuck Berry), disgraced (Jerry Lee Lewis), in holy orders (Little Richard) or otherwise obsolete. The Everly Brothers were less than a year off enlisting as marines when Elvis was demobbed, now a sergeant and "all-round family entertainer". The hit parades of North America and everywhere else became constipated with insipidly handsome boys next door, all doe-eyes, hairspray and bashful half smiles, matched by their forenames (mainly Bobby) and piddle-de-pat records. If they faltered after a brace of Hot 100 entries, queuing around the block would be any number of substitute Bobbys raring to sing any piffle put in front of them.

However, in this twee morass, there were few sparkles. Without compromising their rhythm and blues determination, Ray Charles and Fats Domino were still chart contenders, while a Texan named Roy Orbison transformed 'Only The Lonely' – a trite Bobby exercise – into an unprecedented epic with a voice that combined hillbilly diction with operatic pitch and breath control.

No Beatle would equal Orbison's *bel canto* eloquence, but John, George and Paul together could produce distinctive vocal arrangements of The Marvelettes' 'Please Mr Postman', Barrett Strong's 'Money' and other records on Tamla-Motown, a promising black label from Detroit that had manoeuvred its first fistful of signings into the Hot 100. Of all Tamla-Motown acts, George listened hardest to The Miracles, whose leader, Smokey Robinson, had an "effortless butterfly of a voice"[59] that he would never bring himself to criticise.

John was fonder of Chuck Berry, whose celebrations in song of the pleasures available to American teenage consumers would remain prominent in the repertoire of almost all young vocal-instrumental groups on Merseyside, with Berry's incarceration and lack of major British hits only boosting his cult celebrity. Although more popular Yanks dominated British pop, groups within Liverpool's culturally secluded hinterland – as well as those outside the region who went to Hamburg – didn't lean as obviously as others on chart material. Unless specifically requested, most of them scarcely bothered with numbers by British stars, as only a few were up to US standards.

Although Gerry And The Pacemakers prided themselves on embracing everything in each week's Top 20 in their act, they were as competitive as any other professional Merseyside group in seeking out more obscure numbers. "If a rhythm and blues record – say, something by Chuck Berry – was issued, then I'd rush down to the shop and buy it straight away, and chances were I'd see somebody like Paul Lennon [*sic*] of The Beatles in the same queue. Then there'd be a big rush to see who could get their version of it out first."[60] In exchange for the words to The Olympics' 'Well (Baby Please Don't

Go)', John Lennon scribbled the ones to Gene Vincent's 'Dance In The Street' for The Big Three.

Tony Sheridan praised The Beatles' "great talent for finding unusual records",[52] as did Bill Harry and Chris Curtis, The Searchers' drummer. Some musicians and disc jockeys were on the mailing lists of untold US independent record companies, many of which, said George, "were not even known there".[59] A goldmine of such erudition for The Beatles and Gerry was the collection of Bob Wooler, a master of ceremonies on "jive nights" at Wavertree's Holyoake Hall. Along less exclusive avenues, groups might tune in to some static-ridden rarity on the BBC's overseas service or, more often, on the late evening programmes in English on the continental commercial station Radio Luxembourg.

The Searchers and The Beatles were particularly adept at adapting songs by American girl groups to a different set of hormones. Both tried The Orlons' 'Shimmy Shimmy' (less far-reaching a dance craze than Chubby Checker's Twist variations), while The Beatles' 'Boys' from The Shirelles' catalogue was a favourite with the ladies, because it was one of Pete Best's infrequent vocal outings. In Rory Storm's Hurricanes, it came to be sung as a duet by Ringo and Swingin' Cilla, a typist by day who'd made her debut as a chanteuse at the Iron Door, a former jazz club that had cautiously readjusted itself to pop after the trad boom declined. This was paralleled in a wider world via Dick Lester's film *It's Trad, Dad!*, in which performances by Gene Vincent, Chubby Checker and schoolgirl pop star Helen Shapiro were juxtaposed with those by Acker Bilk and other jazzmen.

As a solo by some New Orleans dotard would be revered as definitive by trad dads, so a certain song might be so worthily executed by this or that Liverpudlian pop outfit that it would be shunned by rivals. Few, for instance, were assured enough to take on 'You'll Never Walk Alone' after Gerry had brought the house down with it at the Vincent show, and similar criteria applied to such diverse items as The Merseybeats' gauchely sentimental 'Hello Young Lovers' and black vocal group The Chants' arrangement of The Stereos' 'I Really Love You'.

Only fractionally more than just a name than The Stereos was James Ray, a New Yorker whose 'If You Gotta Make A Fool Of Somebody' was among those numbers that became Merseybeat standards. Another was Richard Barrett's 'Some Other Guy'. While Jack Good *protégés* Little Tony And His Brothers – expatriate Italians – would simply mimic Chan Romero's 'Hippy Hippy Shake', the intention in Liverpool was to make that song, 'Money', Larry Williams' 'Slow Down', The Clovers' 'Love Potion Number Nine' and all the rest of them sound different to any other group's version. Hence the calm precision of The Searchers' rendering of The Isley Brothers' 'Twist And Shout' and The Beatles' frantic work-out of the same, just one step from chaos. Sometimes a song like 'Up A Lazy River' or Brook Benton's 'Hurtin' Inside' would be heard all over Merseyside before being dropped quite inexplicably, never to be played again.

Allegedly, it wasn't until Paul noticed Earl Preston's TTs performing a self-penned song that The Beatles risked any Lennon-McCartney originals in their stage repertoire. Other Mersey Beat musicians – such as The Zephyrs' Geoff Taggart and ex-Liobian Stuart Slater of The Mojos – also came up with items superior to some of their respective groups' non-originals, while The Big Three knocked together 'Cavern Stomp', immortalising the club that, taking its cue from the nearby Iron Door, had allowed pop and trad bands to share the same bill before hosting its first all-pop event in May 1960.

Despite an essence of disinfectant and cheap perfume in its subterranean rankness, to Liverpool footballer Tommy Smith, the Cavern was "the dirtiest place on Earth",[61] with its arched bricks, sweating with slippery mould, and the suffocating heat growing by the minute as more teenagers descended its narrow stone steps toward the metallic beat of either a group or a record spun by one of the club's resident disc jockeys, be it Billy Butler, who occasionally sang with The Merseybeats, or Bob Wooler, uttering his catchphrase: "Hi there, all you cave dwellers. Welcome to the best of cellars."

This sodden oven in a ravine of lofty warehouses would become as famous a Liverpool landmark as the Pier Head. All manner of future worthies, from government minister Edwina Currie to television actress Sue Johnson, would proudly recall how they'd been among the massed humanity bobbing up and down in the blackness as The Beatles entertained on its wooden stage beneath white light-bulbs. The infrequency of the violence that still marred or supplemented pop evenings elsewhere said much about the Cavern's clientèle. Hatchet-wielding hooligans with grievances against Derry Wilkie converged on the Iron Door while his new group were on stage. Of the same mentality were those who wrecked Knotty Ash Village Hall the night on which The Big Three appeared.

At the Cavern, "It wasn't just kids going to a thing with music in the background," explained Bill Harry. "They were interested in the individual musicians. 'I liked the solo Johnny Guitar did on "Doctor Feelgood".' 'Isn't so-and-so a good singer?' They used to compare the abilities of the different musicians and talk about the tunes they used to play. They were quite an intelligent crowd."

Devoid of the complicity of Mona Best or the anxious disapprobation of Aunt Mimi, Louise Harrison was as fanatical about The Beatles and Mersey Beat as any cave dweller young enough to be her grandchild. Frequenting the Cavern even after The Beatles ceased playing there, she accepted honorary membership of the fan club created for The Hideaways, who performed at the Cavern more times than any other ensemble. Without embarrassment, she'd be down there, clapping and cheering, foremost among those blamed by John's tight-lipped auntie for encouraging "the stupid fool" and his so-called group.

As a "rock and dole group" – Wooler's words – no obligations to regular employment had hindered The Beatles making their Cavern debut in February 1961 during one of the new lunch-time sessions that were further maximising the club's profits since it had gone pop. It was still predominantly a jazz venue then, and its main concession to pop was a weekly off-peak evening with The Swinging Blue Jeans, who walked an uncomfortable line between trad and the blandest of pop. Their days as the club's resident pop group were numbered, however, when The Beatles were rebooked on 21 March as the Jeans' guests. By loudly voicing their preferences, 60 extra customers abused this hospitality. In their striped blazers and pressed denim hosiery, the swinging combo failed to see how anyone could respect a group whose lead guitarist had almost been refused entry for his slovenly turn-out.

The Beatles performed there more than 200 times over the next two years, as much a fixture at the Cavern as The Searchers at the Iron Door, The Undertakers at Orrell Park ballroom and, later, Michael McCartney's Scaffold at the Blue Angel. All Mersey Beat groups that counted had a full work schedule. On the evening of George's 18th birthday, The Beatles crammed in two separate engagements, which was a common undertaking now that hard-nosed promoters had smelled the money to be made from all these young bands happy just to have somewhere to make their noise for the many silly enough to pay to hear them.

On one chronicled occasion, George slipped Cavern doorman Paddy Delaney a few shillings – "but don't tell her I gave it to you"[62] – to pass on to an impoverished fan loitering with vain hope outside. George must have been unusually well heeled that day, because his average turnover was only "a couple of quid a week".[22] Typical, too, was one midsummer evening at Orrell Park when, of the net takings of £67, only £19 was split between three groups.

Church halls, social clubs, village institutes, pub function rooms, ice rinks and even riverboats now offered beat sessions. Eventually, there would be a Junior Cavern Club on Saturday afternoons. The managements of larger places, such as the Locarno and the Grafton Rooms (both in West Derby) and the New Brighton Tower Ballroom, were capitulating to older teenagers. After tussles with the Municipal Parks Committee, open-air promotions catered for pop, too, commencing with an event featuring more than 20 groups amid the playing fields of Stanley Park.

George Harrison's earliest remark in the national music press was, "You know, we've hardly done any touring in England. Working in and around Liverpool keeps you busy throughout the whole year."[63] Other areas couldn't duplicate that unique brand of pop enthusiasm that was Liverpool's, but, other than a smattering of venues like the Beachcomber in Bolton and Cardigan's Black Lion, nowhere else in Britain engaged Mersey Beat outfits. Each locality felt a certain territorial superiority towards other bastions of beat. One agency was "formed with the sole intention of stopping Brum groups playing at Worcester venues".[64] However, such embargos were relaxed for visitors of qualified fame like Screaming Lord Sutch And The Savages or Johnny Kidd And The Pirates, on the understanding that local heroes were to be given support spots.

For The Beatles, that left only Hamburg. Thanks largely to Mrs Best's badgering and Peter Eckhorn's assurances of their good behaviour, the West German Immigration Office allowed firebugs Paul and Pete back so that The Beatles could begin a four-month season at the Top Ten in March. Paul had transferred to bass guitar at last because Stuart – now a student at Hamburg's State Art School – had for all practical purposes left the group. His last duty on their behalf would be to write to Allan Williams, repudiating their professional association with him. The grounds for this schism were that, since The Beatles' ignominious return to Liverpool in December, Williams had negotiated only two bookings for them; the rest had snowballed from those found by either themselves or by Mona Best. Saddened by what he saw as the group's disloyalty – although they'd never really been his – Allan found it in him to offer to take them back, after making token legal threats.

What wounded them more was his barring them temporarily from the Blue Angel, where the bands were inclined to congregate after an evening's work while the rest of Merseyside slept. Johnny Hutch would brag of Paul McCartney's face draining of colour when The Big Three supposedly "blew off" The Beatles one night, but rivalry would dissolve into ribald camaraderie as musicians small-talked and had a laugh or a cry if the booking had gone badly – even if most, so it was frequently put about, were triumphs in retrospect. George's propensity for gossip was as profound as the next guitarist's, but, remembering how The Silver Beatles had borne disdain from other groups, he tended to champion those in need of a break. It was through his recommendation that dexterous barrelhouse pianist Terence O'Toole became a Mojo. George was also sincerely loud in lauding fellow Cavern regulars The Roadrunners.

The best-known example of Mersey Beat's *ésprit de corps* was a merger of The Beatles with Gerry And The Pacemakers, as The Beatmakers, one evening at Litherland Town Hall, but it wasn't unusual for, say, Rory Storm to leap on stage for a couple of numbers with Faron's Flamingos or Gerry to deputise for John Lennon at a Beatles Cavern bash, where it was noticed that, like John and The Searchers' John McNally, he had copied Tony Sheridan's high-chested guitar stance.

Back at the Top Ten, the most piquant memory of The Beatles' first, truncated residency was an extra-long extrapolation of 'What'd I Say' with Sheridan's departing Jets. For their second coming, the Liverpudlians would be replacing Dave Dee And The Bostons, whose leader, on receiving this information, said, "'And what are they called?' The Beatles. 'What a bloody silly name that is.' You make a statement like that and you always remember it. Then, of course, we ended up with a name like Dave Dee, Dozy, Beaky, Mick And Tich."[47]

In the Reeperbahn's bierkeller jollity, Dee And The Bostons had evolved from a clumsy Wiltshire group into perhaps Hamburg's most popular attraction. Crucially, they'd become celebrated exponents of the pounding *mach schau* beat that years later would underpin 'Hold Tight', their first big hit under their more ludicrous name. Now that links with the UK had been established, the Freiheit provided training for other British hit-parade contenders among the many streaming in to serve its clubs. "Germany boosted our morale," said West Drayton vocalist Cliff Bennett. "For the first time, we seemed to be making a solid impression on our audiences." As well as a Merseyside faction so pronounced that the bar staff's English was infused with Scouse slang, from further afield came the likes of Birmingham's Rockin' Berries, Bern Elliott And The Fenmen from the ballrooms of Kent and, sons of Weybridge, The Nashville Teens, with no fewer than three gyrating lead singers.

Although the undisputed Presley of the Reeperbahn, Tony Sheridan faced tough opposition whenever British stars of the same vintage were brought over. Prevented by their stage images from going Bobby-smooth were Lord Sutch with his cartoon horror, Johnny Kidd, and Hounslow's king rocker Vince Taylor – although, during one unhinged evening at the Paris Olympia, the latter floated on stage in atypical white vestments to preach a repent-ye-your-sins sermon to a mystified and then furious *yé-yé* audience.

More formidable than any Limey rock 'n' roller, however, was Gene Vincent, then domiciled in England. When asked by the Kentish instrumental sextet Sounds Incorporated what Hamburg was like, he replied, "Oh, it's OK there. I had a nice band backing me up. They're called The Beatles."[65] As well as signing an autograph for Lennon, the Screaming End also recalled "how desperately they wanted to make records!"[65] There was, however, a single recorded during their second stay in Germany, for which they'd been merely Tony Sheridan's accompanists. They weren't even credited as "The Beatles" on the label because, as George informs us, it was too close to "*die pedals* – whatever little kids' terminology would be for it – that's German for 'prick'."[32]

With Sheridan, they'd shared the Top Ten's skylit bunkroom. In order to reach the lavatory, four floors below, they risked an affray with Asso, Eckhorn's truculent boxer dog, whose teeth had sunk into the ankles of both Paul McCartney and Alex Harvey, among many others. Since The Jets' farewell, Tony had had no fixed backing band, using instead whoever happened to be also playing the club. Most felt honoured to be on the same stage, learning the tricks of the trade from one nicknamed "the Teacher" – although David Sutch likened him more to "a sergeant-major. He was really snappy towards them." Throughout the spring of 1961, the Teacher's class featured Rory Storm's Hurricanes, The Jaybirds (the Nottingham group who preceded them) and his star pupils, The Beatles, who'd been on stage with him when they were heard by Alfred Schlacht, a publisher associated with Deutsche Grammophon, with whom Sheridan had signed in Germany.

At Schlacht's urging, Bert Kaempfert, a power on Polydor, the company's pop subsidiary, invited the thrilled Beatles to be one of two groups – both to be called The Beat Brothers – who'd cut tracks with Sheridan from which a single and probably an album could be selected. Thirty-six-year-old Kaempfert was best known for conducting 'Wonderland By Night', a million-selling orchestral sound-painting of Manhattan, and although his music might not have been to The Beatles' taste he had co-written Presley's recent bilingual Number One, 'Wooden Heart', which they'd prudently included in their club set when Bert came by.

One May morning, after snatching a little rest from the night's Top Ten shift, Tony and The Beatles were transported to their first session. With a Deutschmark sign over every fretful crotchet in a proper commercial studio and a minimal budget, the taping took place on the stage of an infant school (the children were on Whitsun holiday) with equipment that Sheridan reckoned "was a leftover relic of the British Army occupation from some sort of radio station they had".[66]

Each number was punched out in three takes, at most, but the mood was sufficiently relaxed for Kaempfert to lend critical ears to some of Paul and John's songs and an instrumental that George – with John's executive clearance – had constructed to fool Rory Storm into thinking that it was the latest by The Shadows. Homing in on a simple phrase, and with generous employment of the tremolo arm – the note-bending protrusion on some electric guitars – George's joke sounded much like a Shadows out-take. As it was more in keeping with current trends than anything Lennon and McCartney had on offer, Kaempfert allowed The Beatles to record it as one side of a possible single in their own right. Given a title and enlivened with barely audible background yelling, 'Cry For A Shadow' – or 'Beatle Bop', as it was informally known – thus became the first Beatle original to be released on record, appearing in June 1962 on Sheridan's *My Bonnie* LP, named after the 45 that had taken him high up in the German charts. Unhappily for them, The Beatles had settled on a standard session rate rather than a stake in Sheridan's royalties.

As shown in its use by Dr Fuchs' skiffle group and Ray Charles' 1958 recording, 'My Bonnie' was one of those semi-traditional songs that never go away. (I remember being forced to pipe it out in an uncertain treble at a primary school concert in 1961.) Like 'Up A Lazy River', it was more in the air than actually popular that year. The same applied to Sheridan's B-side, 'The Saints', and the tearjerking 'Nobody's Child', which, with 'Sweet Georgia Brown' and two other numbers, was taped a week after the first session.

Producer Kaempfert also spared time to record The Beatles' 'Ain't She Sweet' to go with George's instrumental, but neither track was issued outside Germany until they acquired historical interest. When the group's time came, Bert would recount, "It was obvious to me that they were enormously talented, but nobody – including the boys themselves – knew how to use that talent or where it would lead them."[67]

Although he was persuaded in 1963 to re-record his vocal to 'Sweet Georgia Brown', inserting Beatle references, Tony Sheridan didn't exploit his connection as others less qualified would later. He all but crossed paths with three of his former colleagues in 1964, when all were benighted in the same Australian hotel, but he claimed to the one journalist who asked him why there'd been no reunion that he "wasn't trying to jump on their bandwagon".[68] Yet he continued to look up individual members, as he did Pete Best in 1978, when both chanced to be in Los Angeles, Pete there to talk about the old days on a television show.

A sadder Beatle casualty was Stuart Sutcliffe, who'd been a spectator at the Kaempfert sessions. Within a year, he would die at the age of 21 in a Hamburg ambulance of a cerebral haemorrhage that lay opinion would trace to the night he'd been worked over outside Latham Hall in 1961. After he quit the group, Paul's and – to a lesser degree – George's animosity towards him had diminished, both issuing an open invitation for him to sit in with The Beatles whenever they were in Hamburg.

'My Bonnie' appeared in German shops in June 1961. The final weeks at the Top Ten became very long, simmering as The Beatles were to get back to Liverpool to impress everyone with their marvellous achievement. Calling on Arthur Kelly, George and Paul had literally danced with excitement, leaving footmarks on the freshly scrubbed kitchen floor. To Barbara Kelly's deflationary scolding, Paul's riposte was that she'd regret her blunt words when he was famous. With John assuming Tony's lead vocal, The Beatles rubbed it in on stage. Bob Wooler plugged 'My Bonnie' relentlessly, for all it signified rather than its sound. He'd received his copy from George, who'd made sure his relatives and friends got one as well, even if Red Bentley, among others, wasn't that struck with it.

For the Harrisons, home would shortly be 174 Mackett's Lane, a council house again but this time the other side of Woolton from the McCartneys and a more select area than Speke. That three of the group lived so near each other was handy for the van pick-up for bookings. The Beatles' first true road manager was Frank Garner, who doubled as a Casbah bouncer. He was also their official driver, but, since both Harrison and McCartney had gained their licences, they would clamour for a turn at the wheel, the older Paul bullying his way most often into the driver's seat.

This unpleasantness was representative of the discord and intrigues that make pop groups what they are. The Beatles' history was and would be punctuated with unresolvable rows, prima-donna tantrums, *ménages a trois* and bouts of sulking. In spite of his 'Cry For A Shadow' coup, George was still not sure enough of his position within the quartet to impose unsolicited ideas upon the status quo established by John and Paul, who were so hand-in-glove that the two blew a birthday cheque from John's rich Aunt Elizabeth on a fortnight in Paris while the other two cooled their heels. When the chief Beatles came back with *pilzenkopf* haircuts, which they wore boldly around Liverpool, George nerved himself to do likewise.

Unspoken as yet was the desire of all three to be rid of Pete Best as soon as someone more suitable came to light. His dismissal in August 1962 may be ascribed to an inability to conform to the mores of his peers, shown by his maintenance of a shaped cockade instead of what became known locally as a "Beatle cut". More serious was his continued refusals of the amphetamines consumed by the rest during their Reeperbahn residencies. Neither did he contribute much to the group's studentish restricted code, superstitions and folklore.

Almost as much part of the act as their music was The Beatles' informal knockabout clowning, directives to the audience to shut up, coarser language in heated moments, private jokes and, for the girls, Pete's Brooding Intensity and film-star handsomeness. "Pete was the most popular member of the group," recalled Bill Harry. "Fans used to sleep in his garden. He was in such demand that they finally had to give way to all the girls' wishes and put Pete right at the front." With McCartney on drums, pensive Best would sing and demonstrate the Peppermint Twist, but "all the kids came up and dragged him from the stage".

Pete didn't have to try as hard as the less well-favoured Paul, scuttling to and from microphones, and John, who, scoffed Bob Wooler, "gave the impression of being so hard".[44] Brought forward for his 'Sheik Of Araby', George might have cultivated a Cheeky Chappie persona, but, loquacious as he was in the van, at the Cavern, said his mother, he "never used to say anything or smile. George used to say that it was because he was the lead guitar. If the others made mistakes through larking about, nobody noticed, but he couldn't make any." Nevertheless, the concept of John cementing George's runs with rudimentary chord-slashing had become rather a mistaken. Nowadays, lead and rhythm guitars often merged in interlocking harmony, evolved over hundreds of hours on stage. As Lennon elucidated, "I'd find it a drag to play rhythm all the time, so I always work out something interesting to play, [although] I never play anything that George couldn't do better – but I like playing lead sometimes, so I do it."[44]

The interaction of Harrison's *Play In A Day* virtuosity and Lennon's good-bad rawness was compulsively exquisite, even to more proficient guitarists like Colin Manley And The Roadrunners' Mike Hart, who could hear what was technically wrong. "George was regarded as a good guitarist," disclosed Bill Harry, "but he didn't rank with Adrian Barber and, later, Brian Griffiths [both of The Big Three]. People like that were rated and talked about."

Most of them also gilded their fretboard skills with a grinning vibrancy. George didn't always look glum but he was no natural show-off. His main and most imitated stage gesture came to be "the Liverpool leg", a rhythmic twitching of the said limb as if grinding a cigarette butt with the heel. All the same, John McNally affirmed, "You'd think somehow George would get left behind, but he didn't, and he developed his own style – a bit shy – and the girls really liked that."[58]

A perk of being a Beatle was readier access to female flesh than most of the blokes who'd paid admission to shuffle about in the gloom past the burning footlights. A kind of *droit du seigneur* prevailed as short-skirted "judies" with urchin faces and pale lipstick fringed the stage front, chewing, smoking and ogling. In the days before the birth-control pill, pre-marital sex was a bigger step to take than it was when the '60s started swinging, and The Beatles and other famous groups were showered with paternity suits. Many of them emanated from the Freiheit, where bartering in sex was less sheepish than in Liverpool. Giving in to nature's baser urges, free-spirited *frauleins* would simply lock eyes with a selected musician up on stage and point at him while flexing a phallic forearm. Do you reckon he got the message?

The Beatles' third Hamburg season would pass at the new Star-Club, which had given no quarter during a ruthless campaign to outflank the Top Ten as the district's premier night spot. When American pop stars of the calibre of Jerry Lee Lewis and Fats Domino began including the Star-Club on their European itineraries, a desperate tactic of the Top Ten was to bill a Glaswegian duo who impersonated The Everly Brothers as the genuine article.

During The Beatles' seven weeks at the Star-Club, they warmed up for three visiting US idols: Ray Charles, Little Richard and the ubiquitous Gene Vincent. At first, they were starstruck, but, "Backstage afterwards," Charles recollected, "we would sit and bullshit and say we loved each other's music, the typical thing that people in our musical brotherhood all do."[69] George hit it off straight away with Billy Preston, Little Richard's organist. Although only 15, Billy had been performing in public from his earliest youth in Texas and then California. He was a scion of a showbusiness family, and his prodigious command of keyboards led to his playing with many eminent black gospel artists. It was during a television show with Mahalia Jackson that the ten-year-old was spotted by a film producer, who cast him as the juvenile lead in 1958's *St Louis Blues*, which also starred Nat "King" Cole as blind "father of the blues" WC Handy. However, acting was incidental to Billy's chosen vocation. As well as his gospel work, he also ran his own dance band, which was much in the Nat "King" Cole/Ray Charles milieu. On leaving school, he joined what was supposed to be a gospel tour of the world, but with Little Richard and Sam Cooke involved it had become a straight pop presentation when it reached Europe, where Richard's band plugged a gap in the tour with dates at the Star-Club.

Neither Billy nor his new-found friend George knew the extent to which their careers would interweave. As far as George was concerned, they were only likely to meet again if Preston found himself on Merseyside or the Reeperbahn – which, for The Beatles, was all there was. Of the two stamping grounds, Hamburg seemed the better financial bet. Virtually resident in the Fatherland now, Kingsize Taylor, Ian And The Zodiacs and even obscure Liverpool outfits like The Georgians were making a good living there. Both Adrian Barber and Nashville Teens singer Terry Crowe had opted to pursue secure jobs in Freiheit clubs rather than waste a lifetime back in Britain trying to become stars.

Rather than modestly coming into their own on foreign soil, The Beatles preferred to return to Liverpool, even if some groups there had overtaken them on certain fronts. Fontana had just released The Seniors' debut single, while The Remo Four had broken into the US air base circuit and Rory Storm still had Butlin's, and The Beatles almost envied their Quarry Men past, when there was far less to prove. McCartney's forecast in reply to a fan letter – "the first one I had" – was founded in wishful thinking: "We will be making some records soon and will get them released in Liverpool as soon as possible."[70]

There was also a strong argument that self-contained groups were on the wane. You only had to look at Merseyside's crop of outstanding showmen like Rory, Freddie Starr, Lee Curtis, Ambrose Mogg or Bill "Faron" Russley, dubbed "the Panda-Footed Prince of Prance". All Liverpool girl singers like Barbara Harrison (no relation) and Beryl Marsden needed was to be in the right place at the right time. Although Swingin' Cilla had absented herself on the day through stage-fright, she had landed an audition with Kenny Ball's Jazzmen, then in the middle of their four-year chart run. Perhaps The Beatles ought to find themselves a female Johnny Gentle?

On the plus side, they were "the biggest thing in Liverpool", as Ringo Starr testified. "In them days, that was big enough."[57] In concurrence, George added, "We were recognised there, too, only people didn't chase us about."[56] Fans had no qualms about telephoning them at home to request numbers to be played during Cavern sets that would veer fitfully from the merry 'Sheik Of Araby' to Paul's torchy 'September In The Rain' to a stomping, elongated 'Money'. Copying their repertoire and off-hand stagecraft were units like the younger Merseybeats, who, as their Tony Crane admitted, hired a second guitarist "to make the band more like The Beatles".[2]

As unaware as his interviewers were of The Beatles' distant thunder, Roy Orbison – in London in 1962 – conjectured that "you don't seem to have the kind of rhythm groups that we have in the States, and I'm sure that is what the kids want: strong, beaty rhythms that make them jump".[71] Nobody at Roy's press conference could predict that soon native British "rhythm groups" would be jumping up the hit parade in abundance. One of them would end 1963 as arguably more popular than Cliff Richard And The Shadows, with records as competent and attractive but played with guts, like.

5 The Mersey Beatle

With The Beatles as principal carriers, the bacillus of Mersey Beat had spread down river. Touted as "Manchester's Beatles" were The Hollies, a quintet built around Ricky And Dane. The music-hall element of The Beatles' Cavern act was to have a beneficial effect upon another fan, a certain Peter Noone, who also regularly negotiated the 36 miles from Manchester to catch this Scouse group that everybody was talking about.

Before he became the Herman in Herman's Hermits, young Noone found work as a television actor. One of his more celebrated parts was that of Len Fairclough's son in ITV's *Coronation Street*, a gritty soap opera set in a fictitious northern town. An episode in late 1961 had "Eddie", a local rock 'n' roller, performing at the social club, while besotted teenager Lucille Hewitt incurred parental wrath by having his name tattooed on her forearm.

How aware were the scriptwriters of locally produced alternatives to mainstream pop? Like provincial football teams, artists like Eddie would acquire a tremendous grass-roots following of those who'd recount bitterly how, with chart success, this singer or that group later betrayed them by defecting to London. As far geographically from the Cavern as he could be, George Harrison would one day explain to Australian journalists, "When rock 'n' roll died and ballads and folk music took over, we just carried on playing our type of music. When at last we succeeded in cutting a record, the people were ready for a change, and we clicked."[72]

Before the storm broke, puppyish American Bobbys were not as easily hoisting their discs above the Number 20 mark in the UK hit parade. Nonetheless, although The Shadows ruled 1962's spring charts with 'Wonderful Land', their reliance on massed violins to do so buttressed record moguls' theories that groups with electric guitars were *passé*. Almost the only groups worth fussing over we those like The Kestrels – "Britain's *ace* vocal group" – and The King Brothers, whose records were glutinous with orchestration and their producers' ideas. Their moderate chart entries were regarded as secondary to earnings in variety revues.

Other outfits specialised in commercial folk. The best remembered of this bunch were The Springfields, whose panda-eyed singer, Dusty, achieved spectacular solo success when the trio split up. Of the same ilk were Peter, Paul And Mary, a product of New York's Greenwich Village, where the civil rights movement had fused with folk song to be labelled "protest". This trio first intruded upon the UK singles chart with 'Blowing In The Wind', an anti-war opus written by another Village protest singer, Bob Dylan, whose plaintive debut LP was acclaimed in the *NME* as "most exciting".[73] George, however, expressed little enthusiasm for Dylan's down-home intonation, untutored phrasing and eccentric breath control, until John proclaimed himself a convert.

Harrison and Lennon were also the keenest of The Beatles on the record productions of a weedy young New Yorker named Phil Spector, who was hot property in the music business for his spatial "wall of sound" technique, whereby he'd multi-track an apocalyptic *mélange* – replete with everything, including the proverbial kitchen sink – behind ciphers who'd submitted to his master plan. Styled "the Svengali of Sound", Spector was known in the early 1960s for hits with beehive-and-net-petticoat female vocal groups The Crystals and The Ronettes, the latter of whose lead singer, Veronica "Ronnie" Bennett, he would marry.

George swore by him: "He's brilliant. There's nobody who's come close to some of his productions for excitement."[57] Others – me included – ranked British console boffin Joe Meek far higher for inventiveness in his striking juxtaposition of funfair vulgarity and outer-space aetheria. From his Holloway studio in 1962 came 'Telstar', the quintessential British instrumental, by Meek's house band The Tornados. Unbelievably, it topped the US Hot 100, where no Limey group – not even The Shadows – had made much headway. Although a capitalising tour of the States by The Tornados was unwisely cancelled, 'Telstar' played Eric the Red to the British Invasion of America's charts in 1964.

Three years before, there were signs of resistance to the USA's domination of British pop. At large were Mark Wynter, Jess Conrad and Craig Douglas among a mess of blow-waved UK heart-throbs in the Bobby mould. Owing less to Americana, Joe Brown and his Bruvvers swept into the Top 30 with a blend of rock 'n' roll's country end and gorblimey Cockney music hall. On Parlophone, staff producer George Martin had scored his first Number One in 1961 with The Temperance Seven's period recreation of a 1920s dance tune with a stiff-upper-lip refrain from "Whispering" Paul McDowell, who was briefly George Harrison's favourite vocalist. A year on, Parlophone did it again with 'Come Outside', sung in Cockney by Mike Sarne and "dumb blonde" actress Wendy Richard.

Striking back harder was British television. Quickly shutting down *Wyatt Earp* and *Route 66* in the ratings war were home-produced serials. Most popular was *Coronation Street*, but close behind was *Z-Cars*, which was also as ingrained with northern working-class realism as censorship would allow. From the same environment rose playwrights such as Stan Barstow and Shelagh Delaney, novelist John Braine and others with names as uncompromisingly stark. On celluloid, Delaney's *A Taste Of Honey* was shot on location in Merseyside dockland, while the new young turk of British cinema was Liverpudlian Tom Courtenay as *Billy Liar*.

Charming some and sickening others with his "swinging/dodgy" thumb-sign mannerisms, in 1962, fellow Scouser Norman Vaughan had taken over as compere on ITV's long-running variety showcase *Sunday Night At The London Palladium*. A long way from bus workers' social clubs, now, was shock-headed Ken Dodd, "Squire of Knotty Ash" and a television fixture since 1960. With the coming of Richard Hamilton and David Hockney dawned the realisation in the spheres of fine art that, as Royal College student Vivian Stanshall commented, "Clever people could have Geordie and Mancunian accents." Indeed, they could have Liverpudlian ones, too. To crown it all, why not a northern pop group?

With boys combing their hair like John, Paul and George and iron-bladdered girls arriving ridiculously early in the front row at the Cavern to better gawk at Pete, The Beatles had taken local impact to its limit. They were becoming as peculiar to Liverpool alone as Mickey Finn, a comedian unknown nationally but guaranteed well-paid work for as long as he could stand on Merseyside. As one of the area's key pop attractions, The Beatles' triumphs and tribulations were chronicled in *Mersey Beat*, a fortnightly journal edited by Bill Harry. That the first edition sold out within a day demonstrated the strength of demand for its venue information, news coverage and irregular features, such as John Lennon's Goonish "Beatcomber" column. For the publicity it gave to deserving groups, *Mersey Beat* also served as a stepping stone between rehearsing in front rooms and playing the Cavern for the myriad amateur groups bending over backwards in their hyperbole.

Even the professionals they revered stooped to bulk-buying December 1961's edition, with its voting coupon for a poll to find the region's most popular group. By means as fair and as foul as other contenders, The Beatles came out on top in this tabulation, as they would every year.

An obtuse speculation is that, if, in some parallel universe, The Beatles hadn't gained record company interest, they might have been superseded in *Mersey Beat* stakes by younger acts such as The Riot Squad or The Calderstones. By late 1961, the four must have been aware that they were either the same age as or older than those already famous, like Phil Spector, all those Bobbys and Cliff Richard, who'd been just 17 when first he donned his pop star mantle. Was it time to thrust aside adolescent follies and settle down to a steady job, a mortgage, maybe wedding bells? The consolation of a full workload within easy reach was wearing rather thin.

If there was a storm centre of The Beatles' operation, it was surely the house in Hayman's Green, where promoters would telephone Mona Best to book her son's group. She was even organising Beatles showcases herself in halls in the suburbs of Tue Brook and Knotty Ash.

"Mrs Best wanted to manage the group," reflected Bill Harry. "She'd send the letters to get them on the radio and all the rest of it. She was one of those people born to manage, have control, do the business."

Campaigns for engagements beyond Merseyside yielded little but a further Hamburg residency and a Saturday one December in the Palais Ballroom in Aldershot, where all 18 patrons stayed until the last number, transfixed by The Beatles' racket, their funny dialect and endearing lack of arranged routines – quite unlike Aldershot's own top group, Kerry Rapid And The Blue Stars. This expedition had been the brainchild of Sam Leach, a maverick among Merseyside impresarios, who had hoped that what had enraptured Scouse teenagers would prove as alluring to those nearer the heart of the UK music business. However, continuation of the Aldershot project was aborted, even though over 200 turned up at the Palais the following week, via word of mouth, to see Rory Storm And The Hurricanes, another of these here Liverpool groups.

The lesson of this statistic was that there was a potential market for The Beatles beyond Merseyside and Hamburg. Groups in other areas who drew from like influences thought that the same applied to them. So parochial was provincial pop that there seemed to be no halfway between obscurity and the Big Time. From Mansfield, Shane Fenton And The Fentones had managed the quantum jump to a regular spot on *Saturday Club*. Also yet to make a record, Essex quintet Brian Poole And The Tremeloes would garner some national recognition on this programme when its producer, Jimmy Grant, sounded them out in a Southend ballroom.

As no one that The Beatles knew had the clout to enchant Grant and his sort north of Birmingham to catch them at the Cavern, they mailed a tape of one of their recitals over the edge of the world to the BBC Light Programme. Although John – and, by implication, George – disliked the galloping propulsion of Joe Meek's first chart-topper, 'Johnny Remember Me', sung by John Leyton, a package was also dispatched to the great man's Holloway address. However, no summons to report for audition came from Grant, Meek or any other big shot. They'd had quite enough guitar groups already, thank you.

It wasn't back to square one, however, because The Beatles'

undimmed ring of confidence had caught the eye of Brian Epstein, a local businessman, shortly before their poll victory in *Mersey Beat*. The eldest son of prominent Jews, Epstein had had a sheltered upbringing in which, from car windows, he'd noticed but never spoken to rough boys and girls hopscotching and footballing in grey streets and catcalling in that glottal accent you could cut with a spade. From his birth in 1934, and throughout a public school education that he endured rather than enjoyed, he knew nobody who lived much differently from his own family in the genteel Liverpool suburb of Childwall, with its weeded crazy pavings leading across gardens full of daffodils to front doors with silver letterboxes, where the bell would chime and an aproned maid might answer. Eminently satisfactory to Brian was the orderly way in which his mother kept house – the sugar in its bowl, the milk in its jug, the cups unchipped on their saucers on an embroidered tablecloth.

Before every home in Childwall had them, the Epsteins had long possessed a refrigerator, television and overhead bathroom heater as a requital of the family firm which had grown into a respected Merseyside department chain, specialising in furniture and electrical appliances. Brian followed his father into I Epstein & Sons, beginning as a trainee salesman. Apart from a term of National Service and a happier period at the Royal Academy of Dramatic Art, he stuck it out in the family business. 1961 found him in charge of the record department of the city-centre branch of NEMS (North End Music Stores), named after a smaller suburban shop taken over by the firm during his grandfather's time.

While Brian might have despised his own innate and fastidious talent as a shop-keeper, older employees regarded him as a chip off the old block, a hard-working supplier of sound goods. Straight as a die was young Mr Brian. Old Mr Epstein had run a tight, old-fashioned ship, but when his grandson inherited the firm he would drag it into the 20th century. Through his imaginative administration and absorption of modern techniques of commerce, Brian had already turned NEMS into what he could justifiably advertise in both the *Liverpool Echo* and *Mersey Beat* as "The Finest Record Selection In The North". Although he wasn't particularly enamoured with pop *per se*, the 27-year-old had an instinct for a hit, as shown by his bold requisitioning of 250 copies of 'Johnny Remember Me' when rival dealers, hearing a flop, didn't order any. Sometimes the chart performance of a single would be the subject of a small bet between Epstein and his sales assistant, Alistair Taylor.

Along with other central Liverpool stores that sold records, NEMS was on Bill Harry's *Mersey Beat* delivery round. When a gross of them disappeared like hot cakes from NEMS' counter, Brian – "an inquisitive bugger," according to Bill – invited its editor to join him in a sherry in the back office. After expressing his amused astonishment, he heard himself agreeing with Harry's proposition that he, Brian, should write a record-review column in *Mersey Beat*. While perusing consequent editions, he must have noticed the frequency with which The Beatles' name recurred, if only in the banner headlines.

One Saturday afternoon in October 1961, a couple of customers independently asked for 'My Bonnie'. They'd read about it in *Mersey Beat* and heard it down the Cavern in nearby Mathew Street. As a sealed batch of 25 was the minimum that Polydor could profitably export, WH Smith and other dealers couldn't be bothered with either the financial risk or the paperwork. Could the finest record selection in the north help? On one of his hunches, Brian ordered 200.

While these wended their way across the North Sea, Brian, intrigued, decided to investigate these Beatles. Far from thinking of records as mere merchandise, he was more conscious than he needed to be of the artistic and entrepreneurial aspect of their creation and marketing. As a teenager, he'd been privileged – through family connections – to be a fascinated spectator at a recording session by Geraldo's Orchestra. He'd also been interested enough in the spectacle and presentation of pop to pay exploratory visits to two or three "scream-circuit" shows. During an intermission, he'd encountered Larry Parnes, who, warming to the Liverpudlian's enthusiasm, had led Brian backstage to meet Marty Wilde and Billy Fury.

Through Bill Harry, it was arranged that Mr Epstein would be spared the giggling indignity of queueing for admission to a Beatles lunch-hour session with Cavern regulars ten years his junior. With the grace of a palace courtier, Paddy Delaney indicated the worn, slippery stairwell to the approaching gentleman in his conservative suit, sensible shoes, briefcase and "square" haircut. Only Brian's age set him apart, superficially, from many youths – among them absconded Liverpool Institute pupils – also milling about in the semi-darkness. Their appearances, too, were governed by work conditions. Clusters of girls in fishnet, suede and leather studied Brian as they did every reasonably good-looking newcomer. Assessing that he was a bit mature, they resumed their excited chatter until Bob Wooler announced The Beatles.

Merging into the shadows, Brian was torn between the sordid thrill of being out of bounds and a desire to flee the enveloping fug and sticky heat, never to go there again. He was still procrastinating when a thunderous cheer and squeal of feedback heralded the start of The Beatles' performance. Much has been written about Brian's homosexuality and his erotic attraction to The Beatles, especially John, but what struck him first was the volume that precluded conversation and the show's ragged dissimilarity to the slick Parnes presentation he'd seen. The four louts up there in their glistening leathers sounded like nothing he'd ever heard. Marty Wilde had indulged in a little scripted playfulness but this lot were downright uncouth in their verbal retaliations to bawled comments from the crowd.

Hitting all their instruments at once at a staccato "Right!", they'd barge into a glorious onslaught of pulsating bass, spluttering guitars, crashing drums and ranting vocals. Then the one addressed as "Paul" lunged into a sentimental ballad which Brian recognised as coming from the soundtrack of a musical he'd reviewed in *Mersey Beat*. Next they tried a song that Paul said he'd written with John, the guitarist with the loudest mouth. Between Paul and John stood the other guitarist, who spent most of the time between songs fiddling with the controls of his own and the other's amplifiers.

Brian, over his initial shock, tuned into the situation's epic vulgarity as The Beatles walked what seemed to him to be an artistic tightrope without a safety net. Dammit, they were great! When they stumbled off after exacting their customary submission from whoever hadn't wanted to like them, what could Brian do other than struggle through the crowd to congratulate them?

After the second set, Brian had a spot of lunch. With the Cavern odour in his clothes and temporarily deaf to even cutlery on plate, he pondered the laconic question that a Beatle – George, it was – had put to him when he'd poked his head into the bandroom: "What brings Mr Epstein here?" He'd know why when he was drawn back to another Cavern sweatbath a few days later. For reasons that included vocational boredom and frustrated aspirations to be a performer himself, Brian wanted to be The Beatles' Larry Parnes.

The group weren't as nonchalantly indifferent as they appeared to the intensifying and obsessive overtures made to them by this "executive type". Three had arrived late but arrived all the same when, after researching the professional history of his would-be clients, Brian suggested a formal discussion with them at NEMS after one Wednesday half-day closure. Finally, all four assembled for a second meeting – the day after the Aldershot fiasco – where Brian was informed by leader Lennon that he was the man for them. He lacked the know-how of a Parnes or even an Allan Williams, and there was also the likelihood of conflict with the volcanic Mona Best, who still saw herself as patroness of the group, but they were willing to trust his personal abilities and contacts to at least get them off the Liverpool-Hamburg treadmill.

As Harrison and McCartney were minors, Epstein had to secure the signatures of their respective fathers for the official contract that he drew up a year later, in October 1962, when he'd formed NEMS Enterprises as a management company for The Beatles and – not putting all his eggs in one basket – the other acts that he'd subsequently taken on. Until then, a makeshift agreement would suffice, but, determined on the utmost correctness, Brian called on each Beatle's parents to affirm his own sincerity and faith in the group. The Harrisons had fewest reservations about him, reassured that such an elegant, nicely-spoken gent was taking their youngest in hand. In The Beatles' present state, George would be the least of Epstein's worries.

As Larry Parnes would have advised him, Brian's first task was to make the group altogether smoother pop entertainers. They had to become what a respectable London agent or recording manager in those naïve times expected a good pop outfit to be. They had to be compelled to wear the stylish but not-too-way-out uniform suits he'd bought them. Playing to a fixed programme, punctuality and back projection were all-important. Stage patter must not include swearing or attempts to pull front-row girls. They weren't to eat or smoke on the boards any more. John was not to sing, "Oh me, oh my, I've got infection" to rhyme with, "Cast an eye in my direction" in 'Ain't She Sweet'. Paul was to stand nearer the razor when he shaved.

When George followed John's lead in loosening his matching tie during a performance, he'd be ticked off afterwards, as John would be for setting a bad example. Weren't they aware that, beyond the scruffy jive hives of Liverpool, there were strict limits of "decent" behaviour imposed by town councils upon places of entertainment in a prudish Britain that had compelled Billy Fury to moderate his sub-Elvis gyrations before he could be allowed on television?

Their new manager scuttled about like a mother hen, bringing about and enforcing the transformation, being met with irritated shows of resistance. These lessened after Epstein's string-pulling as a major retailer caused Dick Rowe, Decca's head of A&R, to send his second-in-command, Mike Smith, to the Cavern in mid December 1961 to judge The Beatles. It was the first occasion that any London A&R man had visited Liverpool for such a purpose. Smith thought them a lively enough act in their natural habitat, but only his boss could decide whether they'd come over on vinyl. Could the boys come down for a test in Decca's west Hampstead recording studio? Shall we say 11am on New Year's Day?

A quorum of A&R chiefs at EMI – Brian's first choice – hadn't been prepared to go that far after dutifully listening to 'My Bonnie'. According to company chairman, Sir Joseph Lockwood, the attitude was, "Well, we've got plenty of groups, and how can you tell what they're like just from the backing?"[74]

Decca it had to be, then. On 31 December, The Beatles crawled down south, some with amplifiers on their laps to make more room in the overloaded Commer van. At the wheel was Neil Aspinall, a ledger clerk and ex-Liobian who lodged with the Bests. The further he drove, the thicker the snowfall, the duller the wit as the cold and anxiety about the audition took its toll. After checking in at the Bloomsbury guest house where Brian had booked beds for them, the group and Neil ventured out to see the New Year in around the fountains of Trafalgar Square. It was flattery of a kind, they supposed, when two fellows eyed them up and decided they looked disreputable enough to know what pot was. The pair wondered if the Liverpudlians would care to join them in sampling some. It was packed into a large cigarette called a reefer and smoked communally in a hidey-hole like, say, Neil's van. The Beatles were all too aware of Preludin and other stimulants, but pot sounded a bit too cloak and dagger. Besides, they had to be fresh for the Big Day.

Nonetheless, The Beatles weren't at their best when, for a tardy Mike Smith, they ran through 15 songs selected by Brian to demonstrate their versatility as "all-round entertainers" rather than their individuality as a group. As he would later, in an unimagined future, George stole the show by default from John and Paul. Crippled with nerves as Smith issued commands from his glass-fronted booth of tape spools and switches, McCartney seemed too eager to please with misjudged extemporisations, while Lennon executed his lead vocals with a cautious politeness far removed from the bloodcurdling dementia with which he'd invest 'Money' on the boards at the Cavern.

Blotting out the solemnity of the occasion, George was inspired to sing Bobby Vee's latest hit, 'Take Good Care Of My Baby', with an edge that was missing from the original. He also injected the required humour into 'The Sheik Of Araby' and, after all these years, 'Three Cool Cats'. For the most part, his guitar playing – on a new Gretsch Jubilee model – was accurate, if unadventurous, even when simultaneously lilting Buddy Holly's 'Crying, Waiting, Hoping', backed by Paul and John's chiming responses. Furthermore, while fright muted the others, garrulous George came across to Smith as the Beatle with most "personality".

With as many vocal showcases as John, George might have been more of a prime candidate for election by Rowe and Smith as the group's figurehead, for, when British records charted in the early 1960s, it was usually with solo stars. Unless a hit instrumental unit like The Shadows, backing groups skulked in grey mediocrity beyond the main spotlight. Perhaps the compromise of "George Harrison And The Beatles" flashed across Smith's mind.

Such a suggestion proved hypothetical, however, as Dick Rowe, just back from a business trip to New York, reached wearily for the 1 January session tape while ploughing through the backlog accumulated in his absence. Among Dick's critical prejudices was that the last thing anyone – from a teenager in a dance hall to the director of the Light Programme – wanted to hear was a home-made song, and The Beatles had included three. Composers have to start somewhere, but, apart from B-sides of no real musical value, the possibility of a group developing songwriting to any great extent was unheard of. Even the exceptions, like Cliff Richard's 'Move It' and the climactic 'Shakin' All Over' from Johnny Kidd, began on the backs of either US cover versions or "professional" songs.

How, then, could Rowe appreciate how formidable the Lennon-McCartney partnership had become by 1962? After Decca joined EMI in turning them down, other companies offered The Beatles were just as blinkered.

Even without a record deal The Beatles were now a cut above most other Mersey Beat outfits. Although they weren't yet beyond the odd engagement back at the Casbah, Brian had moved them up to more salubrious venues with plush curtains and dressing-room mirrors bordered by light-bulbs (not all of them working). During a week dotted with Cavern bookings, there were now side trips to maybe a golf-club dance in Port Sunlight or on the bill with Rory and Gerry at Southport's Floral Hall, with its tiered seating. Lennon would spend the evening following his wedding to Cynthia Powell with The Beatles in Chester's Riverpark Ballroom.

No more were they changing in men's toilets or being paid in loose change. When supporting a hit-parade entrant, Brian ensured that his Beatles appeared second to last, as if to imply that they were only one rung below even Americans like Bruce Channel and Little Richard, as well as Emile Ford and Shane Fenton – who, incidentally, began a courtship of Iris Caldwell in 1962, after a period when she'd been "talked of" with Paul McCartney.

The next step up was to the ballroom circuits controlled by Jaycee Clubs and, even better, Top Rank, a leisure corporation that had belatedly clasped rock 'n' roll to its bosom. Reputations were made in these ballrooms, a link to recording contracts and nationwide theatre tours. Having scant seating on purpose, dancing was encouraged, and Top Rank expected its bands to provide action-packed music and the generation of a happy, inoffensive on-stage atmosphere.

Cleaned up, The Beatles rose to the challenge and became a dependable draw as their work spectrum broadened to Yorkshire, Wales and as far south as Swindon. Often they'd appear with other proficient groups who'd likewise broken loose of local orbits and compare notes, among them Sounds Incorporated, Sheffield's Jimmy Crawford And The Ravens, the diverting Barron Knights from Leighton Buzzard and The Rebel Rousers, whose X-factor, Cliff Bennett, could sing updated American R&B without losing the genre's overriding passion.

The same could be said of John Lennon and Paul McCartney, whose respective baritone and tenor were the Beatle voices heard most during the show. A hybrid of the two, George was no slouch on vocals now, either, although he was brought to the fore slightly less frequently these days. John and Paul still took most of the weightier material, leaving comic relief, Bobby drivel and no less than three Joe Brown numbers – including an embarrassed 'I'm Henery The Eighth I Am' – to George. When dancers wanted something from the charts, it would be George who'd give 'em passing joys like Tommy Roe's 'Sheila'. Nevertheless, John had handed him Chuck Berry's 'Roll Over Beethoven', and he'd been permitted to slow things down Paul-style with 'Devil In Her Heart' by The Donays, another obscure US girl group.

A reliable standby when McCartney and Lennon's voices needed a rest in the ballrooms, George was rarely allowed a lead vocal for less run-of-the-mill events, such as The Beatles' first radio broadcast, recorded before an audience at Manchester's Playhouse on 7 March 1962. Afterwards, the four were shocked when they were mobbed by libidinous females not much younger than themselves. Most were after Pete, who, pinned in a doorway, would lose tufts of hair to clawing hands while the other three bought their freedom with mere autographs. Despite himself, taciturn Pete was becoming a star. Watching the frenzy sourly was Paul's father, who would unjustly berate the drummer for stealing the limelight.

However, Mr McCartney couldn't have complained about George, who'd answered the knock of two girls at Mackett's Lane. Unrecognised, he'd been promptly left alone on the doorstep when they realised that it wasn't Paul's residence. Yet neither Paul nor rough diamond John would ever oust Pete as the ladies' dream Beatle for as long as he stayed with them. For a while, Best and his pushy mother had been unconscious victims of sardonic *bons mots* by the McCartneys and Lennon. Bill Harry "couldn't see him being at the root of it", but George joined in the underhanded dissection of Pete. To insiders like Harry, Best had long been a being separate from the others: "Pete would be right in the corner all by himself. George, Paul and John all mixed well. Paul was very smooth and easy to get on with. John was only abrasive if you let him be. George would be very polite, a very warm personality."

George's principal gripe was musical. Although Epstein might have been at fault in choosing the wrong material, Pete's unobtrusive but limited drumming at Decca became another focus for discontent. While Harry insisted that The Beatles were "a lot more raw and raucous with Pete Best", perhaps this was because, as Jackie Lomax of The Undertakers said, he "could only play one drum beat, slowed up or speeded up".[75]

Epstein, too, was a scapegoat. By mid 1962, he still hadn't landed that elusive record deal for his ungracious Beatles. EMI alone had signed up The Barron Knights and, via Joe Meek, Cliff Bennett. With John's wilful sarcasm pricking him, Brian embarked on one more traipse round the record companies of London, this time with a copy of the Decca tape as well as, for display only, a few 'My Bonnie' singles.

Two days after arriving, he had a lucky break. To gild his sales pitch, he decided to transfer the Decca session onto acetate reference discs at the cutting studio within EMI's busy Oxford Street record shop. There he'd arranged to see Robert Boast, its general manager, who he'd met at a retail management course the previous year in Hamburg, of all places. On learning what had brought Epstein to London, the genial Boast said that he might be able to help.

The next morning, in one of EMI's Manchester Square offices, Brian was sitting opposite George Martin, of the one EMI subsidiary that hadn't given The Beatles a thumbs down. Parlophone traded in comedy and variety rather than outright pop, and consequently it was less dogged with fixed ideas than other labels. Adam Faith and The Temperance Seven aside, it had produced few even marginally consistent hit-makers compared to rivals, but a number of Parlophone's records had done well enough without actually making the charts. Those that did were generally short-lived novelties by artists such as The Goons and Irish chat-show host Eamonn Andrews. Mostly, Parlophone ticked over on steady-selling LPs by Scottish dance bands, television spin-offs and light orchestral outings, some by George Martin himself, whose elevation to headship of the label in 1954, at the age of only 29, was no mean achievement.

One such as Epstein couldn't have guessed Martin's lowly origins in a north London back street, because service in the Fleet Air Arm during the war and, later, the BBC had raised his social standards and refined his elocution. A self-taught pianist, George gained a scholarship to the Guildhall School of Music that held him in good stead when he began on the ground floor at EMI in 1950.

Not letting personal dislike of teenage pop music deter him, Martin and his assistant Ron Richards had sought to provision Parlophone with some sort of equivalent to whatever sensations other labels threw up. Among those tried so far were Dean Webb (a dishwasher from the 2I's who resembled Marty Wilde) and Shane Fenton And The Fentones. As a musician, Martin had been more taken with Bill And Brett Landis, a duo who wrote their own songs. However, none of his finds could match Johnny Kidd And The Pirates on HMV or Columbia's precious Cliff Richard And The Shadows. Although a Parlophone artist, Adam Faith was someone else's production baby, and even he was waning when into George Martin's life came a chap called Brian Epstein.

What Martin heard of Epstein's group didn't excite him much, but they weren't obvious no-hopers and Brian himself was more believable than others who'd pressed their clients on Parlophone. It would do no harm, George supposed, to try The Beatles out in one of EMI's St John's Wood studios. As Ron Richards handled most rock 'n' roll, he could take charge of the session, which was set for 6pm on 6 June 1962.

The Beatles had been back from their third visit to Hamburg less than a week when, on that unseasonably cool evening, Neil Aspinall's white Commer bounced into the asphalt car park of 3 Abbey Road, after he'd ascertained that the building, with its Victorian *façade*, actually housed a recording complex. He and the group lugged in the equipment, which was even worse for wear – as were The Beatles themselves – after a seven-week beating in the Star-Club, shortly to be as well known in Germany as the Cavern was about to become in England.

In the crowded but cosy hotel accommodation laid on by the Star-Club, George Harrison had been the only Beatle awake when the telegram arrived with Epstein's news about Parlophone. Basking later on Timmendorf Beach, he seemed to have already counted his chickens as he outlined to Klaus and Paul all that he was going to buy with his share of the royalties from The Beatles' first hit – a house with a swimming pool for himself and a bus for his Dad.

After an eyeful of what other studio staff had told him was a funny-looking band with gimmick haircuts, George Martin sloped off to the Abbey Road canteen, only to be recalled to the console shortly after The Beatles began recording. Like Mike Smith before them, Richards and engineer Norman Smith wanted a second opinion. Taking over, Martin called the group into the control booth when they'd finished to hear a playback.

Towering over them as they lounged about the room, he then explained the technical functions of the studio and suggested that, before – or, rather, if – they returned to Abbey Road, they ought to invest in better amplification. The Beatles digested his words in unresponsive silence. Was there anything they didn't like? There was some fidgeting and poker-faced glances at one another. Suddenly,

George Harrison, lolling on the floor, piped up, "Yeah, I don't like your tie," and the ice broke.

More than their music, Martin was won over by the humour that nerves had suppressed that wintry morning at Decca. Unharnessed by Harrison's cheekiness, it was not unlike the ex-undergraduate satire that was infiltrating television. Martin had lately recorded an album with the team of BBC's *That Was The Week That Was*, a late-evening topical series that nurtured such future balusters of British comedy as John Cleese and Bill Oddie.

After The Beatles left, George Martin re-ran their tape. Cautiously, he decided to take them on for an initial two singles with an option on further releases if these gave cause for hope. All four songs on the tape were fairly mordant and at odds with the group's hilarious corporate personality. He'd have to grub around publishers' offices for a vehicle to project this. The notion of drafting in an outsider to be their Cliff Richard was dismissed.

When they returned to record their debut single in September, they'd done some structural tampering on their own account. The trickiest part of this manoeuvre hadn't been so much the heartless sacking of Pete Best – that they'd delegated to Epstein – but retaining the services of Neil Aspinall as general dogsbody, as well as his van. Not only was he one of Pete's best friends but he was also close to Mrs Best. He'd been disgusted by the cowardly fashion in which the group had cast out Pete, but, surprisingly, it was the drummer himself who convinced Neil that it would be in his best interests to stay on, as "The Beatles are going places".[76]

Because they were doing just that, their change of personnel couldn't be overlooked as simply another switchover in the Merseyside group scene, as incestuous a game of musical chairs as anywhere else. With the truth that Pete hadn't "left the group by mutual agreement",[77] as Brian had informed *Mersey Beat*, the vexation of his many devotees spilled over into "a lot of trouble",[78] as George wrote to a girl fan. This embraced damage one night to George's second-hand car, petitions calling for Best's restoration and an interrelated and very real riot in Mathew Street as The Beatles entered the Cavern with their new member.

George's appearance on stage that day with a black eye, however, resulted not from the Best affair but a jealous swain's vendetta caused by jealousy because of his girlfriend's inordinate fondness for The Beatles.

The bruise still hadn't healed in time for the publicity photographs taken during the group's second visit to Abbey Road, and he compounded this blemish with a sullen expression for the first that Britain at large would see of George Harrison. More welcoming was the wan smile on the homely visage of 22-year-old Ringo Starr, who'd been one of Pete's deputies and then his successor.

Equal to Best as a percussive aggressor but with neater hand-and-foot co-ordination, the ambidextrous Johnny Hutch had been headhunted for The Beatles but declined the post, mainly through loyalty to The Big Three. A requirement that he may have found burdensome was the lighter touch necessary to accentuate vocal harmonies more complex than those of his trio.

More pliant a character than Johnny or Pete, Ringo was prepared to look the part by brushing his hair forward and shaving off his beard. Unlike the hapless Best, Starr was "lucky to be on their wavelength when I joined. I had to be, or I wouldn't have lasted. I had to join them as people, as well as a drummer."[79] It has been said that, if Pete Best was the unluckiest musician in pop, the luckiest was Ringo Starr, even if Lennon later mused, "Ringo's talent would have come out one way or another."[80]

Born Richard Starkey, Starr had had an unsettled boyhood in the Dingle, a depressed Liverpool suburb backing onto the docks. Through his parents' marital unhappiness, he had spent much of his early years minded by other relations. Domestic conditions stabilised when his mother remarried, but long spells in hospital marred the sickly child's schooling. Nevertheless, despite his hangdog appearance, the solitary Richard remained cheerful, philosophical and blessed with a ready wit as guileless as John Lennon's was cruel.

Since rat-a-tat-tatting a tin drum in an Orange Day parade while at primary school, Richard discovered that he had a natural sense of rhythm. For occupational therapy while recovering from pleurisy, he'd bashed percussion in a ward band. This interest was encouraged by his step-father, who bought Richard a second-hand drum kit for his 16th birthday.

By then, British Rail had taken him on as a messenger boy, seconding him to Riverdale Technical College to complete basic education. Unimpressed by his prospects, he resigned to become a Mersey ferryboat barman until he was fired for insubordination. He was then persuaded by his Youth Employment Officer to start an apprenticeship at Henry Hunt Limited, manufacturers of school climbing frames.

With other joiners, he formed The Eddie Clayton Skiffle Group before drumming with other local outfits. With two of The Hi-Fi's, he amalgamated with Alan Caldwell and Johnny Byrne – after George Harrison's failed audition – in what evolved into Rory Storm And The Hurricanes. When the Butlin's offer came up, Richard was considering emigrating to the United States, but after much deliberation he collected his cards from Hunt's. On the rebound from a broken engagement, among other incentives beckoning him to The Hurricanes' booking at Pwllheli were increased opportunities to fraternise with girls.

It was then that he agreed reluctantly to adopt his stage name to facilitate Rory's introduction of a section of the set known as "Starr Time", which included a five-minute drum solo. He first noticed The Beatles when George was giving Stuart a bass lesson in the Jacaranda basement. Even after the shared experience of the Kaiserkeller, Ringo didn't feel that he knew them well enough to ask them to his 21st birthday party, although he became closer to The Beatles during that second Hamburg season, when, from that unfavourable first impression, George especially found him a bit of a card.

By January 1962, Ringo's worth as a drummer was such that, tempted by a huge fee and use of a car and flat, he left Rory Storm for Hamburg to back Tony Sheridan, re-enlisting as a Hurricane three months later for a tour of US military bases in France, followed by another few weeks at Butlin's in bracing Skegness. He seemed to be marking time, even debating whether to quit showbiz to finish his apprenticeship and settle down with Maureen Cox, his 16-year-old girlfriend. Another possibility was returning to Germany as either the Star-Club's resident drummer or as one of Ted Taylor's Dominoes. However, when Lennon and McCartney turned up at Skegness offering a fractionally higher wage, Starr gave Storm three days' notice and became a Beatle.

At the second session for the group's single, Ringo was dejected when George Martin hired a more experienced player to ghost the drumming. At Ron Richards' insistence, George Harrison left out most of the repetitive guitar phrases in an opus entitled 'Love Me Do', a harmonica-led Lennon-McCartney original that The Beatles preferred to the perky and "professional" 'How Do You Do It' that Martin thought tailor-made for them. 'Love Me Do' had been presented to their producer as, recalled John, "a slower number, like Billy Fury's 'Halfway To Paradise', but George Martin suggested we do it faster. I'm glad we did."[81] He later admitted, "We all owe a great deal of our success to George, especially for his patient guidance of our enthusiasm in the right direction."[82]

Perhaps they might have been better off with a remake of 'Like Dreamers Do' or another of the breezier items from the Decca tape. Nonetheless, 'Love Me Do' – still less than mid tempo – had an unusual atmosphere, with no obvious precedent. Not long after its release on 4 October 1962, a few scattered airings crackled from Radio Luxembourg. Tipped off about the night but not the time of the first of these, George sat up to listen. His mother waited, too, until she could scarcely keep awake. She rose from bed, however, at George's shout when 'Love Me Do' finally filled the airwaves. As his wife and son crouched downstairs, straining to hear the guitar work, Harold groaned. He had to be at the depot, fresh and alert for the early morning shift.

An avid surveyor of the hit parade, George was elated when, spurred on by plays on the Light Programme and the buzz from the northwest, 'Love Me Do' began its yo-yo progression to a tantalisingly high of Number 17 in the *NME*'s Top 30. With nothing on file about this "vocal-instrumental group",[83] the newspaper made much of their hailing "from Liverpool, birthplace of such stars as Billy Fury, Frankie Vaughan, Norman Vaughan and Ken Dodd".[83] They'd done well, for first-timers, but who would assume that The

Beatles were anything other than a classic local group who'd caught the lightning once and would probably be back on the factory bench by this time next year?

The Beatles, you see, couldn't sing – not real singing, like Frank Ifield, a yodelling balladeer at the height of his fame, with no fewer than three singles concurrently in the Top 20. Already there'd been a sign that The Beatles were perishable, when the redoubtable *Peterborough Standard* reported that they'd "failed to please"[84] in the mismatched support spot Epstein had procured them to Ifield in that town's Embassy Cinema.

Responding to a request, The Beatles approximated Ifield's 'I Remember You' when, under protest, they disturbed their UK chart campaign by honouring two short seasons outstanding at the Star-Club. Into the bargain, as 'Love Me Do' had fallen from the hit parade, they were considered less deserving of the red-carpet treatment in Hamburg than Johnny And The Hurricanes – nothing to do with Rory Storm – on their first European tour.

It was noted that the American quintet had added vocal items to what had been a purely instrumental repertoire. Similar adulterations were taking place in Britain, as fewer instrumental units were making the charts. By the time The Beatles recorded their second single, 'Please Please Me', in November 1962, the swing towards vocal instrumental – or "beat" – groups had become permanent. This tendency was most keenly felt up north, where, charged Lennon, "other groups are pinching our arrangements",[85] but elsewhere local musicians were latching onto the concept that a group alone, without a featured singer, could be a credible means of both instrumental and vocal expression. In Birmingham, The Jaguars added a singer and became The Applejacks, while north London's Dave Clark Five – contracted to Mecca, Top Rank's rival – shifted their stylistic bias from sax-dominated instrumentals to vocals.

Younger groups sang in public from the outset. One formed by a lad named Kevin Manning was a typical case. Spending a school holiday in Liverpool with Irish relatives, Kevin's path became clear after an evening at the Cavern. On returning to his Hampshire secondary school, he was going to form his own group. They'd call themselves "The E-Types", because it wouldn't be just him and a backing group but a proper one, like The Big Three or The Beatles.

As Kevin carried the Olympic torch of Mersey Beat to his neck of England, its principal ambassadors' 'Please Please Me' was scudding up the charts, after they'd mimed it on *Thank Your Lucky Stars*, TV's main pop showcase. This prestigious slot was the ignition point for The Beatles' continued advancement, rather than a drift back to Merseyside obscurity. The change of colour of Parlophone's labels at this point from red to black was an apt herald of a new pop generation.

The studio audience had screamed indiscriminately at The Beatles, as it did at all male performers, but viewers, cocooned at home during that severe winter, would gauge more objectively from *Thank Your Lucky Stars* and later 'Please Please Me' TV promotions that The Beatles weren't like other groups. Musician Barry Booth, who was to be veteran of many a Beatles package tour, would reminisce, "One of the novelty aspects of The Beatles was that each member of the group was required to present a different identity, and they didn't have choreographed movements on stage. Each man's persona was different, so that John's movement would be up and down, Paul used to shake his head from side to side and George was a bit more still than the other two. Ringo was a law unto himself. There was a complete absence of any organised footwork and patter."

As dirge-like in embryo as 'Love Me Do', the arrangement of 'Please Please Me' had, on George Martin's instructions, been simplified and accelerated, with tight harmonies and responses behind John's lead vocal. Ringo was allowed to drum throughout the session this time, and the Harrison guitar – and voice – were more in evidence than before.

When Bob Wooler announced the momentous news that 'Please Please Me' had tied with Frank Ifield's 'The Wayward Wind' at Number One in the *NME* chart, the Cavern crowd – and, therefore, the rest of The Beatles' possessive Liverpool following – weren't particularly thrilled. After February 1963, "the newest British group to challenge The Shadows"[86] would never play another Cavern lunchtime session, as they were spirited even further away from the trivial round of local engagements. Driving, driving, driving to strange towns, strange venues and strange beds, with more bookings than they could possibly keep, they led what the economist would call "a full life". Five days spent pottering around Scottish town halls might be followed by four in Channel Island ballrooms and a one-nighter back on Merseyside. Often, they'd have to drop everything to fit in photo calls, press interviews and radio or television transmissions. So scrupulously hectic was their schedule that, caught off guard while snatching a quick snack, George spurted a mouthful of hot-dog on air when called to the microphone on an edition of *Saturday Club*.

More pleasant a shock were the considered ovations that unfurled into screams when the group were second billed to Helen Shapiro for an around-Britain tour that spring. By the final night, Helen was still closing the show, but the *de facto* headliners by then were The Beatles, with their "clipped negro sound".[86] She hadn't a prayer from the start. Her last two singles had flopped badly, while The Beatles, buoyed mid tour by their chart-topper, were, according to Barry Booth, "very new news. They'd just appeared from Hamburg. There were buzzes of conversation about this new quartet. The unusual spelling of 'Beatles' was causing comment."

Helen conducted herself with observed good humour when eclipsed by these Liverpool lads, who were as bewildered by their sudden fame as she'd been by hers in 1961. They'd been flattered but not quite comfortable when she chose to travel with the supporting bill in their coach rather than be chauffeured like the star she was. After a while, John became familiar enough with Helen to play practical jokes, while "George asked me lots of showbusiness questions. He is just about the most sincere of the four...and the most professionally intelligent. By that, I mean he's keenest to know all the mechanics of the music industry. Mind you, I was way out of my depth much of the time, because I don't get involved with royalties and things like that. I stick to my music, and so does George, most of the time."[87]

Space restrictions and the laugh-a-minute ambience of the tour bus circumscribed serious guitar practice for George and composition for John and Paul, although flashes of inspiration could be revised and developed in hotel-room seclusion. "The words are written down, but the music is never," elucidated Paul, "because we can't read music. We play it to each other and soon pick it up and fool around with it a bit. George suggests something extra, then John adds a new idea, and so on."[88] First refusal of the freshly-concocted 'Misery' was given to Helen, but it appeared in the shops by Kenny Lynch, another singer on the tour. "The song is very attractive," exclaimed the *NME*, "with a medium-paced beat."[89] It was also the first-ever cover of a Lennon-McCartney song.

The Beatles also left their mark on Kenny's own composing efforts, as exemplified by his 'Shake And Scream', modelled on 'Twist And Shout', soon to be regarded as their signature tune. This had been literally an eleventh-hour addendum to the overworked group's debut LP, issued to cash in on their 'Please Please Me' breakthrough. Legend has it that *NME* scribe Alan Smith, present with them for the "whole day"[90] it took to record, suggested 'Twist And Shout' to George Harrison during the last coffee break of the sessions, after hearing The Isley Brothers' version the day before. Just as the studios were about to close for the evening, the fatigued Beatles picked up their instruments and smashed out the raver that had stopped the show on their last night at the Star-Club, Lennon rupturing his throat with a surfeit of passion on what was, after all, only doggerel about an already outmoded dance.

It became one of those tracks that surface as being Worth The Whole Price Of An Album. The rest of the record was also of a high standard in a year when, geared for singled, LPs containing best-selling 45s were haphazardly programmed, short on needle time and padded with hackneyed chestnuts, stylised instrumentals and unoriginal "originals". As they always will be, good looks and "personality" were sufficient to sell sub-standard produce.

Compared to the electronic ventures of a less innocent age, The Beatles' early Parlophone recordings were crude affairs. "*Please Please Me* we did straight onto a two-track machine," Harrison had deduced from his comprehensive shadowing of George Martin's production methods, "so there wasn't any stereo as such."[32] A more complicated approach would have emasculated the raw drive of 'Twist And Shout', 'Boys' and other crowd-pleasers that George Martin had logged on a field trip to a Beatles bash at the Cavern.

Over half of the *Please Please Me* album was written by Paul and John, an extraordinary production choice when – as The Big Three would discover, to their cost – groups were forced to record material that bore little relation to their own musical inclinations. It was often presumed that, when an artist said he was recording all his own songs, his producer or manager had hired professional composers to come up with items exclusively for him. Even after they'd written dozens of hits for both The Beatles and others, Lennon and McCartney would still be damned by such faint praise as "reasonably good 'amateur' composers, greatly assisted by the poverty of British pop composing standards".[91]

Fusing industrious pragmatism with fertile imagination, John and Paul's originals on *Please Please Me* encompassed concessions to current taste. The melody of 'Please Please Me' itself was not unlike that of 'Charmaine', revived in 1962 by The Bachelors, while more than a touch of Frank Ifield prevailed in 'Do You Want To Know A Secret', George's only lead vocal on the album. Conscious that Lennon especially would knowingly warp the tunes of others to his own ends, it dawned on George that this particular opus was "actually a nick, a bit of a pinch"[59] from The Chants'/Stereos' 'I Really Love You'.

For all his sterling performances at the Decca audition, George was given 'Do You Want To Know A Secret' because, in Lennon's lordly estimation, "it only had three notes and he wasn't the best singer in the world".[80] Whereas Frank Ifield might have lustily yodelled its hookline, "I am in love with yoooooou," George got by with a thin falsetto, boosted with reverberation.

Only a slightly better job of it was made by Billy Kramer, the third act in Epstein's stable to reach the Top Ten, after Gerry And The Pacemakers. Lennon had advocated dividing "Billy" and "Kramer" with a non-signifying J and accepted a commission to provide him with another made-to-measure smash. Another beneficiary of Lennon and McCartney's creativity was Swingin' Cilla, now Cilla Black. Unsolicited covers from *Please Please Me* included a version of 'There's A Place' by The Kestrels' – less than Britain's ace vocal group, now.

They raised a few screams by association, but by 1963 The Kestrels and their kind were lost as The Beatles set the ball rolling for self-created beat groups. Tearing chapters from The Beatles' book, musicians in other outfits were having a go at writing their own songs. A personal triumph for Gerry Marsden was when his own 'I'm The One' was prevented from topping the hit parade only by 'Needles And Pins', The Searchers' third Top Ten single.

One of *Mersey Beat*'s many laudable aims was to foster group members' self-expression beyond merely hammering out 'Money' down at the Iron Door. As well as Lennon's prose, the journal's pages included others' cartoons and travel notes from home and abroad. Further extra-curricular activities encouraged by Bill Harry included a mini pantomime which The Roadrunners put on one Christmas.

On one evening in 1963, Harry fell in with George Harrison, who was just leaving the Cabin Club in Wood Street. The two strolled around the corner to the *Mersey Beat* office, where Bill invited his companion to climb its narrow stairs for coffee. Just in from Germany were review copies of a record by Kingsize Taylor. The conversation got around to The Beatles' Hamburg sessions with Sheridan. Bill recollected George's 'Cry For A Shadow'. Had he written anything else since? Why not? Had he thought about collaborating with Ringo?

From that day on until George actually wrote a song, Harry would embarrass him by bringing up the subject of songwriting each time they met. The steady drip of Bill's incitement impelled George to forego the Liverpool clubs on some of his few nights off to stay in and give this composing lark a whirl. For months, however, everything he tried sounded the same. He didn't have the confidence for the public trial and error that John and Paul endured without a thought when they pieced together The Beatles' third single, 'From Me To You', on the coach during the last leg of the Shapiro tour.

A bare week after this jaunt was finished, the group were thrust into another such trek. On the posters, their name was in smaller type than Tommy Roe and Chris Montez, Bobby-ish Americans both with singles currently in the UK Top 20. Assuming that they'd have a walkover, each went through the motions when the tour opened in east London with stock "wonderful-to-be-here" vapourings and, sneered one reviewer, "no semblance of a stage act".[92] What was a minor sales territory like England to them? Who needed its cold and the snow still on the ground in mid March?

Worse still, right from the first night, the running order was reshuffled as audience response had dictated that the home-grown Beatles play last, even on the three stops when they appeared as a trio, owing to John's absence with 'flu. To Paul's chagrin, the press were referring to Lennon as "lead singer" these days, but the group ably covered for him, with George manfully taking the lead in 'Please Please Me', as well as 'Do You Want To Know A Secret'. The Big Three managed without the almost-compulsory second guitar, so why shouldn't The Beatles? Besides, who could appreciate that a bit was missing in all that screaming?

The one-nighters that were The Beatles' bread and butter between tours were quite ticklish operations now. While Lennon was showering with sweat those crammed closest to the front of one low ballroom stage, "a fan grabbed hold of my tie and [laugh] the knot got so tight I couldn't take it off".[93]

Whether or not John was actually as benign about the incident at the time as he appeared, Beatle fans chose to believe that he was. They also didn't doubt George's humility when, at an engagement in Exeter, he apologised for the group's late arrival but hoped that "our fans were not disappointed with the show we put on".[94] To Jenny Walden, a teenager of the city, The Beatles were loved as "the most natural of all the groups, because they have not got big-headed and are just themselves. If they feel like putting their feet up, they do."[95] Bereft of the practised sincerity of a Bobby, their unabashed, light-comedy irreverence towards both girls like Jenny and music-industry bigwigs was as winsomely irrepressible as Ken Dodd's or Jimmy Tarbuck's, the latter of whom had become an established young comedian, now that he'd succeeded Norman Vaughan as master of ceremonies on *Sunday Night At The London Palladium*.

There was, apparently, no company in which The Beatles couldn't feel at home. The strangest booking of 1963 was at Stowe public school in Buckinghamshire, where 'Twist And Shout' *et al* precipitated only polite clapping from the seated pupils and their with-it headmaster. Noted photographer Dezo Hoffman's lens caught the four as they "talked with the Stowe boys as if they'd always mixed with people like that".[96]

During high tea, it was pointed out to The Beatles that school rules were so liberal that you weren't marched directly to the barber's if your hair touched your ears. Almost everywhere else, you'd risk suspension for cultivating a Beatle fringe, especially in grammar schools, where the formation of intellectually stultifying pop groups was regarded at best with malevolent neutrality – although, since Mr Edwards' retirement in 1961, treading warily at Liverpool Institute was a jazz club which dared to devote a meeting to "blues- and jazz-influenced pop singers".

A simple image – The Beatles in mid-air leap, like on the cover of the 'Twist And Shout' EP – could trigger a ten-year battle with Authority over hair. Back from school or work, you'd shampoo the combed-back flatness required to avoid persecution here and, with your sister's drier, restyle it as close to a Beatle moptop as possible. As he was the most androgynously hirsute, the ultimate objective was to look like George, whose dislike of haircuts went back to his thrifty father's cack-handed way with scissors at Upton Green.

Long hair wasn't a red rag to just teachers and parents. In Aldershot Magistrates Court in 1965, a labourer accused of assaulting a complete stranger offered the plea, "Well, he had long hair, didn't he?" as a defence. Even when it became acceptable for studs to have moptops, you could still get beaten up by members of the armed forces obliged to maintain short backs and sides. Nonetheless, it made your day if some Oscar Wilde bawled, "Get yer 'air cut!" from a passing car while his grinning mates twisted around in the back seat to register the effect of this witticism on you. You weren't insulted; you were proud to invite trouble. At last, you'd pulled wool over the eyes of parents and teachers long enough for it to show.

The Beatles visited the hairdresser more often than their detractors imagined. In Liverpool, the place to get trimmed was Horne Brothers, where the group were said to go on Epstein's recommendation. You'd sit before the mirror there as the wielder of the scissors would sculpt a Beatle cut from a gravity-defying quiff or a Bobby blow-wave. As it neared completion, your eyes would widen and your jaws would cease chomping their Anglo-Beatmint ("a real cool chew"). Such was the glamour of The Beatles and all things Liverpudlian that *Mirabelle*, a girls' comic, appointed as feature writer a lad named Pete Lennon (later a highbrow journalist), largely on the strength of his talismanic surname. From Mersey Beat slang, words such as "fab", "gear", "grotty" and even obscurities like "duff gen" (false information) spread across *Mirabelle* and similar literature and into the mouths of young Britons.

Even more influential were The Beatles' clothes on and off stage. Few teenagers did not adhere to prevalent fashion, various steps behind Carnaby Street (off Oxford Circus), that would soon become a wellspring of male Mod sartorial conformity, hinged vaguely on Cuban-heeled "Beatle boots", which looked like blunted winkle-pickers – high-buttoned jackets with narrow lapels or none at all, thigh-hugging drainpipes and either roll-necked pullovers or denim shirts with button-down collar and tie. The latter, being the cheapest, was the most variable, ranging from knitted plain to op-art slim-jim to – later in the 1960s – the eye-torturing kipper.

Except at set-piece bank-holiday clashes at seaside resorts, enmity between Mods and Rockers was never as virulent as newspapers made out. Usually they'd just congregate at opposite ends of a cafe. Mods dominated the beat boom, but The Beatles were "Mockers",[79] as Ringo quipped, Rockers in Mod clothing. As they and other Scouse upstarts thumbed noses at the wrong-headed London record business, some of the old guard began paying heed. Like Kenny Lynch, Johnny Kidd had seen what was coming and had injected his Pirates with a massive shot of rhythm and blues. Zooming in sharpish, Eden Kane and Adam Faith made smooth switches from lightweight ballads to ersatz Mersey Beat. Accompanied by visible beat groups – Kane with Earl Preston's TTs – their respective appearances on new BBC showcase *Top Of The Pops* was one in the eye for all these bloody bands who were making it just because they had the right accent and hairstyle. Adam had had his hair scraped over his forehead for the past four years.

Television commercials and episodes in serials like *Z-Cars* were given beat-group slants and negotiations began for The Beatles to top the bill on *Sunday Night At The London Palladium* – although, as John Lennon insisted, "We don't feel we are ready."[97] He was the first Beatle to pass judgement on the releases on BBC TV's *Juke Box Jury*.

The last was George, who, according to Barry Booth, was already coming across as "the most introspective of the group. He seemed diffident, shy. I wouldn't have thought he was overwhelmed, but he wasn't a looper. He was just very self-contained."

George was also the Beatle most inclined to oversleep. On the quartet's third major tour in four months, he shared this trait with a jet-lagged Roy Orbison: "George and I missed the bus a lot. They left without us."[98] Flattered to be told of Liverpool's Blue Angel club, named after one of his hits, Roy also enjoyed chatting about music with George. As his own style was "derived from true country music",[99] he was delighted that young Harrison was such an expert on the genre's obscurer trackways as well as sharing a spectator's enthusiasm for motorcycles.

Like his poorly received compatriots Montez and Roe, Orbison had embarked on a long-awaited British tour, understanding that he would be its foremost attraction. After the soundcheck at the Slough Adelphi, where the tour opened, Roy had just sat down in his dressing room when Lennon and Epstein asked if he'd got a minute. "They said, 'Who should close the show? Look, you're getting all the money, so why don't we [The Beatles]?' I don't know whether that was true or not, whether I was getting more than they were. It wasn't that much, and the tour had sold out in one afternoon."[58]

The source of this quick profit, 'From Me To You', would be at Number One for the tour's five-week duration. Just before screaming pandemonium greeted even compere Tony Marsh's attempts to keep order, Gerry Marsden presented The Beatles with a silver disc for this latest triumph. Not far ahead lay the first all-British Top Ten.

Relinquishing his bill-topping supremacy made sense to Orbison, as long as he got paid as per contract. Although aware of the chasm into which even he might fall, Roy, at 27 rather an elder statesman of pop, stood his ground to sustained and rabid cheering. Typifying the underlying affability of British pop's most optimistic period was Roy's initiation into its spirit. "I remember Paul and John grabbing me by the arms and not letting me go back to take my curtain call. [The audience] were yelling, 'We want Roy!' and there I was, held captive by The Beatles, [who were] saying, 'Yankee, go home.' So we had a great time."[58]

Roy was no lamb to the slaughter like Roe and Montez. Bar the remote Elvis, he came to command the most devoted UK following during a lean time for American pop stars, meriting respect for his unostentatious act and artistic consistency.

Headlining over him in 1963, The Beatles were relieved that they could still whip up screams that were growing louder every time they played. At first, Orbison considered them pretty rough and ready, "Just a rehash of rock 'n' roll that I'd been involved with for a long time, but it turned out to be very fresh and full of energy and vitality. So I recognised it at the time."[98]

Coming to recognise it too was an older British public in one of those periodic spasms when it would, as George put it, "get so bloody virtuous all of a sudden"[57] about indiscretion in high places. Throughout the summer, a flow-chart of immorality had unfolded via the trial of osteopath Stephen Ward and Fleet Street's intricate investigations of John Profumo, the unhappy cabinet minister whose disgrace and resignation had rocked the Tory government. His "sex romps" with a call girl who also enlivened the bedtimes of an official at the Russian Embassy in Park Lane led to another tearsheet and her upper-crust clientèle being winkled out. Soon, anyone connected with politics or the aristocracy was in danger of being accused of sundry corruptions, ranging from organised crime to a Pandora's box of kinky sex.

Next up were Congolese rioters ransacking the British Embassy in Leopoldville and, leading into autumn, further heavy headlines with the Great Train Robbery, in which a gang of thugs, since romanticised as 20th-century highwaymen, made off with swag worth more than £2 million.

Come September, adults were no longer failing over themselves from bedroom to doormat for first grab at the morning paper and its pungent disclosures. Saturated with wickedness, only a different kind of news could reactivate their interest. Anything would do, as long as it could hit. From their pop columnists, editors finally got to hear of

The Beatles, just as teenagers were wondering if the group had got into a rut, with 'From Me To You' having much the same overall sound as 'Please Please Me'.

Their tour with Orbison was causing scenes as uninhibited and contagious as those that had accompanied concerts by Johnnie Ray back in the 1950s. All pop music was rubbish but, by God, these Beatles were *British* rubbish. Theirs was a human-interest story of Poor Honest Northern Lads Who'd Bettered Themselves. Furthermore, they were good copy – plain speaking, coupled with quirky wit delivered in thickened Scouse.

John and Paul's comedy act had long been a diversion from the daily grind of road, dressing room, stage and hotel. George was on more solid ground when able to steer discussions with journalists away from "what's-your-favourite-colour" trivia to music, but there were moments when he exploded with succinct repartee. In fact, some of his backchat was even erroneously attributed to John. Joined by Ken Dodd for an interview on ITV, The Beatles were invited by Dodd to think up and earthy forename for him, as he wished to become a rock 'n' roller. "Sod?", suggested George the second the commercial break started.

A stooge-announcer was provided by the BBC to indulge their horsing around in *Pop Go The Beatles*, a radio series in which they held sway over such "special guests" as Johnny Kidd, The Searchers, and Brian Poole And The Tremeloes, who have been accorded an historical footnote – erroneous, as Brian himself told me in 1995 – as the ones that Decca chose instead of The Beatles. Every recording manager outside EMI was alighting with nitpicking hope on the remotest indication of The Beatles' fall. They'd surely had enough revenge on those who'd spurned them when at last they agreed to star on *Sunday Night At The London Palladium*. Could anyone get more famous than that?

Viewing figures were at their highest ever when, straight after the prescribed hour of religious programmes that October evening, The Beatles kicked off the next hour with a teasing burst of 'I Saw Her Standing There' during a single rotation of the Palladium's revolving stage. Before the four reappeared for five numbers that they could hardly hear themselves play, the seated majority of teenagers fidgeted through endless centuries of formation dancing, an American crooner, a singing comedian and the famed "Beat The Clock" interlude, in which a woman was scolded by Jimmy Tarbuck for producing a large toy beetle from her handbag, thereby setting off another orgy of screaming.

Parents in living rooms might have remarked how lowbrow it all was, but children noticed how their eyes were still glued to the set for the traditional finale, when the cast lined up to wave a cheery goodbye as the platform once more turned slowly while the pit orchestra sight-read the show's 'Startime' theme tune. Whenever The Beatles hoved into view, 'Startime' would be swamped in screams that would ebb abruptly as the group were carried off to the back of the stage.

The next day, the media was full of the "overnight sensation" and its aftermath as a police cordon with helmets rolling in the gutter held back hundreds of clamorous fans who'd chase The Beatles' getaway car into Oxford Street. A pressured journalist chronicling the mayhem came up with the word *Beatlemania*. The phrase stuck, but Beatlemania as a phenomenon was to have less to do with the group itself than with the behaviour of the British public, who, once convinced of something incredible, would believe it with an enthusiasm never displayed for mundane fact.

Before it had a name, the madness had rebounded on Liverpool, where those too young to have spent lunchtimes with The Beatles would huddle in blankets for days outside the Cavern to be sure of being first inside when the group came home. A few weeks before their final date in their old stomping ground, the four also played the Tower Ballroom for the last time. Their set over, they changed into casual wear – jeans and leather jackets – and were slipping unobserved through the dancers when, mere yards from the foyer, a female cavorting in the murk let fly a shriek and brought an adoring mob down on them before their pace could quicken.

The Beatles' old schools passed more coherent comment. In an article devoted to the doings of old Liobians, the Institute's termly magazine included a "less serious note" to the effect that "Mr G

Harrison (1956) and Mr P McCartney (1956) have found success as members of 'The Beatles' singing group and have had a number of television and local stage appearances. They recently made their second record to top the national Hit Parade."[100]

In the same publication, another stuffy compiler mentioned that CW Manley and DM Andrew were "displaying versatility in the realm of music",[99] too. The implication that The Beatles were more famous but no better than The Remo Four was also acknowledged by those Mersey Beat musicians who hadn't forgotten a callow group called Johnny And The Moondogs. Geoff Taggart of The Zephyrs had burrowed his way backstage at the Manchester Odeon to demonstrate some of his songs to Roy Orbison. Afterwards, he handed his camera to Paul McCartney to take a souvenir photograph of him with the great American. He didn't think to ask Roy to snap one of him with Paul.

There were at least five other Merseyside outfits that Geoff considered superior to The Beatles. Among these was Gerry And The Pacemakers, who, like The Beatles (and Billy Fury), were the sole subjects of a glossy monthly magazine. Matching *Pop Go The Beatles*, The Swinging Blue Jeans had their own Radio Luxembourg showcase every Sunday.

What, then, was so fantastic about The Beatles? For less than half the cost and discomfort of seeing them when they condescended to appear in Liverpool nowadays, you could scan *Mersey Beat* and amble over to Maggie May's, the Peppermint Lounge and any other of the new clubs that had sprung up. On the opening night at Warrington's Heaven and Hell, for instance, admission was half a crown for The Mersey Monsters, Rory Storm And The Hurricanes and The Pete Best All-Stars.

6 The Moptop

In the *NME*'s popularity poll for 1963, The Beatles would win the British Vocal Group section with more votes than everyone else put together. After 'From Me To You', 'She Loves You' shifted a million copies in Britain alone. In some overseas territories, it was retitled 'Yeah Yeah Yeah'. Succeeding it would be 'I Want To Hold Your Hand', with sufficient advance orders to slam it straight in at Number One. That Christmas, The Beatles occupied the first two places in both the singles and LP charts. Harrying the singles Top 20 too were no fewer than three EPs. Even re-promotions of their Sheridan recordings sold well. Such was anticipation for the group's second album that an ITV public information series warned of black-market copies under London shop counters a week prior to its release. The EMI pressing plant from which they'd been stolen could barely cope with demand for Beatles discs, anyway.

The only direction after that should have been down. By definition, pop stars weren't built to last, were they? With two smash hits in rapid succession since their record debut that summer, The Searchers, second in the *NME* ballot, were causing The Beatles nervous backwards glances. As Gerry And The Pacemakers had been the first Liverpool outfit to unarguably top all UK singles charts, so The Searchers were the first honoured with a gala reception by Merseyside Civic Council.

The figment of publicists' imagination, the "Mersey Sound" or "Liverpool Beat" had germinated in May, when 'From Me To You' eased Gerry's 'How Do You Do It' from Number One, while on their way up were debut singles by The Big Three and Billy J Kramer.

Waiting in the wings were The Merseybeats, who required police protection from the crowd killing them with kindness at Manchester's Oasis club. For the rest of 1963, Gerry, The Beatles, Billy J and The Searchers would slug it out for chart suzerainty, interrupted only by usurping Brian Poole And The Tremeloes, who – partly through the implications of Brian's surname – were promoted as the southern wing of the movement.

If this Mersey Sound was as transitory as any other craze, then as much of it as the traffic would allow ought to be marketed while the going was good. After an all-Liverpool *Thank Your Lucky Stars*, commercial expediency sent even the slowest-witted London talent-scout up north to plunder the musical gold. After all, The Beatles' lead guitarist had said that they were "typical of a hundred groups in our area. We were lucky. We got away with it first."[63] If this was true, why bother with positioning research? All you did was grab other peas from the same pod, groups with sheepdog haircuts who didn't temper their Scouseness and could crank out 'Money', 'Hippy Hippy Shake' and the entire Chuck Berry songbook. One of these could be recorded in a few takes – as was The Swinging Blue Jeans' definitive 'Hippy Hippy Shake' – and smacked out as a single. Why shouldn't it catch on like all the others? The Star-Club was concerned about customer complaints that all Liverpool groups sounded the same nowadays. Why waste resources trying to prove otherwise?

In the rush to the Holy City, unheeded was George Martin's cry that, "In my trips to Liverpool, I haven't discovered any groups with a similar sound."[60] Nevertheless, most of the groups signed were variations on the format of two guitars, bass and drums, such as The Undertakers and The Mojos, who substituted saxophone and piano respectively for lead guitar. Sticking out like sore thumbs were The Chants and three Toxteth schoolgirls christened The Orchids by Decca and proffered as a Mersey Beat "answer" to The Crystals.

Some behaved as though they were visiting another planet, but most A&R reps were discriminating enough to leave their scotch and Cokes half drunk in clubs after eliminating such-and-such a band from the running for, if not *The* New Beatles, then *A* New Beatles. Rory Storm was much loved, but how much studio trickery was needed to improve his dull voice? Like The Chants, Derry Wilkie was black, and in 1963 that presented marketing problems.

Most Mersey Beat groups with the faintest tang of star quality had at least a brief moment of glory as London – with little notion of how to project them – got in on the act. With mobile recording units, some record companies hired Liverpool ballrooms for a couple of days to tape as many groups from the region as could be crammed onto a cheap compilation album with a title like *This Is Merseybeat* or *It's The Gear*. Others cheated by using London session players, who probably bitched about The Beatles during tea breaks. As "Casey Jones", Brian Cassar – now based in the capital – actually moved south, where he assembled the short-lived backing group The Engineers to promote the single that resulted from his Scouse-talking his way into a one-shot deal with Columbia.

When The Hollies were snatched by Parlophone, the contract-waving host pounced on Manchester with the promptness of vultures. There, EMI also snared Freddie And The Dreamers, fronted by trouser-dropping singer Freddie Garrity, who figured, "We definitely succeeded on our visual appeal. We were on *Thank Your Lucky Stars* and just did a routine to take the mickey out of The Shadows. Next week, the record [a version of 'If You Gotta Make A Fool Of Somebody'] went to Number Three. We reckoned it must have been the dance, kicking our legs forward, so for our next record we did a routine kicking our legs back."[101]

More likely money-makers were processed for the hit parade in other northern towns. While Bolton's boss group The Statesmen were bypassed, Sheffield band The Cruisers backed spider-fingered Dave Berry and knocking 'em dead in Newcastle were The Animals. The pride of Nottingham, meanwhile, was the "Trentside Beat" of The Jaybirds, whose high-speed guitarist, Alvin Dean, was "considered by many the best in the Midlands".[102] Midway betwixt Liverpool and London, Birmingham was high on every grasping A&R chief's hit list. Not blessed with hits but adored locally, Mike *Sheridan* – like Brian *Poole* – had a negotiable Mersey Beat/Beatle-associated surname and a versatile backing group, whose ranks would include a teenage guitarist named Jeff Lynne.

Not for nothing would Lynne, Roy Wood, Steve Winwood and other precursors of the second city of pop's coming of age *circa* 1967 spend years mastering their assorted crafts in the ranks of outfits like Sheridan's Nightriders and The Spencer Davis Group. In late 1963, however, *Midland Beat* magazine – modelled on *Mersey Beat* – would bawl in an editorial, "Why has the Brum Beat failed to gain a place in the Top 20?"[103] Although Birmingham's beat boom was as unstoppable as the Black Death, it had mushroomed on the crest of a craze, growing in impact after rather than with Mersey Beat.

In all regions, whether they were deemed to have a "beat" or not, you didn't have to look far for the principal blueprint. The Grasshoppers were "Meridan's answer to The Beatles" while Church Crookham had The Termites. According to John Lennon, Gerry And The Pacemakers also suffered "terrible copying", but, infesting every borough, hundreds of groups had been formed in The Beatles' image, "and down to the last note at that".[84] While some used insectile appelations, others would work the word *beat* into their titles – Beat Ltd, The Beatstalkers, The Beat Merchants, and so on. Back-of-beyond youth club groups now wore moptop hairstyles and suits, and instead of a Hank Marvin lookalike they had an unsmiling guitarist with a Liverpool leg who – in imagination, at least – played a black Rickenbacker through a Marshall amplifier, just like George Harrison.

While grass-roots amateurs grappled with 'She Loves You', their older siblings might yearn for a return to the old ways. "Are you going to let Britain's king of talent be beaten by a flash-in-the-pan group like The Beatles?"[104] inquired a Cliff Richard enthusiast of *NME* readers. Apparently they were. Nevertheless, grinning indulgently, Cliff didn't bother to compete with the rearing four-headed monster.

Other old-timers beat a calculated retreat. Although he may have weathered the storm, Shane Fenton and his wife, Iris, metamorphosed into a song-and-dance act. In closer contact with The Beatles than most, he'd declined a management offer from Brian Epstein, who had used Lennon's 78rpm acetate of 'Do You Want To Know A Secret' as bait. In August 1962, he'd headlined over The

Beatles at the Cavern. Almost a year later, he was supporting them at a "Swinging '63" extravaganza at London's Royal Albert Hall.

In the front row sat The Rolling Stones, a group who'd sprung from an Ealing club as earnestly devoted to blues as other cliques were to yachting or numismatics. Aggressively untidy students and middle-class bohemians would come forth from the audience to thrash guitars and holler gutbucket exorcisms with house band Blues Incorporated, in which two future Rolling Stones were semi-permanent fixtures. Among the frayed jeans, beatnik beards and CND badges in the watching throng were subsequent Kinks, Yardbirds and Pretty Things, who would try to emulate the Slim Harpos, Muddy Waters and Howlin' Wolfs of black America. The results (especially vocal) were generally nothing like it but, after they – like the Stones – had sucked Chuck Berry into the vortex of blues, all three would appear on *Top Of The Pops* within a year of the Stones doing so.

No more a Blues Incorporated splinter group by spring 1963, the motley Rolling Stones were resident at the Crawdaddy, which convened in the back room of a Richmond pub. Descending on the club in droves were Rockers and Mods under a flimsy flag of truce, plus a *nouvelle vague* of "youths" and, half a class up, "young people". No longer appreciating blues with knotted brows, girls crowded around the front spotlight, their evening made if they caught the attention of Stones lead singer Mick Jagger, with his half-caste singing and grotesque beauty, or the general factotum, Brian Jones, who sported an exaggerated blond moptop. With both blues credibility and teen appeal, the group's cash-flow was such that Bill Wyman, their married bass player, was able to think seriously of packing in his day job as a storekeeper.

Through knowing Brian Epstein, club promoter Georgio Gomelsky engineered a visit to the Crawdaddy by The Beatles after they'd recorded a *Thank Your Lucky Stars* at nearby Teddington studios. It would be a fillip for the Stones if they impressed an act who, in April 1963, were bigger than Frank Ifield. Yet, though they attracted a small prattle of fans, The Beatles were not yet so well known around London that they couldn't be steered safely by Gomelsky through his crowded club to the side of the stage.

As Georgio had foreseen, their more revered peers took a shine to the Stones, and the cordiality between the two groups after the customers departed led to Jagger *et al* receiving complimentary tickets and backstage passes for the Albert Hall show. Less incidental to the Stones' future was George Harrison's judging of a "Battle Of The Bands" tournament at Liverpool's Philharmonic Hall a month later. On the panel, too, were Bill Harry and soul-tortured Dick Rowe. Decca seemed to be gorging itself with beat groups now in the hopes that one might be as successful as its failed Scouse supplicants had to teeth-gnashing effect with EMI. From Merseyside alone, Rowe had contracted Kingsize Taylor, The Long And The Short (with Les Stewart), The Big Three and – for who he was, rather than what he did – Pete Best.

Whispering to George sitting next to him, Dick thought that even the likely winners at the Phil – a group containing Ringo's cousin – were no better than any other Beatle-style group to be found anywhere in the country. Civilly, George agreed. Because Rowe had been honest in not over-justifying his mistake over The Beatles, George decided to help him out. There was, he said, this southern group he'd seen. Musically, they were "almost as good as The Roadrunners"[105] but far wilder, visually, and having the same effect on their audience in a provincial club as The Beatles had had on theirs at the Cavern. "Dick got up immediately," observed Bill Harry, "and caught the next train back to sign The Rolling Stones."

The Beatles' largesse extended from endorsement to a gift of – as the Stones' stabilising second single – a song by John and Paul, 'I Wanna Be Your Man', bestowed prior to its appearance on autumn 1963's *With The Beatles* album. Virtually every other track, too, was covered by another artist, from Mike Sheridan's 'Please Mr Postman' to 'Little Child' by a Billy Fonteyne. All were either Beatles' arrangements of non-originals from their concert repertoire or new Lennon-McCartney compositions. The one exception was 'Don't Bother Me', rehashed for Pye by Gregory Phillips with an "oo-aah" girlie chorus, the only digression from

Beatle precedent. This opus was the first published solo composition by George Harrison.

During an intermission at the Phil talent contest, Bill Harry had nagged George, as always, about songwriting. Backstage at Blackpool's ABC theatre, three months later, George would thank Bill "for keeping on and on about me writing songs. I would think about going out, but it was, 'Oh, Christ. I'll bump into Bill Harry and he'll go on and on about these songs.'" The week before, see, while suffering from influenza George had completed 'Don't Bother Me' from his sickbed at the Royal Spa hotel in Bournemouth during The Beatles' six nights there at the Gaumont. Its lyrics portrayed one still carrying a torch for an old love. His refusal of another's comfort may be reflective of George's ill temper that he wasn't unwell enough not to be hauled from fevered quietude for the evening's two performances.

With John as its main champion, the good rather than great 'Don't Bother Me' had been accepted as worth recording when, midway through the Bournemouth season, the group spent hurried daylight hours mixing those *With The Beatles* items already on tape. Even George Martin, who seemed to regard Harrison as a mediocre musician at most, would vary a diet of Lennon-McCartney with 'Don't Bother Me' on *Off The Beatle Track*, his LP of orchestrated Beatle tunes. In a prosy *Times* article that discussed Paul and John's "pandiatonic clusters" and "Aeolian cadence", mention was made of their lead guitarist's little number as "harmonically a good deal more primitive, though it is nicely enough presented".[106]

Against, say, nine takes for 'Not A Second Time' (the one with the Aeolian cadence), the less honed 'Don't Bother Me' needed 19. To pep it up a bit, Ringo, John and Paul overdubbed a loose polyrhythm of minor percussion. Although not an outstanding contribution to *With The Beatles*, a publishing division – Jeep Music – was created to gather its not-insubstantial royalties.

George didn't follow up speedily on this tentative exercise in composition, undeserving of inclusion in the stage act. Instead, he fell back to his accustomed role of being one of Paul and John's sounding boards, one whose advice wasn't taken as seriously as that of George

Martin. Nonetheless, they'd let him have three *With The Beatles* lead vocals to Ringo's one. "In The Beatles days, I was always very paranoid, very nervous, and that inhibited my singing,"[59] George said, but still he managed a painless 'Devil In Her Heart'. Although smoother than Lennon's might have been, his 'Roll Over Beethoven' emerged as a single – and hit, to boot – in many foreign parts.

It was a year when The Beatles could have topped charts with 'Knees Up Mother Brown'. Some listeners, however, weren't that snowblinded. At this most public and prolific phase of the four's recording career, it was easier for journalists and photographers to infiltrate the sessions regulated by the Musicians' Union that The Beatles were yet to challenge by running over into the small hours. When outsiders were scheduled to be present, George would forsake his usual jeans and open-necked shirt for clothes less casual. However, no amount of sprucing up for the cameras could prevent George Martin from stopping run-throughs to point out errors. In front of one scribbling reporter, he criticised the guitar tuning, "and you, George, should be coming in on the second beat every time instead of the fourth." "Oh, I see,"[107] replied Harrison, his hackles rising slightly.

Also noted were the jumbled solos that George would insert into some backing tracks. Those ignorant of advancing recording techniques might or might not be told that George had invented them on the spot for reference only. Later, he'd re-record the parts in less public circumstances, combining his and, most of all, George Martin's further thoughts about them.

Self-contained enough to disassociate the instrument from Martin's schoolmasterly perseverance, "A day doesn't pass without me having a go on the guitar."[108] His ambition, he said, was "to design a guitar myself and have it called 'the Harrison'. I'd like to play as well as Duane Eddy or Chet Atkins, and I wish I could compose like John and Paul."[109] George was, nevertheless, the Beatle whose musical competence was most questioned. Derided for the publicity stunt it was, an allegation that The Beatles used a substitute lead guitarist on recording dates was made by an expatriate Texan entertainer befriended by the group. The changeling was even named as session *wunderkind* Jimmy Page. Although such practices are common in pop, this suggestion can be refuted by documentary evidence that Page must have been in two places at once if he did play on Beatles discs. Moreover, the lead-guitar sections on sufficient Parlophone tracks are identical to those on extant early Beatles recordings, as demonstrated by consecutive hearings of the Decca release of "Til There Was You' and the 1963 treatment.

George also picked the song very prettily when it was second in the group's subdued four-song segment in the *Royal Variety Show* in November. On the boards, however, he wasn't generally so hot. It could be that his best moments were never immortalised on tape, and plausible excuses can be found for those that were. He'd been the worse for alcohol when Ted Taylor's tape recorder captured The Beatles' last stint at the Star-Club. Yet, although the intro was fumbled, George's solo on 'Roll Over Beethoven' was how it would be on *With The Beatles*, bar an unclean note or two. An indifferent improviser, he'd often double up with John, as plainly heard on 'I Saw Her Standing There' during five October days in Sweden, the group's first true overseas tour.

In his defence, however, it must be stated that, at that particular recital in Stockholm, George was about to be almost yanked offstage by rampaging fans as unrestrained as they'd be for The Beatles' first proper headlining tour of Britain. Setting the mood was the heroes' welcome accorded them on their homecoming from Scandinavia. Just over 1,000 teenagers on half-term holiday had ignored the heavy drizzle to converge on Heathrow Airport's upper terraces. From their morning flight, the baffled quartet were met by the unison banshee scream they'd mistaken for engine noise on touchdown.

All 4,000 seats for two shows at the Leeds Odeon had gone in a record three hours, with two 16-year-olds starting the queue four days before the box office opened. At every proposed stop on the tour, hundreds likewise ringed themselves around theatres, cinemas and city halls to guarantee admission. Those lacking such clubbable stamina recoursed to buying tickets from touts at up to eight times their market price.

As their respective Beatles nights crept closer, auditorium directors like Portsmouth Guildhall's David Evans grew "really alarmed at the prospect of getting The Beatles into and away from the hall in safety, because of the big crowds we anticipate. I shall call in every burly and able-bodied man on the staff to keep order and make a pathway, as well as extra police. I shall be glad when it's all over."[110]

Beatlemania was pop hysteria at its most intense. Even in sedate Cheltenham, streets surrounding the Odeon were closed to traffic as police, linked by walkie-talkies to the building, coordinated the group's admittance. Entrances elsewhere weren't as grand, as The Beatles smuggled themselves in through lofts and, in Plymouth, by groping along underground tunnels leading from Westward TV's studios two blocks away to a narrow lane beside the ABC. At a given signal, a fire exit was flung open and a support act ambled out to divert attention from The Beatles' dash across the passageway. Even so, they were still spotted, and a girl's fingers were crushed in the slammed door.

Once inside, they'd be incarcerated until, with the last major sixth of 'Twist And Shout' still reverberating in the pandemonium, they would bolt pell-mell to a waiting limousine in a back alley. They'd be halfway down the road by the end of the national anthem, when the crowd realised that there wouldn't be an encore.

The hours awaiting escape might have been passed carousing in the artists' bar, if there was one, or relaxing in the dressing room. Whereas the supporting programme made do with standard spartan facilities, The Beatles would often subside into freshly-redecorated rooms with television and, perhaps, individually-monogrammed hand-towels and champagne on ice. The comestibles laid on were edible enough for the four not to have to resort to the toaster and electric kettle packed as insurance against their ever being needed by Neil Aspinall's new assistant, Malcolm "Big Mal" Evans, ex-Cavern bouncer. When one venue's caterer read of The Beatles' humble dietary predilections in an *Evening Standard* exclusive about George's disappointment with his first mouthful of caviar, he uncovered for them a hugely appreciated platter of jam sandwiches cut in crescents, diamonds and other exquisite shapes.

Babbling like an idiot relation in the corner, *Take Your Pick*,

Dixon Of Dock Green or other early evening television programmes might be switched off and the Dansette record player plugged in. On instant replay throughout that autumn's jaunt was either the latest Bob Dylan LP or 'Do You Love Me' by The Contours, whose original Tamla-Motown version was pleasanter to George's ears than any of no fewer than three British covers. As they'd just left the Top Ten with a workmanlike 'Twist And Shout', Brian Poole's boys' version of 'Do You Love Me' had an edge over the hitless Dave Clark Five. Faron's Flamingos' adaptation was so vanquished that it was relegated to a B-side.

Other than themselves, no representatives of Mersey Beat were present on the tour, unless you count The Vernons Girls, who paraded their latest single, 'We Love The Beatles', on a nightly basis. An ex-member, Lyn Cordell, had just released a version of the jazz standard 'Moanin'', which was the most common number played during the post-soundcheck bashes that also occupied the time before the show. Although Paul seldom missed opportunities to jam, George was less ready to unwind that way with musicians of the exacting calibre of Peter Jay And The Jaywalkers or Sounds Incorporated. Apprehensive about showing himself up, he'd settle for rhythm guitar or simply rattle a tambourine. Neither was George that active in the off-stage larks during the show itself, such as John and Paul's tormenting interruptions of comperes' patter.

It was hard enough without smart-alec antics in the wings from the main attraction. As the announcement for her troupe was swamped in audience roar on opening night, Vernons Girl Maureen Kennedy panicked, "Oh, God, I can't face that. Them shouting for The Beatles, I mean. I think the boys deserve all this, but it's a bit rough on the other acts."[111] The Girls and other unhappy artists on the bill would soldier on as the eclipsing howls and chants for The Beatles welled up to a pitch where you drowned in noise.

Somehow, the already ear-stinging decibels climbed higher when The Beatles sauntered on, outwardly enjoying their work. The girls went crazy, tearing their hair, wiping their eyes, rocking foetally and flapping scarves and programmes in the air. The volume rose momentarily to its loudest, as if they'd all sat on tin-tacks, when Paul and George zoomed in on the right-hand microphone for the Isley Brother-esque "oooooo" in 'She Loves You'.

The circle stall buckled and the walls trembled, but no one was seriously hurt, as the havoc was tinged with good nature and British reserve. At Doncaster, a boy wriggled through the barrier of stewards to leap on stage for no other purpose than to dance self-consciously for a few seconds before meekly stepping down again. Somewhere further south, another buffoon yelled, "Down with The Beatles!" during a sudden lull between acts. His portly girlfriend swiped him with her handbag and everybody laughed. Girls would go into pretend faints after practising in the queue, their friends catching them under the armpits.

Still able to take greater celebrity in their stride, there was merriment rather than annoyance when The Beatles came upon two youths who'd hidden themselves in a hotel room for hours just to fraternise with the group when they flopped in after the show in Coventry. This wasn't the only such incident. More than once, roadside cafes served mixed grills on the house in exchange for autographs. An Exeter theatre manager's fawning was rewarded when all four Beatles scratched their signatures on a stairway brick for him to sellotape over for posterity. On the previous night, their Torquay hotel hideout had been rumbled and 100 or so fans – mostly truants – had collected in its lobby. Amused, the group had signed their books while strolling out to the limousine the following afternoon.

It was still possible for a Beatle to take the air after breakfast without public fuss, although, warned Lennon, "it's a bit dodgy if you all go out together."[112] Stopping at traffic lights would now attract the beginnings of a crowd, and certain factions desired more than autographs. Sheffield students planned to kidnap the group for a Rag Week stunt. Unwilling to play along, The Beatles cheerfully compromised with a donation to funds.

"At first, when we went on the road as a famous group, it was good fun,"[55] George would later remember. His main grumble was, "We could only sing our hits and none of the old rock things we'd loved doing in Liverpool and Hamburg."[55] Nevertheless, their music was being taken semi-seriously. Before *The Times* caught on, Derek

Taylor, northern showbusiness correspondent with *The Daily Express*, had seen the light and, after covering the Manchester stop on the Orbison tour, had become "very boring about it around the office".[74] When briefed to do a hatchet job on The Beatles' agreement to appear on *The Royal Variety Show* "for the middle-aged middle class",[74] Taylor could only praise them.

After Fritz Spiegl's Mozart pastiche, 'Eine Kleine Beatlemusik', a random B-side would be analysed as if it was a Beethoven symphony in highbrow *Music And Musicians* magazine. As it was estimated that more words had been written about them than about Shakespeare, newspapers no longer put sniffy inverted commas around their name, followed by "the Liverpool 'pop' group" or similar explanatory phrase. Soon, the first of more Beatle biographies than anyone in 1963 could ever have comprehended was in preparation.

The Socialist Worker might vilify Beatlemania, but overall a wider cross-section of the populace "knows how fab they are" – as The Vernons Girls sang – than any pop act before or since. Deb of the year Judy Huxtable was snapped entreating Ringo for his autograph, while swingin' radio vicars would slip them into *Five To Ten*, an incongruous religious broadcast linking *Uncle Mac* and *Saturday Club*. At a school speech day in Havent, Lady Nancy Bridge recommended, "If you feel you cannot do what is asked of you, think of The Beatles. They have got where they are by sheer hard work."[113]

As it had for Tommy Steele, so their fabled appearance in the 1963 *Royal Variety Show* rendered them harmless and lurched the weather-vane of adult toleration, if not approval, in The Beatles' direction. Short haircuts would still be imposed on sons of provincial Britain, and pop was not yet an acceptable career option, but parental blood had not run cold over Lennon's chirpy "rattle yer jewellery" ad lib to the royal balcony as it had over loutish excesses. When two Beatles shook their heads on the "oooooo" in 'She Loves You', it was like spun dishmops, but there was none of this hip-swivelling lewdness.

No distant Beatle could be imagined passing wind or urinating, any more than could a sexless cartoon character or teddy-bear. As a 1960s teenager, actress Kim Hartman – Helga in BBC's *'Allo 'Allo* –

fell in love with George, with his "suffering cheekbones, which made him look so poetic".[114] He was singled out as 'Gorgeous George' in The Vernons Girls' tribute, but Lancastrian comedienne Dora Bryan claimed "Ringo, John, Paul and George – they're all the same" in her 'All I Want For Christmas Is A Beatle'. Sung in a vile "baby" voice, the fact that even this yuk-for-a-buck made the hit parade exemplified the national obsession. Apparently beside herself with excitement, publicity-conscious Dora – no spring chicken – had pursued a terrified George after The Beatles' floorshow at a charity function at London's Grosvenor House Hotel. "Twist and shout! Twist and shout!" she kept yowling, clinging to him like a barnacle. However, other personalities weren't as demonstrative about their bandwagon jumping. Hoping that John and Paul might toss them a song, some would worm their way into the Beatle dressing room to pay artist-to-artist respects. Among the least transparent such visitor was the late Alma Cogan, whom the group liked enough to accept an open invitation to the liberty hall that was her Kensington flat. It was during a *soirée* there that George was introduced to Carl Perkins.

Alma was a mainstay of early editions of ITV's epoch-making pop magazine *Ready, Steady, Go!*, which, when it began in August 1963, was presented by a besuited interlocutor in his 1930s called Keith Fordyce and featured occasional send-ups of current hits by comics of the same age. The pruning of these unhip distractions kept pace with the series' elevation to the most atmospheric pop showcase of the decade. The programme also monitored the mounting isolation that their adoring public inflicted on The Beatles. In October 1963, they walked from make-up to the podium without hindrance to mime 'She Loves You', while on their second *Ready, Steady, Go!* appearance they needed an outside security force of 80 police and a headlong flight through the corridors of the adjacent London School of Economics. By their fifth and final booking, a separate and heavily guarded area would be set aside for the group's performance while the rest of the show took place in the usual Studio Nine.

Absorbing this accelerating adulation, George was initially the Beatle least unsettled by it all. For a while, he remained his old, selectively amiable self, although "old" was a little inappropriate.

Some of those reporters who'd figured out which one was which would refer to him as "young George". He didn't yet behave older than his years. To the group's long-serving publicist Tony Barrow, he lagged behind the other three "in terms of physical appearance and general sophistication".[15] He was the one sighted most often preening himself before dressing room mirrors, perhaps applying lacto-calamine lotion to spots that no hit record could prevent from appearing on an otherwise comely adolescent complexion.

With no steady girlfriend, he seemed perpetually on the look-out for an unsteady one. Fame is a powerful aphrodisiac, and to many within The Beatles' cabal George was something of a lothario on the road. Time which hung heavy between one concert and the next wasn't only killed with practising guitar and watching *Take Your Pick*. As *omerta* is to the Mafia, a vow of silence concerning illicit sex persists among bands of roving minstrels. A strong motive for a red-blooded lad to become a pop star is that, no matter what you look like, you can still be popular with young ladies. Look at Ringo and his nose. Look at spindly Freddie and spotty Herman.

Quite used to demure requests to meet a certain type of female admirer in, say, the romantic seclusion of a backstage broom cupboard, George wasn't quite so sure of himself with more ladylike judies. They were more likely to be won over by a Beatle who dropped names like Segovia or limp and tasteful Stan Getz than anything as coarse as The Isley Brothers or Duane Eddy. "I like most music if it's good" was a truism that George would qualify with "I like classical music on a guitar. I'm not so keen on classical music played on a piano."[115] At the Swinging '63 spectacular, he'd started chatting up a dashing young actress of good breeding named Jane Asher, but before the evening was out she seemed more taken with the suaver charms of Paul McCartney. "Society" Londoners like Jane were often intrigued to meet real "wackers" now that Liverpool was where more happened than just dock strikes. More fascinating was that some of them were suddenly rich enough, like George, to "get a Ferrari and bomb about".[116]

He could also afford well-deserved breaks in faraway places. With Ringo and Paul, he'd limbered up for the Orbison tour with twelve days in Tenerife. On 16 September 1963, the day after a second Albert Hall showcase, George was the first Beatle to set foot in the United States, when he and brother Peter flew via New York and St Louis to stay for a fortnight with their married sister, then living in Benton, Illinois. With a day in hand before the internal flight, they paid the seven-dollar fare from Idlewild to the Pickwick Hotel in New York, and to the taxi driver they were just another pair of long-haired Englishmen. They soaked up the sights like any tourists, and the highlight of the trip was a visit to the Statue of Liberty.

Benton was a restful interlude after the holocaust of Beatlemania. As his face hadn't been plastered over magazine covers in America for the past six months, as it had been at home, George was treated as Mrs Caldwell's youngest brother, some sort of musician. How unexpectedly pleasurable it was to be a nobody again, not to have to steal into a cinema – one of these "drive-ins" – after faded dimmers had guaranteed shelter from the stares and approaches of fans, to wander anonymously the boulevards of east St Louis or picnic on the cottonwood banks of the Mississippi. (See Appendix II.)

Professional interest found him in Benton's record store, thumbing through wares unreleased outside the States. Among albums that would return with him to England was James Ray's *If You Gotta Make A Fool Of Somebody*, which turned out to be "really terrible" on repeated listening, though he half enjoyed two tracks also composed by Ray's regular songwriter, Rudy Clark, 'It's Been A Drag' and 'Got My Mind Set On You Part One'/'Part Two'. Despite its title, the latter "didn't have a break in between. It was coming out of the old jazz/swing era, and it had these horrible screechy women's voices singing those back-up parts."[58] America was still taking saccharine sounds to its heart, but also clogging the ether was Californian surf music. Ruling this genre were The Beach Boys, who celebrated surfing and its companion sport, hot-rod racing, with chugging rock 'n' roll backing overlaid with a chorale more breathtaking than that of The Beatles.

Naturally, sister Louise had been kept posted about George's exploits with his group and had collected all of their Polydor and Parlophone records, plus the two or three issued in North American on labels of no great merit. Through her, some had been played on local radio, but these few spins had the impact of a feather on concrete in a continent whose wavelengths were overloaded with yapping disc jockeys with lurid *noms de turntable* – Wolfman Jack, Murray the K, Magnificent Montague – all unmindful of whatever was gripping a backwater like Britain.

"I don't know. What do you think?" was the spirit that pervaded the eventual unleashing of 'I Want To Hold Your Hand' by EMI's American outlet, Capitol. Although this ensured a better chance of airplay than earlier Beatles singles had with smaller companies, the group and Epstein could not yet assume that they'd be much more than a strictly European phenomenon, like Cliff Richard. Why should America want them? With The Beatles' deepest musical roots in US culture, it might be like taking coals to Newcastle. Besides, what about The Beach Boys, publicly as wholesome and all American as The Beatles were wholesome and British?

Why should The Beatles want America? George hadn't minded Illinois, but a lot of British musicians loathed what glimpses they'd had of the Land of Opportunity. "When The Dave Clark Five started," outlined their drummer/leader, "we used to play the American air bases in England. It was hell, because the American servicemen kept getting pissed. It was the only side of America I'd seen, and I didn't care for it."[117] Food for thought, however, were reports from the Star-Club of how well Dave Dee And The Bostons' medley of the entire *Please Please Me* LP went down with US ships' crews.

If the States were to be off limits, The Beatles had plenty to do elsewhere. They'd made sustained chart strikes in other parts of the world, from Eire to Australasia, although there were rare instances of local talent checkmating them with sly covers. Ray Columbus And The Invaders' single of 'I Wanna Be Your Man' sold more in New Zealand than those released there by both the Stones and The Beatles. Nevertheless, Brian Epstein was deliberating whether to commit The Beatles to a lengthy antipodean tour for as soon as September 1963. Hardly raising a liberal eyebrow then was another plan to send them to South Africa.

They always expected it to end. NEMS' general manager, Alistair

Taylor, recalled that the party line was, "If we can last three years, it would be marvellous."[118] To Pete Murray, Light Programme disc jockey and recurrent *Juke Box* jurist, their records "do not improve"[119] since they'd gone off the boil with 'From Me To You'. By 1964, preceding them on a British stage was less onerous "now that The Beatles have found their own level" – so said the most frequent of their guest stars, Kenny Lynch, in an article headlined "Is The Beatles Frenzy Cooling Down?"[119] Although a concert at the Prince of Wales Theatre – scene of their *Royal Variety* grand slam – had been standing-room only, everyone on a bill which included The Chants and a less fraught Vernons Girls "went down very well without interruptions by people shouting, 'We want The Beatles,' like they used to".[120]

This was London, where Kenny calculated, "The Rolling Stones may be just as big as The Beatles now."[120] Innocent of the capital's *sangfroid*, unabated screaming in the shires indicated that the Moptop Mersey Marvels were just as "gear" as ever. Many children had been as aghast as their parents at the Stones' transfixing androgyny, but in a nonplus of repelled bewitchment they also filled to overflowing venues starring "the Five Shaggy Dogs with a brand of 'shake' all their own",[121] as one local rag had it.

While 1963 was The Beatles' year, the Stones were still scrimmaging round the unsalubrious beat clubs that were now littering British towns – the Cubik in Rochdale, Swindon's X, or R&B night in Norwich's St Andrew's Hall to name but three. A shoal of Caverns abounded, too, from Leicester Square to Manchester to another in Birmingham that was lent an authentic sheen by dim lighting, an arched ceiling and The Searchers' presence at its inauguration.

The Searchers, Gerry and a few more Mersey Beat outfits were still able to take chart placings for granted, although, as Freddie And The Dreamers discovered, "There's only three ways you can kick your legs, and we never had another hit."[101] On Merseyside itself, there was a sense of impending hangover. As a beehive can function for a while after losing its progenitive queen, so did two-guitar-bass-drums combos continue to thrive in Liverpool. Clothed by London-style boutiques now operational in the city centre, the luckiest would gain a slot on the weekly *Sunday Night At The Cavern* broadcast by

Radio Luxembourg.

As the record companies weren't coming around so much any more, far-sighted Liverpudlian musicians realised that their very dialect was shortly to be a millstone around their necks. Too late to squeeze any blood from the Mersey Sound, more than one Scouse group attempted to dilute their accents and pass themselves off as Londoners.

The Beatles had become a London-based outfit when NEMS Enterprises uprooted itself late in 1963. Until then, they'd attended to their recording and broadcasting duties in the metropolis by commuting from wherever their concert itinerary found them. If benighted there, they'd bed down in hotels or avail themselves of the hospitality of old acquaintances like Ken Brown, who put them up the night before a *Saturday Club* recording in March 1963. A more regular port of call was the Shepherd Market flat of the programme's co-producer, Bernie Andrews, shared with George's friend and Beatles business associate Terry Doran. With a palate coarsened by chips-with-everything meals in wayside snack bars, and prevented by fame from frequenting such eateries in central London, George developed a fondness for egg and chips, as fried by Doran. "He didn't want to know about cooking it himself,"[122] recalled Andrews.

But a few streets from Shepherd Market, George began his London domicile by renting briefly a *pied à terre* in Green Street, just off Park Lane and handy for West End nightclubbing. By the time 52 sacks of mail were dumped on his parents' doorstep the day he came of age, he and Ringo were sharing what became an untidy flat beneath Brian Epstein's mews apartment in Whaddon House, Knightsbridge. Paul's billet with Jane Asher's family in Wimpole Street was not yet common knowledge, but Whaddon House and the Lennons' Kensington bedsit were targets for graffiti and marathon vigils by London fans.

Liverpool couldn't reclaim The Beatles, except perhaps if the bubble burst. Sniffing beyond northern counties now, EMI's opponents were still throwing down gauntlets – the laughable Severnbeats, "Hertsbeat" from Unit 4 + 2 and The Zombies, 'Blarney Beat' from The Four Aces, the "Solihull Sound" of The

Applejacks... It was a challenger from another EMI subsidiary that would seem to bring The Beatles to their knees and signal a finish to traipsing up north for pop news. Wowing 'em four nights a week at Tottenham Royal Ballroom, The Dave Clark Five went for the jugular in January 1964 when their sixth single, 'Glad All Over', ended The Beatles' unbroken seven weeks at Number One and sparked off a jubilant Fleet Street field day in which a prototypical headline was "Has The Five Jive Crushed The Beatle Beat?".

7 The Serious One

In foreign climes, The Dave Clark Five would rack up heftier achievements than their solitary UK Number One. Although hits at home didn't mean that much financially, Britain was about to become the world's prime purveyor of pop, and Liverpool – quoth post-beatnik bard Allen Ginsberg – "the centre of the consciousness of the entire universe"[123] after The Beatles instigated a large-scale re-run of British beat hysteria in February 1964, when 'I Want To Hold Your Hand' topped the US Hot 100.

A reason given for the Five's relegation to also-rans was "If you go off Dave, you're off the group".[124] As The Beatles had no obvious leader, fans could be fickle in affections towards individuals yet still maintain overall loyalty. The coherence of the group's image presented what had seemed at first glance to be a single focus for adoration, but by 1964 this Midwich Cuckoo regularity was balanced by the paradoxical realisation of inevitable differences between them – Ringo's harmless wit was especially benefical to the North American breakthrough.

"My part in The Beatles," figured George, "was I never wanted to be the one at the front."[52] This had indeed been acknowledged in a *Mersey Beat* headline, "The Quiet Beatle". He was also the Serious One, the Shy Beatle whose "replies might not be so memorable as Ringo's or John's but they often contain more sense".[125] Following some particularly pragmatic interviews, he also became the Money or Business Beatle, titles that would become more appropriate in the years to come. None of the group was markedly tight fisted, but all would pester Tony Barrow for minute-to-minute record-sales and chart information. "We'd be idiots," said McCartney, "to say that it isn't a constant inspiration to be making a lot of money."[57]

Certain contingency plans were already in force so that, should The Beatles' time be up, all four would recoup more than just golden memories. Harrison and Starr's main source of income was their quarter share apiece in Beatles Ltd, a budgetary receptacle for all net income from concerts. "Ringo and I are constantly being reminded that John and Paul make so much more money than us,"[126] snarled George, who didn't need reminding that the two songwriters each owned 20 times as many shares as he in Northern Songs, their publishing company. Although his eyes would glaze over during the quartet's quarterly meetings with its accountants ("confusing and boring and just like being back at school"[127]), it would be George who prodded most about where this percentage came from or why so-and-so had been granted that franchise. Indeed, it was his questioning that led to Brian Epstein re-examining the three-year-old German record contract. His vocabulary filling with phrases like "tax concession" and "convertible debentures", George's attitude was, "It's easy to get blasé and think we're making plenty and somebody's taking care of it, but I like to know how much is coming in, where it's being put, how much I can spend. I'm no more money mad than the others. I've just persevered and found out."[127] As the others made ready to go, George would stay put for a natter about his private investments, the most interesting of which was a stake in Sybilla's, a London night club. With Lennon and ex-Quarry Man Pete Shotton, he was also co-director of a Hayling Island supermarket until he resigned in 1969.

With most group earnings likewise tied up, George's wallet held little real capital, obliging him to borrow small amounts from Beatle menials, usually the road management. Larger bills were settled through the NEMS office. Like any backstreet lad abruptly rich, his consumption was more conspicuous than those for whom wealth was second nature. Though he'd later rein in his extravagance, purchasing a succession of flash cars was beyond rapture for a youth who for too long had had his nose glued to showroom windows. After an E-Type Jaguar came an Aston Martin DB5 and – motorised epitome of the 1960s – a Mini. When he spotted a maroon-and-black vintage model, he sold his Rolls Royce to Brian Jones. There was much bowing and scraping by a Hammersmith dealer as George paced up and down rows of gleaming Mercedes fitted with one-way windows and all the latest electrically operated gadgetry. Six days later, a black one was delivered, delayed by the personalising of the number plate and adjustment of driving-seat contours to George's – not his chauffeur's – measurements.

Because George had a Mercedes, Ringo and John had to have one, as George himself had earlier coveted Paul's Aston. Their uniformity before the public applied off duty, too: "We have the same number of suits in our wardrobes, and when we order new ones we order three, four, six at a time from the same tailor."[126] From nowhere, crazes would unburden themselves on all four. Cine-photography was one that lasted longer than most, and George's speciality was filming crowds as the group's limousine glided nearer each sold-out theatre.

On tour, they'd become practised at forging each other's signatures – as had Neil and Mal – to more rapidly dispose of the hundreds of autograph books left at stage doors for their attention. Back at the hotel, they usually doubled up in suites provided, George more often than not with John, whose sense of humour was closest to his own. "Sure, we all get on well together," Ringo has assured fans. "Most people call us offbeat. John writes a little poetry, which is the weirdest you ever saw, but it stops him going mental."[63] When Lennon was requested to collate his verse, stories and drawings for two immediate best-sellers, the second, *A Spaniard In The Works*, proved more difficult, as "it was starting from scratch. With the first book, I'd written a lot of it at odd times during my life."[44] As the completion date loomed, so he picked other brains. George, for instance, assisted with 'The Singularge Experience Of Miss Anne Duffield', an inventive corruption of Conan Doyle.

For reasons to do with the closed shop of his songwriting partnership with John, Paul saw George's greater social attachment to John as no threat. Nowadays, it was John and George – rather than John and Paul and Ringo – who were scrutinised through spyholes at the doors of clubs out of bounds to those not yet eminent enough to frequent them. It was George and John together who were interviewed on the first all-live *Ready, Steady, Go!*. With John taking the lead, their replies on these occasions sometimes had an antiphonal effect. When tackled about an inordinately high admission charge at one concert, John's "I wouldn't see anyone for five quid" was followed by a daring "I wouldn't see you for five bob." "Why don't you let the kids into the airport?" demanded John of a security officer after The Beatles landed in Adelaide. "Yes, we want to see the kids,"[68] echoed George.

In cold print, George's repartee often seemed inanely sarcastic or wantonly pedestrian. "Why aren't you wearing a hat?"[68] he cracked back when asked why he'd once dressed differently from the other three. His favourite meats? "Beef, pork...oh, mutton, yes."[68] In mitigation, a lot of questions he endured from ill-informed, patronising journalists were as banal and repetitious as a stuck record. At the New York press conference given after the group's tumultuous arrival on 7 February 1964 for their first US performance, when they were asked about how time passed when cooped up in hotel rooms, he said, "We ice skate." What would you have been if The Beatles hadn't become stars? "A poor Beatle." Do you guys think there'll be another war soon? "Yeah. Friday."

Chronologically, he'd grown to man's estate, but there remained a strong streak of the adolescent in him. At a party, he got so giggly over a quip about "pack up Mick Jagger in your old kit bag" that he had to write it down. In July 1964, at London's Dorchester Hotel, Princess Margaret laughed off as Beatle cheek his entreaty for her to leave so the company could begin the buffet celebration, following the première of The Beatles' first film, *A Hard Day's Night*. On an edition of *Juke Box Jury* showcasing the whole group, he switched the name plates so that, for years, my friend Kevin was under the misapprehension that George was John.

No Beatle was baited by the others as Stuart and Tommy had been, but George was often treated with less than respect by John and Paul. Sometimes he asked for it. One of his most irritating traits was butting into their conversations with some flat line as if trying to imprint his importance to the group on outsiders. Insecure and only

21, his ears strained to catch murmured intrigue and a glimmer of the more intense limelight in which McCartney and Lennon basked. "What are you talking about?" "Mind your own bloody business,"[128] barked John, helping himself to a cigarette from George's top pocket. Interrupting Paul and a *Melody Maker* interviewer, George "was thinking, 'How about something like Little Richard's "Bama Lama Bama Loo"?'" "You just write daft things, George," snapped Paul before turning back to the reporter. "As I was saying, about writing a rocker – I'd liken it to abstract painting..."[129]

Since 'Don't Bother Me', George had composed not a single "daft thing". Even Paul and John went through a bad patch in 1964 during the Australasian tour, which by many accounts was little more than a heavily subsidised debauch.[69] After the *Hard Day's Night* quota of 13 Lennon-McCartney originals, half of 1964's Christmas LP, *Beatles For Sale*, regurgitated old rock 'n' roll standards and songs buried since The Quarry Men. Striking an unfathomable chord for me, however, were the few bars of instrumental play-out on a minor track, 'I Don't Want To Spoil The Party', which somehow caught the essence of The Beatles.

George's undervalued guitar style was as rich a legacy for other artists as any other Beatle innovation. Because his solos and riffs were constructed to integrate with the melodic and lyrical intent of each song, they seemed unobtrusive – even bland – in contrast to those within the year's crop of groups who'd ditched Beatle winsomeness for denim taciturnity. Musically, the main difference lay in the lead guitarist, who, unlike Harrison, would step forward into the spotlight to react with clenched teeth and intellectual flash to underlying chord patterns rather than the aesthetics of the song.

Containing such an exquisite, The Yardbirds secured a support spot at The Beatles' 1964 Christmas season at Hammersmith Odeon. During their allotted ten minutes, they curtailed the extended instrumental "rave-ups" that had made them the toast of the Crawdaddy, where they'd taken over from the Stones. This streamlining cramped the style of their 19-year-old guitarist, Eric "Slowhand" Clapton, who'd briefly been one of Brian Cassar's Engineers. While sharing the self-immolatory tendencies of some of his black icons, Surrey-born Eric was steeped more than most in the note-bending dissonance of the blues. This distinction did not register with George Harrison, who passed the time of day with the Yardbird along backstage corridors "but didn't really get to know him".[32]

For as long as Clapton, Alvin Dean and other would-be virtuosi fermented hitless in the specialist clubs and college circuit, George would continue to win polls as top guitarist. Deservedly, he – and The Searchers – can be credited for introducing the twelve-string guitar to the common-or-garden pop group: "It's gear. It sounds a bit like electric piano, I always think, but you can get a nice fat sound out of it."[129] From an actor friend of Bob Dylan, he learned the rudiments of playing it finger-style, but he always reverted to the plectrum. While it was still a novelty at home, George had procured a Rickenbacker semi-acoustic model – with the four lowest sets of strings tuned in octaves – during The Beatles' first trip to the States. Limited as a solo instrument, its uniquely circular effect powered a flip-side, 'You Can't Do That', on which John played lead, although George's new twelve-string took the resounding bass passage in the title song on *A Hard Day's Night*.

Another American acquisition of George's was also heard in Abbey Road studios. Manufactured by Gretsch, the Chet Atkins Country Gentleman was also heard on the album *Chet Atkins Picks On The Beatles*, for which George was delighted to pen respectful sleeve notes. To his pleasure and embarrassment, a more venerated hero, Carl Perkins, chanced to be there during The Beatles' October evening session for Carl's own 'Everybody's Trying To Be My Baby', swamped in "flutter" echo. On *Beatles For Sale*, this constituted George's one lead vocal. The last Lennon-McCartney number he'd ever record was on *A Hard Day's Night*. Short and with the composers' backing "ooh-oohs" prominent, 'I'm Happy Just To Dance With You' was George's, because John "couldn't have sung it",[78] even though he'd been responsible for most of its lyrics. As a US single, it had sneaked to a lowly Number 95 for, although there was no serious sign of wavering, the impetus of The Beatles' conquest of America had relaxed slightly by late 1964. They'd been in France when Capitol had launched the 'I Want To Hold Your Hand' spring offensive on a Hot 100 rife with Bobby ballads and surf instrumentals. After the first night of their season at the Paris Olympia, they'd needed cheering up.

To a degree, the French way had been paved with Petula Clark's hit translation of 'Please Please Me' (rendered as 'Tu Perds Ton Temps' – "you lost your chance") and the inclusion of 'Money', 'You'll Never Walk Alone' and further Mersey Beat set works in the repertoires of Johnny Hallyday and other Gallic pop luminaries. Nonetheless, The Beatles got off to a bad start on a late-running bill, co-headlining with Trini Lopez and Hallyday's singing wife, Sylvie Vartan. Although he'd tried some nonsensical schoolboy French continuity ("John est sur le table"), George's remarks in English grew less jocular as the set wore on with equipment persistently malfunctioning and the outbreaks of barracking to which the yé-yé – nearly all male this time – were prone. A year later, after the Stones, Kinks and Animals had done well in France, The Beatles would be able to work up their accustomed pandemonium to justify closing the show two nights running at Le Palais de Sports.

By then, they had spearheaded what has passed into myth as the "British Invasion" of the New World, an eventuality predicted in May 1963 by Roy Orbison with English screams still ringing in his ears: "These boys have enough originality to storm our charts in the US with the same effect as they have already done here."[130] As British pop had long been regarded as merely furbished of nine-day wonder, like The Tornados, few believed him, However, even Roy would say, "As a male, I personally don't like feminine hair on men, and I imagine women don't like it either."[131] When a clip of a Beatles concert was shown on his nationwide TV chat show a month prior to their messianic descent on Kennedy Airport, Jack Paar – a US Wogan – wisecracked, "I understand scientists are working on a cure for this."[132] Not so amused, however, were factions in the crew-cut Bible Belt down south.[133]

Dallas, Texas was "a place not known for war", as Jerry Lee Lewis sang in 'Lincoln Limousine', his MacGonagall-esque requiem to president John F Kennedy, assassinated there in 1963 on the same November day that British pop papers proclaimed The Beatles' forthcoming US visit. Some would predicate that the four's American success was an antidote to the depressing Christmas that followed the Dallas tragedy. John Lennon's more forthright theory was "that kids everywhere all go for the same stuff and, seeing as we'd done it in England, there's no reason why we couldn't do it in America, too."[57] They could scarcely miss in a maternally-minded society that was later to indulge in the adoption of Cabbage Patch dolls.

Their confidence might have wobbled in Paris, but The Beatles were quite unruffled in New York. "If anyone dried up," said George, "there was always somebody else there with a smart answer. There was always a good balance, so nobody could quite nail us."[32] The Beatles were boys next door, but not like Bobby goo-merchants, who now couldn't get hits to save their lives. "I don't think they expected musicians playing rock 'n' roll to have any wit or repartee at all,"[134] reckoned Mike Smith of The Dave Clark Five, who likewise disgorged themselves from a Pan Am jet a few weeks later.

The Five would be televised on *The Ed Sullivan Show* – America's *Sunday Night At The London Palladium* – more times than any British group before or after, but it was The Beatles' pulse-quickening slot on 9 February that would be remembered more than that of any other Sullivan guest since Elvis in 1956. George hadn't made the dress rehearsal for the excellent reason that he was flat on his back in the Plaza Hotel, sweating out a high fever, his throat wrapped in a towel and cradling a portable wireless tuned to a commentary on the fans stationed outside. His increasing trepidation about flying may have exacerbated the illness – and sour mood – contracted in Paris. Not likely to improve his constitution either was bumptious Big Apple disc jockey Murray the K, who was trying to blag his way into rooming with George to tape his thoughts on waking and just prior to sleep. George conducted those interviews that couldn't be put off from his bed but, spared Murray the K, he was able to go the distance on Sullivan's show, thanks to quick-acting medication and nursing by sister Louise, who'd extended her visit from Benton to so do. (See Appendix I.)

All About The Beatles, Louise's interview LP, was released in 1965. Another small label – the first of many – had got hold of poor old Pete Best. With his group, he was hauled over to milk his connection with The Beatles via a sell-out North American tour at odds with fading interest in him, even in Liverpool. Backtracking to 'Love Me Do' and the antique Sheridan tracks, so insatiable – and uncritical – was demand for anything on which The Beatles had ever breathed that, for one glorious week, they occupied nine places in the Canadian Top Ten and accounted for 60 per cent of record sales in the States over a twelve-month period. At home, each new Beatle release was, noted Derek Taylor, "a national event",[135] but with most of the Union's 50 states comparable in size to the British Isles it did no harm for US companies with rights to Beatle products to hurl at such a wide sales region singles of any album cuts that took their fancy. George therefore suffered no loss of prestige when the year-old 'Roll Over Beethoven' and the more ancient 'Do You Want To Know A Secret' hovered around the middle of the Hot 100. "Just about everyone is tired of The Beatles," groaned *Billboard* magazine, "except the buying public."[136]

Alighting in Midwest towns in the graveyard hours, The Beatles' aeroplane would still be greeted by hundreds of hot-eyed teenagers, many chaperoned by parents who had not chastised them for squandering their allowances on a six-dollar can of "Beatle Breath" or for neglecting their homework to ogle a TV "documentary" of the group's first US visit (with surreptitious hand-held shots of Ringo's ear for minutes on end). To less determinate purpose, invasions of privacy were enacted by such as "the Torpedo", one of an assortment of female fans notorious for skills in evading the most stringent barricades to impose themselves on The Beatles and other UK beat groups now being fully exploited in the States.

"Britain hasn't been so influential in American affairs since 1775," read the same *Billboard* editorial as fascination with all things from our sceptred isle peaked during that 1964 week, when two-thirds of the Hot 100 was British in origin, although one Capitol executive would caw, "I tell ya, Elmer, you heard one Limey group, you heard 'em all." Most of Britain's major pop acts – and some minor ones – succeeded to varying extents in the unchartered States, but, anticipating this, many Yankee entrepreneurs had crossed the

Atlantic to stake claims in the musical diggings, among them the self-important Phil Spector, who said he wanted to produce The Beatles. Years before they let him, his encounters with them left George with an idea of someone "a bit outrageous, but he was very sweet. He was like a giant person inside this frail little body."[137]

While such big shots were in Britain, a common complaint back home was that of Frank Zappa, of Los Angeles' Soul Giants: "If you didn't sound like The Beatles or Stones, you didn't get hired."[138] By 1965, a host of American groups had grown out their crew-cuts and cowlicks as much as they dared and seized upon whatever aspect of British beat they felt most comfortable with. In The Byrds' case, it was Beatle harmonies and the twelve-string sound pioneered by The Searchers and George Harrison. Moulded less successfully to breadwinning UK specification were the likes of The McCoys, The Wackers, The Remains, The Knickerbockers and, resident on Jack Good's networked *Shindig* show, The Shindogs. Although their debut 45, 'The Peppermint Beatle', was a miss, The Standells' Gary Leeds later drummed with The Walker Brothers, who found greater rewards in Britain itself.

Far behind all of them were The Sundowners, a Florida outfit formed after 13-year-old Tom Petty saw The Beatles on television: "I thought I could be a farmer or I could do that."[139] If teenagers like Tom had to emulate British beat groups, reasoned adult America, let it be ones like The Beatles and Herman's Hermits, as a palatable compromise to hairier monsters like The Rolling Stones and The Pretty Things. Demonstrating this acceptance of The Beatles as good, clean fun was an episode of *I Love Lucy* in which stooge Mr Mooney tries to book for $100 "that English combo everyone's talking about" for a firm's dinner and dance. Now that America had capitulated, the rest of the world was a pushover. Soviet Russia threw up a group, The Candid Lads, whom *The Daily Express* reckoned were The Beatles' opposite numbers. In the back streets of Hong Kong, you'd come across a local outfit with a set consisting entirely of deadpan Beatle imitations. Down Under, where even 'Cry For A Shadow' had made the Top Ten, New Zealand's Shadows clones, The Librettos, made the transition, as did The Bee Gees, regulars on

Australian TV's *Bandstand*. This was broadcast from Sydney, where, despite torrential rain, The Beatles were welcomed by the biggest crowd since aviator Amy Johnson landed there after her solo flight from England in 1932.

For much of this leg of 1964's world tour, The Beatles weren't quite the full shilling. Qualified mainly by his playing on *Beatlemania*, a budget LP of anonymous Beatles covers, freelance drummer Jimmy Nicol was thrust into transient stardom as temporary substitute for Ringo, then under the scalpel for acute tonsillitis. Paul and John had been amenable, but George had dug in his heels – if Ringo couldn't go, neither would he. As it turned out to be The Beatles' only visit to Australasia, it was fortunate for their distant fans – watching defiance, hesitation and final agreement chase across George's face – that Brian Epstein talked him around.

Brian had become accomplished at calming down unruly youths. He'd plenty of opportunity to practise these days as time ran out for many of his clients. Gerry, The Fourmost and Billy J had all borne their first serious flops, while other of his acts had never had hits anyway. After The Big Three's first set at the Blue Angel one night, another drummer took over when Johnny Hutch collected his pay and went home. While his Mersey Beat groups were cashing in what chips were left, Epstein had overloaded himself with trendier non-Liverpool signings like The Moody Blues, a Birmingham quintet who, under their previous handlers, had already topped the UK charts.

However manifold his other undertakings, Brian's primary concern would always be The Beatles. For his "boys" – his surrogate children – he did whatever energy and willingness could do to help their careers, to make him prouder of them and them of him. He took their gratuitous insults, their piques, their flagrant cohabitation with their lady-loves and their headline-making misbehaviour like the loving father he should have been. In language that George could understand, he'd unravel those complexities that still befuddled him after a session with the accountants. Knowing that George was generally grouchy first thing in the morning, Brian had been all sympathy when his "favourite son" (as he called George during a US press conference) had thrown orange juice at Brian Somerville, a publicist that neither of them liked much. As he'd once taken John on a Spanish holiday while Cynthia recovered from child-bearing, so George and a new girlfriend – a model named Pattie Boyd – accompanied Brian to the south of France. Solicitous as usual, he deferred to the couple's wishes about how they spent their leisure but could be relied upon to suggest diversions. A bull fight in Arles, however, wasn't a wincing George's notion of a pleasant afternoon.

When self-confessed Beatlemaniac Derek Taylor approached Brian with a view to ghosting a Beatle's day-to-day ruminations for *The Express*, it was thought that it would be "a nice thing for George, give him an interest in life because the others have their songwriting and Ringo is rather new".[74] In return for an agreed fee of £100 a week, all the newspaper wanted was permission to credit George with the column that Taylor was to submit for twelve Fridays.

Under the editorial lash, he hammered out the first article, but before handing it in Derek felt it was polite to show it to his subject. At Whaddon Court, he read it to Epstein, the Lennons and a bemused George. Uneasily tracing that fading Mersey Beat scent, Derek admitted that, "because the assumption was that George hadn't been to school, it was like a jolly docker would have talked".[74] One tortuous Scouse-ism, "big green job" (for Corporation bus), stuck in Taylor's throat as one that had never reached the lips of a Beatle or anyone else. As George had no wish to be portrayed as the definitive wacker (or, indeed, the definitive anything), he decided that the ghost had to be partly exorcised. He could string a sentence together as well as any ex-Liobian, couldn't he? Taylor and he would collaborate. Thus was laid the foundation of a lasting friendship, strengthened soon afterwards when Derek, a fellow Merseysider, was put on NEMS' payroll as Brian's personal assistant and then The Beatles' press officer after Somerville's outraged exit in October 1964, partly over stipulations in a contract of employment that he saw as implying a lack of trust.

The job was no picnic for Taylor, either, as his job often went *ultra vires* just answering telephones, writing publicity hand-outs and organising press conferences. At one US airport, he became embroiled in a running argument with security officials as The Beatles were bundled into limousines. Riled by his "girly" English accent, a guard punched Taylor in the stomach. Meanwhile, the group's motorcade slid away, leaving Derek gasping for breath on the tarmac.

After thuggish America, a tour of dear old England was a bagatelle. Patrolling round-the-block queues that had formed days before box offices opened, police kept eyes peeled for a girl runaway from Massachusetts believed to be following The Beatles. Otherwise, no bother was expected from the occupants of the sleeping bags that lined the pavements with their transistor radios and comics. Once they might have wrung their hands, but now mums and dads would bring provisions to their waiting daughters. Well, it was only The Beatles, ritualised and cosy.

Once inside, the girls let rip their healthy, good-humoured screams. Sure, there was fainting, and heightened blood pressure brought on nose bleeds. The odd tip-up chair would snap off its spindle, too, but after 'Long Tall Mandy', or whatever it was called, the screeching would cease for the national anthem, resuming half-heartedly before the audience filed quietly out.

Only fire-hoses could quell the riots at shows by those sinister Rolling Stones. A judgement on them was that among the 22 unconscious after one such fiasco lay their guitarist, Keith Richards, stunned by a flying lemonade bottle. On the sodden carpeting, auditorium cleaners would come across soiled knickers among smashed rows of seating.

Fun for all the family, The Beatles' TV appearances were always special, and Christmas wouldn't be Christmas without the "Fab Four" at Number One. Under parental pressure, some West Country headmasters reshuffled lunch hours so that senior pupils might rush to railway stations to glimpse The Beatles when they were shunted to and from Paddington and Devon for four days for some of the train scenes in *A Hard Day's Night*. Hell, they were an institution, weren't they? How could anyone old enough to have fought Hitler have guessed that The Beatles would be more than a passing phase? Like Tommy and Cliff before them, when they were overtaken by a newer sensation, they'd be set up in pantomime, cabaret, charity football matches and all that. Their unforced Scouse urbanity would be ideal for children's television, wouldn't it? "Who'd want to be an 80-year-old Beatle?"[140] laughed John Lennon. Being Liverpudlian, comedy was the obvious path to take. Any fool could see that in *A Hard Day's Night*.

The Beatles' celluloid career could have got under way with them headlining an all-styles-served-here conveyor belt of lip-synched ephemera linked by some vacuous story-line in the tradition of *The Girl Can't Help It* and *It's Trad, Dad*. In August 1963, more than 40 scripts considered had been of this disposition, but, although punctuated with musical breaks and concluded with a concert sequence, The Beatles were more than a monochrome sideshow in *A Hard Days Night*. With no highbrow pretensions, however, they were not required "to other be". That was left to the supporting actors.

Before co-stars were deemed unnecessary, among big names discussed was that of Peter Sellers, who so admired The Beatles – as they did him – that he'd recorded the film's main title as a cod-Shakespearian recitation and scurried into the Top 20 with it, too. A romantic sub-plot was on the cards briefly, until producer Walter Shenson realised how much the group's female following might resent it. Visualised for this role had been 16-year-old Hayley Mills, a pert, snub-nosed miss who'd been in films since the late 1950s. George was the Beatle who'd drawn the short straw for the pleasure of squiring her to the Regal in Henley-on-Thames for a showing of the Hitchcockian *Charade*. At this charity midnight matinee, he was as impressed with the cinema's art-deco interior as he was with *Charade* and Miss Mills.

A one-off date was enough to set tongues wagging about Harrison and Hayley, but rumours about him and Pattie Boyd had infinitely more substance. Pattie was then consistent with George's taste, which "runs to small blonde girls who can share a laugh with me".[141] Their backgrounds, nonetheless, were poles apart. The eldest of six children, Patricia Anne Boyd was born in Somerset in 1945, but one of her father's RAF postings obliged the family to move to Kenya four years later. When they returned to England after half a decade, Pattie was sent to boarding school. By 1962, however, anyone peering through the window of a certain Wimbledon hairdressing salon might have seen her putting the finishing touches to some aged crone's blue rinse. Noticing Pattie's willowy figure and avalanche of wavy hair, another customer – a writer for a women's magazine – asked if she'd ever thought of becoming a photographic model. This hadn't been the first such compliment paid to her, but it was the incentive for Pattie to broaden her horizons beyond shampoo and curlers.

When she met George, she was in the same mini-skirted league as Twiggy, Celia Hammond and Jean Shrimpton, the new face of *Vogue*, *Seventeen* and the fashion pages of Sunday supplements. With the relative girth of middle life, Pattie would later confess to possessing "a couple of minis which I still try on if I can get into them, but, God, I can never believe we wore them so short".[142] Mary Quant, Shrimpton's *haute couture* Diaghilev, noted how mandatory it had become for 1960s dolly-birds "to look like Pattie Boyd rather than Marlene Dietrich. Their aim is to look childishly young, naïvely unsophisticated, and it takes more sophistication to work out that look than those early would-be sophisticates ever dreamed of."[143]

It was fitting, therefore, for 20-year-old Pattie to land a bit part as a schoolgirl in *A Hard Day's Night*. Its director, Richard Lester, had remembered her toothy grin and lisp from an ITV commercial for Smith's Crisps he'd made a few months earlier. With her and three other uniformed and giggly girls as the audience, The Beatles mimed 'I Should Have Known Better' in a studio mock-up of a guard's van. "I could feel George looking at me," recalled Pattie, "and I was a bit embarrassed. Then, when he was giving me his autograph, he put seven kisses under his name. I thought he must like me a little."[143]

He liked her a lot, as did John, whose subliminal signals to her would intensify as his marriage deteriorated. At first, George, the unencumbered bachelor, came on as the rough, untamed Scouser, but even when this was moderated he was still very different from Pattie's previous *beaux* in London. Loyally, she clung to her latest boyfriend until his persevering Beatle rival – whose brash outer shell, she discovered, contained surprising gentleness and sensitivity – prised her away: "I said I was loyal, not stupid."[144] When her flat was burgled, listed on the police inventory was George's *A Hard Day's Night* gold disc.

This real-life courtship made up for the sentimental element that *A Hard Day's Night* thankfully lacked. Although it was, said Lennon, "The Beatles at their most natural",[141] Paul was self-conscious about many lines he had to utter. However, if no Laurence Olivier, the so-called Serious One coped so well with "acting" his big scene – making disparaging remarks about an array of "grotty" shirts – that Shenson demanded another, but the scene became John's instead of George's.

The Beatles' zany farce brought the curtain down on the old teenpics regime of neo-musicals full of cheery unreality. More dated a film than *A Hard Day's Night* was *Ferry Across The Mersey*, set in the fast-waning "Nashville of the North" and starring Gerry And The Pacemakers, whose evocative title song extended a Top Ten farewell for the Mersey Beat movement in January 1965. From the Cavern's battered stage, some musicians were fly enough to spot even those American tourists ungarlanded with cameras. It was a look in the eye, as though mentally ticking off a "gen-u-ine" Liverpool beat group from a list of attractions that also included the Changing Of The Guards and Morris dancers.

Nearing the end of its run, *Mersey Beat*'s saga aligned with that of a buoyant local scene singled out as a pop centre and then gutted of its principal talents by London predators. Like Liverpool itself, Mersey Beat was desecrated and the culprits pardoned. The Beatles could be exonerated from most of the blame, although a *Mersey Beat* editorial in April 1964 would complain, "Maybe we don't get many of our home-grown stars appearing too often these days."

Nevertheless, who wouldn't come out when, for the northern première of *A Hard Day's Night*, The Beatles passed in triumphal Rolls Royces through cheering streets from Speke Airport to a civic reception at the City Hall? Outside, a police-massed band pounded out 'Can't Buy Me Love', their fifth Number One.

At the Odeon, as the projectionist waited, they were brought on stage to say a few words. "All my people are here!" boomed George over the cinema tannoy, and so most of them were. Before he was famous, George didn't realise that he had so many relations and family friends. Although his mother's Australian pen-pal had been persuaded by a journalist with a cheque book to part with snapshots of George as an infant, no one had turned up with open hands like John's long-lost father. However, plenty of bogus cousins, neighbours who'd known him as a boy and the like had been refused entry at stage doors, and a *bona fide* uncle had been sent away with a flea in his ear from one Canadian theatre.

For his nearest and dearest, George was the indirect fount of gifts that fans parcelled to The Beatles' fan club to thank them for having him, including home-made "gonks", honorific plaques and childish daubs. Most were less than ornaments, but from those with more money than sense came complete dinner services and even silverware. Ideally, the most inquisitive among us would like to sample with our own sensory organs, say, the older Harrison brothers' feelings about Our Kid's popularity and wealth. Whatever the complicated emotional shades among them, neither could deny the material benefits of kinship to a Beatle. As well as expensive birthday presents, there were transfusions of cash for the asking. It was, however, the Harrisons' very stability as a family that forbade each from presuming too much upon George's good fortune. From sunning themselves on a Caribbean strand, Louise and Harold returned to Mackett's Lane, instead of spending more of his money by coming along for the ride on The Beatles' Australasian tour. This was in spite of Harry's earlier announcement of it "being good for George that we are going along. We will probably be able to take a load off his shoulders by dealing with fans out there."[68] Also figuring in their decision not to go, perhaps, was the fact that that Lennon's aunt – who'd never recanted some sharp words to Louise at the Cavern – had been invited along, too.

In crushed-velvet seats at the Odeon, the parents had listened to master of ceremonies David Jacobs' build-up to the film's unveiling. To spatters of applause, he'd popped in a couple of *bons mots* at the expense of The Rolling Stones. For weeks, 'A Hard Day's Night' and the Stones' 'It's All Over Now' had monopolised the first two positions in Britain's hit parade, necessitating the avoidance of such revenue-draining clashes in future. Although The Beatles would snipe at the Stones in the press (hardly ever *vice versa*), they'd send Mal

Evans out mid-session to purchase their competitors' latest LP and both groups socialised outside working hours; Jagger and Richards – the Stones' Lennon and McCartney – were among party guests after The Beatles' concert at New York's Shea Stadium in 1965.

In terms of attendance figures, this was to be The Beatles' zenith, but George at least was not so swollen-headed by it all not to drop in on The Merseybeats as they recorded a new single or gravitate back to Liverpool, albeit with decreasing frequency. Long a nightbird by vocation, he'd haunt the Blue Angel, with its anecdotes about what Billy Kramer said to Sam Leach in 1961. George was nobody's lion there but still one of the lads. Seizing the initiative, he ambled over to a Roadrunner with, "Hi, Mike, how's the band?" "Great, George," began Mike Hart's crushing riposte, "How's yours?"

When The Roadrunners ground to a standstill, Mike would be among the founders of that mixed-media aggregation known as "the Liverpool Scene" who drank from much the same pool as The Scaffold. By 1965, however, more and more Scouse artists were seeking their fortunes down south. An example was Gibson Kemp, Ringo's replacement in Rory Storm's Hurricanes, who became one third of Paddy, Klaus And Gibson with Paddy Chambers and Klaus Voorman. Before Voorman left in 1966 to join Manfred Mann, the trio were resident at the Pickwick on Great Newport Street.

The Pickwick was one of about ten fashionable London niteries from which the chosen few could select a night out, with "night" defined as around midnight to dawn. "Fashionable" meant that the supercool Ad-Lib would be "in" for a while, before the inscrutable pack transferred allegiance to the Speakeasy or the Bag O' Nails, off Carnaby Street, before finishing up at the cloistered Scotch of St James, within spitting distance of Buckingham Palace. Talking shop continually, pop's male conquistadores would hold court, with only their equals contradicting them. Close at hand would be a whiskey and Coke and, depending on their status, a variable abundance of skinny, Quant-cropped birds with double-decker eyelashes.

Since pairing off with Pattie, George became less of a West End clubman, but his record collection still reflected an advanced awareness of the American soul music that forever filled the downstairs disco's deafening dark at the Scotch. His record player would pulsate to the Betty Everetts, Don Coveys and Chuck Jacksons, as well as the better-known Marvin Gayes, Nina Simones and Wilson Picketts. Before saturation plugging on Britain's new pirate radio station put them into the charts' lower rungs, George had long been *au fait* with eruditions like 'Harlem Shuffle' by Bob And Earl, Edwin Starr's 'Headline News' and the originals of such British covers as The Hollies' 'Just One Look' (Doris Troy) and The Fourmost's 'Baby I Need Your Loving' (The Four Tops). George had persisted in his advocacy of Mary Wells, who was then Tamla-Motown's foremost female singer, touring Britain as The Beatles' guest star. Most nights, he clapped her three-song spot from the wings, even her unwise choice of the smoochy 'Time After Time', which was better suited for cabaret than a mob impatient for the Fab Four.

George imagined himself quite refined by now, but he would never be snooty about mainstream pop. His tastes again were largely American, running to the post-surf Beach Boys, The Byrds and New York's Lovin' Spoonful, who had roots in rural blues and Memphis jug bands. Both The Byrds and the Spoonful had been classified as "folk-rock", as was Bob Dylan, who'd also offended folk purists by going electric, *circa* 1965. Because it exposes a point of view, even 'Can't Buy Me Love' may be construed as political, but Dylan sang stridently through his nose about myriad less wistful topics.

Nor was he still going on about war being wrong. With The Beatles' Aeolian cadences, Dylan's rapid-fire stream-of-consciousness literariness was jolting pop's under-used brain into quivering, reluctant action. First of all, beat groups dipped into his stockpile of songs, with The Byrds, The Animals and Manfred Mann notable among those having hits. Next, the hunt was on for more Dylans, as it had been for more Beatles. In Britain, the job went to a crumpled Scot named Donovan who, with harmonica harness and nasal inflection, began on *Ready, Steady, Go!* as a more beatific edition of the master. Although it involved sweating a bit over lyrics, Tin Pan Alley composers put their minds to Dylan-type creations, thereby rendering 1965 the golden age of all-purpose protest songs like PF Sloan's 'Eve Of Destruction' for Barry McGuire, a former New Christy Minstrel.

Lennon and McCartney weren't in complete agreement on the issue of Bob Dylan. While Paul had reservations, John's moptop was often covered these days with a denim cap like Dylan's, and some of his newer songs – especially 'I'm A Loser', from *Beatles For Sale* – betrayed an absorption of the American through constant replay of his albums. Time would come when George would be even more hooked on Dylan than John. "Even his stuff which people loathe I like," he'd boast, "because every single thing he does represents something that's him."[145]

As an individual, Dylan was "the looniest person I've ever met".[145] The Beatles were first introduced to him in a New York hotel suite during their first North American tour, and when offered refreshment Bob asked for "cheap wine" rather than any finer beverage in the drinks cabinet. While Mal went out for the requested *vin ordinaire*, it transpired during the intervening chit-chat that The Beatles – contrary to their guest's assumption – had never had much to do with marijuana. "It's as if we're up there pointing down at us,"[118] tittered McCartney to Derek Taylor when Dylan passed round a rectifying joint laced with the narcotic that no longer terrified John, George and Paul like it had with those peculiar blokes the evening before the Decca audition. Paradoxically, if they'd still been worried after inhaling it, then it couldn't have been marijuana.

Dylan grew as heartily sick of explaining his songs as The Beatles were of answering questions about haircuts and how they found America ("turn left at Greenland"). "They asked one question eight different times,"[146] George snorted after another mind-stultifying press conference. What kind of a world was this, where hotel chambermaids would sell their stories to journalists before the group had even checked in? *Beatles Monthly* answered an enquiry about hairs on George's stomach. Actually worth writing about was The Beatles' harrowing visit to brighten the last hours of a Melbourne police chief's terminally ill niece, or the few savoured minutes of ordinary behaviour when, *en route* to a concert, the group's Austin Princess stopped outside a village shop in Devon while they purchased sweets.

It was less trouble to drive rather than walk the shortest distance now. When interruptive fans in restaurants spoiled too many meals, the four took to "ones where people are so snobby they pretend they don't know us".[146] Even an R&B jamboree in Richmond was no sanctuary, as an excursion by George and John to see The Animals there fired an outbreak of Beatlemania and the pair's hasty departure. George's rather optimistic summary of his privations is worth quoting at length: "This poverty of ours – if that's what it should be called – applies to the things we've been deprived of as a result of what we are. For instance, we can't go window shopping. We can't browse around a department store. We'll have this for four or five years or a few more. In the meantime, we'll wait, and it's not bad, really. We're making money while waiting."[126]

There are worse ways of making a living, but for George touring was becoming the most onerous obligation of Beatlehood. Some fans not close enough to maul him as he dashed past would resort to extreme emotional blackmail, threatening to jump off buildings, throw themselves under car wheels or swallow poison. Aspiring to an orgasm at the thrust of a Beatle, one single-minded woman actually slashed her wrists in frustration. Other girls had better luck, for, although admirable young men in many ways, The Beatles also had their share of young men's vices. A natural prudity discourages me from going into detail, except to say that the group's casual and unchallenging procurement of sexual gratification was not brought to public notice by a press who judged any besmirching of the Fab Four's cheeky but innocent image as untimely when no one wanted to know that they were any different from the way they'd been in *A Hard Day's Night*. Save the scandal for The Rolling Stones.

Dressing-room scenes were often how susceptible fans might have imagined them – a card or board game on the middle table, George tuning up, Paul shaving at the wash-basin. Sometimes, it really would be like *A Hard Day's Night*, when they cleared the decks to rehearse acoustically John and Paul's latest opus, with Ringo slapping the table or cardboard-box drums. Who could think ill of boys who, smothering inner revulsion, were charming to the chain of handicapped unfortunates wheeled in by credulous minders deluded that a "laying on of hands" by the four pop deities would bring about a cure? In Beatle parlance, *cripple* came to mean anyone they wished to be shooed from their presence.

Not everyone adored them. Priggish hoteliers would be at pains to stress that no minor was to be served liquor, their faces falling when George produced his passport. Armed with scissors, posses of manly yahoos would attempt raids on the group's quarters, assuming that they'd receive leniency from a regional justice who frowned on male hairstyles longer than a crewcut. None succeeded, but in such areas The Beatles were subjected to insulting placards and rarer peltings with decayed fruit, most of which were thrown by jealous boyfriends. As bullet-holes in the undercarriage of one Beatle chartered flight testified, some were sufficiently maddened to lie at the end of an American runway, shotguns at the ready.

With his nose in the aircraft company's digest, George had been blissfully unaware of the danger. Now and then, he'd be awed by the ego-dissipating effects of high altitude. Staring down on the Arctic's icy tundra, he was heard to mutter, "looking at that lot makes you feel very humble, somehow."[148] Nonetheless, some of the paint-peeling antiquities hired to lift them from A to B bolstered acute misgivings about flying. Billowing with tongues of flame, one such death-trap carried The Beatles and a retinue that included The Ronettes and Phil Spector over the Rockies to Seattle. Haunting George perhaps were the ghosts of Buddy Holly and Jim Reeves. As The Beatles continued to fly in the face of superstition, he fretted in royal plural that, "We've done so much flying without really any incidents that the more we do, the more we worry. If we can go by road, we do."[149]

The Beatles usually hurtled through the British countryside by train or in their Austin Princess, customised with headrests, radio, record player and extra seat. New driver Alf Bicknell had loaded the necessary tools to tackle problems from snowdrifts to overcharging alternators, but he had no remedy for George's Gretsch tumbling from an unsecured boot into the path of a lorry. Rather than bawl out Alf, George withdrew into a resigned silence. Later, he drifted back into the small-talk that always sprang up when the late-night radio station went off the air, disagreeing with Paul over the aesthetics of pylons. Even when too fatigued for deeper dialogue, they preferred not to fall asleep upright with the road roaring in their ears.

In concert, they heard the relentless screaming no more than a mariner hears the sea. As far as guesswork and eye contact would allow, they adhered to recorded arrangements, but, sighed George, "It was impossible to know which song they screamed for most."[150] Before stage monitors and mega-watt public-address systems, Ringo beat his drums without electronic assistance, while the guitarists' three 60-watt Vox amplifiers were less a sound than a presence. Virtually gulping the microphone, The Beatles' singing would strain against the horrendous barrage of noise. Even in Britain, hysterical fans were now subjected to arbitrary manhandling by a cordon of bouncers so exultantly brutal that Lennon reprimanded them from the footlights.

McCartney dealt with the bulk of the patter, which was becoming predictable to the syllable, although sometimes he'd appeal vainly for discontinuance of the rain of votive offerings cascading onto the stage. Because George had mentioned in *The Daily Mirror* that he was partial to them, jelly-babies would shower The Beatles in Britain. As different from these sweets as hailstones are to snow, their harder equivalents would hit them overseas. Through the medium of *Melody Maker*, George begged "a favour for us. Write down that we've had enough jelly-babies now. Thank the fans very much, but we'd like them to stop throwing them."[129] Almost as commonplace were toilet rolls inscribed with messages of undying love, but nothing that thudded onto the boards surprised them any more – cake, tubes of lipstick, combs, binoculars, even a hateful five-inch nail.

Up there, they endured the mixed blessings of their vulnerability by jesting amongst themselves. For devilment, they'd mouth songs soundlessly or slam deliberate dischords. For the wrong reasons, concerts could still be a laugh. "We must have been hell to work with," George would smile in another decade. "We'd always be messing about and joking, especially John."[151]

Who could keep a straight face in the madness? Socialites, civic dignitaries with their hoity-toity children and everyone who was anyone were failing over themselves to be presented to four common-as-muck Liverpudlians. At a famous-names-in-a-good-cause gala held in The Beatles' honour after their first show at the Hollywood Bowl, you could pass a dozen showbusiness legends on a single staircase. Cassius Clay and Ringo would spar playfully. Zsa Zsa Gabor would have her picture taken with George, who concluded, "Meeting everybody we thought worth knowing and finding out they weren't worth meeting, and having more hit records than everybody else and having done it bigger than everybody else – it was like reaching the top of a wall and then looking over and seeing that there's so much more on the other side."[152]

Soon to disappear was the jubilant youth who, clad only in a bath towel, waved at worshipping masses from a hotel balcony in Sydney. What had been the point of travelling so far and seeing nothing but what he could remember of, say, a stolen afternoon driving a borrowed MG sports car in the Dandenong Mountains or a bowling alley somewhere in Quebec, re-opened for his private use at midnight? He'd seen only glimpses of the places where his blinkered life with The Beatles had taken him. When asked what such-and-such a city had been like, he was damned if he could even find it on a map.

8 The Member Of The British Empire

George's prosperity granted Harold and Louise a dotage rich in material comforts. Indeed, nearly all Beatle parents were suddenly able to retire early. It was like winning the Pools. From Mackett's Lane, the Harrisons uprooted themselves to an isolated bungalow in three acres by a golf course in Appleton, where Merseyside bleeds into Cheshire. If short on neighbours, there were plenty of letters to answer, although by this time 1964's daily vanload had subsided to a steady couple of hundred a week. Mr and Mrs Harrison made the most of their second-hand celebrity, travelling as far as Wiltshire to open fêtes, judge beauty contests and, once, attend a fan's wedding. Most who wrote received some sort of response, usually one of the printed newsletters or signed photographs collected every month from Liverpool's fan club headquarters by Louise. She especially devoted tireless hours to answering selected fan mail. Her warm, chatty style often encouraged surprise visits, such as that of an American family whose daughter's whingeing caused them to interrupt a European holiday by flying from Paris to Manchester to be taxied to Appleton. Louise and Harold always made fans welcome. If not the fans, who else was responsible for their present ease?

Once, The Beatles' relations could slip quietly backstage after a show to exchange a few fleeting words in a bustling dressing room. Now the child you'd known all your life was influencing the minds of millions. He was no longer able to mooch down to the newsagent's without raising a riot, and seconds after finishing the last number his group's dressing room would be as deserted as the *Marie Celeste*. These days, you couldn't enter or leave a Beatles concert yourself without nicotine-stained fingers jotting down everything you said. It would be in the newspapers the next day, and The Beatles might or might not be annoyed.

Out in force when the group's 1965 tour of Britain reached the Liverpool Empire, waiting journalists were well rewarded when George's parents arrived with Pattie Boyd in tow. She was staying at Appleton until Tuesday – and George would be too! Did it mean he'd soon be making an honest woman of her? The world knew they'd been on holiday together, and some editors were itching to break the more distressing news that the shameless hussy had been living with him in his posh new house for months.

Indifferent to success rather than celebrating it, George had been seeking – as he'd articulate later – to "try to stop the waves, quieten them down, to make myself a calm little pool".[24] Rather than joining John, Ringo and Mr Epstein in their Weybridge stockbroker's estate, he'd chosen instead a place called Kinfauns, an exclusive property in wooded Claremont Park in Esher, a few miles nearer the metropolis. Surrounded by high walls, it was not as exposed to fans' attentions as his Knightsbridge flat, but George was, nevertheless, the first Beatle to equip himself with electronically operated gates. It was aggravating enough that the fans picked the roses he was cultivating along the inner driveway, but the last straw had come when he'd been startled awake one night when his arm dangled from the bed to touch one of two wretched girls hidden beneath the mattress. As they'd already stolen items of clothing as souvenirs, instead of fishing autograph books from handbags the pair wisely took to their heels as their idol switched on the light and yelled. Fright had become rage when he returned to bed after a pointless chase. Recovered from her own shock, Pattie indicated the window, left open for the Persian cat.

Little inside Kinfauns revealed its owner's profession, apart from the guitars and the juke box. With its pine furnishing, garden pond and home help, it might have been the bungalow of a young marketing executive so admired by his office superiors that he could get away with the Beatle fringe that would render slightly less able men ineligible for promotion.

Very much the junior partner in The Beatles, George's songwriting explorations thus far were of less value than the power he gave to Lennon and McCartney's patterns of chords and rhymes. Formidable even before the Parlophone contract, John and Paul's headstart had been a hard yardstick for Jagger and Richards, Ray Davies and other British beat composers. Nevertheless, artists were now courting Davies for numbers he felt were unsuitable for his Kinks, and, likewise, Jagger and Richards for Stones leftovers. As they'd found their feet as composers, the albums and demo tapes of The Yardbirds, The Who and even Unit 4 + 2 were searched for potential hits. No would-be Gershwin in a beat group would be able to equal the sales of Lennon and McCartney's chart-toppers for Billy J, Cilla and Peter And Gordon, but the 150 recorded versions of Ray Davies' compositions certainly put George's solitary 'Don't Bother Me' and its forgotten cover by Gregory Phillips in the shade.

Neither of the two albums that had passed since *With The Beatles* contained additions to the Harrison portfolio. He was under no commercial discipline to compose. "When I first started at it," he confessed, "I used to forget to keep going and to finish things off. It's like washing your teeth. If you've never washed your teeth before, it takes a bit of time to get into the habit."[153] If he lost heart, it didn't matter, as Paul and John's endlessly inventive and swelling stockpile could fulfil the group's contractual load many times over already.

All the same, as he'd struggled to teach himself guitar, so he strove to ensure that his one or two lead vocals per album would be songs of his own from now on. As much a part of his touring luggage as his cine camera was a transistorised reel-to-reel tape machine, a forerunner of the cassette recorder, on which he would note flashes of inspiration. In hotel-suite seclusion, he'd "play or sing phrases for perhaps an hour. Then I play it all back and may get three or four usable phrases or runs from it."[153] From these doodles, a song might grow, but sometimes he'd tinker into the night on a guitar that might as well have been a coal shovel. By 1966, however, he was able to work at home on less portable but more sophisticated equipment, "so what seemed on one machine to be a waste of time sounded possible when mixed and recorded and perhaps dubbed".[154]

Melodies came easiest. Lyrics were almost always "the hardest part for me. When the thing is finished, I'm usually happy with some parts of it and unhappy with others, so then I show it to John and Paul, whose opinion I respect."[154] He'd clear his throat and start chugging chords, take a deep breath and launch into the first line. When the song died, he'd blink at his feet before glancing up with an enquiring eyebrow. Sometimes he'd realise it was no good as soon as he opened his mouth. At other demonstrations, he couldn't comprehend his two listeners' amused indifference: "The hang-up of my playing my songs to John and Paul always used to hold me back, because I knew how it would sound finished and I had to try to convince them in one play. For that reason, there are a lot of numbers of mine that I decided not to do anything about. It was a shyness, a withdrawal, and I always used to take the easy way out."[153]

Lennon lent the most sympathetic ears when George presented two possibilities for inclusion on the soundtrack to the next film, Help!. A week prior to the recording dates in February 1965 (and, incidentally, the day before Ringo wed Maureen), John and George spent half the night polishing up 'I Need You' and, with a country-and-western tinge, 'You Like Me Too Much'. Much of George's adolescent awe of John would never fade. Although he could never hope to penetrate John and Paul's caste-within-a-caste, he loved occasions like these, when he had big John's solicitude. Utterances unamusing to anyone else would have them howling with hilarity on the carpet and waking baby Julian Lennon. Back to work, they'd cudgel an unshaven objectivity on 'You Like Me Too Much' as milk floats braved the dawn cold. "Well, it was 4.30 in the morning when we got to bed," enthused George, "and we had to be up at 6.30. What a fantastic time!"[155]

Much as George appreciated his help, John began to resent his tacit obligation: "He came to me because he couldn't go to Paul... I thought, 'Oh, no. Don't tell me I have to work on George's stuff. It's enough doing my own and Paul's."[156]

McCartney was the only Beatle still residing in London, but geographical inconvenience wasn't the reason why George "couldn't go to Paul". Partly it was his very familiarity with Paul since school that had provoked in George an attitude like that of a youngest child viewing a middle sibling as an insurmountable barrier to prolonged intimacy with an admired eldest brother. Since Stuart's departure, Paul had had no rival for John's attention, and such was their artistic alliance that The Beatles might have been as successful with any competent drummer and second guitarist. To John, anyway, George would be "like a bloody kid, hanging around all the time. It took me years to start considering him as an equal."[156]

To fans, George was as much the public face of The Beatles as John, and matters had gone far enough for any fears of him going the way of Pete Best to vanish. Although he was no match for John as a verbal intimidator or Paul as a diplomat, the concept of a Beatles without him or Ringo was now unthinkable. Nevertheless, the chemistry of the four interlocking personalities apart, he was expendable. In 1966, George could still be made to do as he was told.

In the studio, Norman Smith witnessed how Lennon and, especially, McCartney treated the other two as mere tools for their masterworks, "because George would have done two or three takes that seemed perfectly all right but Paul wouldn't like it and he'd start quoting American records, telling George to play it like it was such and such a song, like this Otis Redding riff for 'Drive My Car'. We'd try again, and then Paul would take over and do it himself on the left-handed guitar he always brought with him. Later I found out that George had been hating Paul's guts for this but didn't let it show. It says a lot for George that he took so much stick from Paul."

On 'Another Girl' from *Help!*, Paul on celluloid crossed what outsiders had understood as the group's demarcation line. As well as singing the cocky verses about "all the girls, and I've met quite a few", Paul hogged the lead-guitar role, eyeing its neck as if stupefied by his own dexterity. In the middle distance, George fretted staccato chords on the offbeat. Before this sequence had thundered from world cinema screens, none would have supposed that George hadn't played the main riffs and solos on other tracks, too. The promotional clips for television still paid lip-service to John on rhythm, Paul on bass, George on lead and Ringo on drums, even though the latest single, 'Ticket To Ride', had Paul on both bass and lead.

The single's B-side, 'Yes It Is', and 'I Need You', taped at the same session, were more taxing for George, as they kept his feet as well as hands and voice occupied. Mistaken in a *Music And Musicians* critique for a harmonica were the tearful guitar legatos achieved by George on both songs with a volume pedal. The precursor of the wah-wah effect, this device had been first employed by veteran session player Big Jim Sullivan in the previous autumn on Dave Berry's heartbreak ballad 'The Crying Game' and its follow-up, 'One Heart Between Two'.

Another absorption of a rival's idea was the dentist's-drill feedback that had introduced the previous Beatles 45, 'I Feel Fine'. This echoed its in-concert – although unrecorded – use by The Yardbirds and The Kinks. Rendering the circle unbroken, The Kinks would approximate the start of 'I Feel Fine' on a 1965 flip-side which also happened to bear the standardised title 'I Need You'.

Their camouflage nets sparkling with dawn dew, Centurion tanks guarded The Beatles as they mimed George's 'I Need You' for the film cameras on Salisbury Plain scrubland. Only a mild exaggeration of the protective bubble surrounding the group in real life, this scene was to be Harrison's big moment in *Help!*. Nothing of the magnitude of the shirt sketch had been written in for him, but if nothing else 'I Need You', for all its simplistic libretto and suspensions *à la* 'One Heart Between Two', was more immediately attractive than some of Paul and John's offerings on the *Help!* LP. While issued as a foreign single, its presence was felt by proxy in the Australasian charts, for which it was covered by the ubiquitous Ray Columbus And The Invaders.

No such synchronisation was applied to 'You Like Me Too Much', which was placed on the non-soundtrack side of *Help!*. Lyrically more substantial than 'I Need You', it might have described one of the tiffs that punctuated the otherwise happy domesticity at Kinfauns. Until it was resolved over the telephone, an argument with Pattie just before the outward flight had jaded the Australian tour for George, who was observed by Adelaide promoter Kevin Ritchie "wandering around the hotel feeling desperately homesick".[68] George felt her silence most when the other three rang home every night. Back in Esher, it would wound Pattie to give up her two dalmatians because they bothered the cat. Nevertheless, love rode roughshod over such differences, and most assumed that George – following fellow northerners John and Ringo – had settled down and that marriage was the next step.

The jealous character assassinations and physical threats that had fanfared Pattie's public entry into the Beatle "family" had abated by now. George's female fans still envied her but could now stomach Pattie's wasp waist, her lisping confidence, her finger on the pulse of fashion. She'd never be accorded a fan club of her own, like John's Cynthia, or be subject of a novelty record, like The Chicklettes' 'Treat Him Tender, Maureen'. Like Jane Asher, she wasn't a Liverpool "steady" from before 'Love Me Do' but an intruder daring to combine care of a Beatle with a separate career and income. In as late as 1968, she'd be consulted as "top model-girl Pattie Boyd"[157] by girls' annuals about clothes and make-up. Perhaps her advice on these was sound, for tolerance gave way to acceptance and, as George Harrison's girlfriend, she'd be commissioned to write a regular "Letter From London" for *16*, a US magazine that never probed deeper than her favourite colour, what food she served when the Lennons visited and whether she thought Ringo's smile was gorgeous. Pattie's report on her and George's evening cutting a rug with Mick Jagger in a London discotheque was also detailed by Mick's then-girlfriend, Chrissie Shrimpton, in *Mod*, *16*'s sister journal.

Their social circle extended beyond The Beatles and even pop, but, as Pattie discovered, "All wives and girlfriends were made to feel that we shouldn't leave the 'family' at all. We mainly went out with each other. It was just the eight of us and the people involved with The Beatles' company. We were cocooned."[44] Crucial to this insularity was the personal unity of the four principals. Never did it occur to The Beatles not to eat together in studio canteens. "We were good friends," said George, "though we were caged animals for most of the time."[158] Although they'd been within earshot of each other during every working day since 1962, blood ties counted for less than Beatlehood, then. No one, not even The Rolling Stones, could appreciate how the four's common ordeals and jubilations bound them, they supposed, for always. In qualification, George would add, "It's wrong to say we're inseparable. When we're on holiday, for instance, we may head for different places. But even then it could be two of us going together."[126]

Disguises, decoy tactics, false names and secret destinations were as essential as spare underwear when a Beatle and his missus decided to go on holiday. Without these precautions, today's deserted beach would become tomorrow's media circus. Curtains in hotel bedrooms would be drawn to reveal a sea of faces and camera lenses between the main entrance and the silver strand where palms nodded. Holed up in one such ruined paradise, Pattie and Cynthia had to be smuggled to the airport in a laundry basket.

Another vacation was cut short when the "quiet Beatle" and the "sexy Beatle" (as the local newspaper dubbed them) were run to ground and besieged in the Royal Hawaiian Hotel on Waikiki oceanfront. Pursuing an exclusive, one brazen disc jockey nosed through the babbling crowds in limousine, wig and affected Scouse accent in an attempt to breach hotel security by impersonating Paul McCartney. Finally, the Royal Hawaiian's advertising director put up the Beatle couples in his Oahu beach house, but three short hours of serenity there ended with a fresh onslaught of fans and reporters. Fleeing to Tahiti, George and John were delighted to wander the quayside streets of Papeete virtually unnoticed, possibly because the place was in the last throes of its monsoon.

Despite the interruptions, Pattie would recall "so many laughs".[142] The idiosyncratic humour that had sustained George and the others before she knew them was still potent. On the Madrid stop of the 1965 European tour, they pulled swimming trunks over their heads to greet ballet dancer Rudolf Nureyev, another hotel guest, who met fire with fire by deadpanning the subsequent platitudes. Such diversions were to George "always the best bit about being in a band, rather than like Elvis, who, being one, suffered things on his own".[158]

They might have been offhand with Nureyev, but The Beatles were speechless at first when brought to Presley in his Beverly Hills mansion late one evening in August 1965. A prelude to this had been an after-hours jam session with a group led by his ex-bass player Bill Black when both acts were in a Key West hotel a year earlier. There'd also been an exchange of presents when The Beatles dropped by at the Hollywood office of Presley's manager, Colonel

Tom Parker. Because of some now-forgotten quarrel that day, George was in a foul mood when he arrived with the others for the audience with the King. This, however, was put on hold when Elvis received them like deified Caesar had the Gallic peasants. It was Elvis who broke the silence, wondering whether The Beatles intended to stare at him all night. He'd met Herman's Hermits a few weeks before. They'd been shy, too.

Then followed an obligatory blow with Presley on bass, McCartney on piano and the rest (bar Ringo) on guitars. Three hours later, the visitors left, one clutching a signed boxed set of their host's albums. In the flesh, Elvis had been gracious enough. "We know Elvis is great," George said while bemoaning his artistic decline. "Basically he's got such a great bluesy voice." Fancifully, he went on, "It would be great if The Beatles and Elvis could get together for an album, it really would."[27] When Presley returned to the stage in the late 1960s, the group telegramed their felicitations, but in an astounding and ramblingly respectful letter to President Nixon in the early 1970s Elvis asked to be enrolled as a Federal Agent in order to combat "that hippie element" of which he then considered The Beatles to be a part.

Beneath it all, George would always believe that Elvis was on the same wavelength. According to Presley's stepbrother, David Stanley, in spite of mixed feelings about The Beatles *per se*, Presley thought, "George Harrison was all right. Harrison was a seeker of truth, just as Elvis was, and that gave them a special bond."[159] Oblivious to the idol's reactionary leanings, George would, in 1972, insinuate his way backstage to pay respects after an Elvis show in New York. The epitome of all that Nixon and, evidently, Presley loathed, "I had my uniform – the worn-out denim jacket and jeans – and I had a big beard and long hair down to my waist. He was immaculate. He seemed to be about eight feet tall and his tan was perfect. I felt like this grubby little slug and Elvis looked like Lord Siva."[160]

Lord Siva is a Hindu demigod. The journey to a George Harrison almost unrecognisable from the yeah-yeah-yeah moptop had started a few months before that first meeting with Elvis in 1966. The turning point had been an occasion when George and Pattie had, as usual, paired up with the Lennons. A mischievous dentist with whom George was friendly – "a middle class swinger",[155] reckoned John – concluded an otherwise pleasant evening around his house by slipping into his guests' coffee a mickey finn of LSD (Lysergic Acid Diethylamide), an hallucinogenic drug manufactured from *ergot* disease derivatives and known in the Middle Ages as St Anthony's Fire. Learning that they'd been spiked, the four left hurriedly in George's Mini. In the Ad-Lib an hour later, the mental distortions of the drug became all too hysterically apparent as they crossed from reality into a wild dream. His psyche boggling with paranormal sensations and surreal perceptions, George at the steering wheel was guided by street lamps flickering like never before as he inched back to a Kinfauns that was "like a submarine", gasped Lennon. "We were only going about ten miles an hour but it seemed like a thousand."[156]

LSD had been "turning on" factions within London's in crowd for about a year before it was outlawed for recreational purposes in 1966. The Moody Blues and The Small Faces knew it well. So did The Pretty Things, if the worst was thought of song titles like 'Trippin'' and 'LSD'. Its use had become so widespread that Dave Dee insisted to *Melody Maker* that, as far as the clean-minded lads in his group were concerned, LSD still stood for pounds, shillings and pence.

With the same exonerative intent, George eventually admitted to taking it unknowingly, while claiming, "I'd never heard of it then."[161] There is, however, speculation that Brian Epstein had indulged and that some of his charges had quizzed him about it prior to John and George's visit to the dentist. Brian could only elucidate in broad terms – it was a stimulating experience, but its effects varied from person to person, from trip to trip. Pattie had been in a nonsensical frenzy while coming down at Kinfauns. Cynthia surfaced from a quagmire of horror. For her husband, it was the start of a fantastic voyage that would carry him to untold heights of creativity.

George compared it to a mystic purging akin to an extreme religious reverie: "Up until LSD, I never realised that there was anything beyond this state of consciousness, but all the pressure was such that, like the man [Dylan] said, 'There must be some way out of here.' I think, for me, it was definitely LSD. The first time I took it, it just blew everything away. I had such an overwhelming feeling of well-being, that there was a God and I could see Him in every blade of grass. It was like gaining hundreds of years' experience in twelve hours."[162] On one hand was a George of whom he'd hitherto been unaware. On the other, the new profundities were already known – it was just that LSD "happened to be the key that opened the door to reveal them. From the moment I had that, I wanted to have it all the time."[3]

Full of their chemically induced glimpses of the eternal, he and John conducted themselves with smug superiority before Ringo, Paul and others yet uninitiated. However, in California, in the month they met Presley, Neil Aspinall and Ringo also "turned on" when George and John underwent a second trip. Joining them at the rented nerve-centre of this particular US tour were members of The Byrds. As The Beatles' dabbling in drugs was not yet public knowledge, Aspinall was instructed to usher another guest – a *Daily Mirror* reporter – from the premises.

The Mirror's principal source of pop news was through an agreement with *Melody Maker*, who, if they knew about LSD, likewise kept mum. Nonetheless, its interviewers couldn't help but perceive the change in George. Although his replies to questions were unfailingly to the point, any witticisms were oddly sour and would provoke but a puffy smile where there used to be a chuckle. After a facetious prediction that George, barely 22, would "probably end up being a bald recluse monk",[163] a scribe presumed that it was just a phase of growing up that would pass.

Whatever was left to enjoy about the screaming ecstasy, the luxury, the imprisoned larks in hotel-suite torpor – all seemed shallow and pointless now. In an as-yet unfocused spiritual quest, George took with him for idle hours on tour challenging literature co-related to his new mentality, Aldous Huxley being one favoured author. However, during bouts of self-loathing in this bandroom or on that chartered flight, it would occur to him that he'd scarcely peeked at any book during the entire tour and that the highlight of the day wasn't the concert any more but the building up and winding down.

Gourmet dishes with specious names – trepang soup, veal

Hawaii, *furst puckler* – pampered stomachs yearning for the greasy comfort of fish and chips eaten with the fingers. Wherever they were these days, local narcotics dealers were generally able to contrive a network from the outside to sell their goods to the group who'd puffed joints and giggled through the shooting of *Help!*. Varying strengths of marijuana had been imbibed as carelessly as alcohol since Dylan popped by in 1964. In a higher league (in every sense) with LSD, Harrison "started getting into thinking, actually saw what was happening. Before that, we didn't have time to think. We were just going from one gig to another and into the [recording] studio and TV studios and concerts."[164]

More than any in the entourage, George begrudged Beatlemania. Even before LSD worked its questionable magic, "I was fed up. I couldn't take any more but resigned myself to suffering it for another year."[165] To irregular fellow travellers, his hostility emerged almost overnight, giving vitality to a surliness towards both fans and media. He'd sign autographs with bad grace or refuse altogether. Worse still, a V-sign directed at a lucky photographer anticipated the loutish affectations of punk by over a decade. Revelling in his wickedness when the shot appeared in an American newspaper, Harrison ordered the tracking down of the negative – not so that it could be destroyed but so that it could be enlarged and displayed on the bathroom door at Kinfauns and on the front of a 1965 Christmas card. He seemed oblivious to the consequences of behaviour that would have been tantamount to professional suicide back in 1963. Speaking like some withered pedagogue from the Liverpool Institute, he was "by far the most difficult to deal with" to Tony Barrow, "and the most dangerous, because he was liable to say all the wrong things to the press and damage the clean image of The Beatles".[15] With no axe to grind, fledgling journalist Philip Norman was admitted to one backstage sanctum in late 1965, where he found the group "perfectly friendly and pleasant – all but George Harrison. He was rather withdrawn, but the others just talked away."[166]

Others mistook George's frequent brown studies for sullenness, but during this final tour of Britain those in the know might have attributed them to his longing for the sanctuary of Kinfauns and

Pattie. Just before Christmas, not so much a proposition as a discussion – involving Brian, too – led the couple to tie the knot as quietly as they were allowed at Epsom Registry Office on 21 January 1966. "I got married because I'd changed," George explained at the unavoidable press conference the next day. "Marriage didn't bring this about; I'd already changed." He didn't say how or why. That would come when Paul McCartney, one of the two best men, spilled the beans a few months later.

Winking at the camera in the wedding portrait, Paul proclaimed tacitly that he at least was still "available". Now and then, polls to ascertain who was the most popular Beatle were conducted in teenage magazines. Invariably, the results were arranged in ratio not to marital status but to each member's degree of commitment to performing and public relations: Paul first, George last. Ignorant of the imminent nuptials, one 1965 fan letter ran, "I'd like to love all four Beatles, but John's married, Paul is going out with someone and my friend loves Ringo. That leaves you. So I love you." Low vote counts and back-handed compliments were almost a cause for rejoicing for George, in that they might deflect some of the world's intrusive adoration from him.

The ambition to be unrecognised in a restaurant, unphotographed stepping from a lift and unchased out on the street now seemed more far fetched than getting rich and famous had been back in Liverpool. On rare moments, he got away with it because, in the flesh and minus his on-stage trappings, he looked like someone who looked like George Harrison. On a Los Angeles film set, years of unbroken press visibility later, he disguised himself successfully as a studio janitor for a joke by simply donning overalls and sweeping the floor. Ringo couldn't have managed it.

Beatlemania had not merely robbed him of privacy but had also stunted him artistically. As he cranked out the same 30 minutes' worth of stale, unheard music night after artless night, he weighed up the cash benefits of being a Beatle against his self-picture as a musician. While autumn leaves fell on the group's moptop period, the sound systems at some venues would be loud and clear enough for them to pull themselves together, but mostly they were taking numbers too fast;

transitions from choruses to middle eights were cluttered and lead-guitar breaks wantonly slap-dash. Once, George had taken the trouble to tune both his own and John's guitars. Now, he couldn't care less about the wavering bars of bum notes and blown riffs.

Box-office receipts remained astronomical, but by 1966 there was a perceptible falling-off in attendances, which were sometimes as low as half capacity. Although they'd pruned down their concert schedule ("doing a bit of a Presley",[155] said George) to mitigate over-exposure, they were becoming as common a forthcoming attraction in the States and Britain as they'd been on Merseyside in 1962. Like London buses, if you missed a show, there'd be another along soon, if you waited.

The momentum had slackened, but the screams hadn't. When Paul sang 'Yesterday' from the *Help!* album solo, the racket from the onlookers dropped slightly. Only his own strumming on acoustic guitar accompanied him, for no one saw any purpose in taking on the road a string quartet like the one that had been hired for the recording. Money was no object, but any subtleties crammed into the Beatle's short spot were lost on audiences who'd bought tickets for a tribal gathering rather than a musical recital.

'Yesterday' is an extreme example, but tracks from their newest LP, *Rubber Soul*, were also difficult to reproduce with the conventional beat group line-up, although some sections could be approached by using Paul or John's skills on the Vox Continental electric organ that now travelled with the guitars and drums. One that couldn't, however, was the sitar played by George on 'Norwegian Wood', John's smoke-screening of an extra-marital affair.

The sitar is a nine-stringed Indian instrument with moveable frets and vibrating under-strings. George had stumbled upon one among props strewn about the set of *Help!*. Messing about, he treated it as if it were some fancy guitar. As such, its wiry jangle was imposed on 'Norwegian Wood' as one of many funny noises to be heard nowadays on the records of The Beatles and other so-called beat groups. Some months before *Rubber Soul*, both The Kinks and The Yardbirds had invested respective singles with an Indian feel. The Kinks' 'See My Friends', from 1965, conveyed in pop terms a suggestion of somewhere in India without their lead guitarist, Dave

Davies, thrumming a hastily procured sitar. Centred on beat group instrumentation, The Who's Pete Townshend estimated it to be "the first reasonable use of the drone – far, far better than anything The Beatles did and far, far earlier".[167] Ray Davies' art-school friend Barry Fantoni would recall being "with The Beatles the evening that they sat around listening to ['See My Friends'] on a gramophone, saying, 'You know, this guitar thing sounds like a sitar. We must get one of those.' Everything Ray did they copied."[167] A seated sitarist had also been present on a Yardbirds session, but the group preferred the more exotic twang of Jeff Beck, the guitarist who'd replaced Eric Clapton. A deeper breath of the Orient would be exhaled by The Rolling Stones, with Brian Jones' masterful sitar obligato appearing on their third UK Number One, 'Paint It Black'.

With a seal of approval from The Beatles and Stones, the sitar, with its bulging gourd and quarter-tones, became as essential an accessory for certain harbingers of pop's fleeting classical period as a 'Yes It Is' volume pedal. Both Donovan and Dave Mason (from Steve Winwood's half-formed new group, Traffic) acquired a sitar after an exploratory hour or so on George's newly imported instrument, while Roy Wood of The Move – another up-and-coming Midlands act – invented the "banjar", which combined properties of sitar and banjo.

Beyond gimmicks, Eastern musical theories had long been a trace element in modern jazz and folk, becoming more pronounced in the mid 1960s via the work of British acoustic guitarist John Renbourn, John Mayer's Indo-Jazz Fusions and the "trance jazz" of guitarist Gabor Szabo, as implied in titles like 'Search For Nirvana', 'Krishna', 'Raga Doll' and 'Ravi'. The last was a salaam to Ravi Shankar, a sitarist who, in 1965, recorded an album which his record company released as *Portrait Of Genius* during his seventh tour of the USA.

Better known than Shankar at this time was Subbulakshmi, an Indian diva seen frequently on Western stages. However, it was Ravi who brought about the most far-reaching popularisation of Indian music, when, as he put it, "there was a sitar explosion all of a sudden. I become superstar [*sic*]."[168]

A rather solitary boyhood spent in Banares, holiest of Indian cities, was interrupted in 1930, when ten-year-old Ravi accompanied his family from this muddy arm of the Ganges to Paris, where his eldest brother, Uday, was leader of a Hindu dance company. Able to afford to continue Ravi's private education, his parents were pleased with their sensitive youngest son's balance of bookish excellence and the artistic leaning that, from infancy, had led him to "play with my brother's musical instruments, lose myself in thrilling stories or act out plays in front of the mirror".[169]

No coaxing from Uday was necessary to persuade Ravi to participate in the troupe's productions. As music was his strongest suit, on leaving school Ravi became a *shishya* – a cross between a student and a disciple – of Dr Baba Allaudin Khan, who was then the most venerable figure in Indian music and recipient of a *Padma Bhushan* (roughly the same as a knighthood). Under the *khansahib's* guidance, Shankar submitted to years of intensive tutelage, disciplining himself to practise his chosen instrument for up to twelve hours a day.

At 21, Ravi himself was a master musician and his teacher/guru's son-in-law. Through his cosmopolitan upbringing, he was well placed to return to the West to promote the performing arts of India. By 1965, his name might have been unknown to the European man on the street, but support from a substantial intellectual minority bound Ravi – now also a Padma Bhushan – to a fulfilling career of concerts, composing commissions and conducting university master-classes. After collaborating with the likes of the London Symphony Orchestra and jazz flautist Paul Horn, he was accused inevitably by purists of emasculating his art, but to most of those who'd heard of him he was respected (or at least patronised) as one of his country's leading musical ambassadors.

Shankar came into the life of George Harrison with deceptive casualness. *Portrait Of Genius* and other Shankar records had been recommended to George by Dave Crosby of The Byrds. As with LSD, one individual's reaction to Indian classical music can be markedly different to that of another. Some find it hypnotic while others are bored stiff. Its closest European equivalent is in the droning themes of the Scottish *pibroch*, for they, too, don't "go anywhere". Instead, single moods – many pertinent to particular times of day – are investigated undynamically and at length. More complex than the pibroch's pentatonic variations, the sitar's ragas never contain less than a scale of five notes, all reliant on varying ascending and descending patterns, but always in a set sequence.

George's discrimination about foreign music would always be acute. Once, in a Tunisian hotel, he'd manufactured earplugs from bread rolls to block out the wail of native musicians in an adjacent room. Indian music was, however, immediately transfixing. The subordination of the artist's ego to the music coincided with the spiritual decisions that LSD had thrust upon him and complemented his reading. As mere entertainment, too, the chasm between Ravi Shankar and rock 'n' roll was not unbreachable. The Duane Eddy instrumentals that had captivated the teenage Quarry Man were also based on folk tunes and repeated ostinati. Years later, under Harrison's supervision, Eddy would add a bridge to a Shankar melody, making the composing credit "R Shankar/D Eddy", surely the strangest – but perhaps not so strange – to be printed on a record label.

By chance, the Beatle and the middle-aged Indian virtuoso were first introduced at a mutual friend's London home in the late spring of 1966. Ravi was only vaguely aware of his new acquaintance's stature, but Harrison "seemed so different from the usual musicians I meet in the pop field. He was so simple and charming and kind, and he showed his desire to learn something."[170] Since *Help!*, George had been rending the air in the main living room at Kinfauns, trying to extend past the few notes that had lacquered 'Norwegian Wood'. Ravi put him right about the folly of teaching yourself sitar. Ideally, it was best to be accepted as a shishya under a master like himself. You'd never get anywhere without proper instruction.

Thus began a lifelong amity akin to that of a liberal-minded teacher and a waywardly earnest pupil. In his realisation that "through the musical you reach the spiritual",[171] George was beyond the first rung, but, insisted Ravi, he must visit India, not only for more intensive training but also to get the rhythm of life there under his skin and thereby slip more easily into his new musical tongue. As his Beatle duties beckoned until autumn, however, George would have to get by with Ravi's tape-recorded correspondence course.

His humility in Shankar's presence was not the same as his biting back on the exasperation of being told what to do in The Beatles. Nevertheless, the new LP, *like Help!*, contained two Harrison items. Furthermore, in a plethora of *Rubber Soul* covers, among the three that made the UK Top 20 – just – was George's 'If I Needed Someone' by The Hollies.

Second to The Beatles, The Hollies had survived Mersey Beat's collapse as the most distinguished northern group. If they recorded your song as an A-side, you could be in the money. During a vexing discussion in October 1965 about a follow-up to their last hit, their producer, Ron Richards, mentioned an acetate that he'd been given by George Martin of a Harrison number that The Beatles then regarded as unsuitable for *Rubber Soul*. The Mancunians' ill-advised 'If I Needed Someone' was issued on this understanding. However, the inclusion of this cascading *moderato* on the new album wasn't the only excuse for The Hollies' comparative failure. Disliked as a group by Lennon, they were further hindered by the composer's adverse and public criticism that they sounded like session players earning their tea break. While his frankness was commendable, this latest manifestation of George's bitterness hurt only himself through the resulting diminishment of his royalties. Not only that, but the fuss he made elicited praise for The Hollies in *Music Echo*'s argument that they'd salvaged one of the poorer selections on *Rubber Soul*, and one that had borrowed from the twelve-string figure in The Byrds' 'Bells Of Rhymney'.

In common with Bill Wyman, The Who's John Entwistle and other groups' second-string composers, less time was now spent on George's efforts than on those of the main fount of original material. His material was further undermined by being used as an avenue for loose experimentation. George's other *Rubber Soul* opus, the wordy 'Think For Yourself', hadn't a prayer from the start. It wasn't a terrific number, true enough, but its rehearsals had doubled as a session for ad-libbed banter for The Beatles' 1965 fan club flexi-disc. With the tape rolling throughout, the self-conscious mucking around was no help whatsoever during the few hours set aside for the song. Sound compression lent organ-like sustain to George's guitar, but 'Think For

Yourself' lived less in its oblique melody than in the searing trump of Paul's bass, which had been fed through a fuzzbox, then a newish device intended to make a guitar sound like a saxophone but which assumed a character of its own after its blackboard-scratching hoarseness had electroplated the Stones' million-selling '(Can't Get No) Satisfaction' that summer.

Outside the studio, George reaped some satisfaction by taking a firmer initiative in other matters. John was his principal ally in the campaign to stop touring. Bawling purgative obscenities in the teeth of the screams, his paranoia sharpened by drugs, Lennon had become, to Dezo Hoffman, "like a dog with rabies – you never knew when he would jump and bite".[96] He smiled and waved like he was supposed to, but it was anathema to John when he and the others, soberly attired, were driven through cheering masses to Buckingham Palace for investiture as Members of the British Empire on 26 October 1965.

Camouflaging vote-catching as acknowledgement of The Beatles' contribution to the export drive, the Labour government had awarded these decorations, seemingly taking to heart a March headline in *Melody Maker* that ran, "Honour The Beatles!" No honours list, before or since, has ever been as controversial. "I didn't think you got that sort of thing," exclaimed George, "just for playing rock 'n' roll music."[172] Neither did the disgusted senior civil servants and retired admirals who returned their medals to her Majesty. *The Daily Express* printed a suggestion that, if the group had to be honoured, they should subject themselves to a "decent" short-back-and-sides haircut before setting off for the palace. How many in this trickle of protesters would have held their peace, had they known how unwilling the chief Beatle had been to go through with accepting his MBE?

Nearly two years later, The Beatles would affix "MBE" after their signatures to lend respectability to a petition calling for the legalisation of marijuana. The only other use any of them made of the decoration was Lennon's renouncement of it as a political gesture in 1969.

If John was touchy about "one of the biggest jokes in the history of these islands,"[173] Paul was delighted with his MBE. He was still a cheerful stage performer, keenly rolling up for a behind-the-curtains jam session with The Paramounts, a support group when The Beatles last played the Hammersmith Odeon. Nonetheless, he was no glutton for punishment. Even the road crew had had enough. "I always look forward to tours," said Neil Aspinall, "but when I'm on them, they're a drag."[10] An unlikely scheme for a 1966 trip to Russia that might have re-awakened enthusiasm for the stage was thwarted by an immovable world tour in which The Beatles would visit many territories for the first – and only – time.

Along the way, too, was a Hamburg engagement, their first since that reluctant residency at the Star-Club in 1962. However, their old bunkroom above the Top Ten was vacated for a reunion party before they were driven in state to the city's Ernst Merck Halle in a fleet of glittering Mercedes with *polizei* outriders.

No home venues could yet compare with overseas sports stadia and exposition centres that could rake in the most loot with the least effort by accommodating thousands in one go. This policy also eliminated many (but not all) squalid hours in claustrophobic bandrooms and hotel bedrooms. Mr Epstein had cut down press conferences, too. No more were these interminable sessions of wry shallowness. "Epstein always tried to waffle on at us about saying nothing about Vietnam," John would later confide to a journalist's cassette recorder, "so there came a time when George and I said, 'Listen, when they ask next time, we're going to say we don't like the war and we think they should get out.'"[156]

Brian cringed as zany merriment about mini-skirts and debates about when Paul would marry Jane Asher swung in seconds to two-line debates about inflammable issues. He'd recently had to calm friction at Capitol over a record sleeve that showed The Beatles as white-smocked butchers gleefully going about their grisly business. It hadn't mattered that the limbs and heads of dolls were among the bloody wares when this picture appeared in Britain to advertise 'Paperback Writer', the quartet's new single. Such a scene was comic opera in a country that housed Madame Tussaud's Chamber of Horrors and Screaming Lord Sutch. However, with boy soldiers already blown to bits in Indochina, "the butcher sleeve" was hastily withdrawn from circulation in sensitive America. "All this means," said Paul, "is that we're being a bit more careful about the sort of picture we do." John, the instant pundit, had no time for tact. "Anyway, it's as valid as Vietnam,"[174] he quipped unfunnily as George, his young sidekick, sniggered beside him.

Backstage at the Ernst Merck Halle, someone passed around snaps from 1961 of George and John between quiff and *pilzenkopf*. The bunkroom party had become impractical, but a few old pals had been allowed past the stage-door security. Escorted by Gibson Kemp, Astrid was there to renew acquaintance with the "lovely child" who, big eared and woebegone, had once been exiled from Germany for staying up past his bedtime.

At the same station from which she and Stuart had waved him out of sight, The Beatles had steamed back to Hamburg in style on a train usually reserved for royalty. It was during this journey that they first listened to a test pressing of the successor to *Rubber Soul*. The running order was already decided – it would start with George's new song, 'Taxman', and end with the first song recorded during the sessions, 'Tomorrow Never Knows'. Still being bandied about was an album title. *Full Moon* and *Fatman And Bobby* were two possibilities put forward as The Beatles shot through the forests of Lower Saxony.

In the last weeks of The Beatles' most public journey, the privacy of the recording studio – where mistakes could be retracted – was a more agreeable location to contemplate than the ordeal directly ahead. Particularly dire in concert were the vocal harmonies and tricky guitar riffs on newer numbers such as 'If I Needed Someone', 'Nowhere Man' and 'Paperback Writer'. There'd lingered enough pride and concern for an eleventh-hour rehearsal in a hotel suite prior to the first show in Munich, but there wouldn't be any more.

Apart from a rendition of 'Long Tall Sally' smashed out literally at the last minute, the same songs in the same order were rattled off at every stop, despite John's assurance that, "Before we go, we get a list of hits in any particular country, so we try to include them."[174] On a similar premise, George should have warranted a greater share of the main spotlight in Japan, where he wasn't everyone's least favourite Beatle. His gruff taciturnity was translated as professionalism in a land where The Ventures, New Zealand's Peter

Posa and other old-fashioned or elsewhere obscure guitar instrumentalists were still popular.

Three routine performances in Tokyo preceded two more on Luzon, the largest island in the Philippines, as The Beatles traversed an Earth that was rapidly becoming less and less eye-stretching. A luxury hotel in Belgium was just like one in Tennessee – the Coca-Cola tasted exactly the same. Everywhere was the same. If it's Monday, it must be Manila.

Manila, however, would always be remembered. Unaware that they were required to pay a courtesy call on the family and friends of the Philippines' autocratic President Ferdinand Marcos, the group slept through the arrival and ireful departure of presidential lackeys who had been commanded to bring them to his palace. George recalled his bafflement when, over a late breakfast, somebody "turned on the television and there it was, this big palace with lines of people and this guy saying, 'Well, they're not here yet,' and we watched ourselves not arrive at the party."[175]

On the following day, the expected crowd of fans at Manila International Airport were puzzled that no security measures had been laid on. Close enough to be touched, their agitated idols lugged their baggage up static escalators a few steps ahead of an angry mob of adults who stopped just short of open assault when their prey threaded slowly and in a cold sweat through a customs area resounding with jack-in-office unpleasantness and every fibre of red tape that Philippino bureaucracy could gather. "They were waiting for us to retaliate," said George, "so that they could finish us off. I was terrified. These 30 funny-looking fellows with guns had obviously arranged to give us the worst time possible."[175] Out on the tarmac, The Beatles party scuttled for the aeroplane and escape, which was delayed when Mal Evans and Tony Barrow were summoned back to the terminal to be interrogated over some freshly unearthed paperwork.

This jubilant oppression had started the previous evening, when incessant interference contrived by station engineers had wiped out every word of Brian Epstein's televised apology for his Beatles' unknowing insult to the hallowed person of Ferdinand Marcos. The First Family's honour was further assuaged by vast tax deductions of concert receipts still in the grasp of accountants at the football stadium where the group had performed on the previous night. No one was ready to jeopardise his prospects, and possibly his freedom, by not co-operating with the President's harassment of these long-haired foreigners.

Sent on their way by boos and catcalls from the tyrant's creatures, never had George's arguments against continued touring made more sense, but even the Manila incident would be a trifle when compared to what awaited them on the final leg. Prophetic, then, was his flippant "we're going to have a couple of weeks to recuperate before we go and get beaten up by the Americans".[175]

A psychological rather than physical battering started when off-the-cuff comments about religion made by Lennon were reprinted out of context in *Datebook*, a US magazine in the same vein as *16* and *Mod*. Weightier journals picked up the story that Lennon had "boasted" that The Beatles were more popular than Jesus Christ. If anything, John in the original *London Evening Standard* article had seemed to be bemoaning the increasing godlessness of the times, but more sensational was the American interpretation of "blasphemy".

The most vocal supporters of this latter opinion were "redneck" whites from the Deep South, who laced their right-wing militancy with pious fear, not so much of "God" as of "the Lord". It was here, the heart of the Bible Belt, that thousands of Beatle records were ceremonially pulverised in a tree-grinding machine to the running commentary of a local radio presenter. Other mass protests were just as demonstrative. The group's new LP – finally titled *Revolver* – was removed from 22 southern radio playlists and hellfire sermons preached of the divine wrath that would fall on any communicants who attended forthcoming Beatles shows – although the casting-out of the pestilence by one Memphis station was as much in vengeance for Epstein's dim view of its exposure of a hush-hush – and subsequently cancelled – Beatles session at Sun Studios, where Elvis Presley's recording career had begun.

As the ripples of backlash and moral opprobrium spread, so did real fear of an assassination attempt on Lennon and perhaps the other three, too. Brian offered his personal fortune if only the US tour could be scrubbed. For most promoters, however, the possible in-concert slaughter of the artists was insufficient reason for cancellation. Instead, at a press conference hours before opening night in Chicago, John was trotted out to make a statement that most took as an apology.

Engagements in the north passed without incident, including a lacklustre return to Shea Stadium, where George stood stock still throughout with a face like a Merseyside winter. In the Southern states, counterbalancing the anti-Beatles ferment, "I Love John" lapel badges outsold all associated merchandise. Nevertheless, a firework that exploded on stage in Memphis gave all four a horrified start, following a telephoned death threat that afternoon. Recalling an evening in 1964 when "a kid in Brisbane threw a tin on stage and it freaked him right out", an eye-witness theorised that "George has an incredible fear of being killed—" who hasn't, sport? "—which possibly accounts for the shell he withdrew into".[68]

Even Paul was sufficiently unnerved to vomit with fear as The Beatles headed towards the last showdown at San Francisco's Candlestick Park on 29 August 1966, where they downed tools as a working band. No better or worse than any other concert they'd given on the tour, after two hours spent hanging around in a locker room backstage they ran through this final half-hour any old how, with Ringo forgetting the words to 'I Wanna Be Your Man' and George fluffing his guitar runs as Paul tried to make a show of it. Towards the end, the four posed for an on-stage photograph for a keepsake. "Nice working with you, Ringo," cracked John shortly before the four piled into the nostalgic finale, 'Long Tall Sally', which had been in and out of the set even before George had first tagged along with The Quarry Men.

George's would be the most quoted remark from the flight back to England. "Well, that's it," was his succinct and strangely dejected elegy. "I'm not a Beatle any more."

9 The Shishya

Pattie's modelling fees had escalated through her association with George, but by 1967 she all but gave up the catwalks, as she too identified more and more with Indian culture. While her husband grappled with his sitar, she furrowed her brow over the bowed dilruba. With her sister Jenny, she attended Indian dancing lessons garbed in some of the items that George had bought for her during a two-night stopover in New Delhi immediately after the scramble from Manila.

It must have been gratifying for George when John and Paul decided to follow his lead and join him there likewise to purchase native instruments, along with saris for Cynthia and Jane. Ringo also checked in at the BOAC hotel where a Sikh sitarist dropped by to give George a tutorial. In the interim before the last hurrah in America, Ringo and John sat through a recital at Kinfauns by Ravi Shankar and his tabla player, Alla Rakha. "They liked it," noticed George, "but they weren't as into it as I was."[32]

George's hard listening to Shankar came to the fore in 'Love You To' from *Revolver*. A backing track of himself on sitar and a certain Anil Bhaghat hired to tap the tablas set the mood with a slow *alap* ("introduction"), but rather than sustain this serenity, as Ravi would, they snapped into feverish tempo. Only the English lyrics and, down in the mix, the electric bass and fuzz guitar gave 'Love You To' any semblance of Western pop.

The common chord reasserted itself in other Harrison compositions, such as 'I Want To Tell You' and – with John's "few one-liners to help the song along, because that's what he asked for"[80]

– 'Taxman', the rhythmic bounce of which belied a libretto dark with dry fuming at the ravages of the Inland Revenue. George's tally of three songs on *Revolver* was the highest so far on any album. Delivered from the treadmill of the road, his consequent flowering as a songwriter contributed to The Beatles' eventual self-destruction, but on *Revolver* they were at their most effective as a team. Never again would each member work so fully according to his capacity. John may have bitten his lip when assisting George with 'Taxman', but he'd avow that George's presence had helped when he and Paul were putting together 'Eleanor Rigby', the 'Yesterday' of *Revolver*.

With the LP assured a gold disc before its conception, let alone its release, its creators could well afford the means to turn their every whim into audible reality. "In the past, we've thought that the recording people knew what they were talking about," generalised Harrison. "We believed them when they said we couldn't do this or we couldn't do that. Now we know we can, and it's opening up a wide new field for us."[174] Of all of The Beatles, George had become the most knowledgeable console buff, appreciating both Abbey Road's advancing technology and the reasoning behind seeming inadequacies, like the antiquated Altec playback speakers that "don't flatter the sound".[59]

Even on mediocre equipment, every groove on *Revolver* revealed that, in 1966, the group's three composers had been firing on all cylinders. Its programming squeezed the children's song for Ringo ('Yellow Submarine') and Paul's easy-listening 'Here, There And Everywhere' between the Harrison raga and 'She Said She Said', John's unsettling account of that second LSD trip. On paper, these juxtapositions seem inappropriate, but the liberal non-conformity within The Beatles' fundamental structure strengthened the clarity and balance of their rounded unity and gave them an unprecedented stylistic range. As yet, there were no cracks in the image.

From the verbose but confused 'I Want To Tell You' to the eerie omega that was 'Tomorrow Never Knows' there exuded evidence of half-understood Eastern mysticism and the "psychedelic" inner landscapes of LSD. With an electronically warped vocal, quotes from *The Tibetan Book Of The Dead*, a monotonous percussion *rataplan* and an aural junk-sculpture of tape-loops, 'Tomorrow Never Knows' defied adequate categorisation and stood little chance of superseding 'Yesterday' as the most recorded song of all time. "The Stones and The Who visibly sat up and were interested," said Paul. "We also played it to Cilla, who just laughed."[176]

"Everyone, from Brisbane to Bootle, hates that daft song Lennon sang at the end of *Revolver*,"[177] declared a horrified *Mirabelle*, whose schoolgirl subscribers were mostly opposed or insensible to shifts in parameters of musical consciousness as the watershed year of 1967 loomed. Most groups that carried any weight would be operating ambiguously with experimental fancies on albums and penetrating the singles charts with their most trite or mainstream cuts, as did The Beatles with 'Yellow Submarine' and The Yardbirds with the upbeat 'Over Under Sideways Down', from an LP that was praised by one critic as a "mini-*Revolver*".

The only *Revolver* cover to be a hit was Cliff Bennett's improvement on 'Got To Get You Into My Life', which was ideal for his soul-rock crossover, although his "let-me-hear-you-say-yeah" stage routines with The Rebel Rousers would be rendered *passé* in an era when even the bucolic Troggs would be singing about "the bamboo butterflies of yer mind". Others also either consolidated their abilities without developing them or else adjusted themselves to psychedelia without really getting the point.

Tellingly, The Beatles had been the only Mersey Beat group to play in 1966's *NME* pollwinners' concert, where they'd waved into the baying blackness and vanished from the British stage forever. That spring, too, Rory Storm had headlined at the Cavern hours before Authority closed the place. A telegram from The Beatles would be read aloud when the club was re-opened, with a facelift and proper sanitation, but the place would never be the same. That it hosted arty "events" and poetry readings now best exemplified the passing of the old order, while a few brave anachronisms like The Hideaways and Rory still did 'Money' and 'Some Other Guy' for the few who still remembered.

In an outer darkness of European dance halls, luckier brethren like The Swinging Blue Jeans and The Merseybeats staved off a drift back to whatever local venues were still standing. Although brought to their knees, such outfits maintained flashback dignity, even grandeur. By abandoning the Mersey Beat ferry at the first sign of a leak, other musicians had also clung onto a career in music. In the United States, ex-Undertaker Jackie Lomax had immersed himself in his new group, The Lomax Alliance, despite advice from Brian Epstein that he'd fare better as a soloist. Another ill-fated fresh start was made by former Searcher Chris Curtis in an unlikely role as lead singer with Roundabout, a band formed by his flatmate Jon Lord, ex-organist with The Flowerpot Men. Meanwhile, dying on its feet was The Pete Best Combo, whose figurehead was privately relieved to return to Straightsville from the treachery of showbusiness.

A more hard-nosed drummer/leader had taken a leaf from The Beatles' book by retiring The Dave Clark Five to the studio. Unlike the Liverpudlians, however, he didn't expand his musical horizons. Instead, the Five notched up two fast hits by the same songwriters who'd provided crooner Engelbert Humperdinck with the syrupy 'Release Me', which in February 1967 would keep The Beatles' double-A-sided *meisterwerk* 'Penny Lane'/'Strawberry Fields Forever' from Number One in Britain. Schmaltz, the antithesis of psychedelia, was very much alive.

It had been a waterfront covered on *Revolver*, but on 'Here, There And Everywhere' the melody had been potent enough for jazz flautist Charles Lloyd – resplendent in beads and kaftan – to extemporise it amid strobe lights in New York's Fillmore East auditorium. Other famous "underground" venues, such as London's Middle Earth and Amsterdam's Paradiso, also used lightshows among audio-visual aids meant to simulate psychedelic experience as bands – not groups – played on and on and on for hippies in a cross-legged trance and whirling dancers with eyes like catherine wheels.

A big draw on this circuit were Cream, a trio whose appeal hinged not so much on looks but virtuosity demonstrated in lengthy improvisations of selections from their debut album. The loudest cheers – not screams – were for the over-amplified flash of Eric Clapton, who had been the subject of graffiti claiming "Clapton is God" while with John Mayall's Bluesbreakers. The legend had first been scrawled in the Marquee, and one night in that celebrated Soho club's cramped bandroom, after watching The Lovin' Spoonful, Clapton nodded at George Harrison and John Lennon, who afterwards would only recall a crew-cut Yardbird low on the bill at a Beatles Christmas extravaganza. Eric was left behind when they drove off to a party at The Lovin' Spoonful's hotel. He would learn one day of a pang of remorse when George "remembered thinking, 'We should have invited that guy, because I'm sure we know him from somewhere'... He just seemed, like, lonely."[32]

Both *Fresh Cream* and *A Collection Of Beatles Oldies* were released in December 1966, but the former climbed higher in the LP charts than the latter, by which time George was no longer racking his brains to remember Clapton, who – with American newcomer Jimi Hendrix – was now the most worshipped of pop guitarists, while to *The Sunday Times* George was only "a passable guitarist (say among the best thousand in the country)".[90] Of no less import was an opinion given by a stranger during a concert by The Jimi Hendrix Experience who sidled up to Paul McCartney and, pointing towards Hendrix, muttered, "You ought to get a bloke like that in your band, mate."

Such implied slights on George as an instrumentalist were unfair, as The Beatles' stylistic determination left little space for any extensive extrapolations of the kind popularised by Hendrix and Cream – although, judging by unissued recordings of the four jamming to tedious effect at Abbey Road, this was probably just as well. Nonetheless, George must have warmed to Clapton, who in *Disc* magazine praised the lead-guitar playing on *Revolver*. This accolade was deserved, if only for the technical accomplishment demonstrated by George's idea of superimposing two backwards – and tuneful – guitar overdubs on top of one another to create the apt "yawning" solo and obligato on Lennon's 'I'm Only Sleeping'. This attractive enveloping sound was developed further by other guitarists, notably Hendrix on the title track of his LP *Are You Experienced?*.

It was pleasing to be liked and copied like this, but George wasn't to be as revered a guitar hero in the later 1960s as he'd been in the beat boom. Although he'd always see himself as a lesser guitarist, George was in a different rather than lower league to Clapton and Hendrix, whose fretboard fireworks were then heard night after night on stage.

For long after the armoured car had whisked George from Candlestick Park, his guitar had been played only sporadically. This wasn't because it symbolised all that he'd recently and gladly relinquished; it was simply that his concentration on learning sitar was comparable to that which lacerated adolescent fingers on his first guitar. As once he'd laboured over *Play In A Day*, so, from Indian script, he practised raga exercises hour upon hour.

Via the account that all four Beatles had at the hip Indica bookshop off Piccadilly, the Harrisons were digesting all manner of mystical and philosophical literature to do with the East. George found Paramhansa Yogananda's *Autobiography Of A Yogi* a particularly "far-out"[174] book, proving this to whoever was interested by opening it at random and reading aloud. One journalist was treated to the passage, "'I care not if all things are wrested from me by self-created destiny, but I'll demand of thee my own to God the slender taper of my love for thee'".[171]

Two weeks after Candlestick Park, George and Pattie had flown to Bombay, where they registered as "Mr and Mrs Sam Wells" in a lakeside hotel outside the city. Within a day, the alias was uncovered by local newspapers, who were informed by a rueful George that he was in India to study sitar under their own Ravi Shankar in Banares, 600 miles beyond their circulation area, over jungly valleys, jagged peaks and sun-scorched desert.

For much of this holiday-cum-cultural visit, the Harrisons were let alone. In loose robes and pyjama trousers, George was one of two hundred *shishya* studying under the master. Shankar delegated this day-to-day tuition to Shambu Das, his *protégé*, just as Shankar himself had been the Khansahib's. Looking in to check on his progress, Ravi found George to be "an enthusiastic and ambitious student because he realises that the sitar itself is an evolvement from Indian culture. It might take a lifetime of learning, but, if he progresses in the same way that he has been doing, his understanding will lead to a medium of greatness on the sitar."[178]

George would liken Indian music to "an inner feeling"[153] too intense for satisfactory verbal description: "It's like saying, 'It's soul, man!' You know? All this spade music that's going – it's just the first thing people get into, the soul kick, but when you really get into soul, then...it's God."[179]

To his *shishya*, Ravi Shankar was more than a music teacher; he was also a spiritual guide[180] and something of a father figure. He may not have cut much ice with a younger George in the fleshpots of Hamburg, but in holy Banares the refugee from Beatlemania was open to religious enlightenment. Nothing like an Institute RE teacher prattling on about Yahweh, Shankar's guru Tat Baba was straight out of a Victorian penny-dreadful: "They tell you about these yogis who just don't speak, and you ask them what it's all about and they give you a flower. Well, he's the only one I've seen like that. When we saw him, he sat for about two and a half hours and then just said, like, about four or five words, which [translated] is like a poem but so to the point."[171]

The Harrisons' Cook's tour of Hinduism took in religious festivals in temples towering over narrow alleyways and on the banks of the Ganges, the steps to which were worn as smooth as the the Blarney Stone by pious feet descending into the grimy but purifying bathing *ghat*s, each one dedicated to a different deity.

Rama and Krishna are Hindus' most popular manifestations of God, and they may regard Buddha, Moses and Jesus as others. The words to many of the sitar pieces prescribed for George's training were eulogies in Sanskrit to one or other of these avatars, as was 'Bhajan In Rupak Tal', which tells of a poet chanting Krishna's name every second in order to earn His blessings.

In Banares' Nepalese Temple, Pattie and George saw friezes depicting the 81 sins and their corresponding penances. Thus was illustrated the aspect of the Hindu law of karma, whereby all evil proceeds from antecedent evil and penalties must be suffered in each succeeding incarnation through which the soul must pass. "The living thing that goes on," explained George, "always has been, always will be. I am not really George but I happen to be in this body."[24] If you're godly, you might be reborn in a station better suited to self-realisation and eventual removal from the series of continuous transmigrations.

To keep themselves conscious of this aspiration and pre-empt future punishment, an army of ascetics throughout India devise ingenious modes of self-torture and – like LSD often does – humiliating destruction of the ego. Flocking to Banares, Allahabad and other points along the blessed Ganges are human pin-cushions, flagellants, loinclothed fakirs plastered head to toe with sacred cow dung and others whose fanaticism transcends not only self-inflicted pain and discomfort but also the heat, flies and filth that more common Hindus have to endure.

All good things must come to an end, and the Harrisons returned to Britain's unusually rainy autumn, George with a rakish Imperial beard and both with doctrines and perceptions of deeper maturity than before. Yogananda's was more than merely a far-out book. "Everybody has to burn out his karma," George was saying now, "and escape reincarnation and all that."[152] Values in the West were declining, he reckoned, because "discipline is something we don't like, but in a different way I've found out it's very important, because the only way [Hindu] musicians are great is because they've been disciplined by their guru or teacher and they've surrendered to the person they want to be".[179] The Beatles' wealth was "enough to show us that this thing wasn't material. We all get so hung up with material things, yet what they can give you is only there for a little bit and then it's gone."[181] Unlike John, George would never be rash enough to speak of giving it all away.

George and Pattie had both embraced vegetarianism, and George had even gone through a phase of eating with his hands, Indian style. As well as the expected nut roasts and meatless curries, the Kinfauns kitchen also served dishes that, while common in Banares, were exotic in Esher. On the menu might be pakoras (pasties stuffed with cauliflower and peas, deep fried in ghee), samosas or the consecrated prasadam. For dessert, you could tunnel into a rasamlai (a milk sweet) and wash this down with lassi (yoghurt diluted with rose water).

However scrumptious these meals were, the fact that a Beatle was tucking into them was splendid news for stockists of Indian goods in the West. In provincial Britain, where the 1950s hadn't ended until 1966, a Beatle fan might waste hours outside a record shop debating whether or not to spend three week's paper-round savings on Ustad Ali Akbar Khan's *Young Master Of The Sarod*, for which George had supplied sleeve notes. Youths whose short hair broke their hearts would board trains to London to buy joss-sticks. These would then fill sixth-form common rooms with tinted smoke and thereby lend credence to self-generated and false tales of a wild weekend among hippie friends in Swinging London, where nowadays a man wasn't asking to be beaten up by walking its streets with beads and bells around his neck, embroidered Indian slippers on his feet and an eyesore of tie-dyed kaftan and floral trousers. One hipper-than-thou Hampshire schoolboy, Stephen MacDonald, even came home with a sitar.

MacDonald was also the first at his grammar school to own the debut album by The Velvet Underground, an arty New York outfit in which Brian Epstein was "interested". Some of the sleazy perspectives on this record were underlined not by a bass guitar throb but by a noisy electronic drone that made a melodrama from what was merely implicit in Indian music.

Over in San Francisco, "raga rock" was an ingredient in the psychedelic brew being concocted by The Jefferson Airplane, The Grateful Dead and other acts in a city about to become as vital a pop Mecca as Liverpool had been. Like The Big Three's homage to the Cavern, hit records in 1967 by both Eric Burdon and Scott McKenzie paid tribute to San Francisco's new eminence. Each performed in June of that year at the Monterey International Pop Music Festival a few miles down the coast. There, The Jimi Hendrix Experience – at Paul McCartney's urging – was booked to make a spectacular American debut. Among many other highlights was an afternoon set by Ravi Shankar, which confirmed the larger public's acceptance of him and his instrument.

What had started as a gimmick on *Rubber Soul* now surfaced on vinyl as frequently as rocks in a stream. Dominated by sitar was Traffic's most famous song, 'Hole In My Shoe', also checkmated at a UK Number Two by the oily Engelbert. Record shops were also stocking an album of current hits by a certain "Lord Sitar", whose record company would not deny the erroneous supposition that it was George Harrison in disguise. Even if he hadn't originated Indian sounds in pop, George had definitely instigated what could be construed as a trend.

Ravi Shankar's association with The Beatles had done him a lot of good. Ticket sales for his concerts were guaranteed to pick up if there was a hint that George might be attending. As a recording artist in Britain, his destiny was then bound to the World Pacific label, who even tilted for a hit single with the Punjabi folk tune 'Song Of The Hills', from *Portrait Of Genius*. At first, Ravi took this unlooked-for attention in his stride, seizing the opportunity to publicise a new Indian music centre to be founded in Los Angeles, with George's assistance. A sizeable representation of Fleet Street lying in wait at Heathrow would disperse away happily after noting the amusing spectacle of George in flowing Indian garb greeting a disembarking Shankar wearing a Western business suit.

Although he owed his commercial bonanza to Harrison's patronage, Ravi admitted to disquiet when he and his Hindu musicians were placed on the same bill as loud rock bands with extreme stage antics. Especially appalling was Jimi Hendrix at Monterey: "I liked his music, but when he started being obscene with his guitar and burning it I felt very sad. We come from a different part of the world where we respect, almost worship the instruments."[182]

Hinduism is the most tolerant and gentle of faiths, advocating pacifism, rejection of materialism, kindness to animals and other qualities that had been absorbed by the blossoming hippie sub-culture with its "be-ins", "Flower-power" and, of course, its imported Indian exotica. Mantras were chanted *en masse* at San Francisco's Golden Gate Park, led on many occasions by visiting Indian yogi His Divine Grace AC Bhaktivedante Swami Prabhupada, who had topped the bill over The Grateful Dead at a "Mantra-Rock Dance" at the city's Avalon ballroom. The proceeds went towards the opening of the San Francisco Krishna Temple.

However, Shankar and Prabhupada were disappointed by the interrelated promiscuity and, worse, the currency of psychedelic drugs as an artificial means to greater awareness. "The aim of all Eastern religion is to get high," pontificated flower-power guru and disgraced Harvard psychologist Timothy Leary. "LSD is Western yoga." When Ravi had sat on the Monterey stage before beautiful people of like mind to Leary, his Beatle *shishya* and cohorts assembled at Lennon's house to join him in spirit: "We just took acid...and wondered what it would be like."[183]

That The Beatles were all users of LSD would soon become common knowledge after Paul, the last initiate, admitted as much to *Life* magazine – although some might have guessed already from 'Strawberry Fields Forever', which had issued from the radio with the spooky deliberation of a dream's slow motion. Garish psychedelic patterns had been painted all over the outer walls of Kinfauns and the bodywork of Lennon's Rolls, under the direction of four Dutch theatrical designers whose mediaeval fancy dress matched their work and tradename, The Fool. This amalgam also submitted a frontage that was turned down as too hackneyed for *Sgt Pepper's Lonely Hearts Club Band*, the LP that followed *Revolver*.

"I don't know how we met them," laughed Pattie. "They just appeared one day."[184] As part of The Beatles' perpetual small change of hangers-on, The Fool wormed their way into many of the group's private functions, including a party at Brian Epstein's country house, where Derek Taylor succumbed to George's request to try LSD. "Once you've had it," Harrison explained, "it was important that people you were close to took it too."[10] He and Pattie left Keith Richards' West Wittering lodge two hours before the famous drugs bust by the Sussex police in February 1967, their host believing to this day that he'd have been immune from arrest if George – a national treasure with an MBE – had stayed the night.

Sometimes seeming to be a bit gaga, George would talk openly about his psychedelic escapades, acknowledging no difference now between the straight press and underground journals like the fortnightly *International Times*. He'd mention the "magic eyes"[185] in the beads of his necklace or a grasshopper that only he could see jumping into a speaker cabinet.[171]

He'd also taken to quoting Bob Dylan lyrics, as if they were as unanswerable as proverbs. Illustrating what he meant by "karma" would be a couplet from 'Subterranean Homesick Blues'. With poker face and barbed-wire hair, Dylan had gazed from the sleeve of *Blonde On Blonde*, the odd album out among an otherwise all-Indian selection in George's suitcase for his expedition to Banares. Dylan's increasingly surreal symbolism had left its mark as far back as 'Think For Yourself', in which George had sung of "opaque minds" and "the good things that we have if we close our eyes".

By that time, no one was still booing Dylan for his use of an amplified Canadian backing group; in fact, very much the opposite. Off stage, he traded sillier answers for silly questions before he finally banned press interviews altogether, in self-defence, and stonewalled more earnest fans. Being so enigmatic was tiresome, and some cynics doubted that the motorcycle accident that ended this phase of his career in June 1966 had actually happened. He woke from a week's concussed oblivion with a broken neck, mild paralysis and amnesia. There wasn't a hope of any return to public life for at least a year.

During Dylan's enforced sabbatical, The Beatles acknowledged his influence on them – and, by inference, everyone else – by including his image in the photo montage of characters that festooned the fabled cover of *Sgt Pepper's Lonely Hearts Club Band*. Consisting mainly of each Beatle's all-time heroes, almost all of George's contributions were Eastern gurus and religious leaders. As John's choices of Hitler and Christ were vetoed by EMI, so was George's of Gandhi, although escaping the airbrush were Yogananda and Orientals even more unknown to the average Joe.

Just as erudite were those souvenirs of India with which George fairy-dusted passages of *Sgt Pepper*, among them tamboura and the swordmandel, a cross between a zither and an autoharp. From its mothballs came his electric guitar for instances such as the stinging solo on the title song. Otherwise, he remained as dispensably in the background of John and Paul's creations as Ringo. During the media blitz commemorating the 20th anniversary of the album's release, perhaps it was fortunate that George wasn't present to hear McCartney remark nonchalantly, "George turned up for his number and a couple of other sessions but not much else."[186]

It was true that George had absented himself once to attend a Ravi Shankar concert, but this could be excused as fieldwork for the orchestration of 'Within You Without You', his sole *Sgt Pepper* composition and, interestingly, the only one on which just one Beatle appeared. It was also the longest and most complicated piece on the album. Scored for an assortment of Indian instruments and superimposed violins and cellos, its three changes of time signature were unprecedented in a body of work that, since The Beatles' inception, had rarely deviated from straightforward 4/4.

Despite this gear shifting, 'Within You Without You' was as calmly devoid of surging climaxes as you'd expect from a piece based upon a raga exercise. However, it wasn't written on sitar at Kinfauns but on a harmonium in Klaus Voorman's Hampstead home following an after-dinner discussion of a metaphysical nature. More a psalm than a pop ditty, you could only dance to it if you were desperate, as George philosophised about walls of illusion, love, "the space between us all" and gaining the world but losing your soul. When replaying the LP, those as yet unacclimatised to pop as an egghead activity started to skip the ethereal 'Within You Without You' to begin side two with Paul's jaunty 'When I'm 64', dating from the Cavern days. Yet, however superficially boring it was, many stuck with George's opus, among them Steve Stills, leader of California's Buffalo Springfield, who said that he intended to have its entire libretto carved in stone for display in his garden.

After hearing 'Within You Without You', Juan Mascaro, a Sanskrit professor at Cambridge, was moved to write to George, expressing the hope that it would "move the souls of millions" and foretelling that "there is more to come, as you are only beginning on a great journey".[39] This aged academic enclosed a copy of *Lamps Of Fire*, an anthology of poems and maxims translated by himself, to aid religious self-education.

The Word made vinyl in the comfort of their own homes, many – especially in the States – listened to The Beatles' latest gramophone record in the dark, at the wrong speeds, backwards. Every inch of the cover and label was scrutinised for veiled but oracular messages, something that would turn listeners into more aware, more creative human beings truly at one with The Beatles. Nothing would be the same, not even the past. Thanks in part to *Sgt Pepper*, pop was upgraded from ephemera to holy writ. Although you'd have to look far for a Troggologist, one obsessed New Yorker advertised in an underground journal for a Dylan urine sample in order to prove a pet theory about his lyrics. By 1969, evidence traceable to *Sgt Pepper* supported a widespread rumour that Paul McCartney had been killed three years earlier and replaced by a *doppelgänger*.

Well before *Sgt Pepper*, however, others had also elevated the long-player to a product more than a pig in a poke, slopping with musical swill and a hit single. Inspirational to The Beatles were *Pet Sounds* by a Beach Boys estranged from the surf and the stunning pop-Dada hybrid – with snippets of Varèse, Stravinsky and Holst – that was Frank Zappa's Mothers Of Invention's *Freak Out*. Both groups had created a specific and recurring mood – a concept, if you like – that was more far reaching than simply stringing together a bunch of songs about cars (as The Beach Boys had done in 1963).

With McCartney and George Martin as prime movers, The Beatles had embarked on the next step, theoretically a continuous work with no spaces between tracks and teeming with interlocking themes, segues and leitmotifs. *Sgt Pepper* did indeed contain a reprise of the title number, plus various cross-fades and links, and yet only at its beginning and near the end were you reminded of what was supposed to be Sgt Pepper's show. Technically, it improved on *Revolver*, creating, said George Harrison, "new meanings on old equipment".[32] In this mediaeval period of recorded sound, the Abbey Road mixing desk would seem rather Heath Robinson by today's standards. "Well, we had an orchestra on a separate four-track machine in 'Day In The Life'," explained George. "We tried to sync them up [and] they kept going out of sync in playback, so we had to re-mix it."[32] For all its flaws, however, *Sgt Pepper* sounded stratospheric on 1967's shuddering monophonic Dansette machines.

It was almost the sound at any given moment that counted, rather than the individual pieces. Reduced to the acid test of just voice and piano, the raw material of *Sgt Pepper* couldn't hold a candle to the classic *Revolver*. With retrospective honesty, George would agree: "It was a milestone and a millstone in music history. There are some good songs on it, but it's not our best album." He preferred its two predecessors. "There's about half the songs I like and the other half I can't stand."[25]

He may have moderated this view if his 'Only A Northern Song' – which was about nothing in particular – hadn't been shelved at the last minute. Harrison songs in much lesser stages of completion included 'The Art Of Dying', which was another attempted summary of his newly acquired theological mores, although it intimated – albeit not obviously – that he'd also read relevant pages from the anonymous 15th-century tome *Ars Moriendi*. More topical was 'See Yourself', his reaction to Paul's free admission that he'd taken LSD. "And they asked the rest of us. We said yes, and there was a big outcry saying, 'You should have said no. It's your responsibility.' But it's not; it's the press' responsibility. So the song came from that. It's easier to tell a lie than tell the truth."[25] A further confidence to a gentleman of the very press was "That's how a lot of them work, you know. They just find... Well, rather than go into reality, they just cover over it."[25]

Perhaps The Beatles' least attractive trait was their habit of blurting out what their minds hadn't yet formulated in simple terms Like some Scouse Socrates, George was now going on about "these vibrations that you get through yoga, cosmic chants and things like that – I mean, it's such a buzz. It buzzes you right through the astral plane."[175] The music and underground papers in 1967 would be sodden with sentences just as groovy from George and similar victims of the same passion. One sweet flower from the lips of disc jockey and *International Times* columnist John Peel was, "There are sparrows and fountains and roses in my head. Sometimes I don't have enough time to think of loving you. That is very wrong."[187]

Before pseudo-mystical inanities like this were thought worth publishing, if the average guitarist in a beat group entreated the Almighty at all, it was as a sort of divine pimp with an amused tolerance of boozing and pill-popping, but with enough self-discipline to seldom indulge Himself. Piety had been considered a regrettable eccentricity in 1950s rockers like Jerry Lee Lewis and

Little Richard, who were prone to vigorous bouts of evangelism, while beneath contempt was married Pat Boone, who paraded his beliefs by balking at kissing the leading ladies in his films.

However, in tandem with its growth as a means of artistic expression, pop's contradictory merger with religion had reasserted itself. In as early as 1964, Cliff Richard had undertaken his first gospel tour, and a Salvation Army "beat group" called The Joystrings had used the devil's music to spread the word. Doing the reverse were The Small Faces, The Mastersingers and The Zombies, who in 1966 adapted the respective melodies of 'Ding Dong Merrily On High', the Te Deum and the Nunc Dimittis to secular purposes.

Orthodox pop is as devotional in its boy-girl way as sacred music, and, as George had discovered, the chasm between 'Don't Bother Me' and 'Within You Without You' was not unbreachable: "Singing to the Lord or an individual is, in a way, the same."[32] Although he'd been profoundly affected by Hinduism,[180] George's faith was evolving as a syncretic faith in which "the Lord has a million names". His studies had "brought me right back 'round to understanding Christ",[171] even if "my concept of spirituality isn't Cliff Richard and Billy Graham".[188] After "getting religion" in 1966, George's ideals would compound rather than alter. When the Kinfauns pond metamorphosed from clear tap-water to duckweed and wriggling animation, a visiting Alistair Taylor was drawn into a discussion that "veered off the subject of the pool... With George, everything leads to the cosmic meaning of life".[189] The cruel manner of an older Beatle's passing years later would hurt, but death itself "doesn't really matter. He's OK, and life goes on within you and without you."[190]

He wasn't always so beatific. "Cripples, Mal!" he bawled when The Pink Floyd were conducted in from the adjacent studio to see the masters at work on *Sgt Pepper*. Annoyance became contrition when their producer, Norman Smith, ambled in behind the young group. Although the protection of The Beatles' much-liked former engineer made them feel less like gatecrashers, after a few sheepish hellos the Floyd shuffled out. From this inauspicious beginning, however, after learning of their visitors' high standing in London's psychedelic clubs, George, Ringo and Paul returned the call early one evening when The Pink Floyd were recording their debut LP. "We all stood rooted to the spot," remembered Roger Waters, "excited by it all."[191]

Jaws dropped as well when George descended on Haight-Ashbury, the flower-power district of San Francisco, on a mid-week afternoon in August 1967. Here, more than anywhere else, *Sgt Pepper* was a code for life. "Beatle readings" were as much part of the pageant of its streets as mime troupes, palmists, dancers, painters, spiritual healers (who gave instruction on how to write to archangels), poets and vendors of journals such as *The Psychedelic Oracle*.

"Wow! If it's all like this, it's too much," George remarked politely as, flanked by Derek Taylor, Neil Aspinall and a hanger-on named Alex Mardas, he strolled self-consciously with Pattie and Jenny Boyd through "Hashbury" after parking the limousine a block away. Like a squire on a dutiful walkabout at a village fête, his easy smile did not rest on individuals but was diffused to the general populace. As his coming was unheralded, he was just another sightseer – "half like a tourist, half like a hippy"[161] – for a few yards, before someone cried out, "Hey, that's George Harrison!" As the beglamoured girl panted up to him with her tongue-tied laudation, other passers-by gathered around, "then more and more people arrived and it got bigger and bigger".[161]

A common touch was in order, so the most reticent Beatle borrowed a busker's guitar for an impromptu 'Baby You're A Rich Man', the B-side of the group's flower-power anthem 'All You Need Is Love', currently topping the Hot 100. Although he dried up with embarrassment, within minutes the community's edifice of cool shattered as even those who knew the dignity of labour hurried to Golden Gate Park's sloping greensward, where George had been followed by the buzzing crowd from the alleys. Most arrived too late, for, fearful of the growing commotion, he and his retinue had hastened back to the car with as much grace as they could muster after just over half an hour in the hippy capital.

Anxious to be off, George had extended an intimidated invitation to the president of the local Hell's Angels chapter for his boys to visit any time they were in London. Surely they'd never take him up on it in a million years. Despite their Nazi regalia, the dreaded motorcycle brotherhood then had a special rapport with the equally anti-establishment hippies. All this love and peace nonsense might be grasping the wrong end of the stick, but the stick still existed.

In his heart-shaped sunglasses, dry-cleaned denim jacket and psychedelic flares made to measure by The Fool, George had borne as much relation to the flower children he'd seen as dairy butter does to low-fat margarine. Cluttering the pavements in grubby floral tat, many seemed to be living out part of Timothy Leary's "turn on, tune in, drop out" slogan by begging from the very straights they mocked. "They are hypocrites," was George's gut reaction. "I don't mind anybody dropping out of anything, but it's the imposition on somebody else I don't like. I've just realised that it doesn't matter what you are, as long as you work. In fact, if you drop out, you put yourself further away from the goal of life than if you were to keep working."[160]

From London's den of illusion, he'd been the first Beatle to fly out to the Greek islands to investigate possibilities of setting up a private hippy commune there. This scheme had been mooted partly on the rebound from touring and partly in the euphoria of the Summer of Love. For a practical example of how a utopia could crumble, you only had to look at Hashbury, with its drug pedlars, teenage runaways and traffic snarl-ups as it was clogged with curiosity seekers and weekend ravers, who kept the freshly sprouted record shores, boutiques and restaurants in profit.

A look at the charts told you that the music industry had been at the forefront of this inevitable commercialisation of flower-power. When Richards and Jagger were acquitted of their drug convictions in July 1967, the Stones rush-released their double A-side 'Dandelion'/'We Love You', titles that reflected correctly a pixified musical scenario. Cashing in quick that same month with 'Let's Go To San Francisco' were The Flowerpot Men, who, garbed in chiffony robes, tossed dead chrysanthemums into the audience when appearing at London's Finsbury Park Astoria.

In the eyes of the world, the apogee of the Summer of Love was reached on 25 June, when The Beatles convened before the BBC's outside-broadcast cameras in Abbey Road's cavernous Studio One to perform 'All You Need Is Love' as Britain's contribution to *Our*

World, a satellite-linked transmission with a global viewing figure of 400 million. Even lead singer Lennon gnawed apprehensively at his chewing gum as the allotted time approached. On a high stool, George was more fretful as the amplifier that was to power his Stratocaster for the on-air solo buzzed into life. In the small orchestra that would augment the song, violinists tuned up and horn valves slid prelusively. At The Beatles' feet for the *omnes fortissimo* chorus was a turn-out of selected relations and fashionable friends, including Pattie, Gary Leeds, Mike McCartney and Eric Clapton, whose concert with Cream at Shaftsbury Avenue's Saville Theatre had been attended by all four Beatles. Both of the Harrisons had been impressed, and at a party at Epstein's afterwards it had struck Pattie that Eric's introspective on-stage image wasn't entirely contrived.

Now a periodic dinner guest at Kinfauns, Clapton had felt vague envy at George's apparent contentment with Pattie, "because I was certain I was never going to meet a woman quite that beautiful for myself".[43] In reciprocation, the presence of "God" Clapton a few feet away, rather than the unseen millions watching, drew an apologetic grin from George as he delivered a solo for 'All You Need Is Love' that he thought he'd fluffed but, played back, was safely adequate.

For Brian Epstein, George's uncertain hand in 'All You Need Is Love' encapsulated his role in The Beatles – nothing brilliant and in no danger of rocking the Lennon-McCartney ship of state. To paraphrase a disproved adage of Aunt Mimi's about her nephew's guitar, the sitar was all very well but, in Brian's estimation, George would never have made a living at it.

As Epstein had anticipated, the expiry date of his contract with the group in August 1967 meant a reduction of both his cut and his say in their affairs. There were also rumours of The Beatles bringing in a third party. Paul especially liked what he'd been told of Allen Klein, a cigar-chewing New York accountant – "like the archetypal villain in a film,"[166] according to Ray Davies – whose blunt stance in negotiation had done financial wonders for The Dave Clark Five, Donovan, The Kinks and, latterly, the Stones. Although no love was lost between them, Sir Joseph Lockwood said, "In fairness to Klein, I ended up doing deals that I have never regretted."[74]

One of many Goldwyn-esque homilies attributed to Klein was, "What is the point of Utopia if it don't make a profit?" Brian would never say anything like that, although Colonel Parker might. To Brian's mind, monetary killings were secondary to fair dealing and sound commodities. He'd made disturbing mistakes while learning his craft, but his painful commitment and often severely tested loyalty to his stable were assets more valuable than the ability to drive a hard and unrelenting bargain for Elvis to star in another awful movie.

On that score, The Beatles didn't want another *Help!*. While it was to be, as Lennon said, "a film vehicle of some sort to go with the new music",[192] they were adamant that the next one wouldn't portray them as Beatles. "No, we're not rushing into a film," said George. "We'll wait ten years, if we have to."[174] Two years after *Help!*, it looked as if they were going to do just that. While the Harrisons were in India, John had had a part in *How I Won The War*, a Dick Lester tragi-comedy. One up on the others, it was he who was mooted as main character in *Up Against It*, a rejected development by playwright Joe Orton of *Shades Of A Personality*, a script in which a single person has four separate personalities. Also thrust aside were *The Four Musketeers* and Tolkein's *Lord Of The Rings*, the hippy bible, with George as Gandalf. Another possibility particularly favoured by George – who'd been in cowboy gear for the *Rubber Soul* cover – was a screenplay derived from Richard Condon's western novel *A Talent For Loving*. Mel Brooks, then shooting *The Producers*, a black comedy appreciated only in retrospect, was considered as director.

Paul, meanwhile, came up with a plan to make something up as they went along. When in Haight-Ashbury, George had heard of The Merry Band Of Pranksters, an itinerant multi-media troupe whose press releases promised, advisedly, "a drugless psychedelic experience". They were also the ones who gave Beatle readings. Why not, said Paul, hire a coach and some film cameras and, like The Pranksters, just drive off somewhere – anywhere – and see what happens? Who needed a screenplay?

Group and manager also agreed to a full-length cartoon, *Yellow Submarine*, designed to be written off as a sop to United Artists, to whom a third Beatle film (in which they were required to physically star) was owed. Setting the wheels in motion for *Yellow Submarine* was Brian's last major service to The Beatles for a reason more absolute than a contractual termination. During his television chat-show appearances – frequent these days – his reports on the unseen Beatles' progress assured fans that he was as much the group's clear-headed mentor as he'd always been. To David Frost on ITV, he spoke more of the Saville Theatre in which he'd had a controlling interest since 1965.

The "Sundays at the Saville" pop presentations, which sometimes mitigated the poor takings for the drama and dance productions during the week, had been Brian's brainwave. When their turn came to top the bill there, it seemed entirely appropriate for Traffic to play amidst the cardboard ramparts left from the weekday set of a Shakespeare play. Other Sundays featured acts of such diversity as John Mayall's Bluesbreakers, The Four Tops and The Bee Gees.

Growing their hair and catching up with the latest psychedelic gear, The Bee Gees had arrived in London to be groomed for the big time by another Australian, Robert Stigwood, whose agency had merged with NEMS in January 1967. Also on his books were Cream, and it had been through this connection that George had "started meeting Eric and hanging out with him then at Brian Epstein's house".[32]

Brian had been the other best man at the Harrisons' wedding, and, although his feelings about George's musicianship were lukewarm, they were not indicative of any loss of affection for his "favourite son". Since LSD and India, George didn't ask as much about Beatle finances, but he and Brian – along with Eric Clapton and Pattie – had seen in the New Year together in 1967. Back at Kinfauns, after a later evening at Brian's, Pattie urged her husband to warn him of the dangers inherent in the over-prescribed tablets that he took compulsively to sleep, to stay awake, to calm his nerves and to lift his depressions. Pattie's concern was justified, because, so a coroner would conclude, Brian Epstein was killed by "incautious self-overdoses" on 27 August 1967.

One of the few outsiders present with the Epstein family at the interment in Liverpool was given a single white chrysanthemum by

George to throw in the grave. "Brian was one of us," was George's verbal valediction. "One of the boys, as you might say."[193] He'd have liked to have been. Instead, he was their safety net, a shoulder to cry on – faithful and reliable, so they thought. The Beatles had been far from the first to realise that Brian wasn't in the best of health. He'd been on standby for most of 1967, but still he'd waited, poised to serve his boys whenever they wanted him again.

The professional bond between The Beatles themselves had loosened since the abandonment of touring. Their solidarity over not playing themselves in the next film emphasised the separateness of their activities, now. George had his spiritual safari and John had his acting and Paul had written the soundtrack to the Hayley Mills movie *The Family Way*, while Ringo had been the titular head of his own building firm, before the credit squeeze forced its closure. On their records, even non-fans could differentiate between McCartney, Lennon and, nowadays, Harrison songs by musical and lyrical style, as well as through the simpler conjecture that the principal composer was also the lead singer. On the run around the world, Paul and John couldn't help but get together to work up hits from only a title or melodic phrase, but now John in Weybridge and Paul in London tended to present each other with songs in more advanced states of completion than before. The general polarisation was that Lennon's were the most way out, while the more prolific McCartney's sold more.

If not as inseparable as they once were, The Beatles still tended to keep pace with each other's caprices, being photographed at the same premieres, covering the same exhibitions and sampling the same stimulants. Following George, they were all sporting moustaches when *Sgt Pepper* was finished. Paul, Ringo and George also had to have "nothing boxes", mildly amusing but otherwise useless battery-operated what-d'-ye-call-its that this Alex Mardas chap – a high-born Greek, apparently – would knock up to keep in with John.

United in play, the four were also all determined self-improvers. Through Paul, the pioneering tonalities of Berio and Stockhausen were as likely to blast from their car stereos as Dylan or Shankar. It was George, however, who was to lead the others to transcendental meditation.

In San Francisco, George had surprised the hippies with his refusal of ingratiating tabs of LSD and tokes of marijuana as he strode past. Many of them had only "turned on" in the first place because they'd read that The Beatles had. As they were more than pop stars now, the group reacted to pressure from the world's youth to find "the truth", and, judging by the hollowed-eyed young derelicts that littered Hashbury and elsewhere, it wasn't LSD. "We're influencing a lot of people, so really it's up to us to influence them in the right way,"[178] admitted George. Although individually they either continued or resumed the habit, when The Beatles publicly repudiated the taking of illegal drugs, they never again made an issue of it.

George did not regret his experiences: "It showed me that LSD can help you to go from A to B, but when you get to B, you see C."[160] Notable junctures on his and Pattie's pilgrimage to C were a visit to San Francisco's Krishna Temple and a climb up a Cornish tor one night after digesting a book about cosmic communication. Several hours passed with no sign of any extra-terrestrials.

In February, a friend of Pattie's had persuaded her to attend a lecture at London's Caxton Hall on "Spiritual Regeneration". The novel-sounding doctrines advanced that evening were so imperatively appealing that Pattie became a convert, although the orator had stressed that his words were but a pale sketch onto which only the movement's founder, Maharishi Mahesh Yogi, could splash more vivid hues.

There remains bitter division about the Maharishi. Was he a complete charlatan or a well-meaning sage sucked into a vortex of circumstances that he was unable to resist? Definitely he was smarter than the average yogi. Born plain Mahesh Prasad Varma in 1918, he graduated from the University of Allahabad with a physics degree before spending the next 13 years studying Sanskrit and the scriptures under the renowned Guru Dev. Styling himself Maharishi ("great soul"), he travelled to London in 1959 to set up a branch of the International Meditation Society, which had garnered a British membership of some 10,000 by the time Pattie brought her intrigued spouse to a meeting. A gazer through the window of a passing bus might have discovered meditation on his own, but others needed guidance. Like a Charles Atlas course for the mind, the society promised increased productivity, less need for sleep, greater alertness and sharper distinction between the important and the trivial.

Deeper implications were inherent in the titles of some of its seminars, such as "Philosophy in Action" and the aforementioned "Spiritual Regeneration", and the overall aim – via short, daily meditation sessions – was to eradicate piecemeal all human vices and ego until a pure state of bliss was reached. Moreover, such washing of spiritual laundry was possible without forsaking material possessions (bar the society's membership fee) and, within reason, worldly pleasures. This seemed an excellent creed to a millionaire Beatle.

Practising what he preached, Varma stayed at the best hotels, commissioned the most up-market press campaigns and employed a full-time accountant. While he luxuriated in New York's Plaza before speaking at sold-out Madison Square Garden, handbills distributed by a one-man picket line outside railed against "capitalistic little devils within the holy man's robes". Cross-legged on a Louis XV chaise longue, His Holiness toyed with his silvery beard or a flower from the bouquets banking him while dealing with the North American media. "I deal in wisdom, not money," he replied in a gentle, high-pitched voice when some tried to bully him into talking finance. For all his disarming public attitudes – the tee-hee-hee chuckle, the mirth he invested into his expositions – there was no mistaking the steel underneath.

A few had been led to believe that a tutorial on 24 August at the Park Lane Hilton was to be his last before he disappeared back to his Indian fastness. Dragged along by the Harrisons, Paul, Jane and the Lennons stole into the hushed hotel functions room like children to Santa's grotto. He so lived up to George and Pattie's spiel that, directly afterwards, The Beatles buttonholed the Great Soul and wound up promising – as Pattie had already – to join him the next day at the Society's ten-day initiation course at a university faculty in the seaside resort of Bangor.

While packing, they telephoned others who might want to go.

Brian had made other arrangements for what chanced to be a bank-holiday weekend, but they could half-expect him later, although he wasn't sure he approved of this Maharishi. Also catching the mid-afternoon train from Euston to North Wales would be Jenny Boyd, Mick Jagger and Marianne Faithfull, all of whom had to shove through a crush of fans and journalists who had homed in on what one tabloid named "*The Mystical Special*". Although they'd secured first-class seats, it was an edgy, uncomfortable ride as the party, crammed eventually into the same compartment as the Maharishi, dared not risk a walk down the corridor.

For people who'd viewed the world from the Olympus of stardom since 1963, it was perhaps too much of an adventure. Unused now to actually paying for things with hard cash, they were at a loss the following night when handed the bill after a meal in a Bangor restaurant. George was the first to realise why the waiters kept hovering about the table, and it was he, too, who settled the matter with a roll of banknotes he happened to have about his person.

Neither this imposition nor the hard mattresses in their hostel accommodation on the late-Victorian campus could deflect the pop stars from their iron purpose. Yet, during the press conference that Varma's public relations agent had set up in the main hall, most journalists didn't appear to take The Beatles' preoccupation with meditation very seriously. It was worthwhile hanging around in Bangor, though, because the group still provided good copy, whether it was Lennon putting his foot in it or their cottoning onto another new fad.

One or two sick jokes started to circulate among the press corps awaiting them on Sunday afternoon, as they learned that a lonely life had ended in London. Inside the college, the Great Soul was consoling his famous disciples as the tragedy they'd initially refused to avow inflicted itself upon them. "The Maharishi told us not to be too overshadowed by grief," George reported. "I have lost only a few people who were very close to me. This is one of those occasions, but I feel my course on meditation here has helped me to overcome my grief more easily than before."[193]

As twilight thickened, The Beatles brushed past a pitiless

whoomph of flashbulbs, their mouths moving mechanically as they walked from the university building into a black Rolls Royce. Its interior was their last sanctuary before they would be obliged to respond more fully to their manager's death. "We didn't know what to do," shrugged George later. "We were lost."[29]

10 L'Angelo Mysterioso

Could Brian manage The Beatles from the grave? Time after time he'd turn in it as capital was wasted on too many Billy Bunters whose postal orders never arrived. To The Beatles, experience meant recognising mistakes when they occurred again.

Once, a heading emblem on a NEMS press release had been Epstein in a mortar board in the midst of his clients with their impudent schoolboy grins. Now that Sir had left the classroom, the children started doing whatever they liked. With adolescence extended by adulation, most of their ideas were more intriguing, conceptually, than in ill-conceived practice. In the end, their idyll was threatened not by any external danger but by their own inner natures and desires, and when it dawned on them that not everything they did was great. Long before their partnership was officially dissolved, each Beatle – however reluctantly or unknowingly – would be well into his solo career.

Brian's most tangible legacy was The Beatles' new deal with EMI, which gave them a royalty rate higher than that of any other recording act. All they had to do in exchange was produce 70 tracks for release before 1976. This they would do well within the limit, both as individuals and, to a diminishing degree, collectively.

Four were unloaded onto the soundtrack of *Yellow Submarine*, which, inspected halfway towards completion, had been a pleasant surprise. Without making The Beatles too cuddly, it portrayed them as Sgt Pepper's bandsmen in surreal encounters during a "modyssey" from Liverpool to Pepperland. So charmed were they with this epic cartoon that the real Beatles agreed to appear in cameo for the last scene.

However, as 1967's flowers wilted, so did their enthusiasm for

Yellow Submarine. Significantly, half of the cheapskate tie-in album consisted of George Martin's incidental music and the cancelled 'Only A Northern Song'. The only new items that The Beatles bothered to add were, as they realised themselves, just inconsequential fillers. Even Paul's 'All Together Now' was taped in one session. From George's less unwilling quill had dripped 'It's All Too Much', in which a wide-ranged melody and laughably pretentious symbolism stayed afloat amid a roughcast, noisy backing with a vignette from Purcell's *Trumpet Voluntary* chucked in for good measure. In 1975, it was to be revived by arch-hippy guitarist Steve Hillage.

If it seems twee now, *Yellow Submarine* was loved by Beatles fans, who, in obedience to the non-cartoon John Lennon's exhortation, skipped from cinemas singing 'All Together Now'. Once outside, however, they shut up. By 1968, if you carried on like that, sooner or later you'd get a kicking, even in San Francisco. In London, the likes of The Flowerpot Men had jumped on bandwagons new, and the prevailing gangster chic obliged even a cool cat like Georgie Fame to resuscitate a flagging chart career with 'The Ballad Of Bonnie And Clyde'.

Aided by pirate radio's demise and the cautious programming of the BBC's two new national pop stations, the British Top 30 became generally shallower and less subversive in content. The corporation had already banned two Beatles tracks from its airwaves – 'A Day In The Life', for its "I'd love to turn you on" line, and 'I Am The Walrus', for its sexual innuendo – even though a performance had been screened on the BBC's new colour network on Boxing Day 1967 as part of the group's hour-long spectacular, *Magical Mystery Tour*.

Favourable critical reaction to *Yellow Submarine* served to obscure memories of this laboured project, which wasn't perhaps suitable viewing for a nation sleeping off its Yuletide revels. Other than predictable plaudits from the underground press and the *NME*, the interesting-but-boring *Magical Mystery Tour* was universally panned, a first for The Beatles as artistes. As expressive as the most vitriolic review was discerning ex-Walker Brother Scott Engel's rise from his armchair to switch it off after 20 minutes.

It had been a development of McCartney's pretty idea of a journey with no known destination or outcome. "Everything will be spontaneous,"[194] revealed Tony Barrow when puzzled journalists rang to ask why a coach with "Magical Mystery Tour" emblazoned on its sides and alleged to contain The Beatles was trundling through the West Country with the holiday season still on. In trendy Al Capone suits, George, John and Ringo lent a passing uniformity, but inside the vehicle, too, was a hand-picked cast as variegated as a disaster movie's.

Among those described later as "a motley collection of uncouth and unlikable trippers" were a midget, a fat lady, a funnyman in a bow tie, a courier, a little girl, the omnipresent Alex Mardas, an actress playing Paul's girlfriend and Paul himself, who only needed the knotted handkerchief on his head to complete his parody of a holiday-maker coping with the meteorological whims of a British September. Picked up *en route* were minor characters of such diversity as Spencer Davis and bikini-clad truant Judith Rogers, who was roped in by McCartney because "I decided to use some glamour in the film on the spur of the moment".[195]

Judith was but one of hundreds who'd divined the hotels where The Beatles had been provisionally booked. As well as the chaos that their very presence summoned, the 40-seater bus – now divested of its too-distinctive trappings – failed to negotiate the twisty lanes, thus ruling out such potentially stimulating locations as Widecombe Fair and Berry Pomeroy Castle.

Although the bulk of *Magical Mystery Tour* was drawn from this troubled excursion, many interior scenes were filmed elsewhere, mainly back in London. Putting new moral objections on hold, George sat woodenly next to John in the front row of Paul Raymond's Revue Bar. Before him, a stripper entertained to the accompaniment of The Bonzo Dog Doo-Dah Band, whose eventual modicum of chart success was secondary to their alarming stage act, which earned them a weekly turn on *Do Not Adjust Your Set*, an anarchic children's comedy series on ITV

Not far from Raymond's palace of sin, The Beatles spent six weeks in a darkened room, wading through the formless celluloid miles of improvised dialogue and scenes that had seemed a good idea at the time. As Paul was less uncertain about the finished picture, George and John – uneasy about it from the beginning – and Ringo left him to it. Unless called in to give opinions, they whiled away hours in the adjacent office with such amusements as the clowning of 'Rosie', an old Soho vagrant who'd been immortalised in a hit record by a street busker called Don Partridge.

Magical Mystery Tour wasn't *Citizen Kane*, but its music was a winner. Proof of this was the grapple for UK chart supremacy between their latest single, 'Hello Goodbye', and a double EP for the film's six numbers, which cost three times more. Occupying a whole side of this novel package was George's repetitive 'Blue Jay Way', after the boulevard of the same name where the Harrisons stayed while in Los Angeles. As fog encircled their rented house, a still jet-lagged George had picked out its tune on a small electric keyboard to a lyric concerning a long wait for Derek Taylor and his wife, who were groping through the evening traffic. It wasn't much of a song, really, but when it was recorded the combined effect of guttural cello, monochordal organ and wordless responses behind George's phased singing conveyed the requisite misty atmosphere. So, too, did the clouds of incense that shrouded the 'Blue Jay Way' sequence in the film, with the composer squatting in a lotus position, his swirling image refracted as if seen through a fly's eye.

In *Yellow Submarine*, too, he'd been caricatured as a hazy mystic, and it was no surprise to Joe Public when George emerged as the most vocal supporter of this meditation caper. Although, like the Maharishi himself, he was criticised for plugging spirituality like a new record, George's exposition of his belief that "the world is ready for a mystic revolution"[196] on *The David Frost Show* – with witty asides from John – went down so well that he was invited back the next week: "So you can't say going on television and speaking to the press is a bad way to tell people about meditation."[3]

Since Bangor, a retreat for further study to one of the Maharishi's two *yoga-ashrams* ("theological colleges") in the forested foothills of the Himalayas had been on the cards. This trip had been postponed twice owing to *Magical Mystery Tour* commitments, but George had maintained contact with His Holiness, mainly by telephone, although he had taken a day trip to Sweden with Ringo to confer with him and, with John, accompanied the Great Soul to a Shankar concert in Paris.

The media uproar during The Beatles' curtailed sojourn in Bangor had brought home to Varma what a catch he'd made. Like Ravi Shankar before him, he'd been unaware of the group's stature, but, armed with the relevant records, he underwent a crash-course in their music and began to illustrate his talks with quotes from their lyrics. Flattered though they were, The Beatles were unconvinced by his argument that, if they were sincere about meditation, they ought to tithe a percentage of their income into his Swiss bank account. Because they hadn't actually said no, the Maharishi assured American investors that the four would be co-starring in a TV documentary about him. "He is not a modern man," explained George, as much to himself as anyone else. "He just doesn't understand such things."[197]

Shelving their stronger misgivings, Paul, Jane and the Starkeys followed an advance guard of the Harrisons and Lennons to India, in February 1968, where all were both relieved and disconcerted that, after a long and bumpy drive from New Delhi, the meditation academy was not a compound of mud huts but whitewashed, air-conditioned chalets fully equipped to US standards, with an attached post office, laundry and dining hall. The main lecture theatre was not unlike Bangor's. Across the Ganges stood the shanty town of Rishikesh, where hospitality was more frugal.

"It'll probably turn out like a Butlin's holiday camp,"[197] George had remarked to *Melody Maker* before he left, and so it did for Maureen and Ringo, who went home early. Among the 60 remaining seekers of nirvana were some of comparable renown, such as Mia Farrow, Donovan and – the only one to become a lifelong devotee – Mike Love of The Beach Boys, whose Dennis Wilson had been introduced by George to the Maharishi in Paris. Famous or obscure, all would assemble clothed against the morning heat in the open-air amphitheatre for lessons which included practical demonstrations, such as the apparent suspended animation that His Holiness induced in one of his staff. He also spoke of levitation, but no Beatle would be around long enough to witness any. Gradually, the talks became shorter and periods for individual contemplation lengthened. Later, George bragged of being entranced for a 36-hour period.

The balmy quietness of the campus yielded a long-denied if temporary peace of mind, as all of the day-to-day distractions that hindered creativity were on the other side of the planet. Relaxed and happy, new songs poured from the pop contingent, many of them observations of other students. Donovan dedicated his 'Jennifer Juniper' to Jenny Boyd, while Lennon's 'Dear Prudence' was about Mia Farrow's reclusive sister, who "wouldn't come out. They selected me and George to try and bring her out of her chalet, because she would trust us. She'd been locked in for three weeks and was trying to reach God quicker than anybody else."[80]

Shortly after the celebration of Pattie's 23rd birthday, Jane and Paul threw in the towel and returned to London. Alex Mardas, meanwhile, was torn between his own boredom with ashram life and his desire to maintain his position at John's ear. His problem was resolved three weeks later, when he'd accumulated enough tittle-tattle to speak to John and George of Varma's clandestine and earthly scheming for the downfall of an American nurse's knickers, propositioning her with the forbidden meal of chicken as other cads would with a box of chocolates. With the manipulative Alex urging him on, Lennon confronted the Great Soul with this infamy. Deaf to protestations of innocence, John announced his immediate departure, to the dismay of Cynthia, for whom the trip seemed an opportunity to save their marriage.

Not knowing what to think, the Harrisons chose to wash their hands of the Maharishi, too, although George preserved a vestige of regard for one who'd orchestrated "one of the greatest experiences I've ever had".[144] Still a believer in the soundness of the too-human guru's teachings, he confessed, "It's just that we physically left the Maharishi's camp but spiritually never moved an inch. We still meditate now. At least, I do."[3]

He broke the journey back to England to return a visit by Shambu Das to the ashram and to look up Ravi Shankar. At a press conference the previous August, he'd been addressed as "George" and Ravi had been "Mr Shankar". This was commensurate with the respect held for each as a sitarist. Starting too late in life, and with his pop career precluding daily hours of practice, Ravi admitted that George "realised it demands the whole time, like learning the violin or cello, but he still continues to learn from me as much as he can about Indian music, which he uses in his own work as inspiration".[170] George effectively gave it up one New York night in 1968, when "Jimi Hendrix and Eric Clapton were at the same hotel and that was the last time I played the sitar like that".[32] For years afterwards, "George Harrison (sitar)" would crop up in the Miscellaneous Instruments sections of music-press polls. "People put you in a bag,", he groused, "and nowadays all I've got to do is the slightest unusual rhythm and they say, 'There he goes, all Indian again.'"[145]

An electric sitar was the selling point on The Box Tops' 'Cry Like A Baby', which was in the Top 20 when the Harrisons finally got back to Kinfauns. Just as off-putting was session guitarist Chris Spedding's qualification that "nobody's trying to fool anyone about it being an Indian instrument. It's a sound effect. Every time I use it, I charge £10, apart from my session fee. It cost me £80. When they were new in the shops, they cost about £300."[74]

On BBC Radio 1, John Peel – not as "beautiful" as he'd been in 1967 – no longer inserted 20-minute ragas between progressive fare on his *Night Ride* programme. Instead, he bowed to frequent requests for "that boot-slapping thing" (Zulu step-dancing), "the Russian with the funny voice" (a singer from Azerbaijan, USSR) and further obscurities that he'd chosen from Broadcasting House's sound archives. A national pop station filling off-peak ether with nose-flutes, Romanian *cobzas* and further outlandish examples of what would later be termed as "world music" had been unthinkable three years earlier, when George Harrison had double-tracked the sitar on 'Norwegian Wood'.

Not as directly innovative were Brian Jones' explorations into the ethnic music of Morocco. Regarded as George's opposite number in the Stones, Jones was also admired for his weaving of quaint instrumentation into the fabric of their records. Another affinity with George was an artistic insecurity rooted in the near-monopoly of songwriting from a ruling team within his group. Neither were Jagger and Richards as receptive to the compositions of colleagues as Lennon and McCartney. An emotional disaster area, Brian wasn't as bold as George. However, he'd channelled part of his frustration by scoring the soundtrack for a German movie, *Mort Und Totschlag*.

Work of this kind had fallen into George's lap, too. After viewing its uncut rushes in October 1967, The Bee Gees had turned down the task of providing continuous music to an oddity of a cinema film entitled *Wonderwall*. George's name was brought up enough times during subsequent discussions with its backer that director Joe Massot – who'd met The Beatles during *Help!* – was elected to sound him out. George was more impressed with *Wonderwall* than The Bee Gees had been, but confessed that he hadn't a clue how to go about it. Aware of both the film's low budget and the publicity value of Beatle involvement, Massot felt that any old rubbish would do, as long as the words "George Harrison" could be printed on the credits.

Apprehensive about what he'd taken on, George started by "spotting" each sequence with a stop-watch. Back in the recording studio, he'd then "make 35 seconds, say, of something, mix it and line it up with the scene".[59] Within these tight strictures, he compiled an original soundtrack that many would cite as the saving grace of a film graphically condemned as "a right load of codswallop"[198] about an elderly scientist who spends his leisure hours peeping obsessively through a hole in his attic wall at the antics of a young model – played by Jane Birkin – in the flat next door. His new vista of her erotic mirror-posing, wild parties and athletic sex life is so alien to him that reality dissolves (as does the story-line), until his fantasies become concrete when he saves the girl from suicide.

Wonderwall faded from general circulation soon after its release in 1968. Too much for the ordinary moviegoer – although less so than *Magical Mystery Tour* – it only received occasional showings in film clubs and arts centres. Watching it was an intellectual duty rather than entertainment.

Issued some months before the film, the soundtrack album was worthy in its own right, regardless of imagined visuals and what George himself would dismiss as "loads of horrible mellotron stuff and a police siren", as well as the co-related blowing of mouth-organist Tommy Reilly, more famous for his theme to *Dixon Of Dock Green*.

A sympathetic reviewer mentioned that "the Harrison music replaces dialogue waxing almost vocal like a cinema organist from the silent days".[199] On 'Party Seacombe', a pointed reference to an expression in one of Lennon's books, George's schoolchum Colin Manley's wah-wah guitar indeed "waxes almost vocal" to the Pink Floyd-ish accompaniment of the rest of The Remo Four, who were still functional after years of backing various singers, including Gregory Phillips.

The Remo Four, Reilly and Clapton's parts in *Wonderwall* were taped at Abbey Road, but tracks like 'Gat Kirwani' and 'Guru Vandana' had come from an EMI studio further east. On the top floor of the Universal Building in Bombay, George had toiled for an intensive five days with old mono equipment and soundproofing so poor that it was impossible to record during the evening rush hour without picking up extraneous sounds of traffic and the exodus from the offices below. Nevertheless, these were fruitful sessions for George and the players gathered for him by Shambu Das. Under the Beatle's supervision, Das and his fascinated musicians obeyed Western rules of harmony as their contribution to a film most of them would never see quickly took shape – so quickly, in fact, that there was time in hand for George to produce several backing tracks for purposes that were then non-specific. "I was getting so into Indian music then," he'd recall, "that I decided to use the assignment as an excuse for a musical anthology to help spread it."[59]

As Joe Massot knew, George's Beatle status guaranteed the film some attention, but the soundtrack's elevation to Number 49 in the US album chart testified to more intrinsic virtues in an industry where sales figures are arbiters of success. An additional distinction was that it was the first LP to be released via EMI on Apple, The Beatles' own record label, which would be their most lucrative post-Epstein enterprise, almost despite themselves. It's name had first been tossed around during the *Revolver* sessions, to the extent of giving provisional fruity titles to tracks yet to receive one. 'Love You To', for instance, began as 'Granny Smith'.

Frank Sinatra and trumpeter Herb Alpert are off-the-cuff and all-American examples of performers who reduced the number of middlemen and increased quality control on output by founding their own record companies, albeit under leasing deals with parent firms. Neither, however, shared Apple's initial burst of world-shaking ambition, in which records would be only one division of an "Apple Corps", with tentacles in other spheres such as film, electronics and tailoring. After LSD moustaches and meditation, The Beatles had suddenly latched onto bourgeois greed. With their own struggles niggling still, "We had this mad idea of having Apple there," said George, "so that people could come and do artistic stuff and not have a hard time."[24]

In April 1968 – the beginning of the tax year – advertisements appeared in both national and underground journals soliciting the public to bring "artistic stuff" to the new Apple Foundation For The Arts in London. Not a postal delivery would go by without a deluge of demo tapes and manuscripts thumping onto the doormat. All day long, tongue-tied callers who'd found out Apple's ex-directory number would beg for their cases to be heard. Fingers calloused by guitar string and typewriter key constantly pressed the bell. "We had every freak in the world coming in there,"[24] groaned George.

That very month, I too sent Apple a bundle of my poems in the hopes that they'd want someone with imagination rather than ability. When the operation moved headquarters from Wigmore Street to Savile Row, I decided to pay a call to check whether the Beatle who'd read them had set a publication date yet. Well, I was only 16. Wondering what I'd wear on the dust-jacket photograph, I walked straight past the tall Georgian terrace containing Apple, not even noticing two or three girls hanging around the steps of what looked like a private residence. Its front door was wide open, so, unchallenged, I entered and explained my presence to a friendly receptionist on whose desktop was a tin labelled "Canned Heat". She was sorry no one could see me right now but promised I'd hear from Apple in due course. I should imagine that my teenage verse must be quite near the top of the pile by now.

No stranger could have bowled off the street into NEMS any more than they could have into Balmoral. I could have been some maniac out to get Lennon for shooting his mouth off about Jesus. "If you want George to listen to your tape, you're doing it all wrong," shouted one Apple employee when the first Beatle to arrive that day was smothered in kisses by some French-Canadian girl. Taking George at his word, a pair of particularly invidious Hell's Angels blew in from San Francisco to abuse without hindrance Apple's lavish facilities – and female secretariat – for two nerve-wracking weeks. Apple's house style was based on "complete trust", said Derek Taylor. "I now know that we were foolish."[200]

Because George had convinced, the others that Derek was "on the same trip",[199] Epstein's former assistant returned to the fold as Apple's press officer, but "I didn't realise the tensions underneath until George came back from Rishikesh and reacted with real horror to what was going on in the building".[199] A doorman was appointed to keep out riff-raff like me, although certain moneyed young Americans, glad to breathe the groovy air around The Beatles, were let in to act as unpaid and unrecompensed minions.

Behind that closed door, no one Beatle felt responsible for straightening out a venture that had taken a mere two months to snowball into chaos. To see what it was like, he might commandeer a room at Savile Row, stick to conventional office hours and play company director until the novelty wore off. He might (as George did) hammer at a partition he disliked at one of Apple's two unprofitable boutiques, but bigger policy decisions were more likely to be guided by a hired astrologer of the kind who warned George about the danger of wearing sapphire before August 1975.

As no one actually objected, John put Alex Mardas in charge of Apple Electronics, a post that rapidly became a sinecure as, one after another, the wondrous patents involving force-fields and robotics progressed no further than Alex talking about them. Lennon formulated a plan for ex-Quarry Man Ivan Vaughan (now a Cambridge graduate) to set up a school for The Beatles' children and those of their friends to attend. Meetings were arranged, various properties inspected and the skeleton of a steering committee established before Apple's accountant argued that it was not a viable proposition.

George's jobs-for-the-boys were less impeachable. Terry Doran had landed on his feet as George's general factotum, his face now framed by a beard and Hendrix frizz, and Astrid Kemp (*née* Kirchherr) was commissioned to photograph George for the *Wonderwall* cover. A seat had also been found for Tony Bramwell on the executive board, headed by Neil Aspinall.

With no speaker cabinets left to hump, Mal Evans' donkey-work now extended to minor instrumental roles on records. Once, he was asked by Paul – to John's chagrin – to pen some lyrics for a *Sgt Pepper* track. A lowlier office was travelling with the luggage to the Indian ashram. He was enough of an old comrade to be invited to join his masters on holiday, as he and his wife did with the Harrisons for three days in Corfu.

An even older pal, Pete Shotton, had left his Hampshire supermarket to manage the main Apple boutique in Baker Street. No worse than any other trendy store, it was remarkable only in the manner of its closure in July 1968, when The Beatles decreed that all remaining merchandise was to be given away to the public, who predictably pounced on even the shelves and hatstands like hags at a jumble sale.

All fittings, decorations and stock had been either requisitioned or designed by The Fool through a six-figure float from The Beatles, who'd also hinted that the Dutch clothiers could record an LP. The Fool weren't as daft as they looked. After castigation by Apple Retail for removing "a considerable amount of items as yet unpaid"[201] from the boutiques, they departed from The Beatles' court as mysteriously as they'd arrived, having first secured a contract with Mercury Records, for whom they made their album.

The Fool's album was produced by Graham Nash, now rehearsing in a Kensington flat with Dave Crosby and Steve Stills. Their warblings weren't everyone's cup of tea, but Nash ended up a sight richer than if he'd stayed a Holly. Styled as a "supergroup" by the music press, Crosby, Stills And Nash were approached in 1968 by George Harrison, who wanted to sign them to Apple Records. As none in the trio could extricate himself from existing contracts, the deal fell through, as did Apple's negotiations with another promising group, Fleetwood Mac, whose publicist happened to be Bill Harry. A lesser star in embryo, James Taylor, was taken on, but 20-year-old David Bowie slipped through The Beatles' fingers after an interview with Paul McCartney.

When the first Apple recordings were pressed, in August 1968, no one could pretend that any other division of the organisation was either a money-spinner or of scientific or cultural value. No more qualified to run a business than Brian Epstein had been to play guitar, George was the Beatle least interested in any Apple function beyond making records. Nonetheless, he'd show willing now and then, poking his nose in at the first boutique's launch party, attending a charity showing of *Yellow Submarine* in Los Angeles and appearing on the Smothers Brothers TV show to introduce the film clip of The Beatles miming their inaugural Apple single, 'Hey Jude'.

As they and Gerry had held the UK Number One spot for NEMS in 1963, so it was in microcosm for Apple when, bearing the catalogue number Apple 2, Mary Hopkin's 'Those Were The Days' succeeded 'Hey Jude' at the top. A Welsh soprano with an aura of schoolgirl innocence, Mary had been conspicuous among entrants on several editions of ITV's *Opportunity Knocks*. Keener on her voice than he'd been on David Bowie's, Paul McCartney selected and produced 'Those Were The Days' and most of Mary's subsequent lesser hits. Though she wasn't his *protégé*, her singing so enchanted George, who listened in on one of her album sessions, that he sent Mal out to buy her a better acoustic guitar than the one with which she was accompanying herself. He also submitted songs from his growing portfolio for her and Paul's consideration, two of which were tried out by Marianne Faithfull, under the supervision of George, who perhaps saw her as a more worldly Hopkin.

Another Harrison composition was actually heard by the public as the A-side of the third Apple single, although not as often as 'Hey Jude' and 'Those Were The Days', both of which had more radio play and more appetising titles than 'Sour Milk Sea'. With George at the console, this jittery rocker, taped at a "glorified jam session",[202] was sung by Jackie Lomax, back from the States now that his Alliance had fallen apart there. An acquaintance rather than a bosom buddy, he'd supplicated George via Terry Doran for an Apple contract just as The Beatles were leaving for India.

Looking him up and down, George had decided that it might be worth taking trouble over Jackie. Lean and handsomely hatchet faced, his rock-star potential was supplemented by a lithe if tight-throated singing style, which was much in vogue just then. He also composed a bit, although nothing he played to George was markedly commercial. Agreeing with Lomax that an up-tempo A-side was more his line than a ballad, George returned to Britain with 'Sour Milk Sea', its lyrics inspired by a picture in a religious textbook that he'd understood to mean "if you're in the shit, don't go around moaning about it; do something about it".[38] Expressed more delicately in the verses of 'Sour Milk Sea', it was a similar sentiment to that expressed in the Maharishi's dubious maxim that "people are in poverty because they lack intelligence and because of laziness".[203]

None of the records that he cut with George made Jackie rich. Still, they plodded on, with George sparing no expense. An artist of Jackie Lomax's calibre deserved nothing less than publicity photos by Justin de Villeneuve, a full orchestra if he needed one and even the oscillations of one of these new-fangled Moog synthesisers. McCartney, Starr and Clapton were among the famous musicians namechecked on the sleeve of Lomax's only Apple LP, dog-eared copies of which spoke to casual browsers of deletion racks through its title, *Is This What You Want?*. Few did, however, despite Jackie's most professional vocal projection and George's competent – although occasionally cluttered – production.

Hardly any of Lomax's work on Apple was exceptional, but, paralleling George's kindness to Mary Hopkin, Eric Clapton gave him a relic to guard for life, the Gibson SG heard on Cream's double album *Wheels Of Fire*. Since *Fresh Cream*, the trio had gone from their native turf to grander, more impersonal venues in North America, where their musical sensitivity and subtle ironies were warped by high-decibel *diddle-diddle-diddling* and "endless, meaningless solos", reflected a perplexed Eric. "We were not indulging ourselves so much as our audiences, because that's what they wanted."[105] As long as customers went as ape over strings of bum notes as they did over the outfit's most startling moments, Cream in stagnation broke box office records once held by The Beatles in Uncle Sam's concrete colosseums and baseball parks. The band's calculated disbandment in November 1968 was no surprise to George, who'd arrived at a similar artistic impasse in 1965.

Cream had planned a final LP, *Goodbye*. Most of it consisted of in-concert tapings from the last US tour, although each member also agreed to donate a new composition. Songs had never come as readily to Clapton as they had to bass guitarist Jack Bruce and drummer Ginger Baker. Under pressure because the other had finished their *Goodbye* numbers, Eric now felt close enough to George to seek his assistance. Aid was rendered with none of the reluctance that John Lennon had evinced when helping with 'Taxman'. George was only too pleased to collaborate with "one of those people I get on so well with it's like looking at myself".[204] As well as sharing his Beatle friend's depilatory caprices and dress sense, Clapton wasn't "a leader sort of person. It's the same with me. I need someone to encourage me to do things."[204] With the purchase of Hurtwood Edge, a Surrey mansion, Eric was also on a par with George materially.

The two guitarists had similar tastes in women, too, as Eric's squiring of Paula Boyd for three months appeared to prove. Her big sister "wondered why he'd done it, but it became obvious later on".[44] A line towards the end of the number he composed with George implied a portent for the Beatle-ologist: "Talking about a girl who looks quite like you..." Whatever Clapton may have been trying to say, for his co-writer, "that whole song was quite silly. Ringo was sitting around drinking. We were amusing ourselves."[58] Its bridge reiterated the lyrical thrust of 'Sour Milk Sea', but the verses were merely syllables strung together to carry the tune. Its very title, 'Badge', came from misreading the word *bridge* on Harrison's scribbled draft.

In Cream's hands, 'Badge', with its pseudo-cryptic words, was the nearest *Goodbye* came to a straightforward pop song. It always reminded me of 'Love Potion Number Nine'. As the LP's promotional single, it grazed the lower echelons of Britain's Top 20 over spring 1969, and then three years later it almost repeated this modest triumph when reissued by Polydor as a stop-gap 45 during a period when Clapton had retreated from pop.

Other than a plain chord strummed after each verse, 'Badge' had no discernible hook line; much of its appeal lay in the interplay of Bruce's bass lope and the chopping of guest rhythm guitarist George Harrison, under the *nom de guerre* "L'Angelo Mysterioso" – Clapton's idea and used because such moonlighting on a rival label was frowned upon by EMI. Nonetheless, the mysterious angel's identity was a secret so badly kept that his inaudible presence on one track was a minor selling point for canny Jack Bruce's first solo album.

Baker and Clapton, meanwhile, had amalgamated with Steve Winwood and Rick Grech, the bass player from "progressive" group Family, to form Blind Faith, who, so a letter to *Melody Maker* wrongly predicted, would achieve "almost Beatle status".[205] Rather than an expected stylistic hybrid, there'd be strong evidence of Eric's fondness for an LP of insidious impact, *Music From Big Pink* by The Band, a group from upstate New York. The album demonstrated a True West blend of electric folklore that had been nurtured over many a rough night spent in hick Canadian dance halls before the musicians landed a job backing Bob Dylan.

As John's enthusiasm for Dylan had rubbed off on George, so did Clapton's for The Band. "They had great tunes," concurred George, "played in a great spirit and with humour and versatility".[58] Their professional relationship with Bob Dylan, however, had not ceased during his convalescence, as they recorded with him in the basement of their communal pink house in West Saugerties, not far from Bob's own rural home in Bearsville.

Throughout 1967, Dylan had been as unreachable an object of myth as Elvis. Until a water-testing re-emergence in the following year, he was incommunicado to all but his immediate family, The Band and perhaps a dozen or so of those who were his equals in the hierarchy of pop. They alone appreciated why he remained in seclusion even after he was fit enough physically to hold down another album-tour-album sandwich.

Beginning with an invitation from Band guitarist Jaime Robertson to call on Big Pink, George became the most frequent

Beatle guest at Bearsville during Dylan's shadowy refuge from fame. George had found him as initially aloof as John had been in The Quarry Men, although Bob was closer to him in age and outlook. Sleeping at the singer's manager's house for the first visit, he spent his waking hours at the Dylans', where the paterfamilias "hardly said a word for a couple of days. Anyway, we got the guitars out and it loosened up a bit."[24] Bob emerged – so George liked to think – as a kindred spirit, in that his supposed stand-offishness was no more than diffidence. When you got him on his own, he was quite chatty. Furthermore, as George fought an inferiority complex over lyrics, Bob struggled with melodies, even borrowing that of 'Norwegian Wood' for *Blonde On Blonde*'s 'Fourth Time Around'. With a vague music/words delineation, the youngest Beatle and Dylan formed a desultory songwriting team that would bear sparse, half-serious fruit.

George's cultivation of Dylan's friendship may have been interrelated with the behaviour of Lennon since his confrontation with the Maharishi. Shortly after their return to England, John had left Cynthia and Julian to move in with Yoko Ono, a Japanese-American who was to art what Screaming Lord Sutch was to politics. As some mug with a pocketful of money, John had been first introduced to her in 1966 during a preview of her "Unfinished Painting And Objects" display at the gallery attached to the Indica bookshop. Charmed by the all-white chess set, the apple with the £200 price tag and other puzzling exhibits, he'd funded Yoko's next event, taking a benevolent interest in her activities past and present – for example, her film of naked human buttocks in tight close up, or her "happening" in Liverpool's Bluecoat Chambers, where she'd had different members of the audience picking up pieces of a jug she'd just smashed. It was an Art Statement, like.

Yoko had also tried to make it as a pop singer, actually submitting demos to Island Records, who went in for oddball ethnic material. Her vocal flexibility was not dissimilar to that of Subbulakshmi, but she found a niche in the more distant extremes of avant-garde jazz, walking a highly-strung artistic tightrope without a safety net. In the company of respected figures such as Ornette Coleman and drummer John Stevens, she used her voice like a front-line horn, interjecting screeches, wails, nanny-goat vibrato and Nippon jabber into the proceedings.

Her vocal gymnastics actually owed much to stubbornly chromatic *seitoha* (Japanese classical music) and the free choral babbling and odd tone clusters present in the works of post-serialists like Schoenberg and Penderecki. This knowledge did little to soften a critique of a performance with Lennon and Danish saxophonist John Tchcai in which Lennon was squatting at her feet with his back to the audience and holding an electric guitar against a large speaker to create ear-splitting feedback.[206] Later, he elucidated, "I can't quite play like Eric or George, but then I gave up trying and just played whatever way I could to match her voice."[207]

After nature had taken its course one Weybridge night when Mrs Lennon was out, a writer to *Beatles Monthly* expressed the widespread view that Cynthia and John's subsequent divorce eroded The Beatles' magic even more than the absence of the usual Christmas single in 1966. Annihilating completely any cosy illusions such traditionalists had left was the first of a trilogy of non-Beatle albums by Lennon and Ono. The unmelodious avant-garde ramblings of *Unfinished Music No 1: Two Virgins* might have been anticipated, even tolerated, but the ordinary fan's shocked reaction to its cover photographs – of the couple unclothed – was best articulated in the topical disc 'John, You Went Too Far This Time' by Rainbo, alias Sissy Spacek, who was then a struggling starlet. Her love, she sang, would never be the same. Well, he had a penis, didn't he? Who'd have thought a Beatle could ever possess one of those?

Nakedness closed the first half of the Broadway musical *Hair*, but many of Lennon's blushing peers sought to talk him out of releasing *Two Virgins*, conjecturing that he'd finally flipped his lid. More forbearing than most was George, who was about to be an indirect victim of censorship when EMI refused to distribute a single by one of his discoveries, Brute Force, a one-man-band consisting of New Yorker Steven Friedland. Although 'The King Of Fuh' had been allocated an Apple matrix number, EMI were discountenanced by its tension-breaking chorus that ran "I'm the king of Fuh/I'm the Fuh King".

The company washed its hands of *Two Virgins*, too. However, it didn't mind the next Ono-Lennon LP as much – at least, not the non-controversial sleeve. *Unfinished Music No 2: Life With The Lions* was one of but two albums that appeared on Zapple, Apple's only subsidiary label. Intended as a platform for the spoken word and experimental music, "It seized up before it really got going," sighed George, "as with so many other things at Apple."[59] Zapple's charity did not begin at home, as shown by the preponderance of Americans lined up to declaim *vers libre*, read prose and crack jokes in hip restricted code. A few acetates of 'Listening To Richard Brautigan' by *Rolling Stone* magazine's resident rhymer were actually pressed, but whither the gems of Allen Ginsberg, who, drunk and naked, had met George and a disgusted John at a London party in 1965? Or Ken Weaver, a more permanent member of Greenwich Village's burlesque poetry rock group, The Fugs? Whatever happened about the "street diary" of Ken Kesey, mainstay of The Merry Pranksters? Foundering too was a 24-album retrospective of Lenny Bruce, a man who, to most of those outside the States who'd ever heard of him, was remembered as some sort of blue comedian.

George was especially keen for Zapple to acquire extant recordings by another American, the self-ennobled Lord Buckley, a night-club raconteur admired by Dylan for his unorthodox use of language. George also treasured hopes of a Zapple LP of children's stories related by daffy film actress Hermione Gingold and enhanced by effects from the monophonic synthesiser newly installed in a room at Kinfauns that he'd had converted into a cramped four-track studio.

With commendable honesty, George has said that "both of the albums that did come out are a load of rubbish".[58] Alongside Yoko and John's second soul-baring episode was George's own *Electronic Sounds*, which were exactly that: "All I did was get that very first Moog synthesiser with the big patch unit and keyboards you could never tune, and I put a microphone into a tape machine. Whatever came out when I fiddled with the knobs went on tape."[59] Although these haphazard bleeps and flurries were as far from Mersey Beat as he'd ever be, one side's worth of noise was given the title 'Under The Mersey Wall', after another George Harrison's column in the *Liverpool Echo*.

This opus was realised in February 1969 on George's synthesiser, probably the first to be privately purchased in Britain. Previously, such a device could only be hired domestically from US dealers, which is why the earlier half of *Electronic Sounds* – 'No Time Or Space' – evolved during an exploratory twiddle in a Californian recording complex three months prior to 'Under The Mersey Wall'. Later, engineer Bernard Krause would protest that George had stolen his demonstration performance on this synthesiser for issue on *Electronic Sounds*. This may not have been true, as Krause didn't press any claim for whatever scant royalties could be scraped from an album that, that even by a Beatle, rose no higher than Number 191 in the US chart. Mantovani would never cover 'No Time Or Space'.

Self-indulgence by individual Beatles had infiltrated their collective vinyl output on an unprecedented scale through the eight challenging minutes of 'Revolution 9', the longest track on the group's first LP – a double – on Apple. In a year in which "serious" modern composers like Terry Riley and Steve Reich were being promoted like rock stars, this patchwork of noises not usually thought of as musical was justifiably lauded in the *International Times* as a send-up of John Cage's 'Fontana Mix', a classic of its kind. In evidence on 'Revolution 9' and in other ditties during this round of sessions was Yoko Ono, who had now replaced Paul as John's creative partner, just as she had Cynthia in his affections. So too had commenced John's deviation from the spiritual pathway that George had been testing for him since 1966.

The last two to leave the Maharishi, John and George's appetites for mystical edification were more voracious than those of Ringo and Paul. Such a hunger was not unique to The Beatles, although other pop figures may not have looked to their souls' welfare if the likes of George hadn't been "so thrilled about my discoveries that I wanted to shout and tell it to everybody".[152] Nowadays, Radio 1 disc jockeys were "into" Zen macrobiotic cookery and yoga. Another sign of the times was the pragmatic opportunism of records such as The Lemon Pipers' 'Love, Beads And Meditation' and an inspired adaptation of George Formby's 'Hindu Meditating Man' by Birmingham's Alan Randall. Less superficial were the conversions of guitarists

"Mahavishnu" John McLaughlin and "Devadip" Carlos Santana to the doctrines of Bengal holy man Sri Chinmoy. Adopting the Sabud creed in 1968, Jim McGuinn of The Byrds had also assumed a new name. Purportedly, Gene Vincent had embraced Buddhism. Not committing themselves, Eric Clapton and Manfred Mann's Tom McGuinness would, nevertheless, gather some thoughts on religious matters in the respective hymns 'Presence Of The Lord', on Blind Faith's only album, and 'I Will Bring to You', which found a place in British primary school hymnals.

When united into their search for faith, Harrison and Lennon had alighted on an album that the former had brought back from the States. *Krishna Consciousness* featured the chanting of disciples of Swami Prabhupada, who, under commands from his own guru, had arrived in New York from India in 1965 to bring the maha-mantra to the West. Although disadvantaged by poverty and advanced age, he worked up a small following of acolytes dedicated enough to wear the order's citrus-coloured saffron robes, mark their faces with the white clay *tilak* sign of a servant of God and, if male, plane their scalps to a bare stubble, bar a dangling hank at the back. In crocodile procession, these *bhaktas* would jog the main streets of the Big Apple and, with finger cymbals keeping time, chant their endless mantra, "Hare Krishna, Hare Krishna, Krishna Krishna, Hare Hare/Hare Rama, Hare Rama, Rama Rama, Hare Hare," to a four-note melody that was millions of years old, according to the pamphlet they distributed *en route*. Continual repetition of Krishna's name, it read, would build up the chanter's identification with God, thereby drawing upon divine energy.

"Silent meditation is rather dependent on concentration," so George would learn, "but when you chant, it's more of a direct connection with God."[151] It could be practised even when the mind was in turbulence. Similar to what he'd gleaned from Varma, "I didn't get the feeling that I'd have to shave my head, move into a temple and do it full time."[151] Reaching this conclusion while The Beatles were still dazzling themselves with LSD were those who joined the charismatic Prabhupada and his devotees in the call-and-response group chanting that took place when their daily march terminated in Lower East Side Park. Another regular attendee was Allen Ginsberg, who sometimes accompanied the chanting on harmonium and would later lead The Fugs through a version of the mantra that appeared on their 1968 album *Tenderness Junction*. Back in the nearby temple, Prabhupada's sermons would be punctuated by stories of the all-pervading Krishna's personal incarnations taken from the *Bhagavad Gita*, the Hindu scriptures that predated the Bible. Underplaying his own later contribution, George would "see now that, because of [Prabhupada] the mantra had spread so far...more than it had in the last five centuries".[152]

As the Krishna Consciousness whirled for the first time in Kinfauns, "It was like a door opened somewhere in my subconscious, maybe from a previous life."[151] George began chanting himself, once keeping it up non-stop while driving from France to Portugal. When he listened to George's new album, John didn't go that far, usually chanting only when he was with George. When The Beatles were island hopping in Greece, the two "sang for days with ukulele banjos. We felt exalted. It was a very happy time for us."

The group's authorised biographer, Hunter Davies, blamed "the arrival in John's life of Yoko Ono"[208] for the end of The Beatles. To the general public, Lennon certainly seemed much changed since he'd taken up with her, and funny peculiar rather than funny ha-ha. Yet, although I might have dreamt it, because Yoko – small, bossy and no Madame Butterfly – obviously looked a fair old bit to John, the later 1960s brought an influx of good-looking boys hand in hand with girlfriends not conventionally beautiful onto the dance floors.

It may have been a boom time for wallflowers, but other Beatles may have hoped that, if they ignored Yoko, she would go away. In reciprocation, and contrary to John's jealous imaginings, "She wasn't particularly interested in us, anyway,"[188] said George. Through Yoko, Lennon was out on a limb, and The Beatles were less to him now than the artistic bond with her that was making him a laughing stock.

One day at Savile Row, George could no longer contain his resentment of Yoko's intrusion. Seeing red over a jibe at the other Beatles – "some of our beast friends" – in John and Yoko's contribution to 1968's fan club flexidisc, he burst into the couple's office and came straight to the point. "You know, that game of, 'I'm going to be up front, because this is what I've heard',"[156] sneered John later. Naming Dylan among those with a low opinion of uncool Yoko, Harrison went on to complain about the present "bad vibes"[155] within The Beatles' empire that were co-related with her coming. "We both sat through it," said John. "I don't know why, but I was always hoping that they would come around."[156]

Having let off steam, George did try to come around. Although, like Sissy Spacek, his love would never be the same, he and Pattie of all the other Beatle couples were most supportive of John and the soon-to-be second Mrs Lennon. George's *Electronic Sounds* could have been a gesture of artistic solidarity for John and Yoko's *Unfinished Music* series, while – with all pretensions of the Beatle four-man "brotherhood" gone – Pattie joined Yoko at the microphone for backing vocals on 'Birthday', a track destined to open the third side of the long-awaited successor to *Sgt Pepper*. George and John were the only Beatles heard on Lennon's unreleased 'What's The New Mary Jane', which, though it had lyrics and a tune, was closer to 'Revolution 9' than 'Birthday'.

Abbey Road staff were quite accustomed to half and, sometimes, only a quarter of the group being present at any given session. The Beatles didn't seem much of a group these days. "Except on disc," predicted *The Sunday Mirror*, "they will split up in 1969."[209] *Sgt Pepper* had opened floodgates for concept albums, rock operas and other questionable works requiring months in the studios, and its originators debated whether to make this next effort even more complete an entity. One proposal had been to hang each song on the idea and title of *A Doll's House* – a bit like *Wonderwall*, see, this girl and all the different characters, right, who visit her, kind of thing...

Although it encompassed the odd segue and reprise, all that the new record did was spotlight the talents of each separate Beatle. There had been a taste of this on *Revolver* and *Sgt Pepper*, but now it was out in the open. Perhaps they'd have been wiser to have divided the needle time in four and be damned, as The Pink Floyd planned to do. Instead, they functioned as each other's sessionmen, staying away if they weren't needed. "And that," said George, "was when the rot started setting in, really."[164]

It had become "Lennon and McCartney" rather than "Lennon-McCartney". George would deny it, but he was entering the lists as prime contender for their atrophied suzerainty: "I was starting to write loads of tunes, and one or two songs per album wasn't sufficient for me."[164]

Already, Paul and John had unbent enough to allow a Harrison number to grace a Beatles B-side. His last "Indian" song for the group, 'The Inner Light', parcelled a delightful melody over one of the Bombay backing tracks and a marginal adaptation of a Chinese poem from *Lamps Of Fire*.

The fact that he'd so freely lifted lyrics from another's work fuelled George Martin's long-held and deflating view that "an awful lot of George's songs do sound like something else. There actually was a song called 'Something In The Way She Moves', a James Taylor song, and that was written a long time before [Harrison] wrote his 'Something'."[210]

'Something' was also the name of a John Mayall composition for Georgie Fame that leaked into the UK Top 30 in 1965, but this track bore no more resemblance to the Harrison 'Something' than Taylor's number did. If Martin wanted to nitpick, why didn't he mention 'I'm So Tired', in which John had the gall to quote from James Ray's 'Got My Mind Set On You' or, further back, 'Run For Your Life' off *Help!*, which began with a line from Presley's 'Baby Let's Play House'?

Most of 'Something' had occurred to George when time hung heavy during one of Paul's overdubs for the double album and months, incidentally, before 'Something In The Way She Moves' was released. "I sort of just put it on ice," he'd recall, "because I thought, 'This is too easy. It sounds so simple.'"[211] With 'The Inner Light', an Abbey Road tape operator reported that he'd had "this big thing about not wanting to sing it, because he didn't feel confident that he could do the job justice".[212] So it would be with 'Something'. Momentarily, George considered passing it on to Jackie Lomax, although he felt that it was more the meat of Ray Charles, who'd lately made a gristly meal of 'Yesterday' and 'Eleanor Rigby' and was soon to tour Europe with his *protégé* Billy Preston, the youth from the Star-Club days.

One of the few British vocalists who came close to Ray's strangled vehemence was windmill-armed Joe Cocker, an ex-gas fitter from Sheffield who'd wrenched Mary Hopkin from Number One with a funereal overhaul of 'With A Little Help From My Friends' from *Sgt Pepper*. Figuring that it'd stand a better chance with a hit act than a lost cause like Jackie, George put 'Something' Joe's way "about a year before I did it, and then it took him that long to do it".[212]

The workshop ambience of Abbey Road permitted George to tape demos of 'Something' and other new compositions that were now streaming from him, such as 'Old Brown Shoe', 'Isn't It a Pity' and, from a stay at Dylan's, 'All Things Must Pass', which was inspired by the "religious and country feel" of The Band's 'The Weight'. Not meant for public ears, these weren't much more than guitar-and-voice sketches, but their very starkness often captured a strange beauty, a freshness that was invariably lost when they were reshaped by the group. Superior to the issued version was such a take of 'While My Guitar Gently Weeps', rated by many as George's greatest recording. This haunting melancholia was possibly thrust aside because Paul had just taped 'Blackbird', which was likewise sung to a lone guitar.

George's muse for 'While My Guitar Gently Weeps' appeared through a chance operation, his finger landing on the phrase "gently weeps" in a book opened at random at his parents' house. Back down south on 5 September 1968, he expected an enthusiastic response to his new song from John and Paul but "went home really disappointed".[59] There, he concocted an answer to this and future instances of artistic frustration. He was going to humbug the lads into giving his creations a fairer go. As well as the wives, more guest musicians than ever before were allowed increasingly less minor roles on Beatle recordings, from Jackie Lomax loud and clear on 'Dear Prudence' to Nicky Hopkins of The Jeff Beck Group hammering the 88s on 'Revolution'. George intended to bring in an outside party of such eminence that – like a vicar in a BBC situation comedy – his mere presence would compel the other three to bite back on their nonsense.

This would require delicate handling, though, and so, after

mentally rehearsing what he would say, George telephoned to ask Eric Clapton if he'd mind giving him a lift to the next evening's session. Taken aback by his friend's next request, Eric's gut response was, "I can't come. Nobody's ever played on Beatle records. The others won't like it."[211] Nevertheless, turning a thoughtful steering wheel as they neared Abbey Road, he relented, but still felt a gatecrasher as George escorted him into Studio Two. Within minutes, he realised that there was something rotten in the state of the group. Nothing was seen of John during the entire seven hours that Eric was there. On the previous night, Ringo had returned to The Beatles after resigning a fortnight earlier with more than his fill of sitting on the fence, as the shirtiness and provocative indifference mounted up. Yet he and Paul "were as good as gold",[213] smiled the crafty George as they and their distinguished visitor laid down a version of 'While My Guitar Gently Weeps' that he deemed satisfactory. A bonus – and a sure sign of esteem – was Clapton's gift of "Lucy", his beloved cherry-red Les Paul on which he'd delivered solos that were to be among the high points of the collection that they'd now decided to call nothing as ambivalent as *A Doll's House* but just *The Beatles*.

A more dubious accolade for Eric on *The Beatles* was George's 'Savoy Truffle', which – paling beside the storming 'While My Guitar Gently Weeps' – was notable for its raucous saxophone section and the purpose for which it had been composed, which had been "to tease Eric. He's got this, real sweet tooth, and he'd just had his mouth worked on. His dentist said he was through with candy, so, as a tribute, I wrote, 'You'll have to have them all pulled out after the Savoy Truffle.'"[59] It wasn't so peculiar to Clapton, however, that it couldn't refer to any chocolate addict with self-inflicted toothache.

Why did 'Savoy Truffle' – stuffed with the latest slogans – and, as much of a muchness, 'Long Long Long' make it onto *The Beatles* when stronger Harrison material didn't? Possibly a green-eyed monster whispered to McCartney and Lennon, when he thought about it nowadays, that George – heaven forbid – might catch up on either of them as The Beatles' most self-contained and commercial force. And why not? "He was working with two brilliant songwriters," reasoned John, "and he learned a lot from us. I wouldn't have minded being

George the invisible man."[80] Of the new, clever music coming from inside the old Harrison, George Martin justified his previous condescension towards the baby of the group: "He'd been awfully poor up to then, actually. Some of the stuff he'd written was dead boring. The impression is sometimes given that we put him down. I don't think we ever did, but possibly we didn't encourage him enough."[210]

Whereas John could get away with 'Revolution 9' and Paul with the sugary reggae pastiche 'Ob-La-Di-Ob-La-Da', George, like a travelling salesman with a foot in the door, had to make a pitch with his most enticing samples: "The numbers I think are the easiest to get across will take the shortest time to make an impact [and will] sound the nicest tunes."[213] One that struck the right note for a while – especially with John – was 'Not Guilty'. "Even though it was me getting pissed off with Lennon and McCartney for the grief I was catching during the making of the album, I said I wasn't guilty of getting in the way of their careers and of leading them astray in our all going to Rishikesh to see the Maharishi. I was sticking up for myself, and the song came off strong enough to be saved and utilised."[59] But not on The Beatles, despite ear-catching qualities like odd spasms of syncopation, insistent heavy-handed drumming and the low-down guitar riff that broke into fading canon on the coda.

Glancing up from a newspaper, George Martin pressed the intercom button to warn Harrison that, if he put it up a key, he'd have even greater difficulty with the falsetto bit. It was feasible that everyone at Abbey Road could stand only so many fantastic versions of 'Not Guilty', which ran to a marathon 100 takes.

At least George couldn't complain that this song hadn't had a fair hearing. Now he was being treated more like an equal than a servant. A few months after The Beatles at last made the shops, the rocking 'Old Brown Shoe' became his second Beatles flip-side. Was it so unreasonable for George to hold in his heart the exciting hope that one day his would be the composition chosen to be the hit, like 'All You Need Is Love' or 'Hey Jude'? Only then would he no longer be an also-ran in the eyes of the world, lucky to have gone the distance with John and Paul. 'Wah-Wah', a song he wrote in 1969, said as much: "You've made me such a big star/being there at the right time." 'Don't Bother

Me' had been teased from a shy, ponderous boy by Bill Harry, who still bumped into a "completely different" George Harrison who had "confidence in himself where it wasn't so obvious before. He wasn't under the domination of the others. He wasn't a passenger any more."

11 The Gravedigger

Assessing the decade of which he'd be forever an archetype, George Harrison said, "At the beginning of the '60s, people would think you were a freak if you did yoga exercises, but now a huge percentage of the world does yoga exercises. I think the '60s did help to broaden understanding. When someone [male] liked long hair, people used to think he was from a zoo, but now a lot of barriers have been broken."[214]

Middle-class fathers in breakfast rooms would comment disparagingly about them, but by 1969 hippies were common enough, even in English country towns and the American Midwest.

Better late than never, *New Zealand Truth* reported that a group called The Underdogs had 'Gone To Pot' by performing 'The Inner Light' on prime-time television wearing flower-power get-up at least two years past its sell-by date. With more dignity, Frank Sinatra – the jackpot of all songwriters – was feeling his way through a "contemporary" album of numbers by the likes of Judy Collins and Glen Campbell. More pertinent vinyl artefacts of the year in which Neil Armstrong took his small step were David Bowie's 'Space Oddity' and Don Partridge's 'Breakfast On Pluto'.

There wasn't much to get worked up about any more. On the six o'clock news, terrorised Palestinian children, bombings in Belfast, a stabbing at a free Rolling Stones concert near San Francisco and the Sharon Tate bloodbath now horrified viewers as much as a shoot-out in a spaghetti western. The "death" of Paul McCartney was a mere amusement, with morbid Beatle-ologists seeing the cover of the group's *Abbey Road* LP as a funeral march, with John as the Priest,

Paul the Deceased, scruffy George as the Gravedigger and Ringo as the Sexton. Who Killed Cock Robin? Moptop McCartney Manslaughter Mystery!?

Had it been only the previous October that *The International Times* had exclaimed, "Charlie Manson is just a harmless freak"?[215] He and his "Family" had had *The Beatles* on instant replay as they'd prepared for the Tate murders, having heard revolutionary messages in Paul's 'Helter Skelter' and George's 'Piggies', an attack on clichéd targets "in their starched white shirts". Translated by Manson as a call to arms was the throwaway line "what they need's a damn good whacking", originally suggested by George's mother to rhyme with "there's something lacking".

"Revolution is this year's flower-power"[216] – so Frank Zappa had summed up in 1968, when, with Vietnam the common denominator, kaftans had been mothballed as their former wearers followed the crowd to genuinely violent anti-war demonstrations and student sit-ins to protest against "all these old fools who are governing us and bombing us and doing all that".[178] That was what George Harrison called them in *Melody Maker* last week, wasn't it? Still seen as founts of wisdom, The Beatles had chewed over a Zapple interview album with Daniel Cohn-Bendit, organiser of the New Left *événements* in France that May, even though a screening of *Wonderwall* in Cannes was disrupted by a political rally stoked up by "Danny the Red". Bluestocking girls went cow-eyed over Cohn-Bendit, but not as much as they did over the late Cuban *guerrillero* Che Guevara, who was, said George, another who wanted "to change the outward physical structure when really that automatically changes if the internal structure is straight. Christ said, 'Put your own house in order,' and Elvis said, 'Clean up your own back yard,' so if everybody just fixes themselves up first instead of trying to fix everybody else up like the Lone Ranger, then there isn't any problem."[3]

Although the United States took them as seriously as ever, The Beatles had become less pin-ups than favourite – if slightly dotty – uncles in Britain. Nevertheless, they weren't so far above the adoration of schoolgirls that they didn't have recent group photographs available on request for *Jackie* and *Fabulous 208*. The folded arms and unsmiling demeanour of each detached individual reflected the mood that had permeated sessions for *The Beatles*, which to the critic still snowblinded by *Sgt Pepper* were "joyful music-making which only the ignorant will not hear".[178] More privy to the outfit's internal rifts, *Beatles Monthly* was soon to cease publication, not through falling readership – far from it – but "because they are not The Beatles but four separate personalities. It is comparatively rare to find them together."[217]

They couldn't even manage to be in the same room to tape fan-club flexi-discs any more, hence John's annoying "beast friends" dialogue of 1968, unheard by the others until it was mastered. George could hardly spare time for this annual formality now. All he did that year was introduce a 'Nowhere Man' by the late Tiny Tim, an American entertainer whose castrati warble and doe-eyed eccentricities George found endearing enough to relay the heartening message, "You are a gas," as that exquisite was about to make a UK debut at the Albert Hall. George wasn't even in the country when Lennon and McCartney recorded 'The Ballad Of John And Yoko' as The Beatles' final British Number One – and their worst since 'Can't Buy Me Love'.

Paul and John's congeniality as they piled up this single's overdubs had been at odds with "the most miserable session on earth"[156] – Lennon's words – a few months earlier. This vain endeavour to get back to their Mersey Beat womb had been precipitated by McCartney's raising of the subject of touring again. The quickest to forget how dreadful it had been in 1966, he saw it partly as a means to stop the group's disintegration. George was not so averse to such a scheme now. "I agree with what John says about the old days. We were really rocking. We had fun, you know? We really had fun."[32] In as far back as 1967, he'd expressed hope that "The Beatles will tour again, but...I just couldn't stand all the police and crowds and helicopters in Shea Stadium and the scene that goes with it".[218]

Their rejection of a six-figure sum for 13 American dates in 1969 indicated that maybe a tour wasn't the answer to "the idea of being up there, not knowing what you're doing in front of a lot of people which is the fun of it".[218] George liked the notion of a residency like the one they'd had in Hamburg. "Then you've got your amps and drums set up and got used to the one sound."[218] Shortly after an announcement of Presley's televised comeback over Christmas 1968, *Melody Maker* was first with news of three Beatles concerts before the cameras at London's Roundhouse. There were even stranger stories circulating of impending engagements at what was left of the Cavern, on the steps of Liverpool cathedral, in an asylum and aboard a ship. All that was certain was that, on The Beatles' next LP, there'd be nothing that couldn't be reproduced on stage. "It's the old guitar, bass and drums bit again," explained George. "After going through all those things with *Sgt Pepper*, it'll be a regular simple single LP with about 14 tracks."[219]

Tiring of psychedelia sooner than The Beatles, the Stones had dug down to a raw three-chord bedrock with 'Jumping Jack Flash', perhaps their most enduring single. On *Beggar's Banquet*, the album that followed, it was clear that they – like most of The Beatles – had fallen under the spell of Bob Dylan and The Band's recordings, in which unvarnished arrangements and lyrical directness had steered pop from backward-running tapes, sitars and self-conscious symbolism. Rock 'n' roll revival was in the air as Bill Haley and Buddy Holly reissues sneaked into the charts and classic rock medleys closed the shows of "nice little bands" whose names – Tea And Symphony, Audience, Puce Exploding Butterfly – implied musical insights less immediately comprehensible. Entertaining a truer underground than these denizens of the college circuit were up-and-coming provincial combos led by actual Teddy Boys such as "Crazy" Cavan and Shakin' Stevens. Across the Atlantic, others such as Sha Na Na, Flash Cadillac and Cat Mother were also carrying a torch for the 1950s.

Now George was enthusing about Little Richard again ("that's who I'd love to record"[22]), just as he had about Ravi Shankar. Despite its prosaic title and plain white cover, the music of *The Beatles* suddenly seemed over-produced and too clever. "It's like 'Revolution'," said George. "I still think the best version is the one which we did on a Ampex four-track machine with acoustic guitars and Ringo just bashing on maracas."[220] From the perspective of security and experience gained since 'Love Me Do', he and the other mellowed Beatles hoped to "get as funky as we were in the Cavern".[219] Instead, they only hastened their sour freedom from each other.

They spoke less often of where it would take place, but rehearsals for a concert began in January 1969 in Twickenham Film Studios. Killing two birds with one stone, a film crew was on hand to document every unforgiving minute. If the worst came to the worst, the best bits could be stuck together for the movie still owed to United Artists. Most would watch it to the bitter end, whatever it was like, as they had *Magical Mystery Tour*, although you couldn't help wondering if they'd have been as committed if it'd been Dave Dee, Dozy, Beaky, Mick And Tich bickering, playing old songs and hitting trouble as soon as they tried anything new.

George breezed into Twickenham fully re-adjusted to Greenwich Mean Time after a leisurely crossing from New York just before Christmas. This most productive visit to the States had been principally to record sessions for the Jackie Lomax LP at Western Recording Studios in Los Angeles, where he'd also found time for Tiny Tim's 'Nowhere Man'. With this ineffable gentleman in tow, he and Pattie were the most famous among celebrities who looked in at a Frank Sinatra session, also at Western. Impressing George more than the middle-of-the-road material that the venerable Sinatra was tackling was how much was accomplished in one evening, compared to the months of remakes and scrapped tracks that had had to be endured for *The Beatles*. After only two takes, Frank and his orchestra had 'Little Green Apples' in the bag – no arguments, no overdubs – and on to the next number. At 11pm, they wrapped up. Maybe one of his entourage had had to remind him which Beatle had just been chatting to him, but the photograph of them together might do for the back of the album to show that Ol' Blue Eyes was hip.

On the way home, the Harrisons stopped off at Bearsville, where Bob Dylan was also readying himself for an album interspersed with recent easy-listening standards. Assisting him on this atypical venture – misleadingly titled *Self Portrait* – was guitarist David Bromberg, a Columbia University graduate who, like Dylan, had been drawn into the Greenwich Village folk scene. Before leaving, George supplied a melody for 'The Hold-Up', a song for Bromberg's debut album.

Fresh from this pleasant interlude, George returned to The Beatles with favourable memories of the easy but respectful professionalism of the US session musicians under his command for is *This What You Want* and Sinatra's brisk finesse. So, on a winter's morn, he faced the cameras, his three colleagues and the immovable Yoko in a draughty film set-cum-rehearsal room for Paul's latest wheeze. "Straight away, it was back to the old routine. Being together for so long, one of the problems became that we pigeon-holed each other."[211] Since school, he'd been the guitarist who had been at Paul and John's beck and call, along with their dogsbody drummer.

In every sense, they warmed up every day to whatever anyone – usually Paul – began to play. Like Pavlov's dogs, they reacted instinctively to the prelusive "Weeeeeell" that had pitched them into countless twelve-bar rockers back in the Star-Club. Spanning 15 years, numbers with all the standard chord changes and others long learnt by rote accumulated on footage and tape, most of them resurfacing on numerous bootleg recordings but otherwise unreleased. Sometimes they'd peter out, if bedevilled by a forgotten middle eight or words that the vocalist couldn't be bothered to la-la any more. George led them through a fistful of Dylan songs, but less predetermined was the looser jamming in which Yoko played a leading role. Anything went – 'Three Cool Cats', 'The Harry Lime Theme', 'Michael Row The Boat Ashore', 'You Can't Do That', 'Love Me Do'. Even the once-detested 'The One After 909' now had period charm.

Any euphoria that these ambles down memory lane had wrought would fade when they came up against each other's new compositions. Even Ringo had one. In keeping with both the flagrant spirit of self-interest and the uncluttered production choice, anything that needed thinking about got a thumbs-down. George could only get past quality control with 'I Me Mine' – a dissertation of egocentricity that took longer to explain than write – and 'For You Blue', a straight twelve-bar. The lyrics to 'For You Blue' bore out a recent and extraordinary remark of his that was either tongue in cheek or a vainglorious attempt to align himself with Dylan: "I now want to write songs that don't have any meaning, because I'm a bit fed up with people saying, 'Hey, what's it all about?' It's still all 'Within You Without You', but I don't want to go into that any more, because now I'm being a rock 'n' roll star."[27]

If George was full of himself after his American trip, Paul was there to take him down a peg or two. The self-appointed and barely tolerated leader of The Beatles since John's tacit abdication, McCartney was so purposefully confident that, "when he succumbed to playing one of your tunes, he'd always do good, but you'd have to do 59 [sic] of Paul's songs before he'd even listen to one of yours".[52] Sooner than either could guess, Paul would inform his solicitor that Harrison had actually quarrelled with everybody during these sessions. George actually appeared to derive supercilious amusement as Ringo ran through his little 'Octopus' Garden', and his frankness about Yoko still rankled with John, but it was the Beatle he'd known the longest who drove him over the brink: "The very first day, Paul went into this 'you do this, you do that, don't do this, don't do that', and I thought, 'Christ, I thought he'd woken up by now.'"[221] Frustrated to the point of retaliation, George was no longer prepared to studiously avoid confrontation or continue to be Paul's artistic pawn.

His would be one of the quieter departures that aggravated the absolute one. After the worst *had* come to the worst, the film did come out. Entitled *Let It Be*, after Paul's magnum opus, it contained "a scene where Paul and I are having an argument and we're trying to cover it up. Then, the next scene, I'm not there."[32] Not knowing why this was, the reviewer for *The Morning Star* had still been aware of "George Harrison's shut-in expressions".[222] Up until his temporary disappearance, George's glowering huff at Paul's subtle harangues had welled to overflowing. "You're so full of shit, man,"[223] was his rejoinder to Paul's proposal to play a show amid desert ruins in Tunisia.

The last straw was when it transpired that McCartney had already ordered an aeroplane to be put on standby to carry The Beatles to Tunis. The assumption that they'd bend to his will was but one aspect of – as George's court statement would attest – Paul's "superior attitude". Of course, if it hadn't been Paul, he might have focused his resentment on the early starts, Yoko's screech-singing, John's passiveness or a film technician who hummed all the bloody time. It took a week for him to up and quit the chilly encampment with mains leads fanning out in all directions across the hollow chamber. "I didn't care if it was The Beatles," he said. "I was getting out."[59]

After slamming his car door in Kinfauns' forecourt, he immediately directed his anger to a creative end: "Getting home in the pissed-off mood, I wrote 'Wah-Wah'. I had such a headache with the whole argument."[59] None of the others thought to either remonstrate or plead with him to return, although Ringo called with a reminder of the following week's business meeting. With a less specific grievance, Ringo had been the same during *The Beatles*, and George's walk-out, like Ringo's, was viewed as a registered protest rather than boat-burning.

Although he was over-boisterous, Paul was trying at least to whip the group into action. Who else would? Certainly not George, who, in his self-imposed exile, polished up the epigram, "Resistance to dominance does not determine fitness for leadership."[224] Ringo's meeting was not, however, conducted as if nothing had happened. Paul could no longer believe that he held The Beatles in the hollow of his hand. He and John looked at George with new respect. Who'd have thought it? This was George with an unprecedented glint in his eye, George making a stand, George without his thumb in his mouth.

The disagreement's most beneficial outcome was a transfer to the half-finished but cosier studio in the Savile Row basement. The strained atmosphere, however, could only be alleviated by George employing his 'While My Guitar Gently Weeps' strategy, "because having a fifth person there, it sort of off-set the vibes".[211]

Instead of a guitarist, George's eyes fell on Billy Preston, whom Ray Charles had predicted "will follow in my footsteps".[225] Preston's first LP, *Sixteen-Year-Old Soul*, and a recommendation from Sounds Incorporated had led to a regular spot on *Shindig*, where his jovial personality and energetic keyboard dexterity impressed Charles, with whom he recorded another well-received album, *The Wildest Organ In Town*. This spawned a modest US hit, 'Billy's Bag', and the appreciation by other artists as a "musician's musician".

It was after a Royal Festival Hall concert with Charles that Billy renewed his acquaintance with George Harrison. There was an amicable exchange of telephone numbers and an invitation from George to drop in at Savile Row. On 22 January, he and Paul were about to descend into the Apple basement when "Billy walked into the office. I just grabbed him, and brought him down to the studio."[211]

Preston's coming did, indeed, lift the strike-happy depression. On their best behaviour, the group were more receptive to each other's new material. Constructive advice was offered as the three principal composers demonstrated nascent arrangement of songs destined for either one of the two albums left in The Beatles, or on those that began their lives apart. However, although Paul was keen for it to be the next single, his saccharine 'Maxwell's Silver Hammer' was derided as "granny music" by John and "so fruity"[59] by George. First refusal on some of George's items would be given to Billy, whose catalytic effect on the *Let It Be* sessions was about to earn him an Apple recording contract.

The ideal conclusion to the film had to be some public spectacle. Therefore, with less than a day's notice, cameras and sound equipment were made ready for a Beatles performance on Apple's flat roof. Unannounced, they and Preston shambled onto this makeshift stage to impinge upon the hearing of those as far away as Oxford Street with three-quarters of an hour of 'Get Back', 'The One After 909' and other Lennon and McCartney numbers hatched in the bowels of the building. For this, their last-ever performance, The Beatles reverted to type, John and Paul carrying the show with George and Ringo labouring away behind them. To the many that rapidly clotted along the pavements below, The Beatles were invisible and their unknown music muffled by an icy wind. Lennon, especially, was bouncing with backchat between songs, but those watching from windows opposite couldn't pretend that this was what it must have been like down the Cavern around lunchtime 1961. Some within earshot were less aware than their younger employees that they were being treated to something they could tell their grandchildren about. They weren't square, but there was a time and a place for this sort of row.

The breach of the peace was curbed, the crowds moved on, and

The Beatles wondered what poor sod they could bludgeon to edit, tart up and mix the frayed miles of *Let It Be* tapes for an album to go with the film. Throughout the project, The Beatles had subjected George Martin – no longer the awesome figure he'd been in 1962 – to much the same oafish discourtesies they rendered each other. He'd become as sick of *Let It Be* as they were, and they were tempted to ditch everything to do with it altogether. After perhaps re-reading *Shades Of Personality*, George – under duress – supplied one journalist with news containing less substance than hope. The group, he said, were soon to get their teeth into a film that would be "at least as big as *2001*. It's based on an idea we had a year ago but which fell through because of a lot of technicalities at the time. We've agreed to let each other do exactly what he wants to do with it." To this, he attached the enigmatic addenda: "We've got to a point where we can see each other quite clearly, and by allowing each other to be each other we can become The Beatles again."[226]

Quotes like this and events like the rooftop bash gave few cause to doubt that the group would continue. Like the monarchy, they were part of the national furniture. *Let It Be* had cleared some of the air and, if anything, their drifting apart seemed less inevitable than it had during *The Beatles*, when the mayhem that was Apple had been at its most uproarious. As well as the incompetents and losers they'd taken on board, rampant larceny and embezzlement by unscrupulous staff went undetected or was overlooked. Not that far from the truth would be a scene from 1978's spoof Beatles film biography *All You Need Is Cash*, in which a thinly-disguised Apple Corps' is pillaged by its employees while, in the foreground, its press agent chats to a television news commentator (played, incidentally, by George Harrison).

Enough of the Money Beatle of old remained for George to worry about drainage of the company economy. On legitimate business at Savile Row on the afternoon of the *Let It Be* finale, a freelance publicist chanced to share a lift with Harrison and Billy Preston. Smiling with his palm outstretched, he was momentarily embarrassed when George "wasn't prepared to shake hands and get another Beatle fan out of the way. He wanted to know who I was and what I was doing in Apple."[227]

A letter from the group's accountant disabused George that his financial means were infinite. His overdraft on the corporate account of over £30,000 was light against those of John and Paul, whose composing royalties admittedly gave more leeway for extravagance. Although Pattie hung onto her shares in Northern Songs, George had sold his small stake to form a separate and more personally lucrative publishing division, Singsong Ltd. He was therefore well out of it when ATV – amid impotent howls of rage from McCartney and Lennon – managed to buy a majority shareholding of Northern Songs in the late spring of 1969.

Since the loss of Brian Epstein, some of The Beatles' antics – particularly John's – had given Northern Songs' executive founder, Dick James, pause for agonised wonder, but the root cause of his selling his percentage to ATV was what he saw as their supreme folly: the appointment of Allen Klein as their business manager on 3 February 1969. Former clients were caustic about this American go-getter with a brain that spewed forth estimates at a moment's notice; his Tony Curtis haircut atop a boyish face and Barney Rubble frame; his golf-course clothes; and his forward-thrusting gait. Once so pleased with Klein's bellicose interventions on the Stones' behalf, Mick Jagger now took the trouble to call at Apple to dissuade The Beatles from signing with one he suspected of sharp practice. Klein, however, was already there, spieling in top gear.

Mick later rang John, but, following the latter's lead, George and Ringo had already melted into Klein's contractual caress. Although he'd been the first to champion the new administrator, Paul was now the only dissident. To disentangle Apple's disordered threads, he'd advocated his own father-in-law, who'd turned out to be not Sir Richard Asher of Wimpole Street but a New York lawyer named Lee Eastman.

The Harrisons had been unable to attend Linda Eastman and Paul's wedding celebrations on 12 March. If he'd finished a Jackie Lomax session on time, George had intended to meet Pattie at the reception at the Ritz Hotel. That afternoon, however, he was summoned to the studio telephone. Trying to keep calm, Pattie told him that Kinfauns had been invaded. This time, she wished it was only fans under the bed. Armed with a search warrant, a squad of Scotland Yard officers and Yogi, a sniffer dog, had reason to believe that the premises were being used for the consumption of controlled drugs, contrary to the provision of the 1966 Dangerous Drugs Act, section 42. Unconvinced by Pattie's air of fluffy innocence, Yogi and his colleagues executed their duties under the direction of plain-clothes Sergeant Norman Pilcher, who had busted John Lennon in the previous October. National treasures or not, The Beatles weren't above the law any more.

By the time George's engine died on Claremont Drive, the hunt was over and Pattie was most hospitably serving coffee as her persecutors relaxed in front of the television or listened to records. "It was like a social club,"[144] George thought as he and his wife were charged with possession of 570 grains of cannabis and a quantity of cocaine. Most of this, Pilcher of the Yard would inform Walton-on-Thames Magistrates Court, was uncovered in a wardrobe, a shoe box and Mrs Harrison's handbag. Years later, after Pilcher had been jailed for corrupting the course of justice, George felt at liberty to protest, "I'm a tidy man. I keep my socks in the sock drawer and my stash in the stash box. Anything else they must have brought."[144]

Pleading guilty, nonetheless, he and Pattie were fined £250 each. Then followed a minute of comedy when George asked for the return of a Crown exhibit, an ornamental peace pipe on which had been found traces of illegal resin. It was a present, he added, from the Native American Church of Peyote Indians. The judge couldn't see why not, as long as "Mr Harrison doesn't mind if we first remove the drugs".[228] The more trivial tabloids also stressed the irony of a dog called Yogi bringing the most spiritual Beatle to book.

"You are a very holy man!" a lady in a fur coat had shouted at Lennon as he and Yoko had emerged from their court appearance. Although he was lapsing, John was still seen by many as The Beatles' "official religious spokesman",[57] as George had once called him; the Aaron to the less loquacious George's Moses. To say things most people didn't want to hear, the Lennons had made their lives an open and ludicrous book now that they'd started week-long bed-ins for world peace in posh hotels, holding press conferences from inside king-sized white sacks and engaging in further bewildering pranks too indecent for a family newspaper.

After a new angle as a change from weeks of Lennon's headline-hogging outrage, some journalists wondered if George wasn't just as screwy on the quiet. On the afternoon following his court sentence, he'd received a conveyor belt of press in his Savile Row office after changing from a sober blue suit to jumper and jeans. During his audience, the *Music Echo* correspondent logged the presence in the white room of both an unnamed "weird American woman gibbering incessantly" and "members of a quasi-religious cult calling itself the 'Khrishna [*sic*] Consciousness Society'".[299] As far as *Music Echo* could see, this Khrishna lot were no different from any other in the passing show of lunatics that infested Apple.

These days, it was understood by the receptionist that shaven-headed chaps dressed in orange sheets had something to do with George. Often, he and they would be heard on the roof chanting their unremitting maha-mantra. Even when they left, he'd continue *sotto voce* about the offices, sometimes dirging other bhajans by way of variation. Devotees were welcome at Kinfauns, too, for vegetarian feasts, with such occasions concluding (as was proper) with a bout of Hare Krishnas to synthesiser accompaniment by either their host or Billy Preston. As they didn't squander their appetites on stimulants, George was also striving – with incomplete success – to eschew soft drugs, cigarettes, caffeine and alcohol.

When Prabhupada's movement had extended a feeler into England, it was, to George, "just like another piece of a jigsaw puzzle that was coming together to make a complete picture".[152] His first practical response was to co-sign the lease for the Radha Krishna Temple (named after the avatar's closest earthly consort) in Holborn, which, if rather dilapidated, was handy for the regular-as-clockwork chanting processions up and down the principal thoroughfares of central London, mainly Oxford Street.

"I was never with the Hare Krishna movement," George would insist later. "I was just friends with them."[230] In 1969, however, a tale went the rounds that he'd almost become a full-time *bhakta*, bald head and all, but had cried off because Prabhupada himself had soundly advised that he'd be more useful as a pop star. On his death-bed in 1977, the swami would twist a ring from his finger and instruct it to be delivered to George, whom he called his "archangel". There were reasons aplenty for the expiring Prabhupada's gratitude. From George's purse had poured the means for founding and provisioning many temples and yoga-ashrams, as well as the printing of Krishna books, some of which contained Harrison forewords and interviews. "All part of the service,"[152] he reckoned of his astounding feat of steering the mantra into the Top 20 in September 1969.

As much a freak hit as those of The Singing Dogs or, more appropriately, The Singing Nun, The Radha Krishna Temple's accelerando 'Hare Krishna Mantra' on Apple was a smoother affair than The Fugs' version, with most of its accompaniment – harmonium, guitar, percussion and bass – manufactured by George just before a session for *Abbey Road*, The Beatles' next album. The strangest act ever invited to be on *Top Of The Pops*, the devotees nonetheless held their own amid the likes of Creedence Clearwater Revival, The Bee Gees and instrumental duo Sounds Nice, who were particular favourites of Pattie's.

Some chuckled incredulously when the chanters flashed into their living rooms, but thanks to George the irrepressible 'Hare Krishna Mantra' had encroached on public consciousness to a degree that Prabhupada could never had imagined in 1966. The milkman whistled it, it became fodder for comedians' gags and even a vinyl spoof in Harry H Corbett's 'Harry Krishna'. A rendition was a punch-line in a *Crackerjack* sketch on BBC's children's television.

More satisfying than these dubious accolades were the full houses at the movement's initiatory evenings. Admission was free, but some attendees arrived in anticipation of a pop show or of seeing George Harrison. After the talks, the slide shows, the Indian dancing and the performances by The Vedic Ensemble For Dramatic Arts, they were mollified when the Temple band played the hit – an audience-participation number – and hearty refreshments were served at the end. Nevertheless, there were many new converts and an even bigger increase of sympathisers who no longer regarded a line of Hare

Krishna chanters down Oxford Street with sidelong scepticism or contemptuous amusement.

Doing no harm either was the follow-up single, 'Govinda' – Krishna reincarnated as a shepherd boy – which was an actual verse-chorus song rather than a repeated chant. Its Sanskrit lyrics aside, with its muted but driving beat 'Govinda' didn't sound out of place on the juke box in the greasiest cafe. Although they'd made the charts and Jackie Lomax hadn't, The Radha Krishna Temple weren't pop stars any more than The Joystrings had been. As His Divine Grace would expect of them, it was *Top Of The Pops* today and back on the streets tomorrow.

Teaching by example, the ascetic Prabhupada, author of more than 70 profitable theological books, didn't stint on a vigorous global schedule of lecture tours, allowing himself only the barest minimum of material wants. The "humble servant of the servant of the servant of Krishna"[151] made money but had no wish to own it. In 1969, he and his closest disciples were in England, where they were put up in an annex on Tittenhurst Park, the Lennons' newly-acquired 80-acre estate between Ascot and Sunningdale. It was in these quarters on a cold and rainy afternoon that George, John and Yoko were conducted into the master's presence. Well into his 70s, he was a squat, brown, rather ugly old bloke whose lined features were relieved by an underlying humour. Where the Maharishi might have cackled, Prabhupada only twinkled. He and Yoko did most of the talking, enabling George to note that, although he sometimes lapsed into Sanskrit, "He never came off as somebody above you. He always had the child-like simplicity"[152] His Divine Grace had a feeling that, during his Calcutta boyhood, he had known the unborn Lennon in a previous existence as a businessman/philanthropist. Yet, in his self-inflicted poverty and his devotion to the purity of his ancient creed, Prabhupada seemed more plausible to the wary Beatles than the Westernised Maharishi.

At first, the new guru impressed John more than George, until "I realised later on that he was much more incredible than what you could see on the surface".[152] Whatever the rumoured zenith of George's personal commitment to the Krishna movement, his

perspective just prior to Prabhupada's death was, "He is my friend.
he is my master, who I have great respect for. It's like, if you want to
learn how to ski, you go to somebody who'll teach you how to ski. I
accept Prabhupada as qualified to teach people about Krishna."[32]

"Better than Disneyland"[152] was the Society's Bhagavad Gita
museum in Los Angeles, from which the Harrisons ordered a life-
sized fountain/statue of the demigod Siva to be delivered to their new
home when they found it. There wasn't space at Kinfauns either for
the four-poster bed, still to be collected from an antiques shop. From
a vocational viewpoint, too, "The house isn't really big enough to
have a proper studio. I've got all sorts of equipment together, but
there's hardly room to move."[231] Whatever building George chose
was less important than its surroundings. Although he'd recently
roamed New York backstreets virtually unrecognised in non-descript
denims and crêpe-soled work shoes, he – like John – required
abundant grounds, "because I am seeking the absolute peace of
complete privacy. I am also insisting on a private lake, because water
is very peaceful for the mind."[231]

All four Beatles had been house-hunting of late. As well as being
subject to supertax in the "one big Coronation Street"[231] (George's
phrase) that was Britain, a problem facing all four was that of greedy
estate agents forcing up asking prices for those they assumed had
wealth beyond calculation. The Harrison solution was to send an
Apple subordinate masquerading as a prospective buyer to look
around and report on likely-looking properties on the market. On one
occasion, an ivy-clung manor from the pages of *Country Life* was so
intriguing that they had to inspect it in person. The plan was for
Alistair Taylor and Pattie – in untrendy twin-set and pillbox hat – to
pose as a newly married couple, with George as the liveried chauffeur
of his own white Mercedes. His neglecting to open smartly its doors
for his passengers implanted instant suspicion in the pile's lady owner.
This grew with the frequency of Pattie and Alistair's scarcely
suppressed giggles as they kept contradicting each other. Back at the
front door, she glanced again at the driver, his hair pinned under a
peaked cap, staring fixedly ahead. A great light dawned and she turned
to Pattie to ask whether Mr Harrison wanted to see the house as well.

While George and Pattie's search continued, the Starkeys had moved from Surrey to Highgate after purchasing the home of a friend, Peter Sellers, with whom Ringo was co-starring in *The Magic Christian* in his first major film role. A fascinated observer, George looked on at several location shootings, which varied from Henley-on-Thames railway station to an Atlantic crossing on the *QE2*. This excursion was marred when, intending to stage another bed-in on arrival in New York, the Lennons were denied a visa because of John's drug conviction. Less notorious, the Harrisons had already understood that their own police record "means restrictions on where we travel in future".[228] Sellers' commiseration with them confirmed George's opinion that the distinguished comedian/actor was "a devoted hippy, a free spirit".[59] As a guest speaker at an Oxford Union debate, he'd been applauded for his honesty in admitting that he'd smoked cannabis.

Assisting Sellers with *The Magic Christian* screenplay were fellow humorists John Cleese and Graham Chapman, who were on the team of *Monty Python's Flying Circus*, then in the midst of its maiden series on BBC2. Their humour had similarities with that contained in Lennon's own slim volumes in its casual cruelty and stream-of-consciousness transmogrification, and seemed to be the culmination of all that had tickled George about fringe comedy since The Goons. Watching the first show in the company of Derek Taylor, "I couldn't understand how normal television could continue after that."[188] As was his expensive habit then, he sent a telegram straight away to Broadcasting House: "Love the show. Keep doing it."

Although he wasn't one of those people who re-enacted the Dead Parrot Sketch or the Five-Minute Argument at work, he took to quoting lines from Monty Python as frequently as those of Bob Dylan. Advantaged by his celebrity, he came to mix socially with the outfit that – so it was whispered – were to comedy what The Beatles were to pop.

George's enjoyment of this programme was a minor comfort during a year beset with more than just Beatle traumas. Pattie had been his muse for 'Something' and the beginnings of a song entitled 'Beautiful Girl', but the marriage had floated into a choppy sea. Her absence at that first audience with Prabhupada was a symptom of an increasing disinclination to play Yoko to George's John. Her personality precluded as deep an engrossment in spiritual pursuits as her husband. She wanted a bit of frivolity, for a change – and there were others after a bit of frivolity, too. George – console midwife to 'The King Of Fuh' – had become rather sanctimonious about certain London theatre presentations since the abolition of stage censorship in 1968. Nevertheless, Pattie took her seat in the Roundhouse on the opening night of *Oh! Calcutta*, a musical with much nudity and explicit language. With George's blessing, male companions such as Derek Taylor or Eric Clapton accompanied her on this and like occasions almost like 18th-century *cavaliere servantes*. Clapton, however, tired of always meeting her in public.

While Pattie resisted being alone with Eric, stray mutterings about her spouse's extra-marital picayunes filtered around Savile Row's offices, but the later memoirs of former Apple associates offer scant evidence that George was ever unfaithful to his wife. However, Lennon's confessions to *Rolling Stone* in 1970 about The Beatles' amatory adventures on tour may have provoked some frank exchanges in the Harrison living room. George himself was as indiscreet in 1977, attributing Clapton's coveting of Pattie to "trying to get his own back on me. I pulled his chick [*sic*] once."[32]

George confided the dilution of his marriage to a favoured "Apple Scruff", his nickname for a constant loiterer around its steps. No ordinary fans, some Scruffs were nomads from other continents, mainly America. A handful had clogged the pavement for so long that, in this less hectic phase of The Beatles stardom, they'd understood how privately ordinary, even boring, were the icons they'd once worshipped from afar. Some felt oddly disappointed when George began offering conversation as a preferred alternative to irritably signing his autograph while hurrying from kerb to doorway. Adoration, however, would be years a-dwindling. In February 1969, after George's tonsillectomy at University College Hospital, its switchboard had been jammed with requests for the gruesome excisions.

Through daily contact with the Scruffs, George's presumptions about fans had altered. No longer a screaming mass as amorphous as frogspawn, "their part in the play is equally as important as ours".[226] If he was in the mood and Savile Row was quiet, he'd reserve a little attention for certain Scruffs that he knew by name, asking after their families, noticing whether they'd had a haircut and bringing them up to date with progress on Abbey Road. Somehow, these familiarities were closer to the spirit of the Cavern than *Let It Be* had ever been.

Harrison was still as prone to idolatry as the most devout Scruff. Nonetheless, although he rarely missed Monty Python and played over and over again the same records by Electric Flag, Stoneground or whatever new US combo had briefly captivated him, he was always drawn back to Bob Dylan. As John had been fixated in 1965, so Dylan cropped up in Harrison's music – here a *Blonde On Blonde* chord progression for 'Long Long Long', there a *Highway 61 Revisited* chug for 'Old Brown Shoe'. Most heartfelt a homage was 'Behind That Locked Door', a new number about "the tales you have taught me" and George's apprehensions and hopes for Bob's first major concert since his motorbike calamity.

This comeback was to be a 60-minute set with The Band at the second Isle of Wight Festival on 1969's August bank-holiday weekend. A fortnight earlier, The Band had been among those entertaining the half-million drenched Americans who'd braved the larger outdoor gathering at Woodstock just over the state border from Big Pink. From a distance of years, Woodstock would be viewed as the climax of hippy culture, a vote of no confidence in square old President Nixon and the rest of George's "old fools who are governing us".

By Woodstock standards, the three days of music on the downs above the Isle of Wight's Woodside Bay were quite well organised, in that there were a few more portable toilets, washing facilities and vendors of over-priced food and tepid soft drinks than there were at Woodstock. On the Sunday afternoon, the Harrisons, the Lennons and the Starkeys arrived by helicopter in time for John Mayer's Indo-Jazz Fusions and subsequent acts who primed the massed tribes for the main event. In a special compound before the stage, The Beatles and lesser pop aristocrats sat comfortably apart from the common herd beyond the crash barriers. In the dying minutes before Dylan,

George was taken aback when the strains of 'Hare Krishna Mantra' effused from the disc jockey's turntable. Had Bob himself paused in his backstage pacing to request that particular record for his closest Beatle friend? Mattering almost as much perhaps was whether John believed he had.

As arranged, when the show was over, Dylan boarded the Beatle helicopter to spend the night at Tittenhurst Park. His performance had been more adequate than the festival's lavatory provision and, for many, it was enough that he appeared at all. Minstrel to a generation though he was, no one had really expected the waters of the Solent to part any more than those of the Serpentine in June when Eric Clapton's Blind Faith had made its concert debut free of charge in the Cockpit, Hyde Park's natural arena.

A few weeks later, at the same venue, The Rolling Stones hosted the largest assembly for any cultural event London had ever seen. Supported by Alexis Korner, Family and new sensations King Crimson, the Stones' buckshee bash became a memorial for Brian Jones, who had drowned in his swimming pool two days earlier. George was told of the tragedy while on holiday in Sardinia. "I don't think Brian had enough love or understanding,"[233] he said.

A cohort of Brian's even before the formation of The Yardbirds, Eric Clapton was touring the States with Blind Faith. Those six weeks on the road effectively finished off "the supergroup of a time".[234] The "gentle surprise"[235] of their Cockpit performance was perverted to blaring, ham-fisted resignation when "Acclamation By Riot!" became a typical headline summary of US audience conduct.

There were enough rest days on the tour for the band members to risk flights back to English peace and quiet, but Clapton preferred to kill time by purchasing vintage American cars and shipping them back to Surrey. After dark, he began loafing around with the package's small fry, seeking the particular comradeship of a workmanlike group led by Deep South guitarist Delaney Bramlett, a former Shindog, which also included his wife Bonnie, ex-Traffic guitarist Dave Mason and a faction of Los Angeles session musicians nicknamed "the blue-eyed soul school". That faintly sickening word *funky* was used to describe the economic tightness of their rhythm section.

"They were such down-home humble cats," said Eric. "I started a rapport with Delaney and saw ahead that I didn't want Blind Faith."[236] Eric's disenchantment with the Blind Faith routine and his pleasure at bashing tambourine while hidden in the larger ranks of the preceding Delaney And Bonnie And Friends may have been kindled by press criticism aimed directly at him. By the time "the ultimate supergroup" threw in the towel at the LA Forum in August, half of its number – including Ginger Baker – were slumming it in the Bramlett tour bus.

From Clapton's own pocket came the necessary outlay for the aggressively friendly Friends' European tour in December. He'd be their lead guitarist and, they hoped, a passport to fame. A highlight of the intervening months was Eric's recruitment by John Lennon into the *ad hoc* Plastic Ono Band for a hastily rehearsed performance at a festival in Toronto of old rock 'n' roll classics and Yoko's improvisations. They also had a go at 'Cold Turkey', the second hit single that John's new group had recorded as "an escape valve from The Beatles"[173] – so he put it – from whom he'd cast his net furthest.

Back at Savile Row, George was most sarcastic about the Lennons' latest venture. He didn't care for Yoko's Plastic Ono Band input, but nonetheless felt that John had cold-shouldered him by inviting Clapton to Toronto instead. Once, it might have seemed more of a betrayal, but now The Beatles – like his marriage – were held together only by habit. "When we actually split up," George would later remember, "it was just the relief. We should have done it years before."[211] While none of them were yet brave enough to deliver the *coup de grâce*, they prepared for the eventuality, after their individual fashions, with Ringo consolidating his then-promising film career and, like Paul, recording a solo album; John with his new band and espousal of various causes; and George, apparently, attempting to compose a stage musical with Derek Taylor and the soundtrack to *Zachariah*, a western staring Ginger Baker(!), neither of which came to fruition.

Whatever else he may or may not have had up his sleeve, from 1968 George had been "getting more and more into"[201] record production, which he saw as "psychologically trying to get people to do their best without imposing on them and without letting them freak out".[201] Under his aegis, Billy Preston's 'That's The Way God Planned It' had equalled the 'Hare Krishna Mantra' high of Number Eleven in the British hit parade, although his next smash would be a long time coming. George couldn't repeat Billy's success with Doris Troy, a former *protégé* of "godfather of soul" James Brown. Her early singles had been much-demanded spins on the turntables of the "in" nightclub-discotheques that George and Pattie had frequented in their first flush of romance. Even with stirling backing from Preston, Starr, Clapton, Steve Stills and other top-notch musicians assembled by her new producer, much the same impasse loomed for Doris – no big hits but fine-quality disco fodder. Her first for George, 'Ain't That Cute', would be 1970's Soul Record Of The Year in *Melody Maker*, not far ahead of its double-sided follow-up, fiery versions of 'Get Back' and the traditional 'Jacob's Ladder'.

In hard financial terms, George may have been barking up the wrong tree with Doris, just as he had with Jackie Lomax. As Decca had passed on The Beatles, did he miss something when auditioning and rejecting Bamboo, a Swedish band that would connect genealogically with 70s chartbusters Abba? The Hollies thought highly enough of Bamboo to shanghai its lead vocalist in 1971, when Allan Clarke briefly flew the nest.

Noticeably influenced by The Hollies were The Iveys, a Liverpool-Welsh group who were renamed Badfinger by Paul McCartney. With Paul and George among their producers, they were the only Apple band other than The Beatles to enjoy any measure of chart longevity. Badfinger had descended from The Masterminds and The Calderstones, two minor Mersey Beat acts formed by lads who'd coughed up the one-shilling membership fee to catch The Hollies – and The Beatles – time after time at the Cavern. Amalgamating as The Iveys, they were managed by Bill Collins, who'd rubbed shoulders with Jim McCartney in a dance band and was father to Lewis, a latter-day Mojo and future television tough guy. For a while, the Iveys backed a Scouse operatic tenor turned pop singer who, as "David Garrick", had twice penetrated the UK Top 30 in 1966. However, it was without Garrick that they were spotted by Mal Evans and, with their pedigree an asset, groomed for greener pastures.

The fact that Apple didn't throw down a line to better-qualified supplicants like Freddie Garrity – who was interviewed by Yoko – and The Remo Four may have been because their very names were too directly associated with dear, dead Mersey Beat. Nevertheless, when the latter – shedding Colin Manley – mutated into one-hit-wonders Ashton, Gardner And Dyke, George lent an apt hand on 'I'm Your Spiritual Breadman', a track from their second LP

George also had a tinge of complacent snobbery about who was or wasn't worthy of Apple's attention. Only pop's upper crust were really suitable, by which he meant "The Beatles, Stones, Bob Dylan, Eric Clapton and Delaney And Bonnie and that's it. Who needs anything else? Oh yes, Billy Preston's very good, and eventually he'll get through to the people."[224]

Work on the *That's The Way God Planned It* album had been postponed while George also abetted the Bramletts in their projected rise to superstardom. With Ringo, he'd watched Clapton strutting his stuff with his new-found Friends when the British leg of their tour began at the Albert Hall. A little blinded by Eric's hyperbole, he remembered thinking, "That's a great band. I'd love to be playing with them,"[188] as Delaney *et al* punched out their shrill, simple and neatly dovetailed repertoire, which included club soul in the Doris Troy vein, a Little Richard medley and a sexist original entitled 'Groupie'. Buoyed by big-name approbation, they then commanded the stage of the Speakeasy in the small hours and did it all over again. George was overwhelmed by their freewheeling Southern ebullience and drove home wondering how seriously they'd been when they'd said, "OK, we're coming to your house in the morning,"[59] when he'd spoken his thoughts about their earlier performance. For that matter, how serious had *he* been?

He took the plunge after breakfast, when "they pulled up the bus outside my house and said, 'Come on!' I just grabbed a guitar and an amp and went on the road with them."[59] The last time he'd played Bristol's Colston Hall was just over five years earlier. Beatlemania might as well have been five centuries ago as the adult

Moptop took the stage at the same auditorium amongst Bramlett's rank and file in his re-grown beard, drab denims and lank hair centre-parted like John's and splayed halfway down his back. Delaney And Bonnie's name was on the poster, but it was Clapton that the customers had paid to see. No one in the crowd knew who the extra guitarist was until he was introduced near the finish. Only then was he the cynosure of all eyes. This wasn't a record cover, television or a pin-up; George Harrison of the superhuman Beatles was actually there. Not everyone grasped the magnitude of the moment that they'd been fated to witness as the pale figure continued strumming, partly obscured by those drawling exuberantly into the front microphones.

Because the show could have gone on without him, George's return to the footlights wasn't as earth-shattering as Dylan's and Lennon's had been, and yet he was solidly at the music's heart, unobtrusively ministering to the overall effect. Moreover, so little was expected of him by the band that the trek started to be quite fun, as it progressed up England's spine to engagements in Sheffield, Newcastle and, on 5 December, the Liverpool Empire, where he couldn't prevent himself from addressing the audience with the mutual truism, "This certainly brings back a lot of memories."

Diners in motorway service stations stared at him, but it was Eric who was more often accosted for autographs as he laid into a greasy but obviously satisfying fry-up. Gazing at his chum with benign fascination across the formica table, George picked at baked beans and toffee-coloured chips with less enthusiasm. The rest of the band weren't as down home or humble as Clapton had made out, and their detailing of the previous night's carnal shenanigans and stimulant intake could prove monotonous, but otherwise they were good company. Nearly all were now using the Bramletts as a springboard for better-paid, more prestigious employment. Within weeks, most would stop being Friends to enter the ranks of Joe Cocker's cumbersome big band Mad Dogs And Englishmen. The horn section of Bobby Keyes and Jim Price found it convenient to take up British residency, commuting to fulfil a work schedule that blossomed from pot-boiling sessions with comparative unknowns like Audience and Third World War to proudly augmenting The Rolling Stones. Not so openly on the make was drummer Jim Keltner, who paradoxically emerged as the most in demand of these "super sidemen", as they became known. Also, of all the Los Angeles studio crowd, he was the one with whom George felt most at ease.

While crossing the North Sea for dates in Scandinavia, Delaney And Bonnie crept into the UK Top 30 for the first and only time. Strongly in evidence on 'Coming Home' was the departed Dave Mason's bottleneck-guitar obligato. It made sense to plug this single *en route* round England, and George was asked to supply the missing element: "Delaney gave me this slide guitar and said, 'You do the Dave Mason part.' I'd never attempted anything before that, and I think my slide-guitar playing originated from that."[59]

Tuned to any open chord, the guitar's strings were fretted with a finger-sized glass or metal cylinder around the finger. From sustained shiver to undulating legato, its resonant effects are most commonly heard in the contrasting spheres of blues and Hawaiian music. Although the dobro and pedal-operated steel guitar were instruments manufactured specifically for the slide technique, money-conscious non-specialists generally made do on ordinary guitars with test-tubes, bits of piping and, in George's case, a piece hacksawed from an old amplifier stand by Mal Evans: "I had some glass slides made, also. I find the glass slide tends to be a warmer sound, whereas the metal one is more slippery and is brighter, but I couldn't tell you which one I've used where."[58] Lest we forget, 'Old Brown Shoe' had an undercurrent of bottleneck, and there had been traces of it as far back as *Rubber Soul*. However, like the sitar on 'Norwegian Wood', it had been an inappreciable novelty played on either John's Hawaiian model – bought on a whim – or on his own retuned Stratocaster.

The bottleneck or slide guitar is difficult to play creatively and well, and during the earlier week of the Delaney And Bonnie jaunt George had confined himself to a passable solo on 'Coming Home' before dropping back to hack rhythm for the rest of the set. Gaining confidence, however, he gradually inserted more bottleneck and less rhythm. After this practical experience, he continued to teach himself at home, "thinking maybe this is how I can come up with something half decent".[59] With no Shankar of the slide to instruct him or even a worthwhile manual, he was in virgin territory, but he learned what he could from records and trial and error, just as Brian Jones had in 1962. However, rather than a direct absorption of Elmore James and other black bluesmen, he favoured the almost academic approach of Los Angeles-born bottleneck exponent and music archivist Ry Cooder, with his "good touch and good ear for melody".[59]

Although he copied Cooder by winding his guitar with heavy-gauge strings and heightening its bridge, George's slide playing would become musically as distinctive a signature as the mark of Zorro. Ethnic blues had entered his stylistic arsenal too late. It had been the same with his struggles with the sitar, but to these he'd attribute a quality in his post-Beatle guitar work "that you can't put your finger on".[59]

In Sweden, during the Friends tour, he'd written his first bottleneck song, 'Woman Don't You Cry For Me' (with meagre assistance from Delaney and Eric), which strode a tightrope between skiffle and the country-and-western end of pop. During the band's three nights in Copenhagen, he started another opus, 'My Sweet Lord', in which he imagined "corresponding guitar harmonies to the bedrock slide parts"[58] and East-meets-West backing responses that cleverly alternated hallelujahs with *hare krishna*s. As all artists do sometimes, he borrowed from and disguised his source of inspiration, in this instance by tampering with the chordal accents of 'Oh Happy Day', an 18th-century traditional spiritual that had itself been overhauled to chart-climbing effect in the previous summer by US gospel choir The Edwin Hawkins Singers. Although George removed it many degrees from 'Oh Happy Day', something else about 'My Sweet Lord' remained infuriatingly familiar.

Present in Scandinavia at George's invitation, another temporary Friend, Billy Preston – now a born-again Christian – liked the finished 'My Sweet Lord' enough to want to record it when he got back to London. The Edwin Hawkins Singers, of all people, were available to help with Billy's call-and-response interplay, although nearly all of them were ignorant about what this 'Hare Krishna' bit meant. Perhaps because the final result bore too much of a melodic resemblance to 'He's So Fine', a 1963 hit by US girl group The Chiffons, it was released as a single only in Europe, where it became a medium-sized hit. It might have spared George much grief if the 'My Sweet Lord' saga had ended there.

As there would never be enough room for them on Beatles records, George was foisting more and more of his songs onto his production clients, giving the new 'You' to Ronnie Spector while Preston cut 'All Things Must Pass', but he turned his nose up at the freshly concocted 'What Is Life'.

During The Beatles' last weeks, a new face around Apple was often seen beside George at the mixing desk. Phil Spector and George were to have "a lot of good times, but I had a lot of bad times as well".[164] Although past his best, Spector had been unfortunate enough to be reeled in to cobble together an LP from the *Let It Be* tapes.

Under the Klein regime, Apple had been more inclined to fire than hire. So chilling was this new realism that those employees who'd so far survived the purge dared not clock in late or pilfer so much as a paperclip. Out had gone the luxury items and dead wood like Zapple and Apple Electronics. Jackie Lomax's small retainer was discontinued and Ronnie Spector's 'You' was cancelled. Even the faithful Alistair Taylor – not yet over glandular fever made worse by overwork – was called back to the office midway through a business lunch to be cast adrift with three months' salary. Determined to tell The Beatles of what must surely be some mistake and somehow seek their protection, Taylor and others in the same boat were at a loss to comprehend why all four were "too busy" to come to the telephone or answer letters.

McCartney's deafness to these casualties' pleas, however, was not a sign that he'd accepted Klein, even if the American's radical pruning of staff and the huge royalty deal he'd struck with Capitol for The Beatles had amassed millions within months. Thanks to Klein, too, Paul was no longer flummoxed when someone like Frank Zappa rang to ask him if The Mothers Of Invention could parody the *Sgt Pepper* cover for their next album. The problem was that Paul didn't *want* to trust Klein, a feeling partly expressed in his *Abbey Road* songlet 'You Never Give Me Your Money'. Therefore, why should he excuse the seemingly concrete proof put before him by his in-laws of Klein's frauds, low cunning and high-handedness?

Indirectly, Klein was also blamed for the hash made of *Let It Be* by Spector, who, in the pungent words of engineer Glyn Johns, "overdubbed a lot of bullshit all over it, strings and choirs and yuck".[74] McCartney didn't like it much, either, but his written demand to Klein (not Spector) that the damage be repaired had little effect. Adding insult to injury, the release of *McCartney*, his solo album, was to be held back in order to give *Let It Be* a clearer run. Only by bawling out Ringo – sent to mediate by John and George – was he able to ensure that *McCartney* was issued as first scheduled.

When Paul served his writs to dissolve the group, Ringo took it hardest, but John's private announcement of his own resignation many months before had been hushed up for fear of it cramping Klein's bullying of Capitol. As fatigued as everyone else of the fraternal animosity, Lennon was flunking out of more Beatle commitments as The Plastic Ono Band, his peace mission and his life with the Wallis Simpson of pop took priority. He was even missing at the final Beatles recording session, convened on 3 January 1970 to tie up a *Let It Be* loose end. In skittish mood between takes, George indulged in a little verbal tomfoolery at John's expense: "You all will have read that Dave Dee is no longer with us, but Micky, Tich and I would like to carry on the good work that's always gone down at Number Two."[237]

During an Abbey Road session, a digestive biscuit he'd left on top of a speaker cabinet which was found and eaten by Yoko had been the pretext for George to air again his pent-up exasperation with John. Just before Christmas, John and Yoko trawled what a reviewer would describe as "a jamboree of pop talent"[238] to constitute a sprawling Plastic Ono Supergroup for a charity knees-up at the Strand Lyceum. Joining in the impromptu racket was an artillery of drummers, including The Bonzo Dog Band's "Legs" Larry Smith and The Who's Keith Moon, plus pianist Nicky Hopkins and most of the Bramlett Friends, among them Preston and a cynical Harrison. Like Dylan at the Isle of Wight, it was sufficient that two Beatles were simply there, but after a lengthy and headache-inducing 'Cold Turkey' came Yoko's 'Don't Worry Kyoko'. As it stretched into its

20th howling, cacophonous minute, the jamboree of pop talent exchanged nervous glances.

A stone's throw from the Strand, Messrs Harrison, Lennon, McCartney and Starkey were disassociated formally as a business enterprise one morning in 1971 within the stained-glass High Court, where Mr Justice Stamp presided over their mud-slinging before declaring in Paul's favour and delivering Apple's finances to the official receiver's scrutiny. Although it didn't seem so then, this last measure was a boon to the defendants when they too grew disenchanted with Allen Klein, because, said George, "nobody could spend it".[239]

Back in the winter of 1969, however, George for one was not unhappy with his manager. As Bill Harry said, "It took Allen Klein to get him his first A-side." Its six-note instrumental hook too understated, the arrangement of 'Something' that framed Joe Cocker's tardy belly-aching was but a skeleton of what it had become on side one of *Abbey Road*. That hook alone drove me to distraction when it was whistled by a fellow employee during my sojourn as an office cleaner in the following summer, when it was given a second lease of life in the British Top Ten by Shirley Bassey in one of nearly 200 cover versions. Almost as durable a standard as 'Yesterday', 'Something' was heard as supermarket muzak, in the tinklings of Liberace, Smokey Robinson, Elvis, Bert Kaempfert, Booker T's MGs and, yes, Ray Charles. Of them all, George's favourite was the re-invention by James Brown, who masked the hook with a hollered "I got to believe in something" before burying the song in one of his anguished raps. 'Something' was also the only Beatles number to be recorded by Sinatra, who hailed it as "the greatest love song of the past 50 years".[240]

George would cite later compositions as equal in quality, "but they might not be as popular, because it was The Beatles who made 'Something'".[210] This blueprint had been trimmed down from an eight-minute take, losing a long instrumental fade and – like 'While My Guitar Gently Weeps' – an entire verse. None the worse for that, it sliced to Number One in the States like a wire through cheese. Pop, however, obeys no law of natural justice, which is why, in the UK, 'Something' – coupled with John's 'Come Together' – was stopped in its tracks during the usual Yuletide silly season.

Perhaps Paul was right about 'Maxwell's Silver Hammer', for 'Something' was the first Beatle 45 since 1962 that didn't infiltrate the UK Top Three. This petty dampener on George's triumph could be ascribed to Allen Klein's adherence to US procedure of issuing a single off an already successful album. In the week it came out, *Abbey Road* barged its way to a gold disc, outstripping the latest by pretenders like Led Zeppelin, Ten Years After and the defunct Blind Faith. Also swallowing dust was another hot property, Fleetwood Mac, whose 'Albatross' instrumental had triggered one *Abbey Road* track – John's lush 'Sun King' – as outside sources had triggered George's recent songs, "just to get going. ['Sun King'] never really sounded like Fleetwood Mac, just like 'All Things Must Pass' never sounded like The Band, but they were the point of origin."[59]

The atmosphere during the making of *Abbey Road* had been, if not genial, then more co-operative than it had been during *The Beatles* and *Let It Be*. It was as if the four protagonists had agreed – at least, subconsciously – that *Abbey Road* was to be the last LP and so they might as well go out under a flag of truce. Fanning dull embers, George would proffer the press the faggot of a follow-up to *Abbey Road*, on which "we're going to get an equal rights thing so we'll all have as much on the album". He hedged his bets with talk of "doing an album of my own, mainly just to get rid of the songs I've got stacked up."[220]

These days, he was "doing it a lot. I just get the compulsion – like the other week, when I suddenly had the desire to write a country and western song and I didn't have any idea of its shape, but I just had to do it."[241] The outcome of this urge might have been 'Sunshine Life For Me', a countrified hoe-down written and forgotten about when holidaying at Donovan's Irish cottage while the litigational storms gathered. Its subtitle, 'Sail Away Raymond', referred to one of Klein's legal advisers.

Although not as overtly as on Paul's 'You Never Give Me Your Money', Apple's interminable board meetings also had a bearing on George's second *Abbey Road* composition, 'Here Comes The Sun', One morning in early summer, Harrison awoke nauseated with the thought of another spell in the office. Like a truant, he found a bolt-hole at a friend's house. In Eric Clapton's garden, "it was sunny, and it was obviously a release from the tension that had been building up. I picked up the guitar for the first time in a couple of weeks, because I'd been so busy, and the first thing to come out was that."[211]

'Here Comes The Sun' encapsulated more than the relief of a day off work. In the sparkle of its finger-picked acoustic Gibson and light-hearted verses about melting ice and smiling faces, it caught the moment of emergence after a winter cocooned indoors. "You can almost feel the rays of the sun,"[241] *Melody Maker* exclaimed of the *Abbey Road* original while damning with faint praise its cover by a chap called Paul Munday, who was poised to trouble the forthcoming decade as "Gary Glitter". A younger glam rock executant than Glitter, Steve Harley's better timing would put his version of 'Here Comes The Sun' into the British Top Ten during 1976's extraordinarily warm July.

That George's *Abbey Road* songs were subjected to the most widespread syndication reflected both his commercial peak as a composer *per se* and his ascendancy over both Lennon and McCartney. Although John – with sound reason – continued to ridicule Paul's "granny music", he would demonstrate an alarming capacity for tweeness himself, although he would never reach the depths of McCartney's *Abbey Road* vignette 'Her Majesty', surely the most sycophantic lines ever unleashed on a record. The duo that had soundtracked the swinging '60s wouldn't be able, as solo songwriters and ex-Beatles, to so minister to the '70s. The illusion of reconciliation that was *Abbey Road* still fooled the public into believing that The Beatles had saved not the world, perhaps, but themselves. It was, as Debussy said of Wagner's *Das Rheingold*, "a glorious sunset mistaken for a dawn".

12 The Ex-Beatle

The most emphatic twitch in the death throes of The Beatles was 'Something'. Of its singer, George Martin predicted, "I think it's possible that he'll emerge as a great musician and composer next year. He's got tremendous drive and imagination, and also the ability to show himself as a great composer on a par with Lennon and McCartney."[237] This was praise indeed from the one who, almost to the last, had rated George Harrison midway between lowly Mal Evans and the high command of Paul and John. To the world at large, too, Harrison had been no more than merely half of the Other Two.

George's eleventh-hour victory and the hip circles in which he now moved had left him with a firm footing on which to begin a new career. Little could capsize the supposition that he'd continue as a successful recording artist, either solo or as part of a supergroup like Blind Faith or Crosby, Stills And Nash, who were now the toast of the "Woodstock generation".

On the very release date of 'Something' – 31 October 1969 – George had been at Olympic Studios in Barnes recording with what was, in theory, a supergroup drawn from other supergroups. Heard with him on the since-destroyed tapes were Eric Clapton and Rick Grech from Blind Faith; Alan White, one of The Plastic Ono Band's drummers; and Denny Laine, former leader of The Moody Blues. Whatever the quality of the music realised that day, further development of this contingency plan was thwarted as its participants involved themselves in other projects. Laine, for example, joined Wings, Paul McCartney's new group. Nevertheless, like the Delaney And Bonnie episode, this endeavour had fuelled

George's contention that, "Having played with other musicians, I don't think The Beatles were that good."[239] Perhaps they weren't, but a non-member – even if he could sing like a nightingale or make a guitar talk – couldn't guarantee the same attention as the most ill-judged folly of an ex-Beatle.

While McCartney and Lennon's first post-Beatle offerings were either barrel scraping, slap-dash or uxoriously self-centred, to George was afforded the luxury of sifting through a backlog of around 40 songs – "and some of them I think are quite good"[242] – for a new album, a double if he felt like it. Although he was always inclined to function best within the context of a group, George had decided by 1970 to go it alone. Rather than submit his work to the quality control of equals, he'd work with hired assistance as hand-picked as the songs had been. Although stalwarts like Ringo, Mal and Klaus Voorman presented no difficulties, to call the shots to other of the proficient musical practitioners he knew meant fighting giant inhibitions about his own abilities. Warming up for the next backing track, someone might kick off an instrumental jam and extrapolate it at considerable length. With the likes of Ginger Baker dropping by to indulge in these meanderings, it was thought prudent to keep the tape rolling: "Just blowing, having a ball," to quote a contemporary sleeve note. "What a gas, just blowing, blowing, blowing..."[243] As the other participants immortalised their own arrogance, George confined himself mainly to accompaniment, as he had in the post-soundcheck sessions during The Beatles' package tours.

He was particularly in awe of Clapton, because "there's things Eric can do where it would take me all night to get it right. He can knock it off in one take because he plays all the time."[244] However, if not on equal terms technically, George had plucked the heart-strings harder by integrating his talent to his old group's general good with a supine subtlety untried by flasher Eric.

As a singer, George was no Scott Walker. Even Procol Harum's Gary Brooker (an ex-Paramount) and some of the others he'd enlist for the album outclassed him vocally. Nevertheless, his inability to stray far beyond his central two octaves reinforced an idiosyncratic charm peculiar to certain personable vocalists who warp an intrinsically limited range and eccentric delivery to their own devices. George would be one of this oligarchy, as were androgynous Adam Faith, wobbly Ray Davies, laconic Dave Berry and mesmerically ugly Bob Dylan. A Caruso-loving fly on the wall may well have blocked his ears during a secret twelve-hour Harrison-Dylan recording session, after a special dispensation from the US State Department had allowed drug fiend George to visit New York on, ostensibly, a business trip in May 1970. The nadir of his knockabout musical stumblings there was accompanying Dylan groaning a funereal 'Yesterday'. However, with musicians who'd back Bob on his forthcoming *New Morning* LP, George sang two pieces for which he would find room on his own album, a sketchy 'If Not For You' – that Bob had set aside for *New Morning* – and 'I'd Have You Anytime', complete with pattering bongos, one of their joint composing efforts from a stay in Bearsville.

In common with other British rock 'n' rollers, George was discovering that, mere pop star that he was on native turf, he was considered an Artist in enthusiastic North America, where "there's still more chance of picking up on something fresh, interesting. Maybe because it's a much bigger industry, there's not so much tendency for them to get in cliques. England does tend to get very cliquey, as far as I can see."[145] Every pop generation throws up an inward-looking, privileged in crowd, the innermost of all being Presley's Memphis Mafia and, once, The Beatles' retinue. No cabal, however, was so insufferably smug as that of the early 1970s, which "traded licks" during sessions for George Harrison's new LP, mostly at the Trident complex in London's Soho.

Exchanging smirks over the console were Bobby Whitlock, Bobby Keyes or any combination of those interchangeable "funky cats" from Delaney And Bonnie, plus a smaller handful of "heavy friends" from Britain. It was as if George couldn't work in any other way or with any other people than the self-absorbed elite whose only contact with real life out in Dullsville was through managers, runarounds and narcotics dealers.

Leaning against the wall opposite Trident in dawn drizzle that summer, Apple Scruffs sank into a languid daze induced by the fixity of gazing at the studio door. Inside, while George, the engineers and sometimes Phil Spector were head to head in the control booth, the guys toked marijuana, swigged Southern Comfort and discussed who they were going to "ball" later on. In bad shape, Spector "used to have 18 cherry brandies before he could get himself down to the studio. I got so tired of that, because I needed someone to help. I was ending up with more work than if I'd just been doing it on my own."[59] Drafted in to co-produce with George, after applying his spent "genius" to just under half of the backing tracks, Spector's sudden mood swings and absences became more trouble than they were worth. Although he reappeared for the mix, the ailing Svengali of Sound's principal contribution to the outcome was that he could be included among all the other big names credited on the sleeve on what would be – after the Woodstock soundtrack – pop's first triple album, named after one of the songs George had previewed in the *Let It Be* film – 'All Things Must Pass'.

Other than "Old King Log" Spector's maladies, the completion of *All Things Must Pass* was interrupted by the serious illness of George's mother, which involved constant journeys to the Liverpool neurological hospital, where a brain tumour requiring an operation had been diagnosed. "When I went up to see her," said George, "she didn't even know who I was."[58]

Some of the *All Things Must Pass* personnel also embarked on other projects during its pre-planning, Mrs Harrison's infirmity and the four months' recording time booked. Unperturbed and flattered that they should ask, George was delighted to assist his friends, often appearing on their albums under a weak pseudonym, such as "Hari Georgeson" or just "George H". Most of the Bramlett faction and, briefly, Dave Mason had enrolled in Eric Clapton's new band, but its leader's greater commitment to *All Things Must Pass* was such that Dave would sneer, "Eric would be in London doing George's album and nothing was really happening."[245] It has to be said that Clapton wasn't the easiest person to rub along with since contracting a heroin dependency, as some of his group had already, during rehearsals for the outfit's first concert. Events and Eric's own admission would show that an indirect but major cause of this addiction was George Harrison.

Digging the vibes backstage on the June night of Clapton's debut at the Strand Lyceum, George was among those whose brains had been picked for a name for the group – who were due on an hour ago, but that was cool. Let 'em wait. Finally and facetiously, Derek And The Dominoes sauntered on to unacknowledged acclamation by an unreasonably patient audience who'd aped their inconsiderate heroes and their chicks by dressing down in a flurry of pre-faded Levis embroidered with butterfly or mushroom motifs, clogs, long print dresses, cocaine-spoon earrings, Joe Cocker grandad vests and stars-and-stripes singlets revealing underarm hair. Chatter during the long wait embraced misinformed mention of fads – heroin, Jesus, Stoneground, Buddy Holly B-sides – that the condescending Anglo-American superstars were "into". "I can sing better after shooting smack in both my arms,"[246] boasted Linda Ronstadt in an issue of groovy *Rolling Stone* which reached London one month after its publication in High Street, America.

The petrification of British pop since 1968 led to the top of its singles chart bracketing 1970 with what many heard as the undiggable sounds of faceless session group Edison Lighthouse and 'Grandad' by Clive Dunn, who ended the six-week reign of Welsh guitarist Dave Edmunds' trundling 'I Hear You Knocking'. Better exemplifying the dearth of new original talent was Free's 'All Right Now', *the* hit song of 1970, which had been influenced by the Stones' 'Honky Tonk Women' of the previous year. Its central riff was logged by George for later use: a rehash of a rehash. Beyond *Top Of The Pops*, from college juke boxes would moan other album-enhancing 45s plugging albums by Humble Pie, Black Sabbath and their ilk, whose "heavy" excesses appealed to male consumers recently grown to man's estate. With Deep Purple as the link, this category stretched towards the "techno-flash" pomp rock in the ELP/Yes vein.

Infesting the university bedsit rather than its bar juke box were LPs from the other end of the spectrum. Reaching out to self-doubting adolescent diarists rather than headbangers was the early-1970s school of singer/songwriters, which was called "self-rock" if you liked it, and "drip rock" if – like *Melody Maker's* Allan Jones in a scathing article[247] – you didn't. The genre's ethos was of being so bound up in yourself that every trivial occurrence or emotion was worth telling the whole world about in song.

Most of its perpetrators' drab uniformity was but another symptom of the hungover morning after the Swinging '60s. With all the charisma of sacks of potatoes, solemn James Taylor, sweet Melanie or Linda Ronstadt – a singer/songwriter type, except she didn't write many songs – would whinge "beautiful" cheesecloth-and-denim banalities in sold-out stadiums. No Mick Jagger cavortings were necessary; all you had to do was sit on a stool, sing to your guitar and beam a small, sad smile now and then. More than gruff heavy metal or pomp rock, drip rock epitomised the bland tenor of a decade that, to George Harrison, "seemed a bit grumpier than the '60s".[248] With Simon And Garfunkel's 'Bridge Over Troubled Water' its anthem, 1970 was a re-run of 1967 without colour, daring or humour.

When Joe Average first slotted it onto his stereo on 27 November 1970, *All Things Must Pass* seemed to have caught the overall drift of the early 1970s. Even to its creator, it was modern enough to sound dated and in need of a remix within years. As non-hippies were hardly aware of *Wonderwall* and *Electronic Sounds*, *All Things Must Pass* was the first time George had truly shown his head as a soloist. From both detailed demos and half-formed ideas computed on his mind, it was like "being constipated for years, then finally you were allowed to go. I had 17 tracks and I didn't really want to chuck any away, although I'm sure lots of them, in retrospect, could have been. I wanted to get shot of them so I could catch up on myself."[164]

Unfettered as he was by obligations to the most objective and critical of familiars, George had needed a Lennon, McCartney or Martin to suggest paring down *All Things Must Pass* to a lean single album and reserving the best of what remained for a follow-up. The insubstantial 'I Dig Love' could have been ditched without any hardship. As well as including two takes of 'Isn't It A Pity' (one over seven minutes long), much on the package's first two records was blighted by not so much gratuitous soloing as repeated choruses and extended fades which put some in a mantric (or stoned) trance, while others wondered, "How much longer?" Like many latter-day Beatle tracks, constant replay was necessary to comprehend trifles like what sounded like a motor changing gear in the final seconds of 'Wah-Wah'.

Most fans found that the third record remained in pristine condition while its companions acquired scratches and surface hiss. Although it was a free gift to offset a high retail cost, *Apple Jam* – with one exception – made tedious listening. If anyone was expecting a continuation of ersatz Beatle magic, all they heard were edited highlights – if that is the word – from the interminable jamming that consumed time as late arrivals set up their gear or engineers twiddled. Despite intriguing titles – such as 'I Remember Jeep' – bestowed on these extemporisations of twelve-bar blues and two-chord riffs, the clouds parting on the gods at play revealed nothing more remarkable than any idle session crew's ramblings not intended for public ears. However, I must add the raw information that 'Thanks For The Pepperoni' was among the "amazing sounds"[249] beloved by neil, a hippy-drippy anachronism from the 1984 BBC series *The Young Ones*.

Rick, neil's flatmate – and Cliff Richard admirer – would have preferred the only vocal item on *Apple Jam*, the quirky and brief 'It's Johnny's Birthday', which borrowed the melody of Cliff's 1968 Song For Europe entry, 'Congratulations'. Although an in-joke, with its unusual tonality and wandering varispeed, 'It's Johnny's Birthday' was the most musically adventurous offering on *All Things Must Pass*.

The "Johnny" it celebrated was John Lennon, rather than orchestral arranger John Barham, who'd also worked on *Wonderwall*. As the poly-synthesiser was yet to become common in studios, Barham had to notate the required scoring for *All Things Must Pass* as the composer – who could barely sight-read – *dah-dah-dahed*. A backwash of strings gnawed at many selections either as fairy dusting or, as on 'Isn't It A Pity', assuming a part that could have been allocated to lead guitar or saxophone. There were fierce moments – 'Let It Down', for instance – and a few weird shudders, but *All Things Must Pass* was generally easy on the ear and suited to a year when the likes of James Taylor and Crosby, Stills And Nash still held sway. Because some hip names – including Klaus Voorman's – had been printed on one of his LP jackets, it was cool to dig even a purring Mister Wonderful like Andy Williams, who could have adapted with ease most of *All Things Must Pass* to his style, in which was absorbed just enough of prevailing trends not to turn off older fans. Without making any such concessions, English balladeer Matt Monro covered 'Isn't It A Pity', hoping to repeat the Top-Ten success he'd had with 'Yesterday' in 1965.

However much the predominant blandness may have affected his music, George's contributions to albums by Bobby Keyes, Leon Russell, Jesse "Ed" Davis and his other Bramlett pals left less of a mark than you might imagine. While he may have shared these opportunists' prolixity, he forwent, thankfully, their lyrical preoccupations with snorting cocaine, balling chicks and other overworked myths of the rock-band-on-the-road lifestyle. He devoted several libretti to his intensifying religious explorations, rather than to frustrated eroticism. Updating JS Bach's artistic tenet, he'd decided that "music should be used for the perception of God, not jitterbugging".[250] Of greatest antiquity was 'The Art Of Dying' and – with the Billy Preston versions as helpful demos – the title track and 'My Sweet Lord'. The latter was elongated and given a fatter production, but more uplifting was 'Awaiting On You All', a semi-litany and one of the few *All Things Must Pass* numbers with a succinct ending.

From the overt 'Hear Me Lord' to veiled allusions in 'Beware Of Darkness', George invited mockery by so persistently superimposing tracts about Japa Yoga, meditation, karma, maya[180] and the like onto a pop framework. Much later, it was sent up as *All Things Must Fart* in *neil's Book Of The Dead*, a paperback spin-off from *The Young Ones*. Next to some tortuously rhymed doggerel concluding with "a whiff of friendship, love and lentil", neil's mournful visage was pasted over Harrison's in a reproduction of the album cover. As hirsute as he'd ever be, the artist sits in pastoral contemplation, like a spaced-out Farmer Giles, a posture which seems to amuse mildly four garden gnomes – possibly an allusion to The Beatles – sprawled on the grass around him. A box set, *All Things Must Pass* was a handy working surface for rolling a joint in hip student hostel rooms, where it was as much a fixture as Che Guevara's mug had been.

As an old trouper, George must have gauged that the intangible buzz that had been in the air for months would push *All Things Must Pass* to the top of the album lists for reasons other than still-potent loyalty to the Fab Four, whose regrouping was seen then as inevitable by even the most marginally hopeful outsider to whom the concept of collecting every record The Beatles ever made was not yet economically unsound. It wouldn't be too sweeping to say that religion – especially Christianity – was a turn-of-the-decade craze, just as the Twist had been. In corroboration was a trio who seemed to be approximating The Jimi Hendrix Experience for an appearance at Reading University one evening in 1971. Cutting through their noise were half-heard phrases such as "bless the Lord", "mend your ways", "come to Jesu". Some driven to dance were even crossing themselves and bawling hallelujahs that weren't taking the mickey. Seeking more temporal amusement, I headed for the exit, thanking Christ I'd got in without paying.

In *The Liverpool Echo*, Edward Patey, the dean of the cathedral, lauded the new coalition of religious sentiment and pop as "the best partnership since the mediaeval duetting of clowns and folk singers",[251] even if those responsible were, like George Harrison, not aligned to orthodox Christian worship. With politicians envying the pop star's easy manipulation of young opinion, surely the new fad could cajole more teenagers from pot-smoking depravity into Matins, or at least to God? George, too, was "sick of all these young people just boogying around, wasting their lives".[152] Of the same opinion was Dean Patey's fellow Liverpudlian John Lennon, whose perky but reproachful 'Instant Karma' entered the charts in February 1970 and prompted a *Top Of The Pops* appearance, the first Beatle to do so in four years.

After 'Oh Happy Day', 'Spirit In The Sky' answered the prayers of its singer, Norman Greenbaum. While this song was a worldwide smash in the spring of 1971, Diane Colby's 'Holy Man' was huge in Australia, if nowhere else. With at least three renditions of 'Amazing Grace' about to ascend hit parades in major territories later that year, Tin Pan Alley's quick appraisal of the situation led to abominations like 'The Man From Nazareth', mimed on *Top Of The Pops* by John Paul Joans (*sic*), a bearded herbert dressed in bedspreads.

Past the crap, many consumers and artists found the vogue for saintliness reassuring, a relief almost, stuck as they were between the supposed drug-crazed sensuality of rock 'n' roll and their own stolid compliance to middle-aged values. Born-again fervour saw evangelical marches up high streets and the Scriptures being quoted at parties. The Bible, the Koran and *Chant And Be Happy*[152] now had discreet places on hip bookshelves. Mostly, this was just for show as a reefer was passed around during a conversation pocked with words like "mantra" and "karma" while James Taylor's *Mud Slide Slim*, Deep Purple's *Machine Head* or *All Things Must Pass* poured from the stereo. Behind school bike sheds a few years earlier, it had been "gear" and "grotty" over a Woodbine.

This shallow spirituality tipped the balance for many who were then ripe for religion. In as late as 1982, George would "still get letters from people saying, 'I have been in the Krishna temple for three years, and I would never have known about Krishna [if you hadn't] recorded the *All Things Must Pass* album.'"[152] As the Portsmouth Sinfonia would bring popular classics to those who otherwise wouldn't experience them, so George brought Krishna Consciousness. With lines like those in the crass bridge of 'Beware Of Darkness', George might not have been touched with the same gift for hymnology as, say, Charles Wesley, but he closed the gap on Tom McGuinness' 'I Will Bring To You', when 'My Sweet Lord' became accepted as a *bona fide* gospel song.

The first and biggest-selling 45 to be lifted from the album, 'My Sweet Lord', pulled Clive Dunn off the top in Britain within a fortnight of its release. By February 1971, it was Number One virtually everywhere else, too. From newly converted rock groups murdering it on God-slot television to a rendering by Johnny Mathis for the supper-club market, 'My Sweet Lord' would be that year's most performed work.

Every silver lining has a cloud, however, and both the Harrison re-tread of Preston's blueprint and the vast exposure of 'My Sweet Lord' threw the song's stomach-knotting similarity to The Chiffons' 'He's So Fine' into sharper focus. Allen Klein brought to George's notice a revival of The Chiffons' opus by Jody Miller, onto which was faithfully grafted every detail of the 'My Sweet Lord' arrangement, even the plainly strummed acoustic guitars that had replaced Billy's jazzy keyboards on the introduction and the background chants where The Chiffons' *doo-lang-doo-lang-doo-lang*s had been.

Worries that this was litigational ammunition for Bright Tunes, publishers of 'He's So Fine', brought the same questions up again and again as George groped for reasons why such a case would or would not be pursued. Bouncing his thoughts off Klein, he would build up a damning case against himself before concluding that Bright Tunes either couldn't be bothered or hadn't enough evidence to justify making a fuss. However, with no word from Bright Tunes as the months slipped by, perhaps George was panicking unduly. "Maybe he thought God would just sort of let him off,"[80] John Lennon would laugh after He didn't.

This bad karma, however, was at arm's length as the falling 'My Sweet Lord' collided with the catchy 'What Is Life' (the one turned down by Billy Preston) on its way up. Belying its pensive title, this second single from *All Things Must Pass* seemed to be a straight, lovey-dovey pop song. Driven by Mal Evans' tambourine, 'What Is Life' renewed craftily the simplistic tonic-to-dominant riff cliché. Unissued as an A-side in Britain, where it had already appeared on the flip of 'My Sweet Lord', the rise of a version by Olivia Newton-John – pulchritudinous, middle-of-the-road vocalist from Australia – into the Top 20 was, like Shirley Bassey's 'Something', a wooing of a parallel dimension of pop turned off by all this religious nonsense that hippies liked. George's infiltration of this area by proxy continued with 'Isn't It A Pity', which, when sung by Ireland's Dana as the storm brewed in Ulster, was more poignant than either his own or Matt Monro's version.

Olivia's 'What Is Life' had been preceded by her song 'If Not For You', based on the smoother *All Things Must Pass* rather than the *New Morning* treatment. While George's own multitracked vocals ("The George O'Hara Singers"), blaring horns and battalions of strings bloated many other *All Things Must Pass* tracks, those written by, with and about Bob Dylan veered towards the understated production aesthetic of the latter's comeback album, *John Wesley Harding*, even employing its steel guitarist, the late Pete Drake, for the waltz-time 'Behind That Locked Door'. Appropriately, little more than huffing mouth organ and Spanish guitar accompanied 'Apple Scruffs', in a manner closer to Don Partridge than Dylan. The Scruffs themselves – after having "stood around" for years – were actually invited into the control room to hear a playback of the most intrinsically valuable if belated recognition of a vigil soon to end with adulthood and the realisation that The Beatles as a 1960s myth would long outlive the mere mortals that constituted its *dramatis personae*.

Eric Clapton was human now, too. After his guitar divinity had peaked in Cream, only miracles could have rescued his subsequent projects, even if media build-up forestalled an instant backlash. He either couldn't or wouldn't play like he had in Cream, and neither was he an outstanding singer or composer. Nonetheless, he'd always find sufficient buyers to guarantee a good turn-out for his concerts and chart placings for most of his records. Among the rarest of these was a withdrawn single taped during an *All Things Must Pass* furlough. With producer Spector half-seas over, Clapton served up 'Tell The Truth' in a hoarse smoker's monotone. Content once to fret chords under his mate's soloing, George now felt that it was a feather in his cap when he was allowed a bottleneck obligato on its flip-side, 'Roll It Over'. Still earnestly finding a way with the non-standard tuning and slithering left hand, for George to be so rated by even a below-par Clapton was such that, "for me, if Eric gives me the thumbs-up on a slide solo, it means more to me than half the population".[243]

Before 1970 was out, Clapton's heroin odyssey brought about The Dominoes' dismissal midway through their second album together. He'd made no long-term plans. How could he? His descent into this abyss was hinged on what had now become an infatuation with Pattie Harrison. So far, she'd spurned his advances, which even his friendship with her husband would not rein. Not surprisingly, Eric's muse on several tracks on the first Dominoes album was romantic frustration, notably in the hit single 'Layla', in which he howled about comforting the object of his desire "when your old man let you down".

The Harrisons' marriage muddled on because neither partner had enough motivation to finish it. Yet, although her flirting with his friends didn't appear to bother him, George showed her small fondnesses as he and she posed for an Apple Scruff's camera, smiling like they were happy. Why shouldn't the world at large assume that 'What Is Life' was another lovingly crafted paean to Pattie, rather than something dashed off "very quickly, 15 minutes to half an hour"[39] while driving to a Billy Preston session? As neither was yet the sort to wash dirty linen in public, nothing substantial suggested that the childless couple's life together was less than tolerable.

Pattie's hopes for raising a family were impeded by George's reservations about adoption and his months on end of sexual abstinence. While there was less lust in him now than when he'd first clapped eyes on her toothy charms, his restraint was dictated by a more rigid adherence to religious tenets whereby the purpose of sex was for procreation only. "I think if you do something and you don't really like doing it," he would affirm, "then you're a hypocrite about it. In a way, we all have desires; we must learn either to fulfil the desires or terminate those desires. If you can do it by being celibate and it's easy to handle, it's OK. You can either lose certain desires you had when you were younger or the thing that you have to watch – particularly the sex and things like drugs, too. The problem is, you can go, 'Oh well, I'll just have a bit, then I'll be fulfilled,' but it doesn't work that way. First you have a bit and then you want more."[32]

This well-argued point could as easily have come from a street-corner evangelist warming to a pet theme amid jeers from the few stopping to listen. As common a sight in Oxford Street as the Hare Krishna chanters was ex-civil servant Stanley Green, who paced daily back and forth in a sandwich board that declared his creed of "Less Lust From Less Protein". If asked, he'd tell you, "Protein wisdom changes your whole life, makes it easier. Passion can be a great torment. I've seen some remarkable changes in people. The first thing a woman does when she takes up protein wisdom is change her hairstyle." All the lonely people, where do they all come from?

George's incentive for rising at dawn was not the same as Mr Green's. When an interviewer suggested that it was to avoid wet dreams, George laughed and explained that Krishna devotees regarded sleep as the "little death. Prabhupada sleeps an hour or two hours a day. These yogis don't need sleep at all. The don't need food. They're living on the Divine Energy."[32] After a nice cold bath, he'd settle down to a study of the Bhagavad Gita. At given moments, he'd break into the maha-mantra. As Roman Catholics keep count of Hail Marys, so George would tally his *hare krishnas* with a string of Japa Yoga beads kept in a small bag slung over his shoulder. Unlike Stanley Green, who'd "spoiled my life by being too honest", George found it easier to say he'd shut his fingers in a door. The depths of depravity nowadays were three filter tips per day.

George was accorded considerably greater space and luxury for what were regarded as his eccentricities than Stanley Green in his one-room flat in Harrow. For hours at a stretch, George would meditate in his own temple in the grounds of Friar Park, which Ringo Starr would describe in song as "a 40-acre house he doesn't see".[253] Its purchase in January 1970 had concluded the Harrisons' year of searching for a dwelling that would combine privacy without imprisonment, and close proximity to London.

Catering similarly for other famous names, the region where Berkshire dissolves into Oxfordshire – Hollywood-on-Thames – was centred around the Windsor-Ascot-Henley triangle, throwing together the most disparate of neighbours. Thespians such as Michael Caine and Susan George would fill petrol tanks at the same garage as comedian Ernie Wise or Sir James Carreras, retired head of Hammer Films. Fête-opening "personalities" like Rolf Harris, Freddie Starr or Vince Hill might be vaguely impressed when told that the guffawing drinkers in the next bar of the local pub were members of Deep Purple.

Most of the rock 'n' roll elite ensconced themselves in the rural calm of Hambledon, Middle Assenden, Skirmett and other olde worlde hamlets buried in the woods surrounding a reach of the river where no cascading pylons blighted grassy downs and where sheep nibbled on Saxon battlegrounds. While Ten Years After's organist or Deep Purple's drummer might attend village bazaars in undisguised anonymity, seeing an ex-Beatle dipping into the bran tub might be as profoundly disturbing as finding the Prince of Wales using an adjacent urinal in the gents. George, therefore, was hardly ever seen in Henley, whose town square was two minutes' walk down Gravel Hill from the gatehouse of Friar Park, the estate that was to be as synonymous with his name as the Queen's with Windsor Castle.

Unseen from the Peppard Road, this spired and turreted mansion of 120 rooms on Henley's western outskirts was the creation of Sir Frank Crisp, a prominent and astute City of London solicitor. When completed in 1889, the architectural manifestation of Crisp's personality was dismissed by one contemporary journalist as "a bizarre folly"[254] and lauded by another as "a beautiful example of high-Victorian architecture in the style of Pugin".[255] In as late as 1978, *The Henley Standard* was still discussing "Friar Park: beautiful or a monstrosity?"[246] It depended on whether you shared Sir Frank's sense of humour. In deference to its founding on the site of a 13th-century friary were the many intricate carvings of a monastic nature on its red brick and yellow low-stone exterior. Over the legend "Two Holy Friars" is a friar with a frying pan with holes in it. Get it? Visitors' eyes would pop when they saw that, instead of a conventional light switch, there was a wooden friar's face with a moveable nose.

In 1905, one disgruntled guest, Lady Ottoline Morrell, wondered whether Crisp "was colossally simple and really thought these vulgar and monstrous jokes amusing and beautiful".[257] To his offspring, Friar Park was as tangibly grotesque as a Gothic scenario, "Full of surprises. Around every corner, you could come across a quirky statue, an arbour with a seat inscribed with one of my grandfather's special quotations, a summerhouse sited to obtain a certain vista, and numerous little tucked-away gardens, each with its separate identity."[257] What child of this Coca Cola century would not be deliciously chilled by the three artificial caverns with their wishing wells, distorting mirrors, model skeletons and glass grapes, from which you paddled into the Blue Grotto and out into the lowest of the three split-level lakes. Then there were the mazes, the secret passageways and, dominating the Alpine rock garden, a 100-foot-high replica of the Matterhorn constructed from trainloads of millstone grit.

By the mid 1950s, the manor had returned to the Church. Its new proprietors were nuns of the order of St John Bosco. Among minor adjustments in the mansion's conversion was the overpainting of underpants on naked cherubs depicted on ceiling tableaux. Falling rolls, however, depleted the establishment's resources, causing a gradual withering of the estate, so that even Crisp Street – with houses built from Yorkshire stone left over from the Matterhorn – lay outside its environs when the hard-pressed nuns were forced to sell up in 1969. There were woefully few prospective buyers, too, and the one who looked like Rasputin embodied, at first sight, all that the Catholic Church detested. While being shown round, he deposited a four-armed and pagan poster of Vishnu in an empty fireplace and "it sort of freaked them out a bit".[152]

Trailing along behind their guide, the Harrisons pondered the neglected splendour. The topiary, on which thousands of different varieties of flora, shrubs and trees had bloomed, had been strangled by couch grass and creepers and was littered with broken lavatories from a building site. The house itself was in such a state of dereliction that demolition contractors had been readied, should it be taken off the market. Nonetheless, some instinct intimated to George that the high asking price and the money he'd surely have to lay out on renovations might be cash well spent: "It's like a horror movie, but it really doesn't have bad vibes. It's had Christ in it for 16 years, after all."[258]

Money talks in any religion, and by March 1970 a labourer's cottage sufficed as temporary abode for Pattie and George while the main edifice was an unserviceable no man's land of rubble, planks and tea-drinking artisans. While being restored to near enough its former glory, the mansion was customised to the new owner's specifications. A tweaked nose still flooded a room with light, and the cherubs' pants stayed on, but alien to a Victorian baronet, if not a nun, were the juke box, the cinema, the Tiffany lamps and, ultimately, the recording studio that replaced a suite of two bedrooms, bathroom and dressing room.

Freeing him of the restraints of a hired studio, this electronic den enabled George to potter around with sound, tape the wackiest demos, invite friends around to play and begin a day's recording with nothing prepared. Eventually, every note of his public output would also be hand tooled there. Although he graduated from 16-track to digital 48-track and beyond, playbacks were still heard through crude Altecs, as at Abbey Road, because, "when you play it back anyplace else, it sounds fantastic".[58] The latest transistorised toys came and went. "People were talking about quadraphonic sound, and while I didn't think it'd catch on, I figured I'd better have that, just in case."[59] His instructions to engineers came to be dotted with jargon like "pan pots" (stereo-channel potentiometers), "EQ" and "carbon faders". Often technological steps ahead of even Abbey Road, George's FPSHOT (Friar Park Studio, Henley-on-Thames) was recognised as the world's most sophisticated private recording complex.

While this proved a worthwhile investment, he took less detached pride in marshalling a team of gardeners to do battle against the weeds that had ruined Sir Frank's careful landscaping. However, although bellbine and thistle perished by hoe and bonfire, the rabbits that overran the fields continued to multiply. Left alone, too, were the quaint homilies inscribed in the Park's nook and crannies. Around the sundial, for instance, was the legend (in Latin) "Shadows we are and shadows we depart", but more peculiar to Crisp was the phrase "Herons will be prosecuted". His "Don't keep off the grass" had a meaning other than horticultural in 1970, when a fiver persuaded a London butcher to surrender to Dave Crosby a cardboard "All joints must be weighed" sign.

Such jive-talking inanity might have been stonewalled by one such as Sir Frank Crisp. Nevertheless, as more of his domestic idiosyncrasies were uncovered, the 19th-century knight began to walk a tightrope between craziness and heroism – as John Lennon did – for the Harrisons and their house guests. George's particular friend from the Monty Python crowd, Eric Idle, began researching Crisp's career for a biography, while 'The Ballad Of Sir Frankie Crisp' was a breath of fresh air amid the dicta and aimless jamming on *All Things Must Pass*. Couched in mediaeval expression as it was – "through ye woode, here may ye rest awhile" – George had resisted orchestrating this most Beatle-esque of his new songs with tabor and crumhorn. Instead, a sense of the mysterious was conveyed with 1970s rock instrumentation. Other carved Crispisms would inspire further compositions.

George also took it upon himself to perpetuate the founder's good works, which included financing the erection of Christ Church steeple in Duke Street and more anonymous donations to the upkeep of Henley's churches and listed buildings. He was no Little Englander, but, while some aspects of the late 20th century could be welcomed, the town's wealthiest addressee sought to conserve an older aesthetic. From the five-arched bridge, constructed in 1786, the main street has an oak-beamed gentility that overflows onto the art galleries and olde tea shoppes along the waterfront, where the Thames has straightened for a clear mile and motorboats bump in their moorings. The annual Royal Regatta fills the towpaths and meadows that frame this marina with Henley's most noticeable influx of debutantes, yuppies and sightseers.

On the rim of the old town, new housing estates with concrete garages were beginning to intrude upon the countryside. People have to live somewhere, but disquieting to the Harrisons and other residents were those prongs of modern enterprise – supermarkets, car parks *et al* – that pierced Henley's very heart, to the detriment of its elegant past. George, however, would not immediately put action over debate, even though, "during the time I've been here, one old building after another had been torn down".[259]

It would be years before he risked mingling with the few thousand souls who lived in the town beneath his eyrie. Whereas in Sir Frank's day the grounds had been open to the public every summer Wednesday, a sign in ten languages outside Friar Park's tall, iron-barred gates read "Absolutely No Admittance". Razor-sharp barbed wire crowned the outer walls. Now known more for its pop-star incumbent, British trippers would say "cheese" outside that forbidding boundary and Americans would train cine cameras up the drive before ambling down to the Thameside promenade for an ice cream.

Ringo Starr's less grandiose spread in Compton Avenue, Highgate, was less of a magnet for fans. Most at a loss after the break-up, the "straightest" ex-Beatle had been the pliant executor of others' ideas, until renewed confidence teased from him a plethora of original songs, among them his first solo single, 'It Don't Come Easy', which, in the spring of 1971, outsold current offerings by John, Paul and George. The latter had emerged as Ringo's most willing helpmate, producing and twanging the wires on both 'It Don't Come Easy' and its follow-up, 'Back Off Boogaloo'.

This repetitive opus was registered as a "Richard Starkey" composition, but some made the waspish allegation that it was actually the work of Marc Bolan, who was pioneering a swing back to the cheap thrills of the beat boom. This was encapsulated in *Born To Boogie*, Ringo's first essay as a film director, which used footage of Bolan's group, T Rex, at a British concert deluged in screams. Behind the cameras at stage front, it must have been strange for Ringo to find himself ignored as hysterical girls clambered to get at Marc. Their elder sisters might have fancied George Harrison or James Taylor but, light years away on *Top Of The Pops*, T Rex, Slade, Alice Cooper and other newcomers – who'd never mean half as much in laid-back America – were paving the way for the greater musical and sartorial excesses of David Bowie, Gary Glitter and Roxy Music. Also in the ascendant in the UK charts was a mascara'd Shane Fenton, who, borrowing from Glitter's name, had been exhumed as "Alvin Stardust".

Most ex-Beatles embraced different elements that were anathema to glam rock. Rather than George's *ad hoc* aggregations of semi-famous names, Wings favoured a permanency as cosy as Paul and Linda's "simple life" on their Sussex farm among a growing family. Vinyl reflection of this contentment was Wings' cloying 'Mary Had A Little Lamb' – yes, the nursery rhyme – which nestled uneasily in a British Top Ten in which T Rex's 'Metal Guru' had just toppled a version of 'Amazing Grace' by a Scottish military band. An Hibernian outfit of more mercurial stamp was The Sensational Alex Harvey Band, whose bombastic leader – no longer styling himself as "the Tommy Steele of Scotland" – enquired, "Do you think Paul McCartney makes records just to annoy me personally, or does he want to get up everybody's nose with his antics?"[260]

"Everybody" meant those sickened by Paul's developing Mr

Showbusiness image, which seemed bourgeois when set against his former songwriting confrere's more cathartic projection of himself, which involved singing the f-word twice in the primal scream that was his Plastic Ono Band LP. After Lennon regurgitated his lot in 'Working Class Hero', the artistic gulf between him and McCartney widened, and the sibling rivalry intensified so that they were sniping at each other in the press and even in record grooves. Of these attacks, John's were the most malicious. Not content with airing grievances against Paul in the pages of *Rolling Stone*, further insults effused from 'Crippled Inside' and, nastier still, 'How Do You Sleep' (with a few lines suggested by Allen Klein) from *Imagine*, Lennon's winter album of 1971.

In as much as he'd sided with John in the desperate hours of 1969, so George endorsed on slide guitar and dobro these diatribes and other *Imagine* cuts: "I enjoyed 'How Do You Sleep'. I liked being on that side of it, rather than on the receiving end."[59] Although *All Things Must Pass* had shut down The Plastic Ono Band commercially, George would remain a rank outsider to John in the sense of the artistic competition that forever persisted between the ex-Beatles. In *Rolling Stone*, the snigger was almost audible in Lennon's claim that, to the "rubbish"[156] of McCartney, he preferred *All Things Must Pass*. The fact that he was needling Paul rather than praising George was inherent in the qualification, "I think it's all right, I suppose. Personally, at home, I wouldn't play that kind of music, but I don't want to hurt George's feelings."[156]

John's own feelings were hurt when an incident shortly after the *Imagine* sessions instigated George's gradual isolation from his old idol. However, Lennon was "openly pleased I came"[59] when Harrison's car pulled up at Tittenhurst Park. Although he'd helped on 'Instant Karma', George was relieved that John so beholdenly conducted him into the eight-track studio where *Imagine* was taking form, because "very strange, intense feelings were going on. Sometimes, people don't talk to each other, thinking they're not going to be the one to phone you up and risk rejection."[58] *All Things Must Pass* had conditioned George to dozens of retakes and overdubs, so it was with mild apprehension that he tuned up in a playing area where the exhilaration of the impromptu was prized more than technical accuracy. When his lead break came in 'How Do You Sleep', George, bereft of preconception, "hit a few good notes, and it happened to sound like a solo. We did all that work in one day."[59]

On bass was Klaus Voorman, who, gone from Manfred Mann, had been like the stock Hollywood chorus girl thrust into a sudden starring role with the first of countless spurious rumours concerning The Beatles' reformation. See, as Paul was *persona non grata*, the other three were going to try again with Voorman. "New Beatle Klaus Goes Into Hiding!"[261] *Melody Maker* had bawled that spring when he and his wife spent a few days at Friar Park.

A stronger presence around George's gaff was that of Swami Prabhupada and some disciples who'd outstayed their welcome at Tittenhurst Park. Although devotees had been featured on The Plastic Ono Band's first single, 'Give Peace A Chance', their chanting hadn't been peaceful enough when it recurred at regular intervals on the Lennons' own doorstep. Far from finding Prabhupada's louder devotions disturbing, their new host gladly extended his invitation into 1972, when they were able to decamp to Pickett's Manor, the mock-Tudor theological college – renamed Bhaktivedanta Manor – in Hertfordshire that was to become the most popular Hindu rallying point in Europe. Footing the bill for these 17 acres near Letchmore Heath, not far from the Maharishi's stately meditation centre in Mentmore, was George, who felt "fortunate enough to be able to help at the time".[152]

The faith that had prompted such beatific generosity would never exempt him from the odd loss of cool. Unprepared to bite back his annoyance, he steered his Mercedes slowly but threateningly towards a singularly intransigent traffic policeman in Westminster. Pleading guilty to driving without due care and attention, the sentence – a year's ban – was postponed because the defendant had forgotten his driving licence.

Off the public road, his increased leisure had facilitated the resumption and assiduous pursuance of his long-dormant interest – "apart from watching the odd bit on TV or reading magazines" – in motor racing. Nowadays, rather than perch on a railway embankment to goggle illicitly at distant Vanwalls and BRMs, he could luxuriate in the VIP enclosure at Monaco. It was at such a meet that he was introduced to Jackie Stewart, who'd just regained the sport's world championship. A critical thorn in the flesh of his more staid racing comperes, long-haired Stewart had been admired by George, because "he always projected the sport beyond just the racing enthusiasts".[22]

Partly through Jackie, George came to compound his enthusiasm for circuit dare-devilry, but it was Peter Sellers who "was a considerable influence on my getting into the film world".[59] After dinner at Friar Park, Sellers and Harrison would pass pleasant evenings slumped before the silver screen. The discerning Peter's favourite picture, Mel Brooks' *The Producers*, soon became George's, too, as his understanding of which films were worth seeing and which weren't became more acute.

Tightening the bond between the former Beatle and the ex-Goon was that Sellers was "into" Indian culture to a deeper extent than his oft-mimicked part as a Punjabi doctor in *The Millionairess*, a 1960 film starring Sophia Loren. Under George's influence, he was now wearing kaftans, practising yoga and burning incense. During a frightening account of a high-altitude engine mishap, Peter assured a rapt dining room that only his chanting of 'Hare Krishna' had prevented a crash landing. George might have capped this anecdote by recalling a similar scrape with death as a passenger on a transcontinental aeroplane in 1971, when, after two hours of buffeting, the craft had plummeted, the lights had fused, explosions had rocked the fuselage and "I ended up with my feet pressed against the seat in front, my seat belt as tight as could be, gripping on the thing and yelling 'Hare Krishna' at the top of my voice. I know [that], for me, the difference between making it and not making it was actually chanting the mantra."[152] This terrible journey took George from Los Angeles to New York to co-ordinate what would stand as his finest hour: The Concerts For Bangladesh.

Like most occidentals, he was "not interested in the politics of the situation"[262] which had emerged from the division of East and West Pakistan by both geography and 23 years of worsening antagonism.

In March 1971, four months after East Pakistan – now Bangladesh – had been devastated by a cyclone, General Yahya Khan amassed a Moslem army mighty enough to eradicate the Hindu majority who opposed his military dictatorship in both regions. Prostrated by the tempest's aftermath of homelessness, lack of sanitation, cholera and starvation, the East Bengalis were further traumatised by this reign of terror. Carrying their pathetic bundles, millions of refugees stumbled towards the safety of India, which had received hardly a tenth of the foreign aid needed to cope with the disaster.

Ravi Shankar's own family and friends and those of his guru were among the ceaseless fatalities and exiles. In California, during these unhappy months, from Ravi's distraught helplessness came the notion of a modest fund-raising concert. When George arrived in Los Angeles in late June, a better answer clicked in Shankar's mind like a key sliding into a lock. "He wanted to do something which would make a little more money than he normally made. He gave me all this information and articles on what was going on in Bangladesh, and I slowly got pulled into it. I started getting carried away with the whole idea of doing something good, maybe making $10 million."[211] Officially, he'd flown in to produce Badfinger and to negotiate the release of *Messenger Out Of The East*, an Apple Film study – two years in the making – of Shankar and the land that bore him. When this duty was done, George made his giant leap for Bangladesh.

He held at bay misgivings about treading the boards again and instructed Allen Klein to book no less a venue than New York's 20,000-capacity Madison Square Gardens, where no Beatle had gone before. The most convenient date was Sunday 1 August, which left George just enough time to recruit and rehearse whatever musicians he could muster to support him. "We had to get this together quickly, so I had to put myself out there and hope for friends to support me."[262] The coup of the decade, meanwhile, would have been the regrouping of The Beatles. Contacted in Spain while playing a bandit in a Klein-produced western, Ringo was game, but over in Sussex Paul declined, as 'How Do You Sleep' and the legal turmoil at Apple were still sore points. Although in the midst of promoting a book by Yoko, John seemed keen, even when, despite Klein's assurances to the contrary, there'd be no place for his wife on stage that evening. Exercising his novel power of veto, George wouldn't hear of it – 'Don't Worry Kyoko' at the Lyceum was too hard to forget.

Yoko might have been of greater notoriety than Jim Keltner, Carl Radle and the rest of the West Coast minions that George now gathered about him, but she obviously wasn't boring enough. Neither did she know *All Things Must Pass* – the show's principal source of repertoire – backwards. The rank and file would also include a small choir, three members of Badfinger on acoustic guitars and a horn section, led by Jim Horn. When the call came, all had been only too pleased to help. Bigger names were, however, "terribly difficult. It took me three months [*sic*] on the telephone, really, night and day, trying to con everybody into doing it."[211] Some problems were administrative. Newly domiciled in France, Mick Jagger was prevented from taking part because his visa couldn't be cleared in time. Busy with the post-production of *Being There* in Hollywood, Peter Sellers couldn't make it, either. During a trip to Disneyland made by the odd but amicable trio of Harrison, Shankar and Sellers, the latter had been suggested as an ideal compere. Instead, the task fell to George.

To share his lead guitar functions, who better than Eric Clapton? Unfortunately, Clapton's drug habit had now reduced him to spending many lethargic hours between fixes either asleep or before the television, nourished by fast food. As testimony to his regard for George, however, Eric dragged himself from this pit to cross the Atlantic to do his bit for East Pakistan. He found this no easy job. Hours passed at Kennedy Airport for those appointed to look after him. Plane after British plane would land and Clapton would still be shuttered in Hurtwood Edge. Giving up, they missed him when he finally touched down the night before the reckoning. Dazed and ill, he festered in his hotel room while the poor girl he'd brought with him scoured the city for heroin.

Just as doubtful a participant as Clapton was Bob Dylan, whom George had had in mind to be the 1970s equivalent of "featured popular vocalist". Although unnerved by headlines such as "Dylan's Midnight Flop!"[263] after his Isle of Wight re-emergence, he was nevertheless intrigued enough to turn up with his guitar at George's hotel suite to find out exactly what was required of him. While mulling over the more recent of his songs, Bob's rejoinder to Harrison's earnest proposal that they dredge up 'Blowing In The Wind' was to wonder why they didn't try 'I Want To Hold Your Hand' as well. George seemed to have talked him into appearing, but, "right up until the moment he stepped on stage, I was not sure that he was coming".[210]

With sales of *All Things Must Pass* approaching three million, George alone could have sold out the concrete-and-glass amphitheatre many times over. From the onset, an extra performance had had to be crammed in. In order to mollify further demand (and to battle bootleggers), both shows were to be captured on tape and celluloid. Now there was no turning back, as George stole nervous glances at the increasing depth into which he might plunge should he not live up to the selfish public's expectations.

Rather than Blind Faith's self-conscious iconoclasm or The Plastic Ono Band's pandemonium, George's scrupulous rehearsals in a studio on West 57th Street, near Carnegie Hall, aimed at a slick, professional show with few avenues for excessive improvisatory excursions. There'd be nothing in the set that hadn't been a hit for someone on stage or wasn't well-known enough for applause to burst out and subside over its introduction, whether this was the circular riff of 'Wah-Wah' or the backing harmonies prefacing Ringo's vocal entry in 'It Don't Come Easy'. No matter what his musicians got up to elsewhere, George emphasised punctuality and discipline and provided wholesome Indian dainties when some might have expected beer and hamburgers for meal breaks.

Of the principals under his metaphorical baton, only Billy Preston and Ringo could be relied upon to attend as George drove the band through the umpteenth attempt at 'Beware Of Darkness'. Very much in charge, he'd decided to do that one as a duet with Leon Russell, whose star-studded album credits and production of Dylan's latest single during his stint with Mad Dogs And Englishmen indicated his elevation to hip omnipresence after years of anonymous studio work. This reputation had also earned him a solo spot in George's show, although this could be withdrawn if and when room was needed for Dylan, Lennon or Clapton. On standby, too, was Clapton's understudy Jesse "Ed" Davis, whom Klaus Voorman had subjected to a crash-course of the set.

There was still no sign of Eric during the final run-through on the Saturday. Into the bargain, as the evil hour when her husband was actually going to walk onstage without her crept closer, Yoko Ono's rage had exploded in a tantrum of such violence that her other half, after crushing his spectacles in his fist, slammed out of their hotel to catch the next flight home. Dylan got as far as the auditorium but, pausing in the dusty half-light beyond footlight still being tested, "He freaked out...and he was saying, 'Hey man, this isn't my scene. I can't make this.'"[211] He was persuaded to at least soundcheck, but who knew how seriously his stage fright was to be taken?

At around noon the next day, even those without tickets began milling round the huge lobby entrance to Madison Square Gardens. Bestowing each forehead with pinpricks of sweat, the humidity was what The Lovin' Spoonful had sung about in 'Summer In The City'. And yet, despite the leaden skies and touts richer by 1,000 per cent, the mood of the wilted flower children in the queue was light and friendly. When the audience settled down, rumours were as rife in the euphoric atmosphere as frisbees and balloons. Clapton had been seen, guitar case in hand, panting along the dingy passages of nearby Pennsylvania Station. McCartney was stuck in a traffic jam on Seventh Avenue. Even as the customers filed in, Harrison was outlining the set to Dave Clark amidst the wearisome blues jams, prima-donna piques and the usual dressing-room squabbles.

With credulity stretched to the limit, some were weeping with anticipation when the lights dimmed and George steeled himself to face facts. He needn't have worried. The whole extravaganza was a triumph, because everybody wanted it to be. The vogue for spirituality had already provoked philanthropy in other pop stars. Fleetwood Mac's Peter Green, for example, had commanded his accountant, on pain of a punch on the nose, to redirect incoming monies to the coffers of the needy. Cliff Richard had even made a field visit to Bangladesh in as early as 1968 – although, by his own uncomfortably honest admission, this patronage of the Evangelical Alliance Relief Fund "was to give me a sense of satisfaction and fulfilment, and I don't pretend I felt any heartache for the people in the Third World or anywhere else, for that matter".[264]

Even the humblest equipment-humper would be namechecked on the subsequent album and film, but, whatever the motives of those George Harrison had assembled at Madison Square Gardens, "The whole vibe of that concert was that it was something bigger than the lot of us".[262] The onlookers thought so, too. They had a glimmer of how much George had, did and would have on his plate, and so loved him for wanting to please them before he'd even plucked a string. On the radio for the past week had been his new single, 'Bangla Desh' (sic), written after Shankar came "to me with sadness in his eyes".[265] A slow recitative broke into rushing feverishness as George, singing like he might mean it, appealed for "bread to get the starving fed".[265]

'Bangla Desh' was to be the finale of both shows before George vanished stage left. Descending the escalators to the lobby afterwards, most of the customers would agree that they'd participated, however passively, in making history. If nothing else, it had been a diverting evening's entertainment. Opening the show, Ravi and his three musicians' long 'Bangla Dhun' raga had garnered a fidgety respect as their affinity to the main event ensured an almost palpable wave of goodwill – reminiscent of Monterey – washing over them.

Polite clapping for Shankar gave way to barrages of cheering, whistling and stamping when George and his cohorts attacked song after familiar song. A reluctant interlocutor, the bandleader – in matching white suit and Stratocaster – restricted himself largely to announcing the boys in the band six numbers in, building up the lesser-known of those he'd let take a lead vocal and bringing on his one surprise guest. Via nods and eye contact, he conducted a punchy set in which some *All Things Must Pass* items were actually rattled off in less time than the studio originals, in what might have been an opportunity to correct oversights. Headed by Claudia Linnear, the nine-voice chorale fermented with a passion above and beyond that of The George O'Hara Singers. Wisely, a creaky 'Hear Me Lord' was dropped for the second house, but even so, "We were very lucky, really, as we didn't have full rehearsals, as a lot of people had just come in from England or were on tour in the States. It worked out pretty good, considering."[188]

To many, the essence of the show was Harrison and the thrillingly unrehearsed Clapton breaking sweat on duelling guitars during 'While My Guitar Gently Weeps', one of the rare "blowing" numbers. Extricating himself from his Hammond organ, Billy Preston enlivened his one hit with a flickering dancing display that prodded the right festive nerve, while Ringo's singing was endearing in its distracted clumsiness during 'It Don't Come Easy'. Unlike Ringo, George didn't forget his words, but his larynx hadn't switched immediately into gear. Through either trepidation or a blunder at the PA desk, it had been less conspicuous than the accompaniment during the first minutes of the matinee, but, as the sound balance evened out, his voice shimmered like full moonlight over the sea of heads. He was in good form, edgy and without the irritating embellishments that vocalists like Leon Russell are prone to produce in a concert setting.

For longer than Billy and Ringo put together, The Concerts For Bangladesh became The Leon Russell Show. George's band introduction had purposely enabled an instrumental switchover, whereby minstrels in better accord with Russell's Southern-fried flamboyance could get on stage, with grizzled Carl Radle's throb considered preferable to Klaus Voorman's Teutonic elegance. With no hits of his own, Leon offered a medley of 'Jumping Jack Flash' and The Coasters' 'Young Blood', once a Harrison lead vocal with The Quarry Men. To the relentless snappy jitter that typified the "funky" oeuvre, Russell's up-front encroachment was the epitome of the self-satisfied sexism of the Delaney And Bonnie super-sidemen. In a slobbering Dixie whine, abetted by Claudia Linnear's strident responses, a raunchy monologue that was the pinnacle of male chauvinist piggery segued into the lascivious 'Young Blood', which culminated with the cocksure high velocity of Russell's regular guitarist. The most that can be said for this aberration was that it made a change from the piety of 'My Sweet Lord' and 'That's The Way God Planned It'.

Getting back on course after indulging Leon, George took it down with a 'Here Comes The Sun', in which only he and Badfinger's Pete Ham – each on acoustic six-string – were heard. George was unsure what would follow this lull. On the set list sellotaped to his guitar, "Bob?" had been written, "so I just looked 'round to see if there was any indication if Bob was going to come or not, and he was already there. He was so nervous, and he had his harmonica on and his guitar in his hand, and he was walking right on stage. It was, like, now or never, and so I had to say, '[I'd] like to bring on a friend of us all – Mister Bob Dylan.'"[262]

The timid songbird was backed by a relieved Harrison and Ringo on tambourine and Leon Russell (that man again) on bass through a 20-minute slot that, yes, did include hoary old 'Blowing In The Wind'. Feeling almost as jumpy as Bob, George picked his obligatos without the safety net of the big band's blast. Nevertheless, any apprehension was lost in the mob's silent disbelief as Bob Dylan – the single most reclusive and messianic symbol of hipness – swept aside like dust all that had gone before. What else could come after but The Beatles' last US chart-topper, 'Something?'

After the 'Bangla Desh' playout, the company repaired to a celebratory party at which merry-andrews from The Who and Grand Funk Railroad queued for the buffet with swamis and sarod players. Roaring drunk at the piano, Phil Spector pounded out 'Da-Doo-Ron-Ron' and more from his voluminous back catalogue. Once again, he'd been commissioned by Harrison to co-produce a triple album, and once again the twitchy Spector couldn't abide more than a few hours in the studio as the *soirée* – from 'Bangla Dhun' to 'Bangla Desh' – was readied for vinyl. Starr, Dylan and others who'd been put in the spotlight had been promised that they would not be incommoded "if it turns out lousy".[262] All, however, gave their approval, bar Russell, who insisted on a remix of his bit.

Although the artists involved were contracted to different companies, this was less problematic than the unseemly antipathy preceding the album's release. Blaming Capitol's president, Bhaskar Menon – who happened to be Indian – for unwarranted delay, George passed the prestigious task of its distribution to CBS,

Dylan's label, whose television outlet broadcast concert highlights. The world outside North America would have to wait until the following spring, when the film went on general release via 20th-Century Fox.

In collusion with the director Saul Swimmer, George had compiled excerpts of the night's travail. Adding to his technical knowledge of film as faults were ironed out, he noted "about twelve cuts in the film. Nine of them were fake. We had to get a long shot of me where you couldn't see my mouth moving, because they didn't have the opening segment."[188] Meanwhile, Bob Dylan, present at the editing, got his own way over "not changing camera angles, and it is all grainy, but that was because Bob wanted it like that. It was great to have him in it at all."[262]

The flick would win no Oscars, but the album – out in time for Christmas – earned a Grammy and spent most of 1972 in the Hot 100. More self-interested was a band who nipped in sharpish with a French cover version of 'Bangla Desh' and another who cloned every last lecherous gurgle of Leon Russell's medley in a "Battle Of The Bands" tournament at Reading University. Harrison's 'Bangla Desh' had been only a middling hit, while missing completely was another tie-in single, Ravi Shankar's 'Joi Bangla', which translated as "Be Triumphant, Bangla!" It was more melodiously uplifting than any other of George's Indo-pop productions.

The LP's picture sleeve mentioned the Bangladesh Disaster Fund organised by UNICEF, for whom was earmarked the $243,418.50 generated by the show plus the greater amounts accrued by record, film and other by-products, such as George's Material World Charitable Foundation, created to "encourage refugees to start growing their own food and thereby make the cash go further than it would in outright purchases".[262] However, although record companies might have waived royalties theoretically owing to their artists, George discovered that "the law and tax people do not help. They make it so that it is not worthwhile doing anything decent."[262] The show might have been over, but "just that one decision to help Ravi, it took two years solid of my life",[211] as turgid bureaucracy on both sides of the Atlantic dissected the Bangladesh millions with unhelpful slowness. As George hadn't registered the event as a charity, most of the cash would remain at the mercy of the IRS in Washington until – via a conversation between his hip son and George – President Ford began "to try and help it go through the normal channels and get it solved".[210]

In London, even personal appeals by George failed to reduce purchase tax on the album, although the Exchequer's chief financial secretary, Patrick Jenkin, was "glad to talk with a man who has gone right to the top and has stayed there so long", and who put his case so "very eloquently".[266] Eventually, George had to sign a cheque for £1 million to the British government after he had been quoted "sections, schedules and all the other bullshit which is so much part of the game of politics. Until the [politicians] became human, we must do our service to others without their help."[267]

The only gleam of hope had come from the House of Lords, when Lord Harlech met Allen Klein over a meal. Since hosting a reception for The Beatles at the British Embassy in Washington in 1964, Harlech had taken on – among other posts – the chairmanship of Shelter, the campaign for the homeless. With a daughter lately moved in with Eric Clapton, he was, if not "with it", then more conscious than other upper-class do-gooders that The Beatles were just the tip of the pop iceberg that had made more fortunes than had ever been known in the history of entertainment. When George stepped off the QE2 from New York, he did not deny the Harlech-Klein summit nor further talks with Tory MP Jeffrey Archer, who arranged George's luncheon date with Patrick Jenkin. Some newspapers even named the day – 10 October 1971 – when Harrison would repeat his Madison Square miracle on a grander scale in Britain for Shelter. Not reported, however, were the impossible conditions that Klein had stipulated as *quid pro quo* for this deed. One would require a revision of British law so that Harrison and Lennon's drugs convictions would be quashed.

In one throw, George had outshone all John and his wife's bed-ins, John's repudiation of his MBE and more mystifying tactics to right the wrongs of mankind. Perhaps in a spirit of one-upmanship, Lennon spoke for a while of a Wembley showcase for a worthy cause with him, Yoko and their sort of people, instead of George and his Bangladesh gang.

With no such axe to grind, cells within the general public – not only the young – had taken up George's challenge. "There were a lot of people who gave a lot of money and collected on the streets and were hanging on UNICEF's door saying, 'What can we do to help?' A lot of people don't do anything unless they're inspired, and on that it is important, I suppose, that I inspired a lot of people to do something. I mean, I didn't really want the task in the first place."[262] However unwillingly he'd shouldered the burden, George – as the representative of common folk – contemplated riding roughshod over official interference by travelling personally to India to ensure delivery of what he'd describe in a 1973 B-side as "the rice that keeps going astray on its way to Bombay".[268] Composed the day after the concert, his naïve 'The Day The Word Gets 'Round' had smouldered from the angered question of why a mere pop star rather than a governing body was obliged to pinpoint iniquities.

With The Concerts For Bangladesh shipwrecks as his sea markers, Bob Geldof would be knighted for Live Aid after 1985, but, further back on pop's road to respectability, George's efforts had been rewarded by an elevation to *Playboy*'s "Musicians Hall Of Fame". He'd received an MBE for less. Live Aid was still two years away when he presented a cheque for a fraction of the concert's net proceeds to Hugh Downs of the US committee for UNICEF on an American chat show. Accepting a special citation in return, George told the viewers, "It's nice to know you can achieve these sorts of things, even though the concert was ten years ago and the public has forgotten about the problems of Bangladesh. The children still desperately need help and the money will have a significant impact."[269] It was beneath him to vilify those who, in frozen ledgers and computer run-offs, had super-taxed the starving, the diseased and the huddled masses fleeing from terror.

13 His Lectureship

The Bangladesh spectacular was the George Harrison moment, never to return. During the 15-month hiatus between the film's première and his next album, no time would have been better for a world tour. With its appetite whetted by *All Things Must Pass*, The Concerts For Bangladesh and associated hit singles, the public awaited a carnival of the same magnitude as a Fab Four tour, albeit, as Brian Epstein once said, "not in the context of the previous terms".[270] George was now the most respected and, seemingly, the most capable ex-Beatle. Already the first fan club devoted to him alone – the Harrison Alliance – had sprung up in Connecticut. Dollars danced before his eyes, but the so-called Money Beatle, his own man at last, "wouldn't really care if no one ever heard of me again".[271]

His fortunes were by no means secure, but after a decade on the run he chose the stink of fertiliser to dressing-room fug. While growing to manhood in the hothouse of the beat boom and its endless North American sequel, he'd been treated like a food pigeonhole in a self-service cafeteria. No more could it be taken for granted that George Harrison existed only to vend entertainment with a side-serving of cheap insight. The world wouldn't let him stroll unmolested in a public park, so he'd had to buy one of his own. Unobserved, he'd stride forth on a clear, dew-sodden morning across his lake, whose stepping stones made it look like you were walking on water, and into the woods and pastures of his acres. At one with nature, all of the intolerable adulation that his life contained – the Number Ones, the money down the drain – could be transformed to matters of minor importance.

In the first of many hibernations, he watched Friar Park's flowers bloom again, ended a joyless marriage and was conducted by the head waiter to the best table in the restaurant. Of his celebrity, he'd admit, "There are perks, but it all balances out."[272] Although it wasn't downhill all the way, George's popularity on disc was eroded by an overloading of his artistic canvas with the religious preoccupations that were besetting his private life. Once a real cool cat, he was derided by hippies as one more bourgeois liberal with conservative tendencies, a fully paid-up subscriber to what neil would call "the Breadhead Conspiracy". The economic potential of a damaging re-emergence on stage would outweigh its creative merit. They'd find him out.

His fall was not perceptible in 1971, as 'Bangla Desh' was waved out of sight after a reasonable chart run. Some juke boxes had been more inclined to wear away its B-side, 'Deep Blue', which – sung with veiled resignation – was an articulation of Louise Harrison's final illness. Sent home after her operation, "She recovered a little bit for about seven months and, during that period, my father – who'd taken care of her – had suddenly exploded with ulcers, and he was in the same hospital. So I was pretending to both of them that the other one was OK."[59] That sick-room smell was still in their youngest son's nostrils when 'Deep Blue' came to him "one exhausted afternoon, with those major and minor chords. It's filled with the frustration and gloom of going in those hospitals, and the feeling of *disease* – as the word's true meaning is – that permeated the atmosphere."[59]

For all the dicta that he'd absorbed that trivialised death, George was still shaken by the manner of his mother's wasting away. Although a pitiable invalid, Louise had remained to the end the cheerful, patient ally who'd been unmindful of the din as his youthful fingers had striven to emulate Carl Perkins and Chuck Berry into the witching hour. She'd been his biggest fan, but she'd never had favourites among her offspring. Nevertheless, George's immediate kin had continued to be recipients of his largesse. Taking over from Terry Doran in managing Friar Park for Our Kid was brother Harold, in whose gatehouse office had been installed electronic screening for surveillance of the vast expanse of gardens. Meanwhile, overseer of a squad of full-time gardeners plus a botanist was Peter, who'd also been persuaded to turn south. In a bungalow on the same road as the school established by the recent cowled occupants of Friar Park, his wife cooed over Mark, who, in 1972, had been the latest addition to the Harrison brood.

The new baby's Aunt Pattie grieved for the children that she'd never have – not by George, anyway, as he'd purged himself of all things carnal. An inattentive spouse is apt to provoke extreme strategy in his partner. Thumbing her nose at George's spiritual pursuits, Pattie lowered the Om flag that flew over Friar Park and replaced it with a skull and crossbones. George's behaviour was not so funny after he and Pattie sustained minor injuries when, within days of him regaining his licence, the car skidded off the A4 through Maidenhead. Pattie took to her bed on medical advice, but her recovery was impaired by George's pounding on a drum-kit that he'd set up in the next room.

Worse still would be the embarrassment when, during dinner at the Starkeys', the company almost leapt out of their skins when George suddenly declared his deep love for Maureen. Calculated to wound his wife rather than compliment a bright-red Mrs Starkey, this bombshell would reverberate beyond the tense dining room as Pattie rushed out in tears to lock herself in the bathroom. Although Ringo's knuckles had whitened after George's outburst, Maureen's later reciprocation of her guest's affection wouldn't pain him as much as he'd thought it would. It might have hurt more if Harrison had been underhanded about it. What did it matter? Ringo and Maureen were washed up, anyway. If anything, John – as self-appointed Beatle paterfamilias – was more annoyed, apparently chastising George for this "incest".[273]

Although he "always had a sense of humour, even during my really heavy religious period",[151] his displays of devilment were more skirmishes than jokes as he and Pattie drifted into open estrangement. Alone in New York's Park Lane Hotel, George composed 'So Sad' as a requiem for his marriage.

Almost all of George's next LP was cut at Apple, but he and Ringo were spending increasingly longer spells away, mainly in the ego-massaging environs of Los Angeles, where George maintained a

Beverly Hills *pied à terre* with obligatory swimming pool and tennis court. Living on the West Coast unavoidably affected his vocabulary, although other Englishmen in the Hollywood Raj were more pliant in drawling "can" for toilet and "sidewalk" for pavement. Among them was Dave Mason, who reeled in George to pick guitar on his new album. Further affirming his standing in this firmament of hipness, George's played on an LP track by hippy comedians Cheech and Chong, whose humor (*not* humour) wrung dry what it could from drugs and balling chicks.

Turning out for other sessions, he'd be greeted by familiar faces amidst the many British musicians now seeking their fortunes in California. Badfinger had been over there when George's sure-footed production of their third LP was abandoned when all decamped for Madison Square Gardens. Salvaged from his ministrations was the hit single 'Day After Day', which was propelled by a guitar introduction too singular to have been played by anyone else but the producer. In a more creative role, George left his mark on an eponymous album by Ringo that would temporarily allay the ghost of "the downtrodden drummer. You don't know how hard it is to fight that."[260]

Ringo was the closest The Beatles would ever come to an artistic reunion, embracing as it did compositions of all four, with Lennon's semi-autobiographical 'I'm The Greatest' utilising by chance the Klaus-instead-of-Paul line-up, plus Billy Preston. Both 'I'm The Greatest' and Paul's contribution could have been written asleep, but of greater substance were three by George. As a trailer for the album, his 'Photograph' – co-written with Starr – sold a million. Sweeter, however, was John's affable telegram to Ringo to "write me a Number One tune".[274]

The session for 'I'm The Greatest' had started with only John, Ringo, Klaus and producer Richard Perry grouped around a piano figuring out the unfinished song's bridge when George telephoned to invite himself along. Their concord when recording was so jovial that he was emboldened to suggest to John that they ratify the old rumour by forming a permanent group with the others present. Still peeved, perhaps, over the Bangladesh business, John floored George with a sleight of social judo by shrugging off this idea as a *faux pas* and artlessly changed the subject, pretending not to notice George's pride twist into a frown. Despite the glaring commercial pragmatism of a continued solo career, to be on equal footing with John in a new group had been too sorely tempting for George. Although the idea had been scorned, just as his friendly overtures had been when he had first known John, for a while George would champion Lennon's music and confess, "I'd join a band with John Lennon any day, but I couldn't join a band with Paul McCartney. That's not personal, but from a musical point of view."[275]

Wings' *Red Rose Speedway* and George's *Living In The Material World* – only a single album this time – were both released in summer 1973 and were poles apart. The catchy jingles that were *Red Rose Speedway* only confirmed that McCartney's wispy capacity for "granny music" was bottomless. Always a weak link nowadays were his lyrics, churned out with much the same nonchalance with which Ernie Wise wrote plays.

Whereas *Red Rose Speedway* was starved of intellectual depth, there was no shortage on *Living In The Material World*, on which all of the songs were "about" something – the transience of fiscal cares, the inevitability of death or 'The Light That Has Lighted The World'. Although 'Don't Let Me Wait Too Long' betrayed that George's sublimation of lust was by no means total, its consummation was, nonetheless, "like it came from above". With two numbers inspired by Prabhupada's teachings, buzzwords like "om" and "Krishna" blended with Scouse parlance – world leaders acting "like big girls" – and references to The Beatles. However, his verbosity was offset by humour that was not always obvious, the stodgy arrangement of 'Be Here Now' masking a lyric born of a funny story. George was unable to bottle his mirth on the in-joking 'Miss O'Dell' – written after an Apple employee – which, interspersed with Dylan-esque harmonica, let fly such eruditions as Paul's old Liverpool telephone number.

'Miss O'Dell' hadn't suited the LP, and so was consigned to the B-side of its promotional 45, 'Give Me Love (Give Me Peace On Earth)', which had flowed from George with an ease as devoid of ante-start agonies as a Yoko Ono "think piece". It had been one of those lucky creative accidents in which monetary gain – largely from a US Number One – was out of proportion to basic effort. The line "help me cope with this heavy load" might have touched a raw nerve or two in Britain's dole queues, even if the publishing royalties from 'Give Me Love', along with all but one other album track, were assigned to the Material World Charitable Foundation.

The exception was 'Try Some Buy Some', which was left over from the Spector era. Rather than re-record it, George had simply substituted his own vocal for that of Spector's wife, whose version was now mouldering on deletion racks. Although its lyrics mattered less than the general effect, 'Try Some Buy Some' fitted the ethereal mode of *Living In The Material World*. However, its heavy-handed orchestration was at odds with a self-production criterion closer to the style of George Martin, in that it was much less concerned about inflating songs with gratuitous frills. The looser abundance of *All Things Must Pass* was stripped away in favour of a sparser ensemble from which Jim Horn's solitary saxophone might honk a counterpoint that Spector would have saturated with massed strings. Two thumps of timpani would enliven a middle eight all the better for not being buried in grandiloquence.

This moderation resulted in arrangements flexible enough for the title track to flit smoothly from a verse rocking with clipped guitar and Nicky Hopkins' jangling ivories to its quiet "spiritual-sky" sequence made celestial by tabla and flute. As well as ending with a syncopated blues run-down, this number also contained an interlude in which tenor sax intermingled with George's now quite distinctive bottleneck.

"George is king of rock 'n' roll slide guitar"[164] was the opinion voiced by a musician of such sagacity as Jeff Lynne, of the just-launched Electric Light Orchestra. Others wouldn't rate him as highly as that, but in 1973 George was certainly a contender. With controlled grace, he was as inventive in subtle careen on the downbeat hootenanny of 'Sue Me Sue You Blues' as he was in shinning up the octaves for 'The Light That Has Lighted The World', composed originally for Cilla Black to record. George's new niche was once described as "country and eastern",[275] but his most exotic exploit on *Living In The Material World* was the decorative fingering and harmonics of 'Be Here Now', which was on a par with the acoustic virtuosity of John Renbourn.

Harrison himself applied a flattering comparison to his own singing which unfurled a hitherto unprecedented audacity as he tackled the album's more oblique metaphysics without affectation. In swerving from muttered trepidation to strident intensity in 'Who Can See It', you could appreciate why George would later avow that "it reminds me of Roy Orbison".[39] He may have lacked the Big O's operatic pitch, but 'Who Can See It' was among George's most magnificent performances on record. Veering cleanly into falsetto on other tracks, too, never had his pipes been so adept.

The virtues of George's latest did not prevent some scribes – in Britain, especially – from pulling it to bits, their strongest objections being its preachy overtones. "They feel threatened when you talk about something that isn't just be-bop-a-lula," George countered, "and if you say the words 'God'...or 'Lord' it makes some people's hair curl."[210] With the merest mental athleticism, some lumped *Living In The Material World* with the outmoded works of Deep Purple, ELP and James Taylor. Its mystic flavour was somehow too familiar. Wasn't that "spiritual-sky" bit like 'Baby You're A Rich Man'? Only the most hooked Beatle fan had the time to decipher the concealed messages in the cover shot of George proposing a toast to the other musicians on a Friar Park lawn. Was it a comment on the Last Supper? Among objects positioned in the middle distance were a pram (Mark?) and a wheelchair (his mother?). Further back, a woman dangled her bare leg out of a window, but so what?

Unimpressed by this symbolism (if that's what it was), a British teenager might have still dug the gear worn by Krishna in his chariot on the inner sleeve. Androgynous in beaded kaftan, jewelled fez and peacock feather, and strikingly pretty, the Supreme Personality of Godhead was not unlike some of the new breed of theatrical British chartbusters. On *Top Of The Pops*, a commercially expedient toy windmill twirled on Jeff Lynne's hat when he lip-synched The Electric Light Orchestra's debut single. If the art-college camp of Roxy Music and David Bowie – who'd dressed as a lady for one LP cover – appealed to intellectuals as The Beatles had to Hamburg "exis", The

Bay City Rollers – all bow ties and half-mast tartan trousers – were hyped as "the new Beatles", and for a few months Rollermania was rampant among schoolgirls.

The newcomers' many chart strikes guaranteed that they were despised by the whiskered, denimed buyers of Leon Russell's new live triple album. As one who'd "never read the pop papers now and never listen to Radio Luxembourg",[271] George was unable to comment, because, even in as late as 1975, "I've still never heard The Bay City Rollers."[275] Bowie's clothing might not have been for George, but he must have approved a musical taste which led Bowie to revamp The Merseys' 'Sorrow' in autumn 1973. With a nod to Ringo, he agreed that Marc Bolan had come up with "good commercial songs",[271] as had fellow singer/composer Gilbert O'Sullivan, but the impact of these was adulterated by O'Sullivan's being "made to look a dummy by his management".[271]

The shorts and pudding-basin haircut might have been contributory to Gilbert having more hits than more conservatively-attired Peter Skellern, a Lancastrian whose wittily observed love songs were in the same bag. Skellern, George's favourite of the current crop ("he reminds me of Harry Nilsson, full of potential"[276]) and a former pianist for Billy Fury, was honoured with more than mere praise when his fellow northerner popped in with a guitar to lend a hand on his sixth album, *Hard Times*.

George's assistance on the over-rated Nilsson's unpleasant 'You're Breaking My Heart (So Fuck You)' was a more accurate indicator of preference. British pop had nothing on the more traditional exactitudes of laid-back Yanks like The Allman Brothers Band, who were to New York what the Bramlett mob had been to Los Angeles. As well as such contemporary Americana, a concert by reggae apostles Bob Marley And The Wailers was the "best thing I've seen in ten years".[276] Once ignored by most of the so-called intelligentsia, West Indian pop was now outflanking even blues as the new "twisted voice of the underdog" and student disco accessory. Marley reminded George "so much of Dylan in the early days, playing guitar as if he's so new to it. And his rhythm – it's so simple, and yet so beautiful."[276] For the same reason, George was "still basically in favour of the things I liked in the old days – Smokey Robinson, Stevie Wonder, those sort of things".[276]

So were The Carpenters, the States' major singles export of the 1970s, who hit in 1975 with an overhaul of 'Please Mr Postman'. David Bowie and Roxy Music's Bryan Ferry had cut entire albums of oldies, as Lennon also did in 1975. To a lesser degree, George too would succumb. A lot of his pals, including Kláus Voorman and Delaney Bramlett, were among those invited to London to record with Jerry Lee Lewis. At around this time, also, many artists released tracks with "rock 'n' roll" in the title. Seeing the transparency of it made many pop consumers scour jumble sales, junk shops, deletion racks and charity stalls for overlooked artefacts from past musical eras. At the Parisian grave of The Doors' Jim Morrison, a mourner reasoned that these and later seasons of revivals were because "the '60s' music was much better than stuff now".[277]

At the table head in the Valhalla of the lamented decade's youth culture sat The Beatles. By proxy, their presence was felt still in vinyl respects paid by the likes of Elton John and Eric Burdon's new group, War. That glam rock did not bear the same us-and-them parallel to pop's elder statesmen as punk would was implied in a reverential treatment of 'Tomorrow Never Knows' by 801, an offshoot of Roxy Music. Beatle compilations sold briskly, too, with two double volumes of "greatest hits" qualifying for a gold disc two days before release in 1973.

Timely, then, was a Stuart Sutcliffe art exhibition in a Greenwich gallery and *John, Paul, George, Ringo – And Bert*, a musical play by William Russell which shattered box office records at Liverpool's Everyman Theatre that summer. Its stylised portrayal of The Beatles' fable through the eyes of Bert, a fan, was uncannily close to the bone. Contrasting with Pete Best, sacked and alone beneath the proscenium, was a comedy scene of George – played by Philip Joseph – trying to blow into a sitar when still new to Oriental music. When it reached the West End, the proper George looked in, primarily to see his old friend Arthur Kelly, who was playing Bert. "George found it hard to watch," perceived Derek Taylor, "and I found it hard work sitting with him. It was a genuine form of suffering for him."[276]

The drama's climax was Bert, who'd grown up to become a Gary Glitter-ish performer, deputising for the disbanded Beatles who'd just chickened out of a reunion appearance at the Philharmonic Hall. George didn't see this scene, having shuffled out during the interval, but he knew of all sorts of old groups trying their luck again recently. Rebirths had been attempted by The Byrds, The Small Faces, The Temperance Seven, Dave Dee's lot, The Spencer Davis Group, you name 'em. As if they'd never been away, The Walker Brothers rematerialised in the UK Top Ten after eight years apart. Stranger – and infinitely grander – things could happen.

It had only been George and Ringo at Madison Square Gardens, but still the headlines had shrieked, "Beatlemania Sweeps A City!"[278] and even, "The Beatles Are Back!".[279] Since then, monetary inducement for the whole group to play together just one more time had multiplied until for the taking were millions for half an hour at Shea Stadium and even more for an outdoor show at Aintree racecourse. On top of that would be advances for television coverage, merchandising and closed-circuit cinema by satellite.

The four were still embroiled in the financial horrors of Apple, but socially the ex-Beatles were on friendlier terms with each other. George traipsed along with Ringo to a Stones concert in New York. On another night, John had joined them for dinner with Bryan Ferry. Even George and Paul had been photographed together at a Wings press party and, crucially, John had kept a civil tongue in his head when he and Paul had met for a drink in Los Angeles.

Time had healed, but there lingered memories of the struggle back in Liverpool and the unbelievable outcome. The old days had passed, but, no matter how much they'd feigned indifference, neglected to send birthday cards and traduced each other, each Beatle had stayed in the picture by making circuitous enquiries about the other three's activities. George's mask had slipped during the 'I'm The Greatest' session, and Paul – in a dark hour, professionally – had mentioned that he wouldn't mind working with John again on a casual basis. John was now saying how wrong it had been for the group to have split so decisively.

With hormones raging in a premature male menopause, Lennon

had just left Yoko to fling himself into a 15-month "lost weekend" in the company of hard drinkers like Nilsson, Spector and Keith Moon. With divorce from Maureen pending, Ringo too was sucked into this woozy vortex.

For all the hail-fellow-well-met bonhomie, that all four were losing their grip one way or another wasn't the soundest foundation for a second coming of The Beatles. Pressed on the subject, Gary Glitter hit the nail on the head: "They'll have to come back as a bigger creative force than they did before, which would be very difficult indeed."[280] It had been just as difficult for Muhammad Ali to regain his world heavyweight title in 1975. Possibly The Beatles might have regained theirs, even though the world had become wiser to their individual weaknesses. Inevitably, too much would be expected of them, but whether their first new record was good, bad or – worse – ordinary wasn't the issue. As would be proved by a 1980 event more shattering than any one-off concert, Beatlemania was for life. While 'She Loves You' spun on Radio 1's *All Our Yesterplays*, Mr and Mrs Average became Swinging '60s teenagers again, lovestruck and irresponsible.

The objects of their distant adoration did not, after all, amalgamate once more. Their very vacillation over the matter indicated neither destitution nor any real enthusiasm. "You can't reheat a souffle,"[246] concluded McCartney. Instead, you could – as Wings did – take the market that carried the fiercest torch for the departed Fab Four for every cent.

Oddly, it was the Beatle least addicted to the limelight who, in winter 1974, was the first to undertake a coast-to-coast trek across North America as a solo attraction. Balancing George's dislike of the road was restlessness and a resolution to cover as many prestigious venues as possible to give his forthcoming LP, *Dark Horse*, an extra boost – although, with *Living In The Material World* doing as well as its bulkier predecessor, he was still on much of a winning streak, as demonstrated by a huge turnout for the pre-tour press conference. Set in a Beverly Hills hotel, it was like a parody of some Hollywood B-feature: cameras click like typewriters at the star's tardy arrival in a flash Mercedes; no autographs, please; media hounds circle the star, thrusting stick-mikes at his mouth as he deadpans their usual inane and damned impertinent questions. Mr Harrison, are The Beatles getting back together? How did you find America? Turn left at Greenland. Everyone cracks up because Ringo said that in 1964. Are you getting divorced? No, that's as silly as getting married. Why isn't Eric Clapton in your backing band? Tell us why, George.

It wouldn't take long for the scum press to flesh out the Harrisons' domestic upheavals. Clapton hadn't been the first to cuckold George, had he? One Sunday much later, *The News Of The World* teased some sleazy column inches from Krissy, once the bride of Ron Wood, the newest Rolling Stone. In arm-chaired languor after their roast lunch, many Britons found her tale of Beatle-Stone wife-swapping a soothing read. Across two hemispheres, the Woods and Harrisons had flaunted their shame – Krissy and George on holiday "on a very serious and spiritual level"[281] in Portugal and then Switzerland; Ron and Pattie were in the Bahamas. "If anyone was jealous, it was me,"[281] protested Krissy. No one else was. George and Ron tinkered on guitars and wrote songs together and Pattie hadn't minded when the paparazzi named another of her husband's paramours, a Kathy Simmons, whose previous boyfriend had been Rod Stewart, singer with Wood's old group, The Faces.

Two old friends who used to be lovers, Pattie and George made light of each other's infidelities, understanding that sooner or later one of them would find – in the words of 'So Sad' – "someone who can fill the part of the dream we once had". When at last Eric confronted George with his feelings about Pattie, there was less anger than amusement, with George offering to swap her for the latest of Clapton's long-suffering girlfriends. Because George's disarming wit and rationalisation had defused what might have developed into an ugly showdown, the path to a formal dissolution of the Harrisons' dead marriage on 7 June 1977 began on a summer's day in 1975 in the hallway at Hurtwood Edge during some light banter between the parties. As if watching a tennis match, Pattie's eyes flickered from husband to lover. First it was George with, "Well, I suppose I'd better divorce her," then Eric's, "Well, that means I've got to marry her."[44]

Eric's best-selling solo single thus far had been a version of Bob

Marley's 'I Shot The Sheriff', and he'd been annoyed that George and not he had met the great Marley, who died in 1981. This was checkmated by Eric being in thicker with Bob Dylan than George was then. Despite their continued amity, a striving for one-upmanship persisted between Harrison and Clapton. With retrospective honesty, Eric would discourse to his eulogists of his winning of Pattie's hand. Verified by friend and actor John Hurt is a story of Harrison challenging Clapton to a guitar duet over the woman, trading licks rather than using them as clubs, although this may have been one of George's little jokes.

A combination of fame, wealth and religious education had rendered unto Harrison a greater certainty than before about everything he said and did. Longer and more discursive these days were his stern dissertations about living a godly life. Pottering round the garden, he'd go on about karma – often using floral metaphors – and likening working with the soil to meditation. Gravely, he'd present those he considered spiritually inclined with sacred texts. Once he'd lived for cars, girls and records, but 1974's most exciting experience had been an Indian pilgrimage to the holy city of Brindaban to seek Krishna.

Old at 31, a crashing bore and wearing his virtuous observance of his beliefs like Stanley Green did his sandwich board, he was nicknamed "His Lectureship" behind his back. Visitors to Friar Park tended not to swear in his presence. In deference to their vegetarian host – who, since Pattie's departure, had learned to cook his own meals – some would repair to Henley restaurants to gorge themselves with disgraceful joy on steak and chips, mocking over dessert George's proselytising. Back up Gravel Hill, the place smelled of incense and righteousness. Along corridors where portraits of bearded gurus gazed haughtily, you would just as often bump into a robed ascetic as a *Dark Horse* session musician.

"Compared to what I should be, I'm a heathen"[276] seemed, therefore, a strange admission. Morally, some of his guest appearances on the albums of others – Cheech and Chong, Nilsson, *et al* – had been a bit shaky, and there had been rare excursions to catch prurient films like *Last Tango In Paris*, but the greatest paradox during this most cerebral phase of his life was that George was boozing quite heavily. His consumption became so immoderate that for years small tabloid paragraphs would hint falsely of private clinics where blue devils had been sweated out of him.

When tequila and brandy worked their short-lived magic, they stayed the phantoms of paranoia, mounting business difficulties and personal desolations. There were more fatalities, all of them sudden. Most saddening to the Beatle "family" was that of faithful Mal Evans. Dividends from the investments that Mal had made had been disappointing, and, missing the activity and reflected glory of his previous post, he'd left his wife and children for sunny California, where perks of his Beatles connection included an honorary sheriff's badge, which permitted the carrying of sidearms. Thinking that they needed him, he fell in with Ringo and John on the next barstool. He'd also got in on George's act again, even co-writing 'You And Me (Babe)', one of the Harrison contributions for *Ringo*.

More and more often, he'd wake in his Los Angeles bedroom feeling groggy, having salvaged no contentment from following his former masters. The end came when a girl he'd allegedly invited to his apartment told the police that he'd threatened her with a gun. By the time the squad car arrived, he'd barricaded himself in. The cops bashed the door down and the ex-bouncer faced them with the supposed weapon in his hand. Rather than listening to what he might have had to say, they opened fire. At Mal's cremation, some theorised that it had been a kind of suicide.

That had already been the official verdict on Badfinger's Pete Ham, also riven with vocational frustrations, while yet another deprived of the acclaim he may have merited was Ringo's old boss, Rory Storm, who'd expired after tablets prescribed for a chest complaint had been washed down with an injudicious quantity of scotch. No Beatle attended the funeral or the Stormsville wake, Ringo's excuse being that "I wasn't there when he was born, either".[282] Rory's more fortunate brother-in-law, Alvin Stardust, echoed the general opinion, "Rory was very unlucky. None of us could really sing, but some got the breaks and some didn't."[58]

One that did was Cilla Black, now a middle-of-the-road media personality. Their paths had diverged, but her Beatle mates had kept in touch with Swingin' Cilla, with John and Yoko sending a telegram when she wed, Paul writing a theme song for her first TV series and Ringo guesting on another such show, their rehearsed patter far from that of the 1960s, when she'd had to lean over his kit to share the mike for the 'Boys' duet in the Iron Door.

Ringo's drumming – and Clapton's guitar – figured on Cilla's abortive recording in London of a song written and produced by George Harrison in 1972. 'When Every Song Is Sung', once intended for Shirley Bassey, had already exhausted a provisional title ('Whenever') and attempts by both Ronnie Spector and Leon Russell. Although she'd sacrificed her day off from a summer variety season in Blackpool, Cilla had squeezed in a painful dental appointment earlier in the day and "wasn't in the mood to record, and it was a very hot Sunday".[58] Still, she thought that George's lyrics were "super" and tried again in 1974 with another producer, "but even then it didn't have the magic it deserved. It should have had a 'Yesterday'-type arrangement."[58] Melodically, it was more like 'Something'. Cilla remained keen enough to discuss having another go during a chance meeting with the composer in a Chinese restaurant in London, even after it had been re-titled 'I'll Still Love You' for burial on Ringo's *Rotogravure* in 1976

Not a note had been played or written by George on Ringo's previous LP, *Goodnight Vienna*. Under pressure both to complete *Dark Horse* and to prepare for its attendant tour itinerary, scheduled to begin in Vancouver's Pacific Colosseum on 2 November 1974, George didn't have much time for anyone else's music. Another reason for this came to light at the Beverly Hills palaver, when he spoke of attending preliminary *Goodnight Vienna* sessions with John in 1974 "and we all ended up here, fighting Allen Klein".[275]

Gone were the days of open-handed conviviality around Allen's desk. As Mick Jagger had said they would, the three ex-Beatles were – to put it politely – having doubts about the Robin Hood of pop. He was increasingly less available since the Bangladesh shows, and headlines like *Rolling Stone*'s "Did Allen Klein Take The Bangladesh Money?"[238] were not reassuring. "Some guy in New York got onto the idea of Klein," explained George. "You know, 'Well, if Klein is involved with it, it must be a rip off,' and started the whole thing."[275]

However unfounded the story, it sparked off an intense and unwelcome interest by Messrs Harrison, Lennon and Starr in their manager's handling of their affairs. With sufficient music-industry experience for glibness to defer to probing suspicions, the three mustered legal forces to enlighten them as to precisely how much fiscal wool the *de facto* controller of the lumbering Apple empire had pulled over their eyes. No wool was so white that a dyer couldn't blacken it. The instigator of many such investigations himself, Klein's dogged streamlining had, indeed, recouped a fortune from disregarded record-company percentages to the smallest petty-cash fiddle, but where was it – and Klein – when George was challenged with a tax bill that had snowballed over 15 years of international stardom?

Like never before, George "needed someone to organise me out of all that mess. I wanted someone to help me with my present and future, but unfortunately he would have to get involved with my past."[284] Such an apparent paragon materialised in the form of an American who was temperamentally and physically everything that the portly, brash Allen wasn't. A bald, bespectacled beanpole of a man, Denis O'Brien seemed every inch the stereotyped financier. Retiring and besuited, his methodical approach to his university studies in law and accountancy had led to a favoured position in Rothschild's merchant bank. By the early 1970s, a bluffer, battle-hardened Denis emerged with enough cautious confidence to strike out on his own as a Los Angeles financial consultant.

His first showbusiness commission was to superintend Peter Sellers' *Being There*. Although he'd appreciated that The Beatles had been a cut above the usual bilge, he'd never been crazy about pop, "and the stories I'd heard of record people, I thought they'd crawled out of the gutter".[284] Whatever his disinterest in its artistic worth, he understood that pop's growth as an industry meant that deals between entrepreneurs and artists could no longer be mapped out on a serviette over lunch, as Brian Epstein's had been with Billy J Kramer.

It became prudent for O'Brien to lay aside his preconceptions when George Harrison was brought to him in 1973. As George explained, "a Hare Krishna friend of mine discovered this ruby mine in India and was wondering how he could use it to support the temple. He'd met Peter Sellers, who put him in touch with Denis, and the Krishna guy put us together."[284] Whether or not O'Brien and his new client anticipated more than a practised but detached professional relationship, there grew between them a friendship as each came to know what made the other tick. They had a shared sense of humour, and George respected Denis' good sense: "In 20 minutes, he gets more from a budget sheet than most people do in 20 hours."[284] Recounting their first conversation, O'Brien gushed with rare passion, "The chairman of Shell, of RTZ, of IBM, of Ford – I've met all these people and I've never met anyone as together as George."[284]

Outsiders might have assumed this mutual admiration to be a collision of opposites. Even Eric Idle generalised that it was "a balance between George as an amateur saint and Denis an amateur devil".[285] As Harrison wasn't a drug-crazed boor nor O'Brien an unsmiling pedant, there was enough common ground between the Money Beatle and his business advisor for each to be prone to both thrift and extravagance, as well as frequent distribution of alms to outstretched hands.

Although overshadowed by the Concerts For Bangladesh, a not-inconsiderable percentage of the takings and all proceeds from programme sales for the long-awaited *Dark Horse* tour were annexed for all manner of charities, from the Ethiopian famine to community hospitals in the Mississippi Delta. At the beginning, nothing seemed too much trouble for George, who was always uneasy at the possibility of accusations of arrogance or parsimony, – vices for which the Stones had been denounced by *The San Francisco Chronicle* in 1969. Aggrieved, they had responded with the disastrous free concert at Altamont, an hour's drive from the city. Learning from this corrupted endeavour, George confined himself to a guided visit to Haight-Ashbury's Free Medical Clinic, recipient of that night's profits from the Cow Palace, the same venue at which The Beatles had kicked off their first frenzied tour of the continent.

Ten years on, there was only one Beatle and no screaming. However much George had loathed the uproar that had degraded his musicianship, at least he'd been spared the unsettling hush of those who'd shelled out good money specifically for an evening with George Harrison. However demonstrative his giving, the purpose of his sold-out tour was the same as that of any other rock singer. As such, he was to be judged and, by some, found wanting.

The only *bona fide* pop star joining him this time was Billy Preston with his array of assorted keyboards. No more a one-hit-wonder since signing to A&M in 1972, Billy was fresh from his third US Number One, 'Nothing From Nothing'. If not as well known or as conspicuous on stage as Preston, the other players in George's band had impressive *curricula vitae*. At the core was The LA Express, a sextet led by trumpeter and flautist Tom Scott. A crack session team, Scott's boys had been tempted to hit the road from studios where they were equally at ease reading dots for Frank Sinatra as Frank Zappa. Their pricey but blithe dedication to their craft was refreshing after the shiftlessness of some of those on the Bangladesh shows.

Rehearsals on a soundstage at A&M studios didn't run as smoothly as expected. Since leadership had been thrust upon him after The Beatles split, George had never been out on a longer limb. As well as sweating blood over his LP and attending to day-to-day matters during the Klein-O'Brien interregnum, he'd also been organising a Ravi Shankar Music Festival at the Albert Hall, "and the time I'd allowed myself was too tight to allow for a rest between the album and the Ravi Shankar thing and the tour of the States".[276] Unaccustomed to singing for so long and having to instruct The LA Express, for whom the material was new, his vocal cords weakened to a tortured rasp. "I had no voice for the road and I was knackered. I had a choice of cancelling and forgetting it or going on and singing hoarse."[59] Like a trouper, he took the latter course, after supplementing the band with two old retainers, Jim Horn and Jim Keltner, at the last minute but not in the nick of time.

As the tension built on opening night, a backstage security guard might have glanced at a set list that promised an equilibrium of

Beatles numbers, Harrison hits since and a couple of tunes from *Dark Horse*. With that in mind, it looked like George didn't intend to renege on his past, even if – as Billy Preston informed a nosey-parker from *Rolling Stone* – "George didn't want to do 'Something' at all. I knew he was going to have to do it, and he started rebelling against it by doing it in a different way, rewriting the lyrics."[286] Still vying for John's attention, he'd also coarsened 'In My Life', Lennon's *pièce de résistance* on *Rubber Soul*, imbuing it with oppressive horns and squittering wah-wah from Robben Ford, the Clapton of The LA Express. Over where there'd been baroque wistfulness, Billy's Hammond B-3 now rolled like treacle. Perhaps to counteract the continuing 'He's So Fine' debate, George hustled a not immediately recognisable 'My Sweet Lord' out of the way at breakneck speed.

From the instant criticism detectable in the audience's reaction, there was less eagerness whenever he launched into the three *Dark Horse* numbers. 'Maya Love' had perfunctory lyrics but – like the 'Hari's On Tour' instrumental – was a vehicle for its writer to show off how much he'd improved on slide guitar. More piquant was the title track, if only for the hoarse lead vocal, which, although bubbling with catarrh, was a not unattractive cross between McCartney and Rod Stewart. Half-finished in Henley with help from Starr and Keltner, it had become less amorphous with each succeeding run-through with the tour ensemble. "I decided, because I had to teach the band the song anyway, that we'd mic up the soundstage and record it live. If you listen now, it's sort of OK."[59]

"Sort of okay", too, was the first three-hour show, where matches were lit in trendy approval and a girl in the front row sobbed noisily throughout what she'd convinced herself was a recreation of the Bangladesh magic. At every stop was a faint scent of Beatlemania, as in Oakland, where the stage was aswarm with maverick fans adding to George's heavy load during 'Give Me Love'. "It is really a test," he'd predicted. "I either finish the tour ecstatically happy or I'll end up going back into my cave for another five years."[275]

On the minus side, discomforted snarls had replaced 1971's peace sign as everyone with the same-priced tickets grappled for a good view when the stadium doors were flung open. The "festival seating" at many venues, you see, meant no seating. In another of pop's slow moments, there was no overt focus for adoration in North America in 1974, nothing hysterical or outrageous. With Bowie only a marginal success then, glam rock was but a trace element in the Hot 100. While precedents were being forged by the likes of The Ramones in New York's twilight zone and The Sex Pistols, conducting exploratory rehearsals in London, teenagers and post-psychedelic casualties had to make their own amusements. Spirituality was forgotten like last year's grandad vest. Cheap spirits, Mandrax, head-banging and streaking were among the desperate diversions that caught on during that apocryphal year.

At roughly the same mental level was the high-energy blues-plagiarised brutality of minstrels like Rush, Grand Funk Railroad, Led Zeppelin and Bachman-Turner Overdrive, whose sound pictures of Genghis Khan carnage were ideal for US stadia designed originally for championship sport. Meanwhile, lower on the scale were the likes of The Climax Blues Band and Supertramp. If no one went particularly wild over them, at least they were an excuse for a social gathering, an opportunity for friends to get smashed out of their brains together and hurl urine-filled beer-cans stagewards if the band didn't boogie. However, few of these odious projectiles landed within the spotlight's glare, where matchstick figures with V-shaped guitars and double drum-kits cavorted, oblivious to the squalor before them.

Where did George belong in this? After the fifth show, a flight connection variable obliged him to hang about for two hours. Alone, he ambled round Long Beach Arena, deserted but for a bulldozer scooping residual tons of broken whiskey bottles, cigarette packets, discarded garments and other litter left by the rabble who, at one juncture, he'd admonished, "I don't know how it feels down there, but from up here you seem pretty dead."[286] When animated and volatile, some had bawled for the good old good ones played in the good old way and just plain "boogie!". He'd done neither, because "Gandhi says [to] create and preserve the image of your choice. The image of my choice is not Beatle George. If they want that, they can go and see Wings. Why live in the past? Be here now. Whether you like me or not, this is what I am."[286]

His own enquiries and observations told a different story, but a cutting article in that mighty Cerberus *Rolling Stone* implied that a good few hadn't liked him. George protested, firstly that, from the original critique of the tour, the magazine had "just edited everything positive out".[211] Next, "a lot of people who came, without any preconceived ideas, really loved the show. And it really wasn't that bad. Every show was a standing ovation."[211] Naturally, he wrote a song about it, the first of his "sequel" compositions. "'This Guitar (Can't Keep From Crying)' came about because the press and critics tried to nail me on the 1974-5 tour. [It] got really nasty."[59]

From bootlegs and the one officially issued live recording from the tour, it actually wasn't really that bad, and the rottenest reviews he'd ever had didn't diminish George to loyal fans, who lapped up his mistakes and deficiencies as the prerogative of glamour. Even John Lennon – not then on the best of terms with George – opined, "George's voice was shot, but the atmosphere was good and George's performance was great."[44]

The star's pensive stroll around Long Beach Arena was after a harrowing recital, during which every battered inflection had been dredged from an inflamed throat. No medication or enforced silence could forestall the cruel caption "Dark Hoarse" appearing in newspapers local to the itinerary. When the going got especially tough, up to three instrumental items could be stretched out to give George's voice a few minutes' relief, but "rest was the only answer, and there's no way you can rest in the middle of a seven-week tour. I might have been the odd one out, but I quite liked my voice – it sounded like Louis Armstrong a bit, [and it] got better toward the end of the tour."[276] Putting on the agony for sometimes two feverish shows a night, he certainly got better at capitalising on – rather than shrinking from – his temporary inability to pitch past a gruff vocal compass without cracking. Rather than try and fail to hit that high G in the coda of 'In My Life', he extemporised huskily like a soul singer, as though its sentiment couldn't be expressed through expected melodic articulation.

What many would be unable to pardon, however, was his fracturing – perhaps with one word – of the emotive intent of some of the most nostalgic songs ever recorded, including "something in the way she moves it" and, most vexing of all, "while my guitar gently smiles". "In myyyyyy life," he loved *God* more. For those out for a good time, George's milking the audience with hi-di-hi exhortations to chant the name of God was similarly unendearing. "Krishna! Christ! Krishna! Christ!" he kept hollering as best he could, throwing in the odd "Allah!" and "Buddha!" now and then. Some responded, because they understood it was part of his image, but – hell, what had all this Krishna crap to do with heads-down, no-nonsense rock?

More enraging to bigots and racists was the support act, usually brought on after a musical taster from the headliners. Concert promoter Bill Graham advised that advertising it as "George Harrison and Ravi Shankar" would confuse people, although he conceded that both could have equal space in the programme notes. "I even wanted the ads to read, 'Don't come if you don't want to hear Indian music,'" George later insisted. "I thought it would give people another kind of experience other than just watching Led Zeppelin all of their lives."[221]

As a master of ceremonies, Harrison was no Ken Dodd, and he did Ravi no favours by imploring spectators to "be a little patient"[286] before they'd even heard a note from the 16-piece Indian orchestra. He'd then greet his former sitar teacher with a ceremonious *pranum*. Once, less meekly, he swore that he'd die for Indian music. "But not for this," he continued, tapping the sunburst Stratocaster held to him with a strap adorned with a button badge of a yogi.

It might have defied Led Zeppelin to go down well after a build-up of such priggish solemnity. Although he couldn't win, Ravi steered his musicians as close to Western pop as he'd ever gone with the jazzy 'Dispute And Violence' and his latest single, the toe-tapping 'I Am Missing You (Krishna, Where Are You?)'. However, his reappearance in the second half snapped much of the patience that the audience had been asked to have and they began chattering restlessly amongst themselves or heading for the toilets to partake of various soft drugs on offer. "It's a pity that a lot of people missed out on something that went above their heads,"[211] sighed George.

For this faction, Billy Preston had already stolen the show by then. By injecting his trio of recent million-sellers with fancy footwork and soulman exhibitionism, only Billy – up-front in his sequined suit – was able to give 'em what they knew and wanted to dance to, after a monotony of bamboo flutes and sitars. When they'd let their hair down for Preston, George's return to the central microphone to croak 'Dark Horse' or 'For You Blue' was rather an anti-climax.

Upstaging provoked no friction. Like a managing director doing the twist with a voluptuous typist at an office party, George – in checked trousers and raffish moustache – joined in Billy's frolicking, high stepping like a Tiller Girl and messing up the synchronised hand gestures in 'Will It Go Round In Circles'. During a post-mortem of the Vancouver show, said Tom Scott, "No one wanted Ravi to come out to a hostile audience."[286] Among enacted remedies was George coming on to growl a harmony on 'I Am Missing You'. Rather than ask for trouble after the intermission, Ravi's orchestra combined with the rock band, after a mid-tour rehearsal had produced satisfactory re-arrangements of Shankar pieces.

Another restorative ploy was George's open invitation to Dylan and Lennon – then enjoying his first solo US Number One – to do a turn as a surprise treat for the fans. Each turned up at one or two stops but declined to tread the stage. Also along for the ride was Peter Sellers, who provided George with much-needed hilarity when he was in the mood. "When Peter was up," said George, "he was the funniest person you could ever imagine. So many voices and characters. When he wasn't up, he didn't know who he was."[59] By this time, Harrison and the unpredictable Sellers had less in common. Through Denis O'Brien, they had remained bound by mutual investments (mainly in property development), but Peter's mystical phase had fizzled out, the last straw being when he requested Ravi Shankar to arrange a private recital. As he'd assisted Shankar financially in the past, he was astounded by the huge fee demanded by Shambu Das – now Ravi's business manager – for this service. Soon to die, Sellers was never as close to Ravi and George again after the 1974 trek wrapped up, on 20 December at Madison Square Gardens of blessed memory.

At the post-concert party in a Manhattan club, George, Ringo,

Maureen and John chatted amicably enough. The tour had encapsulated every extreme of what had become, in Lennon's estimation, "a love-hate relationship".[79] John had been the only ex-Beatle to send George a bouquet of first-night flowers at Vancouver. George attempted to more than reward this kindness when hip Jack Ford prevailed upon his father to receive the Harrison party – which included George's own father – at the White House on 13 December, the day of the Washington show. Amid the cocktail platitudes, George asked President Ford if anything could be done for Lennon, whose efforts to settle permanently in the States after leaving England forever in 1971 had been hindered, purportedly, by ceaseless official harassment. As recently as November, he'd been in court to battle yet another deportation notice. Like fellow marijuana miscreant Harrison, he had to keep re-applying for an extension of his H-1 visa to remain on US soil.

Their residency status was not the only topic discussed when, two days after the White House chin-wag, George subjected John to a tongue-lashing in a dressing room at Long Island's Nassau Colosseum. Annoyed because John had procrastinated over signing documents pertaining to The Beatles, George had withdrawn his invitation for Lennon to take part in any of the concerts. More relieved than chastened, John had, nevertheless, attempted to bury the hatchet when he and Yoko popped by to congratulate George on the show. In the Colosseum's backstage disarray, the resulting row was of the where-were-you-when-I-needed-you variety, culminating with Harrison whipping off Lennon's glasses and hurling them to the floor. No more the tough guy that he'd never been, John "saw George going through pain, and I know what pain is, so I let him do it".[44]

Exhausted and foul tempered through being too long out of his depth, George fled to his Henley fastness – after first making his peace with John – to assimilate what good had come from this, the most harrowing public ordeal of his solo career. "You either go crackers and commit suicide or you try to realise something and attach yourself more strongly to an inner strength."[32] If he'd had the inclination, he might have regained lost ground at home, where both

Dark Horse singles had faltered outside the Top 30, the first solo Beatle products to do so. The logistics of shunting the show across the ocean for Christmas dates in Britain was discussed with dwindling enthusiasm until, within a day of the New York finale, the troupe had scattered like rats disturbed in a granary. Although 'I'll Be Missing You' had sold well in Europe, how would Ravi have gone down during the second house at the Glasgow Apollo? For that matter, how would George have fared? His name was sufficient to fill the Albert Hall, but how long would it be before some smart-alec of a reviewer compared him and his "Krishna! Christ!" routine to Vince Taylor's sermon at the Paris Olympia back in 1961?

If *Rolling Stone*'s faint praise hadn't been enough, the now-radical *NME* was making up its mind about whether to categorise George's retinue with dinosaur bands as either over the hill, like The Grateful Dead, or wholesomely Americanised, like Fleetwood Mac, who were as far removed from the rough-and-ready blues quartet they once were as George was from 'Roll Over Beethoven'. The street-level acclaim granted to pub-rockers such as Kilburn And The High Roads, Ace and Dr Feelgood was a reaction against the distancing of the humble pop group from its audience. By definition, "pub rock" precludes stardom and its isolation from the everyday. Instead of paying to see whether the Harrison spectacular was really as terrible as *Rolling Stone* made out, how much more gratifying it was to spend an evening in the warm, jolly atmosphere of licensed premises, where – with no religion, Indian music or lyrics that made you embarrassed to be alive – a band would play with more dignity than any remote supergroup with an ex-Beatle in it, forever in America. With *Dark Horse* joining its singles in British bargain bins, who cared about a born-again millionaire like George Harrison any more?

Some *Dark Horse* tracks had been infected by his laryngitis and not all had the sandpapery appeal of the title song. Like Judy Garland, George could elicit anxiety rather than contempt whenever he was obviously struggling, as in the expiring falsetto in 'So Sad'. Another worry was that the LP contained only nine tracks, which included a non-original and an instrumental that went in one ear and out the other. As with *Living In The Material World*, he'd delved into his portfolio for items first given to other artists. Although his sources were less transparent than before, he admitted later that the refrain of 'It Is He' was a syncopation of a devotional *bhajan* that he, Ravi and a spiritual master had chanted *ad infinitum* when in Brindaban. At the heart of 'Ding Dong Ding Dong' were a few Crispisms, while other libretti fused the obscure, the earnest and the slap-dash, as in 'Far East Man', partly composed as George hurtled from Henley to Ron Wood's house in Richmond Hill. After clearing the decks with *All Things Must Pass*, he'd assumed that his muse – like Allen Klein – wouldn't let him down.

However, his writer's block didn'ot prevent more than a little off-hand breast-beating to intrude on *Dark Horse*, as – like Lennon's – his output tended to be more autobiographical now, one man's vision of his immediate world. Most blatant was his liberty-taking with The Everly Brothers' 'Bye Bye Love'. With its 'Badge' bass sound and sly lyrical digs at Pattie and "old Clapper" – neither of whom were present on the session, in contradiction of the album-sleeve notes – he justified what some saw as a rebuttal to 'Layla' as "just a little joke".[211] In a bluer mood, he emoted 'So Sad' with more compassion than had Alvin Lee (formerly "Alvin Dean" of The Jaybirds and the leader of Ten Years After) in the previous year on an album with Mylon Lefevre. In their less fussy rendering, however, this duo made more of the song's oblique riff.

Dark Horse in general would have benefited from a leaner approach to arrangements. Would the absence of trilling flute on 'Dark Horse' itself have spoiled it? On 'Simply Shady', there were what Frank Zappa might call "redundant piano triplets". "Phil Spector nymphomaniacs"[287] was George's own term for the choir, bells and brass layered onto the guitar-bass-drums bedrock of 'Ding Dong Ding Dong', the single that he hoped would reap a similar harvest as that of 'Merry Christmas Everybody', Slade's seasonal Number One twelve months earlier. 'White Christmas', 'Christmas Alphabet', 'Blue Christmas' – no one had cornered the New Year yet.[289]

'Ding Dong Ding Dong' was a brittle basis for optimism, however. "Repetitive and dull"[289] wrote reviewer John Peel in a column that also accused George of complacency. Two years later, Jethro Tull would be luckier with the only record to celebrate the winter solstice. With a chirpy-chirpy-cheapness worthy of *Red Rose Speedway*, 'Ding Dong Ding Dong' had all the credentials of a Yuletide smash but none that actually grabbed the public.

Despite its non-Christian slant, George might have fared better with the wonderful 'It Is He (Jai Sri Krishna)'. Over an accompaniment with pulsating wobble-board to the fore, the repeated chorus was so uplifting that it scarcely mattered that it was sung (without laryngitis) entirely in Hindi – no more, anyway, than McCartney breaking into French on 'Michelle' off *Rubber Soul*. Just as joyous was the decelerated verse which (in English) dwelt on the glories of "He who is complete".

Programmed to precede it on the album was 'Far East Man', one of the fruits of George's musical concurrence with Ron Wood. From just the title, none would guess its far stylistic cry from 'It Is He'. Recorded by Wood, too, it conjured up – intentionally, on *Dark Horse* – a band winding down for the night in some after-hours cocktail lounge. Although featuring altered lyrics and not as torpid as his co-writer's treatment, Harrison's 'Far East Man' adhered to the same sluggish tempo, underpinned by Andy Newmark, the same drummer who'd serviced Wood.

Dominating the artistic texture of *Dark Horse* was the nonchalant proficiency of Newmark's Californian contingent. It was as if they couldn't accomplish what the rowdier Beatles or Plastic Ono Band – for all their casually strewn mistakes – committed to tape instinctively. Even the tracks that included the old firm of Starr and Voorman were overwhelmed by the squeaky-clean, dispiriting neatness behind George's hit-or-miss singing. Given the circumstances under which it was made, these craftsmen kept pace with their employer's physical weariness rather than his emotional and vocational turbulence.

It was a record of a condition more serious than just a sore throat. Apart from a couple of passable numbers and the startling 'It Is He', *Dark Horse* was a comedown after the less derivative sophistication of *Living In The Material World*. Nonetheless, beneath the premeditated carelessness, the hurried meticulousness and yawning ennui was a non-Beatle, as well as an ex-Beatle in uncertain transition. For that reason alone, *Dark Horse* – an artistic *faux pas* – is worth a listen.

Adapted from the logo of an Indian paint firm, a seven-headed dark horse had reared up throughout the tour – on the stage backdrop, on the T-shirt George presented to US Secretary of State Henry Kissinger, on belt buckles and on necklaces. As well as the album, it also signified Dark Horse Records Limited, a label founded by George in May 1974. As EMI had buoyed up Apple, so Dark Horse was under the aegis of A&M. George and Ringo had considered briefly the possibility of buying up Apple and putting it back on course, "but it seemed logical to get more involved in my own set-up."[209] George's nine-year contract with EMI/Capitol wasn't due to expire until 1976, but he doubted that he'd re-sign, owing to what he saw as the company's avaricious dithering over the Bangladesh album and certain royalty discrepancies. Needless to say, EMI/Capitol refuted this sullying of its good name. Swallowing its ire at his accusations, its representative joined the queue of other major labels submitting their bids to Harrison, who at that time was still hot property. Looking for a new record company was as chancy as looking for a new girlfriend. Partly because Billy Preston got on well with A&M, George tested the water by leasing to the label via Dark Horse "a lot of things I was working on".[209] This liaison was rewarding enough for George to add himself to Dark Horse's roster when his time came, "because of the relationship we were, supposedly, going to have [with A&M], which it turned out we never did."[211]

Before it ended in tears, George's mere endorsement of Dark Horse's output as figurehead and pseudonymous record producer ensured exposure, if not chart success. Like Apple in microcosm, more demo tapes than could possibly be heard piled up in the in-trays of Dark Horse's office in London, Amsterdam and within A&M's block in Los Angeles. From the start, George attempted to be more discriminating than Apple had been. "We'll stick to a few," he declared, with his corporation president's hat on, "and we'll work hard on them. No act we sign is going to get hidden away."[290]

Chief among rescued projects from Apple was a narrative ballet composed by Ravi Shankar that had been performed in the Albert Hall and on continental Europe just prior to his joining George for the US tour. Ravi's Dark Horse LP, *The Shankar Family And Friends*, was a refinement of items from his work with both his usual musicians and an augmentation of what George called "the loony band"[211] – the East-West amalgam formed to placate those unwilling to endure two Shankar sets in one concert. With Ringo's paradiddles blending with sarod and swordmandel, *The Shankar Family And Friends* was a likelier commercial proposition than neater medicine on the soundtrack to *Messenger Out Of The East*, now retitled *Raga*.

Shankar merchandise was a reliable potboiler, but the jewel in Dark Horse's crown was Splinter, a duo from South Shields and another discovery by Mal Evans, who'd been on the look-out for an act to play in a night-club scene for another intended Apple movie. Beginning with George's production of their ' Lonely Man' for this sequence, Splinter came to sound as much like mid-period Beatles as Badfinger had. One member of Splinter, Bill Elliott, had already had a brush with Apple, featuring as a singer on John Lennon's production of The Elastic Oz Band's 'God Save Us', a 1971 single to help raise the defence costs of the celebrated *Oz* magazine obscenity trial.

Whatever their feelings about the end result, Splinter seemed in awe of George's working "for 24 hours straight"[291] at FPSHOT sessions for their debut album. Their mentor played at least four superimposed instruments, including the calculated handclaps on their hit 'Costafine Town', which – with a nagging chorus, further accompaniment by Harrison's heavy friends, the fullest distribution network and publicity that included a press photo of them standing on either side of George – scrambled to Number 17 in the UK hit parade, the same position as 'Love Me Do'.

No 'Please Please Me' equivalent was forthcoming as Splinter's follow-up, 'Drink All Day', slumped well outside the Top 50. Some blamed lack of daytime airings on Radio 1 on account of the fact that it contained the world *bloody*. Although as raggedly carefree as, say, Mungo Jerry's chart-topping 'In The Summertime', 'Drink All Day' was not a masterpiece of song. Neither were Splinter the new

Beatles – or the new Badfinger, for that matter. In a letter to a British pop journal years after Splinter's third and final Dark Horse LP, Peter Coulston judged them one of the worst outfits he'd ever heard.[292] However, far from deserving this accolade, they were appropriate to the mild, harmless nature of mid-1970s pop.

So too were other Dark Horse signings, their deals acquired mainly from either knowing George or though the lobbying of someone who did. Even Jiva, whom George had taken on during a genuine talent-spotting expedition, had once backed Donovan. They had a classic two-guitars-bass-drums line-up, and George noticed "a lot of influences from the '60s",[290] but theirs was more a soul than a Mersey Beat calling. Concentrating on creating a party atmosphere, Jiva were roughly the southern Californian counterpart of Geno Washington's Ram Jam Band, which had been popular on Britain's club circuit in around 1966. Although Dark Horse stumped up a Splinter-sized budget to launch Jiva, they were dropped after a solitary album failed to set the world alight.

Henry McCullough's spell as a Dark Horse artist followed a similar pattern. A veteran of several respected British progressive bands, Irish singing guitarist McCullough had never been short of work. After playing in Joe Cocker's Grease Band, he joined Wings during the *Red Rose Speedway* sessions. In 1973, a tiff with McCartney led to his dismissal. He wasn't prepared to play precisely what Paul ordered. George didn't have to be told what Paul was like, but he listened carefully to both Henry's tale of woe and *Mind Your Own Business*, a self-financed LP the artist had just recorded. Because he'd wanted to like it, George decided to put out the album on Dark Horse. After all, it would've been one in the eye for Paul if it'd made Henry a star. By 1977, McCullough was back on small UK stages as a hireling of the likes of Carol Grimes and Frankie Miller.

Simply to let off steam after tapping out take after take of someone else's song in the drum booths of LA, Jim Keltner decided to lead a casual weekend combo of other session musicians. The Dark Horse supremo only "got to sign Keltner's band from meeting the piano player, which is slightly crazy, when you consider the friendship between Keltner and me".[144] Christened 'Attitudes', not so humble were the aspirations of the group when Dark Horse underwrote and issued two of its albums and a pestilence of singles, the third of which, 'Sweet Summer Music', actually climbed into the 90s of the Hot 100 – but, come 1977, Jim and his pals were once performing for their own amusement in local venues.

Encouraged by Billy Preston, Dark Horse had acquired in 1975 an established act, a black vocal quartet calling themself The Five Stairsteps, who had cut their teeth as regulars at Harlem's famous Apollo Theater and, on Buddha Records, in the US R&B chart. In 1970, they were casting their longest shadow with the million-selling 'Ooh Ooh Baby'. Maybe Billy had given George his very own Isley Brothers. A family affair, too, the group were the children of manager Clarence Burke. When sister Aloha left in 1974, her four brothers chose not to replace her, preferring the simpler expedient of continuing as Stairsteps. The title of Stairsteps' only Dark Horse LP, *Second Resurrection*, was, however, only wishful thinking. Leaving his siblings to fend for themselves, lead singer Keni Burke tried again with what chanced to be the penultimate album by Dark Horse, which by then was no longer affiliated to A&M.

At A&M Studios when it was still all smiles, George had fulfilled his last commitment to EMI/Capitol, as well as the final album release for Apple as *Wonderwall* had been the first. Like a tenant paying overdue rent with bad grace, he turned out "a grubby album in a way. The production left a lot to be desired as did my performance."[59] Even so, his fickle public bought as many copies of *Extra Texture (Read All About It)* as it had of its predecessor. In Britain, of all places, it lasted a month in the LP chart, which was a month more than *Dark Horse*.

Credit for its title – wordplay on a line from Edwin Starr's 'Headline News' – was Attitudes bass guitarist Paul Stallworth, who'd been among the highest quota of slick LA studio casts to figure on a Harrison project, and it showed. Their infallible polish suited the large helping of 'Far East Man'-type lethargy that begged critics to rubbish *Extra Texture*. It was a bedsit record rather than a dancing one, with close-miked vocals floating effortlessly over layers of treated sound. There were touches of Motown here and there, but the backbone of *Extra Texture* dabbled in the more feathery emanations from Philadelphia by the likes of The Stylistics and Jerry Butler. He wouldn't capitulate to the limpid mush of "Philly soul" at its most soporific, but you'd be forgiven for thinking that old George was trying to make it as a "quality" entertainer like Sinatra, whose flop singles were excused as "too good for the charts".

Extra Texture, however, wasn't Harrison's *Songs For Swinging Lovers*. In its contradiction of enjoyable depression, only 'Tired Of Midnight Blue' passed muster. Otherwise, the long, dull melodies on *Extra Texture* were, as far as I'm concerned, on a slushy par with those of Bread and, in the 1980s, the equally smooth Style Council, both studio-centred groups who had moderate success with moderate records of uniform blandness. Some of George's tunes were almost watered-down flashbacks to The Beatles, particularly 'Grey Cloudy Lies' and 'This Guitar (Can't Keep From Crying)'. There was also a 'Badge'-style rhythmic lope in 'Tired Of Midnight Blue'. George later argued, "If something's good, you tend to remember it, and sometimes if it's bad, too. I don't think you can get away with your past, if you want to put it like that."[59]

'This Guitar' and 'You' – the oldest and most up-tempo song of the collection – were the soundest choices for singles. 'You' was even Radio 1's Record Of The Week, but such approbation couldn't crank it above Number 38 in Britain, although it tickled the Top 20 in the States. As with 'Try Some Buy Some', George had grafted his own singing onto the original backing track for 'You', hence its high key and indelible traces of Ronnie Spector's vocal. On some other tracks, he'd chosen to sing straight from the nostrils, as if trying to recapture the inadvertent vulnerability of *Dark Horse*, but in better accord with the material was a melting warble reminiscent of Smokey Robinson, who was then never off the Henley juke box.

The music on *Extra Texture* could not be rescued by the words, which, if sparser than before, were either cursory or in restricted code. Even so, although simplistic, 'You' and 'Can't Help Thinking About You' were the only lyrics that took on a breadth of gesture that was immediately universal, as well as personal – apart from the archaic parlour poetry of 'The Answer's At The End', lifted from semi-legible quotes etched above Friar Park's entrance hall.

'His Name Is "Legs"' was a tribute to "Legs" Larry Smith, who, seldom seen since the Plastic Ono bash at the Lyceum, had re-entered George's life via mutual friend, Terry Doran. So charmed was he by Larry's quaint turns of phrase and dress sense – which embraced toy cows grazing on his shoes – that a song about these idiosyncrasies grew as George doodled on a piano one morning. Smith's officer-and-gentleman tones cropped up intermittently on the recording, but, as the composer acknowledged, "really, you have to know him to find it funny".[59]

It was indeed "a piece of self-indulgence, like some other of my songs about things that nobody else knows or cares about, except maybe one or two people".[39] Did that magazine's editor care because George could "climb *Rolling Stone* walls" in 'This Guitar'? When the stereo arm lifted at the close of side two, the lasting impression for most listeners was that of a man as self-obsessed as any drip-rocker. Only the most zealous Beatle-ologists were bothered about covert vinyl revelations by ex-Beatles, and even some of them listened *before* purchasing, these days. Although few were prepared to disconnect them with their previous incarnation, the days of instant Number Ones had passed with 'The Ballad Of John And Yoko'. Whether the latest by John, George, Paul or Ringo made the charts now depended entirely on its commercial suitability.

Six years after disbandment, John had effectively retired; Paul was basking in rave reviews for Wings' US tour; and Ringo was about to rise up the American Top 30 for the tenth consecutive time. Too far out for the commonweal and not cool enough for hipsters, George had become the laggard of the pack. On the eve of punk, a widespread feeling was summarised by King Crimson's Robert Fripp: George Harrison was "a talented bore".[293] His newest alias, "Ohnothimagen", intimated that the self-denigrating creator of *Extra Texture* was of like mind.

On the album, his artistic nadir could not be divorced from the weighty personal misfortunes that split his concentration. 'Grey Cloudy Lies', for example, "describes the clouds of gloom that used to come over me, a difficulty I had". It slopped over into media interviews, too. On Radio 1, he intoned dolefully, "People who were never really keen on me just really hate my guts now. It has become complete opposites, completely black and white."[294]

He was inflicted with such inflexible polarity himself. Once a hero, Allen Klein was now a villain of the darkest hue. The auditors appointed by the three Beatles had unravelled enough evidence of "excessive commissions" from Klein's mazy balance sheets for a court case. Going in fighting, Klein counter-sued for an eight-figure sum, with a cunning card up his sleeve for the specific trumping of George. Mr Klein, George would discover, was not a gentleman – but perhaps he never had been in the first place. It would take until 1977 for the blizzards of writs to settle into complicated but fixed financial channels whereby the assorted and incoming monies could be divided and sent to the sometimes disgruntled parties.

With Klein on the way out and The Beatles not even a legal partnership now, there was no tangible barrier to prevent Lennon, McCartney, Harrison and Starr from forming a group. Since 1970, hardly a day had gone by without somebody asking one of them when they'd get back together. "No one ever asks me about Rory Storm And The Hurricanes or The Eddie Clayton Skiffle Group," moaned Ringo. "They were good bands, too."[295] With all but Paul flying EMI/Capitol's nest, 1976 was a big year for re-promotion of Beatles singles. In Britain alone, seven had breached the Top 40, all from the second half of their career.

Although he was "always pleased when the other three do something good",[276] who could blame George for eating his heart out when even his old music with them was more acceptable than his current solo offerings? As he seemed to be the only one sagging on the ropes, he was struck by the unreasonable notion that, rather than Paul, it might be he who'd have no place in any plotted Beatles of the 1970s. "The way it sometimes comes across is that there is Paul and John and Ringo, and they are very much together, and there's this fly in the ointment called George Harrison" ran one extraordinary press statement that he felt driven to make. "It's put about that I'm the one who is always missing when the talk is on. What I want to say is this:

if Paul, John and Ringo get together in a room, I just hope they invite me along."[290]

He seemed so defeated that it was fanciful to look to future victories – and, in some ways, the worst was yet to come. However, from this, George Harrison's lowest ebb, the tide, with majestic slowness, had already started to turn.

14 *The Jewish Man In The Kitchen*

During one of his last interviews, John Lennon sighed, "Well, he walked right into it. He must have known, you know. He's smarter than that. George could have changed a few notes and nobody could have touched him, but he let it go and paid the price."[80] Found guilty of "subconscious plagiarism" on 7 September 1976, John's former colleague had been ordered to pay the aggrieved party just over half a million greenbacks – and in days when half a million was worth something.

The plaintiff was Bright Tunes, rather than Richard Self, the composer of 'He's So Fine'. The Grim Reaper had come for Richard in 1967, but the Self-serving accountants of the record company and its British outlet, Peter Maurice Music, remained on the look-out for royalties that they felt were owed to their client's estate, ie his mother, who was suing Bright Tunes for non-payment when the writ against Harrison was served.

Such matters were settled out of court, more often than not, as had been a pay-off to Bill Martin and Phil Coulter for 'It's Johnny's Birthday'. Witty Mr Justice Slade suggested that he should sing 'Congratulations' to the parties[296] when Peter Maurice Music and George decided on such a course over 'He's So Fine', and it seemed once – said the defendant – that "the lawyers in America were going to give the people some money to shut them up".[25]

The two factors that provoked the extremity of Bright Tunes' proceedings were the howling success of 'My Sweet Lord' and the intervention of litigation-loving Mr Klein, who, scenting a financial killing, had "brought the case"[211] from Bright Tunes. When he'd been

George's manager, it had suited him to say that 'My Sweet Lord' had "nothing to do with this other song, and now its the other way 'round, just to get some money off me".[211] As well as Jody Miller's 'He's So Fine', Bright Tunes' objection had been hammered home with a 1975 Chiffons rendering of 'My Sweet Lord' rearranged to stress its affinity to their ancient hit.

At the three-day hearing before Judge Richard Owen, star-struck legal staff employed elsewhere in the building came to watch the fun during coffee breaks. They were delighted when the harassed ex-Beatle was obliged to demonstrate on guitar his counsel's argument, which boiled down to the first three notes of the verse and four – "really want to see you" – in the chorus. Among audio-visual aids used were huge wall-charts of musical staves. An ethno-musicologist under oath even questioned the definitions of the items concerned as "songs", if their central riff was subtracted. Both, he further pontificated, were derived in any case from the chorus of 'Oh Happy Day', which had become public domain – ie "traditional" – 50 years after the death of its composer, Paul Doddridge. However, victory was Klein's, who, it would be pleasant to think, ensured that the bereaved Mrs Self got her cut.

This conclusion to perhaps the best-known civil action of the 1970s exacerbated the music industry's icier ruthlessness where there had once been indolence. Whereas The Lovin' Spoonful had got away with imposing the 1940s melody 'Got A Date With An Angel' onto their 'Daydream' smash in 1966, the outcome of *Bright Tunes versus Harrison* led Little Richard's publisher to claim for breach of copyright in a track on the twelve-year-old *Beatles For Sale* album. In 1981, the music press intimated a howl of artistic ire from Rolf Harris when Adam And The Ants' UK Number One, 'Prince Charming', borrowed the tune of one of his (apparently not so) forgotten singles, 'War Canoe'.

Although his bile may have also risen, George had not taken Roxy Music to task when part of their Song For Europe melody bore an uncanny resemblance to 'While My Guitar Gently Weeps', nor The Jam when someone suggested that this Surrey trio had leaned too heavily on 'Taxman' for their chart-topping 'Start'. Later, George would likewise overlook what he considered to be Madonna's heist of the salient points of 'Living In The Material World' for a best-seller of similar title. That George was so forgiving was demonstrative of how much the 'He's So Fine' affair had agitated him. "Look," he said, "I'd be willing, every time I write a song, if somebody will have a computer and I can just play any new song into it, and the computer will say, 'Sorry' or, 'Yes, OK.' the last thing I want to do is keep spending my life in court."[297] He was unable to listen to pop radio or months before and after without nitpicking vigilance. There was 'Hello Goodbye' in ELO's 'Telephone Line'. Didn't you hear 'Food, Glorious Food' in that Stevie Wonder number? "One of them that drove me crackers," he said, "was 'Tie A Yellow Ribbon Round The Old Oak Tree',"[211] in which he perceived both 'April Showers' and a Gilbert O'Sullivan song.

For a while, too, "it made me so paranoid about writing that I didn't even want to touch the guitar or piano in case I touched somebody's note. Somebody may own that note."[297] You could understand his attitude. Surely every combination of even the chromatic scale must have been used by now. The other day, I detected the melody of 'Simon Says' by The 1910 Fruitgum Company in 'Help Me Make It Through The Night'. By rights, the inventor of the twelve-bar blues ought to be richer than Croesus. Should a plumber receive a royalty every time a toilet he has installed is flushed?

Fortunately, George was able to home in on the humorous aspects of what had been a humiliating episode. After all, it wasn't the only song he'd ever written or would write. Who could weep for a composer for whom 'Something' would always provide a regular and substantial income?

Not as big a hit, yet a hit all the same, was the therapeutic 'This Song' and its one-take B-side, 'I Don't Care Any More', penned in the aftershock of the lawsuit. 'This Song' unburdened itself with lines like, "This song ain't black or white and, as far as I know, don't infringe on anyone's copyright", and "This tune had nothing Bright about it" – a play on words, like. The backing laid it on with a trowel, too, in its Leon Russell-type descending piano inversions and gratuitous instrumental work-outs. No sooner does it occur to the listener that the underlying ostinato sounds familiar than the thought is acknowledged on record by Harrison's court jester, Eric Idle, in his "ratbag" guise, wondering whether it's been lifted from The Four Tops or Fontella Bass.

As strained as 'This Song' itself was the accompanying video, shot over one night in a borrowed Los Angeles courtroom. Perhaps it was trying to mirror the Stones' promotional film short for 1967's 'We Love You', Mick and Keith's riposte to their brush with the law. With Ron Wood cast as a lady juror, director Michael Woodleigh's 'This Song' clip had a bewigged Jim Keltner pounding his gavel at George, handcuffed in the dock. During its editing, as Harrison fired suggestions about rhythm, pacing and camera angles, Woodleigh was astounded by his knowledge of film technique.

'This Song' was the first of two moderately successful US singles and one flop to be taken from the delayed new LP *Thirty-Three And A Third* (George's age, see). The album kept that territory's FM radio in tasteful focus, and at its bedrock were the defiantly spare bass lines of Willie Weeks, veteran of many a velvet-smooth Philly soul recording. Willie had recently worked on David Bowie's "plastic soul" LP, *Young Americans*, and with Steve Winwood, and his was a voguish name to print on your album sleeve. *Thirty-Three And A Third* also conceded to the drowsy "country rock" wafting from California by such artists as John Denver, the ubiquitous Linda Ronstadt and The Eagles,[298] whose *Greatest Hits* collection was ensconced in the North American album lists for most of 1976. Less plausible a setting for the Harrison bottleneck swirl was the discreetly jazzy 'Learning To Love You', the reggae jerk of 'Crackerbox Palace' and a couple of nods towards disco fever – a form that he generally disliked – that was then sashaying its way towards its John Travolta zenith. Bemoaning the predictability of George's pool of hip session players, Dark Horse hopefuls and half-famous friends, an English reviewer dismissed it with "Of course it's not rock 'n' roll. Whatever gave you that idea?"[299]

American progressive radio was amenable enough to *Thirty-Three And A Third*, but in Britain artists of George's stamp were despised by journalists, who fawned to someone called Johnny Rotten, 19-year-old chief show-off with The Sex Pistols. The punk rock thunderclap had resounded, and a disaffected adolescent in Speke or Bognor Regis was more likely to go for the Pistols' 'Anarchy In The UK' than a disc about George Harrison's legal hassles in New York.

The Beatles at the Star-Club might have been as excitingly slipshod, but what counted about 'Anarchy', The Damned's fast version of 'Help!', 'Wild Youth' from Generation X and other bursts of self-conscious racket was that, more so than George's beloved skiffle and rockabilly, anybody could do it. As punk fanzine *Sniffin' Glue* elucidated, all you needed were three chords. Not a week went by without another hot "new wave" group ringing some changes, even if most of them looked and sounded just like The Sex Pistols, whose stage entertainments were notable for gobbets of appreciative spit from the audience rather than Beatle jelly-babies.

In August 1977, news of Elvis Presley's death drew a malicious cheer in a basement club frequented by London punks. Benignly, some Grand Old Men refused to bitch back. Roy Orbison, for instance, saw only "a bunch of fresh, new people trying to do their thing like we did".[300] To George, however, it was "rubbish, total rubbish. Listen to the early Beatles records – they were innocent and trivial but still had more meaning than punk music, which is destructive and aggressive."[214] Punk was also the start of his own – albeit temporary – farewell to pop.

No incentive for any withdrawal was apparent, however, when the new Harrison album qualified for a golden disc within weeks of its release in time for Christmas 1976. Most of the sales were in the States. Although it found enough home buyers to flit briefly into the LP charts, "I get the impression from time to time that England is not particularly interested".[25]

Masking an encroaching creative bankruptcy had been George's more pronounced rummaging through his back catalogue than on *Extra Texture*. As well as 1969's 'Woman Don't You Cry For Me' and 'Beautiful Girl' – related to a new "constant companion", Olivia Arias, whom he intended to marry as soon as his and Pattie's decree absolute was accorded – he'd delved even further back for 'See Yourself'. More telling was 'True Love', the first solo Harrison cover version to be issued as a single – but only in The Sex Pistols' Britain. On the premise that the opposite extreme of the day's dominating force is never completely submerged, his overhaul for Grace Kelly and Bing Crosby's funereal duet – with introductory organ sweep, muted funky twitch and altered chord sequence – soundtracked a weakly humorous video, directed by Eric Idle, capturing an Edwardian mood with the artist in boater and false handlebar moustache.

'Crackerbox Palace', another 45rpm extract, failed in the United Kingdom, too (although it sold more than 'This Song' in the States). Dedicated to hep-cat Lord Buckley, George had scrawled its title – the name of Buckley's Chicago home – after meeting the late monologist's manager, George Greif, in January 1976 at the MIDEM music publishing convention in France. On the preceding *Thirty-Three And A Third* track, Harrison had thanked the Lord – God, not Buckley – "for giving us pure" Smokey Robinson, thus expanding on a homage already paid in 'Ooh Baby You Know I Love You' on *Dark Horse*. In so doing, George was at the forefront of a later tendency for pop stars to buttress their own positions with tributes to credible influences on record. In that same year, Bruce Springsteen had slipped a line about "Roy Orbison sings for the lonely" into one of his songs, while just beyond the horizon was Orbison's own 'Hound Dog Man' to the departed Elvis. These would be only the tip of the iceberg.

John Citizen had even less idea what hero George was on about in 'Dear One' than he had been in 'Pure Smokey'. In a press hand-out, however, it was revealed that 'Dear One' was in praise of Yogananda. George had written it on a guitar tuned to an open chord, whereby – other than its bridge – it rose from a drone more Gaelic than Indian. In straying from habit, he'd arrived at the boldest arrangement and most attractive piece on *Thirty-Three And A Third*.

Like 'Dear One', 'It's What You Value' – with the 'All Right Now' riff – was both a product of a holiday in the Virgin Islands and confusing to those unknowing of its lyrical source. As far fewer had the inclination to plumb the depths of his songs these days, they'd wait for his explanation in a newspaper article that its motor-car allusions were to do with the Mercedes 450 SL that was the price that Jim Keltner had put on his participation in the 1974 tour in lieu of a lump sum. That was what Jim valued, sort of thing. Not as sodden with Aesop's fable imagery was 'Learning To Love You', which closed the album. Another religious tract, this song dwelt on unconditional spiritual love, in which "the goal is to love everyone equally, but it doesn't necessarily work out that way."[301]

To a more worldly end, George had been commissioned to pen an item for consideration by Herb Alpert – the A in A&M – as one of his occasional vocal excursions. That the resultant 'Learning To Love You' came home to roost on an LP by Harrison rather than Alpert was not among the principal causes of discord between Dark Horse and its parent company's high command that had led to the sudden release of *Thirty-Three And A Third* not by A&M but the mightier Warner Brothers conglomerate in Burbank. Although George was finally free to sign himself to Dark Horse in January 1976, this did not mitigate the comparative insolvency of the label's other acts. George blamed A&M's distribution set-up and lack of faith while, having ploughed nearly $3 million into Dark Horse, Alpert and partner Jerry Moss had hoped that, by cross-collateralisation, *Thirty-Three And A Third* would transfuse what had become a disappointing investment. Stipulations in Harrison's contract forbade such a ploy, so they sought to recoup what they could, even if it meant losing their ex-Beatle, who – if *Extra Texture* was anything to go by – was past his best, anyway.

Expected in July 1976, George's album master tapes arrived three months late. Symptomatic of the erosion of rapport between artist and corporation was, first, a remonstrative letter from Moss and then an eight-figure writ against Harrison for "non-delivery of product". George's explanation in a depressingly familiar court – in Los Angeles, this time – was the plain truth, that for most of the summer either his bowels had been exploding or he'd been heaving his guts up with what had been initially diagnosed as food poisoning. When his skin turned yellow, his doctors concluded that it was hepatitis, necessitating a long stay in bed and, for the sake of his liver, total abstinence: "I needed the hepatitis to quite drinking."[274] He called it 'hippy-titis'. When I was poleaxed by this disease myself in 1970, a Department of Health official – damn his impudence – called to ascertain whether I was a junkie who'd caught it via a dirty syringe.

George finally vacated the chilly A&M building with the *Thirty-Three And A Third* artwork already in Warners' clutches. As Warners' out-of-court reimbursement of A&M's Dark Horse money was part of the deal, he was delighted to announce, "We're very excited about our new affiliation."[302] To show willing, he'd subjected himself to an extensive publicity blitz, which included an open-ended interview recorded for radio use – a device particularly favoured by Warners – and a five-city promotional tour of the States, accompanied by Gary Wright, another artist who'd also defected from A&M to Warners, and had played keyboards on *Thirty-Three And A Third*.

More than ever, now, it wasn't sufficient merely to mail a pre-release copy of a Harrison album to *Rolling Stone*; you had to yowl it from the rooftops, despite some who still insisted that there was an unbreachable chasm between rock – which only the finest minds could appreciate – and vulgar pop. Patiently puffing a Gitane, George gave the media unblinking copy, clarifying the album's more obscure lyrical byways, justifying his stand in the Bright Tunes bother and retelling the old, old story of The Beatles for the trillionth time, tormenting some questioners with mischievous hints of a reunion. Recuperated from his illness – thanks, he said, to herbs prescribed by a Californian physician – the subsequent weight loss and beardless pallor made him look for all the world like Dave Davies, the youngest Kink. George's shoulder-length hair was kinked and centre-parted, too, and his teeth freshly capped. There was no doubting it – the boy meant business.

Yes, he'd pencilled in a world concert tour for summer 1977, "but I would pace it better."[299] It would embrace, he promised, neglected markets in Japan and Europe, "because they keep shouting about it."[302] When the campaign actually reached Europe, he wasn't so sure. He didn't wish to "compromise himself".[301] No, he wouldn't even entertain a one-off event on a Bangladesh scale, because it would lack intimacy. At the Hamburg stop, a reunion with Tony Sheridan – over from his San Fernando home for a Star-Club anniversary show with Cliff Bennett and PJ Proby – was one of the less onerous incidents of an itinerary which reawakened George's nausea for the dazzle of flash bulbs, the scratch of biros on autograph books and, even now, screams (which may or may not have been ironic). In Los Angeles, a virago had badgered him to boogie on down with her in an adjacent disco, and a lift door in Boston had opened on a wild-eyed, Beatle-fringed youth grinning as if he had a mouthful of salts. "I play guitar," he'd spluttered, "in a band." Within that awe-struck – and possibly dangerous – gleam, George smothered a likely annoyance, playing Mr Nice Guy with an affable "Keep playing, man! Stay with it!" as a nervous Warners publicist shepherded him away. By recoiling, he might have lost a fan.

As unexpected as the encounter in the lift was the thrusting-together of former Prime Minister Edward Heath and George for a photograph at Manchester's Television Centre. During this British leg of the *Thirty-Three And A Third* marketing quest, George's most significant plug was as a guest on BBC2's "progressive" pop showcase, *The Old Grey Whistle Test*, on 30 November.

Ten days earlier, he'd done more than simply chat when his pre-recorded appearance with Paul Simon on NBC's satirical *Saturday Night Live* in New York had broken the programme's viewing record. As well as putting up with facetious enquiries from the studio audience, George had hunched over a hollow-body Gretsch to sing 'Dark Horse' in dim blue light. From the shadows, Paul Simon had then joined in for 'Here Comes The Sun' and his own 'Homeward Bound', for which his temporary partner required an idiot card. Thus satisfying public presumptions, the pair indulged themselves with 'Bye Bye Love', an unsteady 'Rock Island Line' and Presley's 'That's All Right', all of which had been common to both The Quarry Men and the pre-Simon And Garfunkel duo, Tom And Jerry.

As the show's producer, Lorne Michaels, had once offered a sardonic $3,000 bucks for The Beatles to regroup before his cameras, George called his bluff by asking for his quarter of the fee. By coincidence, in the following month all four ex-Beatles happened to be in New York. As all enjoyed *Saturday Night Live*, American cousin of Monty Python, "they decided to rebound on us," revealed its host, Chevy Chase, a pal of Eric Idle, "and appear on the show. I never dreamt they'd actually take up our offer."[230] Unfortunately (or not) Lennon's chauffeur drove to the wrong studio, thereby capsizing what would have been, had they kept their nerve, the ultimate practical joke.

The ceiling of more serious incentives was now an appeal from the United Nations on behalf of the Vietnamese boat people and from an American who offered $50 million for one Beatles performance. Beyond hard cash were pleas on vinyl like that of an act called People – Americans again – with 'Come Back Beatles'. The solo produce of each former Beatle intimated that what you'd hear might not be magic, just music. Yet, admitted George, "The Beatles was bigger than the four personalities separately – not like The Bee Gees. They make good records, but they don't have whatever it was that The Beatles had."[214]

This was best demonstrated by the brothers Gibb's starring roles in a 1978 musical film based on all of the *Sgt Pepper* songs, minus 'Within You Without You'. George "heard it was dreadful and wouldn't bother watching."[303] No Harrison compositions were included, either, in an earlier Beatle-inspired movie, *All This And World War Two*, which contained among its Lennon-McCartney works two tracks by Jeff Lynne, whose ELO had also reworked 'Eleanor Rigby' in concert. George's role in The Beatles' history was also belittled after post-production on the made-for-TV *Birth Of The Beatles*, for which, according to one bizarre report, Pete Best would play the teenage Harrison. Actually, the sacked drummer had been engaged as the project's unheeded factual advisor. The part of George had gone to a professional actor named John Althan.

Another slight on the Quiet One was when the suit he wore in *Help!* – although a suspected fake – did not fetch its reserve price in an auction at one of the Beatle conventions that had started in Western continents. George had donated saleable artefacts to such a function in Los Angeles, where Jackie Lomax was a guest speaker. On the *Thirty-Three And A Third* campaign trail, however, George shied away from a gathering at London' Alexandra Palace, fearing that, in Britain, at least, "the media are not interested in me as a person. They are only interested in The Beatles."[304] In the Fab Four's footsteps, foreign visitors – mainly Japanese and American – were pouring vast amounts into the English Tourist Board's coffers for conducted treks round London and Liverpool to such golgothas as the Abbey Road zebra crossing and 25 Arnold Grove.

After doing his *Thirty-Three And A Third* duty, George, with Olivia Arias – formerly his personal secretary at A&M – and Gary Wright, had embarked on a pilgrimage of his own: four days in southern India for the wedding of Kumar Shankar, Ravi's nephew, and a Hindu festival, where Olivia feared losing the other two when the sexes were segregated. On to Los Angeles, George and his girlfriend looked in on Prabhupada, then at the city's Krishna centre. Having had no qualms about exalting His Divine Grace even in hardcore rock magazine interviews, George in 1976 had also found it in him to vindicate the Maharishi: "I can see much clearer now what happened, and there was still just a lot of ignorance that went down. Maharishi was fantastic, and I admire him – like Prabhupada – for being able, in spite of all the ridicule, to just keep on going."[32]

When her future husband had first spotted her at a Los Angeles party, Olivia Arias – five years younger than George – had been a devotee of Maharaj Ji, a moon-faced Perfect Master with an adolescent moustache whose sermon before the multitudes at 1971's Glastonbury Fayre had been punctuated by indiscreet glances at his gold watch. Among his thousands of followers was a sound engineer that I knew. In many a shabby hotel room, I would wake to find him cross-legged in meditation beneath the counterpane of an adjacent bed. Such a habit formed common ground between Olivia and George. The fancy-free Harrison had been attracted instantly to the self-possessed, California-reared Mexican whose easy smile showed off her fine teeth. Despite her Aztec forebears, she was not unlike her Liverpudlian suitor, both facially and in her slim build.

George and the second Mrs Harrison plighted their troth on 2 September 1978 in an unpublicised ceremony at Friar Park. Among the few witnesses was their son, Dhani, who had been born the month before in a Windsor nursing home. Called after the notes *dha* and *ni* from the Indian music scale as much as for the name's phonetic proximity to the English "Danny", the infant would be so removed from public gaze that, when he was older, he would be able to walk around Henley unnoticed.

Appropriately clad in a Union Jack coat, Dhani's father had dared a sortie down the hill to a street party during 1977's Royal Jubilee. For greater distances, it was safer to drive. Nevertheless, George was sighted on more than one occasion knocking back a quiet brown ale in one or other of South Oxfordshire's more far-flung pubs or eating in a favoured Indian restaurant in Caversham Park Village, on the outskirts of Reading. Out of the blue, he'd even rolled up with his guitar to jam with an *ad hoc* combo assembled by Jon Lord to the disbelief of the yuppie patrons of a hostelry in the whimsically named hamlet of Pishill.

On a more makeshift stage at Hurtwood Edge, he'd do likewise at the wedding reception of his ex-wife and Eric Clapton on a May evening in 1979. Also among the stars up there to blast out a pot-pourri of classic rock and old Beatles numbers were Paul McCartney and Ringo, plus various Rolling Stones, Jeff Beck, percussionist Ray Cooper – who'd accompanied Elton John as one of the first of Western pop's ambassadors to Russia – and, for one night only, the reunited Cream. It says much for George's self-confidence that he was able to tread the boards with the outstanding Beck, who – more deserving of guitar deity than Clapton – displayed eclecticism and unpredictability in compatible amounts.

Terming himself Eric's "husband-in-law", George went along for the laugh on Clapton's European Tour that year, sitting in for a couple of shows. Through Eric and Elton John, who came too, he'd got over his aversion to organised sport, particularly cricket, as they, with ex-Traffic drummer Jim Capaldi, "got me going to the matches in this nice little English town, drinking beer, laughing. I think we've all had similar times and experiences, and because of that we can just make fun and have a real laugh. You can't ask for much more than that, really."[75]

Rubbing shoulders with professional cricketers such as Ian Botham and Mike Gatting, George's spectator's interest grew, although he was never to be as enthusiastic as Mick Jagger, Bill Wyman – or Phil May. As a Pretty Thing in the 1960s, May had been a social pariah, but, having won the heart of a Stuart and trimmed his girlish tresses, he was among those attending Prince Charles' wedding in 1981.

The Beatles' MBEs had been the turning point in impressing the upper crust that pop was a generator of vast financial power. At first, its younger fledglings had appalled staider swells by dropping into small-talk references of this or that long-haired rock star they knew. Soon, lads like George and Eric came to inhabit a world more exclusive than even that of the Bangladesh superstars. The new pop squirearchy began taking up pastimes recommended by those born into privilege. Steve Winwood, born in a Birmingham semi-detached and owner since 1970 of an ivy-clung manor house not far from the ancestral Cotswolds home of the Mitfords, had an open invitation from one of his monied neighbours to take part in the disgusting aristocratic passion of stag hunting.

Huntin', fishin' and shootin' didn't appeal to the Harrisons, but George dabbled once more in motorcycle scrambling, sponsoring champion Steve Parrish – although in 1979 he declined an approach for £185,000 to run a BMW M1 in the Procar series. Parrish and Harrison had met through both knowing Barry Sheene, who had transferred his allegiance from bikes to racing cars in 1976. Always stimulated by the celebrity of others, George had been introduced to Barry at a 1977 meet at Long Beach. Later, he readily consented to appear on an edition of ITV's *This Is Your Life* that honoured Sheen, on which he'd recall his first circuit of Brand's Hatch when "Barry persuaded John Surtees to let me have a go."[22] In a borrowed helmet and overalls, an apprehensive Harrison followed Surtees' shouted instructions while "just hanging on for dear life. I hadn't even remembered to close my visor. Still, it was a great feeling, [although] I didn't go very fast. I just signed the chit saying that, if I killed myself, it wasn't John's fault."[22]

After this cautious spin, George took part in many celebrity meets, such as a 24-hour run at Silverstone organised by Maltin's, Henley's sports car concessionaires, in aid of a cancer foundation to the memory of Swedish driver Gunnar Nilsson. For the same charity – to whom he'd also donated some record royalties – George, in Stirling Moss's famous Lotus 18, swallowed dust behind the terrifying Jackie Stewart. As they ambled to the royal enclosure afterwards, Stewart in his mandatory corduroy cap commented, "I don't know why I dress like this," to which Harrison replied, "Because you're a twit."[15]

Stewart's chuckling along to such familiarity didn't solely stem from his personal liking for the track's most renowned amateur. Repaying the VIP treatment that was automatically his, George publicised the sport with almost the same fervour as he had meditation. An expected presence at Grand Prix events around the globe, the ex-Beatle resigned himself to "getting too well known at motor races now"[22] as he was besieged by journalist and fans who had just rushed past the victor of the last race. With Stewart in Brazil, where no Beatle had gone before, he was blinded by flashlights the second he stepped off the Concorde at Rio. Only police intervention allowed a safe passage to a waiting limousine. Amid the droning excitement of the Formula One tournament at São Paulo the next day, his tormentors' persistence drew from him a cornered "You should photograph the cars. They're more important than I am."[214] When probed, he spoke with jaw-dropping authority about oversteer and gear ratios, while tipping Jody Scheckter to be 1979's world champion, because he was ready: "It would be good if Grand Prix racing was like the music business, where you can have a Number One hit and then get knocked off by your mate – but, unfortunately, it isn't like that. There is a point where you are just 'ready' to be world champion, and if it doesn't happen it could be all downhill from there."[22]

Like a dog to a bath, George steeled himself for the press conferences and other media slots that he could have sidestepped during what was meant to be a private visit. However, with an eponymous new album imminent, it would do no harm to go politely through the motions. Yes, he liked Brazilian music – "more wild music...rumba, samba, conga drumming, that type of thing"[214] – and intended to tour there real, real soon. Words are cheap.

"We heard your latest record is dedicated to racing," prompted one correspondent. "Only one out of ten," corrected George. "It's called 'Faster', and I think the words are good because it's abstract. It could be about anyone, and not just about cars and engines."[213] With its title taken from Jackie Stewart's 1973 autobiography, 'Faster' was inspired by the injured Niki Lauda's return to racing, although "his wife held back her fears". Like The Beach Boys' more erudite '409' of 1963 or Jan And Dean's 'Dead Man's Curve', buzzing carburettors – from 1978's Grand Prix – riddled 'Faster', but George was right, the lyrics could as easily apply to the Grand National or the Tour de France, and the line "he's the master of going faster" was adapted from Apollo Creed's nickname in the film *Rocky*. The orchestration effortlessly tracks George, who, with his jogalong acoustic guitar and overdubbed bass, catches listeners off guard with unpredictable phrasing.

The first reference in song to his racing mates had been to Elf Tyrrell's six-wheeler in 'It's What You Value', but the attractive 'Blow Away' – the first 45 from *George Harrison* – if nothing to do with the sport was still "a song that Niki, Jody, Emerson [Fittipaldi] and the gang could enjoy".[39] Barely teetering on the edge of Britain's Top 50, 'Blow Away' showed class as a US Number 16 in March 1979. In 1960s' journalese, it might have been described as a "blues-chaser", but shackled to this elevating opus was a Beatle-esque guitar riff that irritated the memory, just as – if you want me to be pedantic – Irish songstress Enya would in her unconscious integration of the 'Blow Away' hook into her 1988 hit 'Orinoco Flow'.

As Enya's rarefied Gaelic *lieder* were forged in the "wild country" of Donegal, so items on *George Harrison* were as referential to their composer's surroundings. Although the album was mostly recorded at Friar Park, a good half was written at George's new home from home on Maui, midway across the northern Pacific. Named after the demigod whose fish-hook wrenched up the ocean floor to form the Hawaiian archipelago, Maui, with its tropic-softened terrain, ranges from lunar-like desert to a lush eastern coastline where a moustache of surf lashes petrified lava cliffs from the vomitings of the extinct Haleakala. Much of Maui – comparable in size to the Isle of Man – remains trackless jungle, particularly in the depths of the volcano's capacious crater.

From the stultifying humidity of a Thames Valley summer, the Harrisons could escape to the purer air of an opulent Maui spread called Kuppaqulua, separated by two miles of gravelled track from the fern-edged coastal road on which mongooses were flattened, as hedgehogs were on the A4155 through Henley. Secluded on this refuge were other stars, such as Dolly Parton, Kris Kristofferson and comedian Robin Williams – with whom George once hiked the Haleakala slopes. Escaping from the facile superficiality of showbusiness, it was most agreeable to mix with the 60 or so islanders who populated nearby Hana, where Hasegawa's General Store served the more immediate needs of stomach and household. Hana's only other major public facilities were a garage, a hotel and a plant nursery, whence George would furnish Kuppaqulua with silversword, poinsettia and other local flora.

Both 'If You Believe' and 'Love Comes To Everyone' on *George Harrison* were finished on Maui, as was the pretty-but-nothing 'Dark Sweet Lady' – dedicated to Olivia – which introduced the harp to Harrison's canon. More obviously born of Kuppaqulua was 'Soft Touch', which transmitted the blue curvature of the ocean via the swoop of a Hawaiian guitar, while the lengthy intro to 'Your Love Is Forever' had a subtler Polynesian flavour. 'Soft-Hearted Hana', however, screamed its origin, its background hubbub taped directly from Longhi's restaurant in Lahaini, only two miles from Hana.

The title was a warping of The Temperance Seven's 'Hard-Hearted Hannah', but from George's own arsenal came 'Here Comes The Moon', which – like the Hana number – came from a naughty-but-nice clifftop flirtation with hallucinogenics, his first in ten years. The Pacific sunset is spellbinding, "even when you're not on mushrooms",[59] but, dazzled by surreal colour formations and even the gambolling of some dolphins, "I was blissed out, and then I turned 'round and saw a big full moon rising. I laughed and thought it was about time someone – and it might as well be me – gave the moon its due."[59]

A tang of sitar, a few "oh yeahs" and a vaguely Dylan-esque vocal also harked back to a 1960s past in 'Here Comes The Moon'. While 'Not Guilty' was an actual artefact of that era, the chord sequences of 'Deep Blue' and 'Run Of The Mill' which had led, respectively, to 'Soft Touch' and 'Hard-Hearted Hana' were from only a couple of years later.

These revisions and leitmotifs may have been contributory to the relatively favourable critical notices for *George Harrison*. Without the niggling preoccupations that shrouded the previous outing, the LP had a more disciplined instrumental attack. George was in strong voice, too. The task of drawing these virtues from him had been assigned to co-producer Russ Titelman, "who was a great help. At that time, I felt I didn't really know what was going on out there in music, and I felt Russ, who was in music day by day, would give me a bit of direction."[59] Then on Warners' payroll, other professional landmarks in Titelman's past and future embraced albums by Ry Cooder (his brother-in-law), Christine McVie, Chaka Khan and, in 1985, his apotheosis, the award-winning 'Back In The High Life' by Steve Winwood, whose penchant for blood sports George had overlooked when inviting him to play on *George Harrison*. Other cronies likewise participated, among them Ray Cooper, Clapton, Wright and the newly wed Kumar Shankar. Anchoring most of the ten selections was Willie Weeks again and his usual rhythm partner, Andy Newmark. The detached and high-waged precision of these two, as Winwood had discovered, did not always reconcile easily with their paymasters' artistic intent.

Theirs, however, was no death touch. With the absorption of punk's more palatable performers into the music-industry mainstream, there'd been a move towards more melodic fare, of which there was no shortage on *George Harrison*. Whereas in Europe and Australia, it did only as well as its predecessor, its steady sales in the States overtook popular favourites of such middling chart variety as Frank Zappa's *Joe's Garage* and the latest from Herb Alpert and Smokey Robinson. Newer to the album list was another bandleader, former Sundowner Tom Petty, who'd grown up a blond stick-insect of a guitarist whose style had been determined by listening to The Byrds.

As his less intense media junket for *George Harrison* intimated, records were now less prevalent a concern. As other of his peers had diversified into back-room branches of entertainment – like, for instance, ex-Animal Chas Chandler into management and Dave Clark's exploitation of the *Ready, Steady, Go!* archives – so George looked beyond music for fun and profit. Scoring only one vote against Ringo's 60 in a 1966 *Melody Maker* poll[305] for best actor in

Help!, George always seemed the Beatle least likely to involve himself in films. However, a fleeting appearance in the specialist *Raga* apart, he'd first dipped his toe into that cultural pool by financing the shooting of the vengeful *Little Malcolm And His Struggle Against The Eunuchs* in the early 1970s. He had seen the stage version – starring John Hurt – with Mal Evans. The movie (also with Hurt) won awards but was rarely seen by the general public.

In netting a rich sponsor, the film's writer, David Halliwell, had been luckier than Eric Idle, who had a heap of original film scripts mouldering unmade in his filing cabinet. After the final series of *Monty Python's Flying Circus* in 1974, among the more successful ventures was Idle's own BBC2 series, *Rutland Weekend Television*, with Neil Innes. On one programme, in December 1975, George was roped in to back Idle on 'The Pirate Song'. Riddled with excerpts from 'My Sweet Lord', the track had an Idle-Harrison composing credit.

With his too-serious singing of the exploits of "Mrs Black" and "Captain Fantastic" while chopping at an electric guitar in *Do Not Adjust Your Set*, Eric Idle had already signalled that he was a frustrated pop star. This inclination was given its head when, as a spin-off from *Rutland Weekend Television*, a parody of The Beatles – The Rutles – was elongated for the silver screen under the direction of Gary Weiss. Premièred in March 1978, *All You Need Is Cash* ran the gauntlet, from an Arthur Scouse sending The Rutles for a season at Hamburg's Rat Keller, their rise to fame, *Sergeant Rutler's Darts Club Band*, formation of Rutler's Corps, and the split following *Let It Rut*. Get the picture? While Idle cast himself as the heart-throb "Paul" character, the part of "Stig O'Hara" (ie George) went to a musician, Rick Fataar, a latter-day Beach Boy. Mainly in cameo were other of Idle's pop-star pals, including George himself, Mick Jagger, Ron Wood and Paul Simon.

So began George's transition from maker of curate's-egg albums to paladin of the British film industry. In with the Python crowd, he'd stayed informed about he follow-tip to John Cleese *et al*'s feature film *Monty Python And The Holy Grail*. Originally called *Jesus Christ: Lust For Glory*, *Life Of Brian* – with Graham Chapman in the title role of the 13th disciple – trod on thinner ice with the scriptures than The Rutles had with the Fab Four. God might have been able to stand the joke, but during pre-production the film's nervous investors elected to wash their hands of it. Prodded by pangs of Lord Delfont's Jewish conscience, as well as a loss just incurred through signing and hastily dropping The Sex Pistols, EMI's withdrawal of financial support was on the basis of blasphemy – although, as George pointed out, "It's only the ignorant people – who didn't care to check it out – who though that it was knocking Christ. Actually, it was upholding Him and knocking all the idiotic stuff that goes on around religion."[59]

Rather than jettison *Life Of Brian*, the Python team investigated other possibilities for raising the budget required. Chief of these were Chapman's drinking buddy Keith Moon and Idle's bit-part player George Harrison. Moon's sudden death precluded that line of enquiry, but Idle's man was not so inconsiderate. Amused by Eric's ideas for the film, George considered EMI's *volte face* regrettable but by no means disastrous. A sceptical Idle, however, "didn't believe you could just pick up a film like that for four million. I didn't know how loaded he was."[23] Loaded or not, Harrison, in conjunction with Denis O'Brien, "pawned my house and the office in London to get a bank loan – and that was a bit nerve-wracking".[23]

Purchaser of the dearest cinema ticket in history, it was only fair that, as well as getting a credit as "executive producer", George should be fitted into the film somewhere. Thus, hanging around the set in Tunisia, he was persuaded to don Arab gear as an extra in a kitchen scene "among a bunch of incurables and women taken in sin" who are supplicating the mistakenly messianic Brian for his curative blessing. As Michael Palin noted, "For George, the shock of finding himself in a crowd mobbing someone else was just too much."[285]

With his own property as collateral, the "Jewish man in the kitchen" was mightily relieved when *Life Of Brian* grossed in excess of $15 million in North America alone. Thus heartened, George reconsidered a view expressed in 1974 that "the film industry is like the record industry ten years ago – very difficult to get a look-in. It needs a kick up the arse."[285] With the *Brian* speculation proving that conventional routes could be circumvented more effectively than anything attempted by Apple, O'Brien and Harrison then ventured further into the celluloid interior with the official formation of HandMade Films in 1980, named "as a bit of a joke"[23] following George's outing to the British Handmade Paper Mill at Wookey Hole in Somerset.

Denis, at least, looked like a movie mogul. Furthermore, apart from the statue of Buddha and a corridor lined with gold discs, HandMade's suite in Cadogan Square off King's Road was just how you might visualise a film company's headquarters: receptionist clattering a typewriter, crenellated wallpaper, glossy magazines under the waiting area's coffee table and workaholic O'Brien standing pensive at his office window, sun-blanked spectacle lenses flashing over Knightsbridge. Sprawled in a button leather armchair is George, his young partner.

The maverick firm developed an adventurous policy of taking on what a major backer would most likely reject or, at best, severely edit, just as the Grade Organisation intended to do with the gangster film *The Long Good Friday*. For its disgruntled male lead, Bob Hoskins, Eric Idle was again the catalyst for Harrison and O'Brien's rescue of a promising flick. Not as immediate a money-spinner as *Life Of Brian*, *The Long Good Friday* was, nevertheless, well received and also facilitated Hoskins' rise to an international plateau of stardom.

Such career opportunities were not extended to any old riff-raff. Unlike Apple, HandMade assured no theoretical glad welcome to would-be directors. It mattered that you could nurture a connection via, say, a friend of a friend to its inner sanctum. It was the time-honoured adage of "it isn't how good you are, it's who you know". Once over this hurdle, it was often easier to get a deal than might be imagined. For a start, you were advantaged by George being "on the other side to the artists, and it's a funny position for me to be in. I hope I can understand their problems and that they can see I do."[8] This praiseworthy sentiment was to be much tested throughout the shooting of *Shanghai Surprise* in 1986.

On the strength of a two-page synopsis, Monty Python's American animator, Terry Gilliam, got the go-ahead for the *Time Bandits* family fantasy, while HandMade's first US film, Tony Bill's

Five Corners, came about because Harrison "liked his restaurant in LA. We'd had a good meal there, and then he came up to the table and said he'd like to make a film for us."[306]

Economic potential rather than artistic worth led George to back *Black And Blue*, a 1980 movie featuring Black Sabbath and other heavy metal acts. With the most irrevocable veto in the organisation, George tended to exercise thrift by encouraging editing at approved screenplay level instead of in the cutting room, but he'd say with quiet pride, "Sometimes I have nothing to do with a film until the rushes."[306] In an age when Hollywood underwriters would fork out $20 million for the average picture, HandMade managed *Time Bandits* on five. The fact that Palin's *Bullshot* was a tale too damn British for the colonials was mitigated by an even lower bill of less than two million.

It wasn't all roses, however, as exemplified by Monty Python defecting elsewhere for *The Meaning Of Life* – the cabal's least pleasing work – evidently through a falling-out over O'Brien's over-ambitious monetary propositions. Of all of the Python *dramatis personae*, HandMade was most at odds with Gilliam, who to George was "eccentric, bordering on genius",[285] just like Phil Spector. When an aghast O'Brien suggested nixing one particular *Time Bandits* sequence of jailed midgets eating rats, Gilliam said he'd burn the negatives of the entire feature. This threat could be tolerated when *Time Bandits* brought in more than $80 million.

HandMade's losses – such as that sustained for 1984's *Water* – were blamed on poor distribution and the faint hearts of many American buyers. At first hand, George pinpointed one US failure: "Everybody who hadn't seen *Withnail And I* was trying to find out where it was on. It had already been whipped off. That's the problem. If you don't pack out cinemas in the first week, that's it."[306] Most administrative functions were therefore doled out to bigger organisations like EMI, while HandMade retained its creative initiative and exploitation.

George put his own eminence at the disposal of HandMade's publicity department after implying to the tabloids that "three old friends *might* act in *Life Of Brian*".[307] He stirred up interest in

HandMade product less crassly on such key forums as BBC2's *Film '83* and, with Bob Hoskins, in a pre-recorded segment on *Good Morning America*.

Although his new position as movie Big Shot had novelty appeal, George was too long in the tooth to harbour pretensions far beyond that of money lender and lay advisor, as there were "some films I wouldn't have done that were really good",[282] such as *Mona Lisa*, a film about an ex-convict's entanglement with a lesbian prostitute. Initially, this film lark had been incidental to his music, because "I don't put in much time, not even into scripts. I can think of project to do and I can put people together, but I'm no good at saying, 'Here, give me five million dollars.' All this firing people and shouting, you know? I'm a sensitive artist."[282] He'd tool along to an odd day's shooting, but ultimately, "I'm just this lad who happens to be standing around watching them make a movie."[272] As with Alfred Hitchcock, the sharp-eyed viewer might espy George in minor cameos – for example, as a Mexican janitor in 1988's *Checking Out*, and singing in a night club band in *Shanghai Surprise*. More pertinent to his calling were soundtrack contributions, like 'Only A Dream Away' – with an insidious nonsense chorus – for *Time Bandits*. In *Water*, with Ringo behind the kit, George and Eric Clapton portrayed themselves in The Singing Rebels Band, sharing a microphone during a concert sequence. Through George, Larry Smith – now a resident of Hambledon and a lesser light in what was becoming known as the "Henley Music Mafia" – gained both a singing and a dramatic role in *Bullshot*.

Increasing respect for HandMade within the industry caused more illustrious thespians to be seen frequently in its productions. As well as Bob Hoskins and Michael Palin, other HandMade regulars included David Warner, Maggie Smith and Michael Caine. Also among those with HandMade service to their credit were Helen Mirren, Paul McCann, Frances Tomelty (first wife of pop-star-turned-actor Sting), the late Trevor Howard and Dennis Quilley, convincingly out of character as the openly homosexual leader of an ENSA concert party in *Privates On Parade*.

The engagement of such comic stalwarts as Leonard Rossiter and the scriptwriting team of Dick Clement and Ian La Frenais enhanced HandMade's image as a saviour of British comedy during its dullest period. In the late 1970s, only the likes of *Fawlty Towers* were oases of rampant hilarity in a desert of "more tea, Vicar?" home-counties sitcoms in which a moptopped and acrylically amiable young man muddled through a weekly half hour in, perhaps, a restaurant, hospital or shared flat, fraught with innuendo about wogs, poofs and tits. HandMade jokes from the Python team attacked these prejudices and often overkilled their perpetrators. Refreshingly tangential to the current vogue altogether were *The Missionary*, a lunge at Edwardian "muscular Christianity", and *Privates On Parade*, with Cleese as Quilley's Fawlty-esque CO. Blacker was the humour of *How To Get Ahead In Advertising*, with, promised director Bruce Robinson, "something to offend everybody".[285]

Films at other points of the HandMade compass were hardly any fun at all, among them the gloomy *The Lonely Passion Of Judith Hearne*. Still grimmer was *Scrubbers*, set in a girls' borstal and directed by Mai Zetterling.

As if in late consolation for his poor showing in *Melody Maker*'s *Help!* tabulation, the placing of *Time Bandits* at Number Three in its Film section was the sole Beatle-associated entry in the magazine's 1979 popularity poll. The only other Beatle still in the running was the irrepressible Paul, who – with or without Wings – was happy to bask in the limelight of what were often hit singles, especially in snug old Britain. At least Paul was no snob. Plugging 'Mull Of Kintyre' and appearing in a comedy sketch on BBC's *Mike Yarwood Christmas Show* were all part of a day's work. If rather subdued after a custodial drugs bust when Wings' world tour reached Japan in January 1980, Paul bounced back with 'Coming Up', which in April was high up international charts, thanks to a promotional video with him in various guises all over it.

As much Mr Showbusiness in his way was Ringo, who had actually been close to death in 1979 with an intestinal complaint. Those who read about it felt sorry for him but were no longer buying his records. The day would soon come when no British or US label was prepared to release his latest album, and his movie career was all but spent. Although in 1980 he met his second wife, Barbara Bach, on location in *Caveman*, this – his last major film – drew all of six customers the night after its London opening.

Until his final weeks, nothing as public could cajole John from his reclusive sojourn as Yoko's house-husband. Now blessed – like the Harrisons – with a son, the Lennons were based in New York's exclusive Dakota block, where they were systematically buying up additional apartments as other tenants departed. Of John's city, George had once observed, "Some of my best songs were written there. It's great, in that it gives you 360-degree vision, New York."[275] Events, however, would convince him that "the lifestyle I lead is more correct than the one [John] chose, to have some peace and quiet, rather than live in the middle of New York, which is – let's face it – a madhouse".[306] Lennon may have found his spiritual home there, but not one melody or lyric had been heard from him commercially since the appropriately premonitory 'Cookin'', a donation to Ringo's *Rotogravure* in 1976. What right had anyone to expect more? He said the same in a reluctantly given press conference a year later, adding that, when Sean was no more such a baby, "then we'll think of creating something else other than the child".[308]

The wanderings of the four ex-Beatles, even ten years after disbandment, did not prevent them from keeping in touch. With Apple finances set to occupy lawyers and accountants into the next century, George, Paul, Ringo and – wearing the trousers – Yoko were obliged anyway to convene on occasions to review progress. Old wounds were sometimes reopened, but at the end of the decade there was a protracted truce.

McCartney's arrest in Tokyo had been instrumental in establishing this concordat. The detainee's week spent pondering his folly in a Nippon gaol elicited a sympathetic telegram from George, even if – though in New York that same night – he had found no reason to attend Wings' show at Madison Square Garden. It also prompted Ringo's realisation that he no longer knew Paul's telephone number. Between Starr and Harrison, however, any bad blood had long been diluted, as shown by George's affectionate cameo in the drummer's made-for-TV spectacular *Ringo*. However, only the rare postcard filtered between George and John. Other than these, Harrison now knew Lennon only via hearsay and tales in the press of him as the Howard Hughes of pop. The same as any other fan, George was "very interested to know whether John still writes tunes and puts them on a cassette, or does he just forget all about music and not play the guitar?".[309]

A chance encounter with John in a Bermudan night club made one newshound report that the Lennon songwriting well was not as arid as might be imagined. This was confirmed a month later in August 1980, when John and Yoko booked sessions in a Big Apple studio to cut enough material for two LPs, the first of which was later scheduled for release in autumn. There were enough songs left over for John to present four to Ringo that November, when they met for the last time.

New records from George, however, were not big events any more. Maybe he also needed to absent himself from pop for years on end, for – as Ringo was already aware – an old stager's album was now less likely to be accepted without comment by a record company's quality control. 1977 had seen Warners' signing of The Sex Pistols and the company's farewell to middle-aged Van Morrison, much admired but tetchy and often long winded, musically. Not as drastic but still unnerving was executive reaction in October 1980 to *Somewhere In England*, George's proposed third album for the label. "If George wants a million-seller," moaned company president Mo Ostin, "it's not on here."[52]

Firstly, Mo didn't like the front cover: with a satellite shot of England superimposed over the back of his head, the artist in profile gazes westwards. As to the music, most of it was sufficiently "current", but some numbers would have to go, such as the opening one about "drowning in the tears of the world". That's a cheerful thought for short-listing on a radio playlist. Just as downbeat was 'Sat Singing'. Depression, however tuneful, didn't get airplay like it had during the drip-rock fad. Also axed from *Somewhere In England* were 'Flying Hour' and – surfacing years later on a B-Side – 'Lay His Head'. Like 'Writing On The Wall', which slipped through the net, both were pleasant but unexciting Harrison fare that he'd earmarked to end side two. What Ostin wanted instead was some up-tempo product to balance the mood. Until then, George's LP was to be postponed indefinitely. In any case, Lennon's *Double Fantasy* album was imminent. Even in 1980, the issue of two ex-Beatle discs within weeks of each other could still be detrimental to the sales of both.

More than anything, Ostin desired not a promotional single that might or might not chart but an unmistakable worldwide smash like 'My Sweet Lord' had been. George had had a good run since then, but now – even in the States – only by pulling such a stroke could he reverse what was an undisguisable downward spiral. Because so many cuts on his latest effort hadn't been up to scratch, this possibility was unlikely. As with Ringo, Harrison's previous handlers had been lucky in milking his calling-card Beatlehood when they did. Amid these glum reflections, an occurrence as the Yuletide sell-in got under way would give Warner Brothers a miracle.

With pride smarting at the company's rejection of the first *Somewhere In England*, George's return to the drawing board for four replacement tracks threw up two potential hits. While the words of 'Teardrops' were as lachrymose as those of 'Tears Of The World', no more did they convey socio-political tenets commercially unacceptable to Mo Ostin. To an ebullient backing and ear-grabbing melody in which the beat lifts for the chorus, George sang of a lonely man's need for love. However, although a stronger song, 'Teardrops' failed to shift a fraction of the units of the first *Somewhere In England* single, 'All Those Years Ago'.

A US Number Two, and placed in most other Top Tens, its lyrical connotations and the affinity of its writer to its subject had bequeathed unto this singalong canter an undeserved piquancy. 'All Those Years Ago', you see, was about John Lennon, who had been shot outside the Dakota in a travesty of legitimate admiration by Mark David Chapman, described in the song as "the Devil's best friend". "Are you John Lennon?" asked one of the cops in whose squad car the victim was rushed to hospital. "Yeah," gasped John. Then he died.

Everybody remembers the moment they heard. In our house the morning after, my wife shouted the intelligence up the stairs after catching it on the seven o'clock news. A few miles away in Henley,

George already knew. Olivia had told him after being wrenched from sleep by a long-distance call from her sister-in-law just before dawn. She shook George gently and came straight to the point. "How bad is it?" he inquired dozily. "A flesh wound or something?" With phlegmatic detachment, he turned over and "just went back to sleep, actually. Maybe it was a way of getting away from it."[306]

When the world woke up, John Lennon still hadn't recovered from being dead. Cancelling the day's recording session, George withdrew indoors with Dhani and Olivia. By late afternoon, he was collected enough to parry calls from the media with a prepared opening sentence: "After all we went through together, I had – and still have – great love and respect for John."[310] Paul's hiring of bodyguards on that strange day contradicted a flippancy of 1964 when asked about security by *Ready, Steady, Go!* compere Cathy McGowan. "What do we want to be protected for?" Paul replied. "We may be popular, but we're not china dolls."[311]

Paul and George had each suffered derogatory remarks from John during the promotion of *Double Fantasy*. His last published thoughts on The Beatles had been sugared with regretful affection, but, apparently, it might not have bothered him that much if he'd never seen any of them again. Among John's valedictions in print to George was some pot-calling-the-kettle-black self-righteousness about the Bright Tunes affair, which ignored his own melodic plundering of The Shirelles' B-side 'Mama Said' for 'Nobody Told Me', one of his final recordings.

His waspishness – as both his targets and John himself realised – could be shrugged off. "I don't want to start another whole thing because of the way I feel today. Tomorrow I will feel absolutely differently. It's not important, anyway."[80] George had been stunned not by the bald fact of John's passing but by the way he died. After catharsis and a dull ache, he wondered why this Mark lunatic had done it. Chapman had been photographed stalking Bob Dylan too. "John's shooting definitely scared all of us – me, Paul and Ringo," admitted George. "When a fan recognises me and rushes over, it definitely makes me nervous."[151] In as late as 1990, George was accompanied in public by a bodyguard, a six-foot-four-inch former

SAS crackshot, but any worries he may have had for his own safety in 1980 were unfounded. Like McCartney, Steve Winwood and Jeff Lynne, he didn't appear to be in the same vulnerable league then as Lennon, Dylan and other possessors of original genius rather than anything as common as mere talent.

On the "improved" *Somewhere In England* – as with George's other albums – it was vice versa. Technical advances – even since *George Harrison* – accorded greater clarity, particularly in the close-miked lead vocals, which blended Dylan-esque whinge with ingrained Scouse more than ever: "I've had my shur of cryin' bookets full of teardrops." Unruffled dispatch was tempered by details such as the slightly heavier snare drum on 'That Which I Have Lost', co-producer Ray Cooper's percussion frills and the oscillating degrees of wah-wah and other artifices on minor guitar sections throughout. All but blocked were avenues for flabby extemporisation of the kind instanced on the lengthy fade of the remaindered 'Tears Of The World'. Once he might have had licence to metaphorically blow his brains out, but now Tom Scott was limited to a fluid, one-verse solo in 'Unconsciousness Rules'.

In keeping with its title, the LP featured George's highest percentage of English musicians since *All Things Must Pass*. From The Albion Dance Band came drummer Dave Mattacks, while other natives included top session bass player Herbie Flowers and – summoned from his Godalming pub – landlord Gary Brooker, whose purring organ stood out on 'Life Itself', a slow waltz extolling George's religious liberalism.

Not as non-sectarian was 'That Which I Have Lost', which, countering its country and western-ish punch, was "right out of the *Bhagavad Gita*. In it, I talk about fighting the forces of darkness, limitations, falsehood and mortality."[151] A worldly ferocity pervaded 'Blood From A Clone'. That this was one of the substitutions was evidenced by nose-thumbing phrases about "beating my head on a brick wall", "nitpicking" (presumably by Mr Ostin) and being "nothing like Frank Zappa", whose drift towards lavatorial "humor" restricted mainstream airplay. However, because it had a popular ska rhythm and, less so, because he was George Harrison, he was excused. Otherwise, the ill-humoured 'Blood From A Clone' was in like vein to 'This Song'. Who but the most uncritical fan wants to pay out to listen to a singer getting his hassles with his record company off his chest?

Appealing more directly to common sensibilities was 'Save The World', the title of which said it all. As much an all-round protest song as 'Eve Of Destruction', any conservationist could appreciate George's laudable anxiety about our abused planet, if not his sometimes clumsy expression. With the impartiality of one long and, perhaps, guiltily isolated from the everyday, he railed against pollution, nuclear weapons, deforestation and other ills motivated by human greed. Driving it home are sound effects of bombs, a cash register, a wailing infant and similar noises when the quasi-reggae tempo slows down. According to the composer, 'Save The World' was "very serious but at the same time...hysterical. The lyrics have a lot of funny things about 'dog-food salesmen' and 'making your own H-bomb in the kitchen with your mum'."[59] Most amusing, I'm sure. As to the snatch of 'Crying' from *Wonderwall* on the play-out, he explained, "I just wanted to let the whole song go out with something sad to touch that nerve."[59]

More subtle a sign on *Somewhere In England* that George's heart was in the right place was the vicarious pleasure he gave many listeners through two chestnuts from his childhood which he sang more or less straight. Both by Hoagy Carmichael, George included these tunes partly because, prior to the pressures that spurred him to write 'Teardrops' *et al*, he'd been fresh out of ideas. Also, Carmichael was much in the air, then; Robin Sarstedt – younger brother of Eden Kane – had soared into the British Top Ten with 'My Resistance Is Low' in 1976, while, even as *Somewhere In England* was shipped to record stores, cool Georgie Fame was planning an entire Carmichael album in collaboration with Annie Ross, one of his smart jazz friends. Most significantly, if Hurtwood Edge was empty, Eric Clapton's Ansafone would croon a customised verse of 'Gone Fishin''. Rather than consume needle time with a pair of sub-standard originals, why shouldn't George – who'd been "nuts for him since I was a kid"[58] – indulge himself with 'Baltimore

Oriole' and a 'Hong Kong Blues', bracketed by the clashing of "old Buddha's gong"?

For all its overhauls and alterations, no one could pretend that George's higher chart position was down to any improved qualities within the grooves since *George Harrison*, which was coming to be regarded as the Serious Beatle's most compelling solo collection. However, ever since Buddy Holly's Number One with 'I Guess It Doesn't Matter Any More' in 1959, it had been understood that a death in pop tends to sell records. Before they'd even wiped away the tears, music-business moguls were obliged to meet demand kindled by tragedy by rush-releasing product while John's corpse was still warm. Indeed, ghoulish Beatlemania had already given the slain Beatle a hat-trick of UK chart-toppers within a month of his cremation. Out of sympathy, too, his widow finally made her Top 40 debut without him. For the first time since *Two Virgins*, Lennon's bum made the cover of *Rolling Stone*.

Inevitably, there were a rash of tribute discs. Head and shoulders commercially above titles like 'It Was Nice To Know You, John' and 'Elegy For The Walrus' and Lennon covers such as Roxy Music's 'Jealous Guy' was George's better-qualified 'All Those Years Ago', the main selling point of *Somewhere In England* and the reason why George – by association – was to end 1981 seven places behind Lennon as tenth Top Male Vocalist in *Billboard* magazine's awards. Another incentive for buyers was the overdubbed presence of Paul and Ringo, who, with Denny Laine and Linda McCartney, had broken off recording Wings' new album in George Martin's Monserrat complex to add their bits when the unmixed 'All Those Years Ago' arrived from Friar Park.

It's futile to hypothesise about John's beyond-the-grave judgement on 'All Those Years Ago'. However, I would submit that, in the same interview as the Bright Tunes barbs, he seemed wounded by the "glaring omissions"[80] of him from George's autobiography, *I Me Mine*, published earlier that year. The roots of what its author admitted was "a little ego detour"[39] lay in a conversation in 1977 with two representatives of Genesis, a publishing concern. Not any old publishing concern, Surrey-based Genesis specialised in beautifully made books of creamy vellum, coloured inks, gold leaf and hand-tooled leather bindings. Limited by cost, it was good going if an edition exhausted a run of a couple of thousand, as did a facsimile of *HMS Bounty*'s log, a snip at £158 apiece.

After the visit to Wookey Hole paper mill, George warmed to the notion of Genesis reproducing his lyrics as a joy forever, "because how it's made was almost more important than what's inside".[58] Derek Taylor, then HandMade's publicist, was commissioned to write a scene-setting introduction, but confessed, "I couldn't, though I'd known him for 15 years. I didn't know enough. I decided that the introduction should be the story of his life as he chose to tell it."[52] Interspersed with Taylor's narrative, therefore, were transcriptions of George's taped reminiscences.

This filled but 62 pages. A photograph section then led to Part Two, which took up the remaining two thirds of the "autobiography". Here, George's original scribblings of rhymes and chords are printed alongside his commentary on each. With a choice of three colours for the cover, the fly-leaf signed by George himself and – via some outlets – sold at a knockdown £116, what discerning fan could resist investing in *I Me Mine*? As only 1,000 were available in this form, its rarity enabled a London radio station to auction a copy for charity at over twice its recommended price.

Easier on the pocket in mass-market paperback, seven years on, its value in my research was not as great as you'd think – although it was more rewarding than a slim Harrison biography by Ross Michaels published in 1977.[312] Although the background to George's songs is quite intriguing, *I Me Mine* is not so much a serious study of his life as a good read. There's little space for in-depth estimation of motive or weighing of experience, but the surfacing of some unfamiliar anecdotes and the recounting of the old yarns in the subject's own laconic words is as relaxed as a fireside chat.

15 The Hermit

Throughout the 1980s, pop's history as much as its present was seized upon as a way of making money. No more the market's most vital consumer group, teenagers were outmanoeuvred by their Swinging '60s parents and young marrieds with high disposable incomes who'd sated their appetites for novelty. No matter how it was packaged – twelve-inch club mix on polkadot vinyl, or whatever – the pop single became a loss leader, an incentive for grown-ups to buy an album, hopefully on more expensive compact disc.

Incorrigible old Mods, Rockers and flower children didn't mind squeezing into the smart casuals that were the frequent norm in citadels of "quality" entertainment and on under-40s weekends where "Sounds Of The Sixties" nights would pull in capacity crowds. Rebooked at the same such venues time and time again, the likes of The Searchers, Herman's Hermits (now minus Herman), Gerry Marsden and The Swinging Blue Jeans – now with Colin Manley in their ranks – had opportunities to form genuine friendships rather than play backstage host to a residue of stargazers.

In the charts, it was often as if time had stopped. The sampler single for US albums would be an act's revamp of an oldie, like Tiffany's 'I Saw Her Standing There' or Van Halen's touching Number Twelve in 1982's Hot 100 with Roy Orbison's 'Oh! Pretty Woman', which the previous year had resounded as part of Tight Fit's 'Back To The Sixties' medley in a Britain that was even more awash with nostalgia for that decade. At one stage, every fourth record in the UK hit parade was either a re-issue or a revival of an old song. Contradicting Billy J Kramer's 'You Can't Live On

Memories' single of 1983, the culmination of this trend was The Hollies' windfall when the 20-year-old single 'He Ain't Heavy (He's My Brother)' shot to Number One in 1988 via the offices of Miller Lite lager, who'd worked it into a television commercial.

Not needing unsolicited snippet coverage, another re-promotion of The Beatles' back catalogue by EMI began well, with 'Love Me Do' and the spliced-up 'Beatles Movie Medley' both cracking the Top Ten. A year earlier, Dutch session musicians Stars On 45 – imitating the Fab Four – had done likewise, as would Siouxsie And The Banshees with 'Dear Prudence' in 1984.

The latter was a one-shot ploy to revive a flagging career, but there were other bands whose *raison d'être* was centred solely on impersonating The Beatles. Foremost among these were Abbey Road, Cavern and – most accurate of all – The Bootleg Beatles, formed from the cast of the West End musical *Beatlemania*. While "Paul" more resembled *Old Grey Whistle Test* presenter Mark Ellen, one Bootleg Beatle watcher was able to confirm to the real Harrison – at a Formula One meet – that actor Andre Barreau's "George" was authentic down to the Liverpool leg.

In that city's Kensington district, where they'd recorded 'In Spite Of All The Danger', a cluster of new streets had been named in the Beatles' honour, with George Harrison Way being the shortest cul-de-sac off John Lennon Drive. In similar ratio, Lennon ephemera drew highest bids among Beatle memorabilia on offer at Sotheby's and other top sale rooms. Although few bothered with *Dark Horse* items under the hammer, a letter to Stuart Sutcliffe from George fetched just short of £2,000 and his first guitar had appreciated by over 1,000 per cent by 1983. Even the Harrison family toilet, removed during modernisation of Mackett's Lane, was displayed and sold as solemnly as if it had been a Duchamp ready-made.

Although a gold 'My Sweet Lord' went for £2,750, comparative indifference towards other artefacts from George's post-Beatle years reflected his standing as a contemporary artist. The goodwill that had propelled 'All Those Years Ago' into the charts was not extended to 'Teardrops' or even to *The Best Of George Harrison*, a budget re-issue from 1968 with a cover photo. While McCartney was accorded

41 lines in the *Who's Who* social register, in 1981 George was stuck between Bill Haley and Noel Harrison in *Whatever Happened To...?*, a publication claiming to be "the great rock and pop nostalgia book".[313]

In commercial decline as a recording artist and with his very competence as a composer questioned by Warners, George had come to loathe public fascination with his "previous incarnation".[8] Ringo's tentative agreement was rumoured, but George would have nothing to do with a multi-million-pound bribe for a one-album collaboration by the Fab Three and the adult Julian Lennon. According to "Uncle George", Julian took most after Cynthia. Although his surname had opened doors and packed out Carnegie Hall for one of his concerts, Julian had become something of a "Tumbledown Dick" among pop stars. Nevertheless, the press produced another rumour – that he and his father's former confreres would perform together at the climax of Live Aid in 1985. Instead, Paul sang a gremlin-troubled 'Let It Be'. As an elder of pop altruism, an invitation merely to attend had been sent to George, but he confessed, "I was just a little worried in case somebody was trying to re-form The Beatles, trying to trick us all into being on it."[188] However, he contributed a vignette to a paperback published in aid of the associated charity, Comic Relief.

To no humanitarian end, George and the other Beatles were more lucratively exploited when an old recording was used to advertise Nike's "revolution" in footwear, supposedly with Yoko Ono's permission. A suit was filed by the surviving Beatles because, predicted George, "If it's allowed to happen, every Beatle song ever recorded is going to be advertising women's underwear and sausages. The other thing is, even while Nike might have paid Capitol Records for the rights, Capitol certainly don't give us the money."[188] To redress similar royalty grievances, a legal battle was joined by The Beatles against EMI in 1984. Four years later, the group slapped a writ for damages on old rival Dave Clark's video company for Beatles clips shown in Channel 4's re-runs of *Ready, Steady, Go!*. Minor matters included an injunction to stop an English independent company from releasing an album of their Decca audition.

In the ups and downs of George's separate business affairs, his rapport with Warners was even less cordial now. On top of the disheartening um-ing and ah-ing over *Somewhere In England*, he'd been miffed over an unimaginative – if justifiable – usage of Beatles stills and footage in the video for 'All Those Years Ago'. That he'd left the making of this to the company rather than intervene personally showed the extent of the disenchantment he'd spelled out in 'Blood From A Clone'. Moreover, like others his age, he concluded, "The Top 40 songs are so bland and trends like hip-hop or rap music are so tedious. I can't wait until we go back to the old days, when the charts were full of good songs by real musicians. These days, there's not an ounce of talent to be seen."[315]

The sweeping lack of sympathy with an ear of commodity over creativity was coupled with a realisation that he'd lost the knack of writing hits, even American ones. Quite simply, George was out of touch. He was not, however, unduly worried. No longer did he explore the same worn-out themes over and over again from new angles in the wrong-headed expectation of finding gold. He'd sit down to compose almost eagerly, but sometimes all he'd hear were vibrations hanging in the air. Glazed languor would set in, and his mind would wander to car-racing tracks, Friar Park gardens, Maui – anywhere but to the job in hand. His, however, was not the same malady that had crept up on John, who, unlike George, was basically lazy.

George had found a full life beyond either cheerful lassitude or the pursuit of hit records. By gripping tightly on the realities of past success and defining his motivations sharply enough, he had reached a level – both professional and personal – where another 'My Sweet Lord' would have been a mere sideshow. It was income from HandMade – which by now averaged three or four films annually – rather than royalty cheques from *Somewhere In England* that kept the wolf from the door nowadays. Despite heavy promotion, there'd still been a few damp squibs, and George had been alarmed by the movie industry's competition and occasional downright thuggishness: "A lot of cinemas down the eastern seaboard of America wouldn't pay over the box-office money. They held it for six or nine months, investing our money, but it's all Mafia connections, and there's nothing you can do about it."[315] Nevertheless, HandMade had gone from strength to strength, from Bob Hoskins' BAFTA Best Actor statuette for *Mona Lisa* to George and Denis receiving from the Duchess of Kent an award for HandMade's services to British film. Before millions of BBC viewers, a jubilant George planted a kiss on the royal cheek.

Such Fab Four-ish sauciness was absent on ITV a few months later, when *News At Ten* showed George among protesters at an anti-nuclear rally in Trafalgar Square. This was one of the less anonymous manifestations of his and Olivia's concern about pressing environmental and human issues that had passed him by during the ebbing bustle of the 1970s. As well as a generous financial gesture to float *Vole* – a green journal launched by Monty Python's Terry Jones – a re-recorded 'Save The World', with specifically adjusted lyrics, was donated to a fund-raising LP for Greenpeace, an organisation dedicated – like *Vole* – to the extirpation of iniquities like whale fishing and radioactive dumping. "As an ordinary member of humanity and of the British public," he explained, "the only vote I have ever cast is Green. The whole planet is operating on the waste of over-indulgence. It's just ridiculous. 'Money doesn't talk, it swears.' Bob Dylan said that years ago."[316]

An appeal from the Cancer Research Fund, who'd noted his involvement in the Nilsson foundation, fired George "to try and get something started"[317] in order to publicise the British leg of Canadian "13-million-dollar man" Steve Fonyo's marathon 'Journey For Lives' sponsored walk. *Leg* is a crucial word here, as one of 22-year-old Steve's had been amputated because of cancer. *En route* from Scotland to London in March 1987, he and his fiancée were joined along the towpath in Henley by the Harrisons. With his collar turned up against a chill spring breeze, George, Dhani and Steve posed in midstride before press cameras, and then all repaired to Friar Park and afternoon tea.

If seldom seen, George continued throughout the 1980s to function as town patrician and patron of Henley events and institutions. Among the pies in which he had a finger was the Kenton Theatre. He was not, however, present when I performed there in 1980, although he'd been sent a complimentary ticket and an invitation to bring his guitar along in case he couldn't prevent himself from joining The Argonauts and me on stage. Maybe he did turn up after all. Certainly, he saw fit to attend a reception for television gourmet Ken Lo in the restaurant above the Angel on the Bridge pub and present a cheque for a charity fun run at a local college.

Of all of George's interventions in parochial affairs, none were as intensely public as those concerning the threatened demolition of Bell Street's Regal Cinema, scene of his date with Hayley Mills and other assignations "long, before I lived in Henley".[318] From its grand opening in 1936 with *Take My Tip*, starring Cicely Courtenay, until its abrupt closure with *Back To The Future* half a century later, this 740-seater theatre had been a popular facet of the town's social life, its attendance figures increasing by almost half during the months preceding the declaration by its owners, Henley Picture Houses Ltd, that it had become "unprofitable" since the advent of video.

To the howl of rage from the 7,000 who signed an opposing petition, the Regal was to be levelled by the John Lewis Partnership's bulldozers in order to extend the adjacent branch of Waitrose supermarket and create a mall of 18 shops – and, if you like, a smaller cinema. "This is rape!"[318] yelled an affronted *Henley Standard* editorial. Furthermore, the turmoil of the proposed reconstruction would exacerbate the already critical traffic problem of – as George complained – "cars and lorries crashing through the narrow streets that were originally built for the horse and cart".[318]

As *éminence grise* behind some of the Regal's weekly offerings, George had needed little persuasion from borough councillor Tony Lane to join the Davids against the John Lewis Goliath in a star-studded show of strength outside the empty cinema on a busy Saturday morning in September 1986. "I'm not doing this for an ulterior motive," elucidated Lane's most powerful convert, raising a placard from the centre of the bunched local celebrities. "I genuinely want to preserve this town. These faceless people who made the planning applications and those who give permission should come out of the shadow. Let us see the faces of the assassins!"[318] Hemmed in by jotting reporters, George snarled further about Waitrose's "Orwellian cynicism" and "concrete monsters",[318] even evoking

Dylan and Liverpool during a debate that simmered on even after Environment Secretary Chris Patten decided against calling a public enquiry in October 1989. This was in spite of crowded Town Hall meetings (some attended by Olivia), offers to the Lewis firm of alternative sites, "Save The Regal" galas and Dhani joining in the booing as a children's protest march passed Waitrose. Lobbying the constituency's unmoved MP, Michael Heseltine, George's sarcastic suggestion of replacing Henley's antique bridge with a wider concrete model was met, allegedly, with a look "as if to say, 'Shut your mouth, you Liverpool git.'"[315]

Also pitching in were the likes of barrister/playwright John Mortimer, actors George Cole and Jeremy Irons and – from up the river, in Wargrave – Mary Hopkin. Others supporting George, among members of what was still technically his own profession, were Joe Brown from neighbouring Skirmett, Dave Edmunds and Jon Lord, who, as squire of the acres round Yewton Lodge, could well afford the thousand quid he put into the "Save The Regal" kitty.

They and other members of the Henley Music Mafia played together, either in the privacy of their own homes or on stages like those in Watlington's Carriers Arms or the Crown in Pishill, with a rambling selection sprung from "old twelve-bars, The Everly Brothers and the odd bit of Django Reinhardt".[187] From these casual unwindings came more palpable liaisons. While house-hunting in the area, The Hollies' Tony Hicks stayed at Kenny Lynch's place near Nettlebed, where owner and lodger wrote songs that would be unveiled on a consequent Hollies album. George composed 'Flying Hour' with Nettlebed guitarist Mick Ralphs – former mainstay of Mott The Hoople – and 'Shelter Of Your Love' with Alvin Lee from Goring. In 1985, he lent Mike Batt a hand on the Womble *führer*'s musical setting of Lewis Carroll's 'The Hunting Of The Snark'. For George, Jon Lord tickled the ivories in the Cascara band in *Water* and manipulated synthesiser on *Gone Troppo*. This album, so George disclosed two years after its release in November 1982, would be his last. He'd had his fill of the music business, thank you. "Once I'd got myself out of that star rat-race, I promised myself I'd never work again. Well I do work – but I want it to be enjoyable, not just a slog."[272]

As a farewell, if it was one, *Gone Troppo* was the sort of record you could leave on instant replay while you put your feet up. Although 'I Really Love You' was conspicuous, it was almost the sound at any given moment that counted rather than individual tracks. Working sensually more than intellectually, it was warm latitudes, dreamy sighs and an ocean dawn from the quarterdeck: a slow boat redirected from China to Maui. After the adulterated *Somewhere In England*, the new LP was a refinement and apparent culmination of the seam mined on *George Harrison* – which means that it was Harrison's most enterprising musical statement since The Beatles.

Pacific culture had been absorbed by George less self-consciously than his Indian studies had been in the 1960s. His slide-guitar playing was now closer to that of Hawaiian virtuoso Frank Ferera than Ry Cooder's. On one number, he even plucked a Javan *jal-tarang*. Nowhere were there raucous and distorted-fretboard pyrotechnics, which were never his style, anyway. Instead, George's obligatos and solos were all the more rewarding for their semi-acoustic restraint in the overall elegance of *Gone Troppo*.

Opening the album was its most laboured song, 'Wake Up, My Love', which dwelt in a staccato unison riff and tension-building chorus, both of which marred by the snotty grating of a synthesiser. These extrovert qualities rather than gentler possibilities were presumably why 'Wake Up My Love' was selected by Warners as the trailer single, which peaked around the middle of the Hot 100 while slumbering in deletion in most other territories.

More deserving of even this slight chart placing was the US follow-up, the charming 'I Really Love You'. Blowing the dust off this favourite from The Chants' Merseyside repertoire, George didn't reconstruct it as he had 'True Love'. To a sparse accompaniment, which included the rhythmic clattering of Ray Cooper's feet – an idea from *Ringo* – George, in street-corner harmony with three other singers, conveyed both the despondency of abused infatuation and – largely through the "fool" grumblings of bassman Willie Green – the feeling that George and his accomplices had exploded with laughter the second that engineer Phil McDonald stopped the tape. More flattering perhaps than its fleeting visit to the US charts was Rocky

Sharp And The Razors' later cover of 'I Really Love You' in Britain.

Vocal interplay was also to the fore in less light-hearted *Gone Troppo* songs such as 'That's The Way It Goes' – another slant on the transience of worldly care – and the less complicated 'Baby Don't Run Away'. Although the melody of The Rolling Stones' 'All Sold Out' from 1967 was buried in the title track, George's tunes elsewhere had never been so wrought with quirks of phrasing and bar lengths. Particularly intriguing are 'Mystical One' and 'Unknown Delight', each serenely unpredictable and of a world more free of pain than could be imagined by a *Gone Troppo* consumer daydreaming through the vapour of a train window on the way to work.

Purposely listless was the performance of the finale, 'Circles', in which a sense of once more going through the old routine suited the world-weary lyrics. "I think you have to be a George Harrison fan to appreciate his music" had been Phil McDonald's excuse. "He does them the way he likes them."[319]

Even if the very president of Warners disliked *Gone Troppo*, George, at the end of his tether, would not brook any demands for amendment this time. There were no 'All Those Years Ago' Godsends on it, but maybe the repercussions of *Somewhere In England* and, of course, The Beatles would be enough to make this new Harrison project a practical proposition. Attractive though they were, the inclusion of a neo-instrumental ('Greece'), a non-original and the previously issued (if remixed) 'Dream Away' attested to the dryness of George's commercial fount. Still irked about *Somewhere In England*, wild horses couldn't drag him from his hideaway to utter the odd word on behalf of *Gone Troppo*: "I didn't want to end up like some famous people, always living in a goldfish bowl, so I just decided not to do all these television talk shows every five minutes and tons of interviews."[151] Besides, he had more important things to do.

If the artist wasn't going to co-operate, neither would Warners' press office. Left to fend for itself, the album – treasured only in retrospect – dithered in the lower reaches of the charts before leaving quietly. As the remaining pressings waited in vain for shipment, Warners' high command may have used its title among politer descriptive tags applied to George.

The phrase "gone troppo", meaning "gone crazy", is one of Australia's florid gifts to the English language. In New South Wales, six months before its release, the expression had been bandied about when George magnanimously invited staff at Warners' Melbourne office out to lunch. This wasn't the only reason for his visit. Since a hush-hush landing at Queensland airport and exit by helicopter to racing driver Bobby Jones' homestead on the Gold Coast, George had been house-hunting after drinking in glowing accounts of God's Own Country from Bobby and other racers, including world champion Alan Jones, another with whom the Harrisons lodged that March.

Unrecognised on a trip with Dhani to Sydney's Sea World, a clean-shaven sightseer with a "pre-Astrid Teddy Boy haircut"[320] also paid his respects at the city's Hare Krishna temple. Nonetheless, it would have been an incurious media that hadn't got wind of an ex-Beatle in their midst. Without revealing why he'd really come to the Antipodes for the first time since 1964, George granted an audience to *Australian Woman's Weekly* as well as a television interview on *Good Morning Australia* where he was most complimentary about the continent he'd dismissed with scant lines in *I Me Mine*. Before flying out, he instructed an estate agent to go up to two million notes for a "crash-hot pad" – as an Aussie might call it – on secluded Whitsunday Island off Repulse Bay and opposite the Great Barrier Reef. It was also close to Barry Sheene's villa on a stretch of Queensland coast known as Surfer's Paradise.

By coincidence, on the market then, for just under £200,000, were two houses on Friar Park manor where, for all the fluctuations of its owner's musical and celluloid undertakings, his toparian ventures had been an unqualified triumph. Recovering from overgrown neglect, the parkland had become once more a fairyland panorama of floral harmony, a unified blending of shape and colour. Dedicating his autobiography to "all gardeners everywhere", George loved "being close to nature; it makes me feel very peaceful",[321] although not when a tractor once ran over his foot. In the expert estimation of Beth Chatto, author of *The Damp Garden*,[322] *Plant Portraits*[322] and other classics, he had "the makings of a very good gardener. He's appreciative of good taste. He doesn't want a gaudy garden. He wants a sensitive garden where plants look natural."[322]

Because he'd taken a fancy to her yellow-flowered bog plant, George had sought out Mrs Chatto during his now-annual visit to the Chelsea Flower Show. Later, he'd drive to her Colchester nursery to purchase further unusual plants. It had been too late for George to become a master of the sitar, but it wasn't too late for him to become a master gardener. Soon he was fraternising as much with the craft's top echelon as he did with the Formula One *côterie*. A bouquet from Friar Park was arranged at Beth Chatto's bedside when she was recovering from an operation. Gardening correspondent Peter Seabrook was pleased to help George identify a white hardy perennial – an antirrhinum asarina, he reckoned – that had sprouted in the Park rockery, and, said Olivia, "We had someone visit us from the Soil Association to teach us how to upgrade the standard of our vegetables."[316] Whatever the field of expertise – music, sport, bookbinding or gardening – George enjoyed associating with those who were good at something and watching them doing it.

With him at an Everly Brothers concert in Adelaide were Ferrari drivers Michele Alboreto and Stefan Johansson, "with their nice clean clothes, such good little boys, and the next morning you see them come down the pit land at 120 miles an hour like these lunatics. That's what amazes me."[315] Contrasting with the quiet of wheelbarrows and hoes were George's ongoing weekends at the races, an enthusiasm now shared with nephew Mark – then a trainee motor mechanic – and Ringo. One Beatle fanzine bleated that he "lives more for car racing than rock 'n' roll",[247] but George wasn't that addicted: "If I had three million to give away, which I haven't, there's probably better things to give it to than motor racing – like the starving, for example."[22] Nonetheless, although a critic of Yoko Ono's apparent Nike error, he allowed the revitalised Chrysler auto corporation to avail itself of 'Something' for a TV commercial. Nobler was a cash incentive allegedly offered to the aging Barry Sheene not to risk death or maiming by racing again.

An older mate accepted a cheaper yet just as valuable present from George in the doleful 'Wrack My Brain', written for Ringo Starr's first album in three years, 1981's *Stop And Smell The Roses*. As songs by Paul and the late John had also been considered, it was possible to guess the identity of the "three brothers" thanked by Ringo on the LP cover. As financiers, however, Yoko, Paul, George and Ringo in 1983 would lock themselves away with champagne and salmon in an eighth-floor suite in London's Dorchester Hotel to talk again of the division of the empire. Also pertinent to the past was Harrison and McCartney's later mulling over the making of "the definitive Beatle story",[324] comprising home movies, scenes edited from *Help!*, *et al*, and new narration. After Dick Lester passed on the scheme, *Back To The Future* producer Steven Spielberg "was far more encouraging".[324] However, another schism between Paul and the others lay close ahead, thwarting for now this and further creative reconciliations.

Business turmoils apart, George was not averse to more sociable reunions. "Paul and I had not been friends for a number of years," he said, "but lately we spent a lot of time really getting to know each other again."[325] Ringo's marriage to Barbara Bach at Marylebone Registry Office in April 1981 was splashed across the front of *The Daily Express*. For the reception in a Mayfair club, a car-rental firm delivered instruments and amplifiers, but most of the conflicting reports intimate that the three former Beatles did not reunite on stage as they'd done at Hurtwood Edge two years earlier. When the party broke up, screams hailed the exit of Paul – still a chart contender – while George and Olivia shuffled out almost unnoticed.

Starring with David Yip in ITV's *The Chinese Detective*, even George's pre-Beatle pal Arthur Kelly was more likely to be accosted by starstruck British teenagers. George still had a lot of time for Arthur, respecting him for not profiteering from his Beatle connection as Allan Williams had done with a digitally touched-up tape of a rough night during the group's final Hamburg residency. As well as issuing this on disc, Williams also cashed in with *The Man Who Gave The Beatles Away*, a book which, if heavy on poetic licence, was an atmospheric chronicle of his *soi-disant* "management" of John, Paul, George and Pete.

Infinitely more acceptable to George was Derek Taylor's *50 Years Adrift*, an autobiography that would have been most odd if it hadn't also contained hefty segments of the George Harrison saga, especially as the lad himself was its editor. George couldn't help liking Derek, whose appointment as Warners' general manager in Europe had been a deciding factor precipitating Dark Horse's transfer from A&M. One of his more burdensome tasks in this post had been to bear the news of Mo Ostin's savaging of *Somewhere In England* to its originator. In the following year, Taylor's promotion to vice-president of Creative Services found him in Los Angeles, where the company honoured him with a *This Is Your Life*-type citation, with George, Ringo and many leading entertainers walking on to tell funny stories from the past.

By autumn 1979, the mercurial Derek had gravitated back to England when HandMade cried out for his unique skills. Happy with the result of both his work and the assistance with *I Me Mine*, George interceded to convince Genesis Publications that Taylor's idiosyncratic story of his first half-century would be viable. With facsimiles of such relics as his *Help!* première ticket physically stuck on the pages, 2,000 hand-numbered volumes of Taylor's prose – completed at tranquil Kuppaqulua in November 1983 – went on sale at £148 each. To the chagrin of Warners, who'd just deleted *Gone Troppo*, Harrison was much in evidence during Derek's promotion of *50 Years Adrift*. At his side at two literary luncheons in Australia, George had been tractable enough to autograph an entire collection of Beatle LPs and patiently request one ill-informed hack to rephrase his question, "Mr Harrison, what prompted you to write this book?"[326]

By letting their contractual option on one more album lapse, any anger at Warners about George's antics had dissipated to apathy. He hadn't a hope of getting back on his perch, had he? Let him do what he liked. To the confusion of those bootleggers still bothered, and what he regarded as Warners' cloth-eared ignorance, Harrison had started thinking aloud to anyone listening in 1985 about including an EP of the four recordings ousted from *Somewhere In England* with another planned *de luxe* exercise by Genesis. Illustrating *Songs By George Harrison* would be appropriate water-colours by Keith West, an artist who had lately entered the Friar Park circle.[327]

That George was contemplating tying up this loose end was one more indication that he had dumped his load, as far as the record-buying populace was concerned. Now that the pressure of making albums no longer loomed, there was just the perverse joy of creating uncommercial music: "I've never stopped writing songs, and I've made hundreds of demos."[328] He also added to a multitude of credits on the LP jackets of others. As well as Ringo's latest and film soundtracks, he was also heard on albums by Gary Brooker and Mick Fleetwood, drummer with Fleetwood Mac and husband for many years of Jenny Boyd. Harrison was at Alvin Lee's service, too, playing slide on his US-only *Detroit Diesel* LP.

A HandMade spokesman in 1982 had pleaded stage-fright "after all these years away"[329] in reply to a call for George to walk the boards again for charity. All the same, he sat in with his guitar when Sean Lennon's godfather, Elton John's world tour reached Sydney that year. On the day after a *50 Years Adrift* bunfight in the city, he was introduced as "Arnold Grove from Liverpool, New South Wales", winner of a competition to play an encore with Deep Purple. It took a minute of a Little Richard number with Jon Lord's reformed quintet before screams of recognition reverberated past the footlights. In contrast, George's was the slightly throaty vocal refrain – in Hindi – on the title tack of Ravi Shankar's eclectic *Tana Mana* album, which also contained a track entitled 'Friar Park'.

Confining such favours to fellow old soldiers, a meeting with Dave Edmunds in 1985 included George's only formal stage appearance in Britain since The Plastic Ono Band 16 years earlier. While producing a soundtrack for the US teen-exploitation movie *Porky's Revenge*, Edmunds was fishing around for contributors whose names would help sales of the tie-in album. Having procured Jeff Beck and Led Zeppelin's Robert Plant, Dave then sounded out George. That his friend had no suitable original material was no problem; he could do a cover. George whittled down his choices to 'I Didn't Want To Do It', one of two obscure Dylan numbers considered. Harrison's response to this humble summons encouraged Dave to prod him into allying with other guest musicians for a TV special he was co-ordinating. Fourteen months in preparation, it was to star one whose songs about clothes, lust and violence had captured George's adolescent imaginings – Carl Perkins.

Fifty-three-year-old Carl had been another of Edmunds' assistants on *Porky's Revenge*. While in Memphis to supervise the recording, Dave had been invited to a party at the much-modernised Sun Studio that climaxed with the taping of a roistering medley for *Homecoming*, an album conceived four years earlier when Sun released a 30-minute sing-song from 1956 supposedly involving the "Million-Dollar Quartet" of Perkins, Jerry Lee Lewis, Johnny Cash and Elvis Presley. This provoked sufficient interest for a premeditated 1980s reconstruction to be organised, with Roy Orbison filling in for the departed Elvis.

Implicit in the presence of Edmunds, Creedence Clearwater Revival's John Fogerty and other younger performers on *Homecoming* was the renewed veneration felt for pop's methuselahs. The 60th birthdays of Fats Domino and Chuck Berry were both sanctified before television cameras with back-slapping attendance by celebrities who'd grown up to their music. Roy Orbison's turn came in 1987 in a glittering extravaganza in Los Angeles with the likes of Ry Cooder, the over-valued Bruce Springsteen and Elvis Costello backing him.

Carl Perkins And Friends: A Rockabilly Special, broadcast on 21 October 1985, had some of the ingredients of a self-congratulatory disaster, but if any of the distinguished rank and file had sought to upstage Perkins this was edited out of the two hours of film before it hit British screens on New Year's Day 1986. On the cutting-room floor lay Harrison's attempt to lead the cast into Dylan's 'Rainy Day Women' and his plug for the latest HandMade movie. George was also very quick to criticise the audience for not clapping hard enough. Few of these sequences had impressed the Teddy Boys who'd queued in the cold outside Limehouse Studios amid London's dockland wharfs. Three hundred quiffs strong, they might have preferred a more typical Perkins recital, unimpeded by the contemporary stamp of approval of his illustrious helpmates. Carl was who they'd mob afterwards.

The Teds were appeased, however, by the homely pub-like

ambience as the players switched on small amplifiers. With grey-haired Perkins close enough for everyone to see, Dave Edmunds and his usual combo were stage fixtures, while among those waiting in the wings were Eric Clapton, two of the revivalist Stray Cats, Rozanne Cash (daughter of Johnny) and Ringo Starr, who was to rattle the traps while singing 'Honey Don't' and, with Carl, 'Matchbox', two Perkins items that had thrust him into the main spotlight with The Beatles.

No one was surprised when George ambled on in a baggy grey suit for 'Everybody's Trying To Be My Baby'. However, as his spot progressed with less familiar pieces from the Silver Beatles era, such as 'Your True Love' and 'Gone Gone Gone', many were struck by his animated enthusiasm and obvious pleasure in performing again. With an ear cocked on the tightly arranged rhythmic undercurrent from two days' rehearsal, George's hopping from shoe to unbearably excited shoe was belied not so much by his vocal confidence as his tough guitar soloing. His picking was certainly truer to the show's driving rockabilly spirit than that of slap-dash Clapton. Both, nevertheless, were delighted to sit with the others in a devout semi-circle at Carl's tapping feet in the finale.

George guaranteed himself a more pronounced stake in the proceedings when he booked Perkins as entertainment for a televised celebration of HandMade's first decade in business. As he was paying for it, George had no qualms about sharing the limelight with Carl. Backed by Joe Brown and Ray Cooper, among others, the pair rampaged through 'That's All Right', 'Boppin' The Blues' and further 1950s favourites while revellers cut a rug in the dancing area of the private sanctum within Shepperton Studios. Master of ceremonies Michael Palin's after-dinner speech had concluded with glasses raised to the founder of the feast. Following this toast, George's opening sentence, to sycophantic titters, had been, "Thank you all for coming. Now fuck off."[285]

A couple spared this amicable vulgarity were Madonna and her husband, Sean Penn. Since completing their roles in *Shanghai Surprise*, an adaptation of Tony Kenrick's novel *Faraday's Flowers*, George hadn't "seen them from that day to this".[315] Neither was he troubling to see Madonna's newest flick. This petulant little madam, you see, had been another pop singer who'd seen herself as a cinema attraction. Like Petula Clark and Cilla Black before her, Madonna was an ordinary-looking but competent female vocalist with a facial mole. Unlike them, she let you know she was a star. That's S-T-A-R! Star! Star! Star! Moreover, she'd saddled herself with a volatile spouse who resented being "Mr Madonna". He was also a competent film actor, albeit one with a face asking to be punched. On a short fuse, Mr Madonna's own fists had already landed him a spell in jail.

In deference perhaps to their hosts' more glorious pop pedigree, the Penns had been genial enough when sampling Friar Park hospitality. "The project got to within a day of being elbowed and then suddenly Sean Penn and Madonna decided they'd be in it. We didn't know all the trouble they were going to cause us."[24] Both had made earlier forays into film, but Madonna's cache of hit records tipped the balance. Although other actresses had been auditioned, George had agreed, "It was obviously good to have her in it, because it's better than having somebody nobody had ever heard of."[330] Nonetheless, after sinking £10 million into *Shanghai Surprise*, HandMade had been "damn lucky to get our money back and not lose our shirts."[151]

George blamed this close shave on "a combination of her thinking she's a star and the way the press was gunning for her".[8] Penn and his wife's Garbo-esque refusal to be interviewed was a provocation to Fleet Street, which disgraced itself from the moment the pair arrived at Heathrow *en route* to the filming location in Kowloon, Hong Kong. Even incarceration in their hotel brought the Penns no peace, as "creative" journalists disguised themselves as staff to get a scoop. Notebook at the ready, one muckraker loitered for hours in the ladies' in order to buttonhole seat-bound acolytes of the Penn entourage.

More than anyone, George could sympathise with the brusque Penns' plight and said so at a London press conference in March 1986. As at the *50 Years Adrift* lunch dates, most questions were directed at George throughout the 45-minute grilling, which ended with Madonna proclaiming, "We're not such a bad bunch of people, are we? Byeeeeee."[330]

Hoping the newspapers might agree, executive producer and stars then split like an amoeba, he to Henley and they to Kowloon, with the press in close pursuit. To the glee of breakfast-table readers everywhere, the situation worsened. Juxtaposed with misappropriated *Shanghai Surprise* stills were both true and untrue tabloid stories of "Poison" Penn's bodyguards assaulting a photographer; a make-up girl's sacking for asking Madonna for an autograph; and frightful quarrels that could be heard all over the set.

While appreciating how the smallest incidents could be embroidered, interruption in day-to-day shooting had become so serious by September that a despairing George was compelled to jet eastwards to sort out the mess. Later, he'd laugh off this "bloody nightmare",[151] even framing one front page – "George Harrison Emerges As A Movie Mogul To Take The Penns In Hand!" – alongside more tasteful prints in Cadogan Square; but, when first he reached Kowloon, "[Sean and Madonna] weren't being very nice to the crew. It's hard work [for the crew], dragging equipment 'round places where it's freezing cold for hours. And while she's in a warm trailer, the crew are trying to drink a cup of tea to keep warm, and a little 'Hello, good morning, how are you?' goes a long way in those circumstances. So when I got there, the crew hated them."[188]

The executive producer's descent into their midst stripped the Penns of enough hauteur for Madonna to propose humouring the malcontented underlings with a party. Disgusted, George had already gauged that such tardy sweetness and light wouldn't wash, "because, to tell you the truth, nobody would show up."[188] For the second time that year, he submitted himself to another paparazzi ordeal for Madonna's benefit. Although he bore himself with his accustomed self-assurance, clicking shutters froze a thunderous countenance in marked contrast to Mrs Penn's smirk.

George's last word on Madonna in *Shanghai Surprise* was, "She doesn't have a sense of humour, which is unfortunate, because it was a comedy."[188] Some had been astonished by his firm and stoical conduct during this episode as he mediated between journalistic malevolence and the Penns' prima-donna snootiness. "I never realised you had it in you,"[331] commented John Peel to George on an ITV chat show.

Harrison also rendered unto *Shanghai Surprise* a soundtrack, which went unreleased "because the film got slagged off so bad".[59] Other than elongated interludes, such as 'Hottest Gong In Town', much of it would reach the public when staggered over the next three years in either album tracks or makeweight flip-sides. Madonna had been mooted to duet with George on the main title theme, but the job went instead to the more affable Vikki Brown, ex-Vernons Girl, wife of Joe and cabaret star in northern Europe.

The song 'Shanghai Surprise' set her with George amid verses clustered with lines about rickshaws, Asia Minor and it being "a hell of a way to see China". Switching musically from the Pacific of *Gone Troppo*, the bright tone colours of *sheng*, *koto*, *erhu* and like instruments common to south-east Asia were simulated in George's Friar Park studio via synthesiser, effects pedals and Western session players. The opus was as accurate and attractive a pastiche as Bryan Ferry's 'Tokyo Joe' or John Entwistle's 'Made In Japan'. A more insidious dose of Yellow Peril, however, was contracted on 'Breath Away From Heaven', a softer-hued piece with fragile zither glissandos and George's "nice words"[59] about smiles and whispers at sunrise "in another life". Also wasted on Madonna's movie was 'Someplace Else', which wouldn't have been out of place on *Gone Troppo*.

In a night-club scene, the drama had continued over 'Zig-Zag', in which George's vocals played as incidental a part as they had in 'Greece'. Smeared with muted trumpet and clarinet, his combo shuffled away at the Kenny Ball end of traditional jazz. Of more long-term import was the attendance on 'Zig-Zag' of Jeff Lynne, whose bond with Harrison was to prove considerably more productive in the months to follow. Finding that, "when you write, perform and produce, there's a good chance of getting lost",[59] George had sought a console collaborator with as much objectivity as percussion aesthete Ray Cooper but with a background more in accordance with his own. He wondered "who would understand me and my past, and have respect for that, who I have great respect for – and then I hit on Jeff Lynne, thinking he'd he good if we got on well."[58] This he mentioned to Dave Edmunds, whose two most recent albums had been produced by Lynne. In Los Angeles, Dave passed on this matter-of-fact information to Jeff. With Edmunds as go-between, the bearded leader of the now-redundant ELO was invited to dinner at Friar Park.

As well as overseeing ELO's explorations of the more magniloquent aspect of The Beatles' psychedelic period, 39-year-old Lynne was a studio veteran with skills perfected from a Birmingham adolescence when he converted his Shard End front room into an Aladdin's cave of linked-up reel-to-reel tape recorders, editing blocks and jack-to-jack leads. Yet, for all the technical refinements since, Lynne's attitude towards recording seemed to have gone full circle. 1980s pop was full of short-cut records in which vocals glided smoothly over perfect time-keeping, sequencers, "twanging-plank" disco bass and other programmed sounds. The Japanese had even invented a drum machine that would make a deliberate mistake within bar lines every now and then to preserve some vestige of humanity. No such allowances had been made on a Steve Winwood album of 1982, on which more machines and sound laboratories received "special thanks"[105] than people.

With ELO, Lynne had never yielded to expensive electronic paraphernalia to anywhere near the same extent, which is why his work was admired by rock 'n' rollers of Dave Edmunds' discernment. George came around too when, while they were getting to know each other, he and Jeff "drank red wine for a year and a half".[332] After confessing to his new chum that a drum machine had been used to "toughen" *Gone Troppo*, George unburdened his own dislike of automation in music. He'd recently added "a few choice modules"[59] to FPSHOT, but admitted, "I prefer the old components and spending a friendly weekend getting the manual mix you want just as much as I prefer my ancient Fender Strat."[59] He wished for "all these whales stuck in ice – namely the music industry – to release all these people from feeling guilty for not using a synthesiser and not being able to programme it," which forthright Lynne crowned with, "Don't even bother learning; just play the bleeding piano."[333]

In Jeff, George found "the perfect choice", while if Jeff "could've picked one guy I wanted to work with, it would've been George."[168] With the compatible Lynne, George prepared to contradict his 1982 retirement statement with a new album – and, although Mr Average would not be made aware of this undertaking until the last minute, the wheels had been cranked into motion long before. Even the thought of publicising it was almost inviting enough to erase flashbacks of how ghastly such a duty could be.

This was all very well, but was a comeback actually tenable? Although George had been quite actively consolidating his other professional and recreational interests since *Somewhere In England*, when he'd materialised to defend Madonna it was as a ghost from the recent past, detached from a life where you got up, went to work, got home and went to bed. Symbolic of grass-roots disaffection with George was the downsizing of a Harrison fanzine from Glasgow that went by the title of *Soft Touch* to a generalised Beatles tract, because, wrote editor David Dunn, "I've found there is no real interest in George Harrison. I personally find the personality of George Harrison most unappealing and depressing. His inactivity has led me to the conclusion that it's just not worth doing a fanzine for him."[334]

Among the Bob Dylan homilies quoted by George was "I become my enemy the instance that I speak."[315] Fuelling rumours that were to paint him in the same psychotic colours as housebound Pink Floyd founder member Syd Barrett were reported remarks like, "I plant flowers and watch them grow. I don't go out to clubs and partying. I just say at home and watch the river flow."[335] Even brother Peter would "hardly ever see George socially these days".[304] Onto George's shoulder, therefore, was pressed Lennon's mantle of the Howard Hughes of pop. Instead of that noted recluse's bottles of urine and yard-long fingernails, bored tabloid hacks had Harrison defecating on a Kuppaqulua khazi customised to play 'Lucy In The Sky With Diamonds' whenever its seat was raised. In as late as 1990, a laughable "investigation" by one Sunday newspaper had George as a cocaine abuser who shied from appeals to help clean up the "floating sea of drugs" with which Henley was awash. Worthy of Peter Sellers was George's insistence on taking herbal remedies for a minor ailment, causing an orthodox MD to snap shut his black bag and storm off testily straight into a Friar Park broom cupboard. When the juke box malfunctioned, it was repaired by an artisan brought blindfold to the mansion by the secretive Harrison's minions. Rabbits would peer indifferently at squealing 140mph burn-ups in either a Porsche or Ferrari racer on a ten-mile circuit winding around the estate.

The latter distortion of a dull truth had grown from George's infrequent spins through the woods, but "It's all very slow speed around the garden, you know – tractors and wheelbarrows and things like that."[22] It was hard fact, however, that George had contested a £50 fine imposed by a Brentford magistrate after he was hooked in his lead-free Porsche 924 for speeding at "only" 84mph – police claimed that it had been over 90mph – on the M4 motorway to London.

Like the Loch Ness Monster, there were unofficial sightings, too, of George sipping tea in a Birmingham hotel lounge with Jeff Lynne, backstage at a Wembley concert by Simon And Garfunkel, and at the respective birthday parties of Elton John and Dot Mitchell, landlady of the Row Barge in Henley. At the height of the revels in this West Street pub, he bade the to hostess close her eyes and hold out her hand. "Have a happy birthday," he said, dropping three valuable rubies onto Dot's palm.

At his other domicile, *The Honolulu Advertiser* noticed his presence at the occasional art exhibition in Hawaii, but more uncaring were those organs in Queensland whose coverage went beyond paragraphs about George watching the Australasian Grand Prix. His comings and goings on Whitsunday Island would "become the world's worst secret. It seems everybody in Australia knows about it and they're starting to come down in droves to stare at it. it's turning into a wallyworld and there's no way I'm going to live in it."[336]

The sale of this retreat narrowed George's domestic options and reinformed the press-inspired concept of him as "the Hermit of Friar Park". Nevertheless, although his so-called seclusion had been aggravated in part by the horrible release of John's spirit, fear for his own safety had mutated to a blithe fatalism that enabled him not only to show up at Dot's party or a sculpture opening in Lahaina but also to pop out to shops around Falaise Square and even from HandMade's office to Chelsea emporia. The years away from the public at large had helped in that. "Thankfully, today's generation really doesn't know much about me or what I look like. Now I reckon I could walk down the high street and there would be very few people who would recognise me, and that's a great feeling."[258]

Prominent in a citrine pullover, he was conducted round Shiplake College, midway between Henley and Reading, by headmaster Peter Lapping. Until he was 13, Dhani had attended the Dolphin School, near Twyford. Representing the antithesis of his father's formal education, this Montessori establishment had a very broad curriculum, including the teaching of French at nursery level, as well as small classes, no uniform and an extremely child-centred set-up. Shiplake had been recommended by Jon Lord and Deep Purple drummer Ian Paice, whose children had gone there after finishing at the Dolphin School. Had Dhani's parents been of Paul and Linda McCartney's self-consciously homely bent, they might have considered one of Henley's state institutions, instead of such a slap-up, fee-paying seat of learning with vast grounds cascading down to a Thameside marina that swelled with supervised aquatic activity during jolly boating weather.

While providing their boy with the best of everything, George and Olivia hoped that "we can instil the right values in our son. It is his nightmare that he should grow up spoiled. No child likes to be singled out."[316] Nonetheless, although it wasn't stressed at home, Dhani couldn't help but become aware of his sire's celebrity, even if – as with John and Sean Lennon – George's "retirement" granted his handsome offspring more paternal attention than most. Most of George's familiars agreed that fatherhood suited him.

Best illuminating the balanced content of the Quiet One in middle life was his authorship of brief forewords to both *Chant And Be Happy*[151] – a learned history of the Hare Krishna movement – and Joe Brown's chirpy autobiography, *Brown Sauce*.[337] With the imposition on his privacy at its lowest level within the parameters of his fame and means, he had "gone about my life like a normal person. Every so often, I see a newspaper saying I'm this, that or the other, but, as Jeff Lynne says, 'It's tomorrow's chip-paper.'"[315]

16 The Trembling Wilbury

The 1980s would end with George as the most engaging and commercially operative ex-Beatle, although the opposition were admittedly both at a personal or artistic low by then. Sibling rivalry had abated with maturity, but it must have been sweet indeed for George not only to score over Paul in the charts but also to hear of his desire to compose with his old schoolmate. It had been a long time since 'Hey Darlin'. After Lennon and Wings, McCartney had teamed up with Elvis Costello, one of the first and most successful new wave ambassadors to make it over the Atlantic. Paul looked at it like this: "George has been writing with Jeff Lynne; I've been writing with Elvis Costello, so it's natural for me to want to write with George...and we're both quite interested in that idea, so if only we could get the shit out of the way and get a bit of sense happening."[338]

The shit to which he referred was the question of how big a chunk of the Beatle money each should receive. Dismissed by one Apple attorney as "a storm in a teacup"[339] was a lawsuit brought by Harrison, Starr and Mrs Lennon against Paul over a deal he'd made whereby six post-Beatle albums he'd delivered to Capitol had rewarded him with increased royalties from the company's Beatles stock. On the line to George in Maui, McCartney twigged that the plaintiffs were "mightily upset – in their minds, it's all for one, one for all."[339]

As well as finding his *Thriller* video "the squarest thing I've ever seen",[187] Harrison was also indignant that Michael Jackson – who'd once joined Paul for two singles – now owned most of The Beatles' publishing rights, feeling that it was "like owning a Picasso". "It was a bit off, the way Michael Jackson bought up our old catalogue when he knew Paul was also bidding. He was supposed to be Paul's mate."[152]

George, Paul and Ringo were also united with Yoko in condemning the ignoble Lennon biography by Albert Goldman, who, having previously dished the dirt on Presley, depicted John as barking mad inside the Dakota after a lifetime of incredible human frailty. Goldman was as twisted in his way as Mark Chapman, but morbid inquisitiveness nonetheless ensured a mammoth return for his *The Lives Of John Lennon*. This was in spite of protests from George – a better authority on Lennon – that its purchasers "don't realise it's the same old clap-trap. People's consciousness is stuck, and the Goldmans of this world can make a hell of a living, a lot of money, for slagging off someone who's dead."[340]

John was missed "because he was so funny"[187] whenever George or any of the others – without prompting now – spoke of past times. Beatle reunions were two a penny these days, not on stage or record but for dinner. Rather than a fashionable Knightsbridge restaurant like San Lorenzo, where whirring Nikons heralded the arrival of professional celebrities, George and Paul – environmental evangelists both – favoured Healthy, Wealthy and Wise in Soho, where plain-clothed Hare Krishna devotees served "proper foods, good balanced stuff – and it's fresh".[151] All three ex-Beatles would dine and chat more often in a Chinese restaurant down London's Finchley Road, where service had once been so much to Harrison's satisfaction that he'd left a tip of £200.

Sustained by what must have been an excellent table, the "reasonably sane"[190] survivors of perhaps the most unique human experience of the century would enjoy companionable evenings of matey abuse, coded hilarity and reminiscence. Removed from financial wrangles, George would "remember a lot of the good stuff. It used to be only the bad, but enough time has gone by for everything to be all right."[315] Everything had long been all right with him and Ringo, but George's relationship with Paul still blew hot and cold. Because he didn't give Paul a bear-hug when both attended an Italian music festival, George felt obliged to affirm on television, "We weren't avoiding each other. Neither of us knew each other was going to be there."[190] Obstructed by journalists when disembarking at Heathrow, George's finding Paul "definitely a bit too moody for me"[341] was more widely quoted.

Back at his place for coffee, Paul was able to fill curious gaps in George's understanding of the Lennon-McCartney pact. Idly singing 'She's Leaving Home' at McCartney's harmonium, George inquired which one wrote what bit. "Then I thought, 'This is stupid. I'm asking Paul about "She's Leaving Home" 20 years later. Who cares, anyway?'"[340] Since a rediscovery of more than 50 of the group's Light Programme recordings, the BBC calculated that there were enough caring listeners to make it worthwhile producing a 14-part Radio 1 series based on these relics.

With Paul and other 1960s icons, mainly American, George was drawn into a television documentary celebrating the anniversary of *Sgt Pepper's Lonely Hearts Club Band*, on which he read a relevant passage from Scott's 'Lay Of The Last Minstrel'. This coincided with the transference of Beatles LPs onto compact disc, on which you could almost make out the dandruff falling from Ringo's hair. The selling of these was but one aspect of the persisting demand for 1960s music and musicians. Beyond re-releases of oldies, there were also *Top Of The Pops* visitations – either on video or in the chicken-necked flesh – by elderly pop stars with their latest releases. As well as perennials like McCartney and Cliff Richard, such old faces as The Kinks, Beach Boys, Steve Winwood and The Bee Gees filled the screens. In 1987, some would try to will Tom Jones to Number One as a verification of the lost value of someone singing a song, as opposed to producing a production. A younger hopeful than that beefcake Welshman, George Harrison had his moment, too.

From the beginning of 1986, his re-emergence as an entertainer became more and more perceptible. A performance in Birmingham's National Exhibition Centre involving Jeff Lynne was a welcome break during sessions for his new album. During the soundcheck, George was hurtling up from Henley in his new black Ferrari to catch what would be no ordinary concert. Also on the bill were other Brum Beat denizens, such as Denny Laine and Robert Plant, all doing their bit for Heartbeat '86, a committee headed by ELO's Bev Bevan to raise money for Birmingham Children's Hospital. As George had discovered with Deep Purple in Sydney, "It's hard to go to a show and just watch it without someone hanging a guitar 'round your neck [and] pushing you on stage."[188] So it was that George – with Plant and Laine – stood stage centre during the finale, belting out 'Johnny B Goode', his fingers barring its over-familiar chord changes.

Not quite a year later, he was up on the boards again whilst on a business trip to Los Angeles in connection with his now-completed album, entitled *Cloud Nine*. Mixing work with pleasure, he and Olivia were in the company of Bob Dylan and John Fogerty, being serenaded by bluesman Taj Mahal in the Palomino Club on Sunset Strip. Emboldened by a few Mexican beers, the males in the Harrison party clambered on stage to delight the other 400 drinkers with an amused rendering of Creedence Clearwater hits, old time rock 'n' roll and Dylan's 'Watching The River Flow', the latter sung by George. A few months later, George was less sure of the words to 'Rainy Day Women' as he intoned them at Wembley Arena during a ragged encore on the last night of Bob's European tour.

George was no stranger to Wembley. On 6 June 1987, 25 years to the day after The Beatles' Parlophone recording test, he made a more formal appearance there among star acts assembled for a show organised by the Prince's Trust, one of the heir to the throne's charities. Contrasting with the processed frenzy of Curiosity Killed The Cat and other young chart-riders, George's spot was as nostalgic, after its fashion, as that of Freddie And The Dreamers on the chicken-in-a-basket trail. Endearingly nervous, in between 'While My Guitar Gently Weeps' and 'Here Comes The Sun', George saluted his *ad hoc* backing quartet of Eric Clapton, Jeff, Ringo, Elton John and Ultravox's Midge Ure on bass. A handshake from the Prince of Wales afterwards had possibly less intrinsic value than "You were good, Dad, you were good"[342] from a round-eyed Dhani, for whom the extravaganza was his first experience of his father as a stage performer. Rather deflating, however, was Dhani's enquiry as to why George hadn't played 'Roll Over Beethoven'.

This was one of the boy's favourite Beatle – and ELO – numbers, because it had been written by Chuck Berry, who'd been discovered obliquely when Dhani heard The Beach Boys' 'Surfin' USA' – derived from Chuck's 'Sweet Little 16' – in the film *Teen Wolf* Applauding his son's taste in pop, George had dug out the 1958 source from his collection while compiling a Berry tape for Dhani's further edification.

The Harrison adults continued to broaden their own cultural and spiritual horizons, respectively booking seats for a South Bank recital of Bulgarian music and a flight to an Indian retreat for deeper penetration into the disciplines of yoga and meditation. The reissue of George's 1969 production of the maha-mantra back in Britain had brought into sharper perspective the threatened closure of Bhaktivedanta Manor. Once on cordial terms with the college's hundred or so incumbents, Letchmore Heath locals had become increasingly uppity about the volume of traffic and noise, especially during the week-long spring festival of Holi. By the mid 1980s, Holi swelled the community by 20,000 worshippers – "But not all at once," protested the manor's president, Akhandadhi Das (Martin Fleming). "Most stay for only and hour or two."[343] When the district council rejected compromise solutions, such as a new approach road, George did not swoop as publicly to the centre's defence as he had over the Regal Cinema matter. His surreptitious intervention hindered but did not prevent the Environment Secretary from ordering the centre's dissolution, just as he had the closure of the Regal.

As well as the tithing of his time and high income to sacred topics, George shared with Cliff Richard a stake in a tax scheme that, launched in 1977, had attracted others in the top income bracket because it enable them to claim a loss of £4 for every £1 invested. Managed by the Southbrook Film Group, the idea was to put money into limited partnerships – called Monday and Tuesday Films – which, with the banks supplying the balance, provided 25 per cent of the finance for three major movies, including 1987 Oscar winner *Platoon*. However, despite appeals to the House of Lords, the Inland Revenue wouldn't allow the depositors to take credit for the entire loss made by the partnerships, thus reducing the chances of similar manoeuvres in the film industry succeeding. For many of those in on it, a decade's interest on the tax due more than doubled the Revenue's claim.

"I hate all the wheeling and dealing,"[272] shrugged George. Leaving more and more poring over figures to Denis O'Brien (who was to leave the company in 1993), he was also adding less creative input into HandMade, which, he'd concluded, hadn't of late "been enormously successful. We have big debts. We can't afford $25 million productions. HandMade Films will continue, but in order to get an audience you have to make one of these big budget blockbuster movies, like *Batman* and *Ghostbusters*, full of crash, bang, wallop."[316] He was nevertheless benevolent enough to accept an invitation to join O'Brien, Bob Hoskins and Michael Palin in a debate staged at the National Film Theatre during a "HandMade On Parade" film season in autumn 1988, although recording commitments necessitated his last-minute absence.[344] It wouldn't be long before George Harrison would wash his hands of HandMade altogether, after a falling-out with the departing O'Brien. However, the partnership was outwardly still a functioning concern when, together with Ringo and another old friend, Donovan, George was scheduled for a cameo in *Walking After Midnight*, a film starring Martin Sheen and James Coburn. Shot partly in Tibet, the Dalai Lama appeared unscripted in one scene.

Harrison and Starr's names cropped up more often in high-society gossip columns than in *Melody Maker* since their most recent albums had failed in the marketplace. With Viscount Linley, they, Steve Winwood, Roger Waters and actor George Hamilton were noticed at a shindig at the Café de Paris. The Queen's nephew was also there when the ex-Beatles were among the vetted guests at Elton John's wife's lavish birthday party in another London night club. However, the royal ears were not there to hear George's after-dinner laudation of Eric Clapton when Elton, Bill Wyman, Ringo, Phil Collins – all the usual shower – gathered at the Savoy Hotel on 7 June 1987 to celebrate old Slowhand's first quarter-century as a professional guitarist. George's best friend was, he enthused, "such a sweet cat. I caught one of his shows just before Easter last year. I stood at the side of the stage, holding up my cigarette lighter for the encore. Really! I love him that much."[59] Although Eric was now estranged from Pattie, both of her former husbands would remain friends with her.

Social diversions apart, George had been so busy on *Cloud Nine* that many exotic plants and shrubs in Friar Park that had been destroyed in an unforeseen hurricane were not immediately replaced. The console labours related to this marginal neglect were not in vain. Released in 1987, *Cloud Nine* was less offensively adult orientated than current offerings by Clapton, Winwood and Dire Straits – a group liked by George. Physically unmarred by baldness or podginess, he brought much of the aura of a fresh sensation to those young enough not to have heard much of him before – especially as, at Warners' request, he'd shaved off a scrappy beard. When he walked into a Burbank record shop, a teenager near the counter cried, "Look! There's that singer!" Turning their heads, her companions saw neither a dotard nor the oldest swinger in town.

Although they'd lately rejected the running order of a Clapton LP as they had *Somewhere In England*, Warners' executives had passed *Cloud Nine* as "a killer sequence of tracks".[162] Selections had been culled from 17 pieces, mastered mostly at FPSHOT. Among these were more "Oriental"-sounding remakes of 'Breath Away From Heaven' and 'Someplace Else'. The only cover version was an update of the James Ray number that George had heard when he visited his sister in Benton in 1963: "I did that song because Jim Keltner got this drum pattern going that was a cross between swing and rock. Gary Wright turned around and said, 'Hey, doesn't that remind you of "Got My Mind Set On You?"' I was so surprised that anyone had ever heard that tune."[59]

Keltner and Wright – who co-wrote 'That's What It Takes' – were but two old hands called to Henley when Harrison "started missing the whole thing of making a record and playing with my mates".[151] Rather than call all the shots, George wanted it to be a group effort, "where you can come up with all your own ideas, and you have other people's ideas and they all mix together and they become a different idea".[277] Also mucking in were comfortable comrades like Clapton, Winwood, Elton John, Ray Cooper, Jim Horn and Ringo, who was "like myself with the guitar. I don't play it that often. Ringo may not play the drums from one year to the next, but...he'll just rock and play just like he played in the old days."[164]

Of earlier antiquity was the Gretsch, dating from the Mersey Beat era, that George – in mirror shades and Hawaiian shirt – gripped on the *Cloud Nine* front cover. The words were not included, because the main writer thought the practice *passé*. This mattered little, however, for George's diction was clear enough. Vocally, he was more consistently strong than he had been before, delving into a hitherto unrealised bass register on the title track, although he still trotted out his Dylanish rasp for 'Devil's Radio'. If his backing singing was not sufficiently "depersonalised", unlimited studio time facilitated the honing of George's every nuance and vibrato as well as the disciplined structuring of instrumental interludes, such as the adroit break in tempo in 'This Is Love'. In its clean breadth of expression, Lynne and Harrison's production was not so pat that listeners were purblind to the quality of the album's raw material, nearly all of which stood tall as basic songs. There was also a healthy tendency for *Cloud Nine* to embrace definite endings rather than fading out.

Pulling from all elements in his musical past, George had come to terms with both The Beatles and his present situation. Other than one more obvious and calculated stroll down Memory Lane, you'd pick up on this "oh yeah", that ascending guitar riff from *Revolver*, a gritty *All Things Must Pass* horn section and a sweep of *Gone Troppo* bottleneck. On the opening track, there were traces of both Cream and a Temptations single from 1969, also entitled 'Cloud Nine', but who minded?

A brake had been applied to the religious lyricism that had hung over him like a mist since 'Within You Without You'. Only 'Cloud Nine' itself – setting human limitations against divine potential – is blatantly spiritual, its title an advance on "Cloud Seven", a pictorialisation of the Seventh Heaven, the abode of God Himself in both Mohammed and Jewish tradition. With the James Ray item and 'Breath Away From Heaven' were two other love songs, 'Fish On The Sand' – with rapid-fire verses – and the brighter 'This Is Love', which had come about when Harrison enlisted Lynne's help on a melody: "He came down with lots of bits and pieces on cassette and almost let me choose. I routined the song with him and we wrote the words together."[59]

Going along when the artist took a breather Down Under for the Adelaide Grand Prix, Jeff also contributed to an opus from a sketchy outline by George on a borrowed guitar with a broken string. The resulting 'When We Was Fab' was a happier invocation and exorcism of The Beatles than the selfish 'Ballad Of John And Yoko' or 'All Those Years Ago'. Unlike 'Blood From A Clone', it was as simultaneously personal and universal as 'Don't Cry For Me, Argentina', 'The Battle Of New Orleans' and other musical encapsulations of historical events both less and more far-reaching than Beatlemania.

To a backing track that included a count-in and period "pudding" tom-toms from Ringo, the composer/producers "overdubbed more, and it developed and took shape to where we wrote words".[59] Interweaved with false clues and negative symbolism – "caresses fleeced you in the morning light" – were odd lines from Dylan, Smokey Robinson and even 'This Pullover' by Jess Conrad, plus "fab! gear!" vocal responses. Musically, it leaned most heavily on the *Magical Mystery Tour* age, with its ELO cellos, a melodic quote from 'A Day In The Life', effervescent 'Blue Jay Way' phasing and a psychedelic coda of wiry sitar, backwards tapes and 'I Am The Walrus' babble. At the song's heart was an F augmented ninth chord common to both 'I Want To Tell You' and Lennon's 'I Want You' off *Abbey Road*. Fab Four trivia freaks will be fascinated to learn that these two numbers are adjacent if you list Beatles songs alphabetically. Moreover, the late Louise Harrison's maiden name was French, while that of 'When We Was Fab' pianist Steve Winwood's mother was Saunders. Like, there's this British comedy duo called French and Saunders. Weird, eh?

The mock significance of 'When We Was Fab' might have overshadowed companion pieces that had more to say, such as 'Devil's Radio', a swipe at tittle-tattlers by one who'd long been one of their victims. Driving Dhani to school, the words "Gossip! The devil's radio! Don't be a broadcaster!" had screamed at George from a church notice-board in Hurst. Another added ingredient as he frowned over the first draft of the song that morning was "that straight-from-the-gate force"[59] of The Eurythmics, a combo whose musical policy and subsequent chart entries had been founded on a truce between synthesiser technology and minor-key human emotion.

George's hook-line sentiment that "it's everywhere that you go/the Devil's radio" was quite sound. Doing most damage is the popular press, which he harangued as "poison penmen" in the middle eight of 'The Wreck Of The Hesperus'. In this musical resistance to dignified aging, George aligns himself to Arkansas blues crooner Big Bill Broonzy, who continued to mature as a working musician until the month of his death.

You wouldn't catch George trudging around European concert halls with an acoustic guitar like Broonzy, but an enthusiastic record company's generous budget guaranteed his active participation in the promotion of *Cloud Nine*. From pretending to be someone else whenever a journalist telephoned, throughout the winter of 1987/8 he – quite often with Ringo – never seemed to be off tabloid pop pages with quotable jocularities and scathing attacks on radio disc jockeys' yap and the latest Top 20. There he was on an ITV chat show with a ponderous quip about the vastness of Friar Park's acreage: "You can stroll 'round my garden in ten minutes – if you're power-walking. If you saunter, it could take half an hour. Swagger? Maybe 45 minutes."[190] He was just as congenial on *Countdown* in the Netherlands and when interviewed by BBC1's omnipresent Terry Wogan. Of more specialist persuasion was a natter about the merits of Rickenbacker guitars over on BBC2.

In America, headlines on the glossy pages of *Newsweek*, *Musician*, *et al*, proclaimed, "Quiet Beatle Finally Talks!" Patiently, he endured three hours of shooting to give 15 minutes' low-down on *Cloud Nine* for CBS television. Worse was an interview for inclusion in a morale-boosting promo clip for the annual Warners sales conference in Miami, where, as a Briton, his interrogator's running joke about baseball was lost on him. Over a beer and Marlboro cigarette after these tribulations, he'd sign and smile for the pushiest autograph-hunters, listening with a glazed expression to long-winded accounts of how they'd seen The Beatles once.

Cloud Nine was nudging the higher reaches of the US chart when George mounted the podium in New York's posh Waldorf-Astoria

Hotel after The Beatles had been inducted by Mick Jagger at the third Rock 'n' Roll Hall of Fame ceremony. Representing what was left of the group, too, were Ringo, John's widow and Julian Lennon. In the opening sentences of his speech, George made light of McCartney's glaring absence. Although he then assured everybody that "we all love Paul very much", he wasn't as friendly a fortnight later on Australian television, when, while acknowledging that the Capitol lawsuit was at the root of Paul's non-attendance, George railed at what he saw as his fellow Liverpudlian's inability to separate business from the citation. Paul should have made his way too onto the Waldorf stage, heaving with celebrities, for the "surprise" jam session at the end. Perhaps in his honour, Jagger, Harrison and Dylan bunched around a single microphone for a raucous 'I Saw Her Standing There'.

Paul also backed out of an apparent agreement to appear in videos for the *Cloud Nine* singles. George had been slightly disappointed that the non-original 'Got My Mind Set On You' was chosen as the first of these. Furthermore, Warners had so disapproved of its attendant monochrome video – a flirting adolescent couple in a amusement arcade with George, Jeff and Ray performing on a nickelodeon – that director Gary Weiss was instructed to film another in which Harrison was more prominent. Hurriedly, Weiss cobbled together a scenario in which furniture came to life around a seated George, who – with help from a stunt-man – seemed to execute gymnastic back-flips at one point. Admitting that teenagers might not identify so easily with this second attempt, Warners let programmers make up their own minds. *Top Of The Pops* used the "furniture" video, which was shown when 'Got My Mind Set On You' touched its British high of Number Two. Over in the States, it went one better, the first Harrison 45 to top a national chart since 'Give Me Love'.

Not as gigantic a smash was 'When We Was Fab', which, nonetheless, still did better than similar singles by less bankable contemporaries, such as Freddie Garrity with 'I'm A Singer In A '60s Band' and 'This Is Merseybeat', a medley from The Merseybeats (who also showcased 'Got My Mind Set On You' in their cabaret act). With greater resources and lingering hip sensibility, George could afford the expensive services of Godley And Creme to direct a video in which he and Ringo donned the *Sgt Pepper* costumes that the older Starkey children had been borrowing for fancy-dress parties.

Along with Elton John, Ray Cooper and a left-handed bass player dressed as a walrus, Jeff Lynne had had a cameo in the video for 'When We Was Fab'. With his part in steering the former Beatle back into the spotlight recognised, Jeff was much in demand these days. A considerable accolade for him was a contract to produce most of *Mystery Girl*, the LP that restored Roy Orbison to the charts. Even during the *Cloud Nine* sessions, he'd worked on an album by Duane Eddy, from the same pop generation as Roy, who'd re-entered the hit parade after a much longer absence than Harrison, thanks to a link-up with The Art Of Noise. For all their wrinkles, hair loss and belts at the last hole, old timers like Orbison and Eddy intrigued the young and artistically bankrupt. The Art Of Noise also had success with Tom Jones, and Marc Almond's duet with Gene Pitney was a UK chart-topper in 1989.

George Harrison needed no such affinity. Nevertheless, he was pleased to put both his musical skills and private studio at the disposal of Duane Eddy, whom he'd listed as "favourite instrumentalist"[345] for the *NME*'s "Lifelines" annotations in 1963. His was the good-measured slide touch-ups on two or three tracks cut by Duane Eddy in Henley. For those who hadn't heard much of Duane since the early 1960s, his Friar Park output – with twangy guitar high in the mix – was much how they may have expected him to sound in the 1980s.

As he'd postponed work on *Cloud Nine* in order to cater for the peripatetic Eddy, so Jeff had left off *Mystery Girl* – and his work on tracks by Tom Petty – to oversee one final and trifling detail of his prior commitment to Harrison, a bonus number for the European twelve-inch of 'When We Was Fab'. Roy Orbison was on the conversation's edge when the two Englishmen discussed this over luncheon in Los Angeles. That Roy was so well versed in the Monty Python genre of British comedy staggered George, with whom Roy had had only sporadic contact since the ravages of Beatlemania. The closest encounter of the 1980s had been when Orbison attended a

Sgt Pepper party at Abbey Road at which George did not show. George was elated, however, when the jovial balladeer volunteered to sing with him on this extra track. Well, it might be a laugh. Fun is the one thing that money can't buy. Anyway, it was doubtful whether anyone would bother playing a throwaway B-side.

It wasn't worth booking anywhere expensive, so George – impressing Roy with his proud familiarity – telephoned the Santa Monica home of Bob Dylan, whose "little Ampex in the corner of his garage"[333] was available the next day.

Duly rolling up late the following morning, Roy shook hands with Tom Petty, whom Jeff and – to a lesser extent – George had assisted in his production of a Del Shannon album in 1987, after Petty's group had backed Dylan on the tour that had terminated at Wembley.

From initially merely providing refreshments, Dylan later lent a hand when Harrison – with his B-side only half-finished – said, "Give us some lyrics, you famous lyricist."[340] To Bob's reasonable enquiry as to the subject matter, "I looked behind the garage door and there was a cardboard box with 'handle with care' on it."[340] At that instance, George may have had a mental flash that 'Fragile (Handle With Care)' had been the title of the first single by Mark Peters And The Silhouettes, with whom his far-distant Merseyside acquaintance Dave May had played.

By the evening, flesh had been layered on the skeleton of 'Handle With Care'. George had added what he called "a lonely bit"[333] for Orbison, who'd long been stereotyped as a purveyor of woe, while Dylan wheezed his trademark harmonica on the fade-out. Cemented with an ascending five-note riff, 'Handle With Care' – about a pop idol's personal vulnerability – could only have radiated from a caste thus cosseted and deprived. At this juncture, the gathering was not intended as any permanent "supergroup", that most fascist of all pop cliques. Fulfilling a suggestion made to George by chat-show host Michael Aspel for "getting a bunch of oldies together",[190] it was more like Roy's 'Class Of '55' on *Homecoming* – just the ancient gods at play over a long afternoon among the cedared slopes of the Hollywood hills. Roy spoke for everyone when he said, "We all enjoyed it so much. It was so relaxed. There was no ego involved and there was some sort of chemistry going on."[346] Apart from certain distinctive voices heard on it, none would suppose that 'Handle With Care' was special. Would they?

On the next day, Roy left for a one-nighter in Anaheim, near Long Beach; Bob carried on preparing for a summer tour; and George slipped over to Warners with the new tape. There it was pronounced too potentially remunerative to hide its light under a twelve-inch 45. In conference with Jeff afterwards over a quantity of Mexican lager, the idea of cutting a whole LP with the 'Handle With Care' quintet surfaced. When the two skidded up to his house with the plan, Petty jumped at the chance while, over the phone, Dylan's affirmative was blunter. That evening, Jeff, George, Tom and their wives drove down the coast to Anaheim to put it to the Big O. "Roy said, 'That'd be great,'" remembered Petty. "We watched Roy give an incredible concert and kept nudging each other and saying, 'Isn't he great? He's in our band.' We were real happy that night."[338]

When intelligence of this new combination spread, other musicians in the Harrison circle wondered why they hadn't been invited to join in, but the album, completed over the summer of 1988, "worked because it was so unplanned,"[346] estimated Orbison. Most of the composing took place at the hospitable LA home of The Eurythmics' Dave Stewart, then Dylan's producer. Nourished by a continuous running barbecue, George's team "would assemble after breakfast at about one in the afternoon and just sit around with acoustic guitars. Then someone would have a title or a chord pattern and we'd let it roll."[340]

With Tinseltown stretching as far as the eye could see under a rind of smog, fraternisation on Stewart's lawn would breed retrospection about the old days. The Beatles may have integrated Roy's 'Oh! Pretty Woman' riff into their concert version of 'Dizzy Miss Lizzie', but would Bob bring up the demo of his 'Don't Think Twice, It's Alright' that Roy had turned down in 1963?

The word "Wilbury" entered the five musicians' vocabulary. It had been an in-joke during *Cloud Nine*, referring to studio gremlins. First, "The Trembling Wilburys" was suggested as a name when, remembered Lynne, he and George had "this fantasy idea. We'd start

inventing a group that would have all our favourite people."
Ultimately, the vote went to "The Traveling Wilburys".

As its instigator, Harrison was the most avid Wilbury plugger,
enthusing about the album at a Warners summit in Eastbourne(!) and
on *Kaleidoscope*, a BBC radio programme usually more devoted to
Etruscan pottery or Bach fugues. Later, he'd chew over the likelihood
of a full-length movie based on the sleeve notes attributed to Michael
Palin from a brainwave of Derek Taylor's.

Masquerading as half-brothers sired by the same philandering
father – Charles Truscott Wilbury, Senior – the five appeared on the
cover under chosen pseudonyms, George's being "Nelson Wilbury".
Entering into the spirit of the elaborate prank, 50-year-old Orbison
– as "Lefty", the eldest sibling – remarked, "Some said Daddy was a
cad and a bounder, but I remember him as a Baptist minister."[340] As
to the group going on the road, discussions only got as far as the
order in which each member would walk out on stage. George made
it clear that he'd "hate waking up in motels in Philadelphia. I'd
rather be home." However, he added that, if the others wanted to
tour, then "I'd be inclined to do something."[340]

Despite a "Volume One" tag on the cover, no second Wilbury LP
was then on the cards, partly because, as Roy explained, "We
couldn't repeat the ploy on the record companies the second time
'round."[346] None of the relevant labels had raised any fuss when *The
Traveling Wilburys, Volume One* was foisted on them as a *fait
accompli*. Nobody wanted to be unpopular. One executive simply
muttered something about not standing in the way of history before
hanging up on the Wilbury concerned.

Out of step with the strident march of hip-hop, acid house, *et al*,
the release of *Volume One* was like a Viking longship docking in a
hovercraft terminal. After the songs had been written, only ten days
could be set aside for the taping, owing to Lucky Wilbury's
forthcoming tour, but any lifting of this restriction might have
detracted from the proceedings' rough-and-ready spontaneity and
endearing imperfections. Close in execution to skiffle or rockabilly,
the items on *Volume One* were for George a V-sign at all that he
detested about 1980s mainstream pop: "They represent the stand

against this horrible computerised music."[316] As producers, he and Jeff had respectively combined the adequate and the pedantic in the mix, with George recognising that his colleague was "a craftsman, and he's got endless patience. I tend to feel, 'OK, that'll do' and go on, and Jeff'll be thinking about how to tidy up what's just been done."[59] Although it was the product of gentlemen who could afford to lark about, minor experiments – such as hired drummer Jim Keltner's whacking a refrigerator's wire grille with brushes – reflected the LP's do-it-yourself air.

Orbison's only contribution as featured singer, 'Not Alone Any More', crystallised the tenor of the production by making its point without the cinematic strings, sombre horns and wailing chorale generally associated with 'Running Scared', 'It's Over' and other of his hits. The chugging guitars, Jeff's one-finger crash-diving fairground organ, some staccato sha-la-la-las and a secondary riff of unison piano and guitar were just as effective. On 'Dirty World', George got Roy to unloosen that querulous 'Oh! Pretty Woman' growl like a conjuror reproducing a popular trick to amuse children.

Not the most prolific of songwriters, the obliging Orbison had contributed least to the ten numbers selected. Nevertheless, these were credited to the Wilburys as a whole, rather than individual members. A study of UK publishing rights, however, reveals that to Harrison was allocated 'Handle With Care', the Beatle-esque 'Heading For The Light' and the appositely titled closing track, 'End Of The Line', which he described as "sort of like Carl Perkins says, '[sings] Weeeeeell, it's aaaaaall right!' If you're going to be an optimist, then it's going to be all right. If you happen to be a peg-legged old pirate who's trying to make an album, it's still all right."[333] Vocally, other than specific the lead singing required on 'Not Alone Any More' or Dylan's 'Tweeter And The Monkey Man', items were communal efforts, with verses, backing harmonies and bridges more or less doled out equally.

When *Volume One* was finished, the personnel returned to individual projects – although, bound by the Wilbury "brotherhood", each performed services for the others. *Mystery Girl* was completed at Friar Park, with George on acoustic guitar. He also assisted on both

Tom and Jeff's first solo albums. As for Bob, George noted that "people close to him say that, since the Wilburys, he's started writing really good songs again".[340] Among these, apparently, was an offering for the follow-up to *Mystery Girl* that was never recorded because of the ill-starred Roy's fatal heart attack in December 1988.

It was to be expected that the morbid publicity would boost the Top-40 placings of both the slipping 'Handle With Care' single and the LP. Whereas the video for 'Handle With Care' had had all five grouped around an omni-directional microphone, in the one for 'End Of The Line' Roy's spiritual presence was symbolised by a guitar propped up in a vacant chair. Certain media folk speculated on who would be the new Wilbury. In the running were Roger (formerly Jim) McGuinn, Carl Perkins, Jaime Robertson and Gene Pitney. "I hope there will be another Travelling Wilburys record," said George. "It was one of the most enjoyable things I've done. I don't really have a desire to be a solo artist. It's much more fun being in the Wilburys."[316] In April 1990, he, Lynne, Petty and Dylan were recording together in a rented house in Bel Air for what was presumed to be *Volume Two* but was actually entitled *Volume Three* when eleven selected tracks were issued later that year, after a mere three weeks spent in the studio.

Apart from a "best of" package yet to come, the Wilburys had seen out George's commitment to Warners. Hot property again, George contemplated options that only one of his means could consider. He could, for instance, sign up for no more than one album at a time, or – cutting out middlemen – press his own records and distribute them by mail order. In no hurry to snap at the heels of *Cloud Nine*, it could be years before the next Harrison album hit the shelves, reckoned HandMade insiders.

As a possible pointer to future methodology, shortly after Warners had released *Cloud Nine*, Genesis Publications quietly made available the long-scheduled *Songs By George Harrison*. This was limited to 2,500 copies, each in a leather box for Keith West's hand-lettered interpretations, with a pull-out wallet for a record of the three tracks axed from the *Somewhere In England* epoch, plus an in-concert cut of 'For You Blue' taped during the 1974 US tour. At over £200 a time, you wondered how anyone dared place a needle on it. "It's expensive, yes," conceded George, "but in a world of crass, disposable junk, it's meant to be a lovely thing."[59] Enough people thought that it was for West to mix his colours for a second volume.

With similarly unassuming commercial ambition, George – with Ray Cooper, The Bee Gees and Eric Clapton – had concocted some music for a BBC series based on a David English story about cricket-playing rabbits. A new composition with Tom Petty entitled 'Cheer Down', deemed unsuitable when put before Clapton, was recorded by George himself, to be heard over the closing credits of the Mel Gibson flick *Lethal Weapon 2*.

The first manifestation of George's post-Orbison Wilbury sessions had been the release of 'Nobody's Child', a cover of the ancient Tony Sheridan And The Beat Brothers standby. This was taped two days after Olivia had asked her husband to consider recording a number for the appeal she'd set up – with assistance from Maureen Starkey, Linda McCartney and Yoko Ono – after the Romanian earthquake in May 1990, which could be felt as far away as Moscow and Istanbul. With help from Joe Brown, George dug the first bit of 'Nobody's Child' from his memory but wrote a new second verse relevant to Olivia's shocked inspection of an orphanage 100 miles from Bucharest, "which had had no food for three weeks, building packed with small children often two to three to a bed, left naked because there is no one to wash or dress them."[349] She and George were to house a deaf Romanian orphan and his adopted British mother on Friar Park Estate. Hot off the press, copies of 'Nobody's Child' were on sale at Henley Regatta Bazaar on 28 July. "If you can't help your own wife," reckoned George, "then it's a pretty bad state of affairs."[349] In support of the compassionate Mrs Harrison's Romanian Angel Appeal was a compilation LP – with 'Nobody's Child' the title track – organised by George and featuring mostly his old musical confreres, among them Clapton, Starr, Dave Stewart, Elton John, Duane Eddy and Paul Simon.

Far less likely than a *bona fide* new Harrison album was George's full-time return to the stage, in spite of Cynthia Lennon suggesting that the remaining Beatles would re-unite for a concert at Berlin's Brandenburg Gate on 9 October 1990, the day on which John would have turned 50. Unlike Paul and Ringo, George had had nothing to do with an international tribute to Lennon at Liverpool's Pier Head in May 1990. Sanctioned and partly compered by Yoko, no Mersey Beat groups who'd "got drunk with him"[350] had been invited to warm up for the likes of Lou Reed or Australia's Kylie Minogue. With sound reason, George considered the event to be "in poor taste".[350] There were, however, plausible reports of the four living Wilburys playing unannounced acoustic floor spots in folk clubs in and around Los Angeles as "The Traveling Ovaries".

Such weapons as programmable desks and graphic equalisers in the war against adverse auditorium acoustics couldn't erase George's memories of touring in 1974 with "people...trying to shove drugs up my nose"[321] and the perturbing psychological undertow compounded by an admirer "going absolutely bananas"[321] feet from the stage at the Prince's Trust gig: "He was so fanatical and kept staring at me with this manic glint in his eye."[321] With gun-toting Chapman and his sort shadowing his thoughts, George had decided that, "even if I had been considering coming back to do large shows, the sight of this guy made me think twice."[321]

From a person or persons with an apparent grudge against Olivia, a series of poison pen letters – signed by "Rosalind" – began to arrive at Friar Park in 1989. As they threatened death – "Time you went", "Your time is up" and so forth – the matter was serious enough to call in the Thames Valley CID, whose Detective Sergeant Robert Harrington would "feel sorry for [George]. He is a recluse and just wants to be left alone."[351] Misinterpreting a 1989 Harrison biography, one of the letters implied that George was an admirer of Adolf Hitler. "The world is full of strange people who do stupid things like this,"[352] commented Peter Harrison, who'd been ignorant of the hate mail until the story was leaked by a London police officer to a national newspaper.

Similarly ugly occurrences of cold terror did not thwart Paul or Ringo, who in 1989 each chanced their first tours since John's slaughter. The show went on for others, too. The diverse likes of Jefferson Airplane, The Who, The Fugs, The Applejacks and the Stones were also poised to do it again. George, however, didn't "really see myself as being out there like the George Michaels or the Mick Jaggers. I'm not putting them down, but they have performing built into them. The most I ever did was the Liverpool leg. Well, I just don't have a desire to be a pop star, and acting – well, that's the most boring job in the world. I just want to be a musician, somebody who writes songs and makes music."[315]

On the telephone during the *Sgt Pepper* anniversary hoo-hah, George Martin – knowing his man – had re-assured him by saying, "Never mind, George. It'll soon be gone and we can go back into our shells."[315]

Cloud Nine and a spot on *Wogan* with Olivia (in connection with the Romanian appeal) had drawn out the agony, but in 'Just For Today', the slowest, saddest song from *Cloud Nine*, George poured out his need to escape these distracted times. At least he was free to run away to Maui, although he wasn't so far gone from the discontent festering on the claustrophobic streets of Brixton in the late 1980s not to comment, "It's terrible. It's like hell."[164]

His comments could also have applied to a seldom-visited Liverpool. Whereas once Daniel Defoe had praised "the fineness of its streets and the beauty of its buildings", boarded-up Georgian houses in its centre awaited flattening to make room for characterless skyscrapers, shopping precincts and multi-storey car parks. Many old haunts – including the Cavern – had either been demolished in the process or refurbished for re-opening as cabaret clubs or restaurants. More profitable than ever were the Merseyside Tourist Board's guided Beatle coach trips around suburbs where the "four lad who shook the world" had spent their formative years. Who'd have cared otherwise about a corporation terrace swallowed in Speke? In 1990, George Harrison was paying £300 less poll tax than pensioners Matthew and Edna Kermode, who moved to 25 Upton Green in 1983. This still-expanding overspill estate might have been home to the heroine of *Letter To Brezhnev*, a film of harsh, dead-end realism that, for George, "resurrected my original belief in the character of the Liverpool people. It is a fantastic example of how someone with no money and no hope can actually get through that."[188]

As always, Liverpool looked after its own. In the Anfield silence in the week after the Hillsborough tragedy, tears filled the eyes of elderly supporters. For some, Gerry's 'You'll Never Walk Alone' – the Kop choir anthem – had been the only pop record they'd ever bought. Their vigil was more widespread than that held outside St

George's Hall in 1980 for John Lennon, or at the Pier Head tribute a decade later that George had ignored. Partly, this was because the 95 ordinary people killed in the swollen away-match stadium had been closer to home than the Beatle spirited away to the New World. Lennon's three mates had long flown the nest, too. Although posters of Paul's 'My Brave Face' single were defaced with a day of their appearing in the city centre, McCartney was the only known Beatle "friend" of the University's Popular Music faculty and other local projects. He was also the only one to bother with a few words of printed encouragement in the souvenir programme for the inaugural evening in May 1989 of Merseycats, a committee formed by Don Andrew to facilitate reunions of Mersey Beat groups in support of KIND (Kids In Need and Distress), a group which provides activity holidays for seriously ill and handicapped local children.

The venue was the Grafton Rooms, scene of many a rough night in the early days. Old friendships and rivalries were renewed as groups and fans united in a common cause. Among those on the bill were The Undertakers, Faron's Flamingos and The Fourmost, each containing some if not all of their original members. Headlining were The Merseybeats, who, like The Beatles, had lost a player to the Grim Reaper. Taking their late drummer's place was Pete Best. After a quarter of a century's deliberation, he'd decided that one of Mr Epstein's suggestions following his ousting from The Beatles – that he join The Merseybeats – wasn't such a bad idea after all.

The ecstatic 2,000-strong audience – possibly the real stars of the occasion – included a high percentage of middle-aged Cavern dwellers rabidly recollecting lunchtimes spent underground. Mike McCartney and members of The Roadrunners, Mark Peters' Silhouettes and like 1960s beat combos were also spotted in the throng. A couple of the acts weren't as wild as they might have been owing, perhaps to years of cabaret taming, but, following the advent of monitors and high-tech PA systems, no Mersey Beat groups were ever so loud and clear. Neither were any seen so well, courtesy of giant video screens erected on either side of the stage, where they played before a mock-up of the graffiti-covered Cavern wall and, to their left, a ghostly photo enlargement of Rory Storm.

Pete Best smoked and chewed gum from a ringside table until his time came. I couldn't help wondering what that solitary mister was thinking as group followed group, particularly when The Undertakers were joined mid set by Lee Curtis, into whose All-Stars Pete had been absorbed immediately after he had left The Beatles. In the All-Stars, too, had been Beryl Marsden, whose unscheduled three-song spot at the Grafton confirmed that she should have represented Merseyside womanhood in the 1960s charts, rather than a lesser talent like Cilla. When the grippingly raw vocals of grey-headed Geoff Nugent brought The Undertakers within an ace of stealing the show, I was also questioning whether in Jackie Lomax they'd chosen the right man to be lead singer back in 1961. Closing the night's entertainment, the venerable "Panda-Footed Prince of Prance" led his Flamingos through 'Do You Love Me', the sure-fire smash that he'd let slip through his fingers in 1963 when, so the story goes, he dictated its lyrics to Brian Poole for the price of a double whiskey.

Hip-shakin' Faron no longer had the figure for such gyrations. He looked his age, even if he didn't act it. Nature had been kinder to Pete Best, however, who enjoyed the biggest ovation of the evening, even eliciting a few screams. Pop is unfair and erratic. Mersey Beat had hinted at a golden future for Best, Faron, Beryl Marsden and Lee Curtis, but, as Bill Harry gloomed, "The cream doesn't necessarily come to the top in this sort of business." Arbitrary isolations, a mislaid telephone number, Larry Parnes' extended lunch break, a drummer's hangover, a flat tyre – all of these unrelated trivialities can trigger changes affecting the entire course of the career of a musician, even one with the tenacity of George Harrison.

A brief chart entry, a one-shot record contract and even an encore were once sufficient to feed hope. Often, without vanity, mere awareness of your worth in the teeth of ill luck was enough, although with every passing day you were less likely to become The Beatles. You had the right haircut, clothes and accent at the wrong time. The bass player leaves. A band who used to support you turns up on *Top Of The Pops*. If only there hadn't been a power-cut when Brian Epstein was there. If only the singer hadn't had a sore throat at New Brighton Tower. If only we hadn't lost our way...

17 *The Anthologist*

After the Romanian Angel appeal, 'Nobody's Child' and an interrelated appearance by the Harrisons on BBC1's chat show *Wogan*, things went as quiet as they had during the post-*Gone Troppo* period. In the following years, George put his head above the parapet rarely, if memorably.

Yet if he'd never been seen again after *Cloud Nine*, George Harrison would still have continued to preoccupy countless devotees, despite certain of them considering that it was his misfortune not to have died after shedding what they could presume to be the bulk of his creative load. However, other believers would feel that he almost owed it to them to reappear as if from Rip Van Winkle-esque slumber, rejuvenated and contemporary, thus debunking the myth of either an artistic death or the spending of final world-weary years in religious contemplation.

Meditation, gardening, recording, watching *Brookside* or whatever else George Harrison gets up to in the privacy of his own home – as long as he doesn't break the law – and the length of time he spends doing it is no more everybody else's business than the activities of Joe Average outside working hours. If everybody else disagrees with that, then it's conceivable that George might envy not so much Mr Average as St Francis with his "hidden solitude where I can listen in loneliness and silence to the secret treasures of God's conversation".[356]

A pop star, however, isn't either a nameless gazer from a commuter train in the rush-hour or a mediaeval anchorite but one whose face peers at you from half-page newspaper advertisements graciously inviting you to worship him on the public stage. If he elects not to bother with in-person appearances, then he'll ensure that record-shop windows bloom with the splendour of every latest disc he deigns to issue – and for his fans, whether there from the beginning or 'Got My Mind Set On You' latecomers, every new George Harrison release remains a special event.

As the substance of these have become progressively more autobiographical, pundits and fans alike have been increasingly more intrigued about what makes him tick, even when he himself wouldn't tell them, as he didn't during the ripplings of *Gone Troppo*. Although Harrison had been a willing enough interviewee in order to allow *Cloud Nine* the best possible chance, he didn't have to be. He could have remained remote and still sold enough records to more than break even. He certainly didn't need the money Why should he have felt bound to give it some showbiz? Why should he have felt obliged to set himself up as a target for media snipers? Was it really incumbent upon him to justify his artistic conduct or clarify more obscure lyrical byways?

Why waste such effort when all you have to do is let someone like me do it for you? However, I can only go so far before the amount of space I've been allocated runs out. If you want any more, you can write it yourself – but if you think you'd derive deep and lasting pleasure from a study and comparison of, say, on-stage utterances of each stop on George's twelve-date Rock Legends tour of Japan in December 1991 with Eric Clapton, please write to a magazine called *Beatlefan* which caters for anyone with an insatiable appetite for all things Beatle as it uncovers the distant past whilst keeping as intricate a pace with the present.

Beatlefan is published in the States,[357] where Beatlemania lasts for all eternity, as opposed to the mere lifetime experienced by the British faithful. Thanks to my authorship of *The Quiet One*, *Ringo Starr: Straight Man Or Joker?* and *Backbeat* (a tie-in to the 1994 biopic of Stuart Sutcliffe), I have been an honoured guest at many US Beatlefests, every one dwarfing even the Merseybeatle event.

The Union's politicians got in on the act, too, during 1996, the year of the presidential election. A well-timed if incredible story was leaked about swingin' Bill Clinton as a University of Oxford student visiting a Liverpool pub and wading in when Ringo was attacked by a crowbar-wielding drinker. To counter this astute attempt at image-polishing, Republican candidate Bob Dole purportedly considered utilising a tape of 'Taxman' in his campaign meetings.

That North America loves the Beatles so demonstratively explains why both George and Ringo had separate cameo roles in the US cartoon series *The Simpsons* in the 1990s and why Starr's aptly-named All-Starr Band – embracing at various times Dr John, Todd Rundgren, Dave Edmunds and key members of bands such as The Who and The Eagles – covered the United States more extensively than any other territory. The troupe was formed in 1989 to join the likes of The Beach Boys, The Who and The Monkees on the nostalgia circuit – for, although the 1992 edition featured a couple of tracks from the new Ringo studio LP *Time Takes Time*, if I'd gone to an All-Starrs recital, what would I have wanted to hear? Ringo's excerpts from his album didn't make him a current challenger again, partly because his fans, old and new, will always clap loudest for the sounds of yesteryear.

In many respects, the future was the past all over again. Whether The Fourmost on the chicken-in-a-basket trail or Ringo Starr, cynosure of 20,000 picnicking eyes in some US stadium open to the sky, all that an act still intact from the 1960s needed to do was to be an archetypal unit of its own, spanning every familiar avenue of its professional life – all the timeless hits, every change of image, every bandwagon jumped.

Opening at the same sold-out Yokohama Arena at which Ringo's ensemble had been just over a year earlier, George Harrison's understanding of this was apparent when, at Clapton's encouragement, he sought to experience what touring was like nowadays by easing into his trek around Japan, a country second only to the USA in the intensity of its passion for the Beatles. This was reflected in gross ticket sales of around £10 million and a naming as International Tour of 1991 by subscribers to *Performance*, trade journal of the concert industry.

With no new record in the shops, the lion's share of George's part of each night's proceedings was fixed solely and unashamedly on nothing that wasn't in either The Beatles' or his solo portfolio of favourites – some, admittedly, re-arranged slightly – up to and including 'Cheer Down'. Into the bargain, Clapton – whose "name and likeness can be no larger than any other sidemen's", according to a memo from his record company – slipped 'Badge' and his 1977 paean to Pattie, 'Wonderful Tonight', into his four songs at the central microphone. "Here's another one of the old ones for you" was a sentence that seemed to recur (along with fragments of Japanese) during continuity by George that was more effusive, witty and relaxed than customers who recalled *The Concerts For Bangladesh* movie might have expected. He was supposed to be the Quiet One, wasn't he?

Although 'Love Comes To Everyone' and 'Fish In The Sand' were dropped by the third show, whatever else carried ovation-earning punch – 'If I Needed Someone' (in The Beatles' Budokan show in 1966), 'I Want To Tell You', 'Here Comes The Sun', 'Something' (with the word "jack" inserted *à la* Sinatra after "just stick around"), 'Isn't It A Pity' (which segued into the long coda of 'Hey Jude'), 'Give Me Love', 'All Those Years Ago' (usually prefaced or concluded with a reference to Lennon), 'Devil's Radio' – you name it, George, sipping herbal tea between each song, didn't miss a laser-lit trick. He was also in excellent form, both vocally and instrumentally, as evidenced not so much in what few reviews there were by Western media ("entertaining if unspectacular" said *Billboard*[358]) as in the subsequent *Live In Japan* double album, extracted from highlights of the Osaka and Tokyo stops.

There was to be no falling off in quality, either, during what amounted to his first full-scale UK concert as an ex-Beatle when it was announced on 1 April 1992 that he'd be heading a surprise extravaganza entitled "George Harrison And Friends: Election Is A Celebration" six days later at the Royal Albert Hall. The Beatles had played this venue only once, at the Sounds '63 bash in 1963. However, the questionable acoustics had been improved so much since then that a season there starring Eric Clapton had become almost as established an annual fixture as the Proms.

The actuality of George's show and its underlying purpose turned out to be no April Fool joke. He was doing it to raise funds for – and sharpen the profile of – the Natural Law Party (NLP), an organisation that had smouldered into form in the previous month after the Prime Minister had called a general election. Its manifesto promised "a disease-free, crime-free, pollution-free society", epitomised by transcendental meditation on the National Health and the cross-legged yogic flying that is the best-remembered sequence of the party political broadcast that delayed BBC 1's *Nine O'Clock News* one evening as the population prepared to cross its ballot papers.

In case you haven't yet realised, the proposals of the NLP were traceable to the Maharishi Mahesh Yogi, now in his 80s, and again in favour with George, whose testimonial on behalf of the party explained, "I want a total change, and not just a choice between left and right. The system we have now is obsolete and is not fulfilling the needs of the people."[359] Hear, hear! 60,000-odd people – including me – voted Natural Law when the time came. This was no mean feat for first-timers. Yet, because proportional representation would be harmful to the Conservatives – who were to continue to cling onto power for another five years – not a solitary one of more than 300 NLP candidates fielded was to make a maiden speech in the House of Commons.

Harrison declined an invitation to stand for a Merseyside constituency, perhaps recalling Swami Prabhupada's advice that he'd be more useful as a musician, and for those who slept outside the Albert Hall box office to be first in the queue, his first solo "home game", was more than just entertainment by a pop star. Veiled in flesh, George Harrison was to materialise before them like Moses from the clouded summit of Mount Sinai to the Israelites. Others were more level headed. However, although it took several days for it to sell out, for those who went or wanted to go, the extravaganza was on the scale of a cup final or Muhammad Ali's last hurrah in Las Vegas – even if George's first announcement on the night was, "It's not all it's cracked up to be." Nevertheless, a small army of his famous acquaintances – including Joe Brown, a couple of Beach Boys and TV-actor-turned-pop singer Jimmy Nail[360] – were out in force. His past life flashed before him, too, via the presence of such as Julian Lennon, Pattie Boyd and – soon to die of leukaemia – a remarried Maureen Starkey.

Against a backdrop of the NLP rainbow symbol and amid a heavy fragrance of joss-sticks, George was accompanied by personnel drawn mainly from Eric Clapton's backing group,[361] still warmed up enough by the Japanese expedition to need few rehearsals. Although it wasn't mentioned over footage of these in television news magazines, other media outlets were to note and speculate upon the non-appearance of Slowhand himself. Had he and George fallen out? During the final show in Japan, they'd seemed the best of wisecracking, bear-hugging mates, George hailing his ex-husband-in-law as *"saiko!"* ("the greatest!") and Eric replying, "You're not so bad yourself."

However, while the two may have been regarded as artistic and commercial equals in the east, the over-valued and more omnipresent Clapton had continued to sweep the board in British music-journal polls, with the underestimated George remaining conspicuously absent, as he was in *Q* magazine's photographic supplement of pop guitarists in 1990. Although there has been very recent reassessment, nothing seemed to have changed since the 1960s, when Eric was god of the Marquee and George only *The Sunday Times*' "passable guitarist (say among the best 1,000 in the country)".[90] In 1992, at Clapton's Albert Hall stomping ground, George may have been aware that there were some determined to originate a myth that his friend had upstaged him, even before the concert. On the other hand, maybe Eric was simply otherwise engaged that particular evening.

In the absentee's stead at the Albert Hall, Eagle and All-Starr Joe Walsh and – heard on the Wilburys' *Volume Three* – Gary Moore[362] – guitarists on a par with Clapton (and Harrison) technically, if not as revered – were to dominate the stage, one after the other, before the intermission, and then pitched in with the main event.

When first the lights went down, however, a short speech about a "new sunshine for the nation" by party leader Dr Geoffrey Clements had summarised both the musical and political significance of the occasion in a telling paragraph: "George's music is the crowning melody of every heart in Britain. Let us build a beautiful new country...to bring joy, just as George's music brings joy to everyone." Laying it on with a trowel, the good doctor then brought, on to a roaring ovation "one of the greatest musicians of all time" to introduce 20 minutes of Walsh and accompanists that included Ringo's eldest son, Zak, on drums.

Before an audience with a preponderance of over-30s – who nonetheless weren't above odd outbreaks of screaming – George, in a plain black suit and white shirt like he'd worn at Yokohama, gave as admirable an account of himself – and delivered virtually the same set – as he had in Japan, but with the additional spice of a dodgy moment at the beginning of 'My Sweet Lord' and spontaneous salvos of applause for specific couplets in 'Piggies' and 'Taxman', the latter's topicality emphasised with an updated libretto name-dropping notable national and world figures (and, like 'Piggies', an additional verse). Less political than sentimental, however, was a clearly moved George calling up Ringo ("a bit of a blast from all our pasts") from a balcony box for the encores, 'While My Guitar Gently Weeps' and a reprised 'Roll Over Beethoven', the latter of which incorporated a drum battle between the ubiquitous Ray Cooper and other percussionists on hand.

Among the next morning's critical dampeners were *The Times*' "middling performance by today's standards"[363] and, worse, *The Daily Express*' complaints about Harrison's "shouted" lyrics as he "massacred" some of the songs.[364] Nevertheless, the London *Evening Standard* reckoned it was "fantastic"[365] and, more cautiously, *The Daily Telegraph* agreed that it "lived up to the hopes of those who had waited 23 years for the moment."[366] However, another "Greatest Night Anyone Could Ever Remember" was, like The Rebels' recital at Speke Legion Hall or The Concerts For Bangladesh, not repeated, despite a still-overwhelmed George's regret expressed in an interview with *Musician* magazine two months later: "Everyone has rehearsed really hard and so much effort has been put into the production that it should be a proper tour." Why it wasn't to be may have had less to do with any disinclination on Harrison's part than the logistics of finding suitable short-notice venues while the other participants were still available.

Among the assembled cast for the finale had been Dhani, now very much a young adult. He had also become a proficient guitarist, so much so that he joined his nervous father for 'In My Little Snapshot Album' from the 1938 film *I See Ice* as a contribution to a George Formby Appreciation Society convention in March 1991 in Blackpool. (Allegedly, Formby songs filled the bulk of an impromptu performance by Harrison *père* to relieve the boredom of fellow passengers during a three-hour delay in a departure lounge at Kennedy Airport.) Moreover, shortly after the NLP recital, Harrison was also heard in nearly as improbable a setting, singing and plinking ukulele on 'Between The Devil And The Deep Blue Sea' in *Mister Roadrunner*, a Channel 4 documentary.

Places where Beatle-spotters would have been more likely to find George were on the stage at London's Hard Rock Cafe, where he sat in with Carl Perkins; on two tracks of *Alvin Lee 1994*, that included a reworking of 'I Want You (She's So Heavy)' from *Abbey Road*; and at Madison Square Garden, where, on 16 October 1995, he was prominent in the jubilee atmosphere of a Bob Dylan tribute concert, paying his respects with 'If Not For You' and 'Absolutely Sweet Marie' (from *Blonde On Blonde*) and then ministering to overall effect when ol' Lucky Wilbury came on in person.

Others with principal roles in the story of the Quiet One had not left its latter-day orbit, either. Far from it. The Shankar family holidayed with the Harrisons in as recently as 1995, and George instigated the resurrection of the Dark Horse label in the following year to issue *Ravi Shankar: In Celebration*, a lovingly compiled four-CD boxed retrospective spanning different aspects of the now quite elderly Padma Bhushan's recording career, from the post-war decade to 1995, and including previously unissued items, some taped at FPSHOT. "Most music-lovers will have heard of Ravi Shankar, the sitar and the classical ragas and talas of India," read George's notes in the 60-page book that came with it, "but how about Ravi the singer, the orchestrator, the innovator or the experimentalist?"

George also turned up at the Oxfordshire home of another innovator and experimentalist, George Martin, to be interviewed for a June 1992 edition of ITV's *South Bank Show* that marked yet another anniversary, marking the quarter-century of the release of *Sgt Pepper's Lonely Hearts Club Band*.

It always boiled down to The Beatles. Yet, nearly two years earlier on BBC2's *Rapido* pop series, George had not only poured coldest water on any idea of a Beatles reunion but had also underlined his boredom with the ceaseless fascination with the wretched group, a fascination that was to escalate with the runaway success in 1994 of *Live At The BBC*, a compilation of early broadcasts. This prefaced an official proclamation of a coming anthology of further items from the vaults. These were to be hand-picked by George, Paul and Ringo themselves for issue over the period of a year on nine albums (in packs of three) as companion commodities to a six-hour documentary film to be spread over three weeks on ITV and presented likewise on foreign television.

Then came talk of the Fab Three recording new material for the project. When asked to comment in a connected news bulletin for London's Capital Radio, I estimated that all they'd be doing was incidental music. Writing in *The Daily Mail*,[367] the late Ray Coleman[368] hoped that it wouldn't go further than this, arguing – with no-one contradicting him – that it wouldn't be the same without Lennon. Six years earlier, George, for one, had been of like mind: "What good are three Beatles without John? It's too far in the past."[355]

After a fashion, Harrison, Starr and McCartney's well-documented regrouping in the mid 1990s wasn't without Lennon. Their labours at Friar Park and Paul's studio in Sussex yielded the grafting of new music onto John's stark demos of 'Free As A Bird' and other numbers on tapes provided by his widow after Paul's conciliatory embrace of her at another Rock 'n' Roll Hall Of Fame extravaganza.

Isn't it wonderful what they can do nowadays? Precedents had been set by the respective superimposition of backing material onto musical sketches by Buddy Holly and Jim Reeves. In 1981, Nashville producer Owen Bradley's skills with varispeed, editing block and sampler had brought together Reeves and Patsy Cline on record with a duet of 'Have You Ever Been Lonely'. A decade later, there arrived a global smash with 'Unforgettable', a similar cobbling together of

Nat "King" Cole and daughter Natalie's voices over a state-of-the-art facsimile of Nat's original 1951 arrangement.

With Jeff Lynne as console midwife, 'Free As A Bird' took shape as near as dammit to a new Beatles record as could be hoped, complete with a bottleneck passage from George, Ringo's trademark pudding drums and both George and Paul emoting a freshly composed bridge as a sparkling contrast to John's downbeat verses. The result was not unlike that of a mordant 'We Can Work It Out'. It was certainly better than certain A-sides released by The Beatles when Lennon was still amongst us.

Yet, for all the amassing of anticipation via no sneak previews, a half-hour TV special building up to its first spin over a remarkable video and the multitudes willing it to leap straight in at Number One as usual, 'Free As A Bird' stalled in second place in Britain's Christmas list when up against 'Earth Song' by Michael Jackson and an easy-listening cover of Oasis' 'Wonderwall' from the amazing Mike Flowers Pops. The follow-up, 'Real Love', reached the Top Ten more grudgingly, having been dogged by exclusion from Radio 1's playlist of choreographed boy bands, chart ballast from the turntables of disco and rave and – despite glaring evidence that they had been fed Beatles music from the cradle – Britpop executants like Supergrass, The Bluetones, Ocean Colour Scene and, most pointedly of all, Oasis.

Who couldn't understand George, Paul and Ringo's mingled disappointment and elation when the million-selling *Anthology* albums paralleled the 'Something'/*Abbey Road* scenario in its affirmation that almost-but-not-quite reaching the top in the UK singles chart was but a surface manifestation of enduring interest in The Beatles that made even their out-takes[369] as viable as any young Britpop outfit's finest work?

Oasis, The Bluetones and all the rest of them were inclined to be more impressed by Lennon and McCartney compositions than anything by the Other Two. This was epitomised by the proud familiarity of Oasis leader Noel Gallagher – and Paul Weller – with McCartney when sharing vocals as The Smokin' Mojo Filters on an arrangement of 'Come Together' for a 1995 charity album for children in war-torn Bosnia.

Yet, for whatever reason, George's *Wonderwall* soundtrack LP caught on too. Oasis borrowed its title for their best-known song, but the influence of *Wonderwall* in particular and George in general was heard most blatantly in the grooves of Kula Shaker, the most exotic of all the new Top-40 arrivals of the mid 1990s, with items like 'Acintya Bhedabheda Tattva', 'Sleeping Jiva' and 'Temple Of Everlasting Light'. Moreover, this London combo's fourth single – issued in November 1996 – was 'Govinda', complete with Sanskrit lyrics and "interwoven through an ancient north Indian folk song", as it said in the press release. More than the stimulus of the Radha Krishna Temple hit on the A-side, the flip, 'Gokula', lived so obviously in a *Wonderwall* guitar riff (from 'Skiing') that permission to use it had to be sought by Kula Shaker from Northern Songs via a direct appeal to the composer himself

Kula Shaker were a further acknowledgment that, as both a Beatle and ex-Beatle, George Harrison's entries in *The Guinness Book Of Hit Singles* count for less than his inspiration for pop musicians from The Zombies to Malcolm McLaren to dip into non-Western cultures. In 1982, a British act called Monsoon had made the Top 50 with 'Shakti (The Meaning Of Within)' and other Indian-flavoured excursions. The impact of Oriental music only seems to hold less allure these days because of the fine line between its ear-catching extraneousness and the real danger of it sounding like a parody of George Harrison, a point driven home in the coda of 'When We Was Fab'.

Beyond pop, where would the Krishna Consciousness Society be without the invocation of George's name and money? Without him, how many of its tracts would be screwed up unread or perused with the same scornful amusement reserved for Flat Earth Society's pamphlets? In a mugger's paradise like Reading, why else is there enough interest for chanting *bhakta*s to process down its main streets on Saturday afternoons now and then and to hold weekly meetings in a church hall also used for judo and amateur dramatics?

From George's lips in 1987 had come a desire "to be able consciously to leave my body at will",[354] but, no matter how far his spiritual wanderings since leaving Liverpool Institute, fellow pupil Charles Shaw would always "see him back in the classroom at break time saying 'Gorra ciggie, Charlie?'". In fastnesses forever unreachable to a bloke like Charlie, George was still as eternally Scouse as any who'd mounted the stage on that ravers' return at the Grafton in 1989 and the other Merseycats functions that have come since. In creating "skiffle for the '90s"[333] in his last studio records, he may have been trying to reach an even earlier epoch. If ever he succeeded, he might just about recognise himself.

However, Harrison doesn't spend as many incognito hours as Paul McCartney in a maudlin haunting of his genesis, although he and Olivia strolled the corridors of the Institute one evening shortly before its conversion – with a massive financial injection by Paul – into the Liverpool Institute of Performing Arts (LIPA).

The one least cut out for showbusiness, George was nevertheless "thankful that The Beatles enabled me to be adventurous. It saved me from another mundane sort of life."[151] What as? An electrician at Blackler's? A "good, medium-weight business executive", as *The Sunday Times* once suggested? A pen-pusher alongside Pete Best at Garston Job Centre? A latter-day Swinging Blue Jean instead of Colin Manley?

I think that, if George Harrison hadn't been a Beatle, he'd have been in the Jeans or in some other Liverpool outfit that may or may not have had hits. At Don Andrew's request, he might have blown the dust from his guitar to belie, for one 1989 night only, some daytime occupation in an office or factory. His moment of glory might have reared up and then subsided until perhaps the next Merseycats function.

Just as fond of hypothesising is George himself, who "would've probably been a better guitarist than I am now, because the fame made me end up playing the same old stuff for years".[189] He'd tell you himself, too, that he "can't write brilliant lyrics – though occasionally some are half-decent – and I can half-decently produce something, but I've never really had any cards to play".[151]

18 The Alien

On Wednesday 29 December 1999, a chilly twilight fell on the small village that is Friar Park. Within the parameters of a remarkable life, it started like an unremarkable night for George Harrison.

All of the staff bar three were away for the Christmas holidays. Dhani was home with a friend from university. The two were staying in one of the lodges. In another still dwelt Dhani's Uncle Harold. George spent most of the evening there before returning to the main house. The mother-in-law had already gone to bed. He and the wife watched some video or other. Olivia lost interest and retired, too. George joined her just after two o'clock.

Whatever the nature of the film and its effect upon his nocturnal imaginings as he climbed the stairs, how could he possibly have suspected that, by dawn on Thursday, his own gore would be splattered and drying on the surrounding walls and carpets, that he'd be half dead in hospital and that Olivia would be raised to unlooked-for heroine status?

Suddenly and unwillingly, he'd be back in even sharper public focus than he'd been during the 'Free As A Bird' episode in 1995. Since then, he'd melted into the background again without quite retreating into neurotically self-conscious seclusion or ostentatious McCartney-esque domesticity.

At an Australian Grand Prix, he took the trouble to amble over to Jenson Button's grid to say, "Good luck" to the young driver for his first Formula One race. They chatted easily, and Button was surprised to be told later by his mechanic, "That was George Harrison, you know." The ex-Beatle was also amenable to speaking learnedly about motor-racing in a *Sunday Times* supplement, *Formula One Handbook*,[375] but "I wouldn't want to be financially involved because only crazy people put their own money into it. It's the many different amazing people and their on-going soap opera that I can view closely without having direct responsibility for. It beats *Coronation Street*." Utterances like this were nevertheless rare, and few apart from regular readers of *Beatles Monthly*, *Beatlefan* and the like could speak with any authority or interest about a seemingly untroubled existence in which nothing much seemed to happen, year in, year out.

As each one passed, the usual hearsay went the rounds. One of the more intriguing rumours was that George had approached Elvis Presley's estate for any unissued tapes of the King singing. The idea was for The Traveling Wilburys to add accompaniment to these as Harrison, McCartney, Starr and Jeff Lynne had to John's 'Free As A Bird' demo (and, since then, The Hollies to an album's worth of Buddy Holly items). Yet, via material given to George by the family, a more likely candidate for ghostly fifth Wilbury is Carl Perkins, taken by a stroke at the age of 65 in February 1998.

A few years earlier, Perkins had recovered from throat cancer. Stray paragraphs in 1997's national tabloids had hinted – correctly – that George had undergone medical examinations for the same malady. Nevertheless, the fragile substance of this particular story was indicated by *The Henley Standard*'s silence about it while chronicling the mundane saga of Friar Park's fraught negotiations with South Oxfordshire District Council about a proposed new swimming pool. Complete with changing rooms and sauna, it was designed to blend tastefully within the exotic waterfalls of the caves. A gesture of defiance against a nosy world was George's refusal to allow the planning committee to inspect the site in person. Why couldn't the application be judged on the basis of the architect's drawings, just as they would be for a householder whose physical presence wouldn't thrill them to the marrow because he was a pop star? Over in Goring, George Michael was up against more or less the same problem, but as a newer comer to both pop and the area he was more co-operative.

Michael also hadn't been famous for long enough to be annoyed rather than flattered by the presence of bootlegs. Despite George, Paul and Ringo's attempts to contain it, the industry of illicit Beatles merchandise thrived as if the *Anthology* albums had never been released. There was even a US magazine, *Belmo's Beatleg News*, devoted solely to unforgiving hours of everything – and I mean everything – on which The Beatles, together and apart, ever breathed. An example germane to this discussion is 1997's *12 Arnold Grove*, conspicuous for George's lead vocal on a demo of 'It Don't Come Easy', an alternative mix of 'Got My Mind Set On You' and 'Every Grain Of Sand', another go at a Bob Dylan obscurity.

At what sort of lunatic were such products targeted? Who had the patience to sit through six takes of the same backing track, a fractionally shorter edit of some Italian flip-side, a false start of 'I Want To Tell You', one more fantastic version of 'It Is He (Jai Sri Krishna)' and then spend infinitely less time actually listening to something like *12 Arnold Grove* over and over again than discussing how "interesting" its contents were?

The overall effect of eavesdropping on such conversations was akin to overhearing a prattle of great-aunts comparing ailments. Yet, to The Beatles' most painfully committed fans, the intrinsic worth and high retail price of a bootleg hardly mattered – and, displayed on the CD rack between, say, *Portrait Of Genius* and *Jacques Brel Is Alive And Well And Living In Paris*, it served as both a fine detail of interior decorating and a conversational ice-breaker.

Beatles talk became more animated among the faithful in 1998 when a borderline case, *The Beatles Live At The Star-Club, Germany, 1962* – the one that Allan Williams had released in 1977 on a vinyl double album – reared up again when Lingasong, a record label of no great merit, announced its intention to reissue it on CD. Reviewing it the first time around, the now-defunct UK pop journal *Sounds* had noted contemporary implications in the back cover photograph depicting 1962 teenagers congregating beneath the club's attributive neon sign, Treffpunkt Der Jugend ("Youth Rendezvous"), before concluding waspishly, "The Beatles couldn't play, either."

That's as may be, but Billy Childish, a leading light of a Medway Towns group scene of agreeably retrogressive bent, had considered it "their finest LP". The artists concerned, however, lacked Billy's objectivity about both the alcohol-fuelled performance and the atrocious sound quality – despite further expensive studio doctoring – of what Kingsize Taylor ("not a friend we hung around with," reckoned George) had taped with a hand-held microphone onto a domestic machine.

So it was that on a mid-week day in May 1998, George Harrison represented The Beatles and Apple in the High Court witness stand before Mr Justice Neuberger, who was to compliment the litigant upon the clarity of his testimony. Leaving his Southport butcher's shop to take care of itself for the duration, Kingsize Taylor for Lingasong had already sworn that he'd been given verbal permission by John Lennon to immortalise The Beatles' late shift at the Star-Club "as long as I got the ales in". Taylor had assumed that Lennon's go-ahead meant that it was OK by the others, too.

That was an easy mistake, smiled George, because "John was the loudest, the noisiest and the oldest [*sic*]. We didn't ask [Kingsize] to do it. We never heard [the tapes]. We never had anything to do with them – and that's the story. One drunken person recording another bunch of drunks does not constitute a business deal or the right to put out a record." Neuberger agreed, and the elaborate press packs of the CD that had been distributed by Lingasong in false anticipation of victory became instant prized rarities.

A less onerous Beatles duty for George was to be promoter-in-chief of a renovated *Yellow Submarine* in summer 1999 – including additional footage, remixed soundtrack CD, video and DVD, along with associated clothing, memorabilia and toys – to the extent of inviting Timothy White, editor-in-chief of *Billboard*, to Friar Park to hear the retelling of the old, old story. Harrison was to relate it in far more detail, and in doing so would earn about £5 million in a single tax year via the publication of *The Beatles Anthology* book[371] in 2000. Despite a cover price of £35, this title accrued enough advance orders to slam straight in at Number One in *The Sunday Times* book chart, a feat duplicated in other publications around the world.

Its weight on a par with a paving slab, this de luxe "Beatles story told for the first time in their own words and pictures" had been several years in gestation. Transcriptions of ruminations and fallible reminiscences dating from the *Anthology* TV series by Harrison, Starr and McCartney, along with archive spoken material by Lennon and a treasury of photographs, documents and further memorabilia were edited by Genesis in consultation with usual suspects of the ilk of Klaus Voorman, Sir George Martin and, prior to his death in 1997, Derek Taylor.

Overall, a likeable and sometimes courageous account – and an intriguing companion volume to this one – passed the litmus test of any pop life story in that it provoked a compulsion in the reader to check out the records. Nevertheless, it was flawed, mainly because there is little if any anchoring text for that Tibetan monk who still hasn't heard of the group; and, while the surviving Beatles were often painfully honest about events that occurred up to 50 years earlier, it was an autobiography aimed at fans who prefer not to know too much about what kinds of people their idols are in private life. Too many illusions are shattered, and the music may never sound the same.

Just as serious a fault was the fact that, like the televisual *Anthology*, it lacked the perspectives of other living key *dramatis personae*, such as Pete Best, Tony Sheridan, Bill Harry, Pattie Boyd, the Maharishi, Phil Spector, you name 'em. But where do you draw the line? By including all the acts on the same label? Everyone who ever recorded a Beatles song? The foresters who felled the trees to make the paper on which they were written?

Anthology remained a bestseller when, with 60-year-old Neil Aspinall still at the helm, a four-strong team at Apple – now run from one of the white townhouses encircling the central gardens in Knightsbridge – helped to co-ordinate EMI's biggest-ever marketing campaign. Its budget was between £1 million and £2 million in Britain alone and eight million copies of *1*, a compilation of The Beatles' 27 UK and/or US chart-toppers (titled originally *Best Of The Beatles*), were shipped around the world.

The fastest-selling CD ever, *1* was just that in Britain, Japan, Spain, Germany and Canada within a week of being issued in autumn 2001, with over 400,000 customers stampeding into Japanese record shops during the first day. At home, it outsold Oasis' *Standing On The Shoulder* [*sic*] *Of Giants* four to one.

Whether or not looking forward to the past is a healthy situation for any artist is open to conjecture, but it was hard fact that Joe Average was more intrigued by the corporate Beatles than George Harrison or any other individual locked in their orbit.* Ringo's acceptance of this was manifest in his preparation for his next US trek with The All-Starr Band. He contemplated daring some tracks from his 1992 album, *Time Takes Time*, but he knew he'd be lynched if the majority of the set wasn't principally the good old good ones played in, approximately, the good old way, like it was the last time, when *The New York Times* had lauded Ringo's as "the better kind of nostalgia tour".

George, however, wasn't ready to go so gently into that good night. If being only instrumental in setting up a Beatles website, he was more directly involved in www.allthingsmustpass.com, personally answering internet users' enquiries, which ranged from "Does Paul still piss you off?"† to the gauge of guitar strings he used in 1965 to the bleedin' obvious.

In this respect, George was friendly, patient and tolerant, but he derived greater pleasure from doing favours for old friends. In 1997, he joined Ravi Shankar on the VH1 television programme *George Harrison And Ravi Shankar: Yin And Yang*[370] to plug *Chants Of India*, the latest Shankar album. A thoroughly diverting production, what might serve as the octogenarian maestro's recording finale balanced sung lyrics as succinct as *haiku* and instrumental passages of a quirky complexity vaguely reminiscent of Frank Zappa.‡

"*Chants Of India* isn't really sitar music," George elucidated. "It's basically spiritual music, spiritual songs, ancient mantras and passages from the *Vedas*, which are the most sacred texts on Earth."[370]

As well as penning a foreword to Ravi's autobiography,[373] George guested on a Radio 2 series hosted by Joe Brown to discuss influential rock 'n' roll records,* and he would also slide some bottleneck for Bill Wyman on a revival of Kitty Lester's 'Love Letters' during a January 2001 session. Initially, he was less inclined to do so on 'I'll Be Fine Anyway' and the funereal 'King Of The Broken Hearts' on Ringo's latest effort, 1998's *Vertical Man*. "He wasn't in the mood," sighed Ringo, "Two weeks later, I phoned him up from LA just to say, 'Hi,' and, 'What are you doing?'

"'Oh, I'm in the studio, playing with the dobro.'

"I go, 'Oooh, a dobro would sound good on my album.'

"So he goes, 'Oh, all right. Send it over, then.' I really wanted that slide guitar. His soul comes out of that guitar. It just blows me away."[374]

As honorary president of the George Formby Appreciation Society, Harrison himself was impressed by Jimmy Nail's ukulele picking on a Formby-type version of 'Something' with another Friar Park visitor, Jim Capaldi, on bongos. Nevertheless, Jimmy chose a less adventurous brass-band arrangement for the version of 'Something' on *Ten Great Songs And An OK Voice*, a collection of cover versions (now a common vocational ploy).

While admiring Nail's way with a ukulele, Harrison was more seriously in awe of U Srinivas, an Indian who was to the electric mandolin what Shankar was to the sitar. George's recreational listening didn't really extend to much contemporary pop. While he contributed a bottleneck obligato to 'Punchdrunk', an album track by Rubyhorse, a young Irish combo of vaguely Britpop persuasion, he regarded Oasis as "pretty average" and rap as "computerised crap". Indeed, he was as unable to distinguish between different rap artists as a shopper dithering between wedges of supermarket Muzak. "I listen to *Top Of The Pops*," he snarled, "and after three tunes, it makes me want to kill somebody."[375]

This was an unfortunate turn of phrase, in view of the events

* This may be illustrated by the raw statistic that, of nigh on 200 Beatles tribute bands in Liverpool alone, only one, Harry Georgeson, pays homage to George alone.

† To which he replied, "'Scan not a friend/With a microscope glass/You know his faults/Then let his foibles pass' – old Victorian proverb. I'm sure there's enough about me that pisses him off, but I think we have now grown old enough to realise that we're both pretty damn cute (!)."

‡ Prior to his death in 1993, Zappa had established himself as a composer in the same league as his "classical" idols Varèse, Stravinsky and Shankar. "Frank was into Ravi Shankar," Mothers Of Invention drummer Jimmy Carl Black told me in May 2000. "'Help, I'm A Rock' [from *Freak Out!*] was a raga."

that followed later, culminating with the agitated oscillations of an ambulance siren two nights before Big Ben clanged in the new century. The horror came to Henley in the likely-looking form of Michael Abram, alias "Mad Mick", a 34-year-old paranoid schizophrenic – from Liverpool, of all places. The wild hair and staring eyes betrayed an inner chaos of delusion and nightmare hallucinations in one deemed "normal" by Lynda, his mother, during an upbringing in a three-bedroom council house.

At 16, he left the local Roman Catholic comprehensive with sufficient qualifications to enter the world of telemarketing. His intentions towards Jeanette, a girl from school, were honourable, in that he stuck by her when she became pregnant with the first of their two children. However, passers-by would hear the couple quarrelling, Michael blustering through rages that climaxed in a Hitlerian screech. There was also something intangibly odd about his behaviour in the streets of Huyton-with-Roby, a twin borough that had descended into seediness since the days when Stuart Sutcliffe had been head chorister in St Gabriel's. Now the church was dwarfed by tower blocks on estates like Woolfall Heights, where a now-jobless Abram lived in tenth-floor squalor after separating from Jeanette.

Their estrangement was traceable to his increased reliance on illegal substances as a form of self-medication. According to Michael, cannabis, LSD, crack cocaine and, especially, heroin helped stay "the spooks" that had been haunting him since he was 18. In collusion with Jeanette, Lynda had made an appointment for him with a psychiatrist at Whiston hospital, where, although diagnosed as psychotic, he remained an out-patient, his afflictions dismissed as curable as soon as he stopped malingering and found the self-discipline to cease his drug habit.

Helplessly, his nearest-and-dearest monitored Michael's accelerating envelopment by a world inhabited by witches, devils and sorcerers. Outsiders gathered that he thought that the Messiah was alive in Marseilles, arriving at this conclusion after poring over *The Holy Blood And The Holy Grail*. First published in 1982,* this

---

* For George, these included the expected set works of Jerry Lee, Elvis, The Coasters, Eddie Cochran and Carl Perkins, plus Richie Barrett's 'Some Other Guy'.

remarkable tome cast uncomfortable light on the origins of Christianity and the very identity of Christ.

Texts that buttressed further unorthodox beliefs included the Bible and the more topical *Centuries*, the 16th-century book of prophesies by Nostradamus, who equated the forthcoming millennium with global calamity. Abram also received Charles Manson-like messages when replaying certain discs by Bob Marley, Cat Stevens and Oasis on his personal stereo. Then he borrowed his mother's Beatles tapes, and his destiny was taken from him.

"Mad Mick", or "the fifth Beatle", became a familiar and grotesque sight – and sound – in Huyton and further afield. Mocked by children, who dubbed him "Sheephead" because of his shocked, pale-yellow thatch, the local Mister Strange would sit chain-smoking for hours – sometimes naked – on an upturned plant pot on his dismal balcony or roam the shopping precincts ululating Beatles numbers to himself and lost in misery, paranoid self-obsession and lonely contemplation. Who were, he pondered, the four phantom menaces, spreading global consternation and plague, as predicted by Nostradamus? Clinging desperately to his fantasies, he attracted comparatively little hostile attention as a seemingly harmless if unsavoury part of the parochial furniture.

Nonetheless, by 1997 so many shreds of human dignity had been torn from Abram that he was admitted into a psychiatric ward, although he was cast back into the community after eleven days, just as he would be two years later, after allegedly assaulting a male nurse. In an advancing state of bewilderment and panic, he sought fleeting shelter with his poor mother, sobbing – with some justification – "Nobody can help me."

"Alarm bells went off," cried Lynda Abram, "but were missed by doctors and social workers."

If such a condition can be quantified, the solar eclipse in August 1999 correlated with gradually more profound insanity, although a perceived directive in a Lennon song caused him to cease use heroin. Conversely, Michael had convinced himself that he was possessed by McCartney, deconstructing the title of 'Let It Be', for example, as

---

* By Jonathan Cape, written by Michael Baigent, Richard Leigh and Henry Lincoln.

"L" for "hell", "et" for "extra terrestrial" – and "It Be" an indication that he (Abram) was about to contract tuberculosis.

By October, he was focusing his persecution complex on George, seeing the line "It's going to take money" from 'Got My Mind Set On You' – albeit not a Harrison original – as a reference to the £80,000 he understood that someone he knew owed a drug dealer. After the game was up, Michael informed his solicitor, "The Beatles were witches, and George was the leader, a witch on a broomstick, who talked in the Devil's tongue, an alien from Hell." Mark David Chapman had grasped the wrong end of the stick, too, but the stick still existed.

As the incarnation of St Michael the Archangel, Mad Mick had been sent to execute George Harrison by God, with whom he was overheard arguing in a police cell on one of the three occasions that he'd been arrested for minor public-order offences since the eclipse.

On 16 December, Mad Mick bought a railway ticket from Lime Street to Henley. Keeping his dark reflections to himself for now, he stood before a church next to a stonemason's at the Reading Road roundabout at the top of Station Road. He'd learned the whereabouts of Friar Park from a clergyman. Yet, like Richard the Lionheart within sight of Jerusalem but declaring himself unworthy to proceed further, Abram peered through concealing shrubbery over a section of disrepaired wall that was neither as high nor as thickly razor-wired as elsewhere and turned away. Down in Falaise Square, in front of the Town Hall and less than 20 feet from the police station, he burst into ranting song, hoping to stir up an uprising to lay "the House" to siege. "Which house?" asked a bemused onlooker.

"Which house?" or "Witch House"? Fixating on the latter, the wheels of the universe came together for Michael Abram, as one of the psychiatrists who were to testify at the trial deduced. "If he did not kill George Harrison," added the good doctor, "he would be sitting on an upturned plant pot in his flat and made a fool of every time he went out."

A man's gotta do what a man's gotta do. Roman Catholic to the bone and full of superstitious terror of punishment for breaking the "Thou shalt not kill" commandment, Mad Mick hoped that something would prevent him from boarding the train for his second and final journey to Friar Park. He carried about his person a two-foot length of cord, knotted in the middle, and a black-handled knife with a six-inch blade. While his prey's awareness of his role in the tragedy was irrelevant, Michael was certain that Harrison knew what was coming. As it had been with the Crucifixion, the world would be saved by the sacrifice of a divine victim in his prime, be he angel or demon.

Spurred on by a voice in his ear as clear as a bell telling him that "God is with you", Michael affected entry to Friar Park in the graveyard hours of 30 December, undetected by the infra-red sensors, the closed-circuit television cameras and further state-of-the-art installations.

Not long after three, Olivia was jerked from slumber by what she'd describe in court as "the loudest crash of glass imaginable". Had a chandelier fallen? In case it was something more sinister, she broke into George's dreams. He toiled groaningly out of bed and, clad in dressing gown, pyjamas and sockless boots, semi-groped his way down the two flights of a wide stairway. A whiff of cigarette smoke and a blast of colder air from the crack under the kitchen door told him that it was no shattered chandelier.

With throat constricting, skin crawling and heart pounding like a hunted beast – which he was – the head of the household hastened back upstairs, where Olivia was attempting unsuccessfully to telephone the entrance lodge, where the video surveillance equipment was supposed to be under constant observation. However, another member of staff was contacted and instructed to ring the police and try to activate the floodlights. Olivia then dialled 999 herself.

Venturing to the balustrades overlooking the hall, George, frowning with astonishment, caught the crunch of footsteps on shards of glass. With a stone lance from a statue of St George and the Dragon in the conservatory, Michael Abram had smashed the double patio doors of the kitchen. Now, his leather-jacketed, black-gloved shape stood foursquare, glaring into the gloom above as his victim's face smouldered into form.

His voice should have been shrill with fear, but George asked almost matter-of-factly the identity of the intruder. In contrast came a bawled "You know! Get down 'ere!"

As he had in that hair-raising flight to New York in 1971 and other ugly moments, George let slip a "Hare Krishna" or two (although perhaps 'Help!' or 'Get Back' may have been more appropriate). For a split second, Abram was dumbfounded before interpreting these exclamations as a curse from Satan. Furiously, he breathed hard and charged onwards and upwards.

Aware of the peril a beat before an eerily silent and strong assailant fell upon him, "My first instinct was to grab for the knife," Harrison was to inform the Crown prosecutor. "I tried to get into a room, but the key was stuck, so I decided to tackle him by running towards him and knocking him over. We both fell to the floor. I was fending off blows with my hands. He was on top of me and stabbing down at my upper body."

The commotion drew Olivia out. Freeze-framed for the blink of a bulging eye, Olivia held her husband's bewildered gaze, "one I had never seen before". The slow moment over, she seized the nearest blunt instrument to hand, a small brass poker, and waded in. A snatch at his testicles sent Mad Mick into a unbalanced half-spin, but, boiling over with pain, he sprang like a panther at Olivia, who dropped the poker and fled vainly into the sitting room next to the sleeping quarters. Abram's grip on the back of her neck slackened as George leapt on her pursuer, "but he continued to strike out and he got the better of me".

George and Michael tumbled, wrestling, onto meditation cushions. Beyond the knobbles of the latter's spine, George saw Olivia grab a weighty glass table lamp and bring it down with all her force. "Even as I was swinging," she later recalled, "I was aware and amazed that I was doing so without a drop of malice in my heart."

"Don't stop!" yelled George. "Hit him harder!"

Heaving violently like an erupting volcano, Abram took a few more indiscriminate blows while fumbling for the light's flex, whipping it around the woman's hands and gashing her forehead in the process. Panting too, George "felt exhausted. My arms dropped to my side. I could feel the strength drain from me. I vividly remember a deliberate thrust of the knife into my chest."

Warm liquid welled up inside his mouth. Blood. Lower down, the knife had missed his heart by less than an inch, but a twice-punctured lung collapsed, and so did its owner. "I believed I had been fatally stabbed," he said later. But, even as the blade had penetrated his flesh, he understood that he would be genuinely mourned by Olivia.

With facial wounds that needed stitching, the fight had gone out of Abram as well. "He slumped over me," Olivia later recalled. "I again took hold of the blade of the knife and wrenched it from his grasp."

At that point, two Thames Valley constables – PC Paul Williams and, only six months in the job, 33-year-old Matt Morgans – turned up, not exactly in the nick of time. "The house was in total darkness," so Morgans related to both his sergeant and *The Henley Standard*.[376] "We jumped out of the car and PC Williams went up to the huge set of front doors while I went around the side to see if someone had broken in there. My first thought was that, in my training, we were told you shouldn't touch anything, but then I heard the screaming, so I shouted for PC Williams and went through the window."

There, in a red haze, a bruised and bloodstained Olivia was staggering to the bottom of the hallway stairs.

"I was so new in training, I just went into automatic mode," gasped Matt. "Since then, people have asked me why I didn't call back-up or put a stab-proof on. I met her, and she said the man was upstairs, trying to kill George. He was my immediate priority.

"I saw a guy running across the landing. I thought he was wearing a mask, but it was just the blood running down his face and in his hair from where Olivia had hit him. He was a bit streaky and wild. I shouted to the man to stay where he was and get down on the floor, which he did. I stood over him, and then saw the bedroom light and George Harrison lying behind the door. I left PC Williams to handcuff the intruder and restrain him.

"George was in a right mess. He had been kicked, punched and stabbed. He was conscious, but his main concern was for his wife. He thought the man thought he was finished and had gone after his wife. I put him in the recovery position and did enough first aid so that he didn't croak."

The officers then checked elsewhere for any accomplices, but there was only Michael Abram, whose ravings you could have heard down at the police station in Falaise Square. "You should have heard the spooky things he was saying, the bastard," he shrieked, before "I did it! I did it!" several times in succession.

Next on the scene was Dhani. He knelt by his prostrate father and was "immediately covered in blood". As well as the lung, the knife had left its mark in George's thigh, cheek, chest and left forearm. "He was drifting," noticed Dhani. "I honestly believed he was going to die. He was so pale. I looked into his eyes and saw the pain. Dad kept saying, 'Oh Dhan, oh Dhan.' He looked even paler in the face, and he was groaning and saying, 'I'm going out.' He made little sense, and I knew he was losing consciousness. It was about ten to twelve minutes – although it seemed like a lifetime – before the paramedics arrived."

Both victim and attacker were rushed to the Royal Berkshire Hospital in Reading. The truth that he may have refused to avow at first inflicted itself on Dhani at this point: "As [George] was taken away in a stretcher chair, he looked back and said, 'I love you, Dhan.' My father's spoken words were broken with coughing and spluttering. He said, 'Hare Krishna,' and closed his eyes. At this point, he drew a very strange breath. It was deep and what I would describe as a death breath. His mouth was puckered, his cheeks were drawn in and he sucked at his bottom lip. I shouted, 'Dad! Dad! You are with me? Listen to my voice. It is going to be OK. Stay with me!' His face was contorted and he had not taken a breath for some seconds. As I finished shouting, he breathed out and opened his eyes. I have never seen another human being, whether dead or alive – and I have seen my grandfather in his coffin – look so bad."

Sooner than expected, George was off the danger list by the following afternoon. He was then transferred to Harefield Hospital, on the edge of London, where he saw in 2000 AD. Gruesomely hilarious remarks and relayed witticisms* hid the shaken man beneath to everyone but Olivia and Dhani, to whom he still had every appearance of being seriously unwell, despite assurances that he was on the mend.

For Olivia, fright had turned to rage towards one who "owes us a thank you for saving him from the karma of murder. We do not accept that he did not know that what he was doing was wrong. We shall never forget that he was full of hatred and violence when he came into our home."

When George's old smile was back by mid January, she accompanied him on a brief convalescence in Ireland as a prelude to a longer stay with Dhani and a lately-widowed Joe Brown in a rented holiday home in Barbados, the expensive facilities of which were less important than the ex-SAS militia who patrolled the grounds around the clock.

From less exotic surroundings, Michael Abram, on remand, sent a letter of apology "for having to face a lunatic like me in their house". Via the Crown Prosecution Service, this reached Friar Park the day before his case came up the following November. Olivia, for one, was not impressed: "I didn't read it properly. What I did read sounded like it wasn't written by him. Given the timing, it sounded convenient."

The next day, in Oxford Crown Court, Abram was smartened up beyond recognition in a pinstripe suit and John Lennon swot spectacles, his hair trimmed to a short crop. A vision of poker-faced sobriety, he denied two counts of attempted murder, causing grievous bodily harm, unlawful wounding and aggravated burglary. Through the oratory skills of his barrister, the jury were persuaded that Society Was To Blame, and in measured tones the defendant was to thank Mr Justice Astill, after being found not guilty on the grounds of insanity. The summit of his life conquered, Mad Mick was escorted away by two male nurses for the first stage of a journey that would terminate in the medium-secure Scott Clinic, a psychiatric wing of Rainhill Hospital, out of harm's way in rural Merseyside. He was to be detained there indefinitely, meaning that he'd be eligible for release if ever a mental health review tribunal decided that he was no longer a risk to the public. The Harrisons' plea to be informed if this should happen was rejected, but Justice Astill intimated that there might be "other channels" they could try.

This was food for thought, as, flanked by bodyguards in the

---

* Such as, "He wasn't a burglar, and he definitely wasn't auditioning for The Traveling Wilburys," and a more measured, "Adi Shankara, an Indian historical, spiritual and groovy-type person once said, 'Life is fragile, like a raindrop on a lotus leaf,' and you'd better believe it."

building's forecourt afterwards, Dhani Harrison read a statement to the gentlefolk of the press. Its most crucial sentence was, "The prospect of him being released back into society is abhorrent to us."

Newspaper reports on what amounted to 22-year-old Dhani's first public address were accompanied by photographs that accentuated his close resemblance to his father at the same age.*

Dhani had preferred not to stand up in court, but his mother had resolved from the start to testify in her own voice rather than "have my statement read by a male police officer in a monotone". Via a half-page interview in *The Independent On Sunday*, she also expressed hopes that "the growing violence in society is controlled and ultimately replaced by the goodness of most people in the world" before putting a full-stop on the affair, with a dramatic "The line is drawn under it all when I hang up this phone."[377]

Yet it wasn't as easy as that. Death threats from other Beatlemaniacs continued to reach George Harrison and unfounded media speculation that he was planning to leave Friar Park because it now had "bad vibes" reawakened parochial opinion that he intended to offer the place to the Krishna Consciousness Society.

"Mr and Mrs Harrison are not merely victims but continuing targets" was the thrust of hired QC Geoffrey Robertson's argument on behalf of George when approaching Home Secretary Jack Straw, one of Judge Astill's "other channels". Straw assured Robertson that to "put victims back at the heart of the justice system has been my guiding preoccupation as Home Secretary. When I read and hear of the experiences of those like George and Olivia Harrison, it intensifies my determination. I believe victims of crime have a right to know that those who have offended against them are released and I propose to introduce new laws to do just that."

These fine words in the run-up to 2001's general election have been thus far the most far-reaching repercussion of the Michael Abram incident, although the amassed publicity did help to pave the way for the release schedule of re-mastered CDs of George's solo back catalogue, complete with tacked-on alternative takes and hitherto-unissued songs, beginning with the 2001 boxed set of *All Things Must Pass*.* Its full-colour variation on the original black-

and-white front cover reflected the 30 years' worth of technology that had been developed since 1971. With the audio fidelity of compact discs, rather than suffer the sweet torment of worn-out vinyl, fans might at last think that they could catch the whirring of George's nervous system. Into the bargain, the new *All Things Must Pass* was made flabbier, with different versions of 'Beware Of Darkness', 'Let It Down' and 'What Is Life', the baleful 'I Live For You' – with a riff too similar to that of 'I Got A Feeling' from *Let It Be* – and the previous autumn's remake of 'My Sweet Lord', featuring Joe Brown's pop-singing daughter Sam† and, less conspicuously, Dhani Harrison on acoustic guitar, along with the ubiquitous Jim Keltner on drums.

"I just made it in the same way as we made it back in the '60s," explained George, "which is [with] analogue tapes, microphones and guitars, bass, drums, piano. The world is going mental, as far as I'm concerned. It's speeding up with technology and everything that's happening. I just liked the idea and opportunity to freshen it up, because the point of 'My Sweet Lord' is just to try to remind myself that there's more to life than the material world. Basically, I think the planet is doomed, and it is my attempt to put a spin on the spiritual side, a reminder for myself and for anybody who's interested."[378]

Plenty were, and the double CD's topping of *The Henley Standard*'s Top Ten was reflected to a lesser extent in lists throughout a wider world. This boded well for CD re-promotions of the more attractive *Living In The Material World* and the Dark Horse catalogue, that had now reverted to its maker. Jumping to the front of the queue, however, may be an album of fresh material that has exhausted two working titles already, *Portrait Of A Leg End* and *Your Planet Is Doomed, Volume One*.

During his stay at Friar Park, Timothy White had listened to home demos of three earmarked tracks, 'Brainwashed', 'Pisces Fish' and 'Valentine'. Once, such a preview might have been an enormous scoop for *Billboard* or any pop-music periodical, but George Harrison's name is now a far less potent tool for holding the front

---

* Eight days later, Dhani was the central figure in a road accident at the wheel of his Audi S3 sports car, purchased from Motor World in Kidlington, some 30 miles northeast of Henley, three weeks earlier. Dhani escaped serious injury, but the 60mph crash tore off the front wing on the driver's side and burst all four tyres.

page, unless he pulls some eye-stretching stroke like nearly getting killed. That had been much bigger news than any new or recycled Harrison disc of which a journalist might or might not have been aware as he cobbled together an editorial tirade about the government's vacillation about curbing the increase of violent crime in these distracted times.

In the aftershock of Michael Abram's homicidal campaign, George had sent a grateful bottle of champagne to the police station in Falaise Square, and both Paul Williams and Matt Morgans had been awarded with commendations for bravery. "We're not heroes," shrugs Matt. "We just happened to be on the right shift. People did say to me afterwards, 'Weren't you the one at George Harrison's house?' I'd reply, 'Well, yes, I was. But you still get your parking ticket.'"

For George, the experience faded, and according to Nick Valner, his London lawyer, he was "in the best of spirits and on top form – the most relaxed and free he has been since he was attacked". This was part of a statement relayed to the press in May 2001, shortly after George Harrison underwent his second operation in three years to remove a cancerous growth on a lung. From his bed in the Mayo Clinic in Rochester, Minnesota, George blamed smoking – a habit he gave up when the condition was first diagnosed.

While George convalesced in Tuscany with Olivia, Valner assured the public that "the operation was successful and George has made an excellent recovery. Although All Things Must Pass Away, George has no plans right now and is still Living In The Material World, and wishes everyone all the very best."

---

* The title track had been used in the 1998 movie *Everest*, as were 'Here Comes The Sun', 'Give Me Love' and 'Life Itself'.

† Sam Brown's greatest hits at the time of writing were 1989's 'Stop' and a revival of Marvin Gaye's 'Can I Get A Witness'.

Epilogue
The Once And Future Pop Star

Between us on the desk is a copy of a new biography of Harrison, called The Quiet One *by Alan Clayson... "God knows why these people bother," he says picking it up gingerly. "To make some money, I suppose."*

The Times, *12 November 1990*

Within my own limits, I am a principled wordsmith. Firstly, I wouldn't have got enmeshed in showbiz life stories if the market for them hadn't been a legitimate creation by the fans who, indirectly, pay the subjects' wages. Secondly, disgruntled reissue specialists who have commissioned me to pen eulogistic sleeve notes will tell you that I never write anything I don't mean, no matter how high the fee. Most crucially, however, I have to feel an empathy with the artists concerned, and a lot of these are not considered potentially commercial enough by those publishers who have even heard of them.

Conversely, there are myriad more renowned pop figures whom I love to hate. Rather than offend their fans with disobliging observations, I prefer not to talk – let alone write – about them. That's why my books tend to hurry through unavoidable passages about...well, certain people. No doubt the fault for such prejudices is mine, but I'm as childishly editorial about the James Taylor/Melanie singing/songwriter school of the early 1970s and virtually all the major rap executants. Catch me in full philistine flood about some new boy band, too, and I sound just like some middle-aged dad *circa* 1966 going on about the Stones.

George Harrison, however, passes muster. While much of his output has been unexceptional, his thwarted ambition as an instrumentalist provokes sympathy, and for all his self-deprecation he has realised some extraordinary visions as a composer. Yet tune into an

459

easy-listening radio station and the orchestral medley of Beatle tunes you'll hear will be all Lennon-McCartney.

The jury is, therefore, still out – and probably always will be – over whether he's a merely adequate musician who was lucky enough to have been a Beatle or, as Leonard Bernstein assured us, "a mystical unrealized talent".[253] He's probably been both, but I'm not convinced that he's the God-like genius that others have made him out to be. What is a genius, anyway? Among the many blessed with that dubious title are Horst 'A Walk In The Black Forest' Jankowski, dart-hurling Jocky Wilson and Screaming Lord Sutch. As often happens with a celebrity who, however inadvertently, catches the lightning and sustains the momentum of public favour, reputation and legend continue to grow with each succeeding year, far beyond what has actually been achieved.

Not helping, either, is an established but too-analytical form of pop journalism that intellectualises the simply intelligent, turns metaphorical perfume back into a rotten egg and tells you what Greil Marcus thinks about such-and-such an album and what Simon Frith thinks he means. Why should I have been any different by not including in this book self-aggrandising sections that dismantle Harrison's music and stick it back together again? Obviously, I wouldn't do so if I didn't feel that it was either a worthwhile cultural exercise, a way of trying to convince people that I'm clever (a genius, perhaps?) or a method of covering the number of words I'd been contracted to write.

Whatever the motivations, I hope that such parts of *The Quiet One* have utilised your time interestingly. But remember that, however I dress them up, they're only my opinions – and not always subjective ones, either – about items of merchandise available to all. Your thoughts about 'Don't Bother Me', 'Something', the 1974 tour, the Wilburys, *Cloud Nine, et al*, are as worthy as mine – and beyond either of us, the only true approbation an artist needs is from those who buy the records and tickets for the shows. As the two singles from *Cloud Nine* demonstrated, given the right song – his own or not – George Harrison's return to a qualified prominence as a pop star can never be ruled out. On his own terms, there's no reason why he shouldn't still be making records in old age at a pace that could involve further long periods of vanishing from the public eye.

Appendix 1
The Big Sister

In March 1995, I was a guest speaker at the New Jersey Beatlefest. One of the calmer periods during this eventful weekend was spent sharing a graveyard-hour pizza on a lighting gantry with Louise Harrison, a lady I'd met the previous August at a similar function in Chicago. We'd communicated in a shallow showbiz way then, but this time around we became friends during the relief that follows the switching off of a tape recorder after a formal interview earlier, in which a thought had flashed through my mind: *It runs in the family.*

"I have the same basic beliefs as my brother," she'd confirmed – and, despite Louise's Scouse drawl being all but vanished after 40 years in the Americas, it might indeed have been George talking. "We are all part of one energy or intelligence, if you like, and if enough of us are in tune with 'All You Need Is Love' and other principles that The Beatles put across, then some of the things that are happening politically could swing more in the direction of caring for each other than of greed, and tolerance for other religions without Spanish Inquisitions. Something my mum told us was about a church – symbolising God – on top of a mountain and all of us trying to reach it. We may all take a different path to get there, but we're all heading for the same goal. You don't have to be a this or a that as long as you care about the Earth and other Earthlings."

Unlike her youngest sibling, however, she is "not really geared for meditation. Like many others, I try to live every moment conscious of the Creator working through me. I know my role is an active one. I've been given the gifts of physical stamina, great determination and a natural ability to speak to people about our problems and to look for sensible solutions."

Neither is Louise a strict vegetarian. "I hardly ever eat meat," she disclosed, "but if I'm in a situation where someone's cooked me a wonderful meal with meat in it, I'm not going to turn my nose up at it. Yogananda reaches non-fanaticism about any of your beliefs. Actually, I hardly ever eat at all. I mostly have a lot of vitamins, herbs and minerals for particular needs, and I never really feel hungry."

Yet this was no skeletal ascetic – although the angular Harrison cheekbones and appraising gaze are prominent in this robust grandmother who is also prime mover of the We Care Global Family, the non-profit-making organisation she founded in 1992 to promote environmental education. Among tenets outlined in its application leaflet is "Determination to Restore Our Planet for our children". The Germanic capitals are deliberate, for We Care members are referred to as "DROPs" in *Newsplash*, the quarterly newsletter, containing items with titles like "Rubbish Soul", a children's section ("Drop-lets") and editorials ("From Me To You") by Louise, known within the DROP hierarchy as "the other Queen Mum". "They were calling me President," she explained. "I remarked that I'd rather they called me Mum. One replied, 'That's a good idea, but in deference to your biological children, why can't we call you Queen Mum?' This humorous title caught on."

She's "Miss Harrison", however, in her office as roving We Care spokesperson to schools, colleges, solar-energy conferences, Earthday functions and university ecology workshops. She also broadcasts "Good Earthkeeping Tips" – a regular feature in *Newsplash* – on more than two hundred US radio stations, with George's 'Save The World' as background music. Another of Louise's concerns is negotiating finance and a suitable director for a We Care-related movie, *The Time Is Now*. Based loosely on salient points from *Yellow Submarine* and Dickens' *A Christmas Carol*, this musical fantasy has already attracted big names. Of Beatle associates, Neil Innes has donated a title song, and Victor Spinetti has given tentative consent to play the villain.

Louise Harrison has therefore travelled more than mere geographic distance from Liverpool where she was born in her paternal grandmother's house in the suburb of Wavertree on 16 August 1931 as the Harrisons' eldest child, twelve years older than George.

Like him, Louise passed the Eleven Plus examination and gained a place at a grammar school known as La Sagesse, which was attached to a convent that buttressed now-old-fashioned concepts of a woman's role in a wider world. "We were asked to draw what we were going to be when we grew up," recalled Louise. "I drew myself on stage in a spotlight. I wanted to be an entertainer. But back in the early 1950s, a woman didn't think of herself as having a career. The only options for a woman was to be a nurse, teacher or secretary. If you were lucky, you got married. You dreamed that some wonderful man would ride along on a charger and sweep you off your feet."

It was her mother's wish for a disinclined Louise to be a teacher. To this end, Louise won a scholarship to teacher training college at St Mary's in Fenham, Newcastle-upon-Tyne. Although specialising in English, Geography and PE, she demonstrated a flair for drama one December when a visiting Father Agnelus Andrews – house priest on BBC radio – heard Louise's soliloquy as Mary musing about the new-born Jesus. Impressed, Father Andrews offered to write a letter of introduction to the BBC Drama department, should the trainee ever wish to pursue this type of career.

To Louise's disappointment, parental disapproval of her living alone in London – because of concern about the then-widespread white slave traffic – nipped this notion in the bud. As her We Care work would prove, she had a talent for dealing with children, but, midway through the course at St Mary's, "I was so stressed about being in something that I didn't want to do that I came down with a series of abscesses on my face." After counselling by an understanding head nun, she went back to a dismayed mother and a job as chairside assistant to a Merseyside dentist.

In 1954, she wed Gordon Caldwell, a dour but gifted engineer from Dundee. Married life began in Scotland, but the couple were considering what might lie further afield. "My whole attitude throughout my life has been that each day is an adventure," Louise elucidated. "My parents didn't foster in us the feeling that we had to be tied to anyone's apron strings. They gave us a solid foundation of self-confidence and self-esteem. Therefore, I didn't feel any trepidation about emigrating. We really wanted to go to Australia, but it just happened that, after Gordon wrote off for jobs, it was one in Canada that came up first."

A son, Gordon, was born there in 1957, followed by his sister, Leslie, in 1959. Their father's vocation took the family to Peru and then back to Canada to Gagnon, a dreary settlement near the Arctic circle. By the time they arrived in Benton, Beatlemania was ravaging Britain and, said Louise, "Mum was sending me clippings from *Mersey Beat* and the national newspapers. I was thrilled for George and did whatever I could to further The Beatles, because it was something in showbusiness, something I would have wanted to do myself. I got their records played on a minor radio station and wrote dozens of letters to Dick James, George Martin and Brian Epstein. When the first record came out in the States, on Vee Jay, I went to a company address in St Louis, but there was nothing there. Swan, who put out the next one, was no better, so I studied magazines like *Billboard* and *Cashbox* and sent Brian the names and addresses of more major labels like RCA, Capitol and Columbia.

"When Del Shannon's cover of 'From Me To You' came out, I was calling all kinds of radio stations and plugging the original version, but the general feeling was that The Beatles were never going to go anywhere over here. Gordon thought I was wasting my time, too.

"Nevertheless, when 'I Want To Hold Your Hand' came out on Capitol, a representative, Vito Samela, called me that January [1964] to say that, in nine days, it'd sold a million in the States. I called George at the George V Hotel in Paris to tell him. Originally, he had been going to come back over to Illinois again between the two *Ed Sullivan Show*s, but everything went so crazy that there was no way in which he could get away. George suggested that I come to New York for the weekend.

"We were going to meet at the airport, but it would have been difficult for us to link up, what with all the media descending on it. George booked a room for me at the Plaza, but he had such a bad throat that the hotel physician, Dr Gordon, suggested that using the already present sister made more sense than hiring a nurse."

Thanks to Dr Gordon and Louise's ministrations, George was able to be seen on Sullivan's spectacular with The Beatles. "My first impression of the other three," recalled Louise, "was that I felt like I had an extra bunch of brothers. As the only daughter of four children, I'd gravitated more towards football with the lads than girly pastimes. As a result, I was very much at ease. Paul was the diplomat, very gracious. He'd been doing tape recordings on the plane, funny fake interviews. Ringo was delightful, too, and so was Cynthia, but I was scared of John, because of his sarcasm, his biting sense of humour. Really nasty. I mentioned this to Mum, but she said that basically he was OK. When he behaved like that, he was covering up for his own insecurities. It was an interesting lesson to me, because it made me better able to cope with a wide variety of people on the right level, because you can understand and empathise with their frailty and, consequently, they respond to you in a much nicer way."

Through her affinity with the Fab Four, Louise's radio career got under way in New York when she played along with a spoof kidnap stunt by "the Good Guys" – disc jockeys on station WMCA. She found herself on the air for an hour that included a call to George at the hotel, where he plucked a few obliging bars on his new twelve-string Rickenbacker.

She was also present in Washington at the British Embassy, "where someone snipped off a chunk of Ringo's hair. He was really furious. When this happened, I was drinking tea at the back of the room with Lady Ormsby-Gore. When I got back home, there was a news item alleging that Lady Ormsby-Gore herself had wrestled Ringo to the ground and cut a lock of his hair off. I was horrified, and I called up the radio stations I'd tried in 1963, because I was so concerned about Lady Ormsby-Gore being made a fool of. They invited me on to talk about it. Initially, I was reluctant, but two days later one station in St Louis, realising its mistake in refusing to play The Beatles in 1963, asked me to tell the truth about other rumours and press garbage. They wanted me to do daily 'Beatle Reports' – anecdotes and ongoing news – for a couple of weeks."

The initial fee for the Beatle Reports would cover costs of replying to the thousands of fan letters mailed to Benton. "George called from

Miami and I told him about this proposal," said Louise. "We made arrangements that I would call Mum each week and she'd tell me the latest goings-on so that I could put together these reports. I ended up doing them for 15 major stations across the country for the next 18 months. It did wonders for radio ratings. Sometimes, I'd travel to do live phone-ins as far away as Minneapolis. I had to hire a housekeeper and secretary to cope with it."

This second-hand celebrity also took in personal appearances, such as that before a crowd of 15,000 at Minneapolis/St Paul winter carnival, receiving the key to the city of New Orleans during 1965's Mardi Gras and a three-week tour of the Midwest as part of a *Dick Clark Caravan Of Stars*, performing a spoken ballad to musical accompaniment.

That wasn't all. "The head of STORZ Broadcasting, that covered five stations, compiled some of my answers to five live-on-air press conferences," recounted Louise, "and pressed them on vinyl. A prize in each of their competitions was attending a hotel press conference with me. These were recorded and edited. A couple of guys who owned a carwash put up the money."

Louise's consequent *All About The Beatles* LP (see Chapter Seven) was released in 1965 on the understanding that "I was going to get a third of the proceeds on sales, but it never came to anything, because there were too many people putting out records with the name 'Beatles' or 'Beetles' on the front, and Brian put some kind of blanket cease-and-desist. All of the pressings left stayed in a warehouse."

Yet, like her parents, Louise still devoted tireless hours to answering mail in her warm, chatty style, although 1964's daily vanload had subsided to a steady couple of hundred a week. Her radio exposure boiled down to hosting a chat show, *Sound Off*, for a station in southern Illinois. At last, Louise became a personality in her own right, because the programme's stock in trade was not The Beatles but sewage treatment plants, education committees and similar parochial issues.

Sound Off ran until 1970, when, following the trauma of her divorce, Louise and the children were invited to live in George's middle lodge at Friar Park. "I had everything packed," recounted Louise, "and our passage booked on the *QE2*, but my kids were scared of the idea of going to England, what with the education system there being so much more advanced. They were worried about being put in classes with younger children, and so we didn't go. I'd like to feel that, had I gone, I'd have worked with rather than for George."

Instead, Louise seemed as if she'd landed on her feet in New York when commissioned to be a co-presenter on the ailing *Dick Cavett Show*. "They felt that I could increase the listenership. It got as far as them asking me what colour I'd like my dressing room painted, but then ABC cancelled the series." Thus was lost a chance to escape further into a public trajectory separate from that of The Beatles.

Four years later, Louise bounced back as vice-president of a marketing firm owned by Walter J Kane, her new husband, 14 years her junior. A move to Florida prefaced an "amicable" parting in 1983 and the sad conclusion that "I wasn't very good at choosing men".

Financial support from George might have granted Louise a dotage rich in material comforts, but rather than retire she chose instead to resume work in radio in 1985, applying 20 years' experience in the medium to continuity, programming, compiling and writing copy, producing advertisements and reading news – not forgetting to sign off with "'Til next time, cheerio!", the catch-phrase from the Beatle Reports era.

She re-entered the Beatle orbit in 1993. "I was at one of Paul's concerts where he was trying to bring fans' attention to environmental problems," affirmed Louise. "I thought it would be nice for this ready-made audience to have their own holistic organisation which looked at the planet as a global family, but it wasn't until I started We Care that I started speaking at Beatle conventions.

"I now realise that these and We Care are outgrowings of my parents' dealing with fan letters in the 1960s, that they'd often sign, "Love from Mum and Dad." At first, I was jealous, but then I saw that, far from losing my parents to Beatle people, they had so much love within them to give freely that they were collecting a lot more goodwill for me, being a sister in this huge family."

For information about how to become a DROP, write to We Care Global Family, PO Box 1338, Tallevast, Florida 34270, USA.

Appendix II
The Fifth Vest

In 1994, Robert Bartel introduced himself to me at a Beatlefest in Chicago. If a business consultant and private investigator by trade, he also functions as a poet and Beatles historian. "They kept me alive in the '60s, when things were not always good," he says of the pop combo that launched a thousand fanzines. Through one of these, Bob Bartel met his future wife, Janice, in 1991, whom he wed on Lennon's birthday two years later. A room in their house in Springfield, Illinois, is a shrine to The Beatles, with every nook filled with neatly displayed memorabilia, including a 1964 bubble-gum card, an autographed limited-edition George Harrison songbook and a signed photo of Sean and Yoko with Santa Claus.

At an equidistant 200 miles from St Louis lies Benton, just Off Interstate Highway 57, where Bob travelled shortly before Christmas, intending to photograph 113 McCann Street, a two-storey residence with a broad front porch and bay window where George Harrison's sister Louise, her then-husband and their two children had dwelt for five years, and where George and his brother Peter had visited in 1963. "I drove by and noticed it was empty," relates Bob. "I did some inquiring and found that the Illinois Department for Mines and Minerals Rescue had purchased it for $39,000 and was intending to tear it down for a parking lot for a nearby administrative building. I feel that Benton is sitting on a gold mine. Beatle fans are very loyal and would love to tour the house that George Harrison stayed in for a month."

As you will have read in Chapter Six, it was much less than a month. Nevertheless, as Louise was to point out when we met in

New York in 1995, "That's the only experience any one of [The Beatles] had of living in this country as a normal human being without anyone trying to pull out tufts of his hair and buttons from his shirt. Nobody had ever heard of him."

During the spring prior to George and Peter's holiday, the Caldwells had moved from Canada to the Franklin County settlement of around 8,000 souls when Gordon, a mechanical engineer, was hired by the Freeman Coal Company. "We arrived by car on 10 March and checked into a hotel," remembered Louise. "Gordon had to go to work the next morning, and I wasn't really prepared to buy a house. All I had was a £5 note and a $2 bill."

Nevertheless, she made an appointment with an estate agent, and "one of the first houses he showed me was the one on McCann Street. He told me that all I needed was $500 down and I could move in that day. I went to the bank and borrowed the down-payment and started moving in. I had to call my husband at work and tell him the address to come home to. He didn't get mad, though; he was used to me doing things like that. The first day we moved in, someone brought us a truckload of firewood and Mrs Lillie Lewis – who lived across the street – brought us a big pot of chicken and dumplings. I will always remember the people of Benton being very nice and kind to me, before I was related to someone famous."

For George, Benton was impressive for a temperature sign in the town square that he filmed when it rose to 105 degrees. "He'd never seen a temperature that high in his life," explained Louise. In a crew-cut continent, he was only conspicuous for his moptop. "I'd never seen any man with so much hair. Everywhere we went, people stared at him," exclaimed Gaby McCarty of The Four Vests, Benton's boss group, who had actually heard (via Louise) the *Please Please Me* LP. With this as a conversational starting point, Gaby and Kenny Welch, the Vests' guitarist, befriended George and showed him around.

Inevitably, chat around a record player would develop into jam sessions, and George was invited to sit in when the Vests played at the VFW dance hall in nearby Eldorado. "Everyone was dancing, until he started playing," recalled Jim and Darryl Chady, friends of the Caldwells. "Then everybody just stopped and watched him play.

He was a great guitarist", to which McCarty – now a sheet-metal worker at Southern Illinois University – added, "I thought he was going to play some of those Beatles songs, but he played Hank Williams tunes."

He delivered them on Welch's particular make of Rickenbacker. "He had never seen one before," said Kenny, "and he liked it really well. He wanted to buy it." Welch wasn't selling, however, so George purchased one from Mount Vernon, a town a few miles north. Kenny remains "unsure whether he bought it from an individual or a business". Around Louise's, he was heard picking at this same instrument, which would be heard on 'A Hard Day's Night' and other Beatles recordings.

Dawn greeted George as the plane landed in London on 3 October. If not yet adjusted to Greenwich Mean Time, he still breezed into Abbey Road that afternoon to resume work on what would become *With The Beatles*. During a break, he may have told a funny story about the Eldorado bash when a man told him afterwards that he'd appreciated George's performance, and that, "if you had the right handling, you could go places".

The man's judgement proved correct, and the next the people of Franklin County saw of George was on *The Ed Sullivan Show* in the following February. "I couldn't believe it," gasped Kenny Welch. "I never mentioned it to anybody, because I didn't figure anyone would believe that I had played guitar with him. I just remember him as a nice guy."

"The next time [we met George]," recounted Jim Chady, "was when the Caldwells invited us to see The Beatles when they performed at Cominskey Park in Chicago on their first US tour. Over 50,000 in a stadium was quite a contrast from the Eldorado VFW."

As the group continued to spearhead what passed into myth as the "British Invasion", Louise undertook radio broadcasts – "Beatle Reports" – from number 113. For this purpose, she would liaise by telephone every day with Brian Epstein for updates. "Many of the news releases that were sent to the national media came from this house," Bob Bartel would remark. "That in itself makes it pretty historical."

That's as may be, but the demolition crew were still awaiting instructions while Bob tried to persuade state authorities that the place may be a lucrative tourist attraction. Seeing visions of "each house on that block as a boutique in four or five years", Bartel put the case to the region's Historical Preservation Society, but there persisted "some question in their mind about the historical value of the house. I think it would be more so than that of the old Franklin County jail. Why not work to save a place where someone famous stayed, rather than where someone infamous stayed?"

The tireless young bard had more luck with the Illinois Capitol Development Board, the state's construction management agency, who extended the 26 February deadline (by coincidence George's 52nd birthday) to allow Benton and Beatles fans time to "come up with whatever their plan would be", said spokesperson Mia Jazo.

The state itself suggested that, at a cost of up to $40,000, the house could be moved to another location, and almost immediately a fast-food restaurant chain offered a low-cost lease. Then there was attorney Gerald Owens' idea of drumming up cash to buy another building nearby that could suffer the wrecking ball instead. He also mentioned a willing local lady with the means to do so.

Further champions joined the fray, among them Envirowood, a company that recycles plastic into plastic wood. It pledged to provide tables for a picnic area, while WXRT-FM's Terri Hemmert – a sort of female Jimmy Saville of Chicago and MC of the Windy City's annual Beatlefest – promised to spread the word on the ether.

Most crucial of all was the support of Louise Harrison, now 64 and living in Sarusota, Florida. In 1992, she'd ventured back into the public spotlight as both a speaker at Beatle-related events and as figurehead of the We Care Global Family Inc. The McCann Street issue seemed to combine both her vocational and her personal interests. "I heard about the wrecking plans from some fans in December," she recollected. "They reminded me that this is a special place from a special time. I would like to see if the redbud tree I planted in the yard is still there." She doubted if George would approve of her involvement: "He'd probably think it's a lot of nonsense, but once we've done it and good things are happening, I'm sure he'll say, 'That's OK.'"

Louise's three-day stay in Benton embraced a few campaign meetings and a press conference attended by most of the St Louis Beatles Fan Club. Apparently, during one of Bob's frequent calls to Florida, Louise had thought aloud about acquiring the wherewithal to install her daughter, Leslie, at number 113, but if this was ever more than mere talk it has since been abandoned.

With and without Louise, Bob soldiered on with petitioning and his dogged badgering of the media – including the BBC – and schemes for a book and even a movie about George in Benton. After much soul-searching, he donated his precious Harrison songbook to a fund-raising auction. "It's a world thing," he contended. "It's in everybody's interest. I don't care if you're from Springfield, China or whatever. It's preserving a part of history."

In the centuries to come, the ghost of George Harrison is perhaps less likely to be observed wading and rattling chains around Benton than, say, the Speke council estate where he grew up. Yet, through Bob Bartel's tenacity, sentences with "museum", "guided tours", "souvenir shop" and "Gracelands" in them were put into the mouths of Benton burghers, and 113 McCann Street was saved. Three Benton couples – including Jim and Darryl Chady – clubbed together and bought the place. They turned it into a guest house – called A Hard Day's Night – with restaurant facilities. "We're naturally in it for the investment," insisted Cindy Rice, one of the speculators, "and to preserve it tastefully and not exploit it."

"Just think, this might be 'Little Memphis'," laughed Jean Chamness, president of both the Chamber of Commerce and the Society for Historical Preservation. "I always liked country music more, but I'm forward-looking enough to realise that this could really be a good thing for us. Our economy is stagnant, to say the least."

Notes

In addition to my own correspondence and interviews, I have used the following sources which I would like to credit.

1. *Arena* (BBC2) 27 November 1989
2. *Zabadak* number eight, July 1989
3. *International Times*, 11 September 1969
4. To Glenn Baker, Sydney radio announcer
5. Even good Homer sometimes nods
6. Letter from Clog Holdings, Burbank, California, 28 February 1989
7. What is written down is permanent
8. *Mail On Sunday*, 4 September 1988
8.1 Officially, George's birth took place on 25 February, but later sources calculated that he actually appeared shortly after midnight on the 26th. Who cares?
9. *Rolling Stone*, 30 December 1976
10. To Hunter Davies
11. An inflammation of the kidneys, sometimes called "Bright's disease". Its treatment includes an unappetising but necessary diet of gruel and tepid milk
12. *Sunday Mirror*, 23 April 1989
13. A reference to noted Liverpool FC footballer Ian St John
14. *Melody Maker*, 29 August 1964
15. *Beatles Monthly*, November 1986
16. *Melody Maker*, 1 May 1965
17. *Liverpool Institute Magazine* volume LXIX, number two, July 1961
18. Arthur Evans to Chris Salewicz
19. Peter Sissons to Chris Salewicz
20. Notably as a newsreader and host of BBC1's *Question Time*
21. Jack Sweeney to Chris Salewicz
22. *Motor*, 28 July 1979
23. *Reading Evening Post*, 7 January 1989
24. *Time Out*, 4 September 1988
25. *National Rock Star*, 18 December 1976
26. *Record Mirror*, 21 January 1956
27. *New Musical Express*, 28 September 1968

28. *Everybody's Weekly*, 3 July 1957
29. *Disc*, 6 January 1971
30. *Daily Mirror*, 8 April 1957
31. "A musicologist" on *Six-Five Special* (ITV), 18 January 1957
32. *Crawdaddy*, February 1977
33. *Melody Maker*, 17 October 1964
34. *Sunday Times*, 27 February 1987
35. *New Musical Express*, 7 March 1958
36. *Everybody's Weekly*, 23 June 1956
37. 'All Those Years Ago' by George Harrison (Dark Horse single, K17807, 1981)
38. *A Twist Of Lennon* by C Lennon (Star, 1978)
39. *I Me Mine* by G Harrison (Simon & Schuster, 1988)
40. Kemp's own dance troupe became prominent in "underground" circles in the 1960s. In their ranks for a while was David Bowie
41. *Liverpool Institute Magazine* volume LXVIII, number one, February 1960
42. *Beatlefan* volume two, number two, 1979
43. This collaboration began prior to George joining The Quarry Men. Until 1970, Lennon and McCartney agreed to take equal credit, even if a given song was the work of only one of them
44. To Ray Coleman
45. Quoted in *Call Up The Groups* by A Clayson (Sanctuary, 1997)
46. *The Man Who Gave The Beatles Away* by A Williams and W Marshall (Elm Tree, 1975)
47. Radio Bedfordshire, 29 December 1985
48. *Fiesta*, May 1975
49. *Greatest Hits*, February 1981
50. *Midland Beat* number 31, April 1966
51. 'Circles', from the album *Gone Troppo* (Dark Horse 923734-1, 1982)
52. *Beatlefan*, volume one, number three, 1978
53. A reference to the 1956 novel by Jack Kerouac, recognised as being among the foremost prose writers of the Beat generation
54. *The Times*, 24 September 1988
55. *Globe Magazine*, September 1969
56. *Melody Maker*, 23 February 1963
57. *Playboy*, 19 October 1964
58. To Spencer Leigh
59. *Musician*, November 1987
60. *Hit Parade*, June 1963
61. *Sunday Times*, 25 February 1990
62. *Apple To The Core* by P McCabe and R Schonfeld (Sphere, 1972)
63. *Disc*, 24 November 1962
64. *Midland Beat* number one, October 1963
65. Vincent's widow in an unidentified British tabloid, 1971
66. *Beatlefan* volume three, number two, 1981
67. Sleeve notes to *The Beatles Featuring Tony Sheridan* LP (Polydor 24-4504, 1971)
68. *Beatles Down Under* by GA Baker (Wild & Woolley, 1982)
69. *Rolling Stone*, 22 January 1981
70. Reply to a fan letter to a girl named Annie (sold in Sotheby's in 1986)
71. Westbury Hotel press conference transcript, 2 June 1962

72. Sydney press conference transcript, 19 June 1964
73. *New Musical Express*, 3 August 1962
74. To Michael Wale
75. *Beatles Unlimited*, February 1977
76. *Beatle!* by P Best and P Doncaster (Plexus, 1985)
77. *Mersey Beat*, 23 August 1962
78. Extract from letter auctioned at Sotheby's, December 1981
79. *New Musical Express*, 1 February 1964
80. To David Sheff
81. *Melody Maker*, 9 February 1963
82. Lennon's sleeve notes to *Off The Beatle Track* by The George Martin Orchestra (Parlophone PC5 3057)
83. *New Musical Express*, 26 October 1962
84. *Peterborough Standard*, 7 December 1962
85. *Melody Maker*, 3 August 1963
86. *New Musical Express*, 1 February 1963
87. *Beatles Monthly*, March 1983
88. *New Musical Express*, 31 December 1966
89. *New Musical Express*, 22 February 1963
90. *New Musical Express*, 19 July 1963. (NB A "whole day" – ie 14 hours – was considered to be a reasonable amount of time to record an LP in 1963. Over at Decca, Mike Smith had been aghast at the eight hours needed for Dave Berry and his nervous Cruisers to record their debut single that summer)
91. *Sunday Times*, 13 November 1966
92. *New Musical Express*, 16 March 1963
93. *New Musical Express*, 19 April 1963
94. *Western Morning News*, 29 March 1963
95. *South-West Scene* volume one, number three, undated (*circa* 1963)
96. *With The Beatles* by D Hoffman (Omnibus, 1962)
97. *Melody Maker*, 15 June 1963
98. Veronica TV (Dutch), 1982
99. *New Musical Express*, 22 March 1963
100. *Liverpool Institute Magazine* volume LXXI, number two, July 1963
101. *The Independent*, 8 February 1989
102. *Midland Beat* number 14, 1964
103. *Midland Beat* number three, December 1963
104. *New Musical Express*, 5 April 1963
105. Quoted in *Back In The High Life* by A Clayson (to be published by Sanctuary)
106. *The Times*, 27 December 1963
107. *Record Mirror*, date indecipherable (*circa* 1965)
108. *Melody Maker*, 21 November 1963
109. *Mirabelle*, 19 October 1963
110. *Melody Maker*, 26 October 1963
111. *Melody Maker*, 16 November 1963
112. *Western Morning News*, 13 December 1963
113. *Havant News*, 2 November 1963
114. *Annabel*, September 1988
115. Brisbane local radio, 28-30 June 1964

116. George Harrison quoted in *Best Of Smash Hits* (EMAP, 1984)
117. Worldwide Dave Clark Fan Club newsletter, summer 1984
118. *The Fab Four* (French magazine), March 1975
119. *Melody Maker*, 23 November 1963
120. *Melody Maker*, June 1964
121. *Watlington Gazette*, 11 March 1964
122. To Kevin Howlett
123. Quoted in *Ginsberg* by B Miles (Viking, 1990)
124. *Sunday Times*, 13 November 1966
125. *Ready, Steady, Go!* (ITV publication, 1964)
126. *Radio Luxembourg Record Star Book Number Five* (Souvenir Press, 1965)
127. *Melody Maker*, 1 May 1965
128. *Melody Maker*, 27 February 1965
129. *Melody Maker*, 17 November 1974
130. *New Musical Express*, 31 May 1963
131. *Melody Maker*, 13 August 1966
132. *The Jack Paar Show*, 3 January 1964
133. I Corinthians xi 14: "Doth not even nature itself teach you that, if a man have long hair, it is a shame unto him?"
134. *Goldmine*, February 1982
135. Sleeve notes to 'Long Tall Sally' EP (Parlophone GEP 8913)
136. *Billboard*, February 1964
137. *Rolling Stone*, 22 October 1967
138. *The Rolling Stone Interviews Volume One* (Straight Arrow, 1971)
139. *Q*, July 1986
140. *New York Times*, 20 December 1963
141. *Jackie*, 13 October 1964
142. *Daily Mirror*, 8 October 1979
143. *Quant By Quant* by M Quant (Cassell, 1966)
144. *The Illustrated Rock Almanac* edited by B Miles and P Marchbank (Paddington, 1972)
145. *Melody Maker*, 6 November 1975
146. *Fabulous*, 31 May 1966
147. George Harrison on *Top Gear* (Light Programme), November 1964
148. *Fabulous*, 6 June 1966
149. *Melody Maker*, 11 December 1965
150. *Melody Maker*, 11 February 1969
151. *Woman's Own*, 21 November 1987
152. *Chant And Be Happy* (Bhaktivedante Book Trust, 1982)
153. *New Musical Express*, 1 September 1969
154. *Melody Maker*, 16 July 1966
155. *Record Mirror*, 1 January 1966
156. To Jan Wenner
157. *Boyfriend '68* (Trend, 1968)
158. *Los Angeles Times*, 6 October 1987
159. *Life With Elvis* by D Stanley (MARC Europe, 1986)
160. *Creem*, January 1987
161. *Melody Maker*, 2 September 1967
162. *Rolling Stone*, 5 September 1987

163. *Melody Maker*, 27 August 1966
164. *Rolling Stone*, 22 October 1987
165. *Disc*, 19 April 1969
166. *Beatlefan* volume three, number four, 1981
167. To Jon Savage
168. Quoted in *Experimental Pop* by B Bergman and R Horn (Blandford, 1985)
169. 1974 concert programme
170. *Radio Times*, 21 May 1972
171. *International Times*, 3 May 1967
172. *Daily Sketch*, 12 June 1965
173. *Student*, May 1969
174. *Melody Maker*, 25 June 1966
175. *Disc*, 16 July 1966
176. *New Musical Express*, 25 June 1966
177. *Mirabelle*, 19 August 1966
178. Ravi Shankar in *New Musical Express*, 5 October 1967
179. *Melody Maker*, 30 December 1967
180. As a devout Hindu, Ravi Shankar's God was not the Western creator of the universe but the universe's very unity, in whose indivisible wholeness he was inescapably involved, rather like an Anglo-Saxon's "weird" – ie not as an infinitesimal cog but, potentially, the spiritual embodiment of the impenetrably mysterious One who is All, no more human than animal or angel – a "no-thing", or, in the truest sense, "nothing". A Hindu's aim is to see through the illusion ("maya") that any person or thing has a reality independent of the One, that everything in life would vanish instantly if no mind was aware of it. The whole purpose of life is to know nothing
181. *Melody Maker*, 31 September 1967
182. *Record Collector* number 120, August 1989
183. *50 Years Adrift* by D Taylor (Genesis, 1984)
184. *Rolling Stone*, 9 September 1967
185. *Disc*, 19 August 1967
186. *Making Music*, June 1987
187. *International Times*, 17 May 1967
188. *Q*, January 1988
189. *Yesterday* by A Taylor (Sidgwick & Jackson, 1988)
190. *The Aspel Show* (ITV), March 1988
191. Quoted in *Pink Floyd* by B Miles (Omnibus, 1980)
192. *Rolling Stone*, 14 December 1967
193. *Western Morning News*, 28 August 1967
194. *Western Morning News*, 12 September 1967
195. *Western Morning News*, 14 September 1987
196. *The David Frost Show* (BBC), 30 September 1967
197. *Melody Maker*, 9 March 1968
198. Elkan Allan in *Movies On Television* (Times Newspapers Ltd, 1973)
199. *Films And Filming*, March 1969
200. *Record Collector* number 108, August 1988
201. Letter from John Lydon, head of Apple Retail, to The Fool
202. *Melody Maker*, 28 September 1968
203. *Rolling Stone*, 9 March 1968

204. *Melody Maker*, 20 December 1969
205. *Melody Maker*, 12 April 1969
206. Cambridge University journal, March 1969
207. *Yoko Ono* by J Hopkins (Sidgwick & Jackson, 1987)
208. *The Beatles* by H Davies (Heinemann, 1968)
209. *Sunday Mirror*, 5 January 1969
210. *Melody Maker*, 4 September 1971
211. To Anne Nightingale
212. Jerry Boys to Mark Lewisohn
213. *New Musical Express*, 1 November 1969
214. Brazilian press conference transcript, January 1979
215. *International Times*, October 1968
216. *Village Voice*, September 1968
217. *Beatles Monthly*, December 1969
218. *New Musical Express*, 27 December 1967
219. *New Musical Express*, 12 September 1968
220. *New Musical Express*, 1 November 1968
221. *New Musical Express*, I December 1976
222. *Morning Star*, 21 May 1970
223. *Rolling Stone*, 9 July 1970
224. Quoted in *Wit And Wisdom Of Rock And Roll* edited by M Jakubowski (Unwin, 1983)
225. *New Musical Express*, 26 December 1969
226. *Disc*, 5 April 1969
227. Well-known British record-reissue specialist
228. *Daily Mirror*, 1 April 1969
229. *Music Echo*, 19 April 1969
230. *Beatles Unlimited*, March 1977
231. *Daily Express*, 11 October 1969
232. *Disc*, 26 December 1969
233. *Record Mirror*, 12 July 1969
234. KRLA radio concert poster
235. *Melody Maker*, 13 June 1974
236. *Rolling Stone*, 15 October 1970
237. *Zabadak* number seven, July 1974
238. *Disc*, 22 December 1969
239. *Melody Maker*, 2 November 1974
240. Sinatra's announcement during a TV special in the late 1970s
241. *Melody Maker*, 11 October 1969
242. *New Musical Express*, 20 September 1969
243. Vivian Stanshall's sleeve notes to *Gorilla* by The Bonzo Dog Doo-Dah Band (Liberty)
244. *Guitar Player*, November 1987
245. *Melody Maker*, 1 August 1970
246. Quoted in *Loose Talk* edited by L Botts (Rolling Stone Press, 1980)
247. *Melody Maker*, 20 March 1975
248. *Beatlefan* volume two, number four, 1980
249. *neil's Book Of The Dead* by N Planer and T Blacker (Pavilion, 1984)
250. *Daily Express*, 27 February 1971
251. *Liverpool Echo*, 16 March 1972
252. It was included in 24 *Super-Great Gospel Songs* (Hansen, 1973)

253. Early 1970 single B-side by Ringo Starr (Apple R 5898-B)
254. Jennifer Sherwood in *Buildings Of England*, quoted in *Henley Standard*, 9 June 1978
255. *Sunday Times*, 29 April 1990
256. *Henley Standard*, 16 June 1978
257. Mrs Jean Broome (Crisp's granddaughter) to *Henley Standard*, 9 June 1978
258. *Sun*, 2 October 1987
259. *Henley Standard*, 29 July 1986
260. *Let It Rock*, January 1973
261. *Melody Maker*, 27 March 1971
262. *Melody Maker*, 30 July 1971
263. *Daily Sketch*, September 1969
264. *Which One's Cliff?* by C Richard (Coronet, 1977)
265. 'Bangla Desh' single by George Harrison (Apple R 5912)
266. Letter from P Jenkin to J Archer, 28 September 1971
267. Letter from G Harrison to Steve Shore, a New Yorker who offered to organise a petition against the tax on the *Bangladesh* album (22 October 1971)
268. 'Miss O'Dell' single B-side by George Harrison (Apple R 5988)
269. *Entertainment Tonight*, October 1982
270. Epstein to Murray the K on WORFM, April 1967
271. *Record Mirror*, 15 April 1972
272. *Today*, 20 March 1987
273. *Sun*, 15 July 1980
274. *Rolling Stone*, 30 December 1976
275. *Melody Maker*, 2 November 1974
276. *Melody Maker*, 6 September 1975
277. *Guardian*, 5 July 1989
278. *Sun*, 2 August 1971
279. *Evening Standard*, 2 August 1971
280. *Melody Maker*, 27 April 1974
281. *News Of The World*, 22 January 1984
282. *Special Pop* (French magazine), November 1972
283. *Rolling Stone*, 6 February 1972
284. To Tim Willis
285. *Movie Life Of George* (LWT), 8 January 1988
286. *Rolling Stone*, 19 December 1974
287. G Harrison in conversation on a bootleg record of a 'Ding Dong Ding Dong' out-take
288. Unless you include Freddie And The Dreamers quoting 'Auld Lang Syne' in counterpoint in 'I Understand' in the UK Top Ten in December 1964
289. *Disc*, 21 December 1974
290. *International Musician And Recording World*, March 1976
291. Bill Elliott in Splinter's Dark Horse press release
292. *Q*, September 1989
293. *New Musical Express*, circa 1976
294. BBC Radio 1, February 1976
295. *Beatlefan* volume four, number one, December 1981
296. *Music Week*, 6 July 1977
297. *A Personal Musical Dialogue* with George Harrison at $33^1/_3$ conducted by M Harrison, October 1977

298. Not the Bristol group who, in 1963, recorded on Pye the imaginative rocking up of the Cornish Floral Dance
299. *Sounds*, 22 December 1976
300. *New Musical Express*, 10 December 1980
301. *New Musical Express*, 7 December 1976
302. Transcript of press conference held at Madison Hotel, Washington, 17 September 1976
303. *Beatles Monthly*, December 1983
304. *Sunday People*, 12 February 1984
305. *Melody Maker*, 14 August 1966
306. *Time Out*, 19 October 1989
307. *Evening News*, 11 March 1978
308. Transcript of press conferences held at Hotel Okura, Japan, 4 October 1977
309. *Songwriter*, May 1979
310. *Daily Mirror*, 19 December 1980
311. *Ready, Steady, Go!* (ITV) 20 March 1964
312. *George Harrison: Yesterday And Today* by R Michaels (Flash Books, 1977)
313. By H Elson and J Brunton (Proteus, 198 1)
314. *Sun*, 11 November 1987
315. To Mark Lewisohn
316. *Daily Express*, 29 July 1989
317. *Evening News*, 30 March 1987
318. *Henley Standard*, 29 July 1986
319. *Beatlefan* volume four, number five, 1982
320. *Beatles Monthly*, June 1986
321. *Sun*, 2 October 1987
322. *The Damp Garden* (Dent, 1982); *Plant Portraits* (Dent, 1985)
323. *Daily Mirror*, 24 January 1983
324. *Daily Express*, 20 August 1986
325. *Midday* (Australian TV), February 1988
326. Press conference transcript after a literary luncheon at Sydney Opera House, 28 September 1984
327. But not the same Keith West who sang 'Excerpt From A Teenage Opera', a British hit in August 1967
328. *People*, 9 October 1987
329. *Beatles Unlimited*, February 1982
330. London press conference transcript, 6 March 1986
331. *Last Resort* (ITV), 16 October 1987
332. *Guardian*, 5 May 1988
333. *Kaleidoscope* (BBC Radio 4), 30 November 1987
334. *Soft Touch*, September 1982
335. *Melody Maker*, 10 March 1979
336. *Daily Mail*, 3 May 1987
337. *Brown Sauce* by J Brown (Collins Willow, 1986)
338. *Q*, July 1989
339. *Sun*, 1 May 1989
340. *Guardian*, 3 May 1988
341. *Daily Express/Sun*, 16 February 1988
342. *Daily Mail*, 4 January 1988

343. *Guardian*, 5 April 1990
344. In May 1990, the HandMade film *Nuns On The Run*, starring Robbie Coltrane, was well-received by critics and moderately successful in general circulation
345. *New Musical Express*, 15 February 1963
346. *Time Out*, December 1988
347. *Sunday Times*, 1 July 1990
348. Olivia Harrison to *Henley Standard*, 22 June 1990
349. *Standard Times*, 10 June 1990
350. *Sunday Times*, 6 May 1990
351. *Henley Standard*, 4 May 1990
352. *Reading Evening Post*, 2 May 1990. In connection with the case, police swooped on a house in Battersea where dwelt an American hippy couple who alleged that they'd had an altercation with Olivia Harrison "on another planet" and felt snubbed by her
353. *Inside Pop: The Rock Revolution* (CBS television), early 1967
354. *Today*, 13 April 1987
355. *Evening Post*, 30 November 1989
356. *The Little Flowers Of St Francis* translated by W Heywood (CEFA, 1974)
357. The address is *Beatlefan*, PO Box 33515, Decatur, GA 30033, USA
358. *Billboard*, 1 December 1991
359. Royal Albert Hall concert flyer, 6 April 1992
360. George Harrison is heard on a track on a 1992 album by Jimmy Nail
361. Which included Andy Fairweather-Low, former frontman of Amen Corner and 1970s solo star. During the Japanese tour, he shared lead-guitar duties with Harrison and Clapton
362. The former member of Thin Lizzy had included George's composition 'That Kind Of Woman' on a recent album. This – along with another Harrison opus, 'Run So Far' – was also recorded by Eric Clapton
363. *Times*, 7 April 1992
364. *Daily Express*, 7 April 1992
365. *Evening Standard*, 7 April 1992
366. *Daily Telegraph*, 7 April 1992
367. *Daily Mail*, 24 June 1994
368. Former editor of *Melody Maker* and biographer of John Lennon and Brian Epstein
369. Significant among the lesser tracks unearthed was 'You'll Know What To Do', a Harrison opus from the *Hard Day's Night* era, remaindered possibly as much for it being "not the greatest thing George ever wrote" (Paul McCartney to *The Independent*, 16 July 1995) as its intrusion on an otherwise all Lennon-McCartney soundtrack LP
370. Transmitted on 24 July 1997. Harrison and Shankar were also interviewed on *This Morning*, CBS, on 12 July 1997
371. Published by Cassell (UK) on 3 March 2001
372. *Raga Mala: The Autobiography Of Ravi Shankar* (Genesis, 2000)
373. www.allthingsmustpass.com
374. *Q*, August 1998
375. *Sunday Times*, 19 November 2000
376. *Henley Standard*, 17 November 2000
377. *Independent On Sunday*, 19 November 2000
378. *Daily Telegraph*, 23 December 2000

Index

Also available from **SANCTUARY PUBLISHING**

THE BEATLES AUDIO BOOKS
Available on CD and cassette

Read by top UK DJ and music-book author Mike Read
The only audio books in existence to focus on the Fab Four

CD £14.99 ISBN: 1-86074-536-9
Cassette £14.99 ISBN: 1-86074-537-7

CD £14.99 ISBN: 1-86074-532-6
Cassette £14.99 ISBN: 1-86074-533-4

CD £14.99 ISBN: 1-86074-538-5
Cassette £14.99 ISBN: 1-86074-539-3

CD £14.99 ISBN: 1-86074-534-2
Cassette £14.99 ISBN: 1-86074-535-0

THE LITTLE BOX OF BEATLES

Bite-sized biographies of each Beatle
Perfect format for those wishing to dip into the Fab Four's musical lives

£10.99 ISBN: 1-86074-515-6

FOR MORE INFORMATION on titles from Sanctuary Publishing
visit our website at www.sanctuarypublishing.com or contact us at: Sanctuary
House, 45-53 Sinclair Road, London W14 0NS. Tel: +44 (0)20 7602 6351

To order a title direct call our sales department or write to the above address. You
can also order from our website at www.sanctuarypublishing.com